The Last Citadel

150th Anniversary Edition

Revised and expanded

Fort Sedgwick, Petersburg, Virginia
Library of Congress

Also by Noah Andre Trudeau

Bloody Roads South: The Wilderness to Cold Harbor, May-June 1864

Out of the Storm: The End of the Civil War, April-June 1865

Like Men of War: Black Troops in the Civil War, 1862-1865

Gettysburg: A Testing of Courage

Southern Storm: Sherman's March to the Sea

Robert E. Lee: Lessons in Leadership

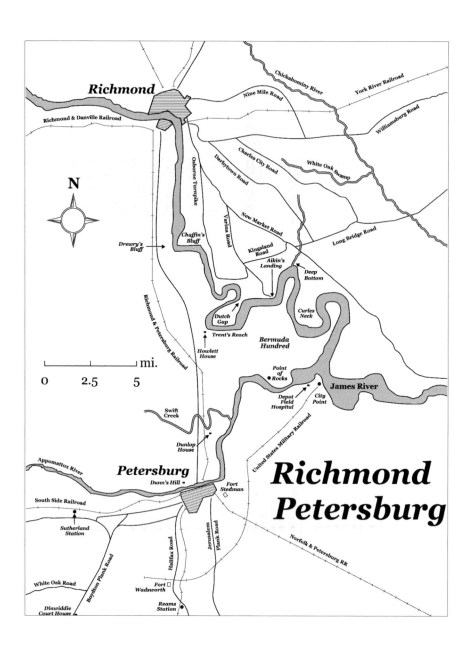

The Last Citadel

Petersburg

June 1864 - April 1865

Noah Andre Trudeau

SB

Savas Beatie

California

Library of Congress Cataloging-in-Publication Data

Trudeau, Noah Andre, 1949-

The Last Citadel: Petersburg, June 1864-April 1865 / Noah Andre Trudeau.

– 150th anniversary edition revised and expanded.

pages cm

Includes bibliographical references and index.

ISBN 978-1-61121-212-9 – ISBN 978-1-940669-56-4 (ebook)

1. Petersburg (Va.)–History–Siege, 1864-1865. 2. Virginia–History–Civil War, 1861-1865. I. Title.

E476.93.T78 2014

973.7'37–dc23

2014019217

SB

Savas Beatie LLC
989 Governor Drive, Suite 102
El Dorado Hills, CA 95762
Phone: 916-941-6896 / (E-mail) sales@savasbeatie.com

05 04 03 02 01   5 4 3 2 1
First Savas Beatie paperback edition, first printing: ISBN: 978-1-61121-705-6

Digital edition by Savas Publishing Company

Savas Beatie titles are available at special discounts for bulk purchases. For more details, contact us at sales@savasbeatie.com, or visit our website at www.savasbeatie.com for additional information.

Grateful acknowledgment is made for permission to quote from the following copyrighted works:

George R. Agassiz, ed., *Meade's Headquarters 1863-1865. Letters of Colonel Theodore Lyman*, copyright 1921 by the Massachusetts Historical Society.
Henry Kyd Douglas, *I Rode with Stonewall*, copyright 1940, © 1968 by The University of North Carolina Press.
Ruth L. Silliker, ed., *The Rebel Yell and the Yankee Hurrah: The Civil War Journal of a Maine Volunteer*, copyright © 1985 by Ruth L. Silliker.

Printed and bound in the United Kingdom

To Christine Malesky,
valued friend, adviser, critic, and fellow author

"To let friendship die away by negligence and silence, is certainly not wise. It is voluntarily to throw away one of the greatest comforts of this weary pilgrimage."

— Samuel Johnson

Contents

Preface   xii

Author's Note   xiv

A Note on the Illustrations   xv

Prologue: A Distant Thunder

1. "Petersburg is to be and shall be defended"   1
2. "It was a marvel of a move"   11

Part I: Enemy at the Gates

3. "Hold on at all hazards!"   27
4. "I have determined to try to envelop Petersburg"   54
5. "The destructive work of the shells was visible on every hand"   88
6. "The saddest affair I have ever witnessed in the war"   96

Part II: Fighting Right, Fighting Left

7. "It was terrible—awful—terrific"   129
8. "Fire low! Low! Low!"   140
9. "Hello! Yanks! Want any fresh beef?"   190
10. Dateline: Petersburg   201
11. "Everything now hinges on the election"   217

Part III: The Last Winter of War

12. "Starvation Parties"   257
13. "We cannot believe Americans can do these things"   262

Contents (continued)

14. "When we weren't killing each other, we were the best of friends"   286

15. "Proper subjects for the hangman"   304

Part IV: An End, A Beginning

16. "The tremendous possibility"   333

17. "I have ordered a general assault along the lines"   359

Epilogue: A Distant Thunder

18. "My kitchen is full of soldiers"   403

19. "I hoped to capture them soon"   416

Notes   426

Note on the Organization of Forces   447

Organization of Forces (1864 - 1865)   448

Bibliography   466

Acknowledgments   504

Index   506

List of Maps

The Richmond-Petersburg Front   iv

Bermuda Hundred/Swift Creek/Petersburg: June 9, 1864   3

The Overland Campaign   13

Crossing the James   19

The First Assaults: June 15-18, 1864   29

Jerusalem Plank Road/Hagood's Assault: June 24, 1864   59

The Wilson-Kautz Raid   84

Petersburg: 1864-1865   89

First Deep Bottom/The Crater   99

The Crater—Competing battle plans   104

Explosion at City Point: August 9, 1864   131

Second Deep Bottom/Reams Station   146

Battles for the Weldon Railroad: August 18-21, 1864   158

The Beefsteak Raid   195

New Market Heights/Fort Harrison/Peebles Farm   205

First Hatcher's Run/Williamsburg Road   221

The Weldon Raid: December 7-12, 1864   265

Petersburg Forts and Siege Lines   289

Second Hatcher's Run   316

Fort Stedman   335

Dinwiddie Court House/Five Forks/Sutherland Station   361

Fort Mahone/Sixth Corps Assault/Fort Gregg   365

Pursuit to Appomattox Court House   418

Photos and illustrations are positioned throughout
the book for the benefit of the reader, with a gallery following page 270.

Preface

The *Last Citadel* is a direct sequel to my first book, *Bloody Roads South*. It picks up the action immediately following the conclusion of Grant's Overland campaign of May-June 1864 and follows it to early April 1865 —the very threshold of Union victory in the East.

No campaign of the Civil War equaled the siege of Petersburg, Virginia. Petersburg was the object of the longest military action ever waged against an American city. More battles were fought and more lives lost in its defense than over any of the other, better-known Southern citadels: Richmond, Atlanta, and Vicksburg.

For 292 days one of the great dramas of the Civil War played out over the fate of the city that historian Fletcher Pratt called "the last bulwark of the Confederacy." "Petersburg…," wrote Richard J. Sommers, was the "guardian of Richmond's lifeline to the Southern heartland." Through it channeled supply lines vital to the Confederate capital. Without Petersburg, Richmond was doomed: it was that simple. Ulysses S. Grant wanted Petersburg; Robert E. Lee was equally determined that it would not succumb. When someone remarked to Grant that the Petersburg siege brought to mind the legendary Kilkenny cats, which fought until only their tails were left, he replied bluntly, "Our cat has the longer tail."

Beyond the story of warfare, the siege of Petersburg is emblematic of the very clash of cultures that brought on the Civil War. Petersburg was the South's Gethsemane, the place where its moral character and its belief in its righteous cause faced their ultimate testing. Time and again outnumbered Confederate armies had won incredible victories. By the summer of 1864, despite a preponderance of men and materiel, despite the attrition brought about by the bloody campaign waged from the Wilderness to the gates of Petersburg, victory for the North seemed no closer than it had been in the spring. It was at Petersburg, Southerners believed, that their God-blessed cause would prove stronger than the North's stomach for further bloodletting. "We heard much about the demoralization of Grant's army, and of the mutterings of discontent at home with the conduct of the campaign," Confederate officer E. M. Law declared, "and we verily believed that their patience would soon come to an end."

Southern hopes had a real basis in fact. Abraham Lincoln faced a difficult reelection in the fall of 1864; his decision to try again for the presidency flew in the face of the popular notion that no President should occupy the office for more than one term. (The last to do so had been Andrew Jackson.) There was reluctance on the part of the Radical Republicans to support him, and even the members of his party's mainstream were uncomfortably aware of newspaper editor Horace Greeley's declaration that "Mr. Lincoln is already beaten. He can never be elected."

Lincoln looked in vain to the rutted battlegrounds of Petersburg for a victory. Press coverage of the campaign was without precedent. Each move and countermove was reported in detail, and each failure exposed in blaring headlines. Public opinion became a force to reckon with as the siege continued for month after month without a major Union victory. The response of the Democratic party was to nominate military hero George B. McClellan for President, on a platform that denounced the war as a failure. So likely did Lincoln think his defeat at the polls that he secretly prepared his administration to relinquish power. More than flesh and blood was on the line at Petersburg—the belief in union itself was given a severe testing.

The human side of the Petersburg siege is a dramatic tale of civilians under fire. The hundreds of men, women, and children in the city learned to cope with shelling, shortages, and the tension of living with the enemy at their gates.

Southern morale was surprisingly high at the beginning of the siege, but the military situation at Petersburg meant a slow death for the once mighty Army of Northern Virginia. Disease, starvation, desertions, and the incremental attrition of trench warfare all combined to sap the living spirit of the Confederate soldier. A sallow-faced Confederate veteran summed up service on the Petersburg front with the comment, "Living cannot be called a fever here, but rather a long catalepsy." By the spring of 1865, thousands of Rebel soldiers had deserted, and hundreds more were leaving every day. In a last, desperate search for men to fill their ranks, the Confederate leaders voted to arm and train slaves. But it was too late—the final actions of the war were at hand.

In spite of its length and the amount of combat activity surrounding it, the Petersburg siege has received remarkably little attention. A number of individual battles have been examined in detail in books and articles, and the overall course of the campaign has been touched upon in general surveys of the war. Yet the great, sprawling mass of events during the Petersburg siege has defied the attempts of more than one modern writer to compress its jumble of oddly named battles into capsule form. Here, then, for the first time, is the full panoply of one of the greatest campaigns of the Civil War.

Preface to the Sesquicentennial Edition

It is both daunting and exhilarating to revisit what I might call (with apologies to the composer Rossini) one of the sins of younger age. My deep personal thanks to Thedore P. Savas of Savas Beatie LLC for his willingness to take on not only a reprinting, but allowing (even encouraging) me to revise the original book.

Those revisions lie in several areas. On a visual level I have reworked all the maps with what I hope is a touch more skill than I possessed when I crafted the originals in 1991 (my first effort in that direction!), and even added a couple. Text-wise, and in my eternal search for perfection, I corrected all errors of fact (thankfully, not many) that were pointed out to me in reviews and conversations about the book, and even a couple I found on my own. I would like to especially thank Dr. Richard J. Sommers, who took time off from his busy schedule to read me through the notes in his annotated copy, which directed me to details I am pleased to have now attended to. Thanks also to historians Chris Calkins and James H. Blankenship, Jr., who passed along corrections. I also took advantage of the fact that Savas Beatie was not merely reprinting the original to add several pages of new material. I'll 'fess up to having learned a few things in the years since the book first appeared, and in some places changed the text to better reflect what I now know, or think I do.

I remain proud of the original version which has stood the test of time and remains the only significant one volume history of the overall Petersburg campaign. I commend this new edition to you with (I hope all) warts removed and text refreshed. Enjoy!

Author's Note

The Union Army of the Potomac and Army of the James and the Confederate Army of Northern Virginia were organized along the same lines. Each was first divided into corps, which were then successively subdivided into divisions, brigades, regiments, and companies. I have generally referred to the various corps, divisions, and brigades of both sides by the names of their commanders: for example, Hill's corps, Gibbon's division, and Bartlett's brigade. This was a common practice in the Confederate armies, but not so in the Union forces. To differentiate between these "official" unit names and my own unofficial designations, the unit name is capitalized in the former case but not in the latter. When the full name of a unit commander is employed, standard grammatical rules are followed. Some Confederate brigades retained the name of a former commander (Kershaw's Brigade, for instance, was led by Colonel John Henagan), while others, such as the Laurel Brigade, enjoyed officially sanctioned nicknames. When it was more appropriate to refer to a brigade, division, or corps by its number, the number is spelled out: First Brigade, Second Division, Fifth Corps. References to regiments are always by number and state, hence 13th Virginia and 32nd Maine.

The armies marched in long columns, four abreast. When it was time to fight, these columns changed into double-ranked lines of battle. Either end of a line of battle was its flank, while the regimental and national flags were usually carried in the center of the line. Geographic directions are always given from the perspective of the side under discussion.

In order to free the text from numerous uses of the qualifier sic, I have adapted a variable rule on spelling. Misspellings that convey a sense of character have been preserved, while those that reflect outdated word usages have been changed. Place names and words that normally appeared in slightly alternate versions (Tar Heel versus Tarheel; entrench versus intrench) have also not been altered.

A Note on the Illustrations

The ten-month-long Petersburg campaign did not lack for photographic coverage, and many images from the siege are familiar fixtures in texts about the Civil War, although the most "famous" one showing huddled Union soldiers in a trench with officers standing above them was actually taken at Fredericksburg. I have opted not to travel over that well-trod ground but have instead chosen (as I did in my first book) to emphasize the work of the Special Artists. These illustrator-correspondents went into the field with the troops and, working from soldiers' accounts and firsthand observations, sketched all aspects of the siege, from the deadly tedium of trench warfare to the violent moments of combat. Their work during the Petersburg siege has generally been overshadowed by the photographic record of the campaign, which is unfortunate as both have their merits. I have selected some of their original field sketches for inclusion, since these images seem to me to capture the vividness of the moment in a way unequaled by any other medium of the time.

The works shown come from the pencils, charcoal sticks, and paintbrushes of ace Special Artists Edwin Forbes, Alfred Waud, and Alfred's equally talented brother William.

Prologue

A DISTANT THUNDER

Petersburg, Virginia: A Rebel battery on outer line of the
Confederate entrenchments, captured on June 15, 1864. *Library of Congress*

Chapter 1

"Petersburg is to be and shall be defended"

Events to June 12, 1864

Ulysses S. Grant
Final Report of Operations, March 1864 - May 1865

I have the honor to submit the following report of the operations of the armies of the United States from the date of my appointment to command the same:

From an early period in the rebellion I had been impressed with the idea that active and continuous operations of all the troops that could be brought into the field...were necessary to a speedy termination of the war. . . .

The enemy had concentrated the bulk of his forces east of the Mississippi into two armies, commanded by Generals R. E. Lee and J. E. Johnston, his ablest and best generals. . . .

In addition to these armies, he had a large cavalry force under [Nathan B.] Forrest in Northeast Mississippi; a considerable force of arms in the Shenandoah Valley and in the western part of Virginia and extreme eastern part of Tennessee. . . .

Maj. Gen. W. T. Sherman . . . was instructed to move against Johnston's army, to break it up, and to go into the interior of the enemy's country as far as he could. . . .

Maj. Gen. George G. Meade . . . was instructed that Lee's army would be his objective point. . . .

Maj. Gen. B. F. Butler [was to] . . . operate on the south side of the James River, Richmond being [his] . . . objective point. . . .

General Butler moved his main force up the James River [and on] . . . the 5th [of May, 1864,] he occupied, without opposition, both City Point and Bermuda Hundred, his movement being a complete surprise. . . .

On the 6th he . . . commenced intrenching. On the 7th he made a reconnaissance.

On the evening of the 13th and morning of the 14th he carried a portion of the enemy's first line of defenses at Drewry's Bluff . . . with small loss. The time thus consumed from the 6th lost to us the benefit of the surprise and capture of Richmond and Petersburg, enabling, as it did, [Confederate General P.G.T.] Beauregard to collect his loose forces in North and South Carolina, and bring them to the defense of those places. On the 16th the enemy attacked General Butler [and he] . . . was forced back, into his intrenchments between the forks of the James and Appomattox Rivers. . . . His army, therefore . . . was as completely shut off from further operations directly against Richmond as if it had been in a bottle strongly corked. . . .

On the 9th of June General Butler sent a force of infantry under General Gillmore, and of cavalry under General Kautz, to capture Petersburg if possible, and destroy the railroad and common bridges across the Appomattox.

*   *   *

War came to Petersburg like the ominous wind gusts of an approaching storm. It lurked just below the horizon, threatening but not yet dangerous.

Even at a distance, the conflict had brought change. Tobacco had helped to make the town's merchants rich in the 1850s, but that trade was doomed once Federal warships anchored in Hampton Roads and blocked access to the sea. Cotton, another big part of Petersburg's prewar economy, boomed, with six mills operating at full capacity. Other industries appeared. There were factories to produce military supplies as well as offices to manage the labor needs of the vital Richmond-Petersburg region. And as a sign of the terrible power of that distant storm, military hospitals were established.

Petersburg, located on the south bank of the Appomattox River, was linked by water and rail to the James River, the Chesapeake Bay, and the Atlantic Ocean. Goods from all around the world came into Petersburg, something the United States government had acknowledged by building a Customs House in the city. That building, once a source of civic pride, now bore silent testament to the fact that the world had changed.

Petersburg's young men marched toward that dark horizon in proud little units; the Petersburg Rifles, the Petersburg Grays, Graham's Battery, the Lafayette Guards, and the Archer Rifles were just some of the seventeen separate units that disappeared into the maw of Mars.

As the "short" war went on and on, the land around Petersburg was refashioned into alien shapes. Captain Charles H. Dimmock came down from Richmond in 1862 with orders to erect an earthen shield for the city. Slaves labored to sculpt the sandy gray soil into trench lines and forts, while stands of trees fell before axes to clear fields of fire. When Captain Dimmock moved on,

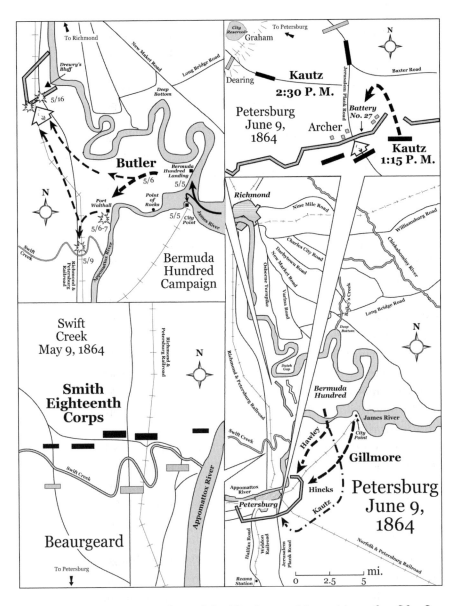

he left behind him ten miles of fortifications, with positions for fifty-five batteries.

The still-distant war caused odd things to happen. One day a warning arrived that the Union gunboat *Pawnee* was coming from Hampton Roads to shell the town. By the time the story (later found to be false) spread into nearby Prince George County, folks were told that the Pawnee "was an Indian tribe sent by the U.S. to ravage the country." Frightened and terrified refugees filled Petersburg's streets for the first time.

There were tangible symbols of the town's proud past that remained despite the war. A visitor traveling along the Jerusalem Plank Road from the southeast passed through the Blandford neighborhood, with its cemetery and its Cockade Monument – erected to honor the Petersburg men who had fallen in the War of 1812. The monument's name came from the rosette that the Petersburg volunteers wore on their caps; such was their dedication to the cause that an admiring President James Madison referred to their home as the Cockade City, a nickname that stuck.

Petersburg's population was 18,266 at the start of the war; an accounting that included 3,164 free blacks and 5,680 slaves. Their city boasted main streets of cobblestone and granite Belgian block, brick sidewalks illuminated by gas lighting, a municipal water system (which included a reservoir on the town's eastern side and the waterworks on St. Andrew Street), two daily newspapers, eight banks, a canal system bypassing the Appomattox River rapids, and well-traveled roads radiating out in all directions.

Petersburg's strategic importance was further emphasized by the five railroads that converged here. The South Side Railroad ran out the city's western side connecting to the state's interior. Materials from the south and North Carolina seaboard arrived via the Petersburg & Weldon or the Norfolk & Petersburg railroads. Petersburg's most direct link to the outside world was the railroad to the east that started at City Point (a port town located where the Appomattox River emptied into the James). Long known as the City Point Railroad, it was properly a spur of the South Side operation, but most residents called it by its old name. All of these routes then funneled northward to Richmond on a single line.

Petersburg passed along more goods to the other parts of the Confederacy during the early war years than it kept. Mrs. Roger A. Pryor, the wife of a Southern military man and former U.S. congressman, moved to her husband's old district from overcrowded Richmond in the winter of 1863. "Petersburg was already virtually in a state of siege," she insisted. "Not a tithe of the food needed for its army of refugees could be brought to the city." By January merchants were selling flour at $200 per barrel, butter at $6 per pound, with bushels of wheat costing $25 and bean bushels $30. Yet a special occasion could still unlock hidden pantries. Young Charles Friend never forgot a dinner his father attended in April 1864 in honor of one of the city's pastors: "The menu for the supper was waffles, oysters and coffee, real coffee, then so rare as to give all who partook a sleepless night."

Suddenly, some might say inevitably, the war was no longer just a distant inconvenience. On May 5, 1864, a great Federal fleet steamed up the James River from Hampton Roads. A brigade of black troops landed late that day at City Point to secure it, putting them not ten miles northeast of Petersburg. But even as City Point was coming under Federal control, soldiers from Major General Benjamin F. Butler's Army of the James were splashing ashore at Bermuda Hundred, a thirty-square-mile peninsula just north of Petersburg, formed by the confluence of the James and Appomattox rivers. More than fifteen thousand Yankees were ashore by dawn on May 6, with more coming.

The next weeks were anxious ones for Petersburg. Train after train arrived from the south to disgorge battalions of Confederate soldiers who hastily formed ranks and marched north to confront the invaders. Directing the defensive operations was one of the South's first war heroes, General P. G. T. Beauregard. Combat erupted on May 7 at Port Walthall Junction, a mere six miles up the Richmond Turnpike from Petersburg's northern corporate limits. At the same time, blue-coated cavalry operating out of Suffolk, to the south, tore up sections of the Norfolk and Weldon railroads. On May 9, units from two Union corps pushed south along the Richmond Turnpike and threatened to cross Swift Creek, the last significant water barrier shielding Petersburg above the Appomattox. This threat evaporated as Confederate forces from Richmond engaged the other wing of the Yankee army at Chester Station on May 10. The Federals concentrated their force northward, and for four days – from May 12 to May 16 – gunfire rattled and cannon boomed around the earthworks protecting Drewry's Bluff.

The mounted Federal raiders returned, this time striking at the South Side Railroad. Then, incredibly, the outnumbered Confederates rolled the enemy back into the Bermuda Hundred peninsula. They frantically scratched a line of trenches across its relatively narrow neck, effectively blocking any further westward movement by Butler's men.

Among the Petersburg soldiers killed during this period was Julian Ruffin, a gunner in Martin's Battery. His body was brought home, where Bessie Callender was among the mourners. "There were no pall bearers," she recalled, "only a few old men and Mrs. Pickrell and myself helped to lift the body in a hearse; only one buggy to follow, the others walked over the hills. I never saw a worse storm than came on when we were in Blandford [cemetery]. We all took refuge in the old church. Thunder and lightning were severe; at the same time shelling was going on at the Point of Rocks on the Appomattox River. It was hard to tell the thunder from the shelling."

Former Virginia governor Henry A. Wise now directed the city's defenses. He found himself in charge of a patchwork force made up of two thin veteran units, one light artillery battery, and two battalions of town militia—perhaps a thousand men in all. Wise was convinced that the greatest threat came from the Union troops at City Point, so he posted most of his command along the eastern Dimmock line to block the direct routes from that quarter.

The optimistic were willing to believe that the worst danger had passed by early June. Butler remained bottled and inactive in Bermuda Hundred. The main combat was north of the James, where the Union Army of the Potomac and the Confederate Army of Northern Virginia had been slugging it out since May 5. Many citizen-soldiers began taking unauthorized furloughs to attend to business in town. During a surprise visit to Major Fletcher H. Archer's militia camp, General Wise asked for the unit's commander and was told he was away in Petersburg. "Yes," Wise fumed, "and if the enemy were to come, you would all be there in less time than it would take a cannon ball to reach there."

*   *   *

"The morning of June 9th came quietly [in Petersburg]," remembered Bessie Callender. Anne Banister recollected the start of this day with a touch more poetry: "The sun had risen that morning over the sleepy old town brightly and except for anxious thoughts of the absent ones, all hearts were happy and bright as the day." Sarah Pryor's first impressions were olfactory ones: "The magnolia grandiflora was in full flower, bee- haunted honey-locusts perfumed the warm air, almost extinguishing the peachy odor of the microphylla roses, graceful garlands of jessamine hung over the trellised front porches."

It was about 9:00 a.m.

Recalled Fanny Waddell, "[A] sound broke upon our ears which palsied our very hearts. It was the sullen roar of cannon and musketry along our lines, and the tolling of the City Hall bell, the signal which summoned grandsires and boys to the defence of their homes." "[Every] bell in the town began to toll and to clang," seconded Anne Banister, "until every household was aroused and alarmed to know what could be the matter."

Standing in the doorway of her home, located on south Jefferson Street along Petersburg's southern heights, Bessie Callender asked a friend what was happening. "There is a heavy force advancing up the Jerusalem Plank Road and few of the home guard are there to prevent their taking the town," was the chilling reply.

Men who had been going about their normal routines dropped everything, grabbed the antique firearms they had been issued, and hurried over crossroads and paths to rally at Major Archer's camp, about two miles out the Jerusalem Plank Road from the city limits. Banker William C. Banister, though too old for military service and nearly deaf, hefted his musket to join the trickle of men, explaining, "This is no time for anyone to stand back." The others who moved toward the threatened point included Anthony Keiley, a young lawyer and legislator who was exempt from military service; Raleigh Colston, a Confederate officer in town awaiting reassignment; druggists George B. Jones and Francis Major; and Bessie Callender's husband, David. The youngest among this scratch force was fourteen; at sixty-one, William Banister was the oldest. By 10:00 a.m. those prepared to fight had cleared the streets. The city now belonged to the women, children, and men who were not able or willing to take up arms.

The next hours passed slowly. It was, Fanny Waddell remembered, a "long weary day." She lay at home in bed, sick with fever, listening. "I could hear the roar and the din of the fierce conflict going on at our very doors nearly; sometimes the firing would be so near, our hearts would stand still expecting every minute to see the enemy rush in."

After watching her husband troop off toward the Jerusalem Plank Road, Bessie Callender waited fretfully for news. A slave who had been working outside in the garden came indoors sometime between noon and 1:00 p.m. and exclaimed, "Missus, don't you hear firing where Master is?" Bessie went out into the garden, the servant following. "Missus," he said, "the Yankees are very near here. Don't you hear them cheering? I see them coming back of the reservoir." If correct, this meant that the enemy riders had overwhelmed the militia line and were entering Petersburg itself. Bessie Callender returned inside and climbed the stairs to an upper window with a commanding view of the open ground east of the reservoir. "I saw that it was true," she remembered thinking, "that the enemy was near the city . . . . I knew the men I saw were Federal soldiers by the caps they wore, our men wearing slouch hats." She ran from the house to spread the alarm.

Other people were gathering near the city waterworks, anxious for news. Then, dramatically, help began to arrive. Graham's Virginia Battery had force-marched seven miles from Port Walthall Junction, and its commander, Captain Edward Graham, was in no mood for polite behavior. Lossie Hill was one of the civilians who scattered frantically as Graham's gunners careened along Bollingbrook and Sycamore streets. "I thought I would be run over," she recalled. "Capt. Ned Graham seeing me, and possibly others in the way, impatiently said to his men, 'Damn the women! Run over them if they don't get out of the way!'"

In E. O. Hinton's drugstore, on the corner of Sycamore and Lombard streets, several city officials had gathered to discuss matters. One of them, Thomas Campbell, scoffed at the idea that a large Federal force could be on the plank road and warranted that if he had 2,500 men, he would "drive every Yankee this side of City Point into [the] James River before sunset." A messenger from the front appeared at that moment and shouted, "Gentlemen, hell is to pay! The Yankees in considerable force have advanced...on the Jerusalem Plank Road, [and] have broken our lines." The discussion group scattered, "and Tom Campbell vanished like a sora," a skittish marsh bird.

Druggist Hinton ran outside in time to see Graham's battery rattle past. He was startled to see one of the cannon barrels slide off its wheels and tumble into a heap. The frantic gunners clambered over the wreckage, replaced a coupling pin, and, Hinton remembered with proud wonder, "on went the gun seemingly as rapidly as before." Hardly had Graham's dust settled when elements of Colonel Dennis D. Ferebee's 4th North Carolina Cavalry, also detached from Bermuda Hundred, galloped by on their way toward the broken lines. Riding with them was Brigadier General James Dearing. These horsemen, and Graham's cannoneers, represented all the help Beauregard could provide in response to Henry Wise's urgent requests for reinforcements. Minutes afterward, Hinton continued, "the welcome booming of the artillery . . . showed that Graham . . . was at work with his guns." Graham's and Dearing's bold defense southeast of town along Lieutenant Run stopped a Federal thrust westward from the Jerusalem Plank Road. A second Yankee group pushing northward along the lane collided with a scratch force of convalescents and veteran units hustled over from the eastern Dimmock line. This swarming defense not only halted the hesitant probe but turned it back on its tracks. By 3:00 p.m., the firing had died down to an occasional shot, and then the blue-coated raiders were gone.

It would be afterwards determined that three strong Union columns had threatened Petersburg this day. A 5,300-man infantry force led by Major General Quincy A. Gillmore moved against the Dimmock line from the northeast, following the City Point road and railroad. These Yankees drew up menacingly before the Confederate earthworks, but beyond some exploratory forays against the line, there was no serious assault. A second body of infantry approached from the east, along Jordan Point Road. This force, made up of 1,300 black soldiers, also did little more than demonstrate. For all intents and purposes, the fighting northeast and east of town was over by noon.

It was around that time when a third Federal column—a 1,300-man cavalry command led by Brigadier General August V. Kautz, which had swung wide to the east and south—pushed north along the Jerusalem Plank Road. Kautz's leading elements hit the town militia guarding the Dimmock line near the point where it crossed the plank road, at Battery 27, not far from Rives' Farm. Major Archer's civilians held their line against those first probings, but a coordinated Union assault at around 1:15 p.m. collapsed the defenses like a row of dominoes. However, Archer's stubborn stand bought enough time for Henry Wise to detach three companies of the veteran 46th Virginia and a detachment of the 7th Confederate Cavalry from the eastern Dimmock line to counter the threat. The citizen-soldiers of Petersburg had made this possible, but at a terrible cost: of the 125 or so who made their stand near Battery 27, fifteen were killed, eighteen wounded, and forty-five captured.

Raleigh Colston, Francis Major, and David Callender survived the action. Anthony Keiley, the exempt Confederate politician, was among those taken prisoner. The list of the dead included John E. Friend, druggist George Jones, and William Banister. It was said that the latter's deafness prevented him from hearing demands to surrender and he fought until the Yankees shot him down. Anne Banister was standing on her porch with her mother and sister "when my uncle . . . drove up in a wagon with my father's lifeless body shot through the head, his gray hair dabbled in blood . . . . [In] a few seconds [my mother] . . . was kneeling by my father in such grief as I had never seen before." Anne's mother was not alone in her sorrow. Recalled Charles Friend, "That evening universal mourning was over the town, for the young and old were lying dead in many homes."

The funerals began the next day and continued into Saturday. Dr. John Herbert Claiborne, a Petersburg native and director of the city's military hospitals, wrote to his wife on Sunday, "Yesterday was a gloomy day here—funerals all day and the enemy constantly looked for in force."

Federal reports claimed to have battled forces many times larger than were actually present, and coordination among the three attacking columns was virtually nonexistent. In a lengthy postwar defense of his actions, Brigadier General Kautz noted the irony that at the very moment his cavalrymen were breaking through the Rebel defenses, Major General Gillmore was marching away from the fighting. It took a teenage Petersburg girl named Margaret Stanly Beckwith to best sum it up, when she wrote: "The hand of Providence was with us."

The surprise victory energized Brigadier General Wise, who, in his Special Orders No. 11, proclaimed, "Petersburg is to be and shall be defended on her outer walls, on her inner lines, at her corporation bounds, on every street, and around every temple of God and altar of man, in her every heart, until the blood of that heart is spilt. Roused by this spirit to this pitch of resolution, we will fight the enemy at every step, and Petersburg is safe."

Wise's order was dated June 12, 1864.

Chapter 2

"It was a marvel of a move"

June 12 - 14, 1864

Ulysses S. Grant
Final Report of Operations, March 1864 - May 1865

The movement of the Army of the Potomac commenced early on the morning of the 4th of May, [1864,] under the immediate direction and orders of Major-General Meade. . . . Early on the 5th the advance corps. . . . met and engaged the enemy outside his intrenchments near Mine Run. The battle raged furiously all day. . . .

The battle of the Wilderness was renewed by us at 5 o'clock on the morning of the 6th, and continued with unabated fury until darkness set in, each army holding substantially the same position that they had on the evening of the 5th. . . . On the night of the 7th the march was commenced toward Spotsylvania Court-House, the Fifth Corps moving on the most direct road. . . . On the 8th General Warren met a force of the enemy which had been sent out to oppose and delay his advance, to gain time to fortify the line taken up at Spotsylvania. . . . The 9th, 10th, and 11th were spent in maneuvering and fighting, without decisive results. . . . Early on the morning of the 12th a general attack was made on the enemy in position. . . . But the resistance was so obstinate that the advantage gained did not prove decisive. The 13th, 14th, 15th, 16th, 17th, and 18th were consumed in maneuvering and awaiting the arrival of re-enforcements from Washington. Deeming it impracticable to make any further attack upon the enemy at Spotsylvania Court-House, orders were issued . . . with a view to a movement to the North Anna. . . . The Fifth Corps reached the North Anna on the afternoon of the 23d, closely followed by the Sixth Corps. The Second and Ninth Corps got up about the same time . . .

Finding the enemy's position on the North Anna stronger than either of his previous ones, I withdrew on the night of the 26th to the north bank of the North Anna, and moved via Hanovertown to turn the enemy's position by his right. . . . On the 29th and 30th we advanced, with heavy skirmishing, to the Hanover Court-House and Cold

Harbor road, and developed the enemy's position north of the Chickahominy. . . . On the 31st . . . General Sheridan . . . reached Cold Harbor, and held it until relieved by the Sixth Corps and General Smith's command, which had just arrived, via White House, from General Butler's army.

On the 1st day of June an attack was made . . . by the Sixth Corps and the troops under General Smith. . . . This resulted in our carrying and holding the enemy's first line of works. . . . The 2d was spent in getting troops into position for an attack on the 3d. On the 3d of June we again assaulted the enemy's works. . . . In this attempt our loss was heavy, while that of the enemy, I have reason to believe, was comparatively light.

I was still in a condition to either move by his left flank and invest Richmond from the north side, or continue my move by his right flank to the south side of the James. . . . I . . . determined . . . to move the army to the south side of the James River. . . . The movement from Cold Harbor commenced after dark on the evening of the 12th.

*   *   *

More than a hundred thousand Union soldiers were moving along dusty roads on the hot night of June 12. The entire Army of the Potomac, wrote one New Hampshire soldier, "was on a wild, night tramp to the James River." For a few tense hours, everything hinged on the actions of a few Federals standing near the north end of a burned Virginia bridge. Their mood was as sour as the smell of the nearby swamplands. Men from Brigadier General James H. Wilson's cavalry division were to cross the Chickahominy River at Long Bridge to screen the advance of Major General Gouverneur Warren's Fifth Corps. The Federal riders, under the command of Colonel George H. Chapman, arrived soon after dark to find that work had not even begun on the pontoon bridge that was needed for them to pass over the river. As Wilson remembered it, the engineer "officer in charge of the pontoons seemed somewhat timid," and "General Warren...would give him no assistance." Lieutenant Colonel Ira Spaulding of the engineers saw it differently, later writing, "Reports as to the nature of the crossing were conflicting, and the enemy's sharpshooters being in possession of the south bank, it was difficult to ascertain the facts." Fifth Corps staff officers had reported that only a hundred feet of stream needed to be spanned at this point, but engineers who had scouted the location "were confident that there were two streams, with an island between." "The latter opinion proved correct," Spaulding added.

The two officers in immediate command of the site began to work together. Major George W. Ford put one of his wooden pontoon boats in the water, manned by a detail of engineers. Colonel Chapman ordered his men to

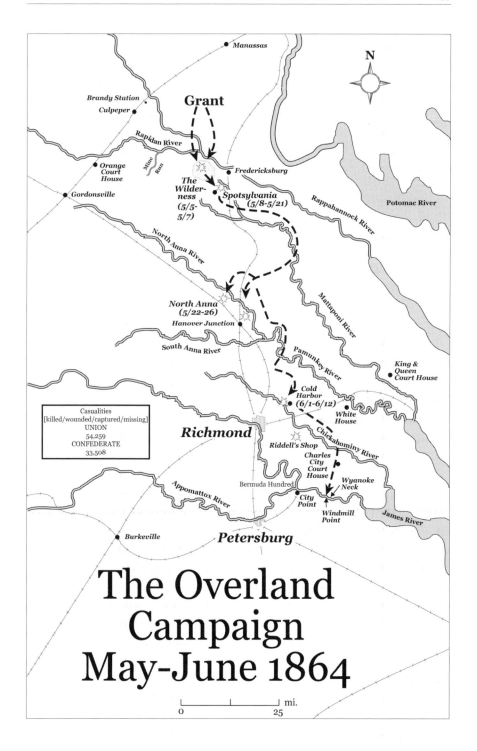

N

Manassas

Brandy Station
Culpeper

Grant

Rapidan River

Orange
Court
House

Mine Run

Fredericksburg

Gordonsville

The
Wilder-
ness
(5/5-
5/7)

Spotsylvania
(5/8-5/21)

Rappahannock River

Potomac River

North Anna River

North Anna
(5/22-26)

Hanover Junction

Mattaponi River

South Anna River

Pamunkey River

King &
Queen
Court House

Cold
Harbor
(6/1-6/12)

Casualities
[killed/wounded/captured/missing]
UNION
54,259
CONFEDERATE
33,508

Richmond

White
House

Riddell's Shop

Chickahominy River

Charles
City
Court
House

Appomattox River

Bermuda Hundred

Wyanoke
Neck

City
Point

Windmill
Point

James River

Burkeville

Petersburg

The Overland
Campaign
May-June 1864

0   25   mi.

dismount at the same time, sending the 22nd New York on a flanking swing above Long Bridge, while a squad from the 3rd Indiana crossed with the engineers. A second boatload of pontoniers and cavalrymen was almost over when the Confederates realized what was happening. For perhaps twenty minutes flashes of gunfire sparkled in the night. One of the Hoosiers later described the firing as "like shaking a pepper-box." The Indiana troopers scrambled ashore on the far bank, formed a line of battle, and cleared away the Tarheel pickets.

Now the engineers got busy. One group dragged three pontoons across the island to bridge the south branch of the river. The remaining engineers corduroyed the approaches to the north branch, cleared away the debris of the old bridge, anchored their wood pontoons in place, and laid the flooring. The remainder of Colonel Chapman's brigade crossed the Chickahominy at midnight; right behind them were the waiting columns of Warren's Fifth Corps. Grant's movement to the James was under way.

Ulysses Grant had made his decision to move south of the James on June 5, two days after his bloody failure at Cold Harbor. In a communication that day to Henry Halleck in Washington, Grant rejected the suggestion that he place the army between Lee's men and Washington. He also instructed Phil Sheridan to take most of his cavalry on a raid against Confederate rail lines northwest of Richmond as a diversionary action. Sheridan departed on June 7, leaving behind just Wilson's division to scout and screen for the infantry.

The plan Grant had determined to follow was a daunting one, requiring disengagement along an almost ten-mile front, a march of nearly fifty miles across swampy, ravine-rippled ground, and the bridging of a tidal river at a point where it was a half-mile wide. To further complicate matters, the crossing place could be reached by Confederate gunboats operating out of Richmond.

Grant dispatched his aides Cyrus Comstock and Horace Porter on June 6 to coordinate the planned movement with Benjamin Butler, whose army held positions south of the James, at Bermuda Hundred and City Point. The lieutenant general instructed George Meade on June 9 to have his Chief of Engineers, Major James C. Duane, "select and intrench a line in the rear of the position at Cold Harbor, to be held while the army was withdrawing." Duane finished the job on June 11. Grant promptly ordered Meade to see "that all preparations may be made for the move tomorrow night."

Robert E. Lee was anticipating the move even before Grant finalized his decision. He warned his corps commanders as early as June 4 that the enemy "is preparing to leave us tonight, and I fear will cross the Chickahominy." Lee's only hope was to catch the Union army in motion. "General Lee is exceedingly anxious to be advised of any movement the enemy may undertake," a First Corps circular noted on June 7. His intentions once the Federal withdrawal was detected had been explained to one of his corps commanders three days earlier. The instant that Grant's army was discovered to be leaving its trenches, Lee would move "down and attack him with our whole force, provided we could catch him in the act of crossing [the Chickahominy]."

Even as he waited for Grant to make his move, Lee's attention was also on the Shenandoah Valley, where Federal activities so threatened the Confederate breadbasket that help was urgently required. Lee sent off 2,100 men under Major General John C. Breckinridge on June 7. Wade Hampton rode out of camp two days later with most of the Confederate cavalry to intercept Sheridan's raiders. Richmond continued its pressure on Lee to send even more men north. Lee grumbled in a June 11 note to Jefferson Davis that it would take at least a corps to properly do the job. He would release that many men if Richmond so ordered, but warned, "I think that is what the enemy would desire." Nevertheless, the next day Lee issued instructions to Jubal Early "to move, with the 2nd. corps, to the Shenandoah Valley." Early's men set out on the morning of June 13.

Horace Porter and Cyrus Comstock returned from their reconnaissance south of the James early that same morning. The two could not give their reports to Grant fast enough to suit him. Porter later reflected that "the general showed the only anxiety and nervousness of manner he had ever manifested on any occasion."

While the music of Federal brass bands "resounded along the whole line," Warren's Fifth Corps began its march southward at around 6:00 p.m. on June 12. His men had been given the assignment of protecting the vulnerable right flank of the multi-pronged Union advance to the James. "With frequent delays we marched to the Chickahominy," recalled Charles E. Davis of the 13th Massachusetts, "where we waited for two hours until a pontoon bridge across the river was completed." A reporter traveling with the corps reminded his readers that the Chickahominy "is a sluggish and muddy stream, resembling a Louisiana bayou more than a river....It runs in the midst of a morass almost as dense as an Indian jungle."

Once over, Brigadier General Samuel Crawford's division, preceded by Chapman's cavalry, swung west, skirting the southern reaches of White Oak Swamp. It was a part of Grant's plan to feint toward Richmond with a small force while the bulk of the army moved quickly to the north bank of the James. Near the intersection of the road from White Oak Bridge, Crawford's men formed a line of battle, threw up breastworks, and endured an enemy shelling. "Our action, of course," noted John H. Dusseault, a Massachusetts soldier, "was a bluff."

Covered by Warren's and Wilson's men, the rest of the Army of the Potomac went into motion on the night of June 12. Major General William F. "Baldy" Smith's Eighteenth Corps moved east to White House, where the men would board river transports for Bermuda Hundred. Private George Buck never forgot the march. "Rapid travelling in the sultry heat induced profuse perspiration, which forming a combination with the dense, suffocating dust, literally encased the men in an earthen armor, and the horrible odors from the dead mules and horses scattered along the road was such to make an occasional breath of fresh air a heavenly luxury."

Hancock's and Wright's men pulled out of their positions soon after dark and fell back to the holding line established by Major Duane. This was abandoned beginning at around 11:00 p.m., when the Second Corps followed in Warren's wake toward the Chickahominy. A short time later, Wright's men moved out. Covering the rear of the withdrawing infantry was another of Wilson's brigades. Wright's destination was Jones Bridge, four miles downstream from Long Bridge. Jones Bridge also had to be rebuilt. Federal engineers began work on the afternoon of June 13 and were open for business an hour and a quarter later.

Once "Baldy" Smith had cleared the roads, Major General Ambrose Burnside's Ninth Corps eased out of its trenches, holding the right flank of the army, and followed the Sixth Corps toward Jones Bridge. "Though the moonlight cheered us," wrote a soldier in the 7th Rhode Island, "the march was unsteady and severe because of our wagon train."

The movement was well under way when Grant joined it. Horace Porter observed: "Although there was moonlight, the dust rose in such dense clouds that it was difficult to see more than a short distance, and the march was exceedingly tedious and uncomfortable."

The withdrawal was carried out smoothly and quietly for the most part. A Connecticut man noted approvingly that "it was not now the custom to inform the rank and file, and the newspapers, and the enemy, of intended movements."

Nearly forgotten amid the great movements of the Union army were the small squads of pickets that held the main trenches until the very last moment.

A detail of troops from the 66th New York and 116th Pennsylvania along Hancock's old Cold Harbor lines "was not notified nor relieved until the army had been gone for some hours." Lieutenant Colonel Hammill, the picket officer, succeeded in forming his men in the dark and, before dawn, led them on a forced march to rejoin the corps.

The newly arrived 187th Pennsylvania, posted along the Chickahominy, was also forgotten in the shuffle. "The pickets could hear our troops moving all that night…but no one notified them to leave." Lieutenant John E. Reilly gathered his men and found a main road, where he had to guess the direction, as the passing wagons had completely obliterated all footprints.

In was a nerve-racking march. At one point a party of Confederate riders threatened to overrun the small column, but it was scared off by a well-aimed volley. Not until nearly midnight did Reilly and his forgotten force find the army. The young officer was spotted by the captain in charge of the division pickets, whose job it was to withdraw the men. Recalled one Pennsylvanian, "He met Lieutenant Reilly with the demand to know where he had been. Reilly's answer was that he had been doing his duty, and that was more than he, the Captain[,] could say."

Robert E. Lee learned at daybreak on June 13 that Grant's army had slipped away during the night. According to Eppa Hunton, one of George Pickett's brigadiers, "It was said that General Lee was in a furious passion—one of the few times during the war. When he did get mad he was mad all over."

Artilleryman Robert Stiles put it this way, "When we waked on the morning of the 13th and found no enemy in our front we realized that a new element had entered into this move—the element of uncertainty…. [Even] Marse Robert, who knew everything knowable, did not appear to know just what his old enemy proposed to do."

Lee's first reaction was to cover the approaches to Richmond south of the Chickahominy. A Georgia soldier named Joseph Fuller scribbled in his diary this day, "At 8 o'clock a.m. we received orders to march immediately." The Army of Northern Virginia—now reduced to just Anderson's First Corps and A. P. Hill's Third—crossed the Chickahominy, moved onto the Charles City Road, and headed toward Riddell's Shop. Remembered J. F. J. Caldwell of McGowan's Brigade, "The day was intensely hot, so that it required unusual vigilance in officers, and unusual exertion in the men, to execute the frequently repeated order to close up and keep in four ranks. As it was, a good many straggled."

"When a great army moves, it fills all the roads," wrote correspondent Charles Page. "It seeks every country cross-road, every farm by-road and uses it, no matter how circuitous the road, no matter what direction it pursues; so that it intersects some road that does make toward the right point, it must be used. Troops often march ten or fifteen miles, and the point reached shall not be five from that of starting."

Almost all the Union commands traveled hard this day. A weary sergeant in Hancock's corps remembered, "It was an awful tramp for us and half the boys' feet were blistered." The forced pace also extracted its deadly price. In the 8th New York Heavy Artillery they mourned Lieutenant Henry R. Swan who died of lung congestion aggravated by the exertion. According to a letter to the regiment's hometown newspaper, he "gave out from sheer exhaustion, and was put into an ambulance, but died during the night." Crossing at Long Bridge after Warren, the Second Corps pushed on southward, and by late afternoon it was drawn up in a defensive position near Wilcox's Landing, on the north side of the James.

Surgeon George Stevens, marching with Wright's Sixth Corps, later wrote that "the men almost suffocated with the dust, which hung over the column like a huge cloud, no halt was made at noon, and the men, deprived of their coffee, choked with dust, and burned with heat, marched wearily toward night."

Wright's men were the first over the Chickahominy at Jones Bridge, followed by Burnside's corps. The crossing was completed by 10:00 a.m. on June 14, at which time orders were given to disassemble the army's bridge. Similar instructions had already been carried out upstream at Long Bridge, where the last elements of Hancock's corps had trooped across late in the afternoon of June 13. A member of the Federal rear guard recalled that as soon as the pontoons had been pulled to the south bank, "horsemen appeared on the [north] shore and fired at us."

Grant's headquarters that night were at Wilcox's Landing, where the view of all the Union activity was invigorating. A Pennsylvanian riding with Grant's escort remembered, "The sight of that grand river—it was a splendid day—the gunboats, steamers and sailing vessels, was a novel sensation. We gazed upon the scene with as much joy and eagerness as if for the first time in our lives." Another member of the headquarters' escort, this one from the infantry, recalled, "It was really a treat, a transformation of things generally, to see this

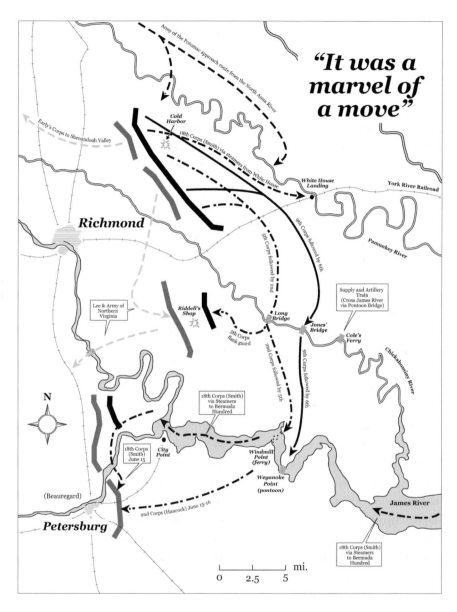

river, with its steamboats and gunboats steaming up and down, and the Stars and Stripes streaming above them."

Army engineer Major Nathaniel Michler had earlier in the day selected a defensive line to cover the proposed Jamea River crossings. General Hancock's men entrenched this line briefly before moving on to their disembarkation point, at which time General Warren's lead elements replaced them. A reporter traveling with Grant watched as the lieutenant general was informed that the passage of the supply wagons would be delayed a several hours. When a member of the headquarters staff began to complain loudly about the delay, Grant silenced him with an unfinished sentence, saying, "If we have nothing worse than this —"

The great army supply train was traveling on a track well to the east of the infantry columns. Grant's planners had hoped that this caravan could cross the Chickahominy at Windsor Shades, but when this was deemed impractical, men and equipment began to gather at Cole's Ferry, not far from the mouth of the Chickahominy. Work on a pontoon bridge here was finished after dark on June 14, and the slow passage of the wagons began. One Sixth Corps soldier who was assigned to protect the train later estimated that it "occupied fourteen hours in passing us." The rear guard and trains were over by June 16 and the temporary span was dismantled.

The Army of the Potomac's objective was now the vital rail hub at Petersburg. Hopes were high. "The capture of Petersburg," wrote Andrew Humphreys, "would leave but one railroad in the hands of the Confederates.... Following the possession of Petersburg would be the turning of Beauregard's intrenchments in front of Butler and an advance toward Richmond."

Robert E. Lee's only solid contact with the withdrawing Federals took place on the southern fringes of White Oak Swamp, where Samuel Crawford's infantrymen and Wilson's cavalry were covering the roads leading east.

Prowling toward Richmond along the Charles City Road at around noon on June 13, elements from Colonel Chapman's Union brigade "came upon the enemy strongly posted in a belt of timber in front of Riddell's Shop." These Virginia and South Carolina troopers from Brigadier General Martin W. Gary's cavalry brigade were, in Chapman's words, "disposed to contest the position with obstinacy." It took a dismounted charge by the 3rd Indiana and 8th New York to dislodge the Rebels.

Gary's men fell back toward Richmond until infantry support arrived from two of A. P. Hill's brigades. Hill's men made contact with Colonel Chapman's line—which now consisted of the 1st Vermont, 3rd Indiana, and 8th New York, supported by the 1st New Hampshire, the 22nd New York, and artillery from Major Robert H. Fitzhugh's reserve brigade—at about 6:00 p.m. According to adjutant Graham Daves of the 22nd North Carolina, some of the regiment "passed at one time over an open knoll, which had been cleared for artillery two years before, where they received the full fire of Wilson's men and lost heavily, but still pressed on."

Chapman's riders retreated to the entrenched position held by Crawford's infantrymen, and the two sides contented themselves with some long-distance shelling and sniping. Federal losses for the day were put at three hundred killed or wounded.

In his postwar memoirs, Union cavalry commander Wilson remembered this day as "a period of extraordinary anxiety and hard work, during which much ammunition was expended and much noise made."

Lee informed the Confederate Secretary of War, James Seddon, of the Riddell's Shop fighting at 10:00 p.m. on June 13. Early the next morning the Federals were found to have faded back from their entrenchments, and the few prisoners who were picked up reported that their comrades were heading toward Harrison's Landing, a position fortified by McClellan in 1862.

Lee weighed Grant's options. He might pull the Federal army back to those old earthworks and hold them with the aid of gunboats on the James. Or he could be planning to move troops south across the river "with the view of getting possession of Petersburg before we can reinforce it." Lee was sure enough of his conclusions by 4:00 p.m. to inform Richmond that Grant "will cross the James River."

The Army of the Potomac began its crossing of the James River at 11:10 a.m. on June 14. Troops from Major General David Birney's Second Corps division clambered onto a motley collection of river craft and were carried from Wilcox's Landing to Windmill Point. It was a cumbersome process. "The means of crossing were very limited," noted Meade's chief of staff, Andrew Humphreys, "and the landing places, wharfs, and roads were incomplete." The transfer of Hancock's corps and four batteries of artillery finished at 5:00 a.m. the next day. "Considering the facilities at hand," reported a Hancock aide, "the troops have been transported across the stream with remarkable promptitude and success." A member of the 108th New York recalled the trip: "It was a grand moonlight evening, and as the boys had not enjoyed the exquisite pleasure of being afloat on the broad bosom of the deep for a long time, their exhilaration, caused by the fresh water zephyrs, was manifested by long and loud cheers."

The defensive pocket around the embarkation area contracted as each corps left the north bank for the south. Major Michler's first position, marked out on June 13, stretched almost twelve miles—from Herring Creek near the old Harrison's Landing line to the upper part of Wyanoke Neck. Three days later the engineer chose a shorter line "to be held by the Sixth Corps to cover the crossing of the remainder of the army and the supply trains." The new position covered perhaps four miles, from the mouth of Queen's Creek to Tyler's Mill.

Work on the very long pontoon bridge across the James began near the tip of Wyanoke Neck at 4:00 p.m. on June 14. A force of 450 army engineers, working from both shores, stretched the floating structure toward mid-stream. The James here was between twelve and fifteen fathoms deep, and the difference between high and low tide was about four feet. Some 101 wooden pontoons were used to cover the span's 2,100 feet. Several large schooners were anchored upriver and lashed to the bridge to brace it against the powerful river current. A stretch of a hundred feet in the center of the pontoon bridge was ingeniously designed to be detached and floated aside to allow gunboats and transports to pass through. Five stone-laden ships were sunk well upstream to prevent Confederate ironclads from interdicting the crossing, a landlubberly act that greatly irritated the USN admiral in charge who "spoke of it as a slur on the navy, as if it could not keep back the rebel war-ships."

The bridge was finished at around 11:00 p.m., though work on the equally important approaches took another four hours. Recalled one of Burnside's artillerymen, "As soon as it was completed the Ninth Corps trains and artillery commenced crossing, followed by the trains and artillery of the Fifth and Sixth corps." One division of the Sixth Corps and all of the Ninth also crossed the river on foot.

Pennsylvanian Allen Albert never forgot the crossing. "The approaches to the river were alive with troops marching here and there or waiting their turn to cross. Drums and brass bands filled the air with martial music." Fifth Corps artillery chief Charles Wainwright found the bridge "very steady," but a Ninth Corps gunner readily admitted that he and his comrades "felt better when we were on terra firma again."

There were problems. Surgeon John H. Brinton was aboard a medical steamer that snagged a section of the bridge. Brinton later recalled that this caused the craft to begin tearing some of the pontoons from their anchorage, "and doing not a little harm in spite of our best efforts.... [Chief Engineer Henry] Benham, who was a high-tempered man...was greatly incensed...and seeing me on the deck of the steamer, in uniform, and apparently in charge, he became fiercely enraged and excited. 'Shoot him, shoot him, shoot the scoundrel,' he shouted. I called to him by name, but he was so angry it was no use, so I prudently disappeared." An army nurse named Anna Holstein sailed past the crossing point on the evening of June 15. She recalled that "signal lights were seen flashing upon the hill-tops…; the shipping was beautifully illuminated with various colored lanterns, and though in the midst of war, the river with its numerous lights, had a gay, holiday look."

The period of June 13-16 was a difficult, anxious time for Robert E. Lee. Most of the reports he received told him what areas Grant had abandoned but offered little real evidence of where he was going. Even though he suspected that Grant's plan was to cross the James, Lee hesitated to commit his army fully until the facts were beyond doubt. General P. G. T. Beauregard was sending increasingly frantic messages from Petersburg for help, but he had been doing that since the current campaign began, and he had yet to offer any firm proof that the Army of the Potomac was in his front. Lee had to face the possibility that Grant's intention was to mount a two-pronged push against Richmond, with the Army of the James south of that river and the Army of the Potomac north of it. Still, Lee detached Hoke's division on June 15 and sent it to reinforce Beauregard.

Lee received a dispatch from Beauregard early the next morning containing the dramatic news that the Creole officer was abandoning his lines across the neck of Bermuda Hundred, opposite Butler, and moving his entire force to cover Petersburg. Nothing in Beauregard's previous communications had suggested that such a high-risk move was in the offing, but Lee now reacted quickly by sending Pickett's Division to cover the abandoned lines. Lee finally crossed to the opposite bank of the James River shortly before 9:40 a.m. He had failed to catch Grant's army on the move. "Thus the last, and perhaps the best, chances of Confederate success…were lost…," bemoaned artillery officer E. P. Alexander. Lee, in an unguarded moment a week earlier, had shared his anxieties with corps commander Jubal Early. "We must destroy this Army of Grant's before he gets to the James River," Lee had said. "If he gets there it will become a siege, and then it will be a mere question of time."

"The movement of the army to the James was one of the most brilliant and successful of the war," declared the historian of one Ninth Corps regiment. Another soldier-historian exclaimed, "It was a marvel of a move." "This memorable operation," Horace Porter echoed, "when examined in all its details, will furnish one of the most valuable and instructive studies in logistics." Reporters covering the movement were almost at a loss for words, one branding it "unparalleled," another praising "the boldness and audacity of its conception and execution."

Substantially all of the Army of the Potomac was south of the James by the morning of June 17. The success of the whole venture amazed everyone, even those most familiar with Grant. War Department observer Charles Dana expressed a sense of this when he wired a progress report to Secretary of War Edwin Stanton on the morning of June 15. Dana began his message, "All goes on like a miracle."

Grant himself had not been idle. He took a steamer upriver on June 14 to confer with Butler about the combined actions to be mounted against Petersburg, and then returned that same day to Wilcox's Landing to oversee operations.

The lieutenant general crossed to the south bank for the final time on June 15, marking the end of his Overland campaign. Before he left he stood for a while on a bluff overlooking the busy scene of troops, wagons, and ships below. "It was a matchless pageant that could not fail to inspire all beholders with the grandeur of achievement and the majesty of military power," recalled his aide Horace Porter. "The man whose genius had conceived and whose skill had executed this masterly movement stood watching the spectacle in profound silence…. After a time he woke from his reverie, mounted his horse, and gave orders to have headquarters ferried across to the south bank of the river."

Part I
ENEMY AT THE GATES

In the trenches at Petersburg: Digging parallels (trenches) near the front. *William Waud*

Chapter 3

"Hold on at all hazards!"

June 15 - 18, 1864

Ulysses S. Grant
Final Report of Operations, March 1864-May 1865

The movement in the Kanawha and Shenandoah Valleys, under General [Franz] Siegel, commenced on the 1st of May. . . . General Siegel moved up the Shenandoah Valley, met the enemy at New Market on the 15th, and after a severe engagement was defeated with heavy loss. . . . Major-General [David] Hunter was appointed to supersede him. . . .

General Hunter immediately took up the offensive, and moving up the Shenandoah Valley, met the enemy on the 5th of June at Piedmont, and . . . defeated him. ... To meet this movement under General Hunter, General Lee sent a force, perhaps equal to a corps, a part of which reached Lynchburg a short time before Hunter. After some skirmishing on the 17th and 18th, General Hunter, owing to a want of ammunition to give battle, retired from the place. Unfortunately, this want of ammunition left him no choice of route for his return but by way of Kanawha. This lost to us the use of his troops for several weeks from the defense of the North. . . .

To return to the Army of the Potomac . . .

Wednesday, June 15

Ulysses S. Grant

The troops no longer cheered him. He had never asked for, or encouraged, their cheers, but they had cheered him anyway. They cheered him after the terrible combat in the Wilderness ended, when his orders were for the army to advance and not retreat. They cheered him at Spotsylvania, despite days of dangerous trench warfare—a cycle broken only by furious assaults that stacked up the dead and wounded on both sides. They cheered him after North Anna, when he led them away from the enemy's formidable earthworks without attacking. But the cheers ended at Cold Harbor.

There was something about the ground there that had made the Confederate trenches seem less dangerous, so Grant insisted upon an all-out assault. On the morning of June 3, some 60,000 blue-coated soldiers charged into a killing ground. Perhaps 7,000 of the Yankees were shot down in the first thirty minutes at Cold Harbor. "Many soldiers expressed freely their scorn of Grant's alleged generalship," John Haley, a Maine soldier, noted in his journal.

That night Grant had confessed his failure to his staff. "I regret this assault more than any one I have ever ordered," he told them. (Afterward, one of his aides observed, the "matter was seldom referred to again in conversation.")

Cold Harbor had been Grant's battle – Meade had seen to that. Two days after it was over, the temperamental commander of the Army of the Potomac confided to an officer that he was fed up with Grant's getting all the credit. Meade, recalled the officer, complained that "he had worked out every plan for every move from the crossing of the Rapidan onward, that the papers were full of the doings of Grant's army, and that he was tired of it, and was determined to let General Grant plan his own battles."

It had taken Grant two days of reflection to chart a new course. Retreat of any kind was not considered. "I shall take no backward steps," he had vowed in mid-May, and he meant it. From the Wilderness to Spotsylvania to North Anna to Cold Harbor, Grant's purpose had been the same: to maneuver Robert E. Lee and the Army of Northern Virginia away from their entrenchments, and to defeat them in a stand-up, open-field fight. That had never happened, however, and Grant now decided to end this deadly dance of death with Lee by striking out for Petersburg.

This time, though, Grant would not pull all the strings. He would issue the orders, but the Army of the Potomac, directed by George Gordon Meade, would carry out these directives.

It was midday, when Grant—having transferred to a steam launch after crossing the James – established headquarters at City Point. Major General William F. "Baldy" Smith, along with 16,000 men from Butler's Army of the James, was attacking the Cockade City a few miles to the southwest. "I believed then," Grant reflected years afterward, "and still believe, that Petersburg could have been easily captured at that time."

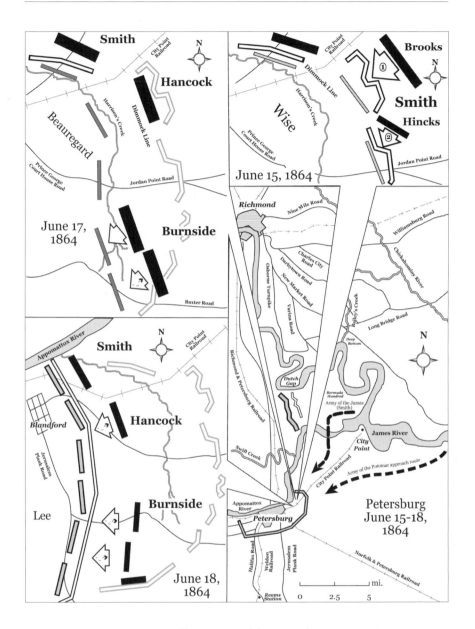

William F. "Baldy" Smith

War offered little mystery to "Baldy" Smith. It was nothing more than a science, and he, in the opinion of many (including himself), was a master scientist.

The curse of Smith's career was the succession of mediocrities he had been forced to serve. He had hungered for an independent command and looked to Grant to provide it. Grant's promotion to direct all the Union armies had come after he broke the Confederate siege of Chattanooga, an operation in which Smith had played an important part. But when orders arrived in April, Smith discovered that he was to be merely a corps commander in Major General Benjamin F. Butler's Army of the James, soon to begin operations against Richmond.

To say that Smith, who had graduated fourth in the West Point class of 1845, despised the crafty, politically powerful Butler would be an understatement. Smith had Grant's ear, and he promptly filled it, saying, "I want to ask you how you can place a man in command of the two army corps, who is as helpless as a child on the field of battle, and as visionary as an opium eater in council?" ("General Smith," Grant later commented in a letter to Henry Halleck, "whilst a very able officer, is obstinate, and likely to condemn whatever is not suggested by himself.")

Butler's campaign against Richmond's southern defenses had been everything Smith had predicted: badly coordinated, poorly conducted, and devoid of substantial results. It mattered not to Smith's way of thinking that as the officer in charge of half of Butler's army, he somehow shared in the blame.

Smith and 12,000 soldiers from the Army of the James had joined the Army of the Potomac in late May at Cold Harbor, just in time to take part in the fighting. Smith found little to like in the way George Meade ran things. Fouled-up orders on June 1 resulted in his men's marching miles in the wrong direction when they were desperately needed at Cold Harbor, and Smith was appalled when he learned what the attack "plan" was for June 3. In his opinion, it "was simply an order to slaughter his best troops." Commanded by Meade to renew the June 3 assault after its bloody repulse, "Baldy" Smith refused point blank. When new orders came on June 11, instructing him to return to Bermuda Hundred, Smith was not sorry to leave. ("Meade is as malignant as he is jealous & as mad as he is either," Smith had groused to a confidant in early April.)

On June 14, Smith and his men had barely returned by means of river transports to Butler's domain when the opportunity he had been seeking presented itself. As Smith recalled, "I arrived at Bermuda Hundred with my aid[e]s about sunset, and was told . . . that I was to proceed at two o'clock a.m. to attack Petersburg."

This time there would be no Ben Butler or George Meade to interfere. This time it would be "Baldy" Smith's show.

P. G. T. Beauregard

Glory had passed through the fingers of Pierre Gustave Toutant Beauregard like fine jeweler's sand. His was a life meant for glory, and he had wandered the Confederacy in search of it. The Creole officer had directed the bombardment of Fort Sumter, and there he began his addiction to fame. Then he was called to Richmond and given command of the Confederate forces near Manassas, Virginia, where he was forced to share the spotlight with another ambitious officer, Joseph E. Johnston.

Manassas had been a great Southern victory, but carping politicians had seen to it that the glory was spread among the senior officers present. Vain and outspoken, Beauregard openly vented his feelings, and in reward was transferred to the West, about as far from Richmond as it was possible to get. Once more Beauregard shared the stage with one of the Confederacy's heroes, this time Albert Sidney Johnston. The two led their barely trained army into the combat holocaust of Shiloh, where nearly 20,000 men of both sides fell in two terrible days. Johnston was killed at the height of the Confederate success; it fell to Beauregard to withdraw the army after Johnston's badly flawed battle plan unraveled.

Acrimonious bickering with subordinates and superiors had marred the next months, and Beauregard had been reassigned to the scene of his unsullied triumph, Charleston. Under his inspired leadership, a major Federal offensive against the city in April 1863 was turned back. Once again his greatness had been made clear. Beauregard now expected to be given command of one of the Confederacy's two major armies.

The orders Beauregard did receive from Jefferson Davis, no friend of his, were almost insulting: he was to take charge of the military department covering North Carolina and Virginia south of the James River. Everyone knew that the decisive actions would take place north of Richmond, not south of it. Even worse, he would again have to share the limelight with a hero of the Confederacy, in this instance Robert E. Lee, an officer whom Beauregard later assessed as having little "Mil[i]t[ar]y foresight or pre-science or great powers of deduction."

Even as Lee's men were grappling with Grant's in the Wilderness on May 5, Ben Butler's Army of the James had landed at Bermuda Hundred, smack between Richmond and Petersburg and within a cannon shot of the vital rail line that supplied both the Confederate capital and the Army of Northern Virginia. For the first few days of this crisis Beauregard remained in North

Carolina, gathering men and material to send north to the fighting. He finally arrived in Petersburg to take personal command on May 10.

The next thirty-six days had been a flurry of frantic maneuvering, furious combat, and petty squabbling as the Creole officer moved men from threatened point to threatened point. Instead of being given the reinforcements he needed, Beauregard was pressured by Richmond to release troops to reinforce Lee, who had taken serious losses during his continuous engagement with Grant's army. Time and again Beauregard used red tape to delay the transfers, but once Butler had been effectively bottled up in Bermuda Hundred, it became much easier for Lee to argue that Beauregard needed fewer men to hold his entrenched line. President Davis agreed, and on May 30 Beauregard grudgingly sent Lee one of his largest veteran units, Major General Robert Hoke's division.

In the stalemate following the June 3 Federal debacle at Cold Harbor, Beauregard had foreseen with startling clarity that he would be the next target. The mishandled June 9 thrust at Petersburg served only to heighten his anxiety, and the telegraph wires to Richmond buzzed with his appeals for more troops. Then Grant's entire army literally disappeared from Lee's front, and the Virginian seemed uncertain of its destination. Soon afterward, the Federal units that had been detached from Butler's Army of the James ("Baldy" Smith's command) rejoined it. Lee may have wondered what Grant was going to do, but Beauregard had no doubts. At 7:00 a.m. on the morning of June 15, he wired Richmond:

> RETURN OF BUTLER'S FORCES SENT TO GRANT . . . RENDERS MY
> POSITION MORE CRITICAL THAN EVER; IF NOT RE-ENFORCED
> IMMEDIATELY ENEMY COULD FORCE MY LINES AT BERMUDA HUNDRED ... OR
> TAKE PETERSBURG. . . . CAN ANYTHING BE DONE IN THE MATTER?

George Gordon Meade

George Meade wanted his army back.

He should have anticipated that Grant would take the Army of the Potomac from him. John Gibbon, a Second Corps division commander, understood the problem: "Gen. Meade occupied a peculiar position at the head of the army. He was a commander directly under a commander, a position at best and under the most favorable circumstances, not a very satisfactory one to fill. . . . [Though] all the details of projected operations are left to the army commander he cannot help but feel that they are under the immediate supervision of another and he must necessarily be shackled and sensible of the fact that he is deprived of that independence and untrammeled authority so necessary to every army commander." Another aide stated the situation even more bluntly with a slip of the pen, heading one set of reports "The Army of the Potomac, commanded by Lieut. Gen. U. S. Grant in person, Major-General Meade second in command."

Second in command. How it stuck in his throat, like a clod of Virginia dirt! Meade remembered how cocksure Grant had been when he came east to face Bobby Lee. The forty bloody days of the Overland Campaign had ended that. "I think Grant has had his eyes opened, and is willing to admit now that Virginia and Lee's army is not Tennessee and [Braxton] Bragg's army," Meade reflected after Cold Harbor. At about the same time, he reacted to an editorial in the *Army Magazine* praising Grant's military genius: "Now to tell the truth, the latter has greatly disappointed me, and since this campaign I really begin to think I am something of a general."

Today Grant had gone on ahead, leaving Meade to oversee the Army of the Potomac's crossing of the James. For the moment, he was alone with his army and able to lose himself in small details. He was still uncertain as to what Grant intended to do with the army once it crossed over, but, he thought with a touch of irritation, Grant would let him know soon enough.

Winfield Scott Hancock

He was a facade—a weary, hurting man trapped within the image of a fearless warrior. He was Hancock the Superb, Hancock the hero of Gettysburg, Hancock the valiant fighter. As U. S. Grant put it, "Hancock is a glorious soldier."

Or had been a glorious soldier. The Overland Campaign finished what a Confederate bullet at Gettysburg had begun. It smothered the fires of ambition and reckless courage that had launched his star on its ascent.

For the past forty days, wherever there had been a tight spot or a need for a decisive stroke, there had been Hancock and his Second Corps. For two terrible days of fighting in the Wilderness, he commanded more than half of Meade's army. Next came Spotsylvania, where Hancock and his men had tense engagements at Todd's Tavern and the Po River and then were engulfed in the nightmare of the Bloody Angle. When Grant decided after Spotsylvania to dangle a corps before Lee as bait, he chose Hancock's Second Corps. After that was North Anna, where, for one heart-stopping afternoon, Hancock and his men were trapped with the river at their backs and Lee's entire army in their front. Unknown to them, Lee had suddenly became too ill to direct the crushing blow, allowing the desperate Federals enough time to entrench and protect themselves. No one could have imagined that things could get worse, but then came Cold Harbor, where Hancock's weary foot cavalry delivered the heaviest assault in that futile action. When someone at Cold Harbor asked Hancock where the Second Corps was, he replied, "It lies buried between the Rapidan and the James."

Hancock was in physical as well as mental distress. That unhealed Gettysburg wound in his groin could be agonizingly painful at times, and his strenuous exertions during the recent campaign had not helped matters. The constant discomfort was like a drug that clouded his thinking and dulled his perceptions.

Fortunately, Hancock's present orders required little analysis. His Second Corps was the first to cross the James River, using a flotilla of Navy ships, river transports, and even some New York ferry boats. It was a tedious process that began on the morning of June 14 and lasted well into the early hours of the next day. As Hancock later recalled, "I had been directed by General Meade ... to hold my troops in readiness to move, and informed that it was probable I would be instructed to march toward Petersburg, and that rations for my command would be sent me from City Point."

But something went wrong. Hancock's dispatches ticked off the delays: at 4:00 a.m. on June 15, "the rations . . . had not yet arrived"; at 6:30 a.m., "no rations." At 9:00 a.m., a rumor that the rations had arrived kept Hancock in place for more than an hour before it was determined to be false. "In consequence," Hancock wrote afterward, "the column did not get in motion until 10:30 a.m."

William F. "Baldy" Smith

A *New York Times* correspondent named Henry J. Winser was near the pontoon bridge spanning the Appomattox River at Point of Rocks, about three and a half miles west of City Point, as Smith's Eighteenth Corps began to cross. He reported that the "air was chilly and a thick mist curled upward from the marshy banks of the stream and floated lazily over the rising ground beyond. Long lines of infantry showed themselves, solemnly issuing out of the mist, and streaming over the hay-carpeted pontoon bridge, which muffled the noise of their marching."

Smith's problems had begun even before his troops arrived from Cold Harbor. His initial orders had called for them to disembark at Bermuda Hundred landing, but once he learned of his new assignment, Smith tried to redirect the transports closer to Point of Rocks. Not every craft received word of the new destination, however, so he eventually found his command scattered at landing places all along the Bermuda Hundred shoreline.

Smith was not pleased. With the transports disgorging their loads at just about any point they chose, "it was impossible for any general to tell what troops he had or would have with him." Still, the prospects of success were intoxicating. His immediate superior, Benjamin Butler, had confidently predicted that "the works protecting Petersburg were not at all formidable" and added that "there was no force of any consequence" defending the city.

The units Smith now commanded consisted of his three-division Eighteenth Corps and 2,500 cavalry led by Brigadier General August V. Kautz. Smith's approach to the Cockade City would be from the northeast. His two white divisions—led by Brigadier General William T. H. Brooks and Brigadier General John H. Martindale—were his power punch. They would advance along the path of the City Point Railroad. Moving on their left would be Smith's all-black division, commanded by Brigadier General Edward W. Hincks, which would march toward Petersburg from City Point following the Jordan Point Road. Kautz's riders were to spread the advancing line to the south and east in order to threaten the enemy positions there.

Kautz's horsemen encountered an unexpected Confederate strong point at Baylor's Farm, several miles northeast of Petersburg, at about 6:00 a.m. Since Hincks's column backed up Kautz here, Smith ordered the hitherto untested black soldiers to clear the way. A portion of the raw force charged without proper supports, only to be smashed by accurate Confederate artillery fire, but another line of black soldiers plunged into the maelstrom and stormed the position, capturing an enemy cannon. A *New York Tribune* reporter, watching the black troops proudly haul away their trophy, wrote that they "fairly hugged it, and feasted their eyes upon it with that kind of satisfaction with which an urchin gloats over his first boots."

The action lasted nearly two hours. This stubborn Confederate defense where no defense had been expected shook Smith's self-confidence. It took another five hours for his force to close up on the main Petersburg defense line. Smith's worries only increased. He nervously messaged General Butler at 1:30 p.m.:

THE FIGHT AT BAYLOR'S HOUSE BROKE UP MY ARRANGEMENTS, SO THAT I
HAVE NOT BEEN ABLE TO STRAIGHTEN MY LINE. . . . HAVE THE
[RAILROAD] CARS I HAVE HEARD ALL DAY BEEN BRINGING [CONFEDERATE]
RE-ENFORCEMENTS [TO PETERSBURG]?

P. G. T. Beauregard

Beauregard's devoted aide Alfred Roman later recalled this period as "never-ending days of unremitting anxiety." As Beauregard himself later summarized the situation: "The Petersburg lines were about seven and a half miles long on the south side of the Appomattox, requiring at least 25,000 men to hold them. On the 15th of June, [Brigadier] General [Henry A.] Wise had still a part of his forces on the north side of the Appomattox, the remainder being in the lines facing the approaches from City Point. My headquarters were at Dunlop's house on Swift Creek, about halfway between Howlett's [House] and Petersburg." All told, Beauregard's defensive force manning the Dimmock line consisted of just 2,200 men, concentrated along the eastern four miles of the ten- mile-long earthwork system. By his accounting he was 22,800 men short of what he needed.

This day brought forth a torrent of communications from Beauregard to Richmond, all directed to Jefferson Davis's chief military adviser, Braxton Bragg. Beauregard neglected to send copies of most of these dispatches to Robert E. Lee.

Beauregard reported at 9:30 a.m. that he was shifting Hoke's Division (just returned to him by Lee) from Bermuda Hundred to Petersburg, leaving only one brigade to watch the lines opposite the "bottled" Butler. A quick follow-up message contained the first news Beauregard's scouts had brought him of "Baldy" Smith's slow advance. According to the scouts, the Federals were engaged in an "on to Petersburg" movement. Half an hour later, the general passed along intelligence confirming the river passage of the Yankee Eighteenth Corps from Cold Harbor. Then the simmering pot of anxiety bubbled to crisis.

Beauregard received word from Petersburg at 11:45 a.m. that the city was under heavy attack. To hold both the Bermuda Hundred lines and Petersburg would be, Beauregard believed, impossible. He exhorted Henry Wise to "Hold on at all hazards!" and then he gave Richmond a stark choice: he could save Petersburg or he could save Bermuda Hundred, but not both.

The first message that he copied Lee on this day went out at 1:00 p.m. Beauregard promised to hold the Bermuda Hundred lines only "as long as practicable." Forty-five minutes later, he was again warning that Richmond must choose either Petersburg and Bermuda Hundred. "I fear my present force may prove unequal to hold both," P. G. T. Beauregard declared.

Winfield Scott Hancock

The march of the Second Corps to Petersburg was a slow, dull affair during which very little went right. "It was intensely hot," recalled a Maine soldier, John Day Smith. "The roads were dusty, and the color of the soldiers' uniforms could not be distinguished. The men suffered for lack of water. . . . Many . . . fell out of the ranks, prostrated by the heat." And unbeknownst to Hancock and his staff, the rough maps they had been given were woefully inaccurate. "Consequently," noted Second Corps aide Francis Walker, "Hancock took a road much longer than that which he would have taken if he had simply been told to go to Petersburg." Hancock's wound was bothering him so much that he spent the day laid out in a wagon instead of on horseback. He still had no cause to press his weary men. "So far as he had any reason to think," continued Walker, "it would be sufficient if he brought up his corps, in good condition, in season to go fairly into camp by nightfall."

William F. "Baldy" Smith

At Cold Harbor twelve days earlier Smith's men had been rushed into the attack without adequate preparation or coordination and had been slaughtered. Now Smith prowled the Union positions confronting the Dimmock line, resolved not to let that happen again. "Wherever I went..." he remembered, "I found a heavy cross-fire of artillery, from the enemy, opened. . . . The reconnaissances were necessarily slow, and, while anxious to lose no time, I was yet determined to take no step in the dark to get my command badly repulsed before such works and in wide, open fields."

Smith carried out his task in spite of the fact that he was suffering from dysentery. He had difficulty riding, and the "condition of my head was such that I could not remain in the sun for two minutes without an intense headache."

He concluded his investigations at about 3:00 p.m. and then spent the next two hours visiting his three division headquarters to thoroughly brief his subordinate officers. He was convinced that the formidable Dimmock line was grossly undermanned. Instead of assaulting these strong positions with heavy columns that would make fat targets for the enemy's artillery, Smith determined to employ a more dispersed formation to do the job. "I think we can carry those works by increasing our skirmish line, making it as heavy as possible, and then charging forward in line," he explained to one division commander.

Smith's attack was to commence with a brief bombardment of the enemy positions, but as he later recalled, "Upon ordering up the artillery, it was found that the Chief of Artillery had, upon his own responsibility, taken everything to the rear and unhitched the horses to water them, and this detained the movement for an hour."

It would be nearly 7:00 p.m. before Smith's attack got underway.

Winfield Scott Hancock

Hancock received two messages at around 5:30 p.m. that changed everything. The first, from Grant, "directed all haste to be made in getting up to the assistance of General Smith." The second, arriving hard on the heels of the first, was from Smith himself, who briefly reviewed the situation and declared, "If the Second Corps can come up in time to make an assault to-night after dark in vicinity of Norfolk and Petersburg Railroad I think we may be successful." Hancock reacted swiftly. "The Corps was then rushed forward to the support of Smith's troops," remembered Corporal J. D. Smith.

Francis Walker later estimated that the head of Hancock's column was about "four miles from Smith's left."

William F. "Baldy" Smith

Smith's 7:00 p.m. assault on the Dimmock line succeeded at almost every point attacked. The Rebel cannoneers, observed Confederate artilleryman and historian E. P. Alexander, held their fire "for the columns which they expected to see. These never appeared, but instead, the cloud of skirmishers overran the works . . . defended by only a skirmish line of infantry." A Connecticut soldier spoke with one of the captured cannoneers who "declared it to be a Yankee sell, to make him keep his guns treble shotted waiting for the line of battle, and then let the skirmish line capture him, guns and all." Black troops assigned to the Eighteenth Corps played a prominent role in this success. A white New Yorker whose regiment relieved some of the Afro-Americans wrote: "If you only saw the forts that those men charged, you would call them brave – yes, very brave."

The powerful redoubts south of the City Point Railroad were captured in rapid succession, and the Confederate defense was rolled up as far south as the

Jordan Point Road—nearly three and a half miles of Petersburg's eastern shield shattered in two hours' fighting. Yet at this moment of great personal success, Smith was overwhelmed by caution. "I had less than nine thousand infantry," he reflected afterward, "and knew that [Confederate] reinforcements had been rushing in to Petersburg. ... I knew nothing of the country in front. My white troops were exhausted. . . . My colored troops . . . could barely be kept in order."

A quick inspection ride along the captured works had confirmed that last point. Smith found his exuberant black soldiers camped, with weapons stacked and dinner fires blazing, on the enemy's side of the earthworks! His sharp orders to the men to put out their fires and take up their guns were met by one bewildered infantryman's complaint, "Why, de coffee am about to bile." (Nonetheless, Smith soon after this told a visitor: "There is material in the negroes to make the best troops in the world, if they receive the right kind of training.")

(Not every Eighteenth Corps soldier agreed with Smith's evaluation of the situation. A young Maine volunteer, George Ulmer, was among those who impatiently awaited the order to advance into Petersburg and finish the thing. "I swore all night," he remembered. "I kicked and condemned every general there was in the army for the blunder I saw they were making. I only wished I could be the general commanding for one hour. But it was no use; I couldn't be.")

"Baldy" Smith believed he had done his job. His men, at small loss, had cracked the hard shell of Petersburg's defenses. "I hold the key to Petersburg," he bragged in a midnight dispatch to Ben Butler. Now it was up to Hancock and his corps to finish the job by attacking on Smith's left.

It was a weary but triumphant William F. Smith who returned to his headquarters sometime after 9:00 p.m. to find Hancock waiting for him. To Smith's amazement, Hancock "informed me that he had [two] divisions . . . near at hand, and that they were ready for any further movements which in my judgment should be made." Hancock ranked Smith, something that the punctilious Smith did not forget. "I had . . . made up my mind that my force could not succeed in reaching Petersburg that night," Smith declared afterward, "and therefore I could not advise Hancock to . . . follow up the success." When Hancock pressed him to clarify a role for the Second Corps, Smith "requested him to relieve my colored troops in the line I had carried—which he did between eleven and two o'clock that night."

(Although the Second Corps commander left this encounter believing that he had done all that was asked of him, a *New York Tribune* correspondent attached to Smith's headquarters later reported that "General Hancock would not cooperate" with Smith.)

Winfield Scott Hancock

In a candid evaluation of the man he faithfully served, aide Francis Walker obseerved that "topographical insight was not one of Hancock's strong points.... [Of] that peculiar form of genius which enables some men ...to know intuitively ... 'the lay of the land' ... Hancock possessed little."

His mind fogged with pain, his sense of position completely disoriented by faulty maps and unfamiliar terrain, Hancock rode back from his meeting with Smith feeling frustrated and edgy. When he encountered a Second Corps division and found it improperly deployed, he tongue-lashed its commander, one of his more capable subordinates. Another of Hancock's divisions—Barlow's—was still wandering over the dark Virginia roads somewhere in the rear. Hancock's final instructions to his two division commanders this night were for them to reconnoiter their new lines, identify the enemy strong points, and attack them promptly at dawn.

P. G. T. Beauregard

Beauregard arrived in Petersburg at about 6:00 p.m., in time to see Smith's successful dusk attack punch a huge hole in the Dimmock line.

Even as some of the routed defenders were spreading panic in Petersburg, the first of the reinforcements dispatched from Bermuda Hundred began to arrive. Beauregard promptly patched together a new position using these troops. The Dimmock line north of the City Point Railroad was still largely in Confederate hands, so he tied his defense to the Appomattox River along those earthworks. Between a quarter-mile and a half-mile west of the lines now held by the Federals ran Harrison's Creek, which roughly paralleled the Dimmock earthworks. Taking full advantage of the high ground along the creek's west bank, Beauregard's engineers established the new defense southward along this ridge, to a point just north of the Baxter Road, where the original Dimmock positions remained in the Confederates' possession.

It was nearly 10:30 p.m. when Beauregard decided to concentrate everything he had to hold Petersburg. Orders were issued to Major General Bushrod Johnson, commanding the Bermuda Hundred lines, to abandon those positions and march south. Beauregard was relinquishing the vital communication corridor linking Richmond and Petersburg. Beauregard informed Lee of what he had done forty-five minutes after issuing those orders, adding, "Cannot these lines be occupied by your troops?"

Beauregard had been incredibly lucky this day. "Petersburg at that hour was clearly at the mercy of the Federal commander," he later wrote, "who had all but captured it, and only failed of final success because he could not realize the fact of the unparalleled disparity between the two contending forces."

George Gordon Meade

Meade's aide Theodore Lyman never ceased to marvel at the great pontoon bridge that the Federal engineers had constructed across the James. "It was very simple," he remarked later. "You have only to fancy a brigade of boats, thirteen feet wide and 2000 long, the whole looking so light as scarcely to be capable of bearing a man on horseback."

At this moment—6:30 p.m.—the bridge was bearing "a steady stream" of Second Corps supply wagons and artillery. After a hectic day spent shepherding the Army of the Potomac across the James, Meade and his staff had settled down to dine with Admiral Samuel P. Lee, commanding the James River flotilla. Dinner had just begun, Lyman recalled, when "came Colonel Babcock with news that 'Baldy' Smith had advanced from City Point before daylight, had struck the enemy . . . and was driving them." It was the first that Meade had heard that Petersburg was to be attacked today.

Continued Lyman, "Orders were immediately given to halt the wagon-train . . . and allow the 9th Corps to pass over and push on towards Petersburg."

Ulysses S. Grant

Grant found time this evening to write his wife, Julia. "We have been engaged in one of the most perilous movements ever executed by a large army," he told her. He summarized the current situation and closed with the comment, "A few days now will enable me to form a judgement of the work before me. It will be hard and may be tedious however."

Thursday, June 16

William F. "Baldy" Smith

Like a hunter stalking his prey, Lieutenant John Davenport staked out "Baldy" Smith's headquarters camp and waited for daylight. Davenport's odyssey during the past twelve hours had been curious indeed.

Davenport, an aide to Ben Butler, had ridden throughout the previous day carrying messages back and forth between Butler and Smith. Late Wednesday afternoon, he brought to Smith Butler's angry dispatch demanding to know why no attack had yet been made on the city. Smith told Davenport that he had just completed a personal reconnaissance and would soon order the assault. At about 8:30 p.m., after Smith reported his successful 7:00 p.m. action, the aide made the trip again, this time with a message from Butler urging Smith to press ahead and asserting that "Petersburg could be taken that night."

Davenport had found Smith talking with Hancock at the Second Corps headquarters. The young aide cornered Smith after the two hard parted and delivered the message. Smith's only reply, Davenport recalled, was that "General Hancock's arrival has left me the junior officer." The implication, as Davenport understood it, was that Hancock called the shots now and had decided not to attack this night. Davenport was surprised by this turn of events and spoke to some Second Corps staff officers, who assured him that Hancock had "waived his rank, [and] placed himself and his command at the service of Smith."

Davenport had reported these affairs directly to Ben Butler. After a few minutes' thought, Butler asked the young aide if he was up to another ride across the Appomattox. Davenport nodded and was given peremptory orders from Butler to Smith to attack immediately and take Petersburg.

The officer had found his way back to Smith's camp "between one and two o'clock on the morning of June 16." Smith was nowhere to be found. His aides claimed to have no idea where he was, though someone suggested that he might be at the Second Corps camp. Davenport checked with members of Hancock's staff, who assured him that Smith was not there. The weary aide returned to Smith's camp and positioned himself so he could see the main road in and out. Setting himself in such a way that anyone passing would wake him, the aide caught an hour of much-needed sleep.

Davenport reentered the camp at dawn. He noticed one large tent set well apart from the others and went over to it. "Opening the fly of this tent,"

Davenport later related, "I came face to face with General Smith who had evidently just risen." The exasperated aide at once asked the general why he had spent the night so isolated from the rest of his staff. "I was very tired," Davenport remembered Smith's replying, "and came here for the purpose of securing rest, and being where I would not be likely to be disturbed."

The incredulous aide then delivered Butler's order to attack at once. Smith responded that "he would look his position over and prepare to attack the enemy."

Davenport returned to Butler's camp between 6:00 and 7:00 a.m. and told him the whole story.

Ulysses S. Grant

U. S. GRANT TO GEORGE MEADE—10:15 A.M.

GENERAL SMITH CARRIED VERY STRONGLY LOCATED AND WELL-CONSTRUCTED WORKS, FORMING THE LEFT OF THE ENEMY'S DEFENSES OF PETERSBURG. . . . HURRY WARREN UP ... TO REACH THE JERUSALEM PLANK ROAD. ... AS SOON AS YOU RECEIVE THIS, AND CAN GIVE THE NECESSARY DIRECTIONS, START YOURSELF BY STEAMER, AND GET HERE TO TAKE COMMAND IN PERSON.

George Gordon Meade

For New Englander Theodore Lyman the trip with Meade up the James to City Point brought a touch of homesickness. "The river is very pretty, or rather fine," he thought, "with banks that remind one of Narragansett Bay. . . ."

The three—Meade's chief of staff, Andrew Humphreys, completed the party—landed at City Point to find that Grant had already gone to the front. The officers quickly followed him. They had ridden, Lyman guessed, "a couple of miles" when they met the lieutenant general and members of his staff.

"Well," said Grant, "Smith has taken a line of works there, stronger than anything we have seen this campaign! If it is a possible thing, I want an assault made at six o'clock this evening!"

Meade's party continued on and presently caught up with the lead elements of Burnside's Ninth Corps. "The men had done awful marching in a dry country, with a hot sun and midst a stifling dust," recorded Lyman, adding, "I hate to see troops so used up."

The command group finally reached Hancock's camp, where "General Meade was soon busy consulting about an assault." Lyman could see in the distance two or three church spires within the city of Petersburg.

Hancock's reconnaissance this morning had not gotten off as early as he had ordered, but his men had aggressively probed the Confederate defenses, even capturing an advanced battery south of the Jordan Point Road. Meade spent the early afternoon hours gathering reports on the enemy positions and conferring with his two corps commanders on the scene.

Ulysses S. Grant

Having handed the battle for Petersburg over to Meade, Grant returned to City Point, where he learned of another great opportunity.

Ben Butler reported at 7:45 a.m. from his Bermuda Hundred lines: "The enemy have evacuated our front." Five hours later, the portly general had troops advanced as far west as the Richmond and Petersburg Railroad, where they began tearing up the tracks.

Grant's chief of staff, John Rawlins, reflected, "This seems a strange move [on the part of the Confederates] . . . and would indicate an intention to evacuate Petersburg. They certainly can't hold it with Butler between it and Richmond."

Yet by 1:15 p.m., Grant was feeling wary. "I do not think it advisable to make an attack in the center of the enemy's line," he cautioned Butler. "It would detain a force from going to Petersburg, but would attract attention to a point where we may want to make a real attack some day hence." Grant was so concerned that he diverted two Sixth Corps divisions from Meade to Butler.

By 5:30 p.m., Butler was positively gloating over his uncontested gains north of Petersburg. "The evacuation," he insisted, "was an enormous blunder."

George Gordon Meade

Following a brief but thunderous bombardment, Federal battle lines again moved against Petersburg at 6:00 p.m. "Baldy" Smith's Eighteenth Corps on the Union right staged a noisy demonstration, hoping to attract Confederate attention away from the main assaults further south. Advancing along a mile-long battle line that stretched south from the Prince George Court House

Road, soldiers from Hancock's three divisions struggled forward in the face of surprisingly heavy Confederate fire.

Grant's aide Horace Porter saw Meade at this time. "His usual nervous energy was displayed in the intensity of his manner and the rapid and animated style of his conversation. ... He was acting, with great earnestness, and doing his utmost to carry out the instructions which he had received."

By dark the Federals had overrun several Confederate outposts, but they had failed to break through Beauregard's Harrison's Creek line. They had suffered some 2,000 casualties doing so.

Confederate counterattacks extended the combat well into the morning hours of June 17—something Meade described in a letter written that day as "another unparalleled feat in the annals of war."

P. G. T. Beauregard

Fortune favored Beauregard this day. Even with Hoke's and Bushrod Johnson's troops, Beauregard had barely 14,000 men defended Petersburg. He was outnumbered at least 3 to 1.

It was the kind of crisis condition that Beauregard relished. He coolly abandoned great portions of his line to concentrate his strength along the most likely avenues of approach. "About four and a half miles of the fortified lines (extending from half a mile east of the Jerusalem Plank Road westwardly to the Appomattox) were entirely unprotected," Beauregard later admitted. But the gamble paid off. "[They] persisted in attacking on my front where I was strongest," he noted, ". . . and the result was that they were repulsed during the day with great loss."

George Gordon Meade

In his report of the day's actions, Meade concluded, "Our men are tired and the attacks have not been made with the vigor and force which characterized our fighting in the Wilderness; if they had been I think we should have been more successful. I will continue to press."

Ulysses S. Grant

Horace Porter recorded, "When I got back to City Point that evening General Grant felt considerably encouraged by the news brought him and spent most of the night in planning movements for the next day." Meade's aide

Theodore Lyman also visited Grant this evening, later recalling that "He sat on the edge of his cot, in shirt and drawers, and listened to my report. . . . He smiled, like one who had done a clever thing, and said, 'I think it is pretty well to get across a great river, and come up here and attack Lee in his rear before he is ready for us!'"

Friday, June 17

George Gordon Meade

Today would be the day.

Meade had received a report during the night from Admiral Lee, whose scout boats had spotted Robert E. Lee's army on the move. "This makes it of great importance to force the enemy's lines before the troops here referred to can join those now in our front," Meade declared.

He had hoped that Burnside's Ninth Corps, now in line on Hancock's left, would launch a moonlight attack, but the dependably slow Burnside had let matters develop at their own pace, and it was almost dawn before his assaulting columns were ready.

The success of the initial Ninth Corps attack seemed to justify the delay. Burnside's men took advantage of a ravine that let deep into the Confederate position and burst forward at 3:00 a.m. In almost no time they took four guns, five flags, 600 prisoners, and 1,500 stands of arms. More than a mile of the Harrison's Creek line now lay in Federal hands.

Meade was pleased but still anxious. "It affords me great satisfaction to congratulate you and your gallant corps," he wired Burnside at 7:00 a.m., adding, "I am satisfied the main body of Lee's army is not yet up, and it is of the utmost importance to do all we can before they get up."

Winfield Scott Hancock

It was almost more than he could bear. This was the moment he had been born for, the time when his very presence on the field could win it all. But it was not to be. "I can hardly walk or ride," Hancock admitted to Meade in a 6:00 a.m. dispatch. George Armes, riding as an aide to Hancock, noted today that the "General's wound has given him a great deal of pain and worry all day, and his want of rest and something proper to eat and drink has been very trying. . . ."

Hancock's leadership on this critical day would be marked by uncertainty, hesitancy, and lackluster inspiration. His corps, assigned largely to support the Ninth Corps's attacks, made small gains and suffered disproportionately large losses.

Hancock's aide Francis Walker noted that his chief's "orders to his division commanders . . . threw upon them much responsibility—not more . . . than is appropriate . . . but rather more than Hancock's habits as a corps commander had usually assigned them."

Ulysses S. Grant

Grant left the battle for Petersburg to Meade and turned his concerns to the north, where the unpredictable Butler and his Army of the James controlled the vital corridor by which Lee would have to send reinforcements to that city. "It seems to me important that we should hold our advantage gained yesterday," he informed Butler at 9:15 a.m. As evidence began to accumulate that Lee was gathering strength to force this passage, Grant directed Meade to return "Baldy" Smith's command to Bermuda Hundred as soon as possible. At 5:15 p.m., the anticipated storm broke. "The enemy have formed in line of battle . . . and advanced to their former line," Butler reported, adding, "Shall we attack them in force?" Grant was out visiting Meade when the message arrived, and not until 6:45 p.m. was a reply sent. "If possible the enemy should be driven back," Grant commanded.

Butler did not enjoy the confidence of his subordinate commanders, and they, in turn, dismissed his grasp of the tactical situation. His orders this day to these commanders to retake the lost lines met with pointed refusals. Butler finally signaled Grant at 11:30 p.m., "I am sorry to say nothing has been done, or even a vigorous attempt made."

Now there was not a thing to prevent Lee from strongly reinforcing Petersburg. Not a thing, that is, but P. G. T. Beauregard.

George Gordon Meade

The follow-up attacks that Meade had directed him to make took time for Burnside to organize. Not until 2:00 p.m. did his men, assisted on their right by one of Hancock's divisions, advance once more. The Confederates were ready and waiting this time. Little ground was gained, and at a stiff price. Yet a third assault went forward at 6:00 p.m.; it enjoyed a brief lodgment in the main Confederate line but was driven back by an evening counterattack.

Warren's Fifth Corps had moved into line on Burnside's left by late morning, but the moody, cautious Warren refrained from fully assisting the Ninth Corps. Meade reinforced Warren's hesitancy with his own indecision as to the role the corps would play. The result: Warren's 20,000 men did very little this day.

Meade observed in a letter to his wife written this day, "We find the enemy, as usual, in a very strong position, defended by earthworks, and it looks very much as if we will have to go through a siege of Petersburg before entering on the siege of Richmond. . . . Well, it is all in the cruise, as the sailors say."

P. G. T. Beauregard

It had been another day of crisis for Beauregard. The Federal attacks had seriously compromised his defensive line, and even he realized that one coordinated push would finish it. By now the high-strung officer was feeling the pressure. His admiring aide Alfred Roman later well recalled "the harassed and almost despairing look that gradually grew upon General Beauregard's bronzed and martial features, as each laborious day and sleepless night passed without bringing the long-expected and often prayed for reinforcements."

Beauregard was not making it easy for Robert E. Lee to send help. Lee worried that Petersburg might be a feint on Grant's part to trick him into leaving the capital under protected; he needed hard evidence to accept that the enemy was indeed before Petersburg in strength. At 9:00 a.m., Beauregard could only advise Lee that "nothing positive [was] yet known of Grant's movements." Two hours later, he passed along an unconfirmed report that the Federal Fifth Corps was on its way north to confront Jubal Early in the Shenandoah Valley. Finally, at 5:00 p.m., Beauregard confirmed to Lee that virtually the entire Army of the Potomac was confronting him at Petersburg. In a 6:40 p.m. dispatch, Beauregard warned, "I shall hold as long as practicable, but, without reinforcements, I may have to evacuate the city shortly."

Beauregard had one last card to play. Anticipating that his defensive line might collapse, he and his chief engineer began at midday to select a final fallback position. This shorter line began at the Appomattox, less than half a mile west of Harrison's Creek, and ran almost directly south to reconnect with the Dimmock line at the Jerusalem Plank Road. They marked it with stakes and briefed every available staff officer in Hoke's and Johnson's divisions "so that each command, at the appointed hour, even at dead of night, might easily retire upon the new line with order and precision, and unperceived by the enemy."

Beauregard then acted as night fell and the gunfire sputtered out. "I had ordered all the camp-fires to be brightly lighted, with sentinels well thrown forward and as near as possible to the enemy's," he later recalled. Beginning a little after midnight, his men fell back some five hundred to eight hundred yards and began to entrench their last ditch line.

William F. "Baldy" Smith

As part of a realignment of troops this evening, one of Wright's divisions marched down from Bermuda Hundred to Petersburg and relieved Brooks's division of Smith's corps.

Smith left with his division for Bermuda Hundred, not bothering to let Meade know he was going. At 7:00 a.m. on the morning of June 18, an exasperated Meade would be reduced to sending an aide to "ascertain who commands that portion of the Eighteenth Corps in our line."

Saturday, June 18

Winfield Scott Hancock

HEADQUARTERS SECOND ARMY CORPS—2:15 A.M.

FOR THE PRESENT MAJOR-GENERAL HANCOCK RELINQUISHES THE COMMAND OF THE CORPS. MAJOR-GENERAL BIRNEY WILL ASSUME COMMAND AT ONCE. BY COMMAND OF MAJOR-GENERAL HANCOCK.

George Gordon Meade

Meade no longer believed that success was possible, but without any orders from Grant to halt operations, he felt he had to press on. "The General was in a tearing humor," Theodore Lyman noted this morning. A member of the headquarters cavalry escort seconded this with his observation that Meade "was in one of his crusty moods."

The attacks went forward at dawn. Instead of facing crashing volleys, however, the skirmishers were met by only a light spattering of picket fire as they probed forward.

On Hancock's front, recalled Francis Walker, the scouts "found the enemy had withdrawn from the position they held the night before to a new line." A report from the Ninth Corps at 8:00 a.m. indicated that "General Burnside is steadily advancing. Has not found anything in his front yet." On the far Union left, where Warren's Fifth Corps held position, advance parties brought back word that the Confederate trenches were "deserted."

In his report to Grant, Meade noted that "the enemy fell back ... to a shorter line." He continued to stress that the Federal troops were exhausted: "The men require rest, and it is probable, unless some favorable chance presents itself, that we shall not do more than develop the enemy."

P. G. T. Beauregard

The van of Lee's Army of Northern Virginia—Joseph Kershaw's division—crossed the Appomattox River into Petersburg at 7:30 a.m. Charles Field's division was two hours behind it. Even as the Federals were groping toward Beauregard's final line, the reinforcements necessary to hold Petersburg were arriving.

Robert E. Lee rode into town and met with Beauregard at 11:30 a.m. "My welcome to General Lee was most cordial," Beauregard remembered, not without irony. "He was at last where I had, for the past three days, so anxiously hoped to see him—within the limits of Petersburg!"

The two rode along the new lines protecting Petersburg, and Beauregard used the opportunity to defend his decision to abandon the outerworks. Lee made no comment other than to approve Beauregard's dispositions. But the Creole officer was not content to have won a defensive battle; "I proposed," Beauregard recalled, ". . . that, as soon as [A. P.] Hill's and [Richard] Anderson's corps should arrive, our entire disposable force be thrown upon the left and rear of the Federal army before it began to fortify its position." According to Beauregard's aide Alfred Roman, "General Lee refused his assent, on the ground that his troops needed rest, and that the defensive having been thus far so advantageous to him against Grant's offensive ... at Petersburg, he preferred continuing the same mode of warfare."

Beauregard had the last word, arguing that the Federals were as exhausted as Lee's men and had yet to entrench. "But," Beauregard later recalled with regret, "I was then only second in command, and my views did not prevail."

George Gordon Meade

The Army of the Potomac had drawn up before Beauregard's final line by late morning, and Meade was desperately trying to coordinate a major assault at noon. "Please telegraph to these headquarters for the [correct] time, in order that the attack may be as simultaneous as possible," he directed the commanders of the Eighteenth, Second, Ninth, and Fifth corps.

It was a futile exercise. Somewhere in the strained machinery of the army, a gear wheel went askew, and the various pieces of the Army of the Potomac and the Army of the James lurched piecemeal into battle, with Meade helpless to affect the course of events. Only portions of the Eighteenth and Second corps managed to advance at the appointed hour; they were hit hard and stopped by Confederate fire. Further down the line, both Burnside and Warren found reasons to delay. Their attacks, when delivered, gained little.

With Smith now at Bermuda Hundred, Brigadier General John H. Martindale commanded.

Grant's aide Horace Porter took a number of messages to Meade and observed him in action. "He sent ringing dispatches to all points of the line," Porter remembered, "and paced up and down the field in his nervous, restless manner, as he watched the progress of the operations and made running comments on the actions of his subordinates."

GEORGE MEADE TO GENERALS WARREN AND BURNSIDE—2:20 P.M.

... MY ORDERS HAVE BEEN EXPLICIT AND ARE NOW REPEATED, THAT YOU EACH IMMEDIATELY ASSAULT THE ENEMY WITH ALL YOUR FORCE, AND IF THERE IS ANY FURTHER DELAY THE RESPONSIBILITY AND THE CONSEQUENCES WILL REST WITH YOU.

GEORGE MEADE TO DAVID BIRNEY— 2:30 P.M.

. . . I FIND IT USELESS TO APPOINT AN HOUR TO EFFECT CO-OPERATION. . . . YOU HAVE A LARGE CORPS, POWERFUL AND NUMEROUS, AND I BEG YOU WILL AT ONCE, AS SOON AS POSSIBLE, ASSAULT IN A STRONG COLUMN.

Time and again the blue lines struggled onto the open ground only to be shredded by Confederate rifle and artillery fire. In one of the last attacks of this day, the nine-hundred-man-strong 1st Maine Heavy Artillery charged from the Prince George Court House Road into the cleared fields near Hare House Hill.

When it reeled back thirty minutes later, 632 men had been killed or wounded—the heaviest battle loss suffered in a single attack by any regiment during the Civil War.

Meade knew it was over by 6:30 p.m. Orders went out to the commands to entrench. He finished his summary for Grant of the day's action at 9:45 p.m., in which he admitted, "It is a source of great regret that I am not able to report more success."

(Grant's military secretary, Adam Badeau, later observed that the lieutenant general "simply gave the general order and Meade directed all details. These were indeed Meade's battles. . . .")

Ulysses S. Grant

A reporter for the *New York Tribune* spotted Grant at this time. William H. Kent had seen the general in Washington when he first came east and thought that Grant was now looking "ten years older." The correspondent was an onlooker for a meeting with several other generals. Grant was a strong presence, "quietly smoking his cigar, suggesting some idea occasionally, asking a pointed question now and then, studying the map carefully, and listening to the conversation and propositions of those around him, as becomes a thinking man." What Grant had to put behind him was that his plan to seize Petersburg had failed. It was time to adjust and adapt to circumstances.

Horace Porter found his boss philosophical this evening. "Lee's whole army has now arrived," the lieutenant general said, "and the topography of the country about Petersburg has been well taken advantage of by the enemy in the location of strong works. I will make no more assaults on that portion of the line, but will give the men a rest, and then look to extension toward our left, with a strong view to destroying Lee's communications on the south and confining him to a close siege."

(Meade's chief of staff, Andrew Humphreys, later put the number of Union soldiers killed or wounded in the fighting from June 15 to June 18 at 8,150, with an additional 1,814 missing, for a total of 9,964. A modern study of these battles estimates Confederate losses at about 4,000 men.)

* * *

The June 15 assault would be "Baldy" Smith's last combat command. On June 21, after being indirectly accused by Butler of "dilatoriness," he replied, with characteristic sharpness, "Your threat of relieving me does not frighten me in the least." Smith immediately forwarded copies of this exchange to Grant and asked to be relieved from duty with the Army of the James.

Grant at first explored the possibility of having Butler reassigned to the Midwest, but Lincoln's military adviser Henry Halleck argued against such a move, claiming that it would probably "cause an insurrection." Grant then issued orders reassigning all of Butler's troops to Smith, while leaving Butler in administrative control of the military department.

Elated over this positive change in his fortunes, Smith paid a visit to his good friend Grant and freely criticized Meade's handling of the Army of the Potomac. Smith then took a ten-day leave prior to assuming command of the Army of the James. Upon his return, he found that Grant had revoked his previous order, restored Butler to full command of the Army of the James, and reassigned Smith to New York to await further orders.

Smith smelled a conspiracy against him. He believed that the fumbled hand-off between him and Hancock had been set-up to "embarrass him." He also later insisted that Butler had forced Grant's reversal by threatening to reveal that the lieutenant general was drinking heavily again. Butler vehemently denied Smith's charge, and Grant ignored it.

On July 19, the day Grant ordered Smith back to New York, his chief of staff, John Rawlins, wrote to Mrs. Rawlins of the matter and said that Smith was being dismissed "[Because] of his spirit of criticism of all military movements and men, and his failure to get along with anyone he is placed under, and his disposition to scatter the seeds of discontent throughout the army."

Chapter Four

"I have determined to try to envelop Petersburg"

June 19 - July 1, 1864

Ulysses S. Grant
Final Report of Operations, March 1864-May 1865

The advantages in position gained by us [at Petersburg following the June 15-18 fighting] were very great. The army then proceeded to envelop Petersburg toward the South Side Railroad, as far as possible, without attacking fortifications.

Sunday, June 19
Union Lines, near Petersburg

Captain J. Madison Drake, of the 9th New Jersey, remembered that this morning "a 'Johnny' in front of the Ninth, sung out: 'Say, Yanks, let's take a rest till night—it's Sunday.'

"'All right, Johnny,' responded a pious Jerseyman, 'we shall feel the better for it.'"

"No operations of importance on the line of Second Corps to-day," noted one unit's official diary, echoing the condition of the other Federal corps before Petersburg. "I now ordered the troops to be put under cover," recorded U. S. Grant, "and allowed [them] some of the rest which they had so long needed."

There was no break for the Union doctors, who struggled to cope with the casualties. "The surgeons had little or no rest during the many days of bloody conflict," a New York soldier recalled after visiting one field hospital. "The mutilated remains of the heroes was piled in heaps and scattered around; the wounded lying on stretchers awaiting for death to relieve their agony." Major

John Chester White in Warren's Fifth Corps felt a special pity for the war's four-legged victims: "One sad feature of these scenes of bloodshed is the poor, wounded horses, whose cries are most heart-rending, as they will raise their heads and glare about them with fast-glazing eyes."

Other Fifth Corps soldiers took out their frustrations by gathering up discarded rifle ramrods and firing them at the enemy. "They went with a terrible screech," noted Austin Stearns, a sergeant in the 13th Massachusetts, "almost frightening ourselves, the first ones we fired; it was great sport for us for a while, but the Rebs did not like it, and opened their great guns, and for an hour or more there was a regular artillery fire duel."

At Army of the Potomac Headquarters, George Gordon Meade's temper was still being felt. "Meade is showing himself up as he really is, a very mean man," Provost Marshal Marsena Patrick grumbled. "There is a great deal of dissatisfaction in the Army about him." Meade spent part of this day trying to arrange for a truce to bury the Union dead and retrieve the wounded who lay between the lines. His aide Theodore Lyman was given the task of delivering the request to the Confederates. After gingerly picking his way along the southern flank of the two armies, Lyman found a Rebel officer who took his message and passed it up the chain of command to P. G. T. Beauregard. "At seven in the evening," Lyman related, "I got the reply and carried it in. The sum of it was: 'Have the honor to acknowledge your favor. As to your proposition—Ah, don't see it!'"

U. S. Grant was not idle this day. He spent some of it with Ben Butler, surveying the James above City Point, looking for a place to establish a staging area on the north side of the river. They found one at Deep Bottom. Instructions were issued for pontoon material to be brought up as quickly as possible. Other orders that went out suggested that Grant no longer expected to storm Petersburg. He wired Washington at 10:00 a.m.:

PLEASE ORDER COLONEL ABBOT'S SIEGE TRAINS FORWARD.

Confederate Lines, Petersburg

More Army of Northern Virginia veterans arrived from Richmond's defenses this day. Virginians from William Mahone's division of A. P. Hill's corps reached town early in the afternoon. "It was to all appearances a doomed city," recalled William H. Stewart of the 61st Regiment, "and the soldiers felt that its rescue from total destruction depended upon their efforts and exertions."

Petersburger Fanny Waddell, her composure somewhat shaken by "all the confusion and noise attending the presence of a large army," ventured out of her house just in time to behold a "grand-looking man riding up the street. ... I knew by intuition that it was our great chief, the Christian warrior, General Lee. I felt as in the presence of royalty."

Lee had come into town to attend services. Mrs. Waddell planted herself outside the church and was rewarded when the military leader emerged. "General Lee, to our great gratification, shook hands with several of us as he left the church. He had a beautiful eye,...a noble countenance, with hair and beard which the terrible burden of a nation's cares seems to have prematurely whitened."

Lee brought Confederate President Jefferson Davis up to date on the military situation in a letter written this day. The general, now recognizing that Petersburg was the critical point, was pulling all but a light covering force away from the north side of the James—which in effect left Richmond's defenses woefully undermanned. However, Lee was quick to reassure Davis, "if we can get early intelligence, and especially maintain the [rail]road from Petersburg to Richmond in running order, I think we shall be able to meet any attack the enemy might make [along the north side of the James]."

Things were quiet at Petersburg now, Lee added, but one matter especially concerned him, and that was maintaining service along the as yet undamaged Weldon Railroad, which ran south from the Cockade City into supply-rich North Carolina. "It will be difficult, and I fear impracticable to preserve it uninterrupted," he warned.

Lee also wrote to his wife today. "Never forget me or our suffering country," he said.

Monday, June 20
Union Lines, near Petersburg

The Sixth Corps soldiers camped near the Jordan House looked with astonishment at the small hill in their immediate front. On it was a structure that was, as soldier W. F. Parish later reflected, a "curious thing"—it had "two very long poles with a cross-beam on top. Underneath was a platform. ... It had an altogether unmilitary look. We have never seen anything like it before." A few recognized it for what it was: a gallows.

The man who had ordered it erected had spent an anxious twenty-four hours preparing things. This was one execution that Provost Marshal Marsena Patrick wanted done right.

The condemned man was a black Union soldier named William Johnson. His crime, according to the reporter for the *Boston Evening Transcript*, consisted of "an attempt to violate the person of a young lady at New Kent Court House." Johnson had been tried, found guilty, and condemned to death. Charged with carrying out the judgment, Patrick had selected a spot for the execution that was in full view of the Rebels. According to W. F. Parish, the "hanging took place in such plain sight of the Confederate lines to show them the detestation we had for a crime like that."

Word of the event caused a gathering of the curious that upset whatever hopes Patrick had had for a quiet, solemn demonstration. "It drew so large a crowd," aide Robert Tilney observed, "that the Rebs commenced shelling." Musician Frank Rauscher was with the regimental band that accompanied the condemned man to the gallows. The procession was passing a fort near the hilltop, he remembered, "when an artilleryman who had just come out with his discharge in his pocket and had started for home, for a moment halted to look at the preliminaries to the execution of the colored man, when a shell struck him and he fell dead on the spot. It was almost a miracle that the band and regiment escaped injury."

Provost Marshal Patrick scribbled in his diary entry for this day, "They arrived, just after a Shelling commenced, upon the very place where the Gallows was erected so that I had to form the troops below the crest & leave as few exposed as possible. The Chaplain prayed with him; he acknowledged that he was a deserter, that he had changed his name & committed the crime charged upon him—the rope was adjusted[,] the bandages placed over his eyes and the drop fell].] He never knew anything after."

Another observer recalled Patrick's losing some of his aplomb. According to a New York artilleryman named W.E. Webster: "The rope was attached to the beam, and a black cap pulled down over his head. The Chaplain commenced his prayer. At the same time the rebels opened with artillery. The Provost Marshal shouted out: 'Cut it short, Chaplain. Cut it short. Pull him off.' And the trap dropped."

The firing died as the crowds dispersed. Soon it was safe enough for photographers from two competing firms—Timothy O'Sullivan's and

Matthew Brady's—to set up their bulky equipment and capture images of the dead black soldier. "It was a funny sight to see Brady, the photographer, dancing around to get a picture," gunner Webster noted, adding that "he finally got it."

Communications among various Union headquarters were especially portentous today. Ulysses S. Grant had decided on a dramatic plan of action. At midmorning he wired George Meade, "As soon as [Brigadier General James H.] Wilson's cavalry is rested sufficiently they should make a raid upon the enemy's railroads." That in itself would make trouble for Confederate forces away from Petersburg, but Grant was not finished. Hancock's Second Corps (still under the command of Major General David Birney) was being relieved from the trenches and would be available as a mobile column. Grant intended to employ it against the two enemy railroads that were not yet under his control.

The Second Corps's move left the Union's Petersburg lines held by (in order, moving south from the Appomattox) the Sixth, Ninth, and Fifth corps. Grant decided that he wanted to add more weight to the mobile infantry column, and so, at 5:40 p.m., he informed Meade that to "give you another corps foot-loose I will order General Butler to extend his lines as to cover the ground now occupied by the Sixth Corps."

Meade made certain at 6:30 p.m. that he and Grant were in accord. "As you propose," he wired, "I will move both corps, Second and Sixth, to the left and endeavor to stretch to the Appomattox." Even as Meade was confirming his understanding of the plan with Grant, the Army of the Potomac's chief of staff, Andrew Humphreys, was explaining to David Birney that the "object is to reach across the Weldon railroad, and finally across the Lynchburg [i.e., South Side] railroad."

From his headquarters near Mount Sinai Church, cavalry commander James Wilson reacted to Grant's note "in regard to a raid upon the enemy's railroads." After summarizing his present supply problems, Wilson concluded, "I don't think it could be well prepared before daylight of the 22nd."

Enough of the plan had taken shape by 6:45 p.m. that Grant could state to Ben Butler, "I have determined to try to envelop Petersburg so as to have the left of the Army of the Potomac rest on the Appomattox about the city."

Throughout the dusty day and well into the dusty night, the various Second Corps units were relieved from the front and allowed to move to the rear. "Out of harm's way," noted a grateful soldier in the 124th New York.

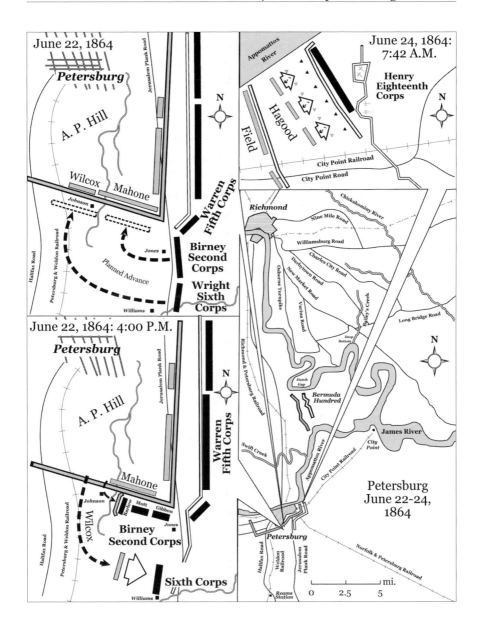

Confederate Lines, Richmond and Petersburg

Gunfire danced along the outer edges of Richmond's defensive perimeter. "Sheridan's raiders are near the city again, followed and preceded by Wade Hampton and Fitz Lee," C.S. War Department clerk John B. Jones wrote in his diary. "The cannon has been heard all the morning."

The Union army had been at Cold Harbor when the Yankee cavalry chief rode north with two-thirds of his men to wreck part of the Virginia Central Railroad, Richmond's lifeline to the Shenandoah Valley. After two days of confused fighting at Trevallian Station, Sheridan returned to the Army of the Potomac instead of riding into the valley to link up with other Federal units.

The march back toward Richmond had been a killing one. A Virginia cavalryman estimated that in eight days of retreat, Sheridan left "on the average, twelve dead horses to the mile."

Today Wade Hampton was near the Federal supply depot at White House, on the Pamunkey River, certain that this was Sheridan's destination. Hampton was anxious to take the place before Sheridan arrived, but if that proved impossible, he wished at least to have enough strength available to pin down the Union's mounted arm. He sent urgent appeals to Richmond for more men, but no help could be sent.

A jubilant Sheridan wired Meade from White House at 5:00 p.m., "I have the honor to notify the major-general commanding of the arrival of my command here. . . ." All Wade Hampton could do was watch.

A Confederate artillerist in Petersburg named James Albright saw Robert E. Lee this day. "A noble, plain old man," Albright told his wife, "toward which every eye is confidently turned."

Rumors of trouble for P. G. T. Beauregard were rife on both sides of the James. The reason was his decision to strip the Bermuda Hundred lines (and thus sever his communications with Richmond) in order to consolidate his strength in the Cockade City. "It is said Beauregard acted contrary to orders," War Clerk Jones observed, "and has been suspended from command by order of the President."

Tuesday, June 21
Union Lines, near Petersburg

George Meade told U. S. Grant at 9:00 a.m. of his progress in carrying out the plans to envelop Petersburg: "[The] Second Corps is moving to take position on the left of the Fifth, the Fifth extending as far as the Jerusalem plank road. . . . Wilson will be ordered to leave at 2. a.m. to-morrow, and directed to proceed as rapidly as possible to the junction of the Lynchburg and Danville roads and do as much damage as possible. . . . Hampton being yesterday at

White House will relieve Wilson of any apprehension of being disturbed, and I trust Sheridan will keep Hampton occupied."

This day began as a cruel joke for the weary soldiers in the Second Corps. "I well remember the sense of relief we felt as our column …filed out of the woods where our position had been, and took the high and open road that led to Jerusalem Plank Road," an infantryman in the 57th New York observed. The men believed they were heading away from Petersburg on some easy mission. "But presently we began to turn to the front and then we understood that we were going to another attack," the New York soldier finished gloomily.

"It was the hottest day of the season and we were nearly suffocated by the dust," a Connecticut soldier complained. The Federal column reached the Jerusalem Plank Road a little after midday and began entrenching a line roughly parallel to it and stretching nearly two miles southward.

Skirmish parties were pushed out to the west, where they scrapped with North Carolina cavalry units screening the Weldon Railroad. A group of U.S. sharpshooters was surrounded and taken, but New Hampshire men from the 5th Regiment returned the favor by capturing Colonel John A. Baker of the 3rd North Carolina Cavalry, along with some members of his staff. "The Confederate colonel, clothed in the finest of Confederate gray, was mounted upon a beautiful, well caparisoned white horse, and one of his staff was securely mounted behind," a soldier in the 5th noted.

The way west to the Weldon Railroad appeared clear for the next day's operation, but the Union men and officers were anything but confident. George Meade worried in a letter written to his wife this day that his army was "exhausted with forty-nine days of continued marching and fighting, and absolutely requires rest to prevent its morale being impaired." Second Corps staff officer George Armes emphatically agreed with this assessment. "I have carefully inspected our entire front line twice to day," he reported, "and the men are completely worn out."

Fred Lockley, a clerk with the 7th New York Heavy Artillery, voiced the fears of the common soldier. "Whatever strategy we practice, Lee always appears with some counter movement—ready to receive us—every advantage we gain is at such a fearful cost of life and limb that we pay the full value for it." Staff officers worried that this cycle was about to occur again. "There seems to be a tremendous force of Confederates in our front," Lockley noted, adding, "we are liable to be charged upon any moment. If so we will be in a bad fix."

Winfield Hancock did little to assuage those fears. Though still resting and not commanding his corps, Hancock chose to accompany the column. He established himself at the Second Corps headquarters, which were set up in the Jones House, just west of the Jerusalem Plank Road. There was a steady crackle of gunfire to the west as the Second Corps skirmishers became engaged with the North Carolina cavalry. Recalled aide Armes, "General Hancock became so excited that he rushed out of his room in the Jones house, and wanted his horse brought up, so as to go to the front line . . . but [the doctors] . . . made him return to his bed with the greatest difficulty. The General keeps saying, 'I am afraid something will happen to the Corps.' "

"[We] were sitting in front of the General's tent," Grant's aide Horace Porter wrote, "when there appeared very suddenly before us a lone, lank-looking personage, dressed all in black, and looking very much like a boss undertaker. It was the President." Abraham Lincoln had left Washington aboard the wooden side-wheeler U.S.S. *Baltimore* on June 20 at 5:00 p.m., steaming down the Potomac, then up the James River, and had arrived off City Point shortly after midday. Lincoln's visit, according to a *New York Herald* reporter on the scene, was "entirely unheralded and unannounced." The correspondent noted that the Commander-in-Chief was at first mistaken for a member of one of the soldier aid organizations and denied access to army headquarters until a "captain upon [Grant's]…staff passing, and recognizing the stranger, set the matter right, and conducted the President to the Lieutenant General's tent."

"I just thought I would jump aboard a boat and come down and see you," Lincoln told Grant as greetings were completed. "I don't expect I can do any good, and in fact I'm afraid I may do some harm, but I'll just put myself under your orders and if you find me doing anything wrong just send me right away."

Grant answered that he would do just that, and then he laughed, though there was a hard edge to his laughter. "You will never hear of me farther from Richmond than now, till I have taken it," Grant vowed, anxious to head off any criticism that might be raised against him for moving the army south of the Confederate capital. Lincoln seemed unconcerned about this point of strategy; his worry was the casualty lists. "I cannot pretend to advise," Lincoln told Grant, "but I do sincerely hope that all may be accomplished with as little bloodshed as possible." The *Herald* reporter termed their discussion "an exceedingly animated conversation, in which the President's gestures were both numerous and awkward."

Grant suggested that they visit nearby troops. "Why, yes," the President answered. "I had fully intended to go out and take a look at the brave fellows who have fought their way down to Petersburg in the wonderful campaign, and I am ready to start at any time."

It was around 4:00 p.m. when the group set out. A somewhat startled artilleryman named Elbert Corbin halted his normal diary entry to scribble, "Old Abe was here and rode along the Lines with Gen. Grant." According to a reporter on the scene, "One cavalry private recognized him on the road. Mr. Lincoln shook him by the hand like an old, familiar acquaintance, to the infinite admiration of the bystanders."

The presidential party dismounted at the Sixth Corps headquarters of Horatio Wright. George Meade and some of his staff were present, as was the band of the First New Jersey Brigade, which played "Hail to the Chief" as the guest party arrived. Meade mentioned the visit in a letter to his wife, with the comment that the President "was so gracious as to say he had seen you in Philadelphia." As soon as Lincoln entered Wright's command center, reporter Sylvanus Cadwallader noted, "Maps were examined, the position of the army explained, its future operations discussed, the steeples and spires of the city observed as well as the dust and smoke would allow... and after a stop of an hour and a half the party started on its return to headquarters."

The route back took them through the camps of some of the black troops. The soldiers "were lounging by the roadside," Cadwallader observed, "and when he approached came rushing by the hundreds screaming, yelling, shouting: 'Hurrah for the Liberator; Hurrah for the President,' and were wild with excitement and delight." Horace Porter was amazed at the actions of the black soldiers. "They crowded about him and fondled his horse; some of them kissed his hands, while others ran off crying in triumph to their comrades that they had touched his clothes....The scene was affecting in the extreme, and no one could have witnessed it unmoved."

Amidst all of these activities and plans, the politics of command were also making themselves known at Union army headquarters. George Meade's mood had not improved in the three days since June 18. Lincoln's visit was a complete surprise; "No one knows what he came for," Meade's son Captain George Meade complained in a letter. The elder Meade found time today to review Washington's official news releases on the June 15-18 fighting. He was not pleased with what he read. "I had exclusive command," he groused to his wife,

". . . and yet in Mr. Stanton's official dispatches . . . my name is not even mentioned. I cannot imagine why I am thus ignored."

The simmering feud between "Baldy" Smith and Ben Butler erupted into the open this day. This evening Smith forwarded copies of his communications with Butler to City Point, along with the request that "I may be relieved from duty in the Department of Virginia and North Carolina." Butler was also nagging Grant's headquarters over his problems with General Quincy Gillmore. The Ohio officer had been relieved of his command after his dismal performance handing the June 9 Petersburg assault and ordered home; but instead of going directly there, he had stopped at the prison camp at Point Lookout where he was seeking to interrogate Rebels captured during that day's fighting. "What action shall I take in this matter, if any?" Butler queried Grant. "General Gillmore refuses to demand a court of inquiry, and yet is preparing his case."

Somehow, despite these distractions, Grant's plan to envelop Petersburg continued to move forward. Throughout the evening, Eighteenth Corps soldiers relieved Wright's Sixth Corps troops, who then marched southward to take station on the left of the Second Corps, along the Jerusalem Plank Road.

Confederate Lines, Petersburg

P. G. T. Beauregard was once more magnificent in defense. Today he forwarded to Braxton Bragg, Jefferson Davis's military adviser, copies of all the messages he had received and sent between June 14 and June 15. Beauregard took pains to point out the great odds he had faced and how, time and again, he had told Richmond that it must decide whether to employ the few forces it had available in holding the Bermuda Hundred lines or in manning Petersburg's defenses. When no decision was forthcoming, Beauregard had made the call. "The result of the concentration of my forces was the successful defense of. . . Petersburg," he concluded, with the triumphal flourish of a wronged man vindicated by history.

In not-so-distant Richmond, War Clerk John B. Jones wrote, "Gen. Beauregard has not been removed from his command,—it would be too great a shock to popular sentiment."

There was action today south of Petersburg, where cavalry units from Brigadier General Rufus Barringer's brigade tangled with Federal infantry feeling their way westward toward the Weldon Railroad. John W. Gordon, a trooper in the 2nd North Carolina Cavalry, wrote in his diary, "To day the Yankees try to take the Weldon Rail road, but after a fight of three hours we repulse them." "We captured fifteen prisoners representing nine different regiments," another Tarheel rider declared.

Backup for the outnumbered cavalrymen came on the run in the form of infantry from Cadmus Wilcox's division of A. P. Hill's Third Corps. "About 2 p.m. the cavalry reported that the enemy were advancing towards the Weldon Railroad and were not far from it," Wilcox later wrote. "The division was ordered out to check this move of the enemy, [and] the Confederate cavalry were found 2 miles from town on the rail road. . . ." In a letter written after the war, Wilcox continued his account of the action: "Two of my brigades were moved forward[,]... the enemy... gave way and were followed...till dark arrested the march, within a few hundred yards of the Jerusalem plank road. . . . The division returned to its position on the Petersburg lines after dark."

Despite the relative ease with which he turned back these Union probes, Robert E. Lee harbored no illusions. He warned in a letter written today to C.S. War Secretary James Seddon that it "will be almost impossible to preserve the connection between this place and Weldon."

Wednesday, June 22
Union Lines, near Petersburg

At 3:00 a.m.—one hour behind schedule—Brigadier General James H. Wilson led his mounted raiding force southwest from the Union lines. His weary cavalrymen had received little rest in the past twenty-four hours, and consequently, one trooper recalled, the slouched men on horseback were "more asleep than awake."

Wilson's 5,000-man division, augmented by the 2,400 riders assigned from Kautz's command from the Army of the James, reached the Weldon Railroad at about midday, cutting it at Reams Station, about seven miles south of the Confederate lines. An Ohio trooper named Roger Hannaford thought Reams Station "a pretty little place. . . . The houses were inhabited, with nice yards & fruit trees around, blooming with flowers." Wilson had no time for such sentimental observations. He ordered the station buildings burned and the rails torn up. His raiding column moved off by early afternoon on a course to the west.

The rugged terrain west of the Jerusalem Plank Road bedeviled Union schemes almost at once. The Second and Sixth corps began this day holding a line that ran roughly parallel to the road. The plan called for that line to swing west as far as the Weldon Railroad and then north, closing on the Confederate lines guarding Petersburg's south side. In this way, the two corps would form a great blue door shutting against the Rebel earthworks, with the Sixth Corps on the outer edge of this new line and the Second Corps (connecting with the Fifth) on the inner portion. The trick was for the two corps to maintain a solid, unbroken front during the maneuver. Any gap between the two might allow Confederate units to break through and launch one of their patented flank attacks.

Second Corps aide Charles Morgan was up early trying to shepherd the moving units, but progress was slow. The Second Corps was pivoting according to instructions, but the Sixth Corps was moving westerly only—when it moved at all. Gaps were constantly opening up between the corps, and time was lost as officers spread the skirmish lines even thinner to reestablish contact.

John Gibbon's Second Corps division was the hinge. Its four brigades crossed to the west of the Jerusalem Plank Road before dawn, turned north, and moved to the edge of the woods fronting Petersburg's earthworks. The ground was difficult to traverse: the men were "in a swamp, covered with a thicket of undergrowth so dense that even in light of the morning sun one could scarcely see from flank to flank of our little battalion, numbering now less than a hundred men," said an officer in the 15th Massachusetts.

Gibbon's line was extended westward by Gershom Mott's command. "The division having deployed into line we again set to work to intrench and before noon we had another strong line of breast-works in front of us and congratulated ourselves that we had so good a protection," recalled one of Mott's soldiers.

It fell to Francis Barlow's division to make the Second Corps's connection to the Sixth, a task that became increasingly difficult as the morning progressed. Wright's men were achieving very little headway in the face of some stiff skirmishing. The soldiers were unfamiliar with the ground, and their first instinct was to dig in, something Wright was disposed to let them do.

Between 9:00 and 10:00 a.m., Second Corps aide Morgan rode down to the Sixth Corps and found that Wright "had made no progress." Returning with his report, Morgan met Francis Barlow, who was directing his division to break its tenuous link with the Sixth Corps and take position on the left of Mott's command. Morgan was aghast; he was certain that this action would "imperil very much the command." He rode back to the Jones House, where he learned that Barlow was following orders. George Meade, impatient with the delays, had commanded David Birney to move the Second Corps into its assigned position "independent of any [movement] by the Sixth Corps." According to Barlow, Meade had declared that "each corps must look out for itself."

Horatio Wright reported at 12:10 p.m. that his skirmish line had at last shaken itself loose from the Jerusalem Plank Road and was slowly advancing toward the Weldon Railroad. Meade's aide Theodore Lyman communicated from Wright's headquarters an hour later that the Sixth Corps's advance parties had "struck the enemy's infantry skirmishers in heavy force. They drove our men a few yards back, but they recovered and now hold without advancing." Wright was stalled.

What everyone had feared might happen had happened. A large gap now separated the right of the Sixth Corps from the left and rear of the Second.

Abraham Lincoln paid a visit today to the Army of the James. The presidential party sailed from City Point at about 8:00 a.m., picking up General Butler and S. P. Lee, admiral of the James River fleet, along the way. "Mr. Lincoln was in excellent spirits," Horace Porter observed, "and listened with great eagerness to the descriptions of the works, which could be seen from the river, and the objects for which they had been constructed." At one place an especially formidable earthwork was pointed out. "When Grant once gets possession of a place, he holds on to it as if he had inherited it," Lincoln joked.

The group went ashore to briefly review the troops. "We were apprised of the fact that our worthy President, Abraham Lincoln, was near us and all that were not engaged on duty were ordered to appear near the regiment headquarters and render a proper salute," was how one New Hampshire noncom remembered the occasion. The cheering of the troops caused the Chief Executive to remove his hat in acknowledgment. "Mr. Lincoln for the rest of the ride [along nearly three miles of lines] was compelled to remain uncovered, with his head exposed to the broiling heat of the sun," *New York Times* reporter Henry Winser wrote. "Such is the penalty of greatness!"

Thermometers were registering well over a hundred degrees in the sun, and Lincoln was showing the strain. A soldier in the 3rd New Hampshire thought the President looked "haggard," while another, in the 6th Connecticut Regiment, described him as "careworn and troubled." This did not diminish the reception Lincoln received: "We greeted the immortal President with enthusiastic cheering," insisted a New Yorker in the 48th regiment.

Lincoln returned to City Point and was soon on his way back to Washington. "His visit to the army had been a memorable event," Horace Porter concluded. "General Grant and he had had so much delightful intercourse that they parted from each other with unfeigned regret, and both felt that their acquaintance had already ripened into a genuine friendship."

Confederate Lines, South of Petersburg

Once again, troops belonging to Cadmus Wilcox's division of A. P. Hill's corps were on the move. As Wilcox later recalled, "I had been ordered out to meet a second advance of the enemy, reported by the cavalry as being directed against the [Weldon] railroad, with instructions to drive this force back to the Jerusalem plank road. The same route was pursued as on the previous day, but attended with more difficulties and delays. The advance from the railroad toward the plank road was in line of battle, preceded by skirmishers; frequent halts were made, and the enemy's skirmishers had to be pushed back." His men were exchanging shots with advance parties from the Yankee Sixth Corps.

Wilcox's slow advance came to a halt at about 1:00 p.m., "at a point some 200 yards short of that reached the evening before....The thickness of the undergrowth rendered it difficult to reconnoiter, but reports from the skirmish line, as well as from prisoners, indicated that the enemy were in force on the plank road, and the officer in command of the skirmishers reported them to be intrenched." Another officer, this one in the 28th North Carolina, afterward attested to the difficulty of moving over this ground, declaring it to be filled with "as many natural difficulties as I ever saw."

William Mahone's men held the lines fronting the Union Second Corps as it cautiously stretched westward from the Jerusalem Plank Road. The officer watched the slow, deliberate procession with mounting impatience, eager for orders to stop it. Even as he was observing Birney's troops "moving in orderly fashion across the Plank Road in the direction of the Johnson House," Robert E. Lee rode up to take a look. Lee, as Mahone recalled it, "expressed a desire that something should be done to arrest the progress of the Federal prolongation.

Mahone knew the local geography well thanks to his pre-war employment as a surveyor for the railroad. He remembered that there was a large ravine that sliced southward out of the Confederate lines at a point about a mile and a half west of the plank road, and he was confident that it would be possible to infiltrate a force down that ravine to strike the enemy in its flank.

Lee gave his approval. Mahone quickly detailed three brigades to "drop quietly to the rear so as to avoid discovery and then [move] … up the ravine." Alabama soldiers from Sanders's Brigade, Georgia troops from Wright's Brigade, and Virginians under Colonel David Weisiger were chosen. A soldier in the 12th Virginia remembered how they "moved out [in] double time in front of the enemy on our left flank and they fired on us all the time, now &c then a man would fall wounded &c some died." Added William H. Stewart, in the 61st Virginia, "we marched across the open field in our front through a deep ravine to a thick wood, which covered our movements and prevented the enemy from observing us."

Mahone was anxious that no opportunity be missed to land a killing blow. Even as his three brigades were filing into their jump-off position, Mahone sent out couriers to find General Wilcox in order to "explain to him what I was about and to request that he bear down on my firing." If all of this force could be brought against the vulnerable flank of the Union line, Mahone believed, the Yankee corps would be crushed. "Whenever Mahone moves out, somebody is apt to be hurt," a fellow Confederate officer observed.

It was about 3:00 p.m. when Mahone was ready to attack.

Union Lines, West of the Jerusalem Plank Road

Major Moncena Dunn awoke with a start. He had fallen asleep in the still, sultry atmosphere of the forest undergrowth along the Second Corps line. His men, all belonging to the 19th Massachusetts, had finished entrenching their position and were getting what rest they could. Dunn cleared his head of a disturbing dream and joined his fellow officers for a hasty lunch. He told them while they were eating of his curious vision. "We were lying just as we are here," he said, "and the rebels came in our rear and captured the entire regiment." According to another officer who heard this tale, "we laughed at his story."

John Gibbon's men had reasons for their confidence. Their north-facing line was already strong enough to repel all but the most determined assaults, and with two full divisions on their left and the Fifth Corps connecting to their right, they felt perfectly secure. The only bother was the enemy artillery fire that was being directed against a small hill on the left of Gibbon's line, which was being prepared for a battery to occupy.

W. D. Robinson was part of the fatigue party detailed to help construct the position for the 12th New York Light Artillery, Captain George F. McKnight commanding. The work was finished after midday, and at 2:00 p.m. McKnight opened fire on the Confederate main line, several hundred yards distant. "[Such] a reply we got," Robinson remembered. "It was awful. Solid shot and shell struck the works, and threw the dirt all over us."

Gershom Mott's division took up the line on Gibbon's left. A soldier in the 57th Pennsylvania recalled marching through the woods to that point, "where we built a line of works with nothing to work with but our bayonets and tin plates." Another of Mott's men noted that "we could hear the enemy chopping and digging in our front and not far away."

Francis Barlow, whose division made up the left of the Second Corps line, was unhappy with his position. "By the movement ordered[,] not only my flank but my rear was exposed to the enemy," he complained. Barlow did his best to secure the flank. "I placed one brigade on the left of General Mott's line and threw back two small brigades at nearly a right angle to General Mott's line as a protection to my flank. I had scarcely got into position before the enemy's skirmishers began pressing into the gap between me and the Sixth Corps."

The time was a little past 3:00 p.m.

Confederate Battle Lines, West of the Jerusalem Plank Road

Artilleryman W. Gordon McCabe rode with Mahone's three-brigade column. As the gunner remembered, "Passing his men quickly along a ravine, which screened them from the enemy's pickets, Mahone gained a point which he rightly conjectured to be beyond the hostile flank. Here, in an open field fronting the 'Johnson House,' he formed line of battle—the brigades of Sanders and Wright in front, his own brigade, commanded by Colonel Weisiger, supporting the right, while McIntosh of the artillery was directed to move with two guns in the open on the left."

"When all was ready," Adjutant L. H. Carter, in the 10th Georgia Battalion, wrote, "the word was given and Wright's brigade, with the deafening Southern yell leaped the fence and dashed into the thick undergrowth, leading the advance. The double line of Yankee skirmishers fled before us as on we pressed, through the dense thicket, making the woods ring with cheers, to the assault of the enemy's breastworks."

"The left of the brigade coming out into an open field before the rest of the line became visible, and the brigade on our left being behind, received a concentrated cross fire from the Yankee works and suffered severely."

The exposed Georgia regiments reeled back, and the advance halted while the battle lines were realigned and Weisiger's men moved up from their support position to Wright's right flank. Then the advance resumed, this time decisively.

According to artilleryman McCabe, "with a wild yell which rang out shrill and fierce through the gloomy pines, Mahone's men burst upon the flank—a pealing volley, which roared along the whole front—a stream of wasting fire, under which the adverse left fell as one man—and the bronzed veterans swept forward, shriveling up Barlow's division as lightning shrivels the dead leaves of autumn."

Union Lines, West of the Jerusalem Plank Road

Charley Barth, a private in Company C of the 116th Pennsylvania, had wandered out in front of his regiment to fill his comrade's canteens. Charley's regiment, holding the extreme left of the Second Corps, had been spared much of the skirmish fire between the front lines. Barth was bent over his task when, according to the regimental historian, "zip! went a ball in the water. Looking up he saw the Confederates not fifty yards away. As he afterwards remarked, he made 'a blue streak for the Regiment!'"

Allen Landis, another soldier in the 116th, writing on June 26, said that the "Rebels…had worked around us and were right in our rear, blazing away and cheering like mad men. Well that was no place for us to offer much of a resistance—we were taken by surprise. You can bet high that there was some 'skedaddling' done about that time." "The attack was to the Union troops more than a surprise," another Pennsylvanian declared. "It was an astonishment."

Barlow's division disintegrated. Explained one New York soldier, "When we think of the many struggles our men had with unseen foes in the woods, and the disasters which often followed, it is easy to account for the distrust we felt as we entered such places…and so it resulted here for, when the enemy flanked us on the left, a panic ran along the line from left to right." A comrade offered this defense for their actions: "Men who can advance upon an entrenched enemy over open fields, or who behind earthworks would defy double their number, can hardly stand still and receive a severe fire from three sides from an unseen foe."

The stampede spread to Mott's division, on Barlow's right. "This was a case of run or be gobbled," a soldier in the 1st Maine Heavy Artillery said afterward. "First the staff officers, then the regimental and company commanders, shouted the command: 'Look out for yourselves; make a stand in the old line.'" "Men were flying in all directions," Maine private John Haley insisted. According to another account, "Colonel R. McAllister, of the Eleventh New Jersey, commanding [one of Mott's brigades] ...is reported to have shouted when he saw his command break: 'Stand fast men!' But when he saw that to remain longer in that position meant certain capture or annihilation, he sang out at the top of his voice: 'Run boys, run! Run like the devil!'"

John Gibbon's division, snug behind its earthworks, was utterly unprepared for an attack from the rear. His leftmost regiments caught the first gusts of the storm as routed troops fled behind them shouting, "Fall back; you are outflanked!" Regiment after regiment faced the perilous decision of whether to fight or flee. In the 152nd New York, the decision was to run: "Every one acted independently, and used their own judgment and legs in getting away," a New Yorker recalled. "A few [ran] into the ranks of the enemy amid the blinding smoke, and were captured."

Disaster struck two small veteran regiments, the 15th and 19th Massachusetts. "With the enemy in front, flank and rear, surrender was inevitable," a soldier in the 15th remembered. "The tattered shot-ridden flag was seized by hostile hands, and the eventful history of the Fifteenth . . . was ended."

Four months earlier, when the men of the 19th Massachusetts had volunteered to extend their enlistments to the end of the war, Captain John G. B. Adams had proudly stepped forward with the rest. Now he raced back from an emergency officers' conference to find his company and regiment surrounded. "I saw my men standing up and the rebels as thick as mosquitoes. A major of a Georgia regiment demanded my sword, [and] I presented it to him, omitting the presentation speech." Just nineteen days earlier, Sergeant Mike Scannell had earned a battlefield commission at Cold Harbor for carrying the regimental flag under a heavy fire. This day, however, patriotism gave way to pragmatism. A Rebel soldier spotted him holding the colors and ran over, shouting, "You damned Yankee, give me that flag." "Well," Scannell replied, "it is twenty years since I came to this country, and you are the first man who ever called me a Yankee. You can take the flag for the compliment." Also rounded up was Major Moncena Dunn, whose prescient warning had not saved his regiment.

McKnight's battery was overrun, its gunners driven off, killed, or captured. Isolated regiments made brief, futile attempts to stem the tide. "There seems to have been no time during this most unfortunate and disgraceful affair when the same promptness and spirit might not have ended the disasters of the day," acting corps commander David Birney wrote.

Staff aide George Armes stopped by the Jones House to tell Winfield Hancock of the rout. "He sprang out of his bed, wild with excitement at the bad news, but, of course, the doctor would not let him go to the front, as he wished to do."

Confederate Battle Lines, West of the Jerusalem Plank Road

"We faced by the left flank & moved down on the enemy & drove them pell mell out of their temporary breastworks made of wood," was how one Virginia soldier remembered the assault. "The old 41st covered itself with glory," another Virginian proclaimed.

William H. Stewart, of the 61st Virginia, recalled, "our regiment ... struck the enemy's newly-made earthworks, and ...we were at once in their front and rear, fighting hand to hand with bayonets, butts of muskets, swords and pistols. And now my spade came into unusual use. I saw a man with his musket to his shoulder, who had not yet realized that we had surrounded them, aiming at one of our men in front of his works. I ran up and struck him a hard blow on the side of his head, forcing him to drop his rifle and surrender unconditionally."

The suddenness with which Mahone's attack had achieved success was now matched by the suddenness with which it came to an end. Mahone rode along the newly captured lines and saw at once that his attacking brigades "had been severely depleted in carrying off prisoners." The wiry Virginia officer had hoped for timely assistance from Wilcox's Division to the south, but it was not forthcoming.

Cadmus Wilcox had his hands full keeping his brigades under control. "The woods and undergrowth were so thick that it was not possible for a Colonel to see his regiment in line," he later explained. Shortly before Mahone's attack began, corps commander A. P. Hill found Wilcox and directed him to detach two brigades to support the flank action. "These brigades moved as directed," Wilcox reported, "but owing to the dense undergrowth the advance was very slow." Shortly after a rising roar of gunfire off to Wilcox's left and rear indicated that the action there was under way, couriers arrived with orders from Mahone for the two brigades to move "in a direction different from that [which] the corps commander had directed." Wilcox hesitated. He had been skirmishing constantly since early morning, and he worried that the large force before him—Wright's Sixth Corps—might advance at any time. Also, his ammunition was almost used up. "I determined to obey the orders of the corps commander," Wilcox remembered.

By the time his two brigades reached Mahone, it was too late for them to do anything. Long after the war, the combative Virginia officer remained bitter about Wilcox's inaction. Had Wilcox come when he was needed, Mahone later insisted to a Union officer, "we should not only have swept from the field all the Federal force west of the Plank Road, but materially disorganized your intrenched line east of that road."

Union Lines, along the Jerusalem Plank Road

The earthworks erected by the Second Corps on June 21 now served as a rallying point for the disorganized units scrambling out of the woods. The corps artillery chief, John C. Tidball, ordered five batteries into line to bolster its defense. Captain A. Judson Clark's New Jersey battery was posted where Gibbon's right touched the plank road; it came under fire from the heavy guns in the Petersburg lines as well as from McKnight's captured cannon. "The air was filled with bursting shells, and death was dancing wildly everywhere in that vicinity," the *New York Herald's* Finley Anderson reported.

When the attack broke, Nelson Miles's brigade, in Barlow's division, had already fallen back to the east in an attempt to connect with the Sixth Corps, and so was able to form relatively unscathed on the Jerusalem Plank Road line. It became the nucleus around which a final defensive line was formed. The few Rebel units that emerged from the woods to test this line were blasted back under cover. "It was fun to see them fall like grass," a Pennsylvania soldier recalled with grim satisfaction, "and the rest run like the devil was after them." "The enemy attacked smartly on two or three points," David Birney afterwards reported, "but were easily repulsed. At 4 p.m. I reported to the major-general commanding that my lines were re-established and the troops again in condition." Birney ordered a counterattack to retake McKnight's battery. The order went to John Gibbon, who passed it to Brigadier General Byron Pierce, commanding his first brigade. Pierce organized a charge that failed; Gibbon later dismissed this action as a "rather feeble effort."

The Sixth Corps, posted to the south, had played a surprisingly passive role. For most of the soldiers wearing the Greek Cross emblem, this was a day of shadowboxing. Throughout the hot afternoon the men thrashed uselessly amidst what one Connecticut soldier described as a "wilderness of woods, bushes, brambles, and vines so thick that a man could hardly see his neighbor."

An advance was finally organized at 7:00 p.m. "We had not gone far, however," a New Jersey soldier recollected, "before the lines were thrown into confusion by the density of the wood, and its character. . . . We struggled back and forth in the woods, until at last we lost our way. . . ." "Night was on us," a nearby New Yorker reflected, "and all we knew was that we were still on the earth."

Darkness ended the fighting. Some Union soldiers were never certain exactly what had happened to them on this day. As one frustrated Federal wrote, "On the 22nd of June occurred what we never dignified with the name of a battle[, but] what has always been known by our men as the 'Petersburg affair'." Army of the Potomac Chief of Staff Andrew Humphreys later tallied Birney's losses at "about 1,700 prisoners, four guns, and several colors. The loss in killed and wounded was not severe." A more careful modern accounting puts the Second Corps casualties at 650 killed or wounded and 1,742 captured, for a grand total of 2,392. Sixth Corps losses, in all categories, came to 150.

Reports coming back to Grant's headquarters at first understated the extent of the disaster. Grant informed Washington in a communication sent at 9:00 a.m. on June 23 that the Rebel attack had "caused some confusion" but that order "was soon restored and the enemy pushed back." Twenty-four hours later he had to confess that the whole matter "was much worse than I had heretofore learned. . . . The affair was a stampede and surprise to both parties and ought to have been turned in our favor." (Writing to his wife, Julia, Grant still exuded confidence: "Our work progresses here slowly and I feel will progress securely until Richmond finally falls. The task is a big one and had to be performed by some one.")

John Gibbon knew why the Second Corps had folded like a house of cards. Using his division as an example, Gibbon pointed out that it had begun the current campaign (on May 1) with 6,799 men and had received, in the course of the next forty days, an additional 4,263. His losses (up to June 30, the next reporting date after June 23) were 6,183—379 of them officers. "Of course, the bravest and most efficient officers and men were those who fell; it is always so," he stated, concluding, "These facts serve to demonstrate the wear and tear on the division, and to show why it is that troops, which at the commencement of the campaign were equal to almost any undertaking, became toward the end of it unfit for almost any."

Confederate Lines, West of the Jerusalem Plank Road

Alabama colonel Hilary Herbert recalled the Federal attempt to retake McKnight's battery. "As soon as we had occupied the works of the enemy, our men expecting an attack provided themselves each with two guns of those captured from the enemy, and loaded them, every man of the 8th (and it is probably true of the other regiments) had not only his own, but two loaded guns besides. Soon the enemy was reformed and made a gallant attack to recapture their works, but they were disastrously repulsed."

Mahone organized a withdrawal to the main lines once darkness fell. "That night every man was required to carry off as many muskets as he was able to tote," remembered James E. Phillips, of the 12th Virginia. "I carried four on my shoulders." The quartet of Yankee cannon was also hitched up and hauled into the Petersburg lines.

Robert E. Lee reported the results of the action to Richmond late this evening. "The enemy's infantry was attacked this afternoon on the west side of the Jerusalem plank road and driven from his first line of works to his second on that road by General Mahone with a part of his division. About 1,600 prisoners, four pieces of artillery, eight stands of colors, and a large number of small arms were captured."

Also this evening, Lee met with E. P. Alexander, the youthful artillery chief of Richard Anderson's First Corps. Lee had a plan in mind that would, he believed, raise the siege of Petersburg. Lee's aide Charles Venable watched as the two men bent over maps and "made arrangements for the disposition of artillery for an attack on the morning of the 24th." Another part of Lee's plan required the services of Alexander's corps commander, R. H. Anderson. Lee tried out a few of his conjectures on Anderson, who replied in a 9:00 p.m. dispatch, "You are certainly right, I think, as to the [poor] condition of the enemy's troops and as to the happy results that may be expected from following up the blow Hill has given them."

Lee was determined to reclaim the strong earthworks lost by Beauregard and to strike another blow against the enemy's morale.

Confederate losses this day were never officially reported, but a modern survey of newspaper accounts and brigade returns puts Mahone s casualties at 421 killed, wounded, or missing, and Wilcox's at 151, for a total of 572.

Thursday, June 23
Union Lines, near Petersburg

"At daybreak on the morning of the twenty-third," recollected a soldier in the 17th Maine, "we were ordered to charge upon and retake the works. . . . We moved in splendid style, in a single line of battle; but we were soon gratified at the discovery that our wary foe had abandoned the line, during the night, and we occupied it without firing a shot, or the loss of a man." "We found all of our dead stripped to the skin," a Pennsylvania soldier grimly added.

The official diary of the Second Corps noted today's actions as "some skirmishing and artillery. Troops engaged in throwing up rifle-pits." However, things were anything but quiet for the corps surgeons. "I am up to my neck in work," one wrote at about this time. "It is slaughter, slaughter."

George Meade was determined that Wright's Sixth Corps would accomplish the mission of reaching the Weldon Railroad. Accordingly, a heavy skirmish line set out, and shortly after 10:00 a.m. Wright informed Meade, "I have possession of the railroad by a detachment, and shall extend the picket-line to it." This detachment, consisting of about ninety picked men, was joined by some fatigue troops from Lewis Grant's all-Vermont brigade, who began tearing up the track. Lewis Grant assumed responsibility for protecting the operation and soon had spread some of his regiments around the working parties in a large square.

The rugged ground was still causing much confusion among the Federal troops, and as a result, Lewis Grant's men were more isolated from the rest of their division than they realized. Confederate infantry appeared in force early in the afternoon, marching south along the railroad. The working parties and sharpshooters quickly scuttled east, back to the main corps line. But portions of two Vermont regiments, which were holding the northern face of the protective square, held their positions in the mistaken belief that supports were nearby. The two regiments were promptly cut off from the rest of the brigade and surrounded, resulting in the capture of 399 men from the 4th and 11th Vermont. Adding to the insult, less than half a mile of railroad track was ripped up before the Federals were chased away.

Whatever plan Wright may have had for a large-scale advance was halted by the Rebel attack. "I have stopped the movement of my main lines forward," he informed Meade at 4:00 p.m. Meade's reply, sent through Andrew Humphreys, was almost a plea, entreating the Sixth Corps commander to "take the initiative and attack the enemy, if in your judgment, this course is advisable. . . ." Wright hesitated. At 5:30 p.m., 5:40, and 6:30, Meade again urged Wright to move forward and engage the enemy, but the Sixth Corps commander was seeing a replay of the Second Corps disaster. "The enemy is evidently in large force, but where he may strike is quite uncertain," Wright replied at 7:00 p.m. "It seems to me that till everything is quiet our role is the defensive." At 7:35 p.m., Meade swallowed the bitter pill. "Your delay has been fatal," he accused Wright. Meade's aide Theodore Lyman was even more blunt, declaring: "On this particular occasion Wright showed himself totally unfit to command a corps."

Writing today to Army Chief of Staff Henry Halleck, U. S. Grant dropped the other shoe. "The siege of Richmond bids fair to be tedious and in consequence of the very extended lines we must have, a much larger force will be necessary than would be required in ordinary sieges against the same force that now opposes us. . . . All the troops [that can be spared from less critical military areas] should be sent here at once."

Confederate Lines, Petersburg

The reporter for the *Petersburg Express* filed this account of the June 23 action along the Weldon Railroad:

Gen. Mahone was speedily despatched at the head of a body of troops, to drive the rascals off. Upon approaching the spot about one hundred and fifty of Grant's horsemen were discovered displacing rails and removing sills. They fled precipitously upon the appearance of our forces, but it was soon ascertained that there was a heavy body of infantry in the woods, east of the track, massed for the purpose of supporting the cavalry.

Gen. Mahone threw forward a heavy line of skirmishers, engaged the attention of the blue coats, and then put into execution one of those flanking movements for which he has become somewhat noted during the campaign. About twilight, Perry's [Florida] brigade, now commanded by Gen. [Joseph] Finnegan, succeeded in swinging around, and brought up in rear of the enemy. . . . We succeeded in securing only four hundred and eighty-three invaders, the remaining running so swiftly that it was found impossible to overtake them.

Robert E. Lee met with P. G. T. Beauregard sometime today to work out plans for an attack on the Union lines. The commander of the Army of Northern Virginia was certain that a section of the Federal trenches lying between the Appomattox River and the City Point Road was the weak link in Grant's defensive scheme. The earthworks themselves were but partially finished and lacked abatis. The Federal lines at that point could also be enfiladed by artillery placed on the north bank of the river, and E. P. Alexander had promised to pull together one dandy bombardment when the sun came up.

South Carolina troops from Brigadier General Johnson Hagood's brigade of Robert Hoke's division held that section of the Confederate line and would spearhead the assault. The strike force needed more weight to do its job, however, so Lee decided to use Major General Charles Field's division, from Anderson's First Corps. Lee issued his instructions through Beauregard, since the latter was technically responsible for Petersburg's defense. Beauregard promptly sent out the following message from his headquarters at Dunn's Hill:

FIRST. THE BATTERIES ON THE NORTH SIDE OF THE APPOMATTOX SHALL OPEN AT DAYLIGHT TO-MORROW ON THE LINES AND BATTERIES OF THE ENEMY IN FRONT OF GENERAL HOKE, AND WILL CONTINUE FIRING FOR HALF AN HOUR FROM THE TIME OF FIRING THE FIRST GUN. THEY WILL THEN CEASE FIRING FOR FIVE MINUTES AS A SIGNAL FOR GENERAL HOKE TO COMMENCE HIS MOVEMENT. THEY WILL RESUME THEIR FIRE, CONCENTRATING IT ONLY ON BATTERIES AND DISTINCT LINES AND MASSES OF THE ENEMY. . . .

SECOND. AT THE SAME TIME ... A SERIOUS DEMONSTRATION . . . SHOULD BE MADE FROM THE RIGHT OF OUR LINE. . . .

THIRD. MAJOR-GENERAL HOKE SHALL . . . SWING AROUND ON HIS RIGHT FLANK, SO AS TO TAKE THE ENEMY'S FIRST AND SECOND LINES IN FLANK, ADVANCING RAPIDLY TO THE ATTACK OF THE ENEMY'S POSITION NEAR HARE'S HOUSE. . . . HAVING TAKEN HARE'S HOUSE HE WILL CONTINUE THE MOVEMENT TO RETAKE OUR OLD LINE OF WORKS BETWEEN THE NORFOLK RAILROAD AND OUR SECOND LINE OF WORKS.

FOURTH. FIELD'S DIVISION . . . WILL BE PUT IN THE BEST POSITION BY LIEUTENANT GENERAL ANDERSON TO SUPPORT HOKE'S ATTACK AND PROTECT HIS LEFT FLANK. . . .

FIFTH. WHEN MAJOR-GENERAL HOKE SHALL ATTACK THE ENEMY ON THE
EAST SIDE OF THE NORFOLK RAILROAD, OPPOSITE TO [BUSH- ROD]
JOHNSON'S FRONT, MAJOR-GENERAL JOHNSON SHALL TAKE THE OFFENSIVE
AND ATTACK BOLDLY THE FORCES OF THE ENEMY. . . .

SIXTH. HE WILL PLACE . . . BATTERIES IN POSITION TO ENFILADE THE
RAILROAD AND TAYLOR'S CREEK AS SOON AS HE SHALL FIND IT
PRACTICABLE.

When Robert Hoke and Charles Field reviewed these orders, each understood them differently. Hoke believed that once his attacking line cleared the enemy rifle pits screening the first Union defensive line, Field's men would then advance to the main position. Field, on the other hand, was convinced that he was not to move forward until Hoke had captured the main Union line. "I was to carry the enemy's second [line] if he should have one, and if not, I was to attack wherever and whatever I found best," he later reported.

Only a handful of officers were briefed. "This precaution was taken, fearing that by some means the enemy might learn our intentions and prepare for us," Hoke wrote.

Friday, June 24
Union Lines, South of the Appomattox River

As the first glimmer of daylight touched the south bank of the Appomattox, Confederate batteries on both sides of the river rumbled to life. One New Hampshire soldier, camped well in the rear of the front line, recalled the cannonade as a "terrific noise, resounding through these deep woods like the roar of continuous thunder." A New Yorker in the target area remembered the moment as well. "The men kept under cover, lay flat on the ground, never fired a gun, while the shells tore through the breastworks or exploded over their heads." The *New York Tribune's* reporter believed that with the "exception of Gettysburg, the war has not afforded another instance of so many guns concentrated upon one point and firing so rapidly for such a length of time. The plain seemed alive with bursting shell, the discharges were as continuous and rapid as the ticking of a watch."

Colonel Guy V. Henry of the Eighteenth Corps, commanding this section of the Union trenches, suspected that the bombardment was a prelude to a ground assault. Should that be the case, he had a few tricks up his sleeve. His skirmishers, occupying the advanced rifle pits, were instructed to fall back to the main line at the first sign of an enemy advance. The troops posted along the main line were told not to fire until ordered to do so. In this way, the first Confederate battle line into the rifle pits would be trapped there.

Confederate Lines, South of the Appomattox River

Major General Robert Hoke was growing frantic. The bombardment had begun at 7:00 a.m., right on schedule. He had serious doubts that the cannonade would do enough damage to justify itself. "Indeed, I fear we were injured more than we gained by the use of the guns, as it notified the enemy of our intended attack," he reflected afterward.

What worried Hoke even more, however, was that none of the troops from Anderson's corps had yet appeared in the main trenches behind his assault spearhead. The artillery barrage lifted like clockwork after thirty minutes, signaling Hoke to advance, and still there was no sign of the heavy supporting columns. Hoke hesitated. At 7:30 a.m., he sent a courier back to look for Field's men, with the message that in "fifteen minutes the attack would certainly take place."

Three regiments from Johnson Hagood's South Carolina brigade would go over the top first. Hagood planned for his advance to proceed in two waves, the first consisting of "400 picked men and officers as skirmishers" and the second containing the remaining 550 men of the 11th, 21st, and 27th South Carolina regiments. Hagood himself would lead the second line, and Lieutenant Colonel Patrick H. Nelson would command the skirmishers.

Some 400 yards separated the two lines. Adjacent to the Union rifle pits, a small oat field rippled in the bombardment's wake. Five minutes after the antipersonnel shelling ended, the anti-battery fire began. Hagood noted the time as 7:42 precisely when he ordered his skirmishers forward.

"Nelson's line responded to his order with energy," a South Carolinian watching from the second line remembered. "Instantly, almost as one man, they mounted the top of their own works and rushed across the wide, open space that separated them from the Federal rifle-pits . . . and not once did they waver or halt until they had captured every pit on the enemy's line from the river to the railroad."

Major General Charles Field would always believe that he did more than his orders required this day. "Although it was not expected that I would move from my position, in reserve, till Hoke had not only vacated his line, but had carried the enemy's, I was so anxious to do more than my duty, that as soon as I saw the first signs of stir in Hoke's line, I rushed forward with my leading brigade . . . and took shelter in Hoke's breastworks with his troops." Field had expected all of Robert Hoke's division to take part in the attack, but to his surprise he found much of it still in the trenches. As Field saw it, "I had nothing to do until they had gotten out of my way and done the duty assigned them."

Johnson Hagood's second line raced across the open plain and went to ground in the oat field "about half-way between the two hostile intrenchments to await Anderson's [i.e., Field's] advance." The enemy's line had come alive with gunfire by now, trapping the first wave on the eastern edge of the field. The captured rifle pits were open to the rear, denying the attacking party their use as cover. Hagood's first line "remained in the oats and behind the embankment of the rifle-pits, exposed to the enemy's heavy fire, hoping every moment to hear the shouts of the supporting brigade," a soldier in the 21st South Carolina noted angrily.

Union Lines, South of the Appomattox River

Reported Colonel Henry, "As soon as my pickets were withdrawn my front line, which up to this time had been silent, commenced a rapid and telling fire on the enemy. The latter found themselves entrapped in my skirmish line, not being able to hold it, neither finding it possible to advance or retreat. Those who attempted to fall back were shot down, those who came forward first threw away their arms in token of surrender. Those who remained were sent for and brought in, either as wounded or prisoners. Hardly a man escaped."

Confederate Lines, South of the Appomattox River

Robert Hoke later estimated it took nearly an hour after the initial forward movement for Charles Field to ready his two brigades to advance, a delay he believed was fatal. "I advised against it," he later reported, "as the enemy had had ample time to make all preparations to receive us. ... At this time orders were received from General Lee for me to report to him in company with General Field, who abandoned the attack after hearing the position of affairs."

Most of the troops in Hagood's second line eased out of the killing field, but the first was too close to the enemy to escape. "At length hope at last fled and the line gradually surrendered," noted one observer.

Johnson Hagood later calculated his loses at 25 killed, 73 wounded, and 208 missing—about a third of the total force engaged. When the time came for him to write his account of this action, First Corps commander R. H. Anderson passed quickly over the matter, stating that Hoke's "attack was repulsed and the enemy having strongly reinforced that part of his line the further prosecution of the affair was abandoned." Robert Hoke declared, "Both the plan of battle and [the plan] of attack were good, but failed in the execution." Some captured South Carolinians were bitter in their condemnation of Hagood's role, and a number of these animadversions were quoted with relish in Northern newspapers. Hagood later felt compelled to defend his actions to the readers of the *Charleston Mercury*. He explained to the newspaper's editor that he had been briefed on his role "a half hour before the action commenced" and stated his belief that "it is considered everywhere to be the duty of the soldier to endeavor to carry out faithfully and unquestioned the commands of his superior."

Robert E. Lee commented in his review of this action that there "seems to have been some misunderstanding as to the part each division was expected to have performed." His aide Charles Venable reflected, "And thus the whole plan, so well conceived and so successful in its beginning, was given up much to the sorrow of the commanding- general."

Union Lines, near Petersburg

Colonel Guy V. Henry reported his losses in this affair as "trifling"—three killed and eight wounded—but he nonetheless took steps to strengthen his defenses so that the enemy would never again have such an opportunity.

After another morning spent trying to nag Horatio Wright into advancing his Sixth Corps toward the Weldon Railroad, George Meade finally threw in the towel. At 12:40 p.m., he wired Wright:

```
YOU NEED NOT ADVANCE BEYOND YOUR PRESENT LINES UNTIL FURTHER
ORDERS.
```

For the time being, at least, the Weldon Railroad remained open to Confederate traffic.

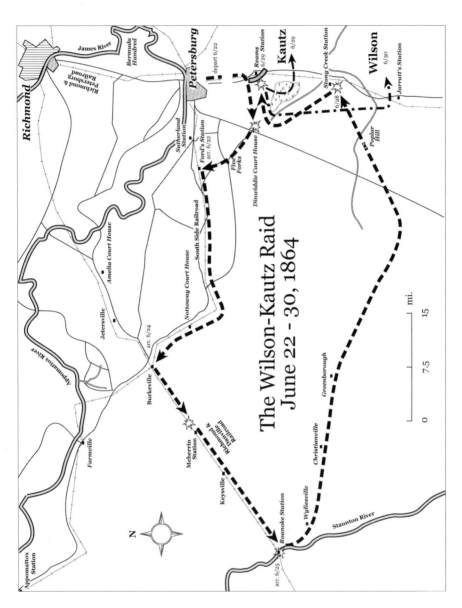

Eight Months Later: Saturday, February 18, 1865
Gravelly Springs, Alabama:
Cavalry Headquarters, Military Division of the Mississippi

Brevet Major General James H. Wilson paused in the midst of planning the greatest cavalry raid of the Civil War—one that would strike deep into the heart of the Confederacy in the last weeks of the conflict—and turned his attention to completing a follow-up report on his Petersburg raid nearly eight months earlier. He had filed an account of the action on July 3 but felt there was a need to explain further the events and decisions that had resulted in his losing nearly a quarter of his command.

HAVING MADE ALL NECESSARY ARRANGEMENTS AND LEFT TWO REGIMENTS ... TO PICKET ON THE LEFT OF THE ARMY, AT 3 A.M. OF THE 22D THE EXPEDITION, CONSISTING OF ABOUT 5,500 CAVALRY AND TWELVE GUNS, BEGAN THE MARCH BY WAY OF REAMS' STATION AND DINWIDDIE COURT HOUSE.

After destroying the depot, thirteen dirt cars, and a few hundred feet of track at Reams Station, seven miles south of Petersburg, Wilson's column wound its way west and north to strike the South Side Railroad at Ford's Station, fourteen miles west of the Cockade City. There his men captured and burned about thirty railroad cars loaded with cotton and furniture.

AT 2 A.M. THE NEXT DAY [JUNE 23] I ORDERED KAUTZ'S DIVISION TO PUSH ON WITH THE UTMOST RAPIDITY FOR BURKEVILLE JUNCTION, AND FOLLOWED WITH THE BALANCE OF THE COMMAND AS RAPIDLY AS IT COULD MARCH AND DESTROY THE ROAD.

Wilson overtook Kautz on June 24, near Burkeville Junction, which was strategically located at the crossing of the South Side Railroad and the Richmond & Danville Railroad, forty miles west of Petersburg. Already Wilson was losing horses at an alarming rate. One Ohio trooper recalled that "we shot on the average one horse every quarter of a mile." To offset theses losses, he sent out detachments to confiscate civilians' horses for his men to use.

EARLY THE NEXT MORNING THE MARCH WAS RESUMED, HEAVY DETAILS ENGAGED IN DESTROYING THE RAILROAD. ABOUT 2 P.M. THE ADVANCE ARRIVED AT ROANOKE STATION, NEAR THE ROANOKE OR STAUNTON RIVER.

Wilson and his columns followed the rail line in a southwesterly direction from Burkeville for another thirty miles. They were now nearly seventy-five miles southwest of Petersburg. The important railroad trestle crossing the Roanoke River at that point was stoutly defended, and after making two costly but unsuccessful attempts to storm it, Wilson fell back.

I DETERMINED TO WITHDRAW TO THE EASTWARD AND MARCH BACK TO THE JAMES RIVER.

Wilson's return march began at about 11:00 o'clock on the night of June 25, and for the next two days it was largely unopposed. The Federal officer faced a difficult decision on June 27, when he had to determine at which point he would recross the Weldon Railroad to link up with the Union army, lying to the east of it. The safest route was also the longest: Jarrett's Station, which was nearly thirty miles south of Petersburg and out of range of the infantry operating from the city. Another possible crossing that was closer to Petersburg and correspondingly riskier was Stony Creek Station, about twenty miles south of the Cockade City. The highest-risk option was Reams Station, Wilson's point of departure. He decided to split the difference.

```
I DETERMINED ... TO LOSE NO TIME, BUT PUSH ON WITH RAPIDITY TO
. . . STONY CREEK DEPOT.
```

A nasty surprise waited for Wilson at Stony Creek: Confederate John R. Chambliss's cavalry brigade, stiffened with about two hundred infantry. Throughout the hot afternoon of June 28, Wilson's weary men tried in vain to break through Chambliss's line.

Wilson up to this point had been able to rely on the fact that the bulk of the Rebel mounted corps, under Wade Hampton, was tied down well north of the James, shadowing Phil Sheridan's cavalry raiding force. But Sheridan's riders had crossed to the south side of the James on June 26 and gone directly into camp, and, unknown to Wilson, Robert E. Lee had promptly put Hampton's men on a course to intercept raiding force.

```
A FEW PRISONERS WERE CAPTURED [AT STONY CREEK DEPOT], FROM WHOM
I LEARNED THAT HAMPTON'S AND FITZHUGH LEE'S DIVISION OF CAVALRY
HAD JUST ARRIVED. ... I DETERMINED TO . . . MOVE BY THE LEFT
FLANK THROUGH THE COUNTRY TO THE ROAD LEADING TO REAMS' STATION.
I HOPED TO . . . REACH THE LEFT OF OUR INFANTRY BEFORE HAMPTON
COULD DISCOVER MY INTENT.
```

When Wilson approached Reams Station, on June 29, he found his way east blocked by two brigades of William Mahone's division. With Hampton pushing up from the south, and Fitzhugh Lee squeezing him from the north and northeast, Wilson was in a box. His command scattered; most of Kautz's division plunged into a nearly impassable swamp and somehow escaped to the east. Wilson, after lightening his column by burning his supply wagons, spiking his cannon, and abandoning his wounded, fell back a few miles to the west, raced south, and then struck east, this time crossing successfully at Jarrett's Station.

> THE ENTIRE COMMAND . . . MARCHED TO THE VICINITY OF CABIN POINT, ON THE JAMES RIVER [TWENTY MILES EAST OF PETERSBURG] . . . ARRIVED AT 2 P.M. [JULY 1] AND ENCAMPED.

Wilson's and Kautz's men had marched over 335 miles between June 22 and July 1. Wilson's losses were 33 killed, 108 wounded, and 674 captured or missing. Kautz's were 48 killed, 153 wounded, and 429 missing or taken prisoner.

Wilson claimed in his immediate after-action report that "Every depot, turn-table, water-tank, and trestle-work between the Sixteen-Mile Turnout on the South Side Railroad to the Roanoke bridge on the Danville road was destroyed." The Confederacy's military railroad chief, I. M. Saint John, later said that it took Southern work crews some sixty- three days to repair the more than sixty miles of track that Wilson destroyed.

Omitted in all of the official assessments of this operation was any mention of the forgotten victims of the raid—the black slaves who had fled their masters and flocked by the hundreds to join what they believed was a march to freedom, only to be cruelly abandoned by their liberators in the scattering at Reams Station.

The July 7 issue of the *Petersburg Express* filled almost two full columns under the banner:

> LIST OF CAPTURED NEGROES ON HAND, JULY 2D, WITH OWNWERS NAMES ATTACHED.

There were more than three hundred slaves named on that list.

Chapter Five

"The destructive work of the shells was visible on every hand"

Petersburg: Summer 1864

The war against the civilian population of the Cockade City began in earnest on June 16. The 10th Massachusetts Battery took an advanced position near the Hare House Hill, from which, one artilleryman later recalled, the "spires of Petersburg were now in full view, though distant, perhaps, two miles." Two days of bitter fighting remained before Union leaders would admit failure in their attempt to storm Petersburg, but the targeting of noncombatants did not wait that long. "By order of Gen. Birney we gave our pieces ample elevation and fired the first shells known to have been thrown into the city," cannoneer John D. Billings noted.

"What a night was the last!" Fanny Waddell wrote the next morning. "Our inhuman foe without a single warning opened their guns upon us, shelling a city full of defenseless women, children and old men." The bombardment that began on June 16 lasted well into the early hours of June 17. "I lay quietly until nearly one o'clock listening to the bursting shells when one exploded so near that the light flashed in my face," Mrs. Waddell recollected. "Ah! the bitterness of that night will never pass from our hearts and memories."

The correspondent for the *Savannah Republican* reported on June 19 that a "number of shells have exploded in the streets, but thus far only eleven persons have been hurt, including one old negro woman killed." A Confederate officer visiting Petersburg shortly after this report was filed thought that everything seemed "exceedingly depressing. The streets were almost deserted, and the

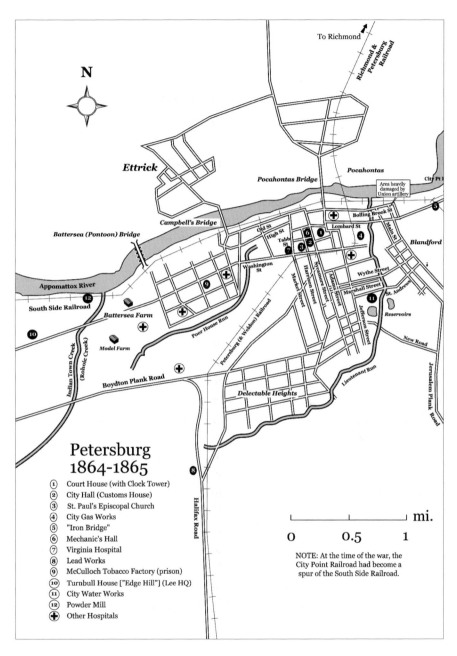

Petersburg 1864-1865

① Court House (with Clock Tower)
② City Hall (Customs House)
③ St. Paul's Episcopal Church
④ City Gas Works
⑤ "Iron Bridge"
⑥ Mechanic's Hall
⑦ Virginia Hospital
⑧ Lead Works
⑨ McCulloch Tobacco Factory (prison)
⑩ Turnbull House ["Edge Hill"] (Lee HQ)
⑪ City Water Works
⑫ Powder Mill
✛ Other Hospitals

0   0.5   1   mi.

NOTE: At the time of the war, the City Point Railroad had become a spur of the South Side Railroad.

destructive work of the shells was visible on every hand. Here a chimney was knocked off, here a handsome residence was deserted, with great rents in its walls, and the windows shattered by explosion; here stood a church tower mutilated, the church yard filled with new-made graves."

Large numbers of civilians fled the Petersburg battle zone within days of Grant's approach. A Virginia artilleryman named James Albright wrote in his diary on June 20, "The vandals are still throwing shell into the city, and it is very distressing to see the poor women & children leaving. It is hard on all; but to see the poor women with the children on one arm and their little budgets on the other seeking a safe place — is enough to move the hardest heart."

The northern and northeastern portions of town came under the heaviest fire. The several Confederate military hospitals lying within that area were ordered to move their three thousand patients to less exposed parts of the city. Sarah Pryor watched the hospital evacuations: "A long, never-ending line of wagons, carts, everything that could run on wheels, passed my door, until there was no more to pass." A diarist writing at the end of June observed that "Most of the families on Market Street have moved away."

The civilian exodus was accelerated by rumors that the Yankees planned to celebrate the Fourth of July with "a furious bombardment of the City." "Most every body is out of the lower part of the Town," wrote Dr. John Claiborne, a Petersburg native and the medical director of all the army hospitals in the city, on July 11, "& I believe two-thirds of the population of the whole city. . . .These people are camped and bivouacked in every form and manner in the surrounding country as far as ten miles." A reporter for the *Mobile Daily Advertiser and Register* noted in July that the "houses, and even the woods and fields, for miles around Petersburg are filled with women and children and old men, who have fled from their homes. Some have provided themselves with tents; others have erected bush arbors, and others are bivouacking under the trees." "What they live on their Heavenly father only knows," Dr. Claiborne reflected. "He who feeds the birds I trust will remember his suffering ones."

Contrary to Dr. Claiborne's estimate, many of Petersburg's civilians had in fact opted to remain. "The enemy shells the city more or less every day," Lee's artillery chief, William Nelson Pendleton, wrote in late June. "The people of the place, ladies and all, bear this outrage upon their pleasant homes with great fortitude and dignity." Another observer, writing on July 9, declared, "I have never known a braver or more patriotic people." A Virginia cavalryman remarked that "it was really refreshing to see ladies pass coolly along the streets as though nothing unusual was transpiring while the 160-pound shells were howling like hawks of perdition through the smoky air and bursting in the very heart of the city, but they didn't mind it a bit; and even the children would stand and watch, at the sound of the passing shells, to see the explosion, and make funny little speeches about them, as if they had been curious birds flying over their heads."

Even as some town residents were fleeing to the surrounding counties, refugees were crowding into Petersburg from areas now under Yankee control. Their numbers were so large that the Petersburg Common Council convened a special meeting on August 16 to decide whether or not the city should "grant supplies to refugee families and to the families of those who had deserted to the enemy." Lacking the wherewithal to assist their own population adequately, the town elders took a hard line, resolving that, first, "this Council does not feel authorized to allow its Agents to grant gratuitous supplies to any person or persons not bona fide residents of this City," and, second, that "the said Committee of Distribution are instructed not to grant supplies to the families of those who have deserted to the enemy."

Old routines began to reemerge by late June, once the Union army had settled into a siege posture. Churches in the more heavily shelled sections of the city continued to hold services, though infrequent ones, while those out of range tried to conduct business as usual. A pastor whose church lay in the target zone decided to forego any bell ringing, fearing that "Gen. Lee might be tempted to come over from his headquarters across the river, and it is too dangerous for him to be riding about the streets." Other operations returned to normalcy. "The trains running out from Petersburg were regularly shelled, but they moved along on schedule time, apparently indifferent to the shots of the Federal artillery," a cavalryman proudly remarked. What he failed to say was that both lines no longer ran into the city center; the Richmond trains halted three miles to the north at Dunlop Station, while the South Side operation no longer ventured east of Campbell's Bridge.

The presence of so many soldiers had its effect on Petersburg's social life. "General Lee allowed a few of the men each evening to pass out to stretch their limbs, bathe in the Appomattox or visit Petersburg, if they wished," an Alabamian noted, adding, "He prohibited anyone in the city selling to the soldiers anything intoxicating, but by paying five dollars for a common cigar, a drink of whiskey was donated by the generous proprietor." For his diary entry of September 5, North Carolina soldier William D. Alexander wrote, "I have had a nice time calling on the ladies." In Kershaw's Brigade, the "soldiers got passes to visit the town on little shopping excursions, notwithstanding the continual bursting of the shells in the city."

The ladies of the Cockade City drew more than their share of accolades. "Petersburg was large enough to admit of every variety of society," artilleryman

Bartlett Napier stated, "embracing, as Pierre Soule once declared, some of the most beautiful ladies he had ever seen anywhere." "The three cotton factories at Petersburg employed hundreds of girls, as they ran day and night," Colonel Hilary Herbert, commanding the 8th Alabama, remembered. "The soldiers married these factory girls, some for life, others for 'during the war.' Dr. J. D. D. Renfro, the Chaplain of the 10th [Alabama], informed me that he married some couples of this class every night while the army was before Petersburg."

In the aftermath of the often bitter battles on Petersburg's perimeter, the bloody debris of combat came into the city. Immediately following one heavy action, Confederate engineer W. W. Blackford recalled, "[the] streets of the town were filled with army wagons and ambulances; the wagons bringing supplies of rations and ammunition; and the ambulances rattling along toward the front and returning with wounded men groaning, cursing and praying, with the drivers sitting on their seats smoking their pipes in a perfectly unconcerned manner."

The almost constant shelling became the dominating feature of Petersburg's investment. "These dreadful missiles fly over and around us like great birds with wild rushing wings, bearing death and destruction in their flight," Fanny Waddell wrote in late June. Another Petersburg diarist noted that during one bombardment "pieces of shell [were] rattling like hail about our house." During an especially heavy bombardment in September, a reporter for the *Petersburg Express* noted that the "explosion of one shell scarcely died away before it was followed by the whistling of another." A postwar visitor who spoke with siege survivors related that when "people heard a shell coming, they used to throw themselves flat on the pavement till the explosion was over, to diminish the chance of being hit by the flying fragments."

Yet these means of destruction also possessed a curious beauty. "As the shells would burst in the air the whole heavens seemed to be raining fire," one resident recollected, "or rather it looked like a flock of fire birds were filling the air."

Dr. John Claiborne believed that he had been singled out by the Federal artillerists. "My ambulance men used to say that the Yankees always knew where my quarters were," he observed wryly. Claiborne regularly changed the location of his base of operations, but his luck almost ran out on the night of August 30. "About ten o'clock I was lying down on a lounge and watching the shells as they flew past the windows. . . . [Suddenly] two planets of the first magnitude seemed to come together right in my face. . . . I felt myself whirling over in the midst of plaster, lathes, glass, broken timber, and the dust of debris indescribable. . . . My first sensible thought was, 'I am not killed, it hurts too badly.'" Claiborne survived this incident with minor injuries.

Fire became a paramount danger. The Petersburg Common Council moved to organize an auxiliary fire brigade soon after the siege began to assist the heavily pressed regular units. One barrage, which began on the night of June 30 and continued into the next morning, ignited multiple conflagrations. There were so many burning structures that one Southern artilleryman angrily declared that the "Yankees appear[ed] to be throwing incendiary shell into the city — as some five buildings were on fire at one time." "The damage [e]ffected in some portions of the city is apparent," a Confederate artilleryman wrote early in July. "Several fires have originated from incendiary missiles and, as yet, the brutal Grant has not notified the authorities to move non-combatants."

At least one Union battery did use Petersburg to test its homemade incendiary shells. These were concocted by Brevet Major Jacob Roemer and thrown into the city in late July, doing "a great deal of damage there." Another heavy Union bombardment on July 28 started a number of blazes, all noted by Union observers.

A soldier from Kershaw's Brigade was present during an especially destructive shelling. "One night," he recalled, "after a furious bombardment the cry was heard, 'The city is on fire; the city is on fire.' A lurid glare shot up out of the very heart of the city, casting a dim light over the buildings and the camps near about. Fire bells began ringing, and the old men rushing like mad to fight the fire. . . . Higher and higher the flames rose until great molten-like tongues seemed to lick the very clouds. The old men mounted the ladder like boys, and soon the tops of the surrounding buildings were lined with determined spirits, and the battle against the flames began in earnest. . . . After the burning of several contiguous buildings, the flames were gotten under control, and eventually the fire was extinguished." To add to the fire hazard, the Union artillery would concentrate its shelling on the burning structures, so that the air around the men battling the flames would be filled with a "perfect storm of shot and shell."

Civilians took countermeasures. Sandbags or cotton bales were placed around the lower floors of some buildings, and bomb shelters (called bombproofs) of all sizes and shapes were constructed. "The Petersburgers had accommodated themselves to the changed conditions with curious completeness," Francis W. Dawson, a staff officer, observed. "Shell frequently fell in or passed over the city, and it was no uncommon thing for old citizens, standing in the street discussing the prospects of the day, to step quietly around a corner until an approaching shell had passed by, and then resume their former place without even suspending their conversation. The basements of houses were used in many instances as bombproofs, the traverses being comprised of mattresses and bedding."

Familiarity began to breed some contempt. A Mississippi soldier named A. L. P. Varin noted in late September that the "enemy frequently shoot very large shells into Petersburg & do some damage to some buildings, but the people are getting used to it, so they don't mind them & the little boys watch for them to fall & if they don't explode they take out the powder & sell it." Spencer Welch, a surgeon with the 13th South Carolina, marveled, "I would often see young ladies sitting on their porches reading quietly while shells were occasionally bursting near by." One of the town newspapers made light of their plight with an editorial ranking "'dodging' as a branch of higher mathematics." Reflecting on Petersburg's adaptation to the regular but random shelling, C.S. engineer Blackford concluded, "It is a curious thing, but nonetheless true, that the constant presence of death familiarizes people to the dread specter and he loses his terrors."

Ominous signs began to appear as summer melded into fall and cool nights began to presage winter. The price of food, which had climbed throughout this period, gave no indication of leveling off. Heating supplies, too, were fast becoming scarce; early in September, the Common Council asked Richmond "to allow the trains on the Richmond and Petersburg Rail Road to haul for the use of our citizens, a sufficient supply of coal to the City, or to some place contiguous thereto." The city leaders even tried to ban the sale of alcohol, an effort that one reporter branded "little more than so much waste paper."

The threat of a health emergency was never far in the background. "There is no little sickness in our city," Petersburger Alexander Brown wrote in early August. "There is no epidemic among us, but Diarrhea seems to be the most fatal of all the diseases." Brown voiced the thoughts of many when he commented that "it is generally agreed that all who can get away ought not to think of wintering in Petersburg."

Federal soldiers in the trenches often viewed Petersburg through eyes clouded with homesickness. A lonely Union picket on duty in late June reflected that he "could hear the town clock strike, a band play and even the dogs bark in Petersburg." Sometimes the familiar sounds had a cutting edge. One Federal diarist wrote on June 30 that the "bells of Petersburg are ringing a merry peal, as though proclaiming the notes of victory." "Later in the day," a nearby artilleryman added, "[it] was learned to have been in rejoicing over the defeat of our cavalry under Gen. Wilson." Another Union soldier summed it all up: "It was an easy matter for us to see the steeples of Petersburg from some parts of our line, and the shrill notes of the car whistle and rumble of moving trains reminded us every day that the beleaguered town was alive and doing business at the old stand."

Chapter Six

"The saddest affair I have ever witnessed in the war"

June 25 - August 1, 1864

Ulysses S. Grant
Final Report of Operations, March 1864-May 1865

General Sherman moved from Chattanooga on the 6th of May [1864], with the Armies of the Cumberland, Tennessee, and Ohio . . . upon Johnston's army at Dalton; but finding the enemy's positions . . . too strong to be assaulted, General McPherson was sent . . . to turn it. . . . This movement was successful. Johnston . . . fell back to his fortified position at Resaca, where he was attacked on the afternoon of May 15. A heavy battle ensued. During the night the enemy retreated south. . . . He was vigorously pursued. . . . On the afternoon of the 25th the [Union] advance under General Hooker, had a severe battle with the enemy, driving him back to New Hope Church, near Dallas. . . .

On the 4th of June Johnston . . . retreated to the strong positions of Kenesaw, Pine, and Lost Mountains. He was forced to yield the two last-named places and concentrate his army on Kenesaw, where, on the 27th, Generals Thomas and McPherson made a determined but unsuccessful assault. On the . . . 3d [Johnston] . . . abandoned Kenesaw and retreated across the Chattahoochee.

General Sherman [resumed his operations] . . . on . . . the 17th of July . . . crossed the Chattahoochee . . . and drove the enemy back to Atlanta. At this place General Hood succeeded General Johnston in command of the rebel army, and . . . made several severe attacks upon Sherman in the vicinity of Atlanta. . . . In all these attacks the enemy was repulsed with great loss.

[In the east, immediately] upon . . . ascertaining that General Hunter was retreating from Lynchburg . . . thus laying the Shenandoah Valley open for raids into Maryland and Pennsylvania, [Major General Jubal Early] returned northward, and moved down that valley. . . . It became necessary, therefore, to find other troops to check this movement of the enemy. For this purpose the Sixth Corps was taken from the armies operating against Richmond, to which was added the Nineteenth Corps . . . .

On the 3d of July the enemy approached Martinsburg. . . . On the 6th the enemy occupied Hagerstown, moving a strong column toward Frederick City. General Wallace . . . met the enemy in force on the Monocacy. . . . His force was not sufficient to insure success . . . yet it detained the enemy and thereby served to enable General Wright to reach Washington with two divisions of the Sixth Corps, and the advance of the Nineteenth Corps before him. From Monocacy the enemy moved on Washington. . . . On the 12th a reconnaissance was thrown out in front of Fort Stevens. . . . A severe skirmish ensued. . . . [The enemy] commenced retreating during the night. . . . I requested Maj. Gen. H. G. Wright . . . should . . . push Early to the last moment. . . . Learning that Early was retreated south toward . . . Richmond, I directed that the Sixth and Nineteenth Corps be got back to the armies operating against Richmond . . . .

About the 25th it became evident that the enemy was again advancing upon Maryland and Pennsylvania. . . . The rebel force . . . on the 30th, burned Chambersburg.

With a view of . . . making [the enemy] . . . wary of the situation of his army in the Shenandoah, and, to take advantage of his necessary withdrawal of troops from Petersburg to explode a mine that had been prepared in front of the Ninth Corps . . . on the night of the 26th of July the Second Corps and two divisions of the Cavalry Corps . . . were crossed to the north bank of the James.

*   *   *

Brigadier

General E. Porter Alexander was a busy man with a suspicious mind. Although he was responsible for all Confederate artillery defenses from the James River to Petersburg, Alexander, except for one visit to the Bermuda Hundred lines, was fully occupied by the situation south of the Appomattox.

Something nagged at him as he prowled a portion of the Confederate position known as Elliott's Salient. There, perhaps half a mile southeast of Petersburg and some 500 yards east of the Jerusalem Plank Road, Rebel and Yankee trenches were separated by less than 130 yards. In one of the final convulsive actions of June 18, blue-coated soldiers from Burnside's Ninth Corps had lunged across shallow Poor Creek (sometimes called Taylor's Creek) and grappled onto a chunk of gently sloping hillside west of it. The Federals had then dug in, and the Confederates had thrown up a four-gun redoubt.

Yankee cannon ranged the open slope from the Jerusalem Plank Road to the Confederate front line, so Alexander's approach to the redoubt was via a ravine that engineers had transformed into a sheltered passage or covered way.

There was something suspicious about this section of the line. Sniper fire had slackened noticeably to either side, but not so near the redoubt. "Here," Alexander noted, "the popping of the muskets rather seemed to increase."

He was convinced that the Federals would begin to push their trenches forward here, in the classic pattern of siege warfare. To counter this, he carefully placed artillery to cover the slopes and each day looked expectantly for signs indicating that regular siege approaches had begun.

Were he a betting man, Alexander would have wagered it all on Wednesday, June 30, as the day the first sap roller would appear. Snaking and ducking his way along the maze of ditches leading to the front, he at last peered carefully over the trench lip. There was no evidence of the large barrel-like cylinders made of wicker, which were filled with dirt and rolled into position to provide temporary protection for working parties extending the trench system toward the enemy. "No fresh dirt now anywhere in that vicinity," he observed with some surprise, "but only that vicious sharpshooting and mortar fire."

Something was not right. Alexander forgot his rounds and stared thoughtfully for a long time across the no-man's land. "Then," he recalled later, "suddenly a light broke in on me. They were coming, but it was not above ground, . . . they were coming underground. They were mining us!"

From Testimony before the Joint Committee on the Conduct of War:

Question to Lieutenant Colonel Henry Pleasants: Were you in the army of the Potomac at the time the mine was sprung before Petersburg, on the 30th of July last; if so, in what capacity?

Answer: I was then lieutenant colonel of the 48th Pennsylvania volunteers. . . .

Question: Will you state who originated the mine, and what was done in regard to it?

Answer: I was then commanding the first brigade of the second division [and]...I frequently had occasion to go to the front line. I noticed a little cup of a ravine near to the enemy's works. I having been a mining and civil engineer many years before the war, it occurred to me that a mine could be excavated there. . . . I spoke to . . . Brigadier General [Robert] Potter, commanding the division, and explained to him what I proposed to do. . . . He received the idea favorably, and wrote a note to General Burnside . . . [who] seemed very much pleased with the proposition, and told me to go right on with the work.

Question: Can you fix the time . . . when you commenced the work?

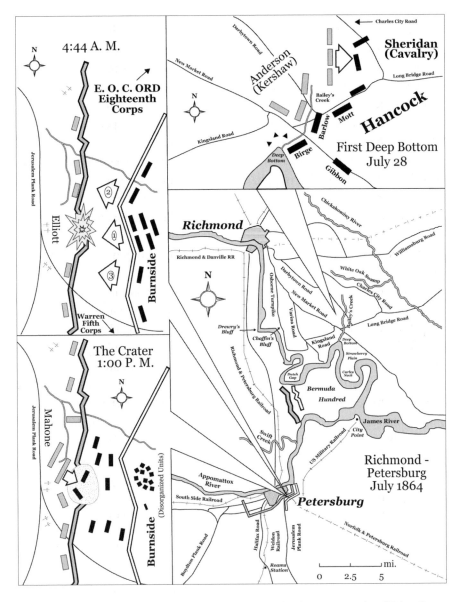

Answer: The work commenced at 12 o'clock noon on the 25th of June, 1864.

The digging began in the sheltered face of a ripple of ground opposite and slightly north of the Confederate redoubt. "We underminded," a Pennsylvanian named George Morgan proudly wrote home afterward. "We had some great old work till we had it done. We used to work 3 hours out of twenty four and then we were done for the day. [We] drawed 2 good drinks of whiskey in [a] day for about a week, then some fellers made fools out of themselves — used to save it till they would get a lot and then got drunk and then it was stopped."

Another member of the 48th noted the dimensions of the project: "The tunnel, or, to use the technical term, 'gallery,' was about four and a half feet high, nearly as many feet wide at the bottom and two feet wide at the top."

An Ohio soldier, observing from the sidelines, remembered, "The men working in the mine had only shirts and drawers on, and some were minus shirt even. I used to watch them popping in and out of the hole like so many brown gophers."

E. Porter Alexander, the Confederate artilleryman, was so excited by his deduction that on his way back to report, he made the mistake of taking a shortcut across some open ground. He was shot in the hand by an enemy sniper.

It was a clean wound, and Alexander gratefully accepted a short furlough to recover. He stopped at army headquarters before leaving "in order to report my conviction that the enemy were mining the Elliott Salient." He spoke with Lee's aide Colonel Charles Venable, who had a guest with him, an English reporter named Francis Lawley. The newspaperman asked the wounded gunner how long a gallery the Federals would have to dig. To Alexander's answer of "500 feet," the veteran combat observer knowingly shook his head. "They could not ventilate so long a gallery," he explained, adding that "the longest military mine ever run was in Delhi, & that about 400 feet was the limit that could be ventilated." Alexander retorted "that in the Federal ranks were plenty of coal miners who had ventilated galleries in coal mines under ground, & that they were up to devices to which 500 feet would be only child's play."

Alexander departed on his furlough, convinced that no one at headquarters was taking him seriously.

From Testimony before the Official Court of Inquiry on the Mine:

Statement by George Gordon Meade, commanding the Army of the Potomac: The mine constructed in front of General Burnside['s] lines] was commenced . . . without . . . any sanction obtained from the general headquarters. . . . [From] the first I never considered that the location of General Burnside's mine was a proper one, because . . . the position [he intended to assault] . . . was commanded on both flanks and taken in reverse by [the

Confederate] . . . position on the Jerusalem Plank Road and
their works opposite the Hare House.

    Question to Major J. C. Duane, chief of engineer corps, Army
of the Potomac: What is your opinion of the mine as a means of
assault?

    Answer: It is a very unusual way of attacking field
fortifications. I do not think that there was any reasonable
chance of success by such an attack.

"I found it impossible to get any assistance from anybody," Lieutenant Colonel Pleasants afterward complained. "I had to do all the work myself."

"There was nothing to do it with except the men," seconded Pennsylvania major Oliver Bosbyshell. "No tools, no planks, no nails, no wheel-barrows. Army picks were made smaller and straightened for mining purposes. Hickory sticks were fastened to cracker boxes so as to make hand-barrows, to convey the material excavated to a place where it could be piled outside the mine."

One of the soldier-miners recalled other problems: "Water was met while not far from the entrance, and for a time gave no little trouble. . . . A quicksand was also met with, and to obviate it the range of the tunnel was carved upward, so that the latter half was several feet higher than at the entrance. . . . The lighting of the tunnel was effected simply by placing candles or lanterns along the walls at a distance of about ten feet apart."

The ventilation problem was ingeniously solved by Pleasants. He later reported, "The mine was ventilated by having the [good air carried to the mine face] . . . in a square tube made of boards [set along the floor]. . . . This tube led to a perpendicular shaft twenty-two feet high out of which [the bad air]. . . escaped. At the bottom of this shaft was placed a grating, in which a large fire was kept burning continually [to draw the bad air up the shaft. Fresh air was kept from going up that same shaft by] . . . placing a partition with a door in the main gallery a little out of the shaft."

Lieutenant Colonel Pleasants had another obstacle to overcome. "The most important thing was to ascertain how far I had to mine, because if I fell short or went beyond the proper place the explosion would have no practical effect. Therefore, I wanted an accurate instrument[, known as a theodolite,] with which to make the necessary triangulations. . . . I could not get the instrument I wanted, although there was one at army headquarters; and General Burnside had to send to Washington and get an old-fashioned theodolite, which was given to me."

GEORGE MEADE TO A. E. BURNSIDE — JULY 3, 1864

THE LIEUTENANT GENERAL COMMANDING HAS INQUIRED OF ME WHETHER AN ASSAULT ON THE ENEMY'S WORKS IS PRACTICABLE AND FEASIBLE AT ANY POINT OF THE LINE HELD BY THIS ARMY. . . . I DESIRE, AT YOUR EARLIEST CONVENIENCE, YOUR VIEWS AS TO THE PRACTICABILITY OF AN ASSAULT AT ANY POINT IN YOUR FRONT, TO BE MADE BY THE 2D AND 6TH CORPS IN CONJUNCTION WITH YOURS.

A. E. BURNSIDE TO GEORGE MEADE — JULY 3, 1864
IF THE QUESTION IS BETWEEN MAKING THE ASSAULT NOW AND A CHANGE OF PLAN LOOKING TO OPERATIONS IN OTHER QUARTERS, I SHOULD UNHESITATINGLY SAY, ASSAULT NOW. IF THE ASSAULT BE DELAYED UNTIL THE COMPLETION OF THE MINE, I THINK WE SHOULD HAVE A MORE THAN EVEN CHANCE OF SUCCESS. IF THE ASSAULT BE MADE NOW, I THINK WE HAVE A FAIR CHANCE OF SUCCESS, PROVIDED MY CORPS CAN MAKE THE ATTACK, AND IT IS LEFT TO ME TO SAY WHEN AND HOW THE OTHER TWO CORPS SHALL COME TO MY SUPPORT.

GEORGE MEADE TO A. E. BURNSIDE — JULY 3, 1864
THE RECENT OPERATIONS IN YOUR FRONT, AS YOU ARE AWARE, THOUGH SANCTIONED BY ME, DID NOT ORIGINATE IN ANY ORDERS FROM THESE HEADQUARTERS. SHOULD IT, HOWEVER, BE DETERMINED TO EMPLOY THE ARMY UNDER MY COMMAND IN OFFENSIVE OPERATIONS ON YOUR FRONT, I SHALL EXERCISE THE PREROGATIVE OF MY POSITION TO CONTROL AND DIRECT THE SAME. . . .

The mine continued to reach toward the Rebel lines in the face of obstructions both natural and bureaucratic. "On the second of July," noted Major Bosbyshell, "extremely wet ground was encountered by the miners, the timbers gave way and the roof and the floor nearly met. It was re-timbered, but a stratum of marl of the consistency of putty was encountered, which made the progress exceedingly slow." Staff officer D. L. Way recalled how the pragmatic Pennsylvanians turned their adversity to profit: "The sappers and miners around the entrance had brought the yellow clay out from under the Confederate fort, put the impression of the Ninth Corps badge on small pieces, cut it out in shape of the badge (a shield) and dried it in the sun, selling them for 25 cents."

"On the 17th of July," reported Lieutenant Colonel Pleasants, "the main gallery was completed, being five hundred and ten and eight-tenths feet in length. The enemy having obtained information of the mine, and having commenced searching for it, I was ordered to stop operations, which were, however, re-commenced on the 18th of July."

Pleasants's subterranean shaft had pushed under and past the Confederate redoubt. Now the Union miners branched left and right, running lateral galleries nearly forty feet each way, parallel to and slightly to the rear of the main Confederate trench line.

The digging stopped on July 23. Some clean-up work remained to be done, but otherwise the mine was ready to be packed with explosives.

From Testimony before the Joint Committee on the Conduct of War:

```
Statement by Ambrose Burnside: The fourth division of the ninth
corps, under command of General Ferrero, [was] composed
entirely of colored troops. . . . During the month of July . . .
I had made up my mind, in case an assault was to be made by the
ninth corps, to put this division in the advance. I had so
informed General Ferrero . . . some three weeks before the
attack was made, on the 30th of July.
```

Noted Lieutenant Colonel H. Seymour Hall, commanding the 43rd United States Colored Troops (U.S.C.T.): "[My] regiment, then consisting of seven companies, was honored by being selected to lead the assaulting column. . . . The work that was expected of me was fully explained, and to do as ordered, my command was to take position . . . as near our front line as possible . . . and when the mine was exploded, was to move quickly forward, pass through the breach in the enemy's works made by the explosion, then turn to our right behind his works, take him in the flank and roll up his line with the bayonet. . . . I practiced these movements till they could have been executed as perfectly in the dark as in the light. . . ."

According to Burnside's plan, the attacking column of black troops would deploy in three sections once the main Confederate line was reached. One would wheel around perpendicular to the main axis of attack and sweep the trenches southward, while another would swing northward on a similar mission. At the same time, the bulk of the column would press westward toward the all-important crest, along which ran the Jerusalem Plank Road.

From Testimony before the Joint Committee on the Conduct of War:

```
Question to Lieutenant General Ulysses S. Grant, commander of
all Union armies in the field: Will you give the Committee such
information as you may deem important in regard to the action
before Petersburg, on the 30th of July last?
```

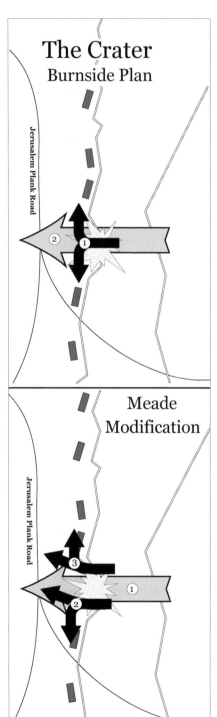

The Crater
Burnside Plan

Meade
Modification

Answer: As you are aware, I made a feint on the north side of the James river, which I intended to convert into an attack if everything should prove favorable. By that movement the attention of the enemy was called to that side of the river, causing them to concentrate there. They were so well fortified there that an advance on that side could not be made without great sacrifice of life. . . . I telegraphed to General Meade that then was the time to charge the mine and explode it, and directed him to make preparations to assault. My dispatch gave no details at all how this was to be done. I left that to him, knowing him as I did to be fully capable of determining when and what ought to be done.

The arming of the mine began at 4:00 p.m. on July 27. Corporal George Allen of the 4th Rhode Island was among those detailed to carry the explosives to the mine. "It was large, coarse blasting powder, and was placed in kegs of twenty-five pounds each. These kegs were then placed in bags and slung over our shoulders. We moved quickly over the space between the teams and traverse to avoid getting a bullet in one of those kegs of powder, as they were continually flying all around us, and left the kegs at the mouth of the gallery. Here they were taken by the miners and carried into the magazine under the fort." In all, 320 kegs of gunpowder were placed in the galleries, which lay some twenty feet beneath the enemy trenches.

After the loading was completed, a detail of 150 men worked on the tamping, designed to keep the force of the blast from dissipating back into the tunnel. "This tamping," one of the 150 recollected, "was about forty feet in length, and consisted of bags of sand placed loosely on one another, with long logs laid diagonally across the gallery, so as to be driven into the sides by the recoil of the explosion."

The work was done by 11:00 p.m.

From Testimony before the Joint Committee on the Conduct of War:

Question to Lieutenant Colonel Henry Pleasants: What amount of powder was used?

Answer: I called for twelve thousand pounds, they gave me eight thousand. . . .

Question: What means did you use to insure the explosion of the powder?

Answer: I used three lines of fuze, called the blasting fuze. I asked for [premium] fuze, and they sent me this common blasting fuze. . . . The fuze I received was cut in short pieces [which had to be spliced together]; some of them were only ten feet long.

Question: Why was that?

Answer: I do not know.

Question: Was [there] not . . . an objection to it?

Answer: A great objection.

Statement by Ambrose Burnside, commanding Ninth Corps: On Thursday, the 28th, when I called upon General Meade . . . he informed me that that portion of my plan which contemplated putting the colored troops in the advance did not meet with his approval; and also, that he did not approve of the formation proposed . . . and that he was of the opinion that the troops should move directly to the crest without attempting these side movements.

Question to George Meade: Will you . . . tell us why it was white troops, instead of colored troops, was placed in the advance to carry that work. . . ?

Answer: . . . [Burnside's] colored division [was] . . . a new division, and had never been under fire — had never been tried — and as this was an operation which I knew beforehand was one requiring the best troops, I thought it impolitic to trust it...

Statement by Ambrose Burnside (continued): [The] three
commanders of the white divisions were then informed of the
changes in the plan, and also that one of their divisions must
lead the assault. Considerable conversation occurred as to the
condition of the different divisions. . . . I finally decided
that I would allow the leading division to be designated by lot,
which was done; [Brigadier] General [James] Ledlie drew the lot
to lead the advance. . . .

According to Major Bosbyshell, of the 48th, "Lieutenant-Colonel Pleasants
was ordered to fire the mine at 3:30 o'clock on the morning of July 30. . . . Who
can ever forget that morning, or the stillness of that hour! The covered ways
were crowded with troops ready to spring into action as soon as the mine was
sprung. . . . [At] 3:30 a.m. [Pleasants] arrived and with quick, nervous strides . . .
entered the gallery and ignited the fuse. Hastening to the surface he stood with
watch in hand mounted on an earthworks awaiting the explosion. . . .

"The time for the explosion passed."

A. A. HUMPHREYS [MEADE'S CHIEF OF STAFF] TO A. E. BURNSIDE —
4:30 A.M.

IS THERE ANY DIFFICULTY IN EXPLODING THE MINE? IT IS THREE-
FOURTHS OF AN HOUR LATER THAN THAT FIXED UPON FOR EXPLODING.

Bosbyshell's account continued: "Pleasants became like a maniac — he
knew where the defect was — those spliced fuses would defeat his great
project!"

A. A. HUMPHREYS TO A. E. BURNSIDE — 4:30 A.M.

IF THE MINE CANNOT BE EXPLODED, SOMETHING ELSE MUST BE
DONE, AND AT ONCE.

"Lieutenant Jacob Douty . . . and Sergeant Henry Reese . . . rapidly ran into
the gallery, and finding a knife would be required, Reese hurried out again to
borrow one, and returning, the two tore away the tamping and came to the
extinguished fuse. . . . Cutting the fuse at the point where the dampness had not
penetrated they relighted it, and regained the outside as rapidly as possible."

A. A. HUMPHREYS TO A. E. BURNSIDE — 4:35 A.M.

THE COMMANDING GENERAL DIRECTS IF YOUR MINE HAS FAILED THAT YOU
MAKE AN ASSAULT AT ONCE, OPENING YOUR BATTERIES.

". . . [It] was sixteen minutes before five when the explosion took place." A soldier in the 57th Massachusetts remembered the blast as a "spectacle . . . of appalling grandeur." "First there came a deep shock and tremor of the earth and a jar like an earthquake," recalled Byron Cutcheon, with the 20th Michigan, "then a heaving and lifting of the fort and of the hill on which it stood; then a monstrous tongue of flame shot fully two hundred feet into the air, followed by a vast column of white smoke, resembling the discharge of an enormous cannon; then a great spout or fountain of red earth rose to a great height, mingled with men and guns, timbers and planks, and every kind of debris, all ascending, spreading, whirling, scattering and falling with great concussion to the earth once more."

Confederates were no less awed. "The earth seemed to tremble," noted one Alabama officer, "and the next instant there was a report that seemed to deafen all nature." A Virginia soldier stationed along the lines southwest of the explosion later wrote, "A deep rumbling sound, that seemed to rend the very earth in twain, startled me from my sleep, and in an instant I beheld a mountain of curling smoke ascending towards the heavens, on the left of our lines."

Of the 300 South Carolina troops manning the trenches directly above the mine gallery and the 30 gunners serving in Captain Richard Pegram's four-gun battery, 278 were killed or wounded in the explosion.

One hundred ten Federal cannon and fifty-four mortars now opened fire along nearly two miles of trench lines. "It was a scene never to be forgotten by those fortunate enough to witness it," declared John H. Rhodes, a Rhode Island gunner, "and beggared description." "The air was filled with whizzing shot and screeching shell," wrote a member of the 115th New York, "reverberation met reverberation and echo struck against echo, until it seemed as if the heavens must be rent with the incessant concussions, and the air blistered by the lightning-like passages of shot and shell." The earth trembled under the recoil of the cannon, and as the sun rose lurid, "the sounds were perfectly deafening," added a New York infantryman. "The men became frantic with excitement."

Clouds of dust and gunsmoke still choked the air as the first Federal troops —Colonel Elisha Marshall's men, who made up the Second Brigade in Ledlie's division—lurched from their trenches and scrambled across the open ground toward the smoldering crater. "One huge lump of clay as large as a hay-stack or a small cottage was thrown out and left on top of the ground toward our own works," an officer in Marshall's brigade noted. The 14th New York Heavy Artillery led the way, one soldier later recalling, "In the pit, powder smoke issued from the crevices; guns were seen half buried; the heads or limbs of half-buried men wriggled in the loose earth." A nearby soldier remembered it as "the awfullest sight that can be conceived – men covered with earth and cut up in every imaginable way." One enterprising noncom began gathering up dazed Confederates, getting them into formation, and sending them to the rear. "Indeed," marveled one observer, "he seemed to be 'drilling troops in squads.'"

With the New Yorkers engaged in impromptu rescue and mop-up missions, it remained for the next regiment in Marshall's attacking column, the 2nd Pennsylvania Heavy Artillery, to push through the crater. These troops formed a line of battle some 150 yards west of the hole.

Close behind Marshall's men were the six regiments of Brigadier General William F. Bartlett's First Brigade, of Ledlie's division. "The explosion produced a crater from one hundred and fifty to two hundred feet in length, about 60 feet in width, and thirty feet deep," remembered one, "the bottom and sides of which were covered with a loose, light sand, furnishing scarcely a foothold, and for this reason, as well as that of the narrowness of the place, it was [only] with great difficulty that the troops could pass through it."

Another unexpected obstacle confronting the first troops to enter the pit was the steep perimeter wall, which had been scoured out of the Virginia clay by the force of the blast. According to an aide of Ledlie's who accompanied the first wave, "owing to the precipitous walls the men could find no footing except by facing inward, digging their heels into the earth, and throwing their backs against the side of the crater, or squatting in a half-sitting, half-standing posture."

The Jerusalem Plank Road lay just 1,600 feet beyond the crater, and only half a mile along it to the north was Cemetery Hill, overlooking Petersburg. Victory was that close. But Marshall's and Bartlett's men hesitated. Spiteful Confederate fire chewed into the flanks of the barely controlled Federal mass occupying the crater, and valuable time was lost as officers deployed men to counter the threat. Adding to the confusion was the fact that the details of Meade's battle plan had not been explained to the field commanders. "Every officer from colonel down to second lieutenant," recalled Massachusetts captain John Anderson, "was giving orders of some kind, most of them being contradictory." "If the division commander had followed us into the rebel lines," insisted Pennsylvanian Clarence Wilson, "the columns of the three leading regiments . . . would have known what the instructions to be followed were." Perhaps thirty minutes had passed since the mine was detonated.

Front Testimony before the Official Court of Inquiry on the Mine:

Question to Major George M. Randall, 14th New York Heavy Artillery: Was the division commander [Ledlie] present during this confusion [in the crater] ?
Answer: Not in the crater.
Question: Is it your opinion that this hesitation affected the result of the action?
Answer: Yes, sir.
Question to Surgeon O. P. Chubb, 20th Michigan: Were you at the assault on the 30th of July?
Answer: I was.
Question: State what you did there.
Answer: . . . I took position in a bomb-proof which had been used as some regimental headquarters, and remained there for the purpose of dressing wounds. This bomb-proof is located at a point about ten rods in rear of our line. Shortly after I took up that position General[s] Ledlie . . . and Ferrero . . . came in and took seats. . . . General Ledlie received orders in my hearing to move his troops forward from where they were then lying [in the crater], . . . General Ledlie dispatched an aide or some other officer to order that done . . . .

A South Carolina artilleryman, Major J. C. Coit, was among the first Confederate officers on the scene after the explosion. "I found the men of Elliott's brigade bravely manning the works up to the borders of the crater," he later remembered, "leaving no front for the entrance of the enemy except such as had been made vacant by the up-heaval of the earth." Coit scurried along the line to a slight elevation some 1,700 feet north of the crater, where Captain Samuel T. Wright's four guns were posted. Continued Coit, "I immediately ordered the battery to open with shrapnel and canister. . . ." Coit was not alone in his actions: one half-formed Confederate counterattack had already struck at the Federal battle lines as they tried to untangle themselves from the hole. The ragged Rebel force lacked the weight to be effective, however, and served only to provide a ready target for confused Federal riflemen. "Our men were literally mowed down," one dazed South Carolinian later remembered. About two hundred survivors stumbled back into the trenches, where they stubbornly held on, blocking any easy Union advance toward Cemetery Hill.

Word of the breakthrough reached Robert E. Lee at his headquarters, just across the Appomattox from Petersburg, at 6:10 a.m. Lee had already begun to suspect that Grant's movement north of the James was merely a feint to draw off strength from Petersburg, and now he reacted quickly. His aide Charles Venable was sent to Brigadier General William Mahone's headquarters with orders for the doughty Virginia officer to pull two brigades out of the line south of the breach to help plug the gap. Then Lee mounted his horse, Traveller, and headed toward Petersburg.

From Testimony before the Official Court of Inquiry on the Mine:

```
Question to Brigadier General Robert B. Potter: Were you in a
position to see the operations of the assault before Petersburg
on the 30th of July, and in what capacity?
    Answer: I was, commanding the Second Division, Ninth Army
Corps.
Question: What time elapsed from the springing of the mine till
the forward movement of the assaulting columns?
    Answer: . . . The First of my regiments commenced to move, I
should think, about 8 or 10 minutes after the mine exploded. My
division was to move third in order, but I took the liberty of
altering the programme a little. . . . I . . . commanded
[Brigadier] General [Simon] Griffin, who had the lead in my
division, to deploy a line of skirmishers to the right of this
crater, and in case the assault seemed to be successful, and
General Ledlie moved forward, he should advance. . . . This
leading division commenced moving and passed into the right of
the crater and turned down to the right.
```

Confederate reinforcements converged on the crater pocket in desperate bits and pieces. The thin screen of South Carolinians barring the direct route to the Jerusalem Plank Road was augmented by North Carolinians pulled out of the line just north of the smoldering hole. "When we reached our position," recalled one Tarheel soldier, "we counted twelve United States flags in the works, and the whole field in front of the Crater was full of Yankees."

In an effort to help Griffin's men push northward out of the pocket, General Potter ordered Colonel Zenas Bliss's brigade of his division forward. But any Federal movement in that direction had to run the gauntlet of Sam Wright's guns. Remembered Major Coit, "The fire from this battery was unremitting from the time it opened until the close of the engagement. . . , having thrown during the time from five to six hundred shell and canister."

Union officers who attempted to lead their men southward out of the crater ran into a patchwork of South Carolina and Virginia troops. "Wise's Brigade threw bullets too thick and fast for them," a soldier in the 26th Virginia later bragged. "So they had to go back [into the crater] . . . again."

More Federal troops now crowded into the crater salient. John Hartranft's brigade of Orlando Willcox's division struggled into the trenches south of the pit, while most of Simon Griffin's brigade grabbed positions along the northern edge of the perimeter. Nearly 7,500 soldiers were battling in and about the crater.

Perhaps an hour had passed since the tremendous explosion first shattered the morning air.

A. A. HUMPHREYS TO A. E. BURNSIDE — 5:40 A.M.

THE GENERAL COMMANDING LEARNS THAT YOUR TROOPS ARE HALTING AT
THE WORKS WHERE THE MINE EXPLODED. HE DIRECTS THAT ALL YOUR
TROOPS BE PUSHED FORWARD TO THE CREST AT ONCE. CALL ON GENERAL
ORD [COMMANDING THE EIGHTEENTH CORPS UNITS ASSIGNED TO SUPPORT
THE NINTH CORPS] TO MOVE FORWARD HIS TROOPS AT ONCE.

From Testimony before the Official Court of Inquiry on the Mine and the Joint Committee on the Conduct of War:

Question to Major General E. O. C. Ord, Eighteenth Army Corps:
Please state what was your command at the assault on the 30th of
July.
    Answer: My command was composed of two divisions to aid in
the assault. . . .
    Question: What were your troops ordered to do?
    Answer: My troops were ordered to a position in the rear of
General Burnside's corps, with a view to supporting it. . . .
Question: Did your troops experience any interference from the
Ninth Corps. . . ?
    Answer: . . . [About] an hour or a little more after the
explosion of the mine, [Burnside] . . . said to me, "Now you can
move your troops forward." In the course of twenty minutes after
the order was sent [it was] . . . reported to me that . . . the
way [was] blocked . . . by the divisions in front.

A. A. HUMPHREYS TO A. E. BURNSIDE — 6:05 A.M.

THE COMMANDING GENERAL WISHES TO KNOW WHAT IS GOING ON ON YOUR LEFT, AND WHETHER IT WOULD BE AN ADVANTAGE FOR [MAJOR GENERAL GOUVERNEUR K.] WARREN'S SUPPORTING FORCE TO GO IN AT ONCE.

A. E. BURNSIDE TO GEORGE MEADE — 6:20 A.M.

IF GENERAL WARREN'S SUPPORTING FORCE CAN BE CONCENTRATED JUST NOW, READY TO GO IN AT THE PROPER TIME, IT WOULD BE WELL.

From Testimony before the Joint Committee on the Conduct of War:

Question to Gouverneur K. Warren, commanding Fifth Corps: Had you any orders to attack the enemy on your front at the time General Burnside made his assault?
Answer: No, sir. . . .
Question: Did the enemy in your front join in the attack upon the troops of the 9th Corps in the crater?
Answer: I think not.
Question: How were you to support the assault of General Burnside?
Answer: To follow his column. . . .
Question: Were there any reasons why you should not have attacked the enemy directly in your front. . . ?
Answer: It was not a part of the programme. . . .

GEORGE MEADE TO A. E. BURNSIDE — 6:50 A.M.

. . . EVERY MINUTE IS MOST PRECIOUS. . . . THE GREAT POINT IS TO SECURE THE CREST AT ONCE, AND AT ALL HAZARDS.

A. E. BURNSIDE TO GEORGE MEADE   [NOT TIME-DATED]

I AM DOING ALL IN MY POWER TO PUSH THE TROOPS FORWARD, AND, IF POSSIBLE, WE WILL CARRY THE CREST. . . .

GEORGE MEADE TO A. E. BURNSIDE — 7:30 A.M.

. . . DO YOU MEAN TO SAY YOUR OFFICERS AND MEN WILL NOT OBEY YOUR ORDERS TO ADVANCE. . . ?

A. E. BURNSIDE TO GEORGE MEADE   [NOT TIME-DATED]

. . . I MEAN TO SAY THAT IT IS VERY HARD TO ADVANCE TO THE CREST. . . . WERE IT NOT INSUBORDINATE I WOULD SAY THAT THE LATTER REMARK OF YOUR NOTE WAS UNOFFICERLIKE AND UNGENTLEMANLY.

It was now 7:30 a.m., almost three hours since the mine had been exploded. Federal troops clung to a perimeter pocket hardly larger than the crater itself, while Confederate reinforcements continued to arrive on the scene. More Union troops stood poised to advance across the no-man's land between what had been the Federal front line and the now demolished redoubt. These were the black troops of Ferrero's division.

Lieutenant Colonel Charles Loring, a Burnside aide who had been observing matters all morning, was so appalled by the prospect of the black soldiers' advancing into the confusion that he countermanded the orders and raced off to report directly to the Ninth Corps commander. Loring found Burnside and told him that throwing additional men into the overcrowded crater salient would do little good. It would be far better, he argued, for the men who were already there to get to work cleaning out the maze of "various lines, traverses between, and bomb-proofs," which the desperate Confederates were employing to halt every attempt to advance. Recalled Loring afterward, "General Burnside did not reply to me, as he usually does to his staff officers, by stating his reasons for disagreeing with them, but simply repeated his previous order."

From Testimony before the Official Court of Inquiry on the Mine:

Question to Brigadier General Edward Ferrero: Did you go forward with your division?

Answer: I went to our first line of works and there remained to see my command go through. I would state that I deemed it more necessary that I should see that they all went in than that I should go in myself.

At 8:00 a.m., the attack orders that Loring had tried to countermand were confirmed.

The officers commanding the black troops now discovered that it was nearly impossible to advance their men in any orderly fashion. Confederate artillery fire ranged all surface approaches to the jump-off point, so compact divisional squares had to be turned into strung-out, four-abreast columns that were then jammed into the two covered ways leading from the staging area to the Union front line. The first troops to use this route found it already occupied: coming back along the same narrow trenches was a tangle of wounded soldiers, couriers, panicked men, and Confederate POWs.

The 30th U.S.C.T. was the first black regiment to advance toward the crater. "The appearance of the regimental colors seemed to be the signal for the enemy's batteries," recalled the regiment's commander, Colonel Delevan Bates, "and it was volley after volley of canister and shrapnel they gave us." All formation was lost in the rush to cross the no-man's land. "The fire at that point was so hot that no one wanted to stay there long," Lieutenant Freeman S. Bowley remembered. "We went on the run for about 100 yards to the crater. . . . I remember seeing a lot of dead white soldiers lying on the slope that we ran over."

Colonel Bates led his men through the smoking crater, gamely pushing out a ragged battle line a short distance northwest of the gaping jagged hole. Coming up behind Bates, the remaining regiments of Colonel Joshua K. Sigfried's brigade filled out Bates's battle line. Then Ferrero's other brigade, Colonel Henry Thomas's, made the dash. "The slaughter was fearful," one of his young regimental officers later recalled in an honest letter home, "but some way I got up to the position but was not safe. After I got there bullets came in amongst us like hailstones. . . . Men were getting killed and wounded on all sides of me."

Thomas got enough of his troops through the crater to extend southward the perimeter battle line begun by Sigfried's men. They found themselves attempting to hold an impossible position. According to Colonel Bates, "The enemy's works on this part of the line was a perfect honeycomb of bomb proofs, trenches, covered ways, sleeping holes, and little alleys running in every direction. . . ."

The soldiers who were crowded into the covered ways leading to the Union front took but little notice of one figure, a "plainly dressed man who was elbowing his way past them so energetically, and whose face was covered with dust and streaked with perspiration." Ulysses S. Grant had been up well before dawn. He observed the giant explosion, then rode anxiously to the front lines, where he perceived that the Union attack plan was already unraveling. His aide Horace Porter accompanied him as he dismounted and moved among the troops near the jump-off point. Grant resolved to find General Burnside, and growing impatient with his slow progress along the crowded trenches, Grant clambered outside the massive protective earthworks. "Shots were now flying thick and fast," recalled his aide Porter. "Scarcely a word was spoken in passing over the distance crossed. Sometimes the gait was a fast walk, sometimes a dog-trot."

They found Burnside in a small fieldwork overlooking the front. Grant wasted no time. "The entire opportunity has been lost," he said, rapidly. "There is now no chance of success. These troops must be immediately withdrawn. It is slaughter to leave them here." Burnside, Porter related, "was still hoping that something could be accomplished."

CYRUS COMSTOCK [GRANT AIDE] TO U. S. GRANT — 9:15 A.M.

I CANNOT SEE THAT WE HAVE ADVANCED BEYOND THE ENEMY'S LINE IN THE VICINITY OF THE MINE. FROM HERE IT LOOKS LIKE THE ENEMY WERE HOLDING A LINE BETWEEN THAT POINT AND THE CREST.

Confederate Brigadier General William Mahone's men held the front about one mile southwest of the crater. The officer commanding the division, a former Petersburg railroad executive, cut an unforgettable figure. "His appearance arrested attention," wrote G. Moxley Sorrel, a staff officer. "Very small in height and frame, he seemed a mere atom with little flesh." Another staff officer, John Sergeant Wise, remembered the 125-pound Mahone as being "the sauciest-looking little manikin imaginable. . . ." One of Mahone's regimental commanders recalled pointing out the bantamweight officer to a Federal general during the truce that followed the Crater battle. "Not much man," was the Yankee's assessment, "but a big general."

Mahone had been along the middle of his line when the explosion occurred. He hurried to his left flank to gauge the situation and, on the way, met "a soldier, who, from thereabouts, hatless and shoeless, passed me, still going and only time to say 'Hell has busted.'" Mahone next encountered Colonel Venable, riding from Robert E. Lee with orders for Mahone to withdraw two of his five brigades to throw back the enemy penetration. "I can't send my brigades to General Johnson," Mahone quickly replied. "I will go with them myself." Leaving orders for his two rightmost brigades — Colonel David Weisiger's Virginia and Wright's Georgia (commanded today by Lieutenant Colonel Matthew R. Hall)—to withdraw quietly and march to Cemetery Hill, Mahone hurried ahead.

He made a brief stop at Major General Bushrod Johnson's headquarters, located at the north side of Blandford Heights. Mahone found Johnson, in whose sector the break had occurred, speaking with General Beauregard, who was responsible for Petersburg's defenses. Johnson, Mahone later recalled with not a little amazement, "appeared to be about ready to take his breakfast," but he readily supplied the Virginia officer with the information he requested as well as a guide to the front.

Mahone and his guide rode south along the Jerusalem Plank Road until they reached the place where a covered way led eastward toward the ravine that in turn branched north and west of the crater. Even as the two began scuttling toward the front, the first of Weisiger's men hauled into sight. Mahone found a vantage point and looked in amazement at the mass of Yankees ("eleven flags in less than one hundred yards"), remarking that they seemed "greatly disordered."

Mahone realized that he would need more men than he had coming, so he sent a courier back to his old lines with orders for Wilcox's Alabama Brigade to come at once. He then deployed the two brigades he had on hand, instructing Weisiger's Virginians to form a north-south line of battle that faced the crater to the east while Hall's Georgians extended the line further north.

Mahone's alignments were still incomplete when a group of Federal officers near the crater were seen gathering men for a charge of their own. Mahone realized that the moment for action was now.

He ordered, "Tell Weisiger to forward."

The time was nearing 9:00 a.m.

A. E. BURNSIDE TO GEORGE MEADE — 9 A.M.

MANY OF THE NINTH AND EIGHTEENTH CORPS ARE RETIRING BEFORE THE ENEMY. I THINK NOW IS THE TIME TO PUT IN THE FIFTH CORPS PROMPTLY.

From Testimony before the Official Court of Inquiry on the Mine:

Statement by George Gordon Meade, commanding the Army of the Potomac: That was the first information I had received that there was any collision with the enemy, or that there was any enemy present.

Weisiger's Virginians, inflamed by reports that the "nigger" troops facing them were giving whites no quarter, burst screaming out of the branch of the ravine that had sheltered them and smashed headlong into the perimeter line stretched by the Federals across the crater's western face. The Rebels hit a mixture of troops from Griffin's, Thomas's, Bliss's, and Sigfried's commands — both white and black soldiers.

Horace Burbank (32nd Maine): "Our men jumped from the trenches and made the best resistance possible. White and black men fought bravely, but, with no division commander within 80 yards of the captured works, and no brigade commander there outside the crater, without formation of any kind to resist such a charge, it was in vain."

William C. Smith (12th Virginia): "Among those who reached the works . . . was Emmet Richardson, a tall, strong, athletic fellow, who, after discharging his gun, did terrible work with the bayonet and with the butt of his gun. No less than five of the enemy fell beneath the terrible strokes of this powerful man."

Freeman S. Bowley (30th U.S.C.T.): "Here it was that our gallant Capt. Seagrave, with a knee shattered by a bullet, unable to retreat, refusing to surrender, fought with revolver and sword, killing six rebels, until he was shot and bayoneted in seven places."

W. H. Etheredge (41st Virginia): "I was among the first to jump into the ditch where the Yanks were as thick as they could stand. The first sergeant of Co. D jumped in about the same time I did, and was killed instantly. Where I was there was a small bomb-proof, and two Yanks squatting down near its mouth to keep out of danger (they were white men with muskets in their hands with fixed bayonets). My feet had not more than touched the ground when they rose up and stood before me. Just then the man that killed the sergeant stepped down and picked up a musket evidently with the intention of killing me.

   I . . . took hold of the two men in front of me and kept them so close together it was impossible for . . . the man that picked up the musket to kill me. . . . Just at that moment our men were jumping into the ditch like frogs. One of them jumped in just behind me, and I sang out to him at the top of my voice to kill the man in front of me. The man . . . stepped one pace to the right of me and killed the Federal soldier as quick as you could wink your eye."

A. A. HUMPHREYS TO A. E. BURNSIDE — 9:30 A.M.

THE MAJOR-GENERAL COMMANDING HAS HEARD THAT THE RESULT OF YOUR ATTACK HAS BEEN A REPULSE, AND DIRECTS THAT, IF IN YOUR JUDGMENT NOTHING FURTHER CAN BE EFFECTED, YOU WITHDRAW. . . .

The frenzied violence of Mahone's first assault, coupled with the confusion and lack of control among the white Federal troops in the crater pocket, was more than the raw black troops could bear.

From Testimony before the Official Court of Inquiry on the Mine:

> Question to Brigadier General S. B. Griffin: Did your command go beyond the crater?
> Answer: I should judge 200 yards. . . .
> Question: Why did you retire?
> Answer: My troops were driven back from . . . the advance position at the time the panic seized the negroes, which more or less affected all our troops, and the negroes rushing through them as they did carried them back. The rebels made a very desperate attack at the same time.

George Meade's aide Theodore Lyman was present at Army Headquarters when, at around 10:30 a.m., Ambrose Burnside and E. O. C. Ord (commanding the Army of the James troops on the Ninth Corps's right) arrived. "The former," Lyman noted, "much flushed, walked up to General Meade and used extremely insubordinate language. . . . Ord was opposed to further attempts. Meade ordered the attack suspended. As Ord and Burnside passed me, the latter said something like: 'You have 15,000 men concentrated on one point. It is strange if you cannot do something with them.' Ord replied angrily, flourishing his arms: 'You can fight if you have an opportunity; but, if you are held by the throat, how can you do anything?' . . . Poor Burnside remarked, quite calmly, 'I certainly fully expected this morning to go into Petersburg!'"

Confederate general William Mahone was still moving with unrelenting purpose to retake the crater. The attack of Weisiger's Virginians had shattered any possibility of an offensive movement on the part of the confused but still deadly mass of Federals clinging to the crater pocket. With his Virginia brigade now spent, Mahone attempted to bull his Georgia troops into a similar attack against the northern rim of the pocket. The Georgians' attack was less well developed, however, and concentrated Federal rifle and cannon fire blasted it apart.

"At this juncture, now a little after 10 o'clock," Mahone recalled later, "Gen. [Bushrod] Johnson came upon the ground and the depression in which my brigade had formed for the charge, and sent for me. . . . I met him there and it was agreed between us that he would have his men in the main line to the south of the Crater push down upon the enemy . . . [there], and that I should renew the assault with the Alabama brigade. . . . He fixed 1 o'clock as the time."

Mahone was aided in his plans by the work of artilleryman John Cheves Haskell, who had a battery of mortars under his supervision. A few of these guns had been in action since dawn, effectively pounding the crater pocket from positions near the Jerusalem Plank Road. Now, with Mahone's fierce approval, Haskell moved a squad of light mortars up the forward most Confederate firing lines. "We got closer and closer to the enemy," Haskell remembered, "until we were throwing shells with such light charges of powder that they would rise so slowly as to look as if they could not get to the enemy, who were so close that we could hear them cry out when the shells would fall among them, and repeatedly they would dash out and beg to surrender."

A Federal in the trenches under Haskell's barrage recalled with horror the weapon's effectiveness: "Dismembered bodies, legs, arms, and heads strewed the ground in every direction, and this horrible butchery explains why the men's clothes were covered with blood and fragments of human flesh and brains to a degree never seen in any other battle of the war." Added Lieutenant Bowley of the 30th U.S.C.T., "I remember one shell that burst and threw two men high into the air. I think they were dead before it burst; I am sure they were dead after it had burst." Conditions in the crater were deteriorating rapidly. One Michigan soldier noted, "The day had been intensely hot, and the men had been exposed in the broiling sun without food or drink since the night before. Many were completely overcome and used up."

From Testimony before the Official Court of Inquiry on the Mine:

Statement by George Gordon Meade, commanding the Army of the Potomac: At the time the order was given to withdraw the troops, the report of Major-General Ord was that the crater of the mine was so overcrowded with men that it would be nothing but murder to send any more men forward there. . . . The impression left upon my mind was that at that time there were as many men in the crater as would enable them to defend themselves. . . . and . . . I presumed that Major-General Ord and Major-General Burnside . . . would see that the men would be properly withdrawn. . . . This conclusion having been arrived at . . . I withdrew to my former headquarters. . . . I remained in total ignorance of any further transactions until about 6 or 7 o'clock in the evening . . .

```
BRIGADIER GENERAL W. F. BARTLETT [IN THE CRATER] TO GENERALS
GRIFFIN AND HARTRANFT — 12:40 P.M.

IT WILL BE IMPOSSIBLE TO WITHDRAW THESE MEN, WHO ARE A RABBLE
WITHOUT OFFICERS, BEFORE DARK. . . .
```

It was, one survivor recalled, "one o'clock, by the watch," when the 628 men of Wilcox's Alabama brigade emerged from the ravine northwest of the crater and attacked.

Robert E. Lee had been observing the changing tides of battle from the Gee House, near the Jerusalem Plank Road. With all but 18,000 of his troops lured north of the James to counter Hancock's move to Deep Bottom, Lee was trying to replace in spirit what he lacked in numbers. Time and again word came to the advancing troops that Lee was watching and expecting them to do their utmost. As Wilcox's men advanced, Captain George Clark spread the word from Lee that "if it were necessary, he would lead them himself."

"We could not see what was before us till we rose the hill," recollected Alabamian Alfred Lewis Scott. The Confederates thought of the crater and its outerworks as a fort to be retaken. "We raised a yell and made a dash to get under the walls of the fort before their artillery could open on us," wrote Captain John C. Featherston, "but in this we failed." "For a moment or two the enemy overshot us and did no damage," continued George Clark, "but as we reached the works, many were struck down. " (According to one incredulous South Carolina observer, "The Yankee cannon seemed literally to tear up the ground under the very feet of the brigade.")

Somehow, the Alabamians made it to the western lip of the crater. Said Featherston, "As soon as this was accomplished we pushed up hats on bayonets and, as expected, they riddled them with bullets, and immediately our men sprang over the walls and were in the fort. Then commenced that awful hand-to-hand struggle of which history tells you."

From Testimony before the Official Court of Inquiry on the Mine:

```
    Question to Brigadier General John F. Hartranft: Did you
remain [in the crater] till the troops retired?
    Answer: Yes, sir.
    Question: Did they retire in confusion?
    Answer: Yes, sir.
```

The fighting in and about the crater pit was chaotic and violent. "This day was the jubilee of fiends in human shape, and without souls," one Southerner later asserted. "Most of the fighting was done with bayonets and butts of muskets," added a North Carolina soldier. "Blood ran in trenches all around." "How the negroe's skulls cracked with the blows," another Tarheel recalled with grim satisfaction. After interviewing some Rebel soldiers involved, a reporter for the *Petersburg Express* wrote that here "the slaughter was terrific."

Some fought with suicidal desperation. Pennsylvania captain R. G. Richards watched one black soldier climb atop a pile of twenty bodies and fire at the approaching Rebels: "[While] hurriedly reloading[, he] was shot in the face; still loading he was shot again in the back of the head, yet loading when the third shot laid him prostrate like those beneath him; all done within the space of a few seconds." "Our men, when shot," remembered aide Charles Amory, "would roll to the bottom of the pit, and there dead and dying lay in a horrible pile." "We had no semblance of an organization," added a Massachusetts officer, John Anderson. "Whites and blacks were squeezed so tightly together that there was hardly standing room. Even many of those killed were held in a standing position until jostled to the ground. . . . It was one seething cauldron of struggling, dying men."

Black troops who were captured in the fighting faced an uncertain fate. "I saw the rebs run up and shoot negro prisoners in front of me," remembered Stephen Weld, a captured Union officer. "One was shot four times." A Georgia soldier, writing home more than a week after the battle, admitted that "some four negroes went to the rear as we could not kill them as fast as they passed us."

A number of captured white officers serving in colored regiments, fearing Confederate retaliation, lied when asked to identify their units. This so infuriated Lieutenant Lemuel D. Dobbs of the 19th U.S.C.T. that when he was asked his unit, he defiantly replied, "Nineteenth Niggers, by —." Young Lieutenant Bowley and a friend also vowed not to deny the brave black soldiers who had fought alongside them. "When our names and rank were taken down," Bowley recalled, "we said 'Thirtieth United States Colored Infantry' and saw the words 'negro officer' written opposite our names on the list."

Groups of Federals — some in organized units, others in no order whatsoever — fled into the deadly crossfire raking the no-man's-land. "It was every man for himself," one New Yorker declared afterward, "some fairly rolling over the earthworks into our lines." "The ground was being ploughed up with shot and shell," another Federal observed, "while a perfect tornado of musket balls swept across with deadly effect."

The fighting continued with no pattern and then ended the same way. A Massachusetts solider, Benjamin Spear, was part of a group of black and white soldiers who gathered around Brigadier General Bartlett. The Federal officer had lost his right leg in 1862, and this day a large boulder dislodged by a shell smashed his cork prosthesis, making it impossible for him to escape the crater. The soldiers around him fought defiantly until they were surrounded. Recollected Spear, "A few blows were struck and a few of the 'niggers' as they called them, were bayoneted. But I heard a rebel Captain shout to his men, 'Hold on there; they have surrendered,' and further acts of this kind ceased."

"By the middle of the afternoon," a Maine soldier in Griffin's brigade noted bitterly, "the affair was over…. The enemy had recovered possession of all the ground we had taken in our first advance, and except for the ugly gap where the demolished redan had stood, their lines were intact, and as strong as before the explosion of the mine." One New Hampshire diarist ended his July 31 entry, "A sad day for our corps. The old story again — a big slaughter, and nothing gained."

R. E. LEE TO SECRETARY OF WAR JAMES SEDDON — 3:25 P.M.

AT 5 A.M. THE ENEMY SPRUNG A MINE UNDER ONE OF THE SALIENTS ON GENERAL B. R. JOHNSON'S FRONT AND OPENED HIS BATTERIES UPON OUR LINES AND THE CITY OF PETERSBURG. IN THE CONFUSION CAUSED BY THE EXPLOSION OF THE MINE HE GOT POSSESSION OF THE SALIENT. WE HAVE RETAKEN THE SALIENT AND DRIVEN THE ENEMY BACK TO HIS LINES WITH LOSS.

From Testimony before the Official Court of Inquiry on the Mine:

FINDING

The causes of failure are:

    1. The injudicious formation of the troops in going forward . . . The troops should have been formed in the open ground in front of the point of attack parallel to the line of the enemy's works. . . .

    2. The halting of the troops in the crater instead of going forward. . . .

    3. No proper employment of engineer officers and working parties [to clear away Union defensive obstructions beforehand]. . . .

4. That some parts of the assaulting column were not properly led.

5. The want of a competent command head at the scene of the assault to direct affairs.

Federals captured in the crater fighting were marched through Petersburg on July 31. Southern soldiers, still angry over the use of black troops in the attack, lined the Union POWs up in alternate rows of black and white. "In this manner we were marched through the principal streets of Petersburg," one Vermont soldier recalled, "and received many taunts and scoffs from the people as we journeyed along." Another captured Union officer remembered, "The people gazed at us as curiosities …and greeted [us] with cries of, 'See the white and nigger equality soldiers!' 'How do you like it, Yanks?' 'Yanks and niggers sleep in the same bed,' etc., Etc."

From Testimony before the Official Court of Inquiry on the Mine:

OPINION

. . . [It] remains to report that the following named officers engaged therein appear from the evidence to be "answerable for want of success" which should have resulted:

I. Maj. Gen. A. E. Burnside . . .
II. Brig. Gen. J. H. Ledlie . . .
III. Brig. Gen. Edward Ferrero . . .
IV. Col. Z. R. Bliss, Seventh Rhode Island Volunteers . . . [who] remained behind with the only regiment of his brigade which did not go forward. . . .
V. Brig. Gen. O. B. Willcox . . . [more] energy might have been exercised . . . to cause his troops to go forward. . . .

A truce was declared at 5:00 a.m. on August 1 so that both sides could retrieve their wounded and bury their dead. "We were not allowed to approach the Crater," a New York soldier recalled. "A confederate guard was posted outside of it and the passed out our wounded." An officer in the 32nd Maine never forgot the horrors of the scene. "Men were swollen out of all human shape, and whites could not be told from blacks, except by their hair. So much were they swollen that their clothes were burst, and their waist-bands would not reach half-way around their bodies; and the stench was awful." A New Hampshire man remembered that not "a shot was heard all along the line.

Officers and men of both armies mingled there, where we were caring for the dead, or sat upon the breastworks on our left and right engaged in friendly conversation." "During the time of removing the dead the Confederates brought a brass band and posted it on their front line of works," continued Pennsylvanian J. R. Holibaugh. "We had a band on our line. So for two hours the bands played alternately, the Federals playing National airs and the Confederate Southern airs."

Lieutenant General Ulysses S. Grant: "It was the saddest affair I have ever witnessed in the war. Such opportunity for carrying fortifications I have never seen and do not expect again to have."

(Following his testimony before the Official Court of Inquiry, Major General Ambrose Burnside left the army on a twenty-day furlough. He was never recalled to duty, and Major General John G. Parke assumed command of the Ninth Corps. Burnside resigned from the service on April 15, 1865.)

Grant: "I blame myself for one thing. I was informed . . . that General Burnside . . . trusted to the pulling of straws which division should lead. It happened to fall on what I thought was the worst commander in his corps . . . I mean General Ledlie."

(On August 6, 1864, Brigadier General James Ledlie left the army on a twenty-day sick leave that lasted four months. Upon returning to the army, in early December, he received orders "to repair to his home and there await further orders." On January 15, 1865, Ledlie tendered his resignation, which was accepted by the War Department on March 6.)

Grant: "General Burnside wanted to put his colored division in front, and I believe if he had done so it would have been a success. Still I agreed with General Meade as to his objections to that plan. General Meade said that if we put the colored troops in front. . . and it should prove a failure, it would then be said, and very properly, that we were shoving those people ahead to get killed because we did not care anything about them."

(Brigadier General Edward Ferrero not only retained a divisional command but in December received the brevet of major general for "meritorious service in the present campaign.")

Grant: "So fair an opportunity will probably never occur again for carrying fortifications; preparations were good, orders ample, and everything so far as I can see, subsequent to the explosion of the mine, shows that almost without loss the crest beyond the mine could have been carried."

(Colonel Zenas R. Bliss continued to direct the First Brigade of the Second Division, Ninth Corps, until August 21, 1864, when he was relieved because of ill health and transferred to administrative duties in West Virginia. Bliss returned to the regular army after the war and retired in 1897 with the rank of major general.)

Grant: "I am satisfied that if the troops had been properly commanded, and been led in accordance with General Meade's order, we would have captured Petersburg with all the artillery and a good portion of its support, without the loss of 500 men."

(Although Brigadier General Orlando B. Willcox was Burnside's logical successor, it was John G. Parke, the corps's chief of staff, who received the promotion. Willcox continued in divisional command until the end of the war and was mustered out of service in January 1866.)

(Union losses at the crater, among the Ninth Corps and Army of the James troops and associated artillery engaged, were officially reported as 504 killed, 1,881 wounded, and 1,413 missing, for a total of 3,798. The most recent estimate of Confederate losses at the crater, among the troops of Mahone's, Johnson's, and Hoke's divisions, Elliott's Brigade, and associated artillery, suggests these figures as minimums: 361 killed, 727 wounded, and 403 missing, for a total of 1,491.)

Part II

FIGHTING RIGHT, FIGHTING LEFT

In the trenches at Petersburg: A covered way. *A Waud*

Chapter Seven

"It was terrible—awful—terrific"

August 9, 1864

Confederate secret agent John Maxwell, described by his service commander as a "bold operator," set out from Richmond on a mission of destruction on July 26. He was accompanied by a fellow operative named R. K. Dillard and armed with an infernal device: an ingenious time bomb of his own invention, which Maxwell proudly dubbed a "horological torpedo." The two men were under orders "to operate . . . against the enemy's vessels navigating . . . the James River."

The small hamlet of City Point, Virginia — located some ten miles northeast of Petersburg, at the confluence of the Appomattox and James rivers — was the river port through which much of the Cockade City's commerce normally passed. At the height of its antebellum activity, City Point, first linked to Petersburg by rail in 1838, had also enjoyed regular steamboat service to and from New York.

The war and the Union naval blockade had choked off most of City Point's business, however, and the once thriving community had fallen into a sharp decline. But its status changed dramatically on the afternoon of May 5, 1864, when a detachment of black troops from the Army of the James splashed ashore to take possession of the area for the United States. Staff officer Thomas Livermore, who accompanied the Federal landing party, recalled that City Point then consisted of "a few shabby houses ranged along two or three short lanes or streets; and the spacious grounds and dilapidated house of one Dr. Eppes."

For the next month, City Point served as an armed camp for the black troops. Then, on June 15, Ulysses S. Grant arrived and turned the formerly quiet settlement into the military headquarters of the United States. "City Point . . . a drummer boy declared, "leaped into worldwide importance in 24 hours in June '64."

City Point underwent a startling transformation by mid-July. "All was activity and movement," a soldier noted on July 12. "Steamboats and sailing vessels, transports and lighters of all kinds, encumbered the river near the improvised wharves on which they were still working. . . . Legions of negroes were discharging the ships, wheeling dirt, sawing the timber, and driving piles. . . . A great village of wood and cloth was erected there, where a few weeks before were but two or three houses." "City Point," wrote a visitor in July, "is as full of hum as a bee hive."

City Point became the central supply depot for all the Union armies operating against Petersburg and Richmond. Munitions, food, and medicines that were off-loaded onto the long wharves lining the James River side of the small promontory were then hauled inland by hand, wagon, or rail. (The army animals alone required six hundred tons of grain and hay per day.) Some forty steamboats, seventy-five sailing vessels, and one hundred barges would be anchored here on busy days. As one observer put it, "City Point became the gateway of the army."

A small metropolis now spread across the teardrop-shaped piece of land jutting into the James and Appomattox rivers. There were offices and quarters for Grant's staff, encampments for the provost units providing security, and administrative bureaus for the personnel needed to operate the facility, as well as vast storage warehouses (where twenty days' forage and thirty days' rations were kept on hand at all times), hospitals (the largest of which, occupying two hundred acres, could handle ten thousand patients), stables, repair shops, a bakery (eventually capable of producing 123,000 loaves per day), chapels, sutler's stores, and a prison known as the Bull Pen. In the last, according to one visitor, were held "various characters, such as deserters, stragglers, cowards and those disgraced for various causes, and now and then a case wrongfully trundled in there."

On August 2, after a roundabout but uneventful trip, Confederate agents Maxwell and Dillard crossed the lower James River into Isle of Wight County, adjacent to Norfolk and Hampton Roads. There the two "learned of immense supplies of stores being landed at City Point." Maxwell decided that this would

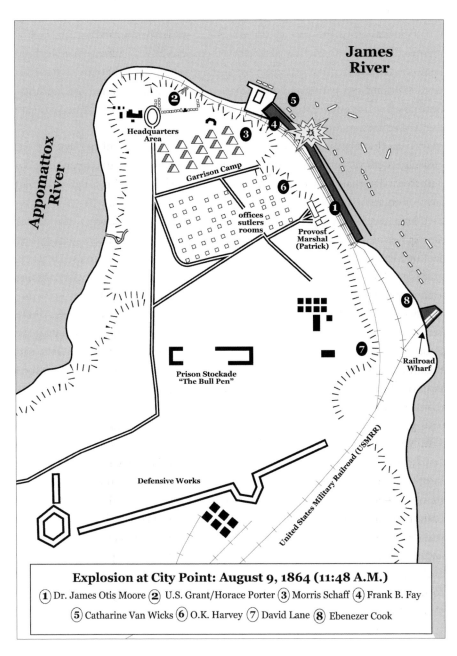

James River

Appomattox River

Headquarters Area

Garrison Camp

offices
sutlers
rooms

Provost
Marshal
(Patrick)

Prison Stockade
"The Bull Pen"

Railroad
Wharf

United States Military Railroad (USMRR)

Defensive Works

Explosion at City Point: August 9, 1864 (11:48 A.M.)

① Dr. James Otis Moore ② U.S. Grant/Horace Porter ③ Morris Schaff ④ Frank B. Fay
⑤ Catharine Van Wicks ⑥ O.K. Harvey ⑦ David Lane ⑧ Ebenezer Cook

be the ideal target for his horological torpedo. Determined to place "our machine upon [one of] the vessels there discharging stores," the pair set out for the place.

"Viewed from the top of the hill[,] City Point presented an interesting picture," a Massachusetts cavalryman remembered. "Everything in sight bore testimony to the fact that war was waging close at hand. A fleet of miscellaneous vessels dotted the James and Appomattox Rivers, and crowded the landings. Several ironclads anchored with their guns trained up the James formed a picket line above the junction of the two rivers."

"City Point was not at this time an inviting place," insisted one of the civilian nurses serving there. A New York soldier who was treated in one of the City Point hospitals disagreed, remarking in his diary, "I think this is a very good place with the exception of too many lice."

There were other problems. "You cannot imagine the great amount of stealing done at City Point," a Fifth Corps officer was complaining as late as January 1865. "We had, for our Corps, sixty wagon loads of boxes last week, and seven out of every ten were broken, and portions, if not all, of the contents were missing."

But there were unexpected moments of beauty as well. A New York soldier stationed nearby recalled how "often, in the evening, when it was quiet, we could hear the colored people, near City Point, who used to hold religious meetings in the open air, sing their quaint but soulful melodies with such volume and earnestness, as to effect listeners even at such a distance."

Tuesday, August 9

It promised to be another scorcher. "The day is going to be intensely hot," Warren Freeman, a Massachusetts soldier, noted uncomfortably, "the thermometer being at ninety-eight now (time half past six a.m.)." A Massachusetts engineer named O. K. Harvey, stationed at the Point of Rocks pontoon bridge, was nevertheless in a good mood. His commander had approved passes for the men to visit City Point, and Harvey was looking forward to the trip "as it was rumored that Gen. Grant and staff were quartered there, and anything in the nature of excitement which might be looked for when the Engineer Corps was not on duty was indeed welcome."

Confederate agent Maxwell openly moved among the tidal wash of laborers surging in and out of the City Point wharf area. No one imagined that he was carrying his horological torpedo, a large box armed with twelve to fifteen pounds of explosives. Harvey and R. K. Dillard had slipped undetected past the

Federal picket line and then paused at City Point's outskirts, where Dillard had hidden himself while Maxwell proceeded alone.

Maxwell observed the dock area for a while and eventually saw one barge captain leave his craft, obviously going on an errand. He promptly moved toward the vessel. "Being halted by one of the wharf sentinels, I succeeded in passing him by representing that the captain had ordered me to convey the box on board," he later reported. "Hailing a man from the barge I put the machine in motion and gave it in his charge. He carried it aboard. . . . Rejoining my companion, we retired to a safe distance to witness the effect of our effort." It was not yet quite 10:00 a.m.

Maxwell's infernal device was now aboard the *J. E. Kendrick*, a barge loaded to capacity with artillery and small-arms munitions.

Dr. James Otis Moore, a physician assigned to a Union field hospital, came to City Point this morning by train to pick up medical supplies. "City Point is situated upon quite a bluff," he wrote the next day, "with space enough between the bluff & the River for the erection of Storehouses and also a road which runs around it." Moore estimated that when he arrived there "was probably a detail of between 2 & 300 men unloading schooners, Steamboats & loading cars." Moore finished his business before boarding the next train headed back down the line. A companion suggested that they ride on top of the car to escape the stifling heat and the rank smell of some hides in a nearby freight car, but Moore preferred the comfort of a seat to the rooftop. His friend persisted until Moore's patience ran out. He snapped that he was not going to move, and that was that. "Well, I can stand it if you can," his companion muttered, and he stared sulkily at the busy wharf not fifty-five yards away.

Passengers who were otherwise disposed settled themselves over Moore's head along the walkboard that ran the length of the car's roof. Among them was a *New York Tribune* reporter who found a comfortable spot "and commenced perusing a letter I had just received from a fraternal youngster in the Prairie State."

U. S. Grant had returned to City Point early this morning following a trip north to confer on operations in the Shenandoah Valley. He moved outside his tent as the day grew hotter to hold court near the edge of the high bluffs, hoping to catch a cool river breeze. Grant listened impassively as Assistant Provost Marshal Colonel George H. Sharpe insisted that Rebel spies had infiltrated City Point several times in the previous weeks. Finishing his report with an emphatic promise to bag the enemy agents, the Union counterintelligence man departed.

U.S. Sanitary Commission official Frank B. Fay had come down to the City Point wharf to post his regular reports. He idly watched as the mail boat, which "had a large number of passengers," pulled away from the shore.

Lieutenant Morris Schaff, who supervised the transfer of munitions from ship to shore, was sitting in his office near the wharf this morning when an old friend paid a call. The two decided to mark the occasion by walking a hundred yards or so to visit with an officer on Grant's staff who always had a well-stocked liquor chest. There Schaff and his companion found a small group of officers clustered convivially "around a pail two-thirds full of claret punch." Before long a game of "seven-up" was going, and Schaff sat in. His luck was good this day. He quickly captured "two tens with a queen" and felt confident that he would win.

Catharine Van Wicks set down her luggage and took off her hat after having boarded the fast steamer *Solomon Rumage*, moored to the City Point wharf. She was booked on the vessel to Fort Monroe, where she would transfer to a Baltimore-bound steamboat. It was hot inside her cabin, so Miss Van Wicks decided to take a turn on the open deck.

Infantryman Ebenezer Cook had come to City Point on a pass to visit some hospitalized friends. "I was much interested in watching the negro stevedores at work transferring ammunition from some of the barges to the army wagons lined up some 10 or 15 feet from the barges," he recalled. "The negroes seemed to be in the best of spirits and were singing as they tossed shells from hand to hand to the army wagons."

Charles Porter, a soldier from the 11th Vermont who had been wounded in June, was convalescing at a City Point hospital. Dinner arrived early today, and after his meal Porter stepped outside the building for a smoke.

Engineer O. K. Harvey and a friend finished an impromptu tour of the busy City Point dockside and resolved to get haircuts and shaves. The two climbed up the steep bluff, found an open barbershop, and settled into the cutting chairs. A coffee grinder fastened to the wall caught Harvey's friend's eye, and he made a joke to the barber about grinding out his taxes.

Hospital attendant David Lane was on his way to the wharf when, about half a mile away from it, he saw something that made him stop and stare. "As I looked toward the landing I saw a lady, mounted on a white horse . . . ride up the bank from the river and turn in the direction of Grant's headquarters. . . . The horse was a spirited one, and I could but admire the ease and grace with which she restrained him and compelled him to do her bidding."

The time was perhaps twenty minutes before noon.

Maxwell and Dillard were a "safe distance" from the City Point wharves when the horological torpedo exploded. "Its effect," Maxwell reported soon afterwards, "was communicated to another barge beyond the one operated upon and also to a large wharf building. . . . The scene was terrific, and the effect deafened my companion to an extent from which he has not yet recovered. My own person was severely shocked, but I am thankful to Providence that we have both escaped without lasting injury."

The *J. E. Kendrick* disintegrated in an instant of incandescence. A newsman for the *Philadelphia Inquirer* recorded the moment as "a stunning concussion . . . accompanied with a sound which some compare to the discharge of a cannon close to each ear." To a New York soldier named Charles Hamlin, posted more than ten miles away, it "sounded more like a clap of thunder than anything." Hospital patient Charles Porter was startled by what sounded to him like heavy cannonading near City Point. "The air to an immense height was filled with exploding shells, and a great cloud of smoke hung over the Point," he recollected. Another New Yorker in the trenches, Uberto Burnham, looked up to see an "immense column of smoke rolling up toward the sky. It seemed to be a mile high and hung in the air for a long time."

The *New York Tribune* man atop the railroad train parked next to the wharf later wrote of a "stunning and deafening shock, as if…the terrible explosion of a monster shell near me, and the concussion of the air, were bending me involuntarily over the deck of the car, as a plant bending before the storm, and it seemed that the concussion would never cease ringing and swaying until it bred more and more danger." Dr. Moore and his sulky companion in the passenger car below were looking toward the river when the explosion occurred. Their eyes, remembered Moore, "filled with cinders. We immediately ran to the end of the car & threw ourselves upon our faces until the noise was all over."

The force of the blast knocked down the Sanitary Commission's Frank Fay, badly bruising his right arm and side. "Curling up in the smallest space, I put my arms over my head to protect it. . . . Missiles of all kinds, shells, Minie balls, pieces of lumber, guns, bayonets, filled the air, and dropped around me." Fay rolled under his supply wagon for protection but had to dodge frantically to avoid the deadly hooves of one of the horses hitched to it. Terrified by the explosion, and by another horse's careening into it, Fay's animal pawed the ground wildly as the equally frightened official scrambled clear.

Ebenezer Cook, who had observed the casual unloading of the ammunition barges, was blown backward and stunned by the furnace blast of air that surged up the bluff face. "I felt myself going up, my hat left my head, and I never saw it again, although, shortly afterwards I found one just as good, and appropriated it." A wagon nearby had been tossed over by the force of the explosion and lay across its team of horses. The trapped, doomed animals, Cook vividly recalled years afterward, "were making cries that seemed almost human."

Catharine Van Wicks came on deck on the *Solomon Rumage* seconds after the explosion. "I saw the guns, shells and men in the air," she later wrote, "and when the dust and smoke cleared away there was nothing left but debris." There was a sickening thud, and a "man's head fell on the deck...at my feet." The redoubtable lady never flinched. "I picked it up by the hair and placed it in the deck bucket of water, which was standing beside the cabin door."

The steep bluff here saved many lives. "Shells, balls and shot of every kind struck this bank in a perfect shower," reported a correspondent, who added that "Had the ground been level the loss of life would no doubt have been far greater than it was." The lovely mounted woman whom young David Lane had been admiring as she rode near the crest disappeared into a whirling eddy of fire and smoke that roiled up the bluff face. "Heavy timbers and other debris flew over and around me," Lane remembered. "I looked for the lady on horseback. For an instant I could see nothing in that direction but a swirling cloud of dust; in another instant I saw, through the dispersing gloom, a white horse clearing the ground with rapid strides, and on his back, cool and erect, a lady."

"As soon as the dense smoke had cleared up," recalled Dr. Moore, "we started to find out the situation of affairs." Moore and his companion emerged from the railroad car into a horrific landscape. Bodies and bits of bodies lay everywhere. The two doctors almost immediately began treatng the injured. "We dressed some of the most hideous and ghastly wounds which [it] falls to the lot of Surgeons to dress," Moore wrote home the next day. In the midst of his labors, he found time to speculate on the decision that had probably saved his life. "Most of the men who were on top of the car were killed," he told his wife. "You. . . . see that it is one of the most clear cases of a special Providence."

The ramshackle barbershop in which O. K. Harvey was sitting literally shook apart around them. "The chair upon which I was reclining turned sidewise. . . . The walls seemed to rock and tremble and collapsed like an eggshell. Windows were shattered into a thousand pieces." Terrified patrons and barbers dashed outdoors and huddled together in the street. "One wagon which I noticed particularly was drawn by a pair of large mules and they were running for dear life; in the bottom of the box clung the most thoroughly frightened negro I ever saw. His face was as gray as ashes . . . he was literally 'scared to death.' "

At U. S. Grant's headquarters, near the bluff edge, "there rained down . . . a terrific shower of shells, bullets, boards, and fragments of timber," recalled the lieutenant general's aide Horace Porter. "The general,. . .fortunately, was not touched by any of the missiles." Several staff officers were injured, however, and one orderly was killed. Continued Porter, "[The] general was the only one of the party who remained unmoved; he did not even leave his seat to run to the bluff with the others to see what had happened." Another staff officer, commissary chief Lieutenant Colonel Michael R. Morgan, saw "Grant at his usual gait, walking up from his tent toward the Adjutant General's tent, taking things coolly and seemingly not thinking anything out of the ordinary was taking place." The telegraph wires managed to survive the falling debris, for five minutes after the blast Grant wired a brief description of the incident to the War Department in Washington. Another aide, Lieutenant Colonel Theodore S. Bowers, had more trouble finding the words to express himself. "It was terrible—awful—terrific," he wrote his wife.

Lieutenant Morris Schaff never finished his winning hand of cards. A twelve-pound cannonball ripped through the tent wall and pulverized a camp chest in the midst of the officers. "In an instant," Schaff recalled, "we were all running for dear life." His first instinct was to move as far away from the wharf as possible, but discipline asserted itself and he turned back to the bluff's edge. "[There] lay before me a staggering scene, a mass of overthrown buildings, their timbers tangled into almost impenetrable heaps." The ordnance officer clambered down to the destroyed area, where he helped drag a badly injured sentry from the wreckage and found the lifeless body of one of the best noncoms assigned to his detail.

Suddenly Schaff heard someone cry, "There it goes again!" "On looking up I saw that the fire which had started on the wharf had just reached a small pile of ammunition, perhaps ten or fifteen boxes. Knowing, or at least thinking, that I could get to it before it could do any harm, I rushed in and with my army hat beat it out."

Sanitary Commission director Frank Fay had heard the same cry of warning. "Starting to run, it occurred to me that there might be men under the crushed building who ought to be removed, and I turned to them. At that instant a tugboat ran up to the wharf, threw out some hose, with one man only to handle it. My [bruised] right arm was helpless, but with the other hand and arm we managed to drag it to the fire, and it was soon extinguished."

In a brief endorsement covering John Maxwell's December 16 report of his and R. K. Dillard's actions, Brigadier General Gabriel Rains concluded, "This succinct narrative is but an epitome of their operations, which necessarily implies secrecy for the advantage of this kind of service as well as their own preservation."

The gruesome job of cleaning up took several days. Every survivor had a story to tell. Morris Schaff looked for the good-natured barber who had operated his chair from a tent perched on the bluff's edge, directly in the path of the worst of the blast wave. "We never saw anything of him or the chair after the explosion," Schaff declared. Catharine Van Wicks swore that "where the big bake house stood nothing was left but the tall brick chimney and over its top was a chain and an anchor evenly balanced." A sight long remembered by one clerk at the wharf was that of the black dockhands who "took gunny sacks and gathered up the shattered bodies of the workers, strewn at least a quarter of a mile about the boat landing."

After viewing the scene, a New York soldier pronounced it the "awfullest mass of ruin I ever beheld." A Massachusetts man, Warren Freeman, noted one great pile of "more than twenty tons of soap, candles, and flour...melted into one immense mass of dough." Freeman also observed that the "trees on the bluff were nearly stripped of their foliage and branches...and suspended from many of the limbs were the intestines and mangled limbs of human beings, who a few seconds before had been breathing, living men." One chaplain reported presiding over "the burial of 12 dead men, and 27 sacks full of pieces of men, heads, arms, hands, legs, bodies, &c., &c., that were picked up over a space of ground as far as a half a mile from the wharf."

It was later determined that two million dollars' worth of supplies and property was lost in the explosion. A recently completed 600-square-foot warehouse had disappeared, and 180 feet of wharf was torn to splinters. According to Morris Schaff's careful bookkeeping, 700 boxes of artillery ammunition, 2,000 boxes of small-arms munitions, and between 600 and 700 blank cartridges were gone as well. The official body count was 43 killed and 126 wounded, though everyone agreed that these figures were too low. An unknown number of unregistered black laborers had simply ceased to exist.

Security was tightened afterward, even though a court of inquiry ruled that the explosion was an accident.[1] The ordnance depot was quickly rebuilt, but at the end of September it was relocated to the end of a large pier, a good distance from the main wharf. Even though the inquiry board found no one to blame for the disaster, Morris Schaff was transferred to Reading, Pennsylvania, where he spent the rest of the war inspecting cannon and projectiles.

The great explosion caused barely a ripple in City Point's operations. In fact, just two months after the catastrophe life there took a decided turn for the better when reporters hailed the grand opening of the Maltby House, offering clean rooms to visitors and "as good a meal as any first-class hotel in the North." By war's end, this once tiny hamlet would boast 280 buildings.

Confederate agent John Maxwell resurfaced just once after the war. In 1872, Horace Porter — then personal secretary to President U. S. Grant — met with Maxwell, who complained that he was not being treated fairly by the commissioner of patents. As evidence of his inventive skills, Maxwell described the horological torpedo that he had used at City Point on August 9, 1864. "I told him that his efforts, from his standpoint, had been eminently successful," Porter noted dryly.

A medical man who had been present at City Point on that August day was less charitable when he learned of Maxwell's achievement, declaring, "It was not war. It was simply butchery."

---

1   However, official Confederate correspondence captured following the fall of Richmond pointed to a sabotage action.

Chapter Eight

"Fire low! Low! Low!"

August 13 - 25, 1864

Ulysses S. Grant
Final Report of Operations, March 1864-May 1865

Sixth Corps, then at Washington, was ordered back to [the Shenandoah Valley to] the vicinity of Harper's Ferry. . . . From the time of the first raid the telegraph wires were frequently down between Washington and City Point..... It took twenty-four to thirty-six hours to get dispatches through and return answers back, so that often orders would be given, and then information would be received showing a different state of facts . . . causing a confusion and apparent contradiction of orders. ... To remedy this evil, it was evident to my mind that some person should have the supreme command of all the forces in the Departments of West Virginia, Washington, Susquehanna, and the Middle Department. . . .

On the 2d of August I ordered General Sheridan to report to the command of all the forces against Early. At this time the enemy was concentrated in the neighborhood of Winchester, while our forces, under General Hunter, were concentrated on the Monocacy . . . leaving open to the enemy Western Maryland and Southern Pennsylvania. . . . [On August] 4th, I left City Point to visit Hunter's command, and determine for myself what was best to be done. ... I issued to him the . . . instructions [to] . . . concentrate all . . . available force without delay in the vicinity of Harper's Ferry.

General Hunter having, in our conversation, expressed a willingness to be relieved from command, I telegraphed to have General Sheridan . . . sent . . . with orders to take general command of all the troops in the field. . . . I remained at Monocacy until General Sheridan arrived on the morning of the 6th, and after a conference with him in relation to military affairs in that vicinity, I returned to City Point by way of Washington.

*   *   *

Ulysses S. Grant and Philip H. Sheridan were of a kind: both viewed the making of war with the same hard eyes. When Grant came east in March 1864 to command all the Union armies, he placed only two of his Western protégés in top positions with the Army of the Potomac. James H. Wilson was given a cavalry division, while "Little Phil" Sheridan got the whole cavalry corps. Sheridan's unconventional views about the proper use of the mounted arm put him on a collision course with George Meade, and the two scrapped constantly during the Overland campaign, with Grant invariably siding with his cavalry chief. Meade endured this embarrassing situation throughout the bloody forty days and the frustrating fumbles before Petersburg in June and July. He longed for an honorable release from his responsibilities, and suddenly one was dangled before him.

Jubal Early's raid through the Shenandoah Valley to the very gates of Washington made it imperative that the scattered Union forces opposing him be joined in a single command not subject to War Department meddling. Meade wanted that assignment, and Grant as much as said that it was his for the asking, but the proud Pennsylvanian could not stoop to request it. In response to Grant's casual offer, Meade replied stiffly that he was "ready to obey any order that might be given" to him. Privately, in a letter to his wife, he confided that "so far as having an independent command, which the Army of the Potomac is not, I would like this change very well." On August 1, Grant told Meade that he was going to send Phil Sheridan north.

Grant made the appointment despite stiff opposition from War Department officials, who felt that Sheridan was too inexperienced for the task. Lincoln himself, however, backed Grant, and Grant backed Sheridan. When Meade cornered him on his turnaround, Grant said that Lincoln had not wanted the Pennsylvanian to be separated from the Army of the Potomac, since such an action might be viewed as expressing disapproval of his leadership. Meade swallowed his disappointment.

Grant left City Point on August 4 and made a quick trip north to put his personal stamp on affairs. When he returned, on August 9, his thoughts remained with Sheridan. He was certain that given a little time to reorganize things, and a fair chance in battle, Little Phil would succeed in his mission to clear Early out of western Virginia once and for all. But Robert E. Lee was equally determined that Sheridan would have neither time nor opportunity.

On August 10, Grant received the summary of a prisoner interrogation containing the disturbing news that "Kershaw's division, of Longstreet's corps" was on its way to reinforce Early. Within twenty-four hours, further intelligence-gathering had listed up to four divisions that might be "now on the way north." There were conflicting reports suggesting that, at most, just one infantry and one cavalry division were involved, but Grant was predisposed to accept the worst.

By August 12, he believed "that the enemy has sent north two if not three divisions of infantry, twenty-three pieces of artillery, and one division of cavalry." If these troops were to join Early, Sheridan would be overwhelmed. "To prevent as much as possible these reinforcements from being sent out from Richmond," Grant later explained, "I had to do something to compel Lee to retain his forces about the capital."

As a counterpoint to the Crater action, just seventeen days earlier, Grant had ordered a large-scale diversionary maneuver on the north side of the James River. It failed to win any combat victories, but it managed to point out Lee's sensitivity in that direction. The Federal expedition consisted of Winfield Hancock's Second Corps and three cavalry divisions, as well as a few infantry units from other commands. When Hancock's men crossed on pontoon bridges from Jones Neck to Curles Neck, near Deep Bottom, on July 26, Confederate strength in that sector was about 11,000 men. Within twenty-four hours of that Union crossing, Lee sent an additional 5,500 men hustling up from Petersburg, and by July 29, Confederate forces north of the James totaled more than 26,000—almost all drawn from the Bermuda Hundred and Cockade City lines. Grant now reasoned that Lee would react to an even stronger move against Richmond by pulling back all the troops that were then in motion for the Shenandoah Valley.

(The area targeted by Grant's operation was named Deep Bottom after the depth of the James River channel at that point. It was located at the northern tip of a two-mile loop in the James, which in turn outlined an appendix off the northeast corner of Bermuda Hundred, known as Jones Neck. Deep Bottom lay about five miles southeast of Richmond's principal defensive lines. Its eastern boundary was abruptly and sharply defined by Bailey's Creek, which came down from the north. About a mile and a half up Bailey's Creek was a large mill pond and, near its southern end, Fussell's Mill. Three major roads fanned out from Richmond toward Deep Bottom, all running in a generally southeastern direction. Nearest to the James was the New Market or River Road. The Darbytown Road was about a mile further north, and equidistant northeast of that was the Charles City Road.

Elements of the Army of the James had held a bridgehead at Deep Bottom since late June. During the First Deep Bottom expedition, Hancock's Second

Corps had marched up from Petersburg via Jones Neck and crossed the James on a pontoon bridge to the east side of Bailey's Creek—an area known as Curles Neck and Strawberry Plain. The plan was for Hancock to then push north along Bailey's Creek, flank the outer Confederate defenses above the New Market Road, and cut loose a mounted raiding force toward Richmond's railroads. Prompt Rebel reaction had stopped Hancock from carrying out the plan; that failure, Grant believed, had stemmed from the amount of time it took the troops to get into position north of the James. This time, things were supposed to be different.)

Saturday, August 13
City Point

Cornelia Hancock (no relation to Winfield Scott) was the delighted center of attention for a literal army of young men. The attractive nurse had served the soldiers of the Second Corps since May, winning the hearts of most of them. Miss Hancock joined the staff of the corps hospital at City Point at the beginning of the Petersburg siege. She was usually forewarned by camp rumor when a major movement was in the offing, but her surprise was complete this morning when she learned that her boys were marching past the river port. "I never spent such a day in the army," Cornelia reflected. "Every person who ever knew me called here as they passed, and they could be counted by hundreds." To a man, Nurse Hancock added, the soldiers "were all jubilant thinking they were going to Washington."

"The troops were in the greatest glee . . . like schoolboys on a holiday," one New Yorker recollected. An inquisitive officer from the provost guard poked around in an effort to determine where the troops were heading. "[General] Hancock declared that he didn't know, Colonel [Francis] Walker, his Assistant Adjutant General, confessed utter ignorance. . . . Half a dozen different destinations were at once suggested and canvassed."

Someone on Grant's staff had had the bright idea of staging an elaborate ruse to disguise the movement. Instead of marching to Deep Bottom, the Second Corps would board transports and move downstream, away from that point. Once it was dark, the vessels would reverse course and swiftly disembark the men at Curles Neck.

The troops marched through City Point and down to the docks, where they clambered onto river steamers. The wearisome process, which began at noon, took nearly seven and a half hours. As each vessel was filled, it pulled away from the wharf and steamed three miles downstream to anchor off Lighthouse Point. Some thirty-two tightly packed transports were clustered there by sunset, awaiting orders. "Suffocatingly hot to-night on board the crowded steamers," noted Hancock's aide-de-camp, Major William G. Mitchell. "Almost impossible to get any sleep. The mosquitoes infernally tormenting."

Amid all the dockside confusion, no one had noticed Winfield Hancock and a few aides slipping away on a small tug that promptly turned its blunt nose upstream, toward Richmond.

General Hancock had profound doubts about the plan's feasibility. "I foresaw that the difficulties of disembarkation would be greater than we apprehended," he later reported. His scout to Deep Bottom confirmed his worst fears; according to Colonel Walker, "Here it was found that the nature of the banks and state of the water would not allow most, if any, of the vessels to land men over a gangplank. The ruins of three wharves were found, which could easily have been repaired with a little previous notice." Hancock ordered men and material to be brought up "to put the wharves in as good condition as might be [possible] in the brief space remaining." The troop-loaded craft were not scheduled to head toward Deep Bottom until midnight, but Hancock moved up the start time by two hours. It was one of the few things he could do to compensate for Grant's overly optimistic plans.

Confederate Defenses near the Howlett House, Bermuda Hundred

The never ending game of cat and mouse was taking its toll on Robert E. Lee. "General Lee was uneasy," his nephew and biographer Fitzhugh Lee later wrote of this period. "He was defending two cities and a line of intrenchments enveloping both thirty-five miles long, and could not know with certainty at what point in them the real blow would be delivered."

Lee had taken it personally when, in early August, Federals on Bermuda Hundred reached across its northwest shoulder to occupy the head of a river loop known as Dutch Gap. "The General did not seem in a remarkably good humor . . . with . . . this impudence of the Yankees in crawling up behind us," one of his division commanders observed. Lee ordered a bombardment this day that blasted futilely at the Union foothold. Its failure was symptomatic of his increasing frustration with the Petersburg stalemate.

The Confederate general had noted with great interest Phil Sheridan's appointment to command the troops facing Early. He had even anticipated matters on August 7 by dispatching Lieutenant General Richard H. Anderson, along with Kershaw's Division, to Culpeper. From that location, just east of the Blue Ridge Mountains, Anderson would be able to move quickly into the Shenandoah Valley if necessary. "Any enterprise that can be undertaken to injure the enemy, distract or separate his forces, embarrass his communications on the Potomac or on land is desirable," Lee instructed Anderson.

On August 11, Lee ordered his cavalry chief, Wade Hampton, to take a mounted division and join Anderson. "It is desirable that the presence of the troops in that region be felt," Lee told Hampton. He played his own game of deception by deliberately leaking the false information that an entire infantry corps was to follow Hampton, in order, as Fitzhugh Lee explained, "to induce Grant to send troops to Sheridan equivalent to [a]…whole corps. In that case Lee would again re-enforce Early and transfer the principal scene of hostilities to the Potomac."

New Market Heights, Confederate Lines near Deep Bottom

Lee's forces north of the James at this time consisted of Charles Field's five-brigade division, a brigade of Tennessee troops, artillery, and a cavalry brigade commanded by Brigadier General Martin W. Gary—perhaps 8,500 men in all. Although these troops operated in the Department of Richmond (which Lieutenant General Richard S. Ewell commanded), it was Field who exercised actual control.

Matters had been relatively quiet here since July 29, when the Federals had withdrawn all but a small force holding a defensive pocket around the Deep Bottom landing. Events elsewhere had taken center stage, and Field was daily expecting orders to follow Kershaw into western Virginia. One of Field's brigadiers caught the mood of the moment when he wrote, on August 12, "We are still lying at rest here although under orders to advance our line and close on the enemy, cramp him . . . in his little jug [i.e., Deep Bottom]. ... It is possible but not probable that our movements will bring on a 'chunk of a fight.' I hope not, for I am enjoying the rest like an old stage horse, resting my weary limbs."

Bermuda Hundred, Union Rear-Echelon Areas

Troops from the First and Second brigades of Brigadier General Alfred H. Terry's Tenth Corps division left their positions along the Bermuda Hundred

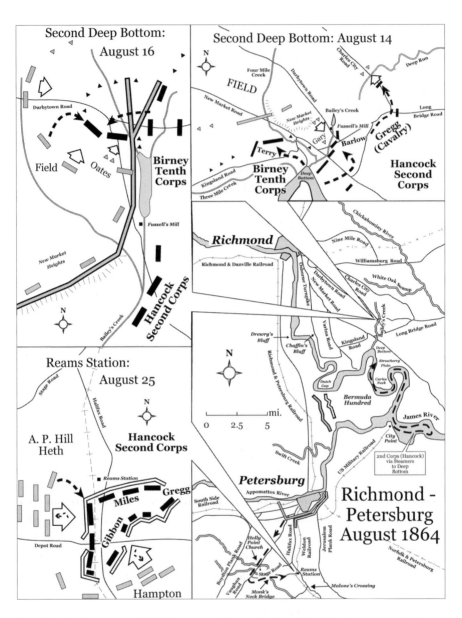

lines beginning around 11:00 p.m. and marched north. Their route took them along Jones Neck to the pontoon bridge connecting with Deep Bottom.

"Somehow an understanding seemed to prevail," recalled a member of the 7th New Hampshire, ". . . that the regiment was to go . . . aboard transports; consequently many men fell into line that were on the sick-list and did not wish to be left behind, yet could not endure a march, and who were obliged to fall out of the ranks after going a short distance."

The head of Terry's column arrived at Deep Bottom at around 2:00 a.m. on August 14, with the last units crossing over an hour later. "The river was full of steamers, gunboats, and transports, laden with troops and war material," one weary Federal marveled.

Sunday, August 14
Deep Bottom

The ships carrying the Second Corps arrived off Curles Neck at about 1:00 a.m., but not for another ninety minutes were the ruined wharves sufficiently reinforced to allow the troops to disembark. Hancock's nightmares came true. "The men had been crowded very closely in the boats," Francis Walker complained, "and in getting off much delay was occasioned by the tedious filing down the narrow stairways between decks. There being but three wharves, steamers had to wait for others to unload. Some of the vessels drew so much water that they could not get up to the wharves at all, but were obliged to unload across others; while the largest steamer, containing a brigade, grounded in the stream and remained there for several hours." Some of the soldiers had fallen asleep during the night expecting to wake up on their way north and instead finding themselves at Deep Bottom with the enemy seemingly waiting for them. "Grant fooled us more than he did the Johnnies," grumbled a New York heavy artilleryman.

Grant's plan called for Hancock's men to be ashore and advancing along Bailey's Creek by 5:00 a.m., but only half the corps was off the boats by that time. It was 7:40 a.m. before the rest of the troops (minus the stranded brigade) were landed. Even then, the advance toward the enemy lines was anything but expeditious. "The day was excessively hot," the corps's medical director later recalled. "The men had been exhausted, and many fell out of the ranks, some insensible or in convulsions, [and] in many cases death resulted."

"I don't like to use God's Holy Day for fighting," one of Hancock's officers muttered. "God forgive our sins. . . ."

The fighting began on the west side of the Deep Bottom pocket at daylight as Tenth Corps troops pressed slowly toward New Market Heights. "The ground over which we passed . . . cannot be described," a New York soldier remembered. "Brush, briars, swamp, ravines, and pits, are but expressions for the surface of this historic soil." Alfred Terry's men had pushed as far as the base of New Market Heights by 10:00 a.m., where they were stopped by strongly manned enemy earthworks along the crest.

Ulysses Grant came to Deep Bottom this morning at 9:30 and rode along the positions that were being developed by both corps. Interrogation of the Rebels taken in the actions up to this point provided a fairly comprehensive picture of Lee's dispositions. "We have captured prisoners from four different brigades of Field's division," Grant noted at 10:00 a.m.; "...Field's division is one that we supposed had gone to the Valley." After ticking off the other units known to be either at Petersburg or at Bermuda Hundred, Grant concluded, "This leaves but one division of infantry to have gone to the Valley. I am now satisfied no more have gone."

Hancock's land actions were supported by ships from the U.S. James River fleet. The wooden side-wheeler USS *Agawam* made quite an impression with its two hundred-pounder Parrott rifles. A Confederate on the receiving end of the *Agawam's* attentions recollected, "The boat threw shells weighing 120 pounds, which would go right through our breastwork and explode away down in the ground, throwing barrels of dirt, rocks, and pieces of shell high into the air, to rain back on us." A Federal sitting near the guns when they went off remembered that they "lifted me right off my seat. You well believe they make a noise." The sound of these shells, another Union soldier observed, "was very peculiar, resembling heavily loaded wagons passing rapidly over a wooden bridge."

Hancock's attack along the east side of Bailey's Creek finally got under way at 10:00 a.m. He had assembled nearly 10,000 men in a striking force under his First Division commander, Brigadier General Francis Barlow, whose instructions were to drive up from Curles Neck in a northwesterly direction to overwhelm the thinly spread Rebel defenses below Fussell's Mill.

Barlow, one of the last of Hancock's trusted inner circle, was not well. He was suffering from physical problems (a Gettysburg wound) and emotional stresses (his wife was seriously ill) that would soon put him on sick leave. Hancock's adjutant, Francis Walker, described Barlow at this time as "more like a dead than a living man."

Barlow's attacks were poorly coordinated. He launched a series of assaults throughout the day, none of which made full use of the forces available to him. Hancock later blamed Barlow's penny-packet tactics for his failure this day: "I must say that had [the troops] . . . been kept more compact they ought to have broken through the line, then thinly held, by mere weight of numbers. . . ." Barlow, in turn, blamed his men. "None of the troops that came under my observation that day behaved with their usual vigor and gallantry under fire," he reported. At the end of this frustrating day, his troops were drenched by a passing rainstorm, "so that the thunder, together with the artillery and infantry fire, made a fine racket," one officer wrote.

Barlow's disjointed attacks were stalled by a few dismounted cavalrymen from Gary's Brigade and stopped altogether by a pair of infantry regiments that Charles Field rushed from New Market Heights to Fussell's Mill. "The conduct of Gary on this occasion was very judicious and gallant," Field stated. Added one of his infantrymen, "As was characteristic of the Federal generals of that day, those in command lost the advantage of their superior numbers by excess of caution and slowness of advance."

Robert E. Lee was worried despite his successes. To Wade Hampton, on his way to join Richard Anderson at Culpeper, Lee wired from Petersburg, "Halt your command and return toward Richmond." He also detached two brigades from the Petersburg defenses and sent them north. "This may be a feint to draw troops from here," Lee cautioned Field.

Even before Barlow's badly directed attacks began, the Tenth Corps troops in the Deep Bottom pocket extended their right flank across Bailey's Creek to link up with the Second Corps. Terry's men overran and captured an advanced Confederate battery as they did so, taking four eight-inch seacoast howitzers.

In other actions, east of Bailey's Creek, two Federal cavalry brigades from David Gregg's division took position near the termination of the Charles City Road, where some light skirmishing cost Gregg a few killed and wounded. Should Hancock succeed in turning the enemy's left, the mounted troopers were to carry out their unfulfilled July mission to wreck Richmond's railroads.

City Point

U. S. Grant continued to monitor the situation north and south of the James. At 7:20 p.m., he approved a suggestion from George Meade to pull the Fifth Corps out of the Petersburg trenches and mass it behind the lines, in preparation "either for a movement or to re-enforce any part of the line if attacked." Ten minutes later, Grant warned Hancock that a "body [of Confederate troops from Petersburg], supposed to be about a division, now seems to be moving [toward you]. . . ."

Deep Bottom

Winfield Hancock made plans for the next day. His goal was to flank the enemy's left, which rested near Fussell's Mill. To accomplish this turning movement, he called upon the Tenth Corps, near Deep Bottom. Accordingly, orders were issued to Major General David Birney (now commanding the Tenth Corps) to leave a small holding force behind and to march the rest of his troops to a point near the mill for a 6:00 a.m. assault.

When Ben Butler, commander of the Army of the James, learned of these instructions, his only comment was, "Pretty far round from left to right."

Monday, August 15
Deep Bottom

Hancock's orders to David Birney proved to be hopelessly optimistic. The Tenth Corps's move from Deep Bottom to Strawberry Plains was not completed until 9:00 a.m., and it took another four hours for these troops to come into position near Fussell's Mill. It was a hard march, and there was much straggling. With his footsore troops in too poor a condition to fight, Birney spent the next five and a half hours scouting the Confederate left. He reported to Hancock at 6:40 p.m. that he had found a weak spot but that it was too late in the day for an assault. "I will make a vigorous one at daylight," he vowed.

There were no significant offensive actions along the Second Corps line this day, though one infantry brigade was detached and sent to the Charles City Road to support Gregg's cavalry when an afternoon reconnaissance began a scrap. The infantry returned to Hancock in the evening, and Gregg's men settled down near Deep Run.

A newspaperman accompanying Birney put a positive spin on matters when he reported the day's events, concluding, "while the results were not of a startling character, still they may be faithfully said to aid us materially, in view of the results to be attained within the next few days."

Recorded Robert E. Lee's aide Walter Taylor, "On August 15th General Lee went to the north side of James River and established headquarters at Chaffin's Bluff, from which point he directed the operations of his troops." In addition to the two infantry brigades already en route to Field, Lee sent along a cobbled-together brigade from George Pickett's Bermuda Hundred force. These reinforcements, Field later reported, "were reaching me at intervals during the 15th."

City Point

Grant's attentions were largely elsewhere today. As his aide Horace Porter later observed, "General Grant was now giving daily watchfulness and direction to four active armies—those of Meade, Butler, Sheridan and Sherman. They constituted a dashing four-in-hand, with Grant holding the reins."

Among the other problems facing him was a panicky mood in Washington over the prospects for the current draft. The Army chief of staff, Henry Halleck, worried that there would be large-scale rioting that could be met only by "the withdrawal of a very considerable [number] of troops from the field." In his response to Halleck, sent today, Grant made it clear that if any trouble occurred, it would be up to the various state governors to restore order. "If we are to draw troops from the field to keep the loyal states in harness it will prove difficult to suppress the rebellion in the disloyal states," he said.

Grant himself later admitted, "It kept me pretty active in looking after all these points."

Tuesday, August 16
Deep Bottom

Gregg's cavalrymen were on the move at first light, pressing hard along the Charles City Road toward Richmond. They were within a mile of White's Tavern by 11:00 a.m., just seven miles from the Confederate capital. Gregg was again accompanied by an infantry brigade from the Second Corps.

The cavalry's advance was sharply contested, and there was constant skirmishing. The Confederacy lost Brigadier General John R. Chambliss during one of these countless little encounters, who was shot from his horse and killed. The Federal soldiers found a valuable document when they searched the body, which was rushed to Hancock by that evening. He pronounced it "a very perfect map, embracing the complete fortifications of Richmond and the surrounding country on both sides of the river."

Once it became light enough for him to see the ground, David Birney concluded that the point he had selected for his infantry attack was not a feasible one after all. The next few hours were spent reconnoitering for a new approach to the enemy lines. One was finally located, north and east of the mill pond, but more time was lost as troops were maneuvered into position. The first attack finally got under way a little after 10:00 a.m.

Even with the help sent to him by Robert E. Lee, Charles Field was hard pressed to cover his sector. He now had two brigades from William Mahone's division under his command, in addition to the five brigades from his own division, two from Cadmus Wilcox's division, and a Tennessee brigade that had been with him since August 14—and there was another pair of brigades on the way from Wilcox and Mahone, bringing the total to nearly 15,000 men, including cavalry from Gary's Brigade and W. H. F. Lee's division.

Field heard the unmistakable sound of an assault against his left flank, near Fussell's Mill, shortly after 10:00 a.m. The firing quickly died down, however, and for the next few hours only the crackle of skirmishing fire was audible. Then the musketry crescendoed to a roar again. Field was so confident that his men could handle the problem that he did not even bother to glance in that direction. As he later recalled, "Major William F. Jones, my Adjutant-General, who was standing up near me and could see all that was going on so near us, suddenly said very excitedly, 'General, they are breaking'; thinking he referred to the Yankees, I replied, 'Well, I knew they would'; but he immediately exclaimed, 'But, General, it's our men.'"

Birney's first attack overran a line of enemy rifle pits posted in a heavily forested area. More troops soon came up, and the Federals regrouped their battle lines. They went forward again at around noon.

The Confederates had cleared a fifty-yard field of fire in their front, and the leading Federal regiments were hit by killing volleys as they burst into the open. "The first division went down like so many tenpins," one regimental commander recollected, but supports were on hand, and the Union soldiers scrambled up to and then over the enemy works. "The first time I ever saw the brigade fighting hand to hand, bayonet to bayonet, over breast-works, was that day," an officer reported.

This time it was Southern troops who were running and Northern troops who were chasing. Another promising Confederate officer, Brigadier General Victor Girardey, was killed as he attempted to rally his men. Rebel prisoners mingled briefly with their Yankee captors. "Confusion for a few minutes followed," one New Hampshire man remembered. "The men of both sides fraternizing and exchanging coffee for tobacco, etc." Matters were finally gotten in hand, and a cautious advance was resumed, but the Union success proved to be two-edged. Enemy riflemen had not been dislodged from their positions below the mill pond, nor had those units posted along the Charles City Road fallen back, so the Confederate flanks on either side of the Union penetration remained firm. At the same time, the head of the Federal column was stunned by a series of fierce blows.

Colonel William Oates led two Alabama regiments forward in a counterattack against the long Federal battle lines. "Some of my men fell dead or horribly wounded at every step," he later wrote, "but the brave fellows . . . pressed forward, driving their enemy…" Oates himself was hit in the arm. "It struck with such force that it turned me half around and stunned me. . . . I was in great pain. One of those large Minie-balls strikes a hard blow."

Other Confederate units were converging from all sides against the now exposed Federal force. Finally, Field got everything organized and choreographed a coordinated action. "[We] advanced against the enemy, and after a hard and well contested battle, drove him back a half mile to our works, which he had captured, over and beyond them, retook our works and continued to hold them forever afterwards."

Affairs along the Charles City Road also took a non-Union turn. Stiff Confederate counterattacks had stopped Gregg's advance a mile short of its goal, White's Tavern, and then Rebel infantry supports had come up and turned the tide. At 1:30 p.m., one of Hancock's aides, riding with the mixed cavalry and infantry force, reported to his commander that they had been attacked "forcibly. Our troops are retiring on the Charles City road, the enemy pressing quite heavily."

The infantry brigade attached to Gregg's command was ordered south at 3:00 p.m. to help Birney. This left the cavalrymen alone to face a growing enemy force on the Charles City Road.

Winfield Hancock exercised little effective control over the fighting this day. His entire plan hinged on turning the enemy's left flank, and with the exception of units sent to support Birney directly, no Second Corps troops seriously threatened the enemy positions in their front. The slow flow of information was not helping matters. "The enemy soon rallied and retook the line," Hancock wrote of Field's counterattack, "but it was several hours before I could ascertain the exact state of affairs." There were worries, too, for his force on the Charles City Road, where Gregg's cavalry had been shoved back across Deep Run "by a superior force of infantry; what command is not known."

Grant visited Hancock's lines again this afternoon. An officer on his staff summed up the situation with the comment that Hancock "does not succeed in finding enemy's left flank, they stretching out apparently, as fast as he does."

It was dark before the trouble spots were stabilized and Hancock could report that the "remainder of the day passed without incident."

City Point

Grant reported to the War Department this evening that the "fighting north of the river to-day has resulted favorably for us, so far as it has gone; but there have been no decisive results."

He was keeping a careful count of the enemy units known to be north of the James, and thinking of Warren's footloose corps. He was also recalling the tempting target that he had been unable to destroy in late June. "If the enemy reduce again to three divisions at Petersburg," he told Meade (referring to the First Deep Bottom expedition and the subsequent assault at the crater), "it will be advisable to move Warren on to the Weldon [Rail]road. . . ." He still had a trick or two up his sleeve that he intended to use north of the James. He wired Hancock at around 9:00 p.m., "I have ordered to Strawberry Plains steamers ostensibly to bring down the Second Corps. It is intended as a ruse to make the enemy believe you are withdrawing, and to bring them out to attack you."

In a public letter written today to his political patron, Senator Elihu B. Washburne, Grant summed up all that had happened at Petersburg with the comment, "We are progressing here slowly."

Wednesday, August 17
Deep Bottom

Neither side was anxious to renew the ground war this day. Hancock reported in a dispatch to City Point that a, "close examination of the enemy's line this morning shows nothing new except that they have been at work all night strengthening their line on our right and extending their intrenchments in that direction."

A truce was arranged late in the afternoon to allow both sides to collect their dead and wounded. The body of John Chambliss was delivered to Confederate authorities during the two-hour pause. After debriefing the officers who had chatted with their enemy counterparts during the truce, Hancock, at 10:25 p.m., passed along to Grant a new count of Rebel units north of the James. "There is no doubt that the enemy have a pretty strong force here to-day," he declared.

Union Petersburg Lines, near the Jerusalem Plank Road

The Fifth Corps commander, Gouverneur Warren, was sent his orders at 2:30 p.m. Warren and his men would "move to-morrow morning at 4 o'clock and endeavor to make a lodgment upon the Weldon Railroad, in the vicinity of the Gurley House, or as much nearer to the enemy's lines of intrenchments as practicable, and destroy the road as far as you can, carrying on the destruction as far south as possible."

Warren's entire four-division corps was to take part in this operation. Also attached to his force was a small two-brigade mounted division commanded by Brigadier General August Kautz of the Army of the James; these cavalrymen would move parallel to Warren's line of march to protect his southern flank.

This was Warren's big opportunity to restore his reputation, which had been tarnished by his lackluster performance both in June and at the Crater. His mission now was clearly defined, and he was to have a practically independent command. "I was exceedingly pleased with my instructions for the movement," he later recalled.

Army of Northern Virginia Headquarters, Chaffin's Bluff

Robert E. Lee was not disposed to let this day pass peaceably. A Union raiding party had landed from the river and seized Signal Hill, about a mile up the north bank of the James from Dutch Gap. Lee sent word of this to the James River fleet at 9:00 a.m., with a request to "Please try and drive him [i.e., the enemy] off." Accordingly, two powerful Rebel ironclads moved down the river, anchored at a bend just above Signal Hill a little after 3:00 p.m., and began a slow bombardment that lasted throughout the night. "Their firing was beautiful!" a Richmond reporter exulted. "Every shell exploded at the right place."

When Confederate infantry advanced the next day, it was found that the enemy raiders had abandoned Signal Hill.

City Point

Reports arriving this evening bumped upward the estimated number of enemy units north of the James. "This leaves the force at Petersburg reduced to what it was when the mine was sprung," Grant informed Meade at 10:00 p.m. "Warren may find an opportunity to do more than I had expected."

Grant was sitting in front of his quarters this evening with members of his staff when he was handed a dispatch from Washington. As Horace Porter recalled, "He opened it, and as he proceeded with the reading his face became suffused with smiles. . . . We were curious to know what could produce so much merriment in the general in the midst of the trying circumstances which surrounded him. He... remarked: 'The President has more nerve than any of his advisors.' He then read aloud to us the following: 'I have seen your despatch expressing your unwillingness to break your hold where you are. Neither am I willing. Hold on with a bulldog grip, and chew and choke as much as possible, [signed] A. Lincoln.'"

Thursday, August 18
Union Petersburg Lines, near the Jerusalem Plank Road

Warren's advance finally got under way at 5:00 a.m., an hour behind schedule. Brigadier General Charles Griffin's division led the way, followed by the divisions of brigadier generals Romeyn B. Ayres, Samuel W. Crawford, and Lysander Cutler. "The moving column was a fine spectacle to behold," a Pennsylvanian remembered. "Ten thousand true and tried soldiers marching[,] . . . their bayonets sparkling in and reflecting the morning sunbeams[,] made a fit subject for the historic painting." The men turned south onto the Jerusalem Plank Road and followed it for three miles, to a crossroad that ran due west. The sweating bluecoats then kept to this sandy trail for almost two and a half miles, finally drawing up before the large white house that belonged to Dr. Gurley. Here Griffin deployed his lead brigade into a double line of battle and, a little after 8:00 a.m., ordered it to continue the westward advance.

Griffin's men crossed the Weldon Railroad at 9:00 a.m., reaching it near the Globe Tavern, a building also known as Yellow Tavern, Six Mile House, or Blick Station. A skirmish line was advanced another five hundred yards beyond the tracks, and then a three-regiment battle line was set perpendicular to the roadbed and moved a third of a mile toward Petersburg. Most of Griffin's remaining troops began ripping up the rails and setting fire to piles of wooden ties.

Deep Bottom

Lee's army had paid a high price in turning back Hancock's expedition. How high became evident today when he tried to organize an all-out push to eliminate the enemy from north of the James once and for all. No one at Lee's headquarters was underplaying the seriousness of the threat; his artillery chief, Brigadier General William Nelson Pendleton, went so far as to declare that ". . . Grant is . . . making a real effort below Chaffin's Bluff."

The Federals had expended great energy trying to turn his left flank, so Lee decided to return the favor and turn their right. His cavalry, now reinforced by Wade Hampton's division, would smash the enemy on the lower Charles City Road. At the same time, his infantry would attack near Fussell's Mill. These actions were to begin at 11:00 a.m.

Nothing went as planned. Through a combination of miscues and miscommunications, the cavalry attack did not get under way until nearly 5:00 p.m. It was successful as far as it went, but darkness quickly put an end to the Southern advances. The infantry assault began sluggishly, at around 5:00 p.m., and made insignificant gains before petering out four hours later.

Hancock's aide-de-camp Major William G. Mitchell noted the day's events for the corps memoranda: "General Barlow taken very ill and gone to hospital. Comparatively quiet until 5 p.m., when the enemy came out of his works and attacked...very heavily on right of Fussell's Mill. . . . He was repulsed. . . . About same time enemy attacked General David McM. Gregg's cavalry ... on Charles City road . . . but were also repulsed. Fighting ceased at dark."

Petersburg

With Robert E. Lee directing operations north of the James, responsibility for defending Petersburg lay with General P. G. T. Beauregard. Beauregard

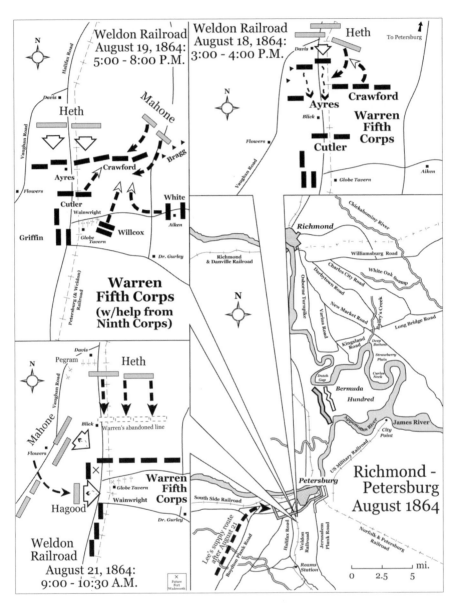

received a dispatch from his cavalry outposts a little after 10:00 a.m. reporting that an enemy force had appeared on the Weldon Railroad near Globe Tavern. Any threat to Petersburg's primary supply link with the south was a serious matter, so at noon Beauregard authorized A. P. Hill to send two infantry brigades to handle the intruders. Lee's transfer of units north of the James had so thinned Beauregard's defenses that he had to insist that Hill's two brigades "must return to-night to their positions."

Weldon Railroad, near the Globe Tavern

The last of Warren's four divisions reached the railroad at about 11:00 a.m. Everyone was moving slowly in the hot weather. "The men give out fearfully in the sun," Warren noted.

Ayres's division headed up the rail line toward Petersburg and deployed, with Brigadier General Joseph Hayes's brigade east of the road, Colonel Nathan Dushane's all-Maryland brigade on Hayes's left and rear, and Lieutenant Colonel Michael Wiedrich's brigade in reserve.

The Halifax Road ran alongside the Weldon tracks. About a mile and a half north of the Globe Tavern, it threw off a branch, the Vaughan Road, which diverged to the southwest. Near this intersection was the Davis house and farm. It was here that a two-gun Rebel battery, with cavalry support, made a stand.

Hayes's men advanced slowly toward the guns, passing through a heavy belt of timber and coming out into the southern edge of the Davis cornfield. Shortly after 2:00 p.m., Hayes's skirmishers forced the enemy artillerists to move their cannon closer to town. Warren was deploying Crawford's division on Ayres's right at the same time. Crawford's men had just begun working their way through a dense thicket, about half a mile north of the Globe Tavern, when a shrill Rebel yell signaled the enemy attack.

A. P. Hill delegated the job of clearing the Yankee raiding party (which he seriously underestimated as "a few regiments of infantry and one or two of cavalry") to Major General Henry Heth, who quickly organized his striking force, calling on Joseph Davis's all-Mississippi brigade (Captain R. W. Thomas commanding) and a newly consolidated brigade of Tennessee, Alabama, Maryland, and Virginia troops led by Colonel William S. Christian. Following after these two was the all-Georgia brigade of Brigadier General Alfred H. Colquitt, which was to be the reserve. One of Colquitt's soldiers remembered that it was "some thing after one" when they started down the Halifax Road after the Yankee raiders.

Heth formed his two leading brigades into battle lines north of the Davis farm, with the Mississippians west of the road and Christian's command east of it. It was not quite 3:00 p.m. when he ordered them forward. "The charge was made with a dash and spirit, at double-quick, for half a mile, and through a corn field a greater part of the way, under a fierce fire of both artillery and infantry," recalled one of Christian's men.

Catching Hayes's brigade well advanced from the rest of Ayres's division, Heth struck it in its front and right flank, sending it tumbling back toward the Globe Tavern. Hayes's retreat uncovered Dushane's brigade on his left. The Maryland veterans, knowing a lost cause when they saw one, broke and raced to the rear.

Once they had cleared the Yankees from the cornfield, Heth's men plunged into the woods and became entangled "by the thick undergrowth and the brush from the large trees which had been felled." Then they were hit by Union supports coming up from Ayres's reserve. The heavy woods made it seem like twilight, "and the volley the enemy poured into our ranks appeared to be a veritable sheet of flame," a Tarheel soldier recalled.

There was a Yankee division forming up on Heth's left, his front was being assailed by fresh enemy troops, and his entire line was taking a pounding from massed Union artillery near the Globe Tavern. The Virginia officer decided that it was time to retire with honors. "I attacked the enemy with three brigades, drove them from two lines of breastworks, but could do no more," he later wrote. It was nearly dark when he pulled his infantrymen back to Petersburg.

Beauregard sent Lee the chilling news at 7:00 p.m. that this had been no small raid. "Over 150 prisoners taken, representing three divisions of Fifth Corps. Heth desires re-enforcements to complete his success. He has already all I can spare."

The panic of Ayres's division was not transmitted to any other commands. The shaken Federals rallied on their reserve, and reinforcements sent up by Warren from Cutler's division helped form the new Union line in the woods that stopped Heth's advance. Crawford's division found its place on Cutler's right, while Griffin's men were told to stop wrecking the railroad and to take up a battle line on the west side of the track bed, facing west.

Warren felt secure enough by 7:00 p.m. to transmit a long message to Meade's headquarters. "It has been a hard day on the men and the fight to-day was severe on both sides....I understand that I am expected to make myself as strong here as I can, hold on till I am forced to leave, and destroy the railroad as much as possible."

Warren's men spent an uncomfortable night. A sergeant in Cutler's division remembered, "It was raining steadily, and ... we lay in the muddy pits, partially filled with water, under orders not to take off our accouterments, and be ready for an attack at any moment."

Army of the Potomac Headquarters, near City Point

George Meade fretted about the mile-long gap between Warren's men on the Weldon Railroad and the rest of the army. John Parke's Ninth Corps held the Union left and should have been in communication with Warren's right, but Parke lacked the troops to fill the space; his men had been spread thin to cover the trenches emptied by Warren on August 14. Cavalry patrols were sent to picket the undefended area, but until infantry could be put there, Warren was out on a limb.

Meade laid out his problem before Grant, who was at first reluctant to consider drawing from the Second Corps to help the Fifth. "Hancock, by detaining a large force north of the James, makes our force at Petersburg relatively as strong as if he were with it," he argued. Grant changed his mind toward evening, however, and authorized Hancock to send one division down to Petersburg. Hancock's men would replace some of Parke's, who would move to Warren's assistance. Then someone remembered that there was a 1,500-man reserve from the Eighteenth Corps on hand. Meade decided to send that to Parke as well to enable him to get help to Warren more quickly.

Grant admonished Meade at 11:15 p.m., "Tell Warren if the enemy comes out and attacks him in the morning not to hesitate about taking out every man he has to repel it; and not to stop when the enemy is repulsed, but to follow him up to the last. We certainly ought to be satisfied, when we can get the enemy to attack us."

Deep Bottom

Troops were on the move this evening. Hancock detached the division requested by Meade at 8:00 p.m. and sent it marching across the pontoon bridge, over Bermuda Hundred, and down to Petersburg.

Lee was also monitoring events outside the Cockade City. Orders went out this evening for W. H. F. Lee to pull his mounted division back along the Charles City Road and move it to Petersburg.

Friday, August 19
Weldon Railroad

Gouverneur Warren was worried about the space between his right flank (Crawford's division) and the left of the Ninth Corps, lying somewhere west of the Jerusalem Plank Road. At 2:00 a.m., a courier arrived at the headquarters of Brigadier General Edward Bragg (of Cutler's division) with orders for the officer to cover the gap.

Bragg had his men mustered within the hour, but it took more than four hours for them to find their way through "a dense tangled thicket" and extend Crawford's line eastward. Bragg stretched as far as he thought prudent and began to dig in. Then, at 7:00 a.m., he was told to extend even further to connect with the Ninth Corps's picket line. "This movement was attended with great difficulty," Bragg later reported. "The nature of the wood, the pelting [rain] storm, and the extended line encumbered and seriously embarrassed the whole operation; but notwithstanding, it was successfully completed at 2:30 p.m."

The two Fifth Corps divisions holding Warren's north-facing line—Ayres's and Crawford's—spent the morning and early afternoon improving their position. Rifle pits were dug, fields of fire cleared, and slashings piled up to slow down enemy attackers. A brigade of Kautz's cavalry was also on hand, and portions trotted south down the Weldon line to within a mile of Reams Station. Other patrols spread out along the dirt paths and cart trails west of the railroad.

Warren received welcome news a little after 10:45 a.m. that nearly six thousand men from Parke's corps were on their way to him. This message also brought a change of mission. No longer was Warren expected to stay on the railroad only long enough to destroy it; now his instructions were to "at all hazards maintain [his]…hold on the Weldon railroad, and, if practicable, extend [his]…line to connect with the Ninth Corps." The Army high command had decided to permanently stretch the Union trenches to the left and anchor the extension on the Weldon line. Warren's reply came at 11:00 a.m. "I think with the force you are sending me it will be safe to trust me to hold on to the railroad." One of Meade's aides, on the ground with Warren, was less sanguine. "It is touching a tiger's cubs to get on that road!" he exclaimed prophetically.

P. G. T. Beauregard could not let the Federal lodgment on the Weldon continue without further challenge. Information gained in yesterday's action made it clear that at least three enemy divisions were present. Scraping together every available unit he could find, Beauregard put together a five-brigade striking force.

Once again, A. P. Hill was tapped to organize the action. Hill gave Henry Heth the same brigades and the same mission as yesterday—he was to press south along the Halifax Road. This time, however, Heth's thrust would be augmented by a flanking force made up of Colquitt's, Weisiger's, and

Clingman's brigades, led by William Mahone – the hero of a similar action near the Jerusalem Plank Road on June 22. Mahone would use much the same route as he had in June, but this time his men would wheel west to strike at the exposed Union right flank.

Both Confederate attack columns went into motion a little after 1:00 p.m.

The first Ninth Corps reinforcements—Brigadier General Orlando B. Willcox's division—arrived near the Globe Tavern at 7:30 a.m. Warren had no immediate use for the men, so they were held in readiness in the fields east of the tavern. "A very unpleasant day was the 19th of August," one of Willcox's soldiers wrote afterward. "All day long the rain poured down in torrents, but we stood to arms, like warlike water-sprites dripping from the sea."

The second wave of reinforcements consisted of the troops that had made up Parke's left flank—Brigadier General Julius White's two-brigade division. These soldiers, relieved at 2:00 p.m. by the Second Corps division sent down from Deep Bottom,[1] were marched south and then west to join Warren. The head of White's column arrived near the Aiken House just before 5:00 p.m., and at that moment, White later reported, "musketry was heard to our right and front."

Heth's battle lines emerged from gloomy mists to strike at Ayres's entrenchments south of the Davis farm. As the Union troops posted east of the railroad waited nervously for the enemy ranks to appear before them, they heard the unmistakable sound of heavy gunfire to their right.

Mahone's three-brigade attack force (with two brigades leading and one in reserve) moved south, following the Johnson Road out of Petersburg.[2] Advancing his men in a tight column of fours, Mahone crashed through Bragg's thin-spread skirmish line. Once the Federal vedettes were scattered, the Confederate officer coolly put his leading brigades into battle lines and wheeled the whole command to face west. Mahone now overlapped the right of Crawford's division, as the Union infantry in the brigade on the end suddenly discovered when screaming Rebel troops appeared on their right and rear. The

---

1   In fact, when Bragg's men finally made contact with the Union left at 2:30 p.m., they found Second Corps soldiers instead of the Ninth Corps troops they were expecting.

2   What is today the Johnson Road was known as Bailey's Road at the time of this battle.

two veteran Pennsylvania regiments that constituted this brigade were surrounded and, within a few confused minutes, captured almost intact.

Mahone wasted little time celebrating his victory, but instead quickly regrouped his men and sent them against the next Federal brigade in Crawford's line.

Union artillery had played only a small role in the fighting up to this point; throughout this day, the guns, under the overall command of Colonel Charles Wainwright, had been relatively silent. Now, as the first panicked soldiers fleeing before Mahone's attack began to appear near the Globe Tavern, the alert Wainwright at once surmised what had happened. Then some of his artillerymen spotted enemy battle lines approaching from the northeast.

Between Wainwright's guns and the enemy troops was a strip of woods in which Crawford's division was posted. Crawford was expected in an emergency to pull his lines toward the railroad in order to unmask the Union cannon. Assuming that Crawford had taken this action, Wainwright ordered his gunners to fire into the woods. Brigadier General Charles Griffin rode over to encourage the cannoneers. "See those Rebs?" he shouted. "Fire on them,—shell, case, solid shot, anything, ricochet them in, give it to them!"

Two of Crawford's three brigades (the third having been, by now, captured) were still in those woods, however, battling enemy troops to their front, right flank, and rear. The sudden barrage of friendly fire only added to their problems. The middle brigade huddled in a defensive semicircle, some of the men even crouching on the north side of their breastworks to escape Wainwright's shells. "We lay flat on our faces while the shot from our own batteries shrieked and howled and exploded over our heads, and even right amongst us," recalled one noncom, "thinking that every minute would be our last, and bewailing the sad fate of being destroyed by our own friends." Somehow, this brigade, though virtually surrounded, maintained its cohesion and successfully withdrew to the Globe Tavern.

Crawford's leftmost brigade, in contrast—pummeled in front by Heth, under attack from behind by Mahone, and barraged by Wainwright—dissolved, some units surrendering wholesale, others scampering through the confusion toward the Globe Tavern.

Crawford's collapse spread to those few of Ayres's units that were posted east of the railroad. These troops were commanded by Brigadier General Joseph Hayes, who was surrounded and captured as he frantically tried to rally his men. Seeing disaster engulf his right, Ayres ordered his whole line to pull back.

Gouverneur Warren now called upon the Ninth Corps troops that had been massed east of the Globe Tavern. With a loud cheer, Orlando Willcox's men stormed toward Crawford's collapsed line as the Union cannoneers lifted their fire. "We met them, and the meeting was terrible," wrote a soldier with Willcox.

Once before, in the June 22 action near the Jerusalem Plank Road, William Mahone had seen a great victory frittered away for lack of a sufficient number of troops to carry out the plan. On this day, as then, the fighting was as confusing to the victors as to the vanquished. "Front and rear seemed to be on all sides," a North Carolinian with Mahone recalled. "The bullets came from every direction." Spotting an enemy battle line approaching from the south, Mahone halted his advance to meet the counterstroke. Gunfire blazed in the dripping forest as Willcox's men met Mahone's, but the fresh Union strength proved to be too much for the Confederates. (There was added pressure from Julius White's division, pushing north from the Aiken House.) Mahone pulled his weary fighters back, using his reserve brigade to cover the movement. At the same time, Henry Heth sent forward one last attack down the Halifax Road; it failed like the others preceding it. Heth would test the Union lines again after dark and again be unsuccessful. The fighting was over by 8:30 p.m.

Gouverneur Warren and his staff assessed the damage throughout the evening and reorganized the battered Fifth Corps. In an 8:15 p.m. message to Meade, Warren itemized his losses: "Nearly all of the Pennsylvania Reserves are missing and a great many in the other brigades of General Crawford. Cutler's division will not be much reduced when we get it together. Ayres has lost very heavily and General Hayes is missing." On the plus side, Warren noted that the enemy had withdrawn to Petersburg, leaving the battlefield in Union hands. In reply to Meade's repeated urging that he strongly reestablish the broken link between his position and the main Union lines, Warren said that it would not be possible this night. He concluded, "We are [as] well disposed as we can be against the enemy if he attack[s] in the morning."

Deep Bottom

Hancock's instructions this day were to watch the enemy. If Lee was seen to be weakening his lines to support his forces near Petersburg, Hancock was to attack. No such movements were observed. One of David Gregg's brigades was sent south in the evening with orders to report to George Meade.

Petersburg

Exhausted but triumphant, the Confederate soldiers returned this night to their Petersburg trenches. "We whipped them bad," one wrote to his mother. With them was an impressive number of enemy prisoners, including a brigadier general. A captured man from Maine never forgot his journey through the Cockade City: "The sidewalks were lined with old men, boys, and decrepit women, who vied with one another in flinging insults and venom. The women were the worst of the lot; they spat upon us, laughed at us, and called us vile and filthy names."

In his report of this day's action, sent early on the morning of August 20, General Beauregard stated that Confederate losses were believed "not to be great." Already plans were in motion to complete the job of driving the enemy away from the Weldon Railroad.

Saturday, August 20
Weldon Railroad

More Ninth Corps troops—Brigadier General Robert B. Potter's division—arrived near the Aiken House this morning. Using Potter's and White's men, Warren was able to restring his line to connect with the main Union positions near the Jerusalem Plank Road.

Additional mounted support also turned up. The cavalry brigade sent down from Deep Bottom reported to Warren at midmorning and was ordered south to assist Kautz's men.

Along Ayres's front, west of the railroad, this day was spent further improving the line under constant sharpshooting by the enemy, now spreading along Warren's left flank, following the Vaughan Road.

Warren was confident. At 2:40 p.m., he assured Army headquarters, "I think we ought to be able to hold against everything."

Beauregard had half hoped that the Yankee troops on the Weldon line would be gone at daylight. However, early-morning scouting reports indicated that the enemy was showing no disposition to move. "Am endeavoring to make necessary arrangements to dislodge him today, if possible," Beauregard informed Lee at 8:15 a.m.

Other scouts had spotted the Second Corps troops back in position along the Petersburg lines. Beauregard put two and two together and reasoned that even more Union soldiers must be near the railroad. The next Confederate attack had to be decisive. It would require every available gun, even if that meant dangerously reducing the trench defenses.

Beauregard began to organize a corps-sized striking force made up of units from his own "army" and from the Army of Northern Virginia. Integrating the two different commands proved more difficult than anyone could have imagined, however, and it took most of the day to withdraw units from their trenches, regroup them into combat commands, and position them.

Beauregard and his staff finished the job at 7 p.m.—too late for any action this day. "Expect to attack early in the morning," he assured Robert E. Lee.

The portents of a coming firestorm were unmistakable. Gouverneur Warren had decided that his battle lines were too extended to be able to effectively meet a heavy enemy assault, so once it was dark, he tightened his defensive alignments to better cover his infantry with his artillery. He abandoned the lines just below the Davis farm and pulled his troops closer to the Globe Tavern. New earthworks were erected and abatis piled up. Squads of Federals unwound spools of telegraph lines to serve as trip wires across their front as an added hindrance to enemy attackers.

Warren's new line was finished well before morning.

Deep Bottom

"Quiet, comparatively, throughout the day; some picket-firing," noted Major Mitchell in the Second Corps log. Hancock began withdrawing his infantry and cavalry across the James at dark. It was hard going. A soldier in Hancock's ranks recalled "marching all night in the rain and over the worst of roads, a distance of seventeen miles." "The rain fell in sheets and the roads were in a frightful condition in the ink-like darkness. The thunder rolled and lightning flashed incessantly," another wrote. Only the Deep Bottom pocket held by the Army of the James remained as a reminder of the maneuver.

Grant summed up the Second Deep Bottom expedition with the comments, "A threatening position was maintained for a number of days, with more or less skirmishing, and some tolerably hard fighting. . . . There was no particular victory gained on either side; but during the time no more reinforcements were sent to the valley."

(The total Union losses at Second Deep Bottom—including Second Corps, Tenth Corps, and cavalry—were later reported as 328 killed, 1,852 wounded, and 721 captured or missing, for a total of 2,901. The total Confederate losses were about 1,000.)

Sunday, August 21
Weldon Railroad

Beauregard's striking force, with A. P. Hill commanding, was in motion at daylight. Henry Heth was once again to advance down the Halifax Road to make a frontal attack. The two brigades that Heth had previously used were now replaced by four—Cooke's, Ransom's, MacRae's, and Kirkland's. The three brigades that had taken part in William Mahone's August 19 action were likewise returned to the Petersburg lines. In their place, Mahone had six brigades—Wright's, Sanders's, Harris's (this day led by Colonel Joseph M. Jayne), Finegan's, Scales's, and Hagood's—plus artillery. This time he would follow the Vaughan Road in an attempt to move past and turn the enemy's left flank.

Rain and early-morning mists delayed the Confederate deployment. Not until almost 9:00 a.m. was everything ready.

Federal scouts came hustling in with word that Rebel columns were moving along the Vaughan Road. None of the advance units had been told about the trip wires, and there was rough laughter among Warren's waiting troops as they watched the scouts go down suddenly, only to scramble back to their feet and hurry, red-faced, into the defense.

Confederate artillery, posted near the Davis House and along the Vaughan Road, opened fire at 9:00 a.m. Although the Southern gunners had Wainwright's cannon caught in a crossfire, the Yankee artillerymen were better protected. Their return salvos soon began to tell on the more exposed Rebel cannoneers. One Virginia battery commander was standing erect, spotting his fire, when an enemy shell burst six or eight inches in front of him. Incredibly, though his pants legs were shredded, the officer himself was unhurt. He remarked to his men in classic understatement, "That was a close shave."

Federal infantrymen took what cover they could, but not everyone got out of the way. One rebel shell neatly decapitated the officer in charge of the all-Maryland brigade, Colonel Nathan Dushane.[3]

Then, through the low banks of gunpowder fog, Union soldiers could see the gray battle lines coming at them from the northwest. Warren galloped along his waiting ranks, shouting, "Fire low! Low! Low!" Mahone's attack fell on the right side of Griffin's division. Once the Federal pickets had been driven in, the troops along the main line had a clear view of the enemy. "We loaded and fired with great rapidity," one of them recollected, "and our rude line of breastworks was wreathed in flame and smoke." Remembered another, "The Confederates came up through the standing corn in four lines of battle. . . . Six times the flag of the first line of Confederates fell, and six times a color corporal picked it up and was killed. . . . The corn stalks were cut off by the bullets as if with a knife."

The Confederate battle line staggered under the fusillade. "It was an explosion in its suddenness, but the metallic peal of the solid shot, the sharp clap and the flat crash of the shell that rose from side to side with rapidity cannot be described in one word," wrote a Mississippi soldier. "This, with the long roll of the musketry, mingled with the yells and cheers of the infantry, was deafening." Mahone's men veered away from the deadly torrent and tried to find the exposed Union flank. This time there was none, however, so the Confederate fighters began to pull back. "General Mahone," wrote one of his soldiers, "...thought he had turned the enemy's left flank when, in fact, we charged square up against their breastworks, and were repulsed with considerable loss."

Henry Heth ordered his lines forward as soon as he learned that Mahone's men were attacking. His soldiers stormed ahead only to find that the enemy positions had been abandoned by Warren during the night. By the time Heth's men realized what had happened and were re-formed, Mahone's attack was ebbing. Freed from the threat to the west, the Union artillery now targeted the enemy to the north, and Heth's men went ducking for cover as canister and case shot scattered deadly anti-personnel loads among them. "I hope that I may

---

3   A fort to be built nearby would bear his name.

never be called on to go through just such another fiery ordeal while I live," one Rebel officer later remarked.

Heth was stalled and Mahone's main force was falling back when a last, tragic vignette unfolded. Brigadier General Johnson Hagood's brigade held position on Mahone's far right flank. Hagood's South Carolinians had seen hard service in the Petersburg trenches, and their commander was of the opinion that they should be used only in an emergency. A. P. Hill had promised as much to Hagood, but Mahone did not agree. The hot-tempered Virginian rode up to the waiting brigade and ordered it forward.

Even as Hagood's men advanced, the rest of Mahone's line was retreating. The forward movement was much broken up by the uneven, swampy terrain, and Hagood stopped his men in the fold of a small rise to re-form them. Learning that the enemy positions lay just a few hundred yards beyond the rise, Hagood ordered a charge. His men were met with a blast of fire as they cleared the hill: more through rough luck than anything else, Hagood's formation had struck the flank of a Yankee brigade that was somewhat advanced from the main line. The South Carolinians got in behind this flank but then found themselves trapped, with the enemy on three sides and vicious cannon fire ripping up the earth on the fourth. "It was surrender or death," a survivor of Hagood's assault wrote.

Everything dissolved into a wild melee, at the height of which an exultant Union officer, Captain Dennis Dailey, rode into Hagood's ranks, grabbed a regimental standard, and shouted at the astonished men to surrender. Hagood came on the run, confronted the officer, and demanded the flag back. When he refused, Hagood shot him. The general's aide caught the standard and carried it from the field. Hagood mounted the fallen Yankee's horse and, calling to his men to face about, led them out of the deadly pocket. Of the 681 officers and men who began the charge, only 292 answered the roll call at day's end.

(Among the prisoners was the standard bearer for the 27th South Carolina who was taken by a Massachusetts soldier named Frederick C. Anderson. Anderson's capture of the man and, more importantly, the flag he carried, brought him a Medal of Honor. He would receive it from Major General Meade in a September 13 ceremony where, a *New York Herald* reporter declared, "everything [was] done to make the occasion one long to be remembered and talked over by those who witnessed it." Anderson survived the Petersburg campaign, though once wounded, and would be present at Appomattox Court House.)

Mahone was frantic with anger and shame at the turn of events. Riding toward Petersburg, he met General Robert E. Lee, who had come down from Chaffin's Bluff to observe the Weldon action. Mahone told Lee that all he needed was two fresh brigades to drive the Yankees from the field. An attempt was made to get Mahone his men, but more troops simply were not available. The fight to keep the enemy away from the vital Weldon supply line was over.

Gouverneur Warren was jubilant. "We have just repulsed an attack of Mahone's division from the west of the railroad," he informed Meade's headquarters at 10:30 a.m. "Whipped it easily." His soldiers shared the mood. "We have no trouble now with the Rebs as we licked them back every time they have tried to drive us from here," one proudly reported to his family. A mortally wounded Pennsylvania sergeant, when asked if he was in pain, replied, "Yes, very much, but we drove them back."

Warren's celebrations were dampened when he received a copy of a message sent to Meade by U. S. Grant. The lieutenant general was not entirely pleased with Warren's defensive victory. Said Grant, "It seems to me that when the enemy comes out of his works and attacks and is repulsed he ought to be followed vigorously to the last minute with every man. Holding a line is of no importance whilst troops are operating in front of it."

Grant's gripe aside, what had begun as a large-scale wrecking expedition now became a permanent extension of the Union lines.

Among the scores of sad letters penned after this fighting was one written on August 22 by A. M. Thrasher to John Stowall, telling him of the death the previous day of his son Robert. The young Georgia soldier had been hit in the groin by a piece of canister, which had severed the main artery. "He was a good boy, a good soldier," Thrasher wrote, and has left many warm friends. . . . I could scarcely mourn the death of a brother more than his, yet while I pay his precious memory the tribute of a tear, I would entertain strong hopes that Bob is today in a better world where his noble spirit will ne'er again be disturbed by war's dread alarms."

It took Robert E. Lee another two days to complete his assessment of the loss of the Weldon Railroad. In a communication to the War Department, Lee reminded the Richmond authorities, "When the army first assumed its present position I informed you that I doubted our ability to keep the road open, owing to the proximity of the enemy, and his superiority in numbers." Lee also believed that the Federal decision to hold on to the rail line suggested a shift in strategy. "I think it evident that the enemy has abandoned the effort to drive us from our present position by force, and that his purpose now is to compel us to evacuate it by cutting off our supplies."

Lee's response was to marshal a small army of wagons and, using various road systems located further west, to reconnect Petersburg with Stony Creek, the closest operating station on the Weldon line. "Under these circumstances," Lee declared, "we should use every effort to maintain ourselves by our remaining line of communications."

(Union losses in the four days of fighting were 251 killed, 1,149 wounded, and 2,879 missing or captured—mostly the latter—for a total of 4,279. Confederate losses in the fighting were never officially tabulated, but one postwar authority estimates them at 1,600. Included were brigadier generals John Sanders, killed, and Thomas Clingman, badly wounded.)

Monday, August 22
Bermuda Hundred

"Chew and choke as much as possible": Lincoln's words echoed in Grant's thoughts as he continued to seek a weak point in Lee's lines.

Early on the afternoon of August 21, even as he waited for news from the Weldon Railroad, Grant had sent a message to Ben Butler asking if something could be done to the enemy's Howlett Line. Butler took a look and by evening had drawn up plans for a four-thousand-man assault along the north bank of the Appomattox River near Port Walthall.

It was to be a Tenth Corps operation, with David Birney in overall command. The troops in the three brigades selected for the assignment began to move into position early on the morning of August 22. Most had participated in the Deep Bottom fighting of August 16, and in one regiment, the 3rd New Hampshire, the marching orders caught a number of three-year veterans just one day before they were due to muster out. "The '61 men looked aghast," a member of the regiment remembered.

An early-morning reconnaissance of the Howlett Line positions showed them to be fully manned. Birney was skeptical about the enterprise, regarding it "as perhaps a doubtful one as to success." Butler promptly forwarded this opinion to City Point; Grant suspended the assault, and the keyed-up troops were told to stand down. "We were like the men set out upon the chess-board—subject to the will of the players in this great game for national existence," one of Birney's men dryly observed.

Weldon Railroad

Gouverneur Warren expected to be attacked again today. Morning arrived, but not the Confederacy. "The enemy seem to have retired toward Petersburg," he informed Meade's headquarters at 7:20 a.m. Scouting parties found that Lee's men had returned to their fortified lines.

George Meade came to the Globe Tavern to meet with Warren. He approved of the defensive position occupied by the Fifth Corps but was dissatisfied with the railroad wrecking. A working party had been sent down from City Point to accomplish the task, but in Meade's estimation, the "railroad men have done very little work, and that very indifferently." His solution was to call upon Hancock's corps, just returned from its Deep Bottom expedition, to supply the needed manpower.

Union Reserve, near the Gurley House

Once the elite striking arm of the Army of the Potomac, the Second Corps was in bad shape. The night march from Deep Bottom "had been very exhausting," an aide reported, and the men had barely broken ranks at their old camps east of the Cockade City when fresh orders arrived, directing the corps[4] to move to support the newly extended lines west of the Jerusalem Plank Road. The troops occupied this position only for "a few hours" before they were again put into ranks, marched further to the Union left, and massed near the Gurley House. "This position was reached later in the afternoon," a bone-tired Pennsylvania soldier recounted, "and the men bivouacked for the night in a muddy field under a downpour of rain."

It was a little after noon this day when Nelson Miles (acting commander of the First Division in Francis Barlow's absence) received orders to advance "on the Weldon railroad [and] . . . assist in the destruction of the same."

---

4   At this time, the corps consisted of two divisions; the third, which had come down two days earlier, occupied front-line trenches formerly held by the Ninth Corps.

Reams Station

Following orders that he received this afternoon, Brigadier General David Gregg took a regiment from his Union cavalry command and rode south along the railroad tracks. His mission was to check out the next main stop on the rail line, Reams Station. "No enemy found," Gregg later reported.

Tuesday, August 23
Army of the Potomac Headquarters, near City Point

George Meade was having a hard time trying to read Grant's mind. The question he posed to the lieutenant general at 10:30 this morning was this: How far down the railroad should Nelson Miles's division be allowed to go while destroying it? Meade tactfully pointed out that the strenuous actions of the past week had reduced the division to four thousand effectives and that, further, the poor road conditions made it impossible for Miles to take with him either supply wagons or artillery. "In my judgment," Meade ventured, ". . . Miles ought not to go beyond support from Warren's position, say Rowanty Creek, some ten miles. . . ."

Grant concurred with Meade's assessment in his reply, sent at 2:15 p.m. Once the roads dried up, a stronger force could be sent as far down as Hicksford, but until then, wrecking the line to Rowanty Creek—perhaps five miles below Reams Station—would suffice.

Along the Weldon Railroad, North of Reams Station

Nelson Miles's men moved from their camps near the Gurley House and resumed the work they had begun yesterday evening. The troops had ripped and burned the line to within one mile of Reams Station by 11:00 a.m. At that hour Francis Barlow returned from sick leave and resumed command of the division, sending Miles back to his brigade. Upon reviewing the situation and learning that no infantry yet occupied Reams Station, Barlow detached a special task force to take possession. Reams Station was firmly in Union hands by 1:00 p.m., and the troops were busy levering up the rails to the north and south of it.

Along the Vaughan and Stage Roads, West of Reams Station

Union mounted patrols now spread west, seeking to locate the enemy. One of Kautz's brigades, commanded by Colonel Samuel P. Spear, stumbled across a strong Confederate roadblock as it pushed down the Vaughan Road toward Hatcher's Run. Spear called for help. In the past few days, this orphan brigade had passed through the command jurisdiction of the Army of the Potomac Cavalry Corps, the Fifth Corps, and the Second Corps; now, when the unit needed assistance, no one felt responsible enough to respond. An angry Spear pulled his men back to the Weldon Railroad and fired off a bitter denunciation of everyone involved.

David Gregg was massing his riders near Reams Station at this same time. He sent a two-regiment combat patrol along the Stage Road late in the afternoon; about a mile and a half from the station, the troopers found an enemy force that Gregg estimated at "more than a division."

Gregg called up the rest of his division while the Confederates moved to the attack. A noisy little fight was raging by 5:00 p.m., with mounted and dismounted units flowing in deadly choreography across the gently rolling landscape. Only after the arrival of Federal foot soldiers (hastily summoned from Barlow's division, near Reams Station) did the Confederate horsemen withdraw.

Army of Northern Virginia Headquarters, Petersburg

Following his recall from Culpeper and the abortive August 18 cavalry operation along the Charles City Road, Wade Hampton returned to Petersburg to take charge of the mounted forces operating west of the Weldon Railroad.

While portions of his command were scrapping along the Vaughan and Stage roads, Hampton was carrying out a personal reconnaissance of the enemy's deployment around Reams Station. His report was in Robert E. Lee's hands by evening. Hampton believed that the Union troops sent to destroy the rail line were vulnerable and could be assailed by a strong attack. The cavalry alone could not do it, however; infantry would be needed. Robert E. Lee mulled over Hampton's proposition and pondered the possibilities.

Second Corps Headquarters, near the Gurley House

Winfield Hancock informed Francis Barlow at 7:00 p.m. that he was sending to Reams Station his other available division—John Gibbon's. The roads south from the Gurley House were so bad that Hancock opted to move

Gibbon's men east to the Jerusalem Plank Road, then south until they could pick up the less-used trails running west to Reams Station.

With two-thirds of his corps either now or soon to be in the field near Reams Station, Hancock decided to accompany Gibbon and take personal command of the operation.

Wednesday, August 24
Reams Station

John Gibbon's men left their soggy bivouac near the Jerusalem Plank Road a little after 3:00 a.m. The head of their column was winding into Reams Station some four hours later. They replaced First Division men, who formed up and were marched down the Weldon line to continue its destruction. Miles's men, one soldier quipped, were "engaged in tearing up the track, burning the ties, and otherwise making things unpleasant for the stockholders."

Also this morning, Francis Barlow departed on a twenty-day leave, putting Nelson Miles back in command of the First Division.

Petersburg

Sending infantry down to challenge the Federals at Reams Station was a risky business. It was one thing for Lee to strike out a short distance from fortified positions; it was quite another to send foot soldiers on a longer expedition, with a sizable force of the enemy between them and their home base.

Yet there were other factors to consider. The longer the section of the railroad that was destroyed, the more difficult and complicated became Lee's supply problems; if unchallenged, the Federals might wreck the line as far south as Stony Creek Station. Also, with the Democratic presidential convention drawing near in the North, Lee needed victories to discredit the Lincoln administration. If Hampton was correct, one beckoned at Reams Station.

Lee made his decision by midday: he would hit the exposed enemy with as many troops as he could possibly spare. An eight-brigade striking force was assembled—two from Henry Heth, two from William Mahone, one from Charles Field, and three from Cadmus Wilcox. A. P. Hill would direct the expedition, which would move southwest out of Petersburg and then swing east toward Reams Station. Once there, Hill would coordinate with Hampton and employ his two cavalry divisions in the operation as well. Lee's instructions to Wade Hampton included the admonition to "do all in your power to punish the enemy."

Most of Hill's force had massed in the southwest corner of Petersburg by 4:00 p.m., not far from the lead works. The main body then passed through the perimeter defenses, following the Squirrel Level Road until it was clear of the Globe Tavern area before turning onto the Vaughan Road and crossing Hatcher's Run near Armstrong's Mill.

Hill's men bivouacked for the night in the vicinity of Holly Point Church.

Near Reams Station

Union cavalry patrols again fanned out to the south and west from Reams Station. To the south, near where Nelson Miles's men labored, a crossroad branched off to the southwest, leading to Rowanty Creek. Its point of intersection with the Halifax Road was known as Malone's Crossing. Colonel Spear's troopers, who had yesterday run into roadblock troubles along this very crossroad, now ran into them again, but this time Nelson Miles responded, sending two infantry regiments in support. The Confederate riders withdrew at the sight of the foot soldiers.

West and northwest of Reams Station, patrols from Gregg's division prowled the roads but found no substantial enemy force.

Miles's infantry tramped back to Reams Station to camp for the night with Gibbon's command. "The impression is that Lee's forces must be weak or he would never allow us to destroy so completely the main and important avenue to the south," one of Miles's soldiers wrote this evening.

Army of the Potomac Headquarters, near City Point

Alert Federal signalmen kept Meade and Grant fully apprised of Confederate movements. A procession of nearly four thousand men was seen marching southward along the Squirrel Level Road at 2:30 p.m. It was followed three hours later by a "column of infantry, extending a mile and a quarter in length, four files deep and well closed up." Fifteen minutes after that, another two thousand men moved in the same direction. Supply wagons and artillery accompanied them. Something was up.

Meade's headquarters issued warnings at 8:20 p.m. to both Warren and Hancock. Hancock's read:

SIGNAL OFFICERS REPORT LARGE BODIES OF INFANTRY PASSING SOUTH
FROM THEIR INTRENCHMENTS BY THE HALIFAX AND VAUGHAN ROADS. THEY
ARE PROBABLY DESTINED TO OPERATE AGAINST GENERAL WARREN OR
YOURSELF—MOST PROBABLY AGAINST YOUR OPERATIONS. THE COMMANDING
GENERAL CAUTIONS YOU TO LOOK OUT FOR THEM.

It took nearly three hours for the message to reach Hancock, and when it
finally did, the Second Corps commander was not pleased at the news. He
complained in his reply that the message had not specified how large the "large
bodies of infantry" were, and he questioned the wisdom of putting the Second
Corps so far out on a limb.

Meade's chief of staff sent a reply at 1:00 a.m. in which he estimated the
total number of enemy troops leaving Petersburg at between eight and ten
thousand. Counting infantry and cavalry, Hancock had fewer than nine
thousand at Reams Station.

A curious lassitude lay over the Union high command this night. Matters
were moving to a crisis, but no alarms were being sounded. Neither Grant nor
Meade issued any orders sending reinforcements to Hancock or giving him the
option of withdrawing his command. Meade's reluctance to act was based in
part on the mistaken belief that Hancock had between sixteen and twenty
thousand troops on hand—more than enough to handle any likely situation.

Hancock's attitude was later expressed by his adjutant Francis Walker: "It
was for [Meade's] headquarters to re-enforce or to withdraw him. Headquarters
alone knew the numbers and the positions of the Confederate troops;
headquarters alone could ascertain how far Lee's lines were being depleted for a
hostile expedition."

Thursday, August 25
Holly Point Church

Field lanterns flickered far into the early-morning hours as A. P. Hill and
Wade Hampton made plans to destroy the enemy. Hill's infantry would move
against Reams Station from the west; Hampton was to assign a small screening
force to operate with the foot soldiers, then take the rest of his riders to strike
the Federals from the south and east.

It was not yet dawn when the orders were issued and the various armed
units began to fall into line. Hampton had a few final words with Hill at 5:00
a.m. before leading his cavalrymen south across the Gravelly Run, then east
toward Malone's Crossing.

Since Hampton's men had a greater distance to travel, the infantry could afford to wait a while before setting out. The head of Hill's column got under way a little after 8:00 a.m.

Reams Station

Winfield Hancock was worried, really worried. He had given provisional orders this morning for John Gibbon's division to take its turn wrecking the tracks near Malone's Crossing, but he suspended the operation pending a security sweep of the roads west of the station. Gregg's patrols galloped out just after 6:00 a.m.

The Union riders spotted nothing beyond a few enemy vedettes, and so reported. Gibbon was instructed by Hancock at 9:00 a.m. "to move down the railroad and continue its destruction." Behind Gibbon, Nelson Miles put his men to work improving the Reams Station defenses.

The works here were about a month and a half old. They had been hastily constructed in late June, when the Sixth Corps slipped out of the Union lines to cover the return of Wilson's cavalry raiders. The defensive works formed an L, with the slightly shorter face lying parallel to the railroad and perhaps twenty to forty yards west of it, and the other face angling toward the northeast. "They had settled down and was too low," one of Miles's men complained. "They was very poor works." Cannon posted along the short leg of the L would be at a serious disadvantage; the lack of space between the elevated railroad bed and the works meant that the battery limbers containing extra munitions would have to park on the east side of the tracks, and soldiers carrying ammunition to the guns would be dangerously exposed as they moved over the line. Also, the cramped setup denied the gunners the ability to hook up and reposition in an emergency. Their weapons had to be rolled into place by hand and could not be easily withdrawn.

Once the tail of Gibbon's column had cleared the area, Hancock decided that he needed another defensive line to cover the southern approaches to Reams Station. Working parties were assigned from Miles's division, and soon the sideways L began to look more like a U, with its new side, the southern one, crimped in toward the northern one.

These "improvements" created new problems. The whole position was so small that a bullet or shell crossing over one face of the U was likely to hit troops clustered behind the others. For men fighting to their front, being hit simultaneously from the rear could be a terrifying experience.

West of Malone's Crossing, South of Reams Station

The advance of Hampton's flanking column struck Colonel Spear's outposts a little before 8:00 a.m.. The Federal vedettes, stiffened by supports, held long enough to see that the enemy was coming in large numbers, and then they pulled back to the crossroad, leaving a few dead and wounded as the price for this intelligence.

Couriers brought the information to John Gibbon, whose infantrymen promptly forgot their track-wrecking and hurried toward Malone's Crossing.

Spear's worn-out cavalry was shoved steadily back as far as the Halifax Road, where the Union colonel tried to make a stand. Enemy horse batteries came racing up to send a storm of shot and shell against the dismounted troopers, who took it for a few minutes before falling back in some disarray to the fields and woods east of the road.

Even as Hampton's officers worked to consolidate their hold on the Halifax Road, John Gibbon's lead brigade began to deploy from the north. While infantry skirmishers bristled forward to send Hampton's outriders scrambling, other Union regiments spread the battle lines east and west of the railroad. The Rebel batteries wheeled to face these new targets and blasted away with such vigor that a few shells overshot the blue lines and burst near Reams Station, prompting one section of Hancock's guns to limber up and hurry down to Gibbon's aid. Soon the boom of opposing artillery was providing a constant undertone for the sharper crack and rattle of rifles, muskets, and carbines.

Wade Hampton managed his mounted forces with cool deliberation, moving small supporting groups forward to block each attempt by the enemy infantrymen either to outflank his line or to overwhelm it with strength. When the Federal foot soldiers entered the arena, Hampton sent word to A. P. Hill that now would be the right time to hit Reams Station. Back came Hill's reply: keep pressing them.

Hampton had nearly two divisions in action by this time. He sent several North Carolina regiments in a sweep east of the railroad, hoping to penetrate the area between Reams Station and the Jerusalem Plank Road. This thrust was stopped only when infantrymen from the station came hustling over to back up Gregg's hard-pressed cavalrymen.

The Federal troops fighting him began to pull back toward Reams Station around 2:00 p.m. Sensing the kill, Hampton organized his scattered units for an advance.

Reams Station

The first warning of trouble for Hancock came at about noon, when Union cavalry outposts along the Dinwiddie Stage Road, west of Reams Station, were rushed by enemy mounted troops. This initial probe was turned back, but when the Rebels again appeared, the Union vedettes saw that they were now facing enemy infantry.

Word of this development sent an electric shock through the men at Reams Station. Nelson Miles ordered one of his regiments out to support the outposts; these Federals marched about three-quarters of a mile to set up a blocking position. Then advanced Union parties along the Stage Road came tumbling back at about 1:00 p.m. to warn that heavy enemy columns were approaching.

The picket line screening the station to the west was heavily reinforced, while other troops were spread along the earthworks, covering gaps and filling in sections of the line. Hancock sent his evaluation of the situation to George Meade at 2:00 p.m. He reported the probings of his position and expressed his worry that he might be cut off from Warren's men near the Globe Tavern. Hancock realized that he was facing a serious threat. "Two prisoners taken at different times say that all of Hampton's cavalry and a part of Hill's corps, or all of it, are in my front," he declared.

A. P. Hill's infantry column had set out at 8:00 a.m., crossing the Rowanty at Monk's Neck Bridge. Then, after a two-hour rest, the troops turned onto the Stage Road, which angled toward Reams Station. Hill called another stop at noon, this time to deploy for his attack.

One brigade went into the woods south of the Stage Road with orders to stretch to the Depot Road and there connect with Hampton's men. Three brigades were formed in the woods north of the Stage Road, preparatory to an attack on the northwest corner of the Reams Station perimeter.

As these movements were being made, several battalions of elite sharpshooters fanned out to cover the western face of the Reams position. Almost immediately they began to press back the Union picket line, a portion of which gave way. This partial collapse convinced the three waiting brigadiers that it was time to attack.

The Confederate battle lines came down from the northwest toward the western face of Hancock's U-shaped perimeter. The Union soldiers waited until friendly pickets had cleared out of the way, before opening a devastating fire. "They had to advance 200 yards over a nice level sod," wrote one Pennsylvanian afterward, "and when they got close enough they screamed that womanlike scream and with fixed bayonets on they came. . . . [We] mowed them with grape and canister…[and] they recoiled[,] fell back[,] and left the sod covered with their dead and wounded."

A. P. Hill's health, increasingly unpredictable at times of great stress, now took a turn for the worse.[5] Even as the survivors of the first attack were returning to their jump-off positions, Hill had to dismount and lie down. Control of the attack now fell to Major General Cadmus Wilcox.

It took Wilcox about an hour to re-form the three brigades that had been stopped by the Federal defenses. Wilcox shifted the axis of the attack to the lower side of the western face. The Confederate infantry again moved forward at around 4:00 p.m.

The foot soldiers were met once again by heavy frontal volleys and punished by oblique fire as well. For a second time, the Confederate advance stopped and receded.

As Wilcox's attack faded back into the woodlands, Hancock digested the contents of a message from George Meade, written at 1:00 p.m. and brought by courier from the Globe Tavern. Meade was sending Mott's division to support Hancock. It would follow the route used by Gibbon's men—south along the Jerusalem Plank Road, then west toward Reams Station. Also, all orders to wreck the railroad were suspended in the face of the enemy attacks, which, Meade surmised, were designed to isolate the Second Corps from the Fifth. Finally, Hancock was to use his own judgment in regard to withdrawing from Reams Station. As Meade's courier turned to leave, he asked Hancock if the Halifax Road north was still open to the Globe Tavern. Hancock nodded, and the courier headed back in that direction.

---

5   It is now known that Hill contracted venereal disease while he was a cadet at West Point. A worsening case of prostatitis often caused him great pain and made it impossible for him to either sit or ride.

For reasons that were never explained, Meade continued throughout the day to use couriers to convey messages between his headquarters and Reams Station, even though telegraphic communication had been established between the two points since 11:45 that morning.[6]

Hancock wired Meade at 2:45 p.m. that he would try to hold Reams Station until dark. Hancock was confident that he could maintain his position and cover the roads leading east to the Jerusalem Plank Road, though he thought it likely that the enemy would interpose between him and Warren.

Another of Meade's couriers showed up after Wilcox's assault had been beaten off. More help was on the way: Meade was sending Orlando Willcox's Ninth Corps division right behind Mott (this despite its commander's request that he be allowed to proceed directly, via the Halifax Road). The promise of all these extra troops confused Hancock. Was it now Meade's intention to hold on to Reams Station? Hancock's question clattered off on the wire at 4:15 p.m. Fifteen minutes later, he reported that his men could hear chopping along the Rebel front, indicating, perhaps, that the enemy was digging in. Thirty minutes after that, another courier arrived, with word that Mott's column had reached the Jerusalem Plank Road turnoff to Reams Station. Help was a few muddy miles and several hours away.

Meanwhile, Nelson Miles was feeling some concern about the northwest corner of his line, where the west face angled to the northeast. There was a gap there where the Weldon Railroad ran through the earthworks. Certain that the enemy would continue to concentrate on this weak point, Miles called on a New York battery to send up a gun to cover the gap. In response, Lieutenant Henry D. Brower arrived with a twelve-pounder Napoleon, which he placed in such a way as to sweep the opening. The young artillery officer seemed worried about his exposed position. He turned to a friend and made as if to give up his watch for safekeeping, but then he thought better of the gesture and pocketed the timepiece.

Major General Henry Heth arrived on the field with two fresh Confederate brigades and assumed tactical control of the operation. He conferred briefly with the stricken Hill, who told him that he "must carry the position." With Heth came Colonel William J. Pegram and twelve artillery pieces. While Pegram

---

6   The Reams Station end of the telegraphic line was actually located at the William Spiers house, about a quarter of a mile north of Hancock's headquarters.

arranged his cannon to bombard the Federals, Heth deployed a three-brigade assault force aimed at the northwest corner of the enemy perimeter.

Pegram opened fire at 5:00 p.m. "[It] was done with a vim scarcely equalled in any battle," one of his cannoneers boasted. Pegram's shells did little damage to the western face of Hancock's position, but many plowed into the backs of John Gibbon's men, holding the southern face of the U.

Pegram's bombardment ended after fifteen minutes. Henry Heth moved to signal the advance by calling for a regimental flag to be brought to him. The standard of the 26th North Carolina arrived, along with its young color-bearer. Heth asked for the flag, but the color-bearer insisted on carrying it himself. Heth smiled and took the soldier by his arm. "Come on then, we will carry the colors together," he said.

Heth and the color-bearer waved the flag for all to see. This was the signal to begin the third assault on Reams Station.

Once again, the Federals seemed to have it all their own way. The enemy lines were blasted the moment they hove into view, and the heavy fire was kept up as the leading Rebel elements scattered the Federal pickets, only to become entangled in the abatis fronting the west face. A few more minutes of this punishment, Nelson Miles thought, and the enemy would have to withdraw.

Suddenly, three of his regiments near the northwest angle panicked, and their once neat battle lines dissolved into a welter of fleeing men. At the same moment, triumphant enemy soldiers began to clamber over the breastworks. Other units along the upper western section of the line soon began to break apart. "This was the turning point of the fight," one of the frightened Federals later recalled, "and here we failed." "I never witnessed such a scene," declared a New Yorker. "It was a second Bull Run." Rebel rifle fire ripped into the battery covering the gap, killing Lieutenant Brower. His cannoneers managed one more blast from the gun before they were driven off and their weapon was captured.

Miles, anticipating just such an emergency, had positioned a reserve brigade across the railroad, immediately behind the front line. He shouted for the men to counterattack, but no one moved. The officer in charge could not be found, and the troops themselves were either cowering or running.

The portion of Miles's line that lay south of the Depot Road was still holding. Miles rode there with orders for the brigade commander to shift troops to the right to meet the new onslaught. For a while, these Federals held their ground in bitter, hand-to-hand combat.

Nelson Miles galloped about the disintegrating perimeter like a man possessed. Now he raced back to the northern face of the line and tried to organize a counterattack from that quarter. A New York battery posted there twisted its gun around to fire into the lost lines even as the regiments supporting it began to catch the panic fever. Once their infantry help fled, the gunners had to run as well, leaving their pieces for the enemy.

Miles rode into this chaotic situation and saw that one regiment was not running. The 61st New York, formed at right angles to the northern face of the U, was stubbornly contesting every inch of ground. Miles personally led these troops to recapture the lost New York battery.

Winfield Hancock was also on hand, vainly attempting to rally his troops. Remembered one soldier, "With sword in one hand and hat in the other, he faced his retreating regiments coming from the center, and exclaimed, 'For God's sake do not run!'" Recalled another, "He looked more like a wild man, or a soldier possessed with a restless and demoniac spirit, than a general commanding in a good cause."

The Union lines below the Depot Road gave way at about the same time Miles counterattacked along the northern face. Union cannoneers posted west of the railroad fought their guns to the last, then had to leave them behind as they raced for cover; many of the horses whose task it was to pull the guns out of harm's way had become early victims of enemy sharpshooters.

Hancock now called on John Gibbon to send help. Gibbon ordered two brigades to retake the western lines, but a combination of panicked Union soldiers and sharp enemy fire stopped this movement. Gibbon's men had the added problem of Rebels in their front, and with Hampton's cavalrymen and horse batteries pressing the southern face of Hancock's line, some of the troops were in fact getting hit from three sides. Once the western face of the perimeter collapsed, dismounted Confederate troopers poured into the lower part of the south-facing earthworks.

Along the northern side of the perimeter, meanwhile, Nelson Miles was far from beaten. As quickly as his officers could reorganize their units, Miles used them to retard and even slightly roll back the enemy advance. This helped to prevent the Southern troops from fully exploiting their breakthrough.

Hancock's U-shaped line had been turned inside out. The easternmost fragments of the northern and southern faces still held, connected by a ragged battle line that bowed dangerously to the east. As it was getting dark, Hancock tried to organize an all-out counterattack to retake the old position; Miles was all for it, but Gibbon said that his troops were not up to the task. Then Gregg reported that his cavalrymen could no longer guarantee the security of the roads running east to the Jerusalem Plank Road. The possibility of encirclement decided the matter: Hancock issued orders at 8:00 p.m. to withdraw. After giving the bitter instructions, he turned to a staff officer and cried, "Colonel, I do not care to die, but I pray to God I may never leave this field."

The Federals had disengaged by 9:00 p.m. and pulled back to the east. In the confusion of this night movement, Hancock's devoted adjutant and postwar biographer, Francis Walker, was captured when he rode into an enemy picket line.

A Virginia reporter visiting the battlefield soon after the fighting ended avowed that anyone "who will…see the character of the work they had to perform, will concur with me in the opinion that the men who carried them in the face of such a fearful fire, from both infantry and artillery, are worthy of being classed among the bravest."

It had been a hard-won victory for Confederate arms, so much so that A. P. Hill decided not to pursue Hancock's retreating corps. His infantry, and Hampton's cavalry, were kept busy rounding up prisoners and captured weapons. Then nature closed the scene with some artillery of its own: a heavy thunderstorm rumbled across Reams Station, bringing vivid flashes of light in the heavens along with a pelting rain that washed over the weary, wounded, and dead alike.

Among those caught in the rain was Captain Joseph Egolf of the 125th New York, badly wounded in the right arm and swept up in the Rebel advance. After his captors relieved him of anything of value (except, fortunately, his Masonic pin), he was waved off to the rear and despite efforts to reach friendly lines he was eventually herded to a field hospital where his wounds were stabilized. A slow ambulance ride carried him to Petersburg where doctors told him that the arm had to come off. "I am aware of it," Egolf replied, "the sooner the better." His recovery took place in Richmond's Libby Prison where his Masonic membership probably saved his life. As an amputee he rated high on the soldier exchange list and some three weeks after the battle was back in Union lines. He returned to upstate New York, where the local newspaper editor took down his story and printed the results in the September 19 edition of the *Troy Daily News*. "He is convinced," wrote the editor, "that the eleventh hour of the rebellion has come."

Hancock's two divisions took a terrible beating at Reams Station. His reported losses were 117 killed, 439 wounded, and 2,046 missing or captured, for a total of 2,602. Total cavalry losses for the period from August 23 to August 25 were about 145. In addition, nine cannon were taken by the enemy. Contrary to the picture painted by official reports written soon afterward, which understated his losses and overstated his corps's combat readiness, Hancock had suffered a heavy personal blow. "The enemy brought everything they could rake and scrape," he wrote to a friend several days after the battle. "We ought to have whipped them."

In the recriminations that followed this affair, Hancock broke with his ambitious protégé John Gibbon, who believed that a complete reorganization of the Second Corps was needed. Only a last-minute apology by the proud Hancock kept Gibbon from publicly resigning his commission.

Hancock's opponent Henry Heth later observed, "If Hancock's heart could have been examined there would have been written on it 'reams' as plainly as the deep scars received at Gettysburg and other fields were visible."

A. P. Hill's men returned to their lines on August 26. Hampton's men covered the withdrawal, holding Reams Station until the foot soldiers had cleared the area, then picketing it for several days afterward. Hampton's losses on August 25 were 16 killed, 75 wounded, and 3 missing, for a total of 94. Hill's total was 720 killed, wounded, or missing. His men took back with them 12 stands of enemy colors, 9 cannon, and 3,100 small arms.

The victory provided Lee's troops with a much-needed shot in the arm. "A few days after the battle I never saw men so much elated by any fight," wrote a Tarheel soldier. "They now think they can storm almost any Yankee's breastworks."

However, more than just wrecking the railroad tracks, Union columns had also wreaked havoc across the land. A correspondent from the *Petersburg Express* who traveled a portion of Hancock's route on August 26 was appalled by what he witnessed. "On both sides of the track, the enemy have swept fences and crops, leaving scarcely a vestige remaining. The crops, consisting chiefly of corn and sorghum, have been fed to men and horses, and the leaves piled up in the railroad sills to assist in the burning." "I never saw such destruction in all my life," a young cavalryman seconded.

Lee had not broken Grant's grip on the Weldon Railroad, but he had loosened the choke hold just enough to keep his supply line to North Carolina intact.

Grant's control of events slipped noticeably after the Second Deep Bottom expedition returned south of the James. His usually robust health now failed him. Writing on August 25, Grant's aide Theodore Bowers observed, "I regret to say that Grant has been quite unwell for the past ten days. He feels languid and feeble and is hardly able to keep about."

Yet the City Point outlook remained essentially positive. Summarizing the view from Grant's headquarters, Horace Porter wrote, "Lee had been so constantly threatened, or compelled to attack around Petersburg and Richmond, that he had been entirely prevented from sending any forces to Hood to be used against Sherman." Or to Early, Porter might have added, to be used against Sheridan.

The feeling at George Meade's headquarters was less sanguine. Reflecting upon his actions in a letter to his wife, Meade found nothing to fault in his own handling of matters. "Hancock expressed himself as confident of maintaining his position, and did not call for reinforcements, which I nevertheless sent as soon as I found how heavily he was engaged," Meade explained. Reviewing his army's operations at Deep Bottom, the Weldon Railroad, and Reams Station, Meade concluded, "These frequent affairs are gradually thinning both armies, and if we can only manage to make the enemy lose more than we do, we will win in the long run, but unfortunately, the offensive being forced on us, causes us to seek battle on the enemy's terms, and our losses are accordingly the greatest, except when they come out and attack, as recently, when they always get the worst of it."

Meade's aide Theodore Lyman marveled at his chief's equanimity under pressure. "[He] doesn't seem to be depressed by that sort of thing," he wrote after word of Hancock's disaster was received. "Perhaps three years of it have made it necessary to his life, just as some persons enjoy a daily portion of arsenic."

Nurse Cornelia Hancock, who had earlier bid a happy farewell to the Second Corps soldiers who believed they were heading to Washington, now faced the bloody aftermath of the past dozen days. She regarded with disgust the Northern newspaper reports that declared Hancock's action at Reams Station a decided "success" for Union arms. "We were whipped badly in the Weldon R.R., no matter what the news," she wrote on August 27.

Theodore Lyman shared her despair. "[When] we have no good chance, or almost none, when our best undertakings fall through, I lose confidence in each move, and, when I hear the cannon, I look for nothing but our men coming back and a beggarly report of loss of prisoners. It is not right to feel so, but I can't help it."

Chapter Nine

"Hello! Yanks! Want any fresh beef?"

September 14 - 17, 1864

Ulysses S. Grant
Final Report of Operations, March 1864-May 1865

[To return to General Sherman in Georgia.] Finding it impossible to entirely invest [Atlanta] ... General Sherman, after securing his line of communications across the Chattahoochee, moved his main force round by the enemy's left flank ... to draw the enemy from his fortifications. In this he succeeded, and, after defeating the enemy near Rough and Ready, Jonesborough, and Lovejoy's, forcing him to retreat to the south, on the 2d of September occupied Atlanta, the objective point of his campaign. ...

General Sherman's movement from Chattanooga to Atlanta was prompt, skillful, and brilliant.

* * *

Regarding the situation in September 1864, Grant's military secretary, Adam Badeau, noted, "The system of field-works which at this time encircled both Richmond and Petersburg, and covered the surrounding country, was complicated in the extreme, and in some respects unprecedented in war." Those rippling lines dramatically defined the principal areas of massed maneuver and combat. Outside those lines—beyond the flanks, well in the rear of both armies, and along the James River—a war of raid and ambush was waged.

Federal control of the James River rested with an unlikely flotilla of converted tugboats, schooners, and ferryboats. Typical of these was the *Commodore Perry*, a wooden, side-wheeled ferryboat plucked from New York

Harbor in 1861, pressed into service, and modified to fit its fore and aft entranceways with a total of six heavy guns. The Perry and others in this river fleet were almost constantly engaged in a deadly little war. As Union admiral David Porter later wrote, "Military and naval expeditions were sent to destroy all grain-fields and other sources of supply within reach, and to pick up deserters from the enemy's ranks. . . . Signal stations were destroyed, their operators captured, and instruments brought away."

Union ships cruising the James River provided troop transportation, landed raiding parties and spies, and were fair game for Rebel sharpshooters. "We never knew," recalled one navy officer, "when a distant crack and puff of smoke might claim another life."

The open and broken country south of the Appomattox, behind and beyond the fortified lines, was a ready arena for irregular operations. John Gordon, whose men took over Lee's right flank in December 1864, described this region as "a dense second growth of pines in which the daring scouts of both armies often passed each other at night and found hiding places during their adventures."

Federal cavalry suffered the most in this war with few rules. "The sanctity of safeguards placed at houses to protect the property of the inhabitants was constantly violated," a trooper in the 3rd Pennsylvania complained. "These isolated guardians, who should have been treated with as much respect as flags of truce, were often taken prisoners, and sometimes murdered in cold blood." Picket posts were especially vulnerable targets. "Our lines were now considerably troubled with guerrillas," noted an officer of the 4th Pennsylvania Cavalry. "These guerrillas were the military outlaws, the cowards and felons of war."

Part of the problem could be traced back to a Confederate military policy requiring its cavalrymen to supply their own mounts. Any Rebel trooper who lost his horse faced reassignment to the infantry, so many tried to steal Yankee replacements. "As a result," declared a soldier in the 11th Pennsylvania Cavalry, "these dismounted cavalrymen would prowl around the picket lines, causing considerable annoyance."

Federal retaliation could be harsh. "Our lines very much annoyed by lurkers of the lowest order or grade," recorded one Union diarist. "But, we'll soon peck-m-out, and get rid of them as we have previously, elsewhere." In an effort to reduce his picket losses, Federal brigadier August Kautz ordered his men to stand their watch posts dismounted, with their horses well to the rear, so that the animals' restlessness would not reveal their position. Kautz further directed that "dismounted [Confederate] cavalrymen, seeking to obtain horses to remount themselves . . . if captured, are not to be sent in as prisoners."

Civilians living thereabouts not only regularly housed these irregulars but also provided them with intelligence—or so Federal authorities believed. A City Point-based reporter for the *New York Times*, writing in October after a mounted Federal patrol departed for a region known for its Rebel sympathies, commented with emphasis, "The present party are entrusted to assure the inhabitants that if they are compelled to make a third visit, it will be to burn every house, destroy every vestige of living and make a perfect desert around us."

Sergeant George D. Shadburne was officially listed as a scout attached to the Jeff Davis Legion. He was described in Union accounts as "a notorious guerrilla . . . well known to the Army of the Potomac as a desperado." He submitted a remarkable report to Wade Hampton on September 5. It sketched with great accuracy the Union defenses east of City Point as far as Coggins Point, and south from the James for about eight miles. Shadburne and his fellow scouts had located the camps of the Federal security forces, noted the conditions of the fords in the region, and identified the various Union corps arrayed against Petersburg. Shadburne also made careful mention of the real object of his little expedition: "At Coggins' Point are 3,000 beeves, attended by 120 men and 30 citizens, without arms."

Brigadier General August Kautz was constantly apprehensive about his ability to protect the Army of the Potomac's rear supply areas. His responsibilities included a three-thousand-head beef herd, which throughout August was penned near Cocke's Mill, some six miles east of Coggins Point.

Kautz's small division was stretched thin to cover the ground. "I was holding a line at the time fifteen miles in length with about fourteen hundred men," Kautz wrote. An officer in one of his overextended regiments was also concerned. As he later recalled, "The portion of the picket line held by the First District of Columbia, now numbering about four hundred effective men, was nearly five miles in length, extending along a road running nearly east and west, mostly through a wooden country."

Although the situation was already precarious, Kautz received orders to spread his force over an even wider area. "I can extend ... to Sycamore [Church]," he warned in early August, "but the force will not be strong enough to be a protection for the cattle herd, for a force sufficient to drive off the cattle could break through the line."

The army high command responded to these complaints by ordering the herd taken closer to City Point. Reported Commissary Department captain Nathaniel A. Richardson, in charge of the animals, "I moved the herd to Coggins' Point, on the James River, on . . . August 29, 1864. The grazing was abundant and good."

Robert E. Lee planted the seed for a Confederate raid on the Yankee cattle pen in a September 3 message to his cavalry chief, Wade Hampton. Lee noted that "the enemy is very open to attack at City Point and other points where his wagons are parked in his rear." Less than two weeks later, Hampton was acting on that suggestion. The various units selected for the operation were quietly staged in readiness with the men kept in the dark as to the mission objective. A gunner in the Stuart Horse Artillery was told they were going after some of the black troops. "We had no intimation nor idea that beeves had any place in the picture at all," he recollected.

"On the morning of the 14th [September]…," Hampton reported, "I moved with the divisions of Maj. Gen. William H. F. ["Rooney"] Lee, the brigades of [Brigadier General Thomas L.] Rosser and [Brigadier General James] Dearing, and a detachment of 100 men from Young's and Dunovant's brigades, under the command of Lieutenant-Colonel [Lovick P.] Miller, Sixth South Carolina Regiment, down the west side of Rowanty Creek to Wilkinson's Bridge . . . where the command bivouacked that night."

"For this raid the whole line was virtually stripped of its protection," one North Carolina cavalryman observed, ". . . but the plans for deceiving the enemy and keeping up appearances were well carried out by the dashing P. M. B. Young, of Georgia, who, by means of camp-fires, bands playing and artillery discharges[,] kept up a constant show of force." Hampton's twenty-mile march consumed all the daylight hours. His riders moved southwest along the Boydton Plank Road for some thirteen miles before swinging to the southeast for seven more miles. "The left of Grant's army was passed," one Virginia trooper recalled, "and our march continued nearly all day along the rear of his lines. In the evening the command was halted, and the men were allowed to unsaddle their horses and take several hours of rest." It was a cold rest, wrote an artilleryman, as they "could not afford to make a smoke."

Continued Hampton, "The command left Wilkinson's Bridge at an early hour on the 15th, and by a rapid march placed itself on the Blackwater [Swamp] at Cook's Bridge." A South Carolinian agreed with Hampton about the pace, remarking that "our horses [were] required to make a brisk walk." "The region through which the expedition passed was flat and marshy," a Virginian added. "The road wound along through occasional pine forests that helped to conceal the strength and design of Hampton's force." A cannoneer with the force wrote that the troopers "were now particularly enjoined not to make a noise. . . . Nothing was heard but the steady tread of the horses and the rattle of sabres."

George Baylor, a trooper in the 12th Virginia, recalled, "The command resumed its march on the 15th, and reached Cooke's Bridge, on the Blackwater, where horses were fed, and we rested until the bridge, which had been destroyed, was repaired. Just after midnight we moved off. . . . " Added a trooper in the 7th Virginia, "There were times when our line of march led through dense forests which obscured the moonlight and left us in comparative darkness."

Hampton had marched his force undetected to within ten miles of the Union cattle pen at Coggins Point. While Confederate engineers repaired the bridge, Hampton gathered together his subordinates and explained his plan.

The command would be split into three parts. The smallest part, consisting of Dearing's men, would advance to Cocke's Mill, there to take a position to block any Federal interference from the east, as well as guard against any Union effort to stampede the herd in that direction. Rooney Lee's division, Hampton's largest unit, would tackle the Federals camped about Prince George Court House and would also make up the western shield for the action. The remaining troopers—Rosser's and Miller's commands—would move directly northward, overrun the small defensive force posted near Sycamore Church, and reach the penned beef.

Wade Hampton's intention was not to scatter or destroy the cattle herd, but to rustle it.

```
HEADQUARTERS SECOND DIVISION, [U.S.] CAVALRY CORPS
DAVID MCM. GREGG TO ANDREW HUMPHREYS - SEPTEMBER 14, 2 P.M.

I HAVE THE HONOR TO REPORT ALL QUIET ON THE CAVALRY PICKET LINE.


HEADQUARTERS SECOND DIVISION, [U.S.] CAVALRY CORPS
HENRY E. DAVIES, JR., TO ANDREW HUMPHREYS - SEPTEMBER 15

I HAVE THE HONOR TO REPORT ALL QUIET ON THE CAVALRY PICKET LINE
FOR THE PAST TWENTY-FOUR HOURS.
```

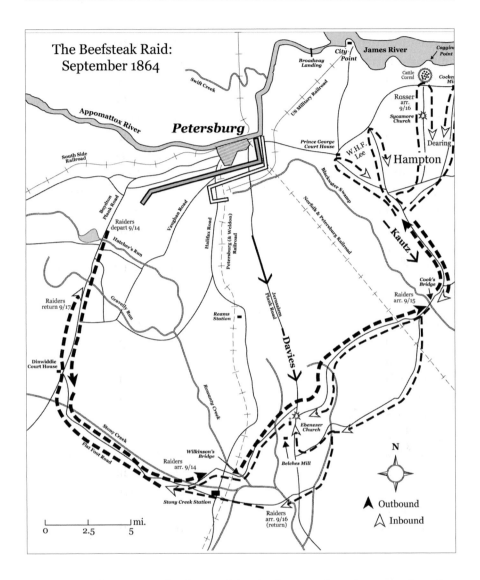

The Beefsteak Raid:
September 1864

"All my dispositions for the attack having been made and communicated to the commanding officers," Hampton reported, "the command moved at 12 a.m. [on September 16]. . . . The three columns all reached the points to which they were ordered without giving the alarm to the enemy, and at 5 a.m. . . . Rosser made the [first] attack."

Hampton allowed the expedition's scouts to lead Rosser's charge and explained his plan of action to the unit's commander. "If the picket does not hear you or fire on you," he said, "try to capture him without firing on him. If he fires on you, follow him closely into the camp, and I will support you." "We went at them in fine order," recalled one, "and when we were within fifty yards of the picket he fired on us and fell back. We charged up and some of us got across the public road when such a volley as alarmed us came from the church and around it. The enemy was reinforced in a few moments, when the firing became intense."

The Confederates had hit an outpost of the 1st District of Columbia Cavalry, a unit armed with sixteen-shot Henry rifles. The picket force, commanded by Lieutenant Albert Spaulding, took cover behind a roadblock of fallen trees, "opened fire with their sixteen shooters with great effect, and quickly repulsed the enemy's advance. . . ."

More Confederate troopers now charged into the fray. According to the historian of Rosser's all-Virginia Laurel Brigade, "A squadron of the Eleventh Regiment was ordered to charge, which it did promptly, the men riding up against the barricade, where heavy volleys were poured into them, it being too dark to see the enemy except by the flash of the discharges. ... A portion of the Seventh Regiment was dismounted and attacked and removed a portion of the barricade in the roadway. . . . The Twelfth Regiment was now ordered to charge. The opening in the barricade was carried, a number of men and horses being killed there."

Four miles to the west, Rooney Lee's men waited to advance. Lee's force had been split by a fork in the road; the westernmost section faced the camps of the 3rd New York Cavalry, while the one to the east came upon a mixed section of the 11th Pennsylvania Cavalry and the 1st District of Columbia. "The firing of Rosser's men was heard before light, and immediately on hearing the sound, our brigade charged down the main road," remembered an officer in the eastern wing. "Most of [the enemy] . . . were cozily sleeping in their tents," recalled a Virginia trooper, "and quite unprepared for so early a visit."

Further east, Dearing's men swept easily into Cocke's Mill and took their blocking position.

Once a path had been cleared through the 1st District of Columbia Cavalry camp, Rosser's men (led by Lieutenant Colonel Elijah White) moved to the cattle pen. Defending the corral was a small detachment from the 13th Pennsylvania Cavalry, commanded by Captain Henry H. Gregg, brother of David McM. Gregg, the overall Union cavalry commander at Petersburg. "By this time it was open daylight," one of Rosser's scouts recollected. "We could see the enemy's cavalry, about a battalion strong, drawn up in a line under the hill, about one hundred and fifty yards off. General Hampton sent Tom Scott, one of our scouts, to demand of the Yankee officer his unconditional surrender."

That reply, as remembered by scout John S. Elliott, was "Give my compliments to General Hampton and tell him that his demand is not the kind of tactics I learned at school."

Cavalryman Frank Myers, riding with the 35th Virginia Cavalry, noted the Yankee response as "Come and get us, if you want us," while the historian for the Laurel Brigade recalled that the answer was "Go to hell!"

Time was critical, and Hampton was not going to waste any more of it. "Come down on them, White!" he commanded. Continued trooper George Baylor, "The enemy fought stubbornly for a short time, but finally broke and fled in confusion." Added scout Elliott, "We overtook a large number of the fleeing cavalry and captured them. Colonel White dashed on and coming up with the cattle ordered his men to surround and stop them. The enemy, seeing our purpose, did their best to stampede the herd by hooting and shooting among them." "In our brigade were quite a number of cowboys," bragged Baylor, "not of the Texas or Western sort, but real Virginia cowboys, who know the habits and dispositions of cattle, and these managed this large drove with skill and dexterity."

Other Confederates found time to enjoy the spoils of war. "Oranges, lemons, cigars, crackers, and good things and useful, were found in great profusion," wrote a *Petersburg Express* reporter, "and not a few of them were secured." "[The Yankee] camp was set on fire," South Carolinian C. M. Calhoun remembered with relish, "and what clothing, blankets, good eating, etc., that our boys could not take off were destroyed, and in a short time the cattle were flying back with new owners." A number of two-legged prisoners were part of the captures, including a 25-man detail from the 8th Connecticut that had been stringing telegraph lines on an assignment that many of the soldiers likely found to be boring.

Hampton's men were driving the captured herd southward by 8:00 a.m., headed toward Cook's Bridge. According to the *Petersburg Express* account, "The cattle stretched out for a distance of four or five miles, but were moved and guarded in the most systematical manner."

August Kautz at first paid little attention to the action. He informed division headquarters at 6:00 a.m. that his pickets had been driven in but blamed a recent outpost incident, "I think the attack is in retaliation for those we killed the other day," he said. An hour later, Kautz cataloged the fighting that was flaring across a wide area in his sector and confessed that he was "fearful that the First District of Columbia [Cavalry] may be entrapped." In his next message, written at 7:30 a.m., Kautz continued to assume that this was a vengeance raid, declaring, "I believe the enemy to have planned the capture of the First District of Columbia Cavalry, which I think was their object, and I fear they have succeeded." Not until 8:30 a.m. would he entertain the notion that the Confederates might have another purpose. "The attack has developed itself as a foray on the cattle and the First District of Columbia Cavalry," he reported.

Kautz related in his postwar memoirs, "I found on reaching Sycamore Church that Wade Hampton with his entire cavalry force had come upon my line . . . and had swept along the line about six miles taking out about three-hundred men, and held the ground until they had got the beef herd…well under way and then retreated." Now, with a force of between five and seven hundred men, he was pressing southward at midday in pursuit.

Federal officers pored over maps and realized that they had an excellent chance of cutting off the Confederate raiders. In order to reach safety, Hampton's men would have to move well south before swinging west; so it might be possible for a fast-moving Federal column to push directly southward out of the Petersburg lines and head off the Rebels. The distance the blue-coated riders would have to cover was about half that for their gray-clad opponents.

Brigadier General Henry Davies, Jr., with a force of about 2,100 riders, galloped south at 12:30 p.m. along the Jerusalem Plank Road on an intercept course.

The head of Hampton's column reached Cook's Bridge at about 10:00 a.m., where the herd was prodded across the rickety temporary structure. The animals were counted as they reached the other side, with the exuberant Confederates who made the tally agreeing on a total of 2,486 head. Once the crossing was completed, the new span was destroyed to delay the Federals' pursuit.

The road forked two miles further south, and here Hampton once again divided his command. The herd, with a small escort, was sent on an even more southerly route, while the bulk of Hampton's command took the upper fork, essentially reversing their approach route. Advance patrols reached the Jerusalem Plank Road and immediately scouted northward. It was about 2:00 p.m. when these advance parties ran into outriders from Davies's force.

Colonel White, of Rosser's command, was the first to confront the Yankees. Noted the Laurel Brigade's historian, "White with characteristic audacity blocked the way with an attitude of defiance that suggested that he had strong backing. It was a fine play of bluff."

Even as Davies brought all his men up and began to overlap White's lines, Hampton had his units converging on that point, near Ebenezer Church and Belches Mill. Recalled one especially cocky Confederate, "The enemy was lavishing profuse attentions upon us in the way of solid shot and shells; but we faced him resolutely and sent back, screaming and glittering like meteors at night[,] shot for shot, seemingly to say: 'Come take your beeves if you can.'"

"I engaged the enemy and held them in their position until 8 p.m.," Henry Davies later reported, "hoping that General Kautz might come up and attack them in rear." For his part, Kautz had gotten his force across the Blackwater, but he stopped once he encountered Hampton's rear guard. "My main hope," he wrote, "was that [Davies] . . . had pushed down the Jerusalem Plank Road to cut off the enemy's retreat." Both Federal forces pulled back at dark. "Leaving four squadrons on picket at the church," wrote Hampton, "I moved the command to their former bivouac, on the Rowanty, halting for the night." Reviewing this sequence of events, one disgusted Pennsylvania cavalryman concluded, "We were ... as usual in such cases, a little too late."

The captured herd was moving westward by dawn. Hampton and his weary men had passed into Confederate lines by 9:00 a.m. In his summary of this action, the writer for the *Petersburg Express* noted that Hampton "brought everything safely with him, losing only some twenty or thirty cattle from fatigue."

The appearance of the cattle was "certainly the prettiest sight I ever saw," a Mississippi surgeon noted. A South Carolina soldier remembered that his friend "looked at them until his eyes watered, and his mouth too, I reckon. I know mine did." One Confederate artilleryman would write home on September 26 that "we are now having Yankee beef every day." In his report of this affair, Wade Hampton listed his losses as "10 killed, 47 wounded, and 4 missing. ... I beg to express my entire satisfaction at the conduct of officers and men."

The view from the Federal side was less congratulatory. "Valuable capture for them," Grant's aide Cyrus Comstock observed dourly. "Very bad for us." "[It] may be supposed that they had a beef carnival," one New York soldier commented, adding, "The Union men in front were jocosely taunted with

'Hello! Yanks! want any fresh beef?'" Along another portion of the line, a New Jersey infantryman recalled, "The rebels taunt[ed] us by bawling and bellowing like cattle." One New York newspaper editorial writer proclaimed that as "a piece of raiding rascality it was perfect."

Grant was away from City Point, conferring with Sheridan, when the raid occurred, a fact that only added to George Meade's worries. "Grant's absence and the usual friendly spirit of the press, will undoubtedly attribute this loss to my negligence," Meade wrote to his wife on September 16, "and I really had as much to do with it as you had, except that I had called attention to the danger of having the cattle there."

Grant ignored the affair in his official report of the Petersburg campaign and made no mention of it in his postwar memoirs. He was confident that Sheridan's actions in the Shenandoah Valley would punish the Confederacy far more than the loss of the herd would affect operations around Petersburg. Fully expecting news of victory in the Valley, Grant responded to a question about the rustling by pulling out and examining his watch with the comment: "They have paid dearly for their beef before this time." Still, it was nettling. A short time after he returned to City Point, when he was asked by a visitor, "When do you expect to starve out Lee and capture Richmond?" Grant replied, "Never, if our armies continue to supply him with beef-cattle."

Chapter Ten

Dateline: Petersburg

September 28 - October 2, 1864

Ulysses S. Grant
Final Report of Operations, March 1864-May 1865

[Sheridan's] operations during the month of August and the fore part of September were both of an offensive and defensive character . . . but no general engagement took place. . . . Defeat to us would lay open to the enemy the States of Maryland and Pennsylvania for long distances before another army could be interposed to check him. Under these circumstances I hesitated about allowing the initiative to be taken. Finally, the use of the Baltimore and Ohio Railroad and the Chesapeake and Ohio Canal, which were both obstructed by the enemy, became so indispensably necessary to us . . . that I determined the risk should be taken. . . .

I left City Point on the 15th of September to visit [Sheridan] . . . at his headquarters, to decide . . . what should be done. I met him at Charlestown, and he pointed out so distinctly how each army lay, what he could do the moment he was authorized, and expressed such confidence of success that I saw there were but two words of instruction necessary—Go in! . . . Early on the morning of the 19th General Sheridan attacked General Early at the crossing on the Opequon Creek, and . . . defeated him, with heavy loss. . . . The enemy rallied and made a stand in a strong position at Fisher's Hill, where he was attacked and again defeated with heavy loss on the [22]d. . . . Sheridan pursued him with great energy through Harrisonburg, Staunton, and the gaps of the Blue Ridge. After stripping the upper Valley of most of the supplies and provisions for the rebel army, he returned to Strasburg and took position on the north side of Cedar Creek.

* * *

Chaplain William Corby of the 88th New York recalled the manner in which newspapers reached the troops at the front: "We were perhaps twelve miles or so from City Point. . . . An enterprising boy would go to the landing on the irrepressible army mule, stay at the landing all night in a dry-goods box or under a wagon, and as soon as the steamer came with the papers he put in front of him his quantum of several hundreds and came galloping out to the camp, crying out at the top of his voice: *New York Herald!* He charged us twenty-five cents apiece for the papers, but even at that price we were delighted to get the news and he sold his papers like hot cakes."

The Union troops at Petersburg generally trusted the news they read. After listening to wild tales of the Crater fiasco, one New Jersey soldier declared, "I will have to wait until I see the New York papers before I draw any conclusions." A Massachusetts officer regularly obtained Richmond papers in order to compare their accounts with those published in the North. "[By] reading the situation as depicted by the papers on either side," he reasoned, "a pretty correct judgment of it could be formed."

Many of the Yankee soldiers had a wide selection of papers available to them. "We now get the 'Washington Chronicle,' 'Philadelphia [I]nquirer,' and the 'New York Herald,'" reported William Boston, of the 20th Michigan, adding that through the mail, men in his regiment also received the "Detroit 'Tribune' and 'Free Press' and the New York 'World.'"

The hometown news sheets had certain attractions, but as one Maine cavalryman observed, "we get our best news through the New York newspapers." "We read the papers when we could get them," a Massachusetts soldier seconded, "principally the *New York Herald.*"

The headquarters for news coverage of the Petersburg campaign was City Point. There the *New York Herald* maintained the largest and best-financed operation, presided over by war correspondent and Grant confidant Sylvanus Cadwallader. With the enthusiastic support of the *Herald's* owner, James Gordon Bennett, Cadwallader established a tented headquarters not far from Grant's own, complete with "a professional cook [and] a tent for his . . . one large hospital tent for a reception room, and another opening out of it for a dining room; an old plantation house servant to always be in attendance on any one who called."

Cadwallader spared no expense to ensure that any noteworthy figure who visited City Point would also spend time with him: "My ambulance would convey a party wherever it wished to go, if that mode of conveyance was preferred. I kept four saddle horses and equipments; and could mount two or three friends for a day at any time. Cigars of excellent quality, stood open and free to all guests, or callers." Concluded Cadwallader, with not a little bit of pride, "In those times of army deprivations, *Herald* headquarters soon became well known and famous."

The *Herald's* strongest challenge came from the far more modest operation run by the *New York Times*. Its field director, J. R. Hamilton, did his best to compete, but it was an uphill battle. "I never go to [Army] Head Quarters without seeing Cadwallader . . . cheek by jowl and hobnobbing with the officers there, from the Adjutant General downwards," he complained to the head office, "while they seem to regard me as some irresponsible nondescript coming among them to pump them. I scarcely blame them for it. The *Herald* puts it in the power of their correspondents to command the attention and consideration due to his position. . . . The *Times* ignores such policy altogether, and compels its correspondents here to make all sorts of ignominious shifts."

Getting news from the front to Washington (whence it was sent by telegraph to New York) in a timely manner required a degree of organization befitting a large-scale military operation. "I rise about six o'clock," Cadwallader explained to his wife, "breakfast immediately, write what I can, look up a special messenger to carry correspondence to Washington, and get ready to supervise the dispatches which two messengers will bring to me from the front by 8:00 or 8:30, at farthest. . . . [After] dinner [these messengers] . . . start back to each wing of the army; learn precisely where to call for correspondence that night; sleep in some camp till three or four in the morning; ride from one correspondent to another, collecting everything written up to that hour; and come to me again."

The *Times's* Hamilton felt outgunned. "I do hope we shall not find ourselves whipped by the infernal *Herald* as we have been on one or two occasions lately," he warned on one occasion. "But really there is no fighting against it, with such machinery as we have to contend against. They send an employee by every boat, to insure their letters going through—while we have to trust to mail agents who may neglect or play us false just when they please without the possibility of detection."

Seeking to overcome the *Herald's* advantage, the City Point representatives for three New York papers—the *Tribune*, the *Times*, and the *World*—joined with the *Philadelphia Ledger's* staff to organize their own messenger service. Cadwallader promptly called upon his friend Quartermaster General Rufus Ingals to raise the fee that civilians were charged to use government transportation between City Point and Washington. "The *Herald* messengers paid these extra charges cheerfully for a month or two," Cadwallader observed smugly, "[until the other papers] became discouraged and abandoned the design." Cadwallader then had the extra traveling charges canceled.

The Petersburg situation, in September 1864, was summarized this way by *New York Times* correspondent and military analyst William Swinton: "The hold gained by Warren on the Weldon Railroad was permanently retained, and a line of redoubts formed connecting his position with the old left of the army, on the Jerusalem plankroad. No further movements of consequence, beyond reconnaissances, were made till the end of September, when General Grant, being resolved to push operations on Butler's front, north of the James River, directed a demonstration to be made on the left, with the view of preventing the transfer of re-enforcements to the troops opposed to Butler."

The news teams were ready. Cadwallader's *New York Herald* force was the largest—made up of correspondents who were veterans all and deployed to cover every contingency. James C. Fitzpatrick, who had been captured and briefly held by Mosby's guerrillas early in May, monitored the City Point scene and Parke's Ninth Corps; W. D. McGregor and William H. Merriam were with the headquarters of the Army of the Potomac and the Army of the James, respectively. In the Army of the Potomac, Solomon T. Bulkley—for two months a prisoner in Richmond's notorious Castle Thunder—rode with the cavalry; L. A. Hendrick, whose reporting had included Antietam and Gettysburg, was with Warren's Fifth Corps; and Finley Anderson, who explained his professional motivation with the words "I want to see . . . what kind of stuff I am made of," traveled with Hancock's Second Corps. In the Army of the James, John A. Brady checked in from the Eighteenth Corps, while Thomas M. Cook—another Gettysburg veteran—covered the Tenth Corps beat.

Other papers had their own coverage crews. J. R. Hamilton anchored the *New York Times* contingent from City Point. Bermuda-born Henry Jacob Winser, who had officered a New York Zouave regiment early in the war, was with the Army of the James, while former British officer George F. Williams, who had risen to the rank of brevet major in the Union army, moved with Meade and the Army of the Potomac. Also in the field were E. T. Peters (covering the Army of the James) and J. L. Rhodes (with the Army of the Potomac), both of the *Philadelphia Inquirer.* These were not the only reporters on the scene, but they wrote for the papers with the largest circulation, and their reports, many of which were copied in syndication, were known all around the country.

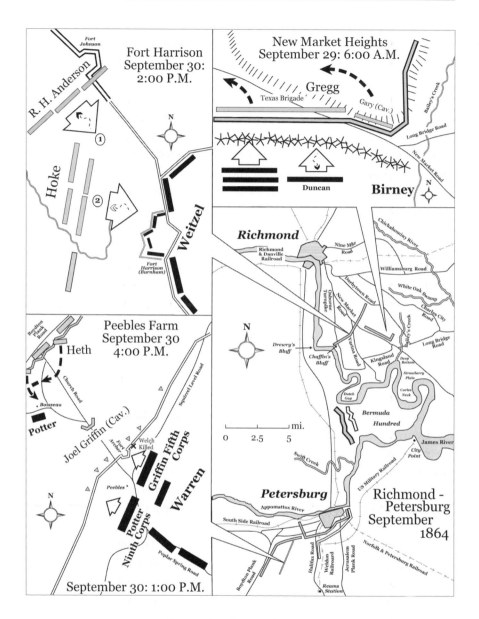

Thursday, September 29

The *Herald's* Fitzpatrick set the mood from City Point: "If the tone of the correspondence from the army expresses any unusual feeling of enthusiasm, it is because that feeling is merely the reflection of the buoyancy of every soldier here."

The night of September 28 had been filled with activity. From hundreds of camps on Bermuda Hundred, the white and black regiments making up the Tenth and Eighteenth corps began to move. "The entire Army of the James is in motion," the *Times's* Winser reported early on the morning of September 29. "As I write and all through the night, the road passing near Gen. Butler's headquarters has echoed to the tramp of infantry and the rumble of artillery and supply trains."

After wrangling his way across the Deep Bottom pontoon bridge, the *Herald's* Merriam paused at Grover's Farm to sketch an overview of the action: "[The] Tenth army corps, Major General D. B. Birney commanding, were ordered . . . to . . . proceed up the south bank of the James to Jones' Neck, crossing to the north bank at Deep Bottom and striking the scene of our operations in August last. . . . The Eighteenth army corps [Major General E. O. C. Ord commanding] . . . moved at one o'clock on the morning of the 29th to the north of the James from the south side of that water course by a pontoon bridge between Jones' and Aiken's landings." Butler's goal, Merriam related without hyperbole, was "Richmond."

The Federal cavalry, which had been massing on the extreme left of the Union line, near Fort Dushane, moved south along the Halifax Road this morning. This was part of Grant's plan to threaten Lee simultaneously north of the James and south of Petersburg. As the *Times's* Winser perceptively observed, the movements of the armies of the Potomac and the James were "coincident and cooperative."

The *Herald's* Bulkley accompanied the Federal riders—a full division, 4,350 strong, commanded by Brigadier General David McM. Gregg. Upon reaching lower Church Road, Gregg sent one of his two brigades (Colonel Charles Smith's) probing westward toward the Boydton Plank Road, now a principal Confederate supply route. Gregg's other brigade (Brigadier General Henry E. Davies's) continued southward to Reams Station to guard against any attack from that quarter.

"Colonel Smith advanced with his column nearly three miles without meeting any large force of the enemy," Bulkley reported. "Upon reaching the [Vaughan] Road regiments were sent out in different directions to ascertain [the enemy's] whereabouts. . . . About one o'clock the various regiments had completed their reconnaissances. The whole brigade then retired a distance of nearly two miles, and took a position upon the east side of a ravine, and awaited the movements of the enemy."

"It is customary for the rebels to make their attacks about five o'clock in the afternoon," Bulkley added prophetically. Shortly before that time, Confederate cavalry and horse artillery, under the overall command of Major General Wade Hampton, struck at Smith's defensive position along a branch of Arthur's Swamp, near the farm of a family named McDowell. A section of Battery I, 1st U.S. Artillery, commanded by Lieutenant Francis Reynolds, came under heavy fire. "The enemy . . . poured the solid shot and shell into him at a lively rate," Bulkley observed, "but he returned shot for shot until an unlucky shell struck one of his caissons, exploding it, killing one man and mortally wounding another."

Both Hampton and Gregg brought reinforcements to the scene. "The country was entirely unsuited to mounted charges, or our cavalry would have had an opportunity of using . . . the sabre," Bulkley wrote. "As it was, they were compelled to rely solely upon their carbines, at short range. The fight continued until it became too dark to distinguish the enemy, when, by mutual consent, the firing ceased, and each side withdrew to count the losses and prepare for the morrow."

North of the James, September 29 was a dramatic day for Union arms. Even though Butler's carefully planned operation had been in the works for several days, not a word of it had leaked out. "In all my experience I never before knew a plan to be kept so profoundly secret," the *Times's* Winser wrote admiringly.

Two great columns, each a full corps, crossed to the north side before dawn. The right wing, consisting of Birney's Tenth Corps with an all-black division from the Eighteenth added, was to assault the New Market Heights position that had twice stymied Hancock. The left wing, Ord's Eighteenth Corps, was to move directly against Richmond's formidable exterior defensive line.

Birney was the first to close with the enemy. After driving Confederate pickets away from the fields just north of Deep Bottom, his men drew up before the enemy's earthworks along New Market Heights. This position, the *Herald's* Thomas M. Cook noted, "in addition to its strong natural character, was rendered doubly formidable by the almost impenetrable slashing that covered the slopes."

The Confederate line was manned by only 1,800 soldiers—Texas and Arkansas infantry from Lee's army, Virginia and South Carolina cavalry (Gary's Brigade), and artillery drawn from units assigned to Richmond's defenses. The Union attack was carried out by the black troops on loan to Birney, all from

Brigadier General Charles Paine's division. The *Herald's* Cook watched the assault. "Their charge in the face of the obstacles interposing was one of the grand features of the day's operation. . . . They never halted or faltered, though their ranks were sadly thinned by the charge, and the slashing was filled with the slain and wounded of their number." E. T. Peters, of the *Philadelphia Inquirer*, took care to note that the "ground was difficult to charge over . . . and the fire from the Rebel rifle-pits was rapid and deliberate, [and] the charging column suffered severely." "It was a wonderful, a sublime sight to see those black men stand up to the rack," the military veteran Winser wrote in the *Times*. "It took 20 minutes to cross the field of death and drive the rebels out of their position."

The Confederate view, expressed in a letter to the *Columbia Daily South Carolinian*, was very different. "Birney's whole corps came against the position held by Gen. Gary's brigade, and was so severely handled that, when the order came for us to fall back, it permitted our thin line, though at close quarters at the time, to retire in order and without injury."

Among the news observers of this affair—which cost the black regiments more than eight hundred casualties—commendation for the U.S.C.T. units was universal. "The behavior of the negro troops . . . was of the most gallant character," the *Herald's* William H. Merriam affirmed. "Who dare say, after this, that negroes will not fight?" the *Times's* Winser asked his readers. "To-day their praises have been on every tongue, and too much cannot be said in appreciation of their courage." Paine's division, declared Thomas Morris Chester of the *Philadelphia Press*, one of the few black reporters present, "has covered itself with glory, and wiped out effectively the imputation against the fighting qualities of the colored troops."

Birney's men now moved west along the New Market Road, heading toward Richmond, where they would join with Ord's troops in a direct assault on the capital's outer defenses. At the same time, Brigadier General August V. Kautz's cavalry division trotted up from Deep Bottom and onto the Darbytown Road, also aiming for Richmond.

"It is well known," the *Herald's* Fitzpatrick wrote this day, "that the rebel capital and stronghold is defended from approach . . . by the most extensive earthworks running in concentric lines from river to river. The lowermost of these works—the outpost it may be called of the citadel itself—commences at the James River, near Chapin's Bluff, and thence . . . deflects to the northwest, covering the Newmarket, Central [i.e., Darbytown] and Charles City Roads." Ord's Eighteenth Corps was marching into the heart of this fortification system.

Only a handful of defenders stood between the Yankee corps and Richmond. As the soldier-correspondent for the *Columbia Daily South Carolinian* explained, "Our line running down the river was so long, and our troops so few in number, that it was impossible to man it along its whole length at the same time, and we were obliged to trust to watching the enemy closely, and hurrying troops to the points threatened."

The major bastion blocking Ord was Fort Harrison. "Stannard's Division of the Eighteenth Corps, was in advance," Winser reported for the *Times*. "They formed in line of battle, and moved up steadily toward the work which was large. . . . With drums beating and colors flaunting, they made a superb charge, carrying the fort under a severe fire." Just at this moment of triumph, however, the Union leadership suffered two sharp blows, noted by the *Herald's* John A. Brady. He reported that "General Ord . . . was shot in the thigh and was compelled to leave the field. . . . Brigadier General Burnham [commanding a brigade in Stannard's division] was killed as he was about entering the fort. He lived a few moments after he was struck, but every attempt to save his life proved futile. General Burnham had but just returned from a leave of absence."

The successful storming of Harrison did not end the combat this day. Federal troops trying to extend their gains south of the fort were stopped, and others were even more decisively repulsed north of the captured position. "About one p.m., a fort or redoubt immediately on the right of those held by General Ord's troops, was attacked by Foster's Division of the Tenth Corps and General Wm. Birney's Brigade of colored troops,[1] both without success," E. T. Peters wrote for the *Philadelphia Inquirer*. The *Herald's* Cook was on the scene as the latter position, the Confederates' Fort Gilmer, was assailed. "The assault was made at precisely two p.m., the men giving a cheer and starting forward on the run. They were met with a most murderous fire of grape and canister, and unceasing volleys of musketry that worked terrible havoc in their ranks." Winser of the *Times* believed that the "colored troops again distinguished themselves here. . . . At least twenty of them climbed on the parapet of the fort, and were shot dead, tumbling back upon their comrades. The rest, it is said, were slaughtered by the enemy with shells thrown among them by hand."

There was one more phase to the actions here this day. Cook of the *Herald* related the details: "General Butler's operations embraced the movement of

---

1   William Birney was the brother of David Birney, commander of the Tenth Corps.

Kautz's division of cavalry on our extreme right. This division, taking the central, or Darby[town] road, dashed boldly up to the very gates of the city of Richmond, and as [William] Birney was making his assault, Kautz's guns could be plainly heard away off to the right. Soon afterwards a courier arrived from Kautz, announcing that he was then within the rebel lines and in close view of the city. Gen. Butler at once ordered a division of infantry to his support . . . but on arriving in the suburbs of the city they found no cavalry there, Kautz having withdrawn. . . . [These troops were then directed] to fall back."

Watching from his perch at City Point, the *Herald's* Fitzpatrick assured his readers that "General Grant gave the battle his personal attention. He left here at an early hour in the morning with his staff and proceeded to the front. All along the road he was greeted with the greatest enthusiasm by the troops. . . . After [Fort Harrison] . . . was carried he entered it and sat down to write a dispatch. . . . [A] hundred-pounder shell burst in the air over the General's head; but it decomposed him none in the least, and he finished his dispatch without any apparent sign of uneasiness at his exposed position or [at] the dangerous missiles flying in such close proximity."

All Union activity north of the James turned to defensive measures as night fell. According to the *Times's* analyst William Swinton, "The position being one very menacing to Richmond, General Butler made dispositions to hold it permanently."

For its part, the Richmond press played down the significance of the loss of Fort Harrison. "The country will be surprised that so much noise had been made and so little damage done," a writer for the *Richmond Examiner*. "The following official dispatch from General Lee tells the balance of the story . . .

> GENERAL GREGG REPORTS THAT HE REPULSED THE SEVERAL ATTACKS OF
> THE ENEMY, MADE AGAINST THE INTERMEDIATE LINE OF DEFENCES,
> CAPTURING MANY PRISONERS. THE ENEMY STILL HOLD BATTERY [I.E.,
> FORT] HARRISON ON THE EXTERIOR LINE. OUR LOSS IS VERY SMALL."

Friday, September 30

Heavy columns of Federal infantry were moving south of Petersburg this morning. The *Herald's* William D. McGregor identified them as "the First and Second division and a brigade of the Third division, of the Fifth corps, with the Second and Third division of the Ninth Corps."

Leaving the Union lines at Fort Wadsworth, the long columns filed onto a narrow country road that led toward the Boydton Plank Road, passing through alternating patches of cleared farmland and cluttered forests. "Grant is earnestly combating the rebellion," James C. Fitzpatrick informed the *Herald's* faithful readers. "Yesterday he let go his right, and inflicted considerable damage north of the James. To-day he brought his left into play, and gave the enemy severe punishment beyond the Weldon Railroad."

With Griffin's division of Warren's Fifth Corps leading, the Federals marched west along Poplar Spring Road and spread into battle lines before the partially finished Confederate entrenchments that snaked southwestward across their path from Squirrel Level Road. Only cavalry and horse artillery manned this Confederate line; Robert E. Lee had pulled most of his infantry into Petersburg to allow reinforcements to go north of the James, and also to create a mobile reserve capable of quickly moving to any threatened point along the Cockade City perimeter.

A lone Confederate strongpoint near Peebles Farm, named Fort Archer, gave pause to the Yankee advance. Warren's men hunkered down along a ravine parallel to the Squirrel Level Road line and waited. Their cautious commander had decided to halt operations until the Ninth Corps troops assisting him cleared the clogged roadway and took up a supporting position on his left. Not until 1:00 p.m. did Warren's attack on Fort Archer begin.

"A more magnificent charge was never made by any troops in any war," Warren later bragged to *Herald* correspondent L. A. Hendrick. The reporter filed this eyewitness account: "The charge was made solely by General Griffin's division. . . . The order being given to charge, the skirmish battle lines soon advanced across the open ground. The charging column pressed steadily, earnestly, persistently forward. Rebel shell and bullets had no dismaying effect.

"'A commission to him who first mounts the parapet of that redoubt,' shouted Col. [Noval E.] Welch, of the Sixteenth Michigan, to his men. He was the first to mount the parapet, where he waved his sword. In an instant a rebel bullet penetrated his brain, and he lay dead."

The outnumbered Confederates finally fled, making a brief stand at a smaller redoubt a short distance northeast of Fort Archer and then falling back to the principal defensive earthworks protecting the Boydton Plank Road. The victorious Federals now worked to consolidate their hold on the enemy's outer line.

Robert E. Lee was doing everything in his power north of the James to recapture Fort Harrison. He had assembled an eight-brigade strike force to accomplish this, drawn largely from the divisions of Charles Field and Robert F.

Hoke. Lee set up a two-pronged assault, with Hoke's men attacking Fort Harrison from the west while Field's troops pressed from the north and northwest. At about 2:00 p.m., even as Warren's men, south of Petersburg, were celebrating their capture of Fort Archer, Lee's attack on Fort Harrison got under way.

The *Herald's* Merriam wrote of this assault as being of "the most desperate, and . . . sanguinary character." Every advantage was pressed, according to Merriam's colleague John Brady. "General Lee in person commanded. . . . The [Confederate James River] rams at the same time opened upon our position, and our line was enfiladed by the fire from the rebel battery on the river." The *Times's* Winser watched the Confederate attack develop: "Formed in three long lines they advanced to the charge, and were met by a murderous fire which sent them staggering back, leaving piles of dead and dying on the field. Rallying again, they renewed the onset, and with such determination that their advance came within two hundred yards of the work. Our men again succeeded in repulsing them, and the slaughter was terrible." The brunt of Lee's attack fell on the Eighteenth Corps. Thomas Cook of the *Herald*, standing with the relatively untouched Tenth Corps, never forgot the "peculiar yell" of the rebels as they advanced. The attack was soundly repulsed in less than an hour.

Field and Hoke had not coordinated their movements, and so each advanced unsupported by the other. A writer for the *Richmond Examiner* explained this failure as a "misconstruction of the order fixing the time of assault by one of the division commanders. He ordered his troops to charge the position twenty minutes before the appointed hour and, of course, received the concentrated fire of the enemy. The men displayed great intrepidity . . . but were compelled to fall back before the heavy fire."

All serious fighting north of the James was over by 4:00 p.m., but south of Petersburg, in the fields west of Peebles Farm, it was starting anew. While the Federals were strengthening their hold on the captured portion of the Squirrel Level Road line, the Confederate Third Corps commander, A. P. Hill, directing Petersburg's defenses in Lee's absence, ordered a counterattack. Four infantry brigades from Heth's and Wilcox's divisions moved out and along the still-untested earthworks defending the Boydton Plank Road. Even as these troops were taking up a blocking position, Federals from Brigadier General Robert Potter's Ninth Corps division began probing cautiously northward from Peebles Farm.

The *Herald's* Fitzpatrick described that advance: "Passing the skirmish line of the Fifth Corps, Gen. Potter moved steadily forward until the enemy, whose skirmishers had gradually fallen back, came to a stand at a point which Gen. Potter now determined to carry by a charge. This charge . . . was met by the enemy in a most decided manner. . . . The charge failed, and, the troops giving way, were countercharged by the enemy, and driven in confusion." Continued George Williams of the *Times*, "The enemy made a flank movement, and succeeded in uncovering our left and doubling it up, and capturing a few hundred prisoners. At this critical juncture, some troops from the Fifth Corps were ordered up, and checked the further advance of the enemy. . . . The rebels failing to make any very serious impression upon our left, sullenly retreated, and our troops busied themselves all night in throwing up intrenchments. Thus closed the . . . day's operations . . . ."

Saturday, October 1

"Mud, rain and dismality—these are the prevalent features," William Merriam of the *Herald* wrote from Butler's headquarters, north of the James. "Almost everybody is drenched," added Henry Winser of the *Times*. Thomas Cook of the *Herald* found the mood in the Tenth Corps upbeat: "Notwithstanding a severe storm of rain that has prevailed since last night, we have been busy strengthening our position, and are now so securely posted that . . . we can safely defy the whole rebel army. . . . The grand feature of the day has been a reconnaissance in force up to the inner line of the rebel works. [Major General David B.] Birney has again pushed his forces up to the very outskirts of the city. . . . The expedition, having accomplished all that was designed, fell back at nightfall to their old position." Winser noted that when the "gallant division arrived in camp there was great cheering to welcome them."

A few reporters interviewed refugees from the enemy capital. Winser spoke to some who "confirmed accounts of confusion in Richmond, non-combatants clearing out, all businesses ended, every male fifteen years of age and over in the defenses of the city." He also took a poke at his "colleagues" on the other side, observing that Richmond's newspapers had been closed down due to the emergency and concluding that "for a time at least, your readers will be spared their high-toned articles."[2]

---

2 `Winser was substantially correct. The *Richmond Whig* alone published throughout the crisis.

Confederate forces were more active south of Petersburg. Yesterday's fighting had been concentrated along the northwestern edge of the Federal incursion; today, a Rebel force struck directly south of Petersburg, at the hinge between the older, better fortified Union line and the new position, which was still being strengthened by soldiers belonging to Romeyn Ayres's Fifth Corps division. Wrote L. A. Hendrick of the *Herald*, "This morning the enemy made two charges upon General Ayres' line, but was handsomely repulsed each time."

At about the same time, other, smaller Confederate units were overrunning the advance Union outposts on Peebles Farm. These actions did not, however, seriously challenge the new extension of the Federal line.

Beyond the ground further south now secured by Warren's and Parke's infantry, Wade Hampton led a three-brigade cavalry strike force along the lower Vaughan Road in hopes of flanking that new line. Hampton ran into Henry E. Davies's brigade of Gregg's division at about 3:00 p.m.

The *Herald's* man with the cavalry, Solomon T. Bulkley, was away from his post when the combat began, but he returned in time to pen a full account for the next issue. "The fight. . . . was terrific. . . . Time and again [the enemy] . . . charged up to within a few feet of the line, when they would receive such a deadly shower of bullets and shot as would send them staggering back.

"The enemy. . . . attempted a flank movement. . . . but General Davies had provided against such a contingency, and gave him such a reception as compelled him to retire."

Sunday, October 2

The situation north of the James remained fairly static today. At about 2:00 p.m., noted the *Herald's* Cook, the "enemy made a desperate attempt . . . to drive in our pickets on the right. . . . Our infantry pickets stood their ground nobly and repulsed them very handsomely."

Prisoners and fleeing civilians continued to spread magnified tales of chaos in Richmond. Their stories seemed so convincing to William Merriam that the *Herald* man now confidently predicted that the "city will undoubtedly fall within the next few days."

The fighting south of Petersburg across the churned-up fields of Peebles Farm was not yet over. Yesterday it had been the Confederates who attempted to shake loose this dangerous extension of the Union line; today it was George Meade who determined to keep the pot boiling. Meade had secretly transferred

Gershom Mott's division of the Second Corps to this sector overnight, and a few hours after daylight, it advanced from the Peebles line toward the Boydton Plank Road, accompanied on its right by a mixed force of Ninth and Fifth corps units.

The *Herald's* McGregor later reported the results of the move: "Two lines of work were found unoccupied, [with] only a skirmish line opposing the advance, which fell back as our troops went forward.

"Near the Boydton road a very formidable line of works was found, behind which the rebels were posted in heavy force. It was not deemed advisable to attack, and our men fell back, and occupy a safe position." Grant's fifth offensive against the Petersburg-Richmond defensive system was over.

What had been accomplished? Newspaper analysts for both sides hastened to provide some answers.

J. R. Hamilton of the *Times* judged the Peebles Farm expedition to have been a partial success. "We carried one line of defenses, but failed in the second, and, as we hold firmly what we got in the first, we have taken one more effective step toward the grand object we have in view." L. A. Hendrick of the *Herald* was more specific about the advantages that the Federals had gained: "Our line has been lengthened a mile and a half; we have driven the enemy from his strong works only recently put up. . . . We are nearer Petersburg, and now securely threatening the Southside Railroad."

The Richmond newspapers put a different spin on the story. A writer for the *Examiner* thought so little of the capture of Fort Harrison that he dismissed it as not even reaching "the dignity of absolute failure. Instead of Richmond, the enemy got Battery Harrison." The writer went on to explain that Battery Harrison was along "the outer or third line of the fortifications around Richmond. It is in no wise essential to the strength of any other battery." The scribe also spoke of Grant's overall plan with contempt: "It is, in fact, his single trick—his sole manoeuver—a demonstration on the north side to make Lee weaken himself on the Petersburg line, and then a sudden dash to the left flank—always to the left."

As affairs on the Petersburg and Richmond fronts returned to normal, both sides had to deal with the battle's aftermath. Wrote W. D. McGregor from Petersburg on October 4, "In passing over the ground where the Second division of the Ninth Corps met with the reverse on Saturday, our dead were found entirely stripped of clothing, and two or three of the bodies were horribly mutilated." Near Fort Harrison—soon to be renamed Fort Burnham, in honor of the general who had died during its capture—the *Herald's* Thomas M. Cook made note of a ravine between the two sides, filled with Confederate dead. "The lines are so close there that the rebels cannot come out to bury them except under a truce, which they have not yet chosen to ask for," he wrote at midnight on October 2, adding, "If they are not interred soon they will become terribly offensive."

Perhaps the final comment on the fighting came from the *Richmond Examiner.* "We have withstood the great shock of Grant's grand army—and still we stand."

(Union losses north of the James, in the fighting from September 28 to October 2, were 1,040 killed or missing and 2,317 wounded, for a total of 3,357. Southern losses, tallied from very fragmentary returns, were approximately 1,700. In the fighting around Peebles Farm, the Federals lost 1,993 killed or missing and 905 wounded, for a total of 2,898. Confederate losses, again an estimate, were about 1,300. Adding in other related casualties, the final cost of Grant's fifth offensive was 6,322 Federals and 3,000 Confederates.)

Chapter Eleven

"Everything now hinges on the election"

October 27, 1864

Ulysses S. Grant
Final Report of Operations, March 1864-May 1865

Having received considerable re-enforcements, General [Jubal] Early again returned to the [Shenandoah] Valley. . . . On the morning of the 19th [of October], under cover of the darkness and the fog, [Early] surprised and turned [Sheridan's] left flank [at Cedar Creek], capturing the batteries which enfiladed our whole line. Our troops fell back with heavy loss and in much confusion.. At this juncture General Sheridan, who was at Winchester when the battle commenced, arrived on the field, arranged his lines just in time to repulse a heavy attack of the enemy, and immediately assuming the offensive, he attacked in turn with great vigor. The enemy was defeated with great slaughter and the loss of most of his artillery and trains. . . . Thus ended the enemy's last attempt to invade the North via the Shenandoah Valley. I was now enabled to return the Sixth Corps to the Army of the Potomac, and send one division from Sheridan's army to the Army of the James, and another to [Sherman].

* * *

Politics began to overshadow military matters in the fall of 1864. All eyes were on the U.S. White House. "The next two months will be the most interesting period of the war," wrote Richmond war clerk John B. Jones in late August. "Everything depends upon the result of the Presidential election in the United States." Many Federal troops would be voting for the first time, and their ballots would serve as a referendum on the Lincoln administration. George B. McClellan, a former commander of the Army of the Potomac, headed the peace-oriented Democratic ticket, with Ohioan George H. Pendleton as his vice-presidential running mate. Abraham

Lincoln, vying to be the first man since Andrew Jackson to serve two terms, carried the Republican banner, with Tennessee's Andrew Johnson selected for vice president.

"McClellan was our first commander, and, as such, he was worshiped by his soldiers," noted Theodore Garrish, a Maine private. But Garrish and others were troubled by the Democrats' contention that the war was lost. Garrish declared that "it was cruel [of] General McClellan to ask us to vote that our campaigns had all been failures, and that our comrades had all died in vain." "As for McClellan I don't think I shall let my love for the soldier do injury to my principles as a man," a New Yorker, Waters Braman, wrote in September, adding that it was "a difficult subject to discuss and I am postponing my decision as long as possible."

A Lincoln plurality from the troops was far from assured. A New Hampshire man in the Army of the James observed in September that the "soldiers are highly pleased with McClellan's nomination & a large portion hopes for his election. The Lincoln men in this reg[imen]t dare not yip. They are scarce and far between in this Brigade." (The same soldier related that one evening, after his comrades cheered at the news of Sherman's victory at Atlanta, Rebel pickets had asked what all the yelling was about. "Our boys answered & said that [Major] Gen. [Benjamin] Butler was nominated for president. The rebels gave 3 moans.")

President Lincoln's issuance of the Emancipation Proclamation also cost him votes in the racially charged atmosphere of the time. A New York soldier wrote to an upstate Democratic newspaper using language that a later age would find unacceptable: "I think I have seen fighting enough to suit me. But I am willing to fight and lay down my life if necessary, in defense of our country, but not for the Nigger; and I think some of the men of the North who are for putting down Slavery, if it takes the last man, had better come down here and shoulder a musket . . . I think Old Abe's time is short, or hope so at least, for I don't want to fight for niggers any longer."

Virginian William Waitt greeted the selection of McClellan and Pendleton with the comment, "May God turn their nominations to a good account, to His glory and to our own benefit." A cavalryman in Barringer's Brigade added his thought: "I hope this war will soon end now and I think will if McClellan is elected, and I hope he will be. It seems to be the general impression if he is elected we will soon have peace." A few Confederates did their part to encourage a Democratic victory. William Hyndman, a New York cavalryman, took note of a "curious circumstance": as he explained it, "Two of our pickets were captured . . . and on being asked who they would vote for, replying that they were McClellan men, they were promptly released by the rebel scoundrels, and allowed to poll their votes at liberty."

Sights became fixed on November 8. "Yankeedom will not stand it much longer," a Virginia soldier reasoned, further predicting that come November, "the war will be well-nigh [at] its end." A New York soldier reported to his hometown newspaper the substance of a chat he had with some Rebel pickets, "[T]hey said if Lincoln was re-elected we would have war for three years longer, if not we would have peace in two months."

Grant's aide Theodore Bowers took the pulse around headquarters and ventured to a friend, "I see no prospect of our doing anything for some time to come. Everything is at a deadlock. We have men enough to make our present positions safe, but none with which to get up 'side shows' or inaugurate new movements. . . . Everything now hinges on the election."

This forecast was not shared by many Confederates. "We are expecting the Yankees to attack us again," Spencer Welch, a surgeon in McGowan's Brigade, predicted early in October. "Grant is evidently doing his best for Lincoln's election." A Virginia infantryman, William H. Stewart, also looked for some Federal action at Petersburg "for the purpose of bolstering up Lincoln's political prospects, hoping for a victory, which would be heralded throughout the North, [and which] would fire the hearts of his supporters."

In fact, Bowers *was* dead wrong; Grant was anxious to continue offensive operations. "Time is passing and Richmond is still not ours," he grumbled to his wife, Julia, in mid-October. Grant was perplexed by the Confederates' resilience. He knew that his recent actions—at Fort Harrison, the Weldon Railroad, and Peebles Farm—had hit Lee's men hard; the Southern army, he believed, was ready to collapse. "I think it cannot be long now before the tug will come which, if it does not secure the prize, will put us where the end will be in sight," he told his wife.

The idea that would become the grand movement of October 27 was suggested to Grant by George Meade, in a conversation they had on the evening of October 23. The Army of the Potomac's commander was acutely conscious that his prestige was at an all-time low: "I undoubtedly do not occupy the position I did just after the battle of Gettysburg," he had written to his wife on October 13. Rumors abounded that he would soon be relieved of his command. "I saw General Grant to-day," Meade related on October 19, "and we had a laugh over the ridiculous canard of my being relieved." There was a bitter edge to Meade's laughter, though, and Sheridan's impressive come-from-behind victory at Cedar Creek did not help matters. With one eye fixed warily on the promotion ladder, Meade wrote home that the success would "place Sheridan in a position that it will be difficult for any other general to approach."

The final straw came on October 23, when Meade got his hands on a ten-day-old edition of the *New York Independent*. He was described in it as hanging "upon the neck of General Grant like an old man of the sea, whom [Grant] longs to be rid of, and whom he retains solely in deference to the weak complaisance of his constitutional commander- in-chief." Meade, furious at what he saw as a "fiendish and malicious attack," appealed directly to Grant, asking him to "furnish me with such evidence as will place it in my power to correct the extraordinary misapprehensions . . . of the *New York Independent*." Grant at once supplied Meade with copies of "every dispatch sent to Washington by me, in which your name was used. These will show at least that I have never expressed dissatisfaction at any portion of your services." Still, the harsh taste remained. "This matter has worried me more than such attacks usually do," Meade explained, "because I see no chance for the truth being made public as it should be."

A victory would silence his critics, Meade believed, and intelligence reports he had received suggested that there was a cheap one to be had. Following the successful Federal lodgment on Peebles Farm, Robert E. Lee had put his men to work extending the Confederate defensive line as far south as Hatcher's Run; the impression gleaned by Federal scouts, and from prisoner interrogations, was that a large section of the lower end of this line was barely scratched out and would provide no obstacle to a serious attack.

Meade that evening suggested to Grant that the Army of the Potomac move against this position and close the ring around Petersburg. The more Grant thought about it, the more he liked the idea. On October 24, he wired Meade:

MAKE PREPARATIONS TO MARCH OUT AT AN EARLY HOUR ON THE 27TH TO GAIN POSSESSION OF THE SOUTH SIDE RAILROAD, AND TO HOLD IT AND FORTIFY BACK TO YOUR PRESENT LEFT.

More specific instructions followed the next day. The greater portion of three corps (the Second, Fifth, and Ninth) would be involved, along with almost all of David Gregg's cavalry division. Each corps would leave a small force behind to hold its position along the siege entrenchments; all other troops

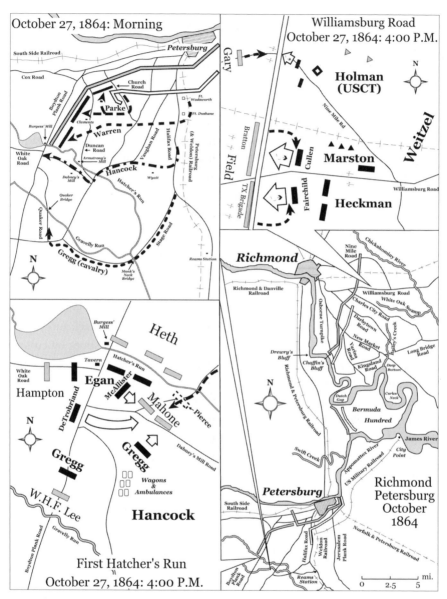

October 27, 1864: Morning

Williamsburg Road
October 27, 1864: 4:00 P.M.

First Hatcher's Run
October 27, 1864: 4:00 P.M.

Richmond
Petersburg
October
1864

(including "clerks, orderlies, and every other man on detached, special, extra, or daily duty") would be put into one of the four mobile columns.

The first column would consist of Major General John Parke's Ninth Corps. It was to swing out of its positions near Peebles Farm and then move directly west to "attack vigorously" the unfinished Confederate line. After breaking through the line, Parke was to pivot to the right and sweep toward Petersburg's inner defensive ring. That was plan A. If Parke was unable to break the line, he would follow plan B, whereby his men would aggressively confront the enemy to divert attention from additional Federal operations further south.

The second mobile column was drawn from Major General Gouverneur Warren's Fifth Corps. It was to march out from its positions near the Weldon Railroad, take station on Parke's left flank, and be ready for either plan A or plan B. In the case of the former, Warren was to "support the Ninth Corps [and] follow up the enemy, moving on the left of the Ninth Corps." If Parke had to resort to plan B, Warren would help the third mobile column.

This would be made up of Major General Winfield Hancock's "foot cavalry," the Second Corps. Its position along the Petersburg front stretched from the Jerusalem Plank Road back to the Appomattox River, so it had to begin moving up earlier, on the afternoon of October 26. Hancock's men were to mass along the Vaughan Road, "just outside the line of rear intrenchments." On the morning of October 27, they would march south and west; after crossing Hatcher's Run, well beyond the extreme right Confederate flank, they would strike west to the Boydton Plank Road, then snake north and west and north again to get astride the South Side Railroad. If Parke's attack succeeded, Hancock would be the one to tighten the noose about Petersburg by cutting both the South Side and the Boydton Plank Road; if Parke was unsuccessful, and plan B was put into effect, then Hancock was expected to turn the Confederate flank and continue his mission to wreck the railroad. Gregg's men, making up the fourth column, were to ride on Hancock's left to screen that flank and protect his rear.

There would also be action north of the James. Since his operations at Deep Bottom and the Crater, Grant had been choreographing offensive moves against both of Lee's well-separated flanks. Until now, these moves had alternated, with a jab north of the James being followed by a stronger blow south of it. This time, Grant was determined to make simultaneous advances above and below the river. "I wish you to demonstrate against the enemy in your front," Grant told Ben Butler on October 24, but he cautioned, "I do not want any attack made by you against intrenched and defended positions, but feel out to the right beyond the front, and, if you can, turn it." The main purpose of Butler's action, Grant stressed, was to "prevent re-enforcements [from] going from the north side of [the] James River to Petersburg."

Grant wrote to Julia on October 26, "To-morrow a great battle will probably be fought. At all events I have made all the arrangements for one and unless I conclude through the day to change my programme it will take place." He signed his letter, "Love and kisses for you and the children, ULYS."

Thursday, October 27
North of the James: Dawn

Benjamin F. Butler took pride in his intelligence-gathering operations. Piecing together newspaper reports, the results of POW questionings, and testimony from deserters, Butler concluded that the main Confederate defensive line confronting him reached northward from Fort Gilmer "only a short distance to the east of the Darbytown Road, certainly not farther than the Charles City Road." He planned his movements accordingly.

After its successful September 29 assault on Fort Harrison, Butler's Army of the James had entrenched (and still held) a line anchored to that river at Fort Brady. The line ran northward along the Varina Road, turned sharply north at Fort Harrison[1], and then bent protectively back toward the southeast along the New Market Road. Cavalry pickets stretched the Harrison spur of the line further north, to the Darbytown Road. Butler's plan mirrored the one Meade was using south of the James. Major General Alfred H. Terry's Tenth Corps would take the Ninth Corps's role in Butler's version: holding Butler's right, Terry's men would extend northward, moving the infantry pressure successively along the Confederate line from the New Market Road to the Darbytown Road to the Charles City Road. As Terry was accomplishing this, Major General Godfrey Weitzel's Eighteenth Corps (acting much as Hancock's Second would in Meade's scheme) was to swing first east and then north, march beyond Terry's right, and, it was hoped, turn the undefended Confederate left, which rested on the Williamsburg Road.

Butler's lead elements went into motion at 4:00 a.m. Over the next ninety minutes, some sixty-two regiments in seventeen brigades shrugged into marching order and left their warm, dry camps. A New Yorker in Terry's column recalled that it was a "dull, misty morning" and that not a "soul knew the meaning or direction" of the march. A reporter at headquarters affirmed that not "even an intimation was received that this corps was so soon to be engaged with the enemy." To further ensure secrecy, the publicity-conscious Butler had embargoed all news reports until the operation was well under way.

Not everyone marched uninformed, however. A New Hampshire officer in the Eighteenth Corps believed that the next twenty-four hours would "bring

---

1   Although officially renamed Fort Burnham, many Union soldiers continued to refer to it by its Rebel name, a practice that will be followed here.

the end of the war in Virginia." Colonel Edward Ripley, commanding a brigade in Weitzel's corps, felt that the "movement had every element of success in it, and I was never so sanguine in my life." Butler shared their optimism. Though not given to fanciful flights, he nonetheless took care to point out to his subordinates that the possibility existed, in his plan, "to enter Richmond." The "prize," declared this master politician, "is large."

Ulysses S. Grant, worried that Butler might allow his ambition to expand the scope of his assignment far beyond what was intended, sent his aide Cyrus Comstock to watchdog the Army of the James. Comstock knew that he had his work cut out for him. Butler, he believed, was "most unscrupulous and would stop at nothing to carry out his ends."

South of the James: Dawn

The 25 brigades containing the 154 regiments assigned to Meade's operation began gathering before dawn in encampments spread throughout the Union left. The mixed infantry and cavalry force was in motion shortly after 3:00 a.m.

Major General John Parke's men held the earthworks erected after the Peebles Farm fighting. These soldiers, in divisions commanded by brigadier generals Orlando B. Willcox, Robert B. Potter, and Edward Ferrero, marched south past Fort Cummings on the rear defensive line and then turned west toward the Boydton Plank Road. The man leading them, John Grubb Parke, had taken over the corps from Ambrose Burnside after the Crater affair. Although he had performed neither badly nor well at Peebles Farm, Parke was given a critical role in this operation. If he could achieve a breakthrough, then the Union plan would reap a rich harvest of victory; if he failed to break through, and was unable to freeze the enemy in place, then the other Union forces involved, especially Hancock's Second Corps, would be dangerously exposed. A perceptive staff officer, Major Charles Mills, assessed Parke as a "perfect gentleman, and an excellent soldier in every respect. His only fault is that he is too modest, and has not quite enough self-assertion or ambition for a very brilliant soldier."

Hancock's corps had come the farthest to be in this maneuver, and it also had the farthest to go. The Petersburg campaign had thus far been a succession of disappointments for Hancock, and his professional prospects, once bright, had grown noticeably dull. Reams Station had been the nadir. A staff officer who saw him three days after the debacle noted that "Hancock's spirits are very low & . . . he says . . . that he now has no confidence in the Corps." Hancock had played only a passive role in the late Peebles Farm actions, and this movement might well represent his last chance to redeem himself.

Hancock had increasingly fallen to quarreling with his subordinates at such stressful times, and his latest target had reopened some old wounds within his corps. The nucleus of his Third Division was the former Third Corps, an organization that had suffered serious losses at Gettysburg and then was broken up in a general consolidation of units that took place in early 1864. The Third Corps had taken its lead from its commander, Daniel E. Sickles, a cocky, profane, outspoken, baldy ambitious and political general who lost his leg and his corps on Gettysburg's second day. As evidence of their stubborn allegiance, these new members of the Second Corps (whose insignia was the trefoil, or clover leaf) still defiantly wore the diamond emblems of their old outfit.

On October 22, Brigadier General Regis de Trobriand—a Third Corps veteran now commanding a brigade in the Third Division—found himself arguing politics with Hancock. De Trobriand, not a McClellan man, wondered aloud about Little Mac's abilities "as a statesman and as a soldier." To illustrate his point, he referred to the 1862 Battle of Williamsburg, in which four generals, Hancock among them, had performed well but only one—Hancock—had been mentioned in McClellan's dispatches. "What can be thought of a general-in-chief capable of such conduct, and of such injustice towards three generals out of four?" de Trobriand mused, with perhaps more honesty than tact. Hancock bridled.

"I understand," he said. "You are all alike in the old Third Corps. In your eyes, you have done everything in this war, and all others nothing."

That meeting had left a bad taste in Hancock's mouth, and as he led his corps southward along the Halifax Road, then west along crossroads to the Vaughan Road, and then south again across Hatcher's Run, he nursed his anger and hoped for a victory.

The man who commanded the pivot position between Hancock and Parke was, in many ways, the most problematic of the three. Gouverneur Kemble Warren was something of a paradox. "The soldiers had confidence in General Warren," a Fifth Corps soldier later remembered, "and regarded him as a prudent and efficient officer." A staff clerk closer to him, however, complained, "Warren is an ugly man to deal with when he gets mad, which he frequently does, by the way."

That Warren still commanded the Fifth Corps was something of a surprise; twice already in this campaign he had come perilously close to being relieved. At

Spotsylvania, on May 12, Grant had actually empowered Andrew Humphreys to take over the Fifth Corps should Warren fail to carry out his orders. In the end, Warren did carry them out – just. Following the failures in June, George Meade had been set on either relieving Warren or charging him "for slowness in the last assault," but this storm also had passed. Warren had limited his actions to holding the Weldon Railroad in August, despite Grant's desire that he move out and attack. And at Peebles Farm, in September, Warren's leadership had been both prudent and lackluster. As Grant's military secretary, Adam Badeau, later observed, "Warren never seemed to appreciate the tremendous importance, in battle, of time. He elaborated and developed, and prepared, as carefully and cautiously and deliberately in the immediate presence of the enemy as if there was nothing else to do, and, while he was preparing and looking out for his flanks, the moment in which victory was possible usually slipped away."

Warren's men now marched after Parke's and Hancock's. Their commander's confidence in them was seriously limited; according to his anxious accounting, of the 11,000 Fifth Corps troops taking part in the operation, some 3,913 – or almost 36 percent – had "never fired off a musket." Yet Warren's aggressive support of Parke (should he break through) or Hancock (should his flank swing prove to be the primary blow) would be crucial to the success of either.

George Meade had assembled perhaps thirty-five thousand men in his strike force. The key would be how quickly each part of it performed its assigned task. "The success of the operation depended upon reaching the objective point by a rapid movement," Grant's aide Horace Porter stated plainly.

At daylight, gunfire began to crackle all along the Confederate lines southwest of Petersburg. It had begun.

From Army Headquarters, near Chaffin's Bluff, Robert E. Lee passed on what he knew to War Secretary James Seddon. A. P. Hill, in Petersburg, was reporting that "the enemy crossed Hatcher's Run this morning at Armstrong's Mill and Monk's Neck Bridge, force unknown." James Longstreet[2] minding the Richmond lines, added his information that "the enemy is moving to our left."

---

[2] Longstreet had been seriously wounded on May 6, at the beginning of the Overland campaign, and had resumed command of the First Corps only a week earlier, on October 19.

Lee concluded that there "thus appears to be a simultaneous movement on both flanks."

Beyond sending this report and others to Richmond, Lee would play no active role in handling these threats. In both cases, the corps commanders on site, and the forces on hand, would have to deal with matters on their own.[3]

North of the James: Dawn–1:00 p.m.

Alfred Terry's role was to deploy his 8,500-man Tenth Corps to "feel along the enemy's lines to the right as far as, at least, the Charles City road." In order to accomplish this, most of his units had to pull back to the east from their lines around Fort Harrison, march north to their assigned jump-off point, get into combat formation, and then press westward toward the Confederate defenses. Lee had begun work on this line after the failure of an October 7 effort to dislodge Butler's troops.

Brigadier General Adelbert Ames's division held Terry's right, lying loosely across the Charles City Road and covering most of the distance between it and the Darbytown Road. The skirmishers who fanned out ahead of Ames's slowly advancing brigades found the Confederate defensive positions lightly but obstinately held. A Connecticut soldier described the inconclusive fighting this morning as "opposition good and plenty."

The middle section of Terry's front was covered by Brigadier General Robert Foster's division, which was stretched just above and just below the Darbytown Road. "We encountered the rebel pickets about daybreak," one Pennsylvanian recalled, "and the ball was opened." Another soldier made note of a pattern that would be repeated all up and down Terry's line: "The skirmishers easily pushed the rebels back, but at length came upon their earthworks and were suddenly checked by a galling fire."

Holding Terry's left, forming a link between the Darbytown Road and the U.S. earthworks just north of the New Market Road, were the black troops under Brigadier General Joseph R. Hawley. A white officer in the 7th U.S.C.T. wrote that his men had to move through "almost impassable undergrowth" as they formed into battle lines. Once they were within sight of the enemy position, the black soldiers hunkered down to await further orders.

---

3 Lee now had sole responsibility for the Petersburg-Richmond front. P. G. T. Beauregard accepted command of the newly created Military Division of the West on October 2.

Butler's hopes this day were riding on the unlikely shoulders of Godfrey Weitzel. The West Point-trained officer had served loyally under Butler since 1862 and learned, firsthand, how generous the Massachusetts man could be to those he favored. Starting as a lieutenant of engineers, Weitzel had moved smoothly up the promotion ladder to brigadier general and now brevet (or acting) major general. His advancement may well have outpaced the self-confidence needed to command a corps of eight thousand or so men.

Speed was to be Weitzel's watchword, but his long column had not been given an easy route. Its circuitous trek ran northeast from Henry Cox's farm, along the Kingsland Road, to the New Market Road, west for perhaps a third of a mile, then north for about a mile and three-quarters to the Darbytown Road, west for more than two miles to the site of a Baptist church, north for a mile and a half to the Charles City Road for another short turn west, and then north for another three miles to the Williamsburg Road. Delays began almost immediately: the "ground, as it thawed, was very slippery for marching," one New Hampshire soldier complained.

The head of Weitzel's column stepped off at 5:00 a.m. It reached the Darbytown Road nearly three hours later and took two hours more to cover the distance to the Charles City Road. Here occurred the first hitch in Butler's neat plan: instead of clearing the way north as far as the Williamsburg Road, the Army of the James's cavalry division, led by Colonel Robert West in the absence of August Kautz, had turned west at the Charles City Road and developed the enemy's position, and was waiting there for further orders.

"[This] villainous Cavalry of Kautz's Division . . . failed us," one of Weitzel's brigade commanders declared. "Where they were to have been ahead two or three hours to have shrouded our march in a cloud of Cavalry dust, we actually ran over them and had to wait for them to get out of the way." Weitzel also discovered that Terry's Tenth Corps was not present in strength on the Charles City Road, as he had expected it to be. "I suppose that . . . you desire me to . . . move on," Weitzel wrote in a dispatch to Butler. "Please send me orders what you wish me now to do."

Butler's original instructions remained unchanged. Weitzel's column was to continue northward, with Colonel Samuel Spear's cavalry brigade skirmishing ahead of it. At about 1:00 p.m., some eight hours after the march had begun, Weitzel's lead elements reached the Williamsburg Road. There, it was hoped, they would find and turn an undefended Confederate flank.

Weitzel's first thoughts upon reaching the Williamsburg Road were of how he would find his way back. "You understand now that I am entirely lost from Terry," he warned Butler.

As he monitored events from his field headquarters on the Darbytown Road, Butler never took his eyes off the prize: Richmond. Even if Lee had somehow moved to block the Williamsburg Road, Butler reasoned, he must have greatly thinned his line to cover the four-mile extension of the front. Here was opportunity beckoning. "Shall I make a trial on this outstretched line?" Butler asked Grant.

Confederate lieutenant general James Longstreet, directing the defenses north of the James, was not fooled for a moment. He was alerted early by a "lively rattle of musketry" as Terry's men cautiously closed on his lines between Fort Gilmer and the Charles City Road. Longstreet watched closely to see if an assault was going to develop. "The delay in making more serious work told me that some other was the point of danger," he reasoned. He was convinced by midmorning that the "skirmishing between the New Market and Charles City roads was but a feint, and that the real move was to flank our position." Longstreet acted at once to meet this as yet unrevealed threat. Major General Charles Field "was ordered to pull his division out of the works and march for the Williamsburg road, [Major General Robert F.] Hoke to cover the line of Field by extending and doubling his sharp-shooters."

South of the James: Dawn-1:00 p.m.

"Early on the morning of October 27," remembered Horace Porter, "General Grant, with his staff, started for the headquarters of the Army of the Potomac, and rode out to the front, accompanied by Meade." (Another aide estimated that the total entourage—including horses, officers, and escorts—numbered "a hundred or more.") Continued Porter, "[the] morning was dark and gloomy, a heavy rain was falling, the roads were muddy and obstructed, and tangled thickets, dense woods, and swampy streams confronted the troops at all points."

Grant and Meade were at the Clements House by 9:00 a.m., about midway along Parke's front. A Ninth Corps soldier, watching the command group splash past, thought that Grant was "the plainest looking General on the field." Already the strong breakthrough envisaged in plan A seemed a forlorn hope. Although his columns had been assembled by 3:00 a.m. and were in motion thirty minutes later, Parke had not made a quick passage. "[The] troops had to move over narrow cross-roads, through dense woods, where felled timber and other obstacles retarded the advance," a Massachusetts officer in Willcox's division complained. Another soldier, in Robert Potter's division, remembered that they moved "over an uneven country, heavily wooded in parts, and quite unfamiliar to the officers in command." Such was the confusion that when Cutcheon's brigade (of Willcox's division) reached the Duncan Road, which ran north-south, it mistakenly established its skirmish line running from east to west, perpendicular to the enemy's position. Some thirty minutes were lost while officers sorted things out and reoriented the combat formation.

Mirroring the case north of the James, Confederate resistance here was initially pesky rather than substantial. Most of the veterans hardly noticed it, but the combination of dismal weather, confusion, and nearby gunfire stretched the nerves of the raw recruits and draftees in Parke's command. Skulkers became a problem in the 50th Pennsylvania, and the fresh-from-the-depot 39th New Jersey, nervously standing downwind in a supporting line, wondered what all the noises and smells meant. "[The] powder smoke was rather unpleasantly strong," recollected George C. Chandler of the 39th. "It was strange to see the effect of the odor on some of the boys' bowels."

Meade's chief of staff, Andrew Humphreys, was anxiously keeping tabs on the operation that it had taken the staff five busy days to plan. He was nudging Parke (on Meade's behalf) at 7:30 a.m. to "push ahead more rapidly and get into position."

Once they drew near to the Boydton Plank Road line, Parke's men discovered that it was anything but unfinished or unmanned. As Orlando Willcox later reported, "every point of the enemy's line [was] carefully felt and examined for a weak point; none such, however, was found."

In a message that was time-dated 9:00 a.m., Meade informed Hancock that Parke had been stymied by the enemy's works and that there was "no chance of his getting into them." Plan A was scuttled after less than four hours of daylight.

Parke's men began to entrench at around noon. Their part in the grand operation had come to an end; if anything was going to be accomplished, it was Hancock and Warren who would have to do it.

Grant, Meade, and their staffs left Parke's sector and rode south along the Duncan Road. They arrived at Warren's headquarters at Armstrong's Mill at about 10:30. Andrew Humphreys had ridden ahead of the group and, upon learning that Hancock was about to reach the Boydton Plank Road, ordered Warren to switch to plan B and send support to the Second Corps. The chief of staff then retraced his steps, met Grant and Meade on the road, and reported what he had done.

Warren's progress report was also disappointing. He had not wanted to march before daylight but had started in the dark as ordered. His men had floundered about in confusion; not until 5:30 had they begun to make even slow headway. At 9:00 a.m., his forward units had struck the enemy outposts north of Armstrong's Mill, and other troops, pushing westward above the mill, had been stopped by "a line of breastworks with abatis and slashing, which was strongly held." (So much for Union intelligence reports.)

With Humphreys's instructions for him to go to Hancock's support still ringing in his ears, Warren decided that the prudent thing to do was to size up the situation. He personally "made a reconnaissance of our front to ascertain the practicability of forcing the enemy back," returning to his headquarters just as Grant and Meade arrived. Meade proceeded to give Warren direct orders to help Hancock, but with one modification: instead of following the Second Corps's route, Warren's men were to cross south at Armstrong's Mill, pivot sharply back to the north, and move toward Hancock along the west bank of Hatcher's Run. Warren would be filling in the gap between Hancock's right and the rest of the Union army, and would also be in position to assist in any general Fifth Corps effort against the Confederate Boydton Plank Road line. Staff aide Robert Tilney was standing nearby when Grant exclaimed to Warren, "If there is an enemy's line there, I want to know it at once."

Brigadier General Samuel Crawford's men were closest to Hancock, so they got the call. "Leaving [Brigadier] General [Charles] Griffin in command, with his division and two brigades of [Brigadier] General [Romeyn] Ayres'," reported Warren, "I started with General Crawford to aid and direct operations in accordance with his movements." At 11:45 a.m., the first troops of Crawford's division crossed Hatcher's Run at Armstrong's Mill, on their way to Hancock.

"After a conference with Warren," continued Horace Porter, "Grant and Meade rode over to Hancock's front, and found that the enemy was there disputing the passage of Hatcher's Run at Burgess's Mill."

Hancock's column had moved out from bivouacs near Fort Dushane at 3:30 a.m. His line of march took him south along the Halifax Road to a point known as Wyatt's Crossing, where his spiky procession turned west to intersect with the Vaughan Road. By 6:00 a.m., Hancock's forward units had reached the Vaughan Road, where they angled south and, at the point where the road crossed Hatcher's Run, got into a serious firefight at about 6:30. The ford was held by a small party of Georgia cavalry in a "strong position across the road, having some works well defended by a slashing, and a deep ditch of water into which brush, &c., had been tangled." A quick rush by a skirmish line of Ohio and West Virginia soldiers was stopped cold. Then the division commander, Brigadier General Thomas Egan, ordered his leading brigade to deploy and clear the crossing. A New York soldier later recalled the action as the men "crossed the run, up to the armpits—the soldiers holding their guns and cartridge-boxes clear of the water—and charged up to and over the enemy's breastworks." "There was one regiment from Georgia that tried to hold the works," a Connecticut soldier added, "but was broken and scattered through the woods."

With the roadblock cleared, Hancock's column crossed south of Hatcher's Run and then turned west toward the Boydton Plank Road, using the road to Dabney's Saw Mill. "This advance of three miles was by a mere path, barely passable for guns, through as thick woods as I [have] seen this campaign," a Second Corps staff officer attested.

Brigadier General David McM. Gregg's cavalry division protected Hancock's left. "It was a most impressive sight to see the sombre looking columns moving so silently in that almost Egyptian darkness," one trooper observed. Gregg's men also found a firefight at their first important creek crossing, Monk's Neck Bridge; it took a dismounted charge by the 1st Maine and the 6th Ohio to scatter the Confederate pickets, from Brigadier General John Dunovant's South Carolina brigade. As his columns pushed steadily westward, Gregg learned from captured couriers that "General W. H. F. Lee's division of cavalry was in camp . . . on my left about three miles distant, and that General Butler's division was . . . in my front." Gregg's men moved west until they reached the Quaker Road, where they turned north. About a mile and a half up that road, a force of Confederate cavalry and artillery under Major General Wade Hampton had taken a strong position on the high ground overlooking Quaker Bridge.

Gregg was in a tight spot. Even as he ordered one brigade to force the crossing, word came that his rear guard was under attack. If Gregg failed to clear Quaker Bridge, he would be in real danger of being surrounded.

When his attack across Gravelly Run went forward, however, it revealed, to everyone's surprise, that the enemy was pulling back. Gregg quickly moved his whole command across Quaker Bridge and burned it behind him. It was not yet 1:00 p.m. when the weary cavalry column reached the Boydton Plank Road.

Hancock's infantry and artillery were deployed and under fire about a half mile ahead of the cavalry, toward Petersburg. The first units had come in sight of the Boydton Plank Road sometime after 10:30 a.m., but it had taken the better part of ninety minutes for the tail of the strung-out column to close up to the front. Perhaps a quarter of a mile north of where Hancock struck the plank road was the intersection with the White Oak Road, and a quarter of a mile beyond that was the site of Burgess' Mill, yet another crossing of Hatcher's Run. The moment Hancock's first regiment hove into view, it came under artillery fire from batteries posted near Burgess' Tavern (at the White Oak Road intersection) and farther west along the White Oak Road.

Hancock's men chased away the battery posted behind a toll-gate barricade near the tavern and advanced to that point. "[The] Virginia highway regulations were not observed," division commander Egan dryly reported. Just then, Gregg arrived with his riders, completing the junction of the two commands. Now, according to plan A (under which he was still operating), Hancock was to move west along the White Oak Road and then head north toward the South Side Railroad. "[Brigadier General Gershom] Mott's division was put in motion for the White Oak Road, and a brigade of cavalry sent down to relieve Egan in order that he might follow Mott," Hancock recalled. "At this juncture, about 1 p.m., I received instructions from the Major-General commanding to halt at the plank road."

Hancock redeployed his units to better cover the position while he waited for further orders. The men in one regiment, the 152nd New York, encountered a local farmer and ex-New Yorker named William Burgess. "Burgess sought protection at headquarters," noted the regimental historian, "while the slaves immediately started in rapid transit."

Wade Hampton was, as one admirer put it, "a born aristocrat. . . . Yet his manners and bearing with the troops were so thoroughly democratic, and his fearlessness in action so conspicuous, that no man ever excited more enthusiasm. He rode like a centaur, and possessed a form and face so noble that men vied with women in admiration of General Hampton."

Robert E. Lee had not acted immediately to fill the command vacancy created by "Jeb" Stuart's death, in May 1864; instead, he had allowed each of his cavalry division commanders to report to him directly. Lee ended this experiment on August 11 by placing the South Carolina-born Hampton in charge of the mounted arm of the Confederate forces.

Hampton's corps, which had been reduced by attrition and transfers from eight brigades to just five, was responsible for picketing the wide-open territory that lay off the Confederates' extreme right flank. Hampton's basic job was to give timely warning of enemy advances and to delay those advances long enough for the mobile infantry reserve, stationed in Petersburg, to come down the line and handle the problem.

To best accomplish this assignment, Hampton parked his brigades close enough to the major approaches so that they could quickly take blocking positions, but not so near that they could be surprised by hit-and-run raids. Nearest to the enemy, usually at stream crossings or other easily defensible points, Hampton stationed small mounted parties (the largest consisting of about thirty men) to give first warning. He also had a dismounted arm, the result of the Confederacy's policy requiring soldiers to furnish their own horses. With no centralized animal depot to make up his losses in horseflesh, Hampton found that more than a third of his men were without mounts. These troopers were grouped into battalions of foot dragoons under Major Henry Farley and used to garrison strong points along Hampton's defensive line.

Hampton later reported that early this morning, "the pickets on my whole line from the extreme left to Monk's Neck bridge road were driven in." "The general impression at first," wrote a South Carolinian in M. C. Butler's division, "was that the demonstration was merely against our picket lines." Hampton quickly identified two strong columns moving against him: infantry (Hancock) "crossing Hatcher's Run at Armstrong's Mill and the Vaughan Road," and cavalry (Gregg) crossing "at Monk's Neck Bridge." His small outposts were unable to do anything more than harass the advancing columns. "[The] enemy's overwhelming numbers and the rapidity of his movements . . . prevented us from managing a successful stand," one of Hampton's troopers admitted afterward.

Hampton had picked Quaker Bridge as the place where he would make a stand. He was confident that he could stall the enemy there long enough to allow W. H. F. Lee's division to come up from its camps a few miles further south and close on its rear. Hampton's one worry about the Quaker Bridge position was that it would leave his rear vulnerable to the infantry column that was moving past Armstrong's Mill. Accordingly, he ordered "[Brigadier General James] Dearing to bring his brigade from the trenches on the north side of Hatcher's Run . . . to protect my rear and guard the roads leading from Armstrong's Mill to the [Boydton] plank road."

The small force that Hampton used to stop the Yankees at Quaker Bridge did its job well. Two guns, commanded by Captain James F. Hart and supported by a mixed mounted and dismounted troop, took position on the high ground overlooking the "bridge across the boggy little stream of Gravelly Run. . . . A sharp fire of musketry was poured into this gallant section at a distance of 150 yards, but a steady fire of canister swept the enemy from the bridge until their efforts to force it had evidently become fruitless." Major Hart was seriously wounded in the engagement, eventually losing his leg as a result.

Then scouts reported that the enemy infantry column had passed Armstrong's Mill and was already nearing the Boydton Plank Road. Dearing either had not moved to cover this route or had been unable to do so, but in any case Hampton's position at Quaker Bridge was no longer tenable. He ordered a general pullback to the White Oak Road. "The skirmish line of the enemy was advancing up this road when we reached it," he later reported, "but it was quickly driven back. I then formed line of battle across this road, my left resting on Burgess' millpond, and repulsed an attack." The combat-wise cavalrymen dismounted and began building "temporary breastworks of fence rails, logs and such material as we could get."

Hampton had unerringly taken a blocking position across the very road that Hancock must use if he was to carry out his mission against the South Side Railroad.

Responsibility for the defensive sector now under attack rested with Major General Henry Heth. Heth, in turn, took orders from Lieutenant General A. P. Hill, but Hill was too sick to leave headquarters in Petersburg today, so tactical control belonged to Heth.

"I had," Heth wrote in his after-action report, "early in the morning of the 27th, under my orders, my own Division [consisting of Davis's, Mayo's, MacRae's, and Cooke's brigades] and two brigades of Wilcox's Division (Lane's and McGowan's), Dearing's Brigade of Cavalry, and about six or eight hundred dismounted Cavalry, the Cavalry occupying the extreme right of the line."

Gunfire began to sound along the whole Boydton line, from Church Road on its northern end to the point where it curled back against the east bank of Hatcher's Run. Fearing for his right, Heth sent Davis's men along the breastworks to reinforce the dismounted cavalry. Even as that order was being executed, Heth heard from Dearing that Wade Hampton wanted him to move out of the trenches to screen the Dabney's Mill Road. "I informed Gen. Dearing that it would be impossible for him to carry out his orders until I replaced his Brigade by an Infantry force," Heth noted. A staff officer, Major

Andrew R. Venable, was sent to inform Hampton of this decision, but he was captured at Armstrong's Mill before he could do so.

Dearing's and Davis's men gathered on the "plateau on the west side of Hatcher's Run, overlook[ing] Burgess Mill, and the bridge across the stream at this point." Earlier this season, Hampton's men had dammed Hatcher's Run farther east, causing the stream to flood the low-lying ground. If the Federals wanted to go north, they would have to use the bridge that Heth was blocking.

One more Confederate column was in motion on this flank today. Major General William Mahone had been ordered by A. P. Hill to take three of his brigades—Weisiger's, Harris's, and Sanders's—and "move with them to the junction of the Cox and Plank Road, there to await further orders." "When you reached that point," one of Mahone's aides later reminded him, "the artillery fire, in the direction of Burgess Mill, already heavy, seemed to be increasing in volume, and you marched toward it following the Plank Road."

More out of combative instinct than preplanning, Confederate units were converging on Hancock in a pattern that could well result in the destruction of the Second Corps.

North of the James: 1:00 p.m.-Dark

It was a little before 2:00 p.m. Godfrey Weitzel had just examined the Confederate earthworks dug across the Williamsburg Road. "I found them . . . ," he later reported, "defended by only three pieces of artillery and a small body of dismounted cavalry." It was the moment for decisive action, but Weitzel, worried about his links back to Terry's Tenth Corps and struggling to define a course of action to cover a situation not in Butler's comprehensive plan, vacillated. He ordered his lead division commander, Gilman Marston, to reconnoiter the enemy position. At about the same time, Weitzel detached Colonel John Holman's all-black brigade, with orders to proceed farther north along Nine Mile Road "until he should come within sight of the enemy's line, and then to halt and report to corps headquarters."

Weitzel probed the Williamsburg Road line for more than two hours and gingerly deployed his troops. Marston's division was placed north of the road, with Raulston's and Cullen's brigades in the advance and Patterson's in reserve. Heckman's division moved south of the road, with Ripley's brigade in the first line while Fairchild's and Draper's (temporarily attached to Heckman's command) supported. Also, two sections of Battery A, 1st Pennsylvania Light

Artillery, were placed one on either side of the road. They promptly began a slow, steady bombardment of the enemy line, eventually firing 523 rounds.

Federal veterans could see a foul-up coming. "We lay there [for] some time," a New Yorker recalled. "There seemed to be but few men in our front at first, but soon the Johnnies began to arrive. Horsemen were seen coming in with an extra man (and sometimes two) on their horses. The extra would dismount, the rider wheel about and soon return with another load." Nobody on Weitzel's staff knew the ground; it was only with the arrival of Lieutenant Colonel Joab Patterson, who had fought here with McClellan in 1862, that the Eighteenth Corps commander was able to ascertain exactly where he was. "Weitzel, if he was to attack at all, took too much time to reconnoiter and get into position," a New Hampshire soldier in Patterson's brigade complained.

James Longstreet used the delay to full advantage. The troops that he had ordered to this point after he became convinced that the actions to the south were a feint appeared in time to blunt Weitzel's first probes. "When the head of General Field's column got to the Williamsburg road the enemy's skirmishes were deployed and half-way across the field approaching our line," Longstreet recalled. "Just behind the trenches was a growth of pines which concealed our troops until a line of sharpshooters stepped into the works. Their fire surprised the enemy somewhat."

While the enemy hesitated, Field's men filed into the trenches that reached across the Williamsburg Road. The South Carolinians of Bratton's Brigade covered the area north of the road, and the Texans and Arkansans of Gregg's Brigade were to the south, with Law's and G. T. Anderson's brigades supporting. Also, as Longstreet reported, "Johnson's and Haskell's battalions of artillery were moved with the infantry and placed in suitable position along the line."

The Confederate defenders were spread out, but their position was excellent. One soldier in Bratton's Brigade remembered their being deployed at "intervals of three to six feet, and no reserves," while a Texan in Gregg's Brigade recalled that the "men stood in a single line, about eight feet apart." Nevertheless, Longstreet was confident. "The open [ground] in front of the breastworks was about six hundred yards wide and twelve hundred in length," he wrote, "extending from the York River Railroad on the north to a ditch draining towards the head of White Oak Swamp on the south. About midway of the field is a slight depression or swale of five or six feet depth." Any attacking force would be terribly exposed.

Godfrey Weitzel had arrived at the Williamsburg Road shortly after 1:00 p.m., leading a seven-brigade column. He sent forward just two of those seven brigades to assault the Williamsburg Road line at about 3:30 p.m.

Colonel Edgar M. Cullen's men attacked along the north side of the road. "We entered a ravine close up to the enemy's works and under fire," a soldier in the 118th New York later wrote. "We saw that the enemy in our front was in force and being rapidly reinforced, and we sent back for reserves, but none came."

"We whipped the Yankees at every point and whipped them badly," a member of the Confederate Palmetto Sharpshooters bragged. "[The] enemy melted away," another South Carolinian exulted. The Federals, as Charles Field later reported, "got in about three hundred yards of my line, when his troops, unable to stand the fire, threw themselves on their faces in a little depression of ground. A portion of Bratton's South Carolina brigade . . . went out in front of my division and captured four hundred or five hundred of them."

One New Yorker never forgot the moment when Bratton's men erupted from their entrenchments: "It was plain enough that we were outnumbered, and finally a confident enemy came out of his works on our flanks and . . . promised our destruction or capture. Word was given for every man to act for himself." James Estes was helping a wounded friend to the rear when the pair became the target of a Confederate battery that loosed two rounds at them. "The first shot struck ahead of us," Estes recalled. "The second shot plowed up the dirt just behind us, nearly throwing me down." Somehow, Estes got his friend to the aide station. "The 5th Maryland, 10th New Hampshire and 96th New York lost their colors," recounted one of the fleeing soldiers, "those of the 118th being saved by our tall colorbearer, Jo. Hastings, who ran with them as fast as his long legs could carry him."

Moving along the south side of the Williamsburg Road was Colonel Harrison S. Fairchild's brigade, of Heckman's division. Fairchild's composite New York and Wisconsin force charged over the "prostrate forms of the men" of Colonel Edward H. Ripley's brigade and advanced into the open plain, where Confederate rifle and cannon mercilessly raked the combat formation. Watching from the supporting line, Colonel Ripley—who had confidently expected to be the first Union officer to enter Richmond this day—now looked on aghast as Fairchild's advancing wave of troops "almost vanished" in the storm of enemy fire. Mixed in with his horror was grudging admiration for the enemy's discipline: "I never saw such magnificent musketry firing," he declared. The lead units somehow managed to get within 150 yards of the Rebel position.

"Here the line became so broken and cut up as to prevent its pushing forward any further, and the men fell upon the ground for protection," a New York officer afterward reported.

Twenty days earlier, Gregg's soldiers had been bloodily turned back in an attack on the Union lines north of Fort Harrison. John Gregg, their popular general, had been killed. Now it was payback time. "Our sharpshooters opened on them at about 700 yards, as also our artillery," Texan Thomas L. McCarty recalled. "As they advanced closer our whole line opened on them, repulsing them with heavy loss." "We repulsed the Yanks at all points easily," another Texas boy, Edward Crockett, wrote in his diary. "Their loss is considerable, ours almost none."

As the battered Federal lines recoiled, one impatient soldier in the 5th Texas clambered over the breastworks in solitary pursuit. Captain W. T. Hill yelled at the soldier to return. "But, Captain, these slow-going generals of ours are going to sit still until night comes, and let those Yankees get away," the soldier protested, continuing his lone chase. Other men scrambled to join him, and by this "unordered advance, several hundred Federals were captured."

The black brigade that Weitzel sent up the Nine Mile Road had an eventful passage. The column had moved only a mile when Rebel cavalry was observed and line of battle formed, with the 1st and 22nd U.S.C.T. south of the road and the 37th north of it. The advance was then continued, but once Colonel Holman spotted what he thought was a large cavalry formation closing on him, he ordered the 37th into a square—a formation better known on the field of Waterloo.

Holman ordered a charge upon catching sight of the enemy's earthworks. The 1st U.S.C.T. went in with a yell and took the position, while the 22nd, on its left, tangled in underbrush and raked by flank fire, "broke and commenced fleeing to the rear."

The Federals, wrote South Carolina cavalryman William Hinson in his diary, "got possession of our line on the . . . Nine Mile Road before we could reach it, but they were driven out by a bold dash [Brigadier General Martin W.] Gary made, having mounted his brigade. It was a bluff game and succeeded."

Along the lines between the Charles City and New Market roads further south, portions of Terry's Tenth Corps advanced at 4:00 p.m., "the object being to ascertain the strength of the enemy and his position." "It had been a dull, drizzly day, the men were chilled, and the long suspense, with nothing to awaken enthusiasm, promoted the result," a member of the 112th New York observed. "It was a terrible place to charge, through thick woods," added young

Hermon Clarke of the 117th New York. "We charged again, but it was useless and against the judgment of our officers. But old Beast Butler ordered it, and it must be done."

The assaulting columns, General Foster later reported, "were met with a severe fire of grape and canister and after advancing to within about eight rods of the enemy's works it was found impracticable to proceed." "We was ordered to halt and lay flat on the ground," Harrison Nesbitt, a soldier in the 203rd Pennsylvania, wrote to his wife afterward. "We lay a few moments and the grape and canister flew over our heads till it made everything rattle. . . . I tell you it took the tree tops off like nothing."

Confusion dogged the probe. The 9th Maine fired into the ranks of the 115th New York and then broke to the rear. A small Virginia household was caught between the two sides when the parents refused to abandon their house. It was afterwards found that "the mother and one of her children were numbered among the victims of cruel war."

At 5:00 p.m., recalled Foster, "I received orders to make no further demonstration that night."

Repulsed at every point, Ben Butler had had enough. "Shortly after dark I commenced to withdraw my command to the Charles City road," Godfrey Weitzel reported, "as directed by the general commanding." Terry's Tenth Corps also disengaged and pulled back.

South of the James: 1:00 p.m.-Dark

Grant, Meade, and their staffs reached the Boydton Plank Road at around 1:30 p.m. A quick survey of the situation revealed to Horace Porter that the enemy's "troops were strongly posted, with a battery in position directly in front of the head of Hancock's corps and another about 800 yards to our left." The large staff group made an attractive target for Confederate artillery, and soon, Porter continued, "the whistling of projectiles and the explosion of shells made the position rather uncomfortable." Even George Meade, normally imperturbable under fire, was heard to remark, "This is pretty hot; it will kill some of our horses." Not until one orderly had been slain and two others wounded did the party draw back under cover.

"Officers of Meade and Hancock now came up to report the situation," wrote Grant's military secretary, Adam Badeau. "Several of Grant's own aides-de-camp were sent to reconnoiter; and Hancock, who had been at the extreme front, also explained what he had seen. But the reports were conflicting."

A cavalry officer who was present later sketched the scene: "General Grant sits upon a rock at the foot of a huge oak tree—His orderly and Horse near him—and about him stood Generals Meade, Hancock, Gregg and Mott. . . . There was high tension easily to be seen—Genl. Grant was smoking— deliberately raising his cigar to his lips, taking a puff or several, then lowering it while he said something I could not understand." One of the things he said, at least according to a soldier standing within earshot, was "Hancock, you are too fast, your whole Corps will be captured."

Grant was growing impatient at the lack of accurate information. "It seemed," observed Badeau, "as if no eyes but his own could ascertain exactly what Grant wanted to know." Calling for Colonel Orville Babcock to accompany him, Grant "galloped down the road to within a few yards of the bridge [across Hatcher's Run]." Horace Porter stood among the onlookers, "expecting every minute to see the general fall." Grant's horse became entangled in a telegraph wire that lay carelessly coiled on the ground, and "Babcock, whose coolness under fire was always conspicuous, dismounted, and carefully uncoiled the wire and released the horse." When he rejoined the command party, the lieutenant general was clucked at by one aide for so exposing himself. "Well," Grant admitted with a smile, "I suppose I ought not to have gone down there."

Grant's personal reconnaissance confirmed everyone's pessimistic assessment. "The rebels were evidently in force north of the creek, with strong defenses," Badeau wrote. "Their entrenched line extended far beyond the point at which it had been supposed to turn to the north. . . . The contemplated movement was thus impracticable." Grant made up his mind shortly before 4:00 p.m. and "determined to withdraw to within our fortified lines." Also factored into that decision, according to Badeau, was Grant's feeling that with the presidential election only ten days off, "the enemies of the nation in the North were certain to exaggerate every mishap. Success at the polls was just now even more important than a victory in the field, and it would have been most unwise to risk greatly on this occasion."

Even though he had given up on his scheme to wreck the South Side Railroad, Grant still hoped to salvage some victory from the operation. Accordingly, he told Hancock to keep his "troops out where they are until toward noon to-morrow, in hope of inviting an attack." Grant was assured that one of Warren's divisions (Crawford's) was in the process of connecting with Hancock's right flank, thereby linking the Second Corps to the Fifth. "This was at four o'clock," Badeau noted, "and Grant and Meade rode back to

Armstrong's Mill, supposing the connection between Hancock and Crawford to have been made."

Even as Grant and Meade disappeared toward the southeast, a courier made his way west and north from Armstrong's Mill, carrying a dispatch for Hancock from Meade's chief of staff, Andrew Humphreys:

> THE SIGNAL OFFICERS REPORT THE MOVEMENT OF THE ENEMY'S TROOPS
> DOWN THE BOYDTON PLANK ROAD. NO DOUBT THEY ARE CONCENTRATING
> TOWARDS YOU.

Throughout that drizzly afternoon, while Grant pondered, Wade Hampton and Henry Heth plotted to destroy Hancock's corps. Hampton's cavalry held the White Oak Road, to the west of Hancock, and W. H. F. Lee's division was slowly pressing Gregg's rear guard (south of Hancock) along the plank road. North of Hancock, a mixed cavalry and infantry force held the high ground above Burgess' Mill. It had already successfully turned back several strong Federal probes pushed across Hatcher's Run.

"About 2 o'clock p.m.," Heth later reported, "I received a message from Lieut. Gen. Hill, through a staff officer, that Maj. Gen. Mahone had been ordered to report to me. . . . Gen. Mahone . . . reported to me about 3 o'clock with two Brigades. . . . It was evident to me that our only chance of driving the enemy from the Boydton Plank Road . . . was to attack him at once with all my available forces. Reinforcing Mahone's two brigades by MacRae's Brigade of my own Division, I directed Maj. Gen. Mahone . . . to attack the enemy, approaching him by . . . a blind path, or abandoned road [that] ran diagonally through dense woods, intersecting the Boydton Plank Road about 1/2 mile south of Burgess Mill."[4]

If all went according to plan, Hancock would be caught in a box. It would all turn on Mahone. Wade Hampton passed on the word that "as soon as the musketry told that our troops were engaged, [Major General M. C.] Butler was to charge with his whole line, while [Major General W. H. F.] Lee was directed to attack on the plank road."

Nothing was going right for Gouverneur Warren, Samuel Crawford, or the soldiers they commanded. Their advance along the west side of Hatcher's Run

---

4   Mahone's third brigade, Harris's, was delayed and arrived late.

took them into impossible terrain. "The denseness of the woods and the crookedness of the run caused great delays in the movement, causing breaks in the line and changes of direction requiring care to prevent confusion," Warren remembered. Lines of battle got separated from one another, flank connections were broken, and no one seemed quite sure of where they were going. When a small firefight broke out at 2:45 p.m., Warren's aide Major Washington Roebling noted, "[the] troops were a little scared, and many stragglers began running to the rear; but few bullets seemed to come from the enemy." By 4:00 p.m., Warren had seen for himself that Crawford's soldiers were "getting lost in great numbers, [with,] in fact, whole regiments losing all idea of where to find the rest of the division."

Over the course of nearly four hours, Crawford's men, thrashing ineffectually northward, had covered little more than a mile and a half. Hancock was less than a mile off Crawford's left, through the trackless forest, but he might as well have been on the moon. Then, shortly after 5:00 p.m., Crawford's skirmishers brought in some Confederates who had been escorting Union prisoners from Hancock's corps. These cocky Rebels bragged that the Second Corps "had been flanked by them and had broken and run."

After Grant and Meade departed, Hancock had moved to tidy up his position. He decided to secure the Burgess' Mill bridge and deployed Egan's division to do the job, supported by McAllister's brigade, from Mott's division (part of the old Third Corps). At the same time, he sent another two regiments from a diamond-emblemed brigade—Byron Pierce's—off into the woods on the right. Firing had been heard in that area for some time; at first it had been thought that it was Crawford's division moving toward a link-up, but Hancock was no longer sure of that. Pierce's two regiments were to "advance well into the wood and ascertain what was there."

The men had hardly disappeared into the gloomy forest before the gunfire there crescendoed to a throaty roar, leaving, as Hancock later wrote, "no doubt that the enemy were advancing."

The time was about 4:30 p.m.

The landscape through which William Mahone funneled his brigades was nearly as bad as that entangling Crawford, but the combative Virginia officer drove his men forward nonetheless. "We were put in line of battle without giving the command, only made signs," a soldier in the 12th Virginia wrote later, "and it was a thick swampy piece of ground [and] as much as we could do to get through the thick undergrowth."

Two of Mahone's brigades—Weisiger's and MacRae's—made it out of the woods and onto the open ground that lay midway between Hancock's northern line, fronting Burgess' Mill, and his southern one, facing W. H. F. Lee's men. In short order, the two Yankee regiments that had been sent to scout the woods were scattered, a Federal battery (Metcalf's) posted near the forest edge was overrun, and the rest of Pierce's brigade was shoved back toward the plank road. Exuberant Confederates rounded up scores of prisoners and hauled away the colors of the 63rd Pennsylvania and the 105th Pennsylvania. Signaled by Mahone's guns, Hampton's battle lines surged forward along the White Oak Road, while W. H. F. Lee's command increased the pressure on Gregg.

The boys in blue later called this battle the Bull Ring or Bull Pen. A New Yorker remembered, "we were completely surrounded, and in so small a cleared spot that the balls from the rebel lines would pass clear over us or stop in our lines on opposite sides." When ordered by Hancock to start digging some breastworks, one confused Federal asked, "General, which way will you have them face?"

Winfield Hancock remained bitter to the end of his life about the failure of Parke and Warren to "hold the enemy close to their entrenchments in their fronts. . . . The troops that attacked me were taken from the entrenchments in front of Generals Parke and Warren, South and East of Hatcher's Run."

Any bile that Hancock may have tasted as Mahone's men burst against his right rear flank, however, was instantly neutralized in a whirlwind of action. Mahone's was a deceptive success. His two brigades had thrust sharply into the east side of Hancock's boxlike perimeter, but unless Confederate reinforcements were available, and unless the other points of attack against Hancock succeeded, Mahone's men would themselves be dangerously isolated and vulnerable.

The task Heth had given to Dearing's cavalry and Davis's infantry was to press across Hatcher's Run to strike the northern face of Hancock's perimeter. "This attack," Heth later reported, "was feeble and without result." W. H. F. Lee's division, pressing Gregg from the south, was also making slow headway. Hampton, moving against the west side of Hancock's box, put everything he had into his action. "The firing was terrible," a trooper in Butler's Division declared. "The battle was now furious," another remembered, with "cannon, and rifles belching forth streams of lead."

Officers and aides dangerously exposed themselves in order to urge their men on, and Union counterfire took a terrible toll on the brave young men. Lieutenant Colonel Robert J. Jeffords, commanding the 5th South Carolina

Cavalry, "fell dead, shot through the head." Two of Wade Hampton's sons served on his staff this day. Lieutenant Preston Hampton was returning to headquarters from the firing line when he was "shot in the left groin, from which he died almost instantly." Shortly thereafter, General Hampton rode up, dismounted, and, ignoring the chaos about him, lifted Preston's head and kissed him, saying, "My son, my son." Moments later, Brigadier General M. C. Butler rode up and saw that something was wrong with Hampton. "I inquired who was wounded," Butler recalled. "I can never forget his expression of anguish and distress as he drew his hand across his forehead, and replied 'Poor Preston!' . . . . Near where we were talking he noticed a one-horse wagon under a shed. He turned and said, 'Butler, I wish you would have that wagon pulled around and have the body moved out of the range of fire.' Wiping away the tears of his pathetic affliction, he returned to his post of duty." Even as these events were occurring, another shot struck Hampton's other son-aide, Wade, seriously wounding him.

Despite these sacrifices, Hampton's attack did not gain any significant ground, nor did it tie down many of Hancock's troops. The Federal Second Corps commander was able to choreograph his own converging attack on Mahone's two brigades. Ironically, it was the old Third Corps that led the way.

Colonel Robert McAllister simply about-faced his battle line and advanced against Mahone's right from the north. "We charged down the hill; the enemy became panic-stricken and gave way," McAllister wrote to his wife after the battle. "We rushed on and received the enemy's front and flank fire. We wavered and fell back. The enemy took courage and followed. We reformed and rolled in the musketry upon them."

It was Brigadier General de Trobriand's men who stood firm and then counterattacked across Mahone's front. "[Up] we went," de Trobriand later wrote, "driving the enemy before us, and clearing the whole of the open field." Portions of Gregg's cavalry division also pitched in, coming up on Mahone's left.

"[We] discovered that we had only knocked a gap out of the Yankee line," a soldier in the 11th North Carolina noted, "and that the two ends were closing together behind us." MacRae, who formed Mahone's right flank, had begun this attack "with the understanding that he should be promptly reinforced by one or more brigades. . . . Awaiting reinforcements, which long since ought to have been with him, he held his vantage ground at all hazards, and against enormous odds. No help came whilst his men toiled, bled and died." "[We] were perfectly surrounded," another 11th North Carolina soldier later wrote to the *Charlotte*

Bulletin, "but we did not falter; we about faced and cut our way out." In the confused fighting, two Tarheel regiments—the 26th and the 47th—left their flags in Yankee hands.

Weisiger's Virginia brigade, on MacRae's left, fared no better. "This fight was rather disastrous to our regiment," William H. Stewart, of the 61st Virginia, declared. He and his friend Tom Murphy found themselves caught with Yankees closing in on all sides. "Tom, let's get out of here," Stewart yelled, and the two raced back into the woods. Another Virginian, this one in the 12th, remembered that when "our men fell back into the woods from which they made this assault, many lost their way in the thick undergrowth, some being captured, others narrowly escaping capture."

Hancock closed his account of this fighting by noting that the "enemy in front had hardly been repulsed when the firing in rear became so brisk that I was obliged to send to General Gregg all of his force I had used to meet the attack in front as well as another of his brigades, which I was about putting in on my right to cover the Dabney's Mill road, constantly threatened by the enemy." Darkness finally put an end to the combat, which would be variously known as the Battle of Boydton Plank Road, of Hatcher's Run, or of Burgess' Mill.

North of the James: Aftermath

The movement of the Eighteenth Corps back to its lines was less a nocturnal tramp than a refugee procession. "This march," Weitzel reported, "owing to the rain, the intense darkness, the muddy and narrow roads, was the most fatiguing and trying one that ever I have known troops to undertake." "Everything is mixed together," a soldier in the 13th New Hampshire wearily observed. "Utter confusion reigns; teams, artillery, ambulances and infantry all jumbled together, and all heavily loaded; mud and water in many places knee-deep in the roads, the night pitchy dark, the rain pouring in torrents . . . wagons are tipped over and smashed . . . horses and mules [grow] ugly, drivers hurrying, noisy, swearing, quarreling, mad." A Confederate scout who crossed this ground after Weitzel's men had passed provided the editor of the *Richmond Daily Examiner* with a "lively description of the roads and fields covered with clothing, small arms, knapsacks, and a truly incredible quantity of ammunition—enough, he thinks, on this part of the field alone to last our whole army for a week."

The Eighteenth Corps finally bivouacked near the Charles City Road, where it rested until 6:00 p.m. on October 28. Weitzel insisted in his after-action report that "I did more than I was ordered to do. I knew my orders were simply to make a demonstration. I probably made a more lively demonstration than was intended."

This "lively demonstration" cost the Eighteenth Corps 1,064 casualties, a high proportion of which, 63 percent, were either captured or missing. The *New York Herald's* William H. Merriam specifically mourned the passing of Captain E. Darwin Gage in the 148th New York. The reporter praised him for the "purity and elevation of his character no less than for his energy and devotion to the cause," and assured his readers that the dying officer spent his final moments on earth "disposing of his personal objects, sending word to this family and friends at home, and attending to the last offices of religion."

In carrying out its part of the operation, Terry's Tenth Corps lost 526 men, with 13 more from the cavalry. The total Union losses for the October 27 fighting at Fair Oaks and Darbytown Road were 1,603; the reported Confederate losses were 64.

Cyrus Comstock, Grant's observer at Butler's headquarters, was apoplectic over the day's events. "Grant's order was imperative that corps commanders should be instructed not to attack entrenched defended lines. . . . This order was not obeyed, at least in spirit—the spirit of Butler's written & verbal orders being to do something." In his only written report on the fighting this day, Butler wired Grant:

```
WE HAVE NOT BEEN ABLE TO TURN THE ENEMY'S LEFT, ALTHOUGH WEITZEL
HAS DEMONSTRATED TO THE LEFT OF THE WILLIAMSBURG ROAD . . .
TERRY HOLDS FROM DARBYTOWN TO OUR INTRENCHED LINES ON THE NEW
MARKET ROAD. HAVE YOU ANY ORDERS?
```

South of the James: Aftermath

Army Headquarters at Armstrong's Mill was leaving the final decision with Hancock: he could withdraw tonight or stand and fight tomorrow. A second Fifth Corps division, Ayres's, had been ordered to reinforce Hancock, but this unit had moved no closer than Armstrong's Mill, and Crawford's men had yet to achieve their promised linkup. "If you think that with Crawford and Ayres joined to your troops you can attack successfully, the commanding general desires you to do so. If not, you can withdraw as directed, and during the night if you consider best," Hancock was told.

One of the aides carrying messages between Hancock and Meade found the Army of the Potomac's commander and his chief of staff at dinner. "I was invited to eat with them and did so," he later recounted, "and pretty soon General Warren arrived and also sat down to supper. I thought this was very considerate of Generals Meade and Humphreys . . . considering my rank and also my hunger, fatigue, and wetness."

Hancock spent the early part of this night moving among his various commands, assessing their condition and combat status. Riding with him was George Meade's son and aide, "in order that General Meade might know all the facts with confidence." Hancock wanted to be absolutely certain there would be no misinterpretation of his actions.

It was, Hancock later wrote, "dark and raining heavily" as he made the rounds. The first stop was at Gregg's headquarters, where the cavalry officer reported that the ammunition supplies for his "breech loading regiments were exhausted entirely and if an amount came he could not issue it before daylight, which promised to be the hour of danger." Checks with the infantry commanders confirmed that their "breechloading regiments (which were few) were practically out of ammunition—[and] the others much depleted."

The narrow, muddy track back to Dabney's Mill was Hancock's lifeline. Already it was "seriously threatened by the enemy, and was becoming very bad." Almost every courier who rode the route had tales to tell of near capture, and some had simply disappeared into the stygian woods, not to be heard from again. The road was a one-way proposition: Hancock could either move supplies and reinforcements forward along it or pull the Second Corps back over it. Entering into Hancock's decision was the fact that he had little faith that Warren's men would join him in time to meet the Confederate onslaught he expected at dawn. "I was of the opinion that the necessary preparations to meet successfully the enemy's attack in the morning could not be made," Hancock later wrote. "Reluctant as I was to leave the field, and by so doing lose some of the fruits of victory, I felt compelled to order a withdrawal rather than risk disaster by awaiting an attack in the morning only partly prepared."

Hancock's movement back to Dabney's Mill began around 10:00 p.m. Mott's division was first, followed by Egan's. Gregg pulled his men back along the Quaker Road, after first rebuilding the bridge he had burned during his advance. These withdrawals were carried out unopposed. The last Federal pickets slipped off the battlefield at 1:00 a.m., October 28.

Hancock did not have enough ambulances available to carry all his casualties, and there was no time to order up extras from Dabney's Mill. Regis de Trobriand was deeply moved by the wounded he saw who "lay along the edge of the road, and, suspecting the fate which awaited them, prayed us with moanings to take them with us. I heard soldiers saying, 'Do not trouble yourselves; be a little patient. The ambulances are going to return; we are here to wait for them.' They well knew that there was nothing of the sort, but they endeavored to spare the poor creatures a few hours of anguish."

"What a march we experienced!" one of Egan's men exclaimed. "Rain had fallen during the latter part of the day and the ground was soft in the timber, and badly cut up by the moving cavalry and artillery that had passed before us." "The mud was ankle- and sometimes knee- deep along the miserable road," added a soldier from the 10th New York.

Even nature seemed to rub it in. According to a reporter present the miseries of October 27 were followed by a morning of October 28 that was "clear and cloudless, with an autumnal glory I have seldom seen equaled." He may well have been the only one there detached enough to enjoy the view.

The Second Corps suffered 60 percent of the Army of the Potomac's total casualties in this operation—1,058 out of an overall loss of 1,758. Other units suffered far less: Fifth Corps, 279; Ninth Corps, 150; cavalry, 271. The Confederate loss was approximately 1,274.

Even as the fighting sputtered out around Burgess' Mill, gunfire flamed alive along the siege lines southeast of Petersburg. Brigadier General Nelson Miles, commanding the Second Corps troops that had been left behind, had decided that a little diversion was in order. Just at dark, a raiding party of a hundred men, led by Captain Jerry Z. Brown, wriggled across the no-man's-land "opposite Fort Morton near the Crater." A historian of the 148th Pennsylvania wrote, "Having formed his men for the desperate work, just at dusk [Brown] dashed forward, thrust aside the dense abatis, drove in the opposing pickets, and scaled the ramparts, carrying a strong work, capturing four commissioned officers and more men than he had led to the encounter." Miles's own report related the end of the affair: "A regiment of the enemy, who had entered a work on the enemy's right of the one thus occupied, immediately charged into it and, by force of superior numbers, our men were driven out, fighting gallantly."

There was more. At 8:30, another raiding party (this one consisting of 130 men and commanded by Lieutenant Colonel D. F. Burke) captured a portion of the Confederate picket line opposite Union Fort Sedgwick. The Federal raiders promptly withdrew, but their action set off a "furious cannonade" that lasted throughout the night. "During this expedition," a member of the 5th New

Hampshire complained, "not an officer or man of the regiment had a moment of sleep."

Miles's casualties for these diversions were four killed, twenty-five wounded, and thirty-eight missing, for a total of sixty-seven. The report of Confederate major general Bushrod Johnson listed the total Rebel losses—killed, wounded, and missing—at fifty-two.

Southern soldiers prowling the Burgess' Mill battlefield the next day saw nothing orderly in Hancock's withdrawal. "Their retreat was a perfect stampede," one crowed. "Their dead were left unburied, hundreds of wounded were abandoned, guns, cartridge boxes, ammunition . . . strewed the ground; three of their ambulances were burned and their videttes were abandoned to be captured." One pragmatic South Carolinian "spied a new red flannel shirt on one of the enemy's dead. Dismounting, he began to disrobe him. . . . As he turned him over on his face he found very little of the Yankee or the shirt either, as his whole back had been torn off by a shell. . . . The rest of us seemed to think it was a good joke and had a hearty laugh at his expense."

Henry Heth had decided to renew the assault this day. During the night he "visited Gen. Hampton's camp and a combined plan of attack was agreed upon." However, as Heth later reported, "On the morning of the 28th it was discovered that the enemy had retreated during the night." Among the nonmilitary decisions made this day was Wade Hampton's determination that once his wounded son Wade recovered, he would be assigned elsewhere. "The agony of such a day, and the anxiety and the duties of the battlefield—it is all more than mere man can bear," the elder Hampton explained.

The face-saving began almost immediately. All the Union dispatches referred to the action north of the James as a simple demonstration, while the fighting south of the river was defined as the result of a "reconnaissance in force." Hancock's action near Burgess' Mill, Grant reported to Washington, was a "decided success. He repulsed the enemy and remained in his position, holding possession of the field until midnight, when he commenced withdrawing."

Few soldiers bought the official line. "Our generals say that they went forth in search of information and returned satisfied," a Rhode Island soldier grumbled. "We suspect the enemy was found in too heavy a force to battle successfully." Four days after the fighting, the Fifth Corps artillery chief, Charles Wainwright, wrote in his diary that the "newspapers try to make the best of our failure last week, taking their cue from Grant's dispatch to Washington in which he calls the move a 'reconnaissance.' This affords a vast deal of amusement in the army, considering there were greater exertions and preparations made for this expedition than any previous one." "As the Mine was to be termed an ill-conducted fizzle," observed Meade's aide Theodore Lyman, "so this attempt might be called a well-conducted fizzle."

Southern newspaper accounts were no less unforgiving. "This was no reconnaissance in force," trumpeted the *Columbia* (Georgia) *Daily Sun.* "It was a serious and determined effort to take Richmond. Grant . . . was notably 'flummoxed.' " From Petersburg, the *Express* added a bit of prophetic irony: "It will probably serve to furnish a glorious theme for a bulletin from [War Secretary Edwin] Stanton, and Grant will undoubtedly report it as a successful reconnaissance."

In his report on these operations, Winfield Hancock lavished praise on the actions of Egan's division while virtually ignoring the substantial contribution made by Mott's Third Division—the old Third Corps. "When a landscape-painter finds his subject for a painting in nature," reflected Regis de Trobriand, "on transferring it to his canvas, he puts in the lights and shadows as pleases him. General Hancock's report was treated somewhat in this manner, and, in the division of light and shade, the relief was for the Second Division, and the background for the Third."

The tension was palpable at Union Headquarters at City Point on November 8, 1864: "Anxious about election," Grant's aide Cyrus Comstock noted in his diary. Grant, meanwhile, did his best to heighten that anxiety. Throughout the evening, he insisted on reading aloud the election returns as they were received from Washington; each time, he solemnly announced that McClellan was leading. Many officers went to bed convinced that "Little Mac" had won. Only after midnight did Grant confess that he had been pulling their legs all along and that, in fact, Lincoln was the clear winner.

When the last ballot was counted, Lincoln had won the popular vote, with 2,203,831 to McClellan's 1,797,019. The disparity was greater in the Electoral College, which went to Lincoln by a margin of 212 to 21. The soldiers, too, backed the incumbent administration, voting 4 to 1 for "Old Abe." Regiment after regiment in the armies of the Potomac and the James showed Lincoln pluralities; typical were the tallies of the 1st Maine Heavy Artillery, where the vote was Lincoln 170, McClellan 72; the 20th Michigan, Lincoln 153, McClellan

35; the 2nd New Hampshire, Lincoln 65, McClellan 4; the 48th Pennsylvania, Lincoln 200, McClellan 30; and the 36th Wisconsin, Lincoln 86, McClellan 51.

"Upon that announcement, not one, nor three, nor nine cheers went up, but cheer upon cheer until they united in one continuous roar, mingled with the sound of drums and the notes of trumpets," wrote a Pennsylvania soldier who used the name "Gamma." Picket firing near Fort Sedgwick was suspended for a while on the night of November 9, "the rebels being extremely anxious to learn the result of the election of the previous day." The "discussion" soon "degenerated into the free exchange of abusive personalities, and the truce was soon brought to a termination by a sudden volley from the rebels."

"Lincoln's triumph was more complete than most of us expected," a Richmond official admitted. "The Yankee election was evidently a damper on the spirits of many of our people, and is said to have depressed the army a good deal." David E. Johnston of the 7th Virginia saw his friend A. C. Summer sitting despondently on the ground after hearing the news. When asked why he was so discouraged, Summer replied, "Don't you know that Abe Lincoln is re-elected and has called for a million men, and that Jeff Davis says war to the knife? What shall we do?" Johnson considered his friend's rumination a "pertinent inquiry."

U.S. Grant concluded in a letter to a friend that the "overwhelming majority received by Mr. Lincoln and the quiet with which the election went off will prove a terrible damper to the Rebels. It will be worth more than a victory in the field both in its effect on the Rebels and in its influence abroad."

October 27 was the last field operation for **Winfield Hancock**. Citing his unhealed Gettysburg wound, Hancock took a leave from the service on Thanksgiving Day, November 26. He turned over command of the Second Corps to Meade's chief of staff, Andrew Humphreys. Following his recuperation, Hancock succeeded Sheridan in command of the Middle Department and oversaw the closing operations of the war in the Shenandoah Valley. "Had I reached the South Side Railroad," he wrote afterward to his trusted aide Francis Walker, "I would have been made a Major General in the regular army, as I was informed. (I was then a Major General of Volunteers.)" Hancock received his coveted promotion in 1866.

Godfrey Weitzel began a public-relations counterattack immediately following the October 27 action north of the James. He reported the next day to Butler that a "Tenth Corps surgeon has circulated a report that my column was repulsed at Williamsburg road. . . . I will report him." On November 17, Weitzel was made a full-rank major general (up till then, he had held a brevet rank). He commanded the troops that first entered Richmond in April 1865.

Benjamin Butler passed over the affair of October 27 almost without comment in his 1,154-page autobiography. His fascination with dramatic schemes eventually proved his undoing. From August 10 to December 30 of 1864, Butler kept hundreds of troops and prisoners busy digging a canal across Dutch Gap, a narrow neck of land on the James River, in the hope of bypassing some formidable Confederate batteries. The final earthen bulkhead was blown on December 31, resulting in what one observer called a "perfect Fizzle!" Not until April 1865 would the Dutch Gap canal be deemed usable for river traffic. A more serious misadventure also took place in December, when Butler directed Union operations against Confederate Fort Fisher, which guarded the entrance to the Cape Fear River in North Carolina. Butler's attack plan called for a ship loaded with gunpowder to be grounded near the base of the fortress and then blown up; the explosion would, it was thought, destroy the fort. The bomb-ship did little more than blacken the fort's walls, however, and Butler's expedition failed. Grant relieved him on January 7, 1865.

Part III

THE LAST WINTER OF WAR

A picket in front of Fort Damnation (Mahone). *A. Waud*

Chapter Twelve

"Starvation Parties"

Petersburg, Fall – Winter 1864

Once the weather turned colder and it became apparent that the active campaigning was ending for the season, Petersburg's refugees began to come back. The *Petersburg Express*, in a passage full of double meanings, observed in September that a "large number of our citizens who left during the early part of the warm season to escape the heats of the summer solstice, have returned."

They found a Petersburg that was much changed. For one thing, the crime rate was up. "Never were robberies so frequent in this community and suburbs," the *Express* had editorialized in July, spotting a trend that showed no signs of abating in the fall and winter. A North Carolina soldier, returning from leave with a collection of food bundles for his regiment, had them stolen from him the instant he and his traveling companions lay down for a short nap. "I would advise all soldiers who arrive with packages entrusted to their care to keep their eyes wide open, and if any should be so unfortunate as to have gold plugs in their mouths, be sure and keep the latter tightly closed, if they desire to retain their masticators," he warned.

The city fathers increased the police force, and a small military detail was also assigned to help keep order. Still, the crime wave grew. Particularly preyed upon were civilians forced to travel the three miles north to Dunlop's Station—which was as close to the city as the Richmond & Petersburg Railroad could operate. The *Express* made a recommendation: "We advise all who walk to Dunlop's by night or day, to go well armed."

The behavior of Petersburg's children was also affected by the siege, as numbers of young people began to react to the violence all around them and the constant threat of sudden death. As late as March 1865, the *Express* reported that "numerous complaints reach us daily of the inconveniences and danger to which citizens are subjected by boys, singly and in crowds, who indulge in the practice of throwing stones about the city. This practice is now carried to such an extent as to have become a perfect nuisance."

Food was the target of choice for many thieves. Shops were frequently broken into, and farm wagons entering Petersburg via the western corridor were waylaid and plundered. "If the farmers cannot be protected in bringing their supplies to market, our people must suffer," the *Express* admonished. Back yard gardens proved such tempting targets that a tongue-in-cheek editorial for the *Petersburg Daily Register* was slugged "Migratory Vegetables."

For the most part, however, food did make its way into the city, and throughout the siege, supplies were more than adequate. But the skyrocketing prices charged for those provisions made siege life difficult for many Petersburg households. "With all our starvation we never ate rats, mice or mule-meat," Sarah Pryor proudly declared. "We managed to exist on peas, bread, and sorghum. We could buy a little milk, and we mixed it with a drink made from roasted and ground corn. The latter, in the grain, was scarce."

A trip to the town market was a daunting experience. "Here," reported the *Express's* town observer, "mingled in one promiscuous, struggling, seething mass, may be seen the old and the young, the grave and the gay, the married and single, white and black, bond and free, male and female, soldier and civilian, beautiful young maidens and buxom matrons, all intent on the one very important object, of procuring something to comfort the 'inner man'."

For refugee families with no relations in town, or those left behind by deserting soldiers, starvation threatened. A visitor named R. P. Scarbrough wrote in January 1865, "I have since I have been around Petersburg, seen many poor women and children compelled to go among the soldiers and beg for bread to eat."

Perhaps the most serious crisis facing Petersburg this winter was the lack of heating supplies. The city council petitioned General Lee in early October "to furnish for the use of the poor of this City 1000 cords of wood at such price as he may think right." When Lee was unable to supply this need (though he did personally contribute $200 for Petersburg's poor), the town elders ordered that all street carts and "hands...not otherwise employed" be used to procure wood. With two armies busy deforesting the city's outskirts, wood could be obtained only at great and greater distances from town, and at higher cost. By January 1865, the town's Wood Committee had overspent its budget by $35,000. Two months later, the *Express's* editor lamented that "nearly every little foot bridge about town has lost half of its timber, while some of them have entirely disappeared. They are stolen at night, and burned as fuel."

Despite these hardships, Petersburg's spirit remained unbowed. "During the winter of 1864-'65," Dr. John Herbert Claiborne wrote, "amidst the sorrow and the suffering, which can hardly be exaggerated, gaiety amongst the young people was rife. There were parties, starvation parties, as they were called, on account of the absence of refreshments impossible to be obtained; ball followed ball, and the soldier met and danced with his lady at night, and on the morrow danced the dance of death in the deadly trenches out on the line." As late as March 17, a foreigner in town attended one gathering and noted that the "manners of these fine fellows to the Ladies was very pretty & their reception most cordial!"

Nonetheless, a great deal of pain lay underneath the gaiety. Dr. Claiborne recalled that a lady still in mourning was present at one ball. "Truly war has no softening or benignant influences," he declared. "If it cultivates any virtues they are the sterner and ruder virtues of courage—endurance & stoicism." "It is passing strange—this disposition to revel in times of danger and suffering," Sarah Pryor reflected afterward. "I think all who remember the dark days of the winter of 1864—1865 will bear witness to the unwritten law enforcing cheerfulness." Christmas 1864 was especially grim, prompting a city native serving on the trench lines to write his wife that the "Yankees have blockaded Old Santa Claus so effectually as to cut off his usual supplies."

Some old routines returned. "Our streets…," the society-oriented *Express* wrote in late November, "were crowded from morning till night—We have not for months before, seen such a mass of people abroad. A large number of ladies were out shopping and promenading, who added greatly to the interest of the moving panorama. Where there was so much beauty displayed, there were, of course, many spectators to behold and enjoy it." Libraries continued to serve patrons, though their hours were anything but predictable, and soldiers were allowed to take out books for a charge of $1 apiece.

Adding to that enjoyment was the presence of music in the air. "The nights are now beautiful," the *Express* enthused in mid-October, "and various military bands around the city are rendering them still more attractive, by the sweet music they discourse." Concert announcements appeared regularly. Mechanic's Hall was one often-used venue; another was the Virginia Hospital, where several charity recitals were given. "Every effort will be made, and no pains or expenses spared in making this one of the most select entertainments of the season," a typical advertisement promised. North Carolina officer Henry Chambers attended one Mechanic's Hall function in late December and pronounced it a "very good one." Another performance, this a Virginia Hospital benefit by "several accomplished musicians connected with the Army of Northern Virginia," was, reported the *Express*, "a complete success."

The war also accelerated the pace of social relationships in this otherwise slow-moving Southern town. "A great many of the soldiers are marrying around and in Petersburg," R. P. Scarbrough wrote, "some for life, some for the war and some for one winter only."

With the exception of a brief pause in early August, the shelling of the city had continued on a regular, if sporadic, basis. Diarist A. J. Leavenworth, writing on November 30, summed up the past month as "nothing remarkable—except frequent shelling on the lines & an occasional shell sent into the city, TO-DAY AT ABOUT 2 O'CLOCK A SHELL KNOCKED OFF ONE OF THE MINARETS FROM THE STEEPLE OF THE BAPTIST CHURCH."

Another resident, in a letter to his mother dated December 6, cataloged the damage to the town: "[Most] of the houses on Bollingbrook Street have been struck and portions of two burned. The houses on Sycamore, Lombard and Old Streets have suffered considerably…. The Courthouse and Jail were each struck several times, one shell passing just under the face of the clock and through the steeple. The two Presbyterian, 1st Baptist, St. Pauls, & I think other churches were struck…. Nearly every store on both sides of Sycamore… [has] been struck."

William Henry Harder, a soldier in the 23rd Tennessee, had marched through town in June. He never forgot the lady, "very beautiful, [who,] from an upper window, threw me a nice present, but another man caught it and I never received it." Harder's regiment marched the same way in late December, and he "of course looked for the pretty face in the window but instead… there was a rent in the wall to the left and to the right that traced the course of one of the shells…. Many houses in that part of the city were pierced by those shots. I shudder to think that maybe that beautiful woman may have been cut asunder by that desperate shell."

Natural forces, abetted by military necessity, also tested Petersburg's mettle. In late January, after several days of heavy rains, a large dam that had been constructed across Indian Town Creek to inundate a portion of the front burst. A roiling wave of water smashed through to the Appomattox, carrying small bridges and trees with it. One observer claimed that the level of the river was raised noticeably as the floodwaters surged into it.

On March 24, 1865, the Petersburg jail yard was the site of a legal execution of a slave named Gilly, who had been found guilty of raping a white woman. (He admitted to robbing her, but no white juryman would believe that a black man would pass up the opportunity for lustful excess.) The next day's *Express* provided the macabre details. "At half past ten o'clock, after the adjustment of the rope around his neck, and a short but earnest prayer by Mr. J. D. Keiley, the criminal stood upon the platform trembling and blindfolded, calling on the Lord for mercy. The drop fell but the rope broke, and the man was stretched upon the ground—more frightened than hurt. A new rope was procured, and at 10 minutes to 11 o'clock, the drop fell a second time and he was launched into eternity. The neck, however, was unbroken. There were some muscular contractions of the body, several attempts at respiration, and all was still."

Even-as the first signs of spring appeared, there were omens that the end was near. A North Carolina soldier named P. B. "Bangs" Heptinstall, after complaining in a letter written in late February about the large number of deserters from Lee's army, concluded with the observation, "I believe that Gen. Lee is doubting his troops for he is having all the tobacco in the city piled in sheds & houses of but little value so that the torch can be applied to a great deal in a short time."

This plan to destroy everything that was of value to the enemy did not escape the watchful eyes of Petersburg's city councilmen, who, at a March 1 meeting, resolved "that a Committee of three be appointed to wait on Genl. Lee and request that, in the event the military authorities shall decide to burn the tobacco in the City [, there] be selected a suitable place or places where the least damage from fire will result to the City."

Chapter Thirteen

"We cannot believe Americans can do these things"

December 7 -11, 1864

Ulysses S. Grant
Final Report of Operations, March 1864-May 1865

General Sherman, immediately after the fall of Atlanta, put his armies in camp in and about the place, and made all preparations for refitting and supplying them for future service. . . .

[Confederate General John B.] Hood, with his army[, succeeded in moving] . . . far to Sherman's right [and in] . . . reaching [Sherman's rail supply line back to Chattanooga]. . . . Seeing the constant annoyance he would have with the roads in his rear if we attempted to hold Atlanta, General Sherman proposed the abandonment and destruction of that place, with all the railroads leading to it. . . .

General Sherman commenced at once his preparations for his proposed movement, keeping his army in position in the mean time to watch Hood. . . . General Sherman sent [two corps] . . . back to Chattanooga to report to Major-General [George H.] Thomas, at Nashville. . . . [There] was little doubt that General Thomas would hold the line of the Tennessee, or in the event Hood should force it, would be able to concentrate and beat him in battle. It was therefore readily consented to that Sherman should start for the sea-coast. Having concentrated his troops at Atlanta by the 14th of November, he commenced his march . . .

Hood, instead of following Sherman, continued his move northward. . . . General Thomas, retarding him as much as possible, fell back toward Nashville for the purpose of concentrating his command and gaining time for the arrival of re-enforcements. The enemy coming up with our main force . . . at Franklin, on the 30th [of November], assaulted our works . . . but were in every instance repulsed. . . . During the night [our forces] . . . fell back toward Nashville. . . . The enemy followed up and commenced the establishment of his line in front of Nashville on the 2d of December. . . . On the morning of the 15th of December General [George] Thomas attacked Hood in position, and, in a battle lasting two days, defeated and drove him from the field in the utmost confusion, leaving in our hands most of his artillery and many thousand prisoners.

* * *

The coming of winter changed the tempo of the war at Petersburg as soldiers of both sides began to prepare for the onset of cold weather.

"I wish you could ride around & see how this great army of N. Va. is housing itself in its various departments for winter," surgeon John Claiborne wrote in a letter to his wife in mid-October. "Here you may see a hut—such as nobody but a soldier ever conceived of—and there a tent of smallest dimensions with a chimney & door—and there a fellow—absolutely burrowing under the ground—and such contrivances for cooking and keeping dry & warm!"

Similar scenes could be seen on the other side of the lines as well. "Winter quarters meant a wall or 'dog' tent, with perhaps two or three logs for the sides," reminisced one Wisconsin soldier, "and if we were in camp any length of time a fire place was made out of the Virginia clay, with barrels or hard tack boxes for chimneys. Some of the fire places were artistically made, [and] were large enough, some of them, to roll a log in."

"Winter is now upon us in earnest," Robert Tilney, a Fifth Corps staff aide, wrote on December 4. "There is not a leaf to be seen on any tree, except the gloomy pines, and we can scarcely call them leaves." Also writing at about this time, a North Carolina officer predicted, "I don't think there is much chance of our fighting any more this campaign, at least about Petersburg . . .for the winter seems to have set in in good earnest."

U. S. Grant, however, was not ready to call it quits. The matter of Confederate supplies still nagged at him. Even though the Union army now blocked the Weldon Railroad and had rendered useless the twenty-mile stretch south down to Stony Creek Station, foodstuffs and war materiel continued to reach the Confederate cities of Petersburg and Richmond. "The enemy still held a portion of the Weldon railroad [between Stony Creek Station and Weldon, North Carolina]," acknowledged one Pennsylvania soldier, "upon which they transported supplies from North Carolina and farther south nearly up to our lines, whence they wagoned them around our left to their camps."

The imminent return of the Sixth Corps from the Shenandoah Valley gave Grant the means to do something about interdicting this tenuous supply chain. No sooner had the first Sixth Corps division reached City Point than it was directed to replace a Fifth Corps division posted along the siege lines. "As fast as your troops are relieved," corps commander Gouverneur Warren was instructed on the afternoon of December 4, "you will mass them at some suitable position in the rear, between the Halifax road and the Jerusalem plank road."

Grant was anxious to move before Lee could react to the influx of Federal veterans to Petersburg, and before the Confederate chieftain's strength was augmented by the remnants of Early's Shenandoah Valley army. On December 5, therefore, Grant informed Meade, "You may make immediate preparations to move down the Weldon railroad for the purpose of effectually destroying it as far south as Hicksford,[1] or farther if practicable."

Once he had settled on a plan of action, Grant brooked no delays. That same day, Meade received word that even as another Sixth Corps division was landing at City Point, Phil Sheridan had decided to hold up transferring the third, George Getty's command, pending clarification of General Jubal Early's intentions. Meade immediately queried Grant, "Does the detention of Getty's division make any suspension of your previous orders?" Back shot Grant's terse reply: "We will not wait for Getty's division. How soon can you move troops?" Meade promptly directed the Second Corps commander, Andrew Humphreys, to take over the position that Getty was to have occupied.

General Warren was summoned to Army Headquarters on December 6 at 1:00 p.m. Meade's orders to him modified Grant's instructions in one important way: Warren was to be "prepared to move down the Weldon railroad to-morrow morning at daylight . . . striking the road below Stony Creek and effectually destroying it from that point as far as Hicksford, *if possible* (emphasis mine)." Besides the three Fifth Corps divisions, Meade added to Warren's striking force Gregg's cavalry division and a division (Mott's) from the Second Corps. Everything depended upon speed; a minimum number of wagons and ambulances were allowed, and only one battery per division would move with the column. In all, 22,000 infantry and 4,200 cavalry would take part in the expedition.

---

1   Modern Emporia, approximately 44 miles south from City Point.

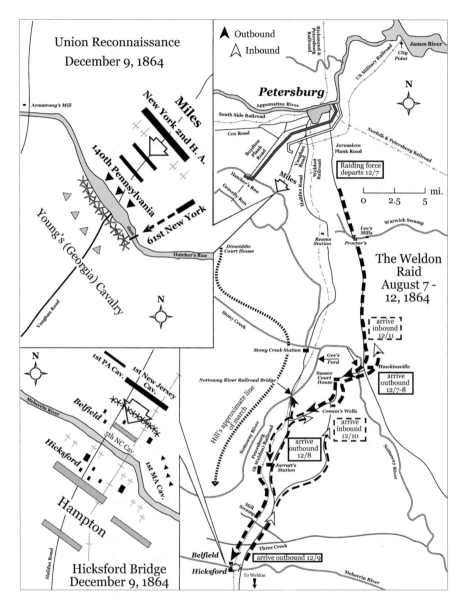

Union Reconnaissance
December 9, 1864

Outbound
Inbound

Petersburg

The Weldon Raid
August 7 - 12, 1864

Hicksford Bridge
December 9, 1864

Orders were held "till the last moment, so as to prevent the information getting to the enemy," but the soldiers' grapevine was as thorough as ever. "Rumors of an extensive raid were circulated," a Second Corps soldier remarked, "and it was considered a matter of course that . . . 'Hancock's Flying Infantry,' would be called upon in such an event; nor were we disappointed."

All day on December 6, and well into the night, troops gathered at painstakingly plotted departure points, where they were issued sixty rounds of ammunition and four days' ration supply. (An additional forty rounds per man and provisions for two more days were carried along in wagons.) It dawned on the men of the 83rd Pennsylvania that their carefully constructed winter camp would be taken over by soldiers who had not done any work on it. "Swearing was indulged in freely, as you can well imagine," one member of the regiment noted.

"The massing of these troops on the Jerusalem Plank Road dispelled the idea of another 'flank movement' to the left," a soldier in the 155th Pennsylvania reasoned. "The supplying of the troops with four days' rations, and the news that the supply trains carried additional supplies of rations . . .caused much conjecture among the troops as to the destination of the impending movement." Fifth Corps staff officer Tilney was philosophical about the prospect of having to tear up more stretches of Virginia railroad. "It would seem that they can't trust any Corps but this for that kind of work," he mused. "Well, all the more laurels for the grand old Fifth. I hope we shall do something worthwhile this time. . . ."

Wednesday, December 7
Day One

"This whole command was on the move at 6 a.m. on the 7th," Warren later stated, "having been located beforehand so as to make a simultaneous start."

Gregg's cavalry began moving out at 4:00 a.m. As the riders passed the infantry camps, a few early-rising foot soldiers called out good-natured greetings. "Don't go out and stir up the Johnnies in such weather," one yelled to C. W. Wiler of the 10th New York cavalry. "The weather was cold, and rainy, and snowy, and the roads very rough and deep," a New Jersey trooper recalled.

The cavalrymen rode south along the Jerusalem Plank Road, splitting into two columns to cross Warwick Swamp Creek at Proctor's and Lee's mills. At Proctor's—perhaps ten miles out—"the enemy's scouts were encountered and two of them captured."

Samuel Crawford's division led the infantry. "It was a dull winter morning as the troops filed out along the Jerusalem plank-road," a Pennsylvania chaplain, William Locke, remembered. A soldier in the 6th Wisconsin made a quick head count of the troops on the move and was satisfied that there were "[enough] men to put up a good stiff fight should occasion have required it."

Next in line was Charles Griffin's division. "At half past eight o'clock a.m., the rain began to fall, and continued with intervals during the day," one New

York soldier later wrote. "The country through which we passed was the first we had beheld since landing in Virginia [that was] undesolated by the horrid tramp of war."

Behind Griffin came the division commanded by Romeyn Ayres. A soldier in the 190th Pennsylvania, Robert McBride, was apprehensive. "With this force we felt quite at home within one day's march of the main army," he declared. "Once across the [Nottoway] river, and at a greater distance, we might stir up all the game we could take care of." Bringing up the tail of the armed procession was Gershom Mott's division, detached from the Second Corps. "I will not say that we left our new quarters without regret," noted Brigadier General Regis de Trobriand, ". . . but all traces of annoyance vanished . . .when it became evident that . . .we were to make an excursion to a new part of the country." Not everyone was so sanguine, however. "This day's work represents an entirely new departure in the tactics of the army," grumbled John Haley, a private in the 17th Maine. "For us to boldly strike out, put a day's march between us and our supports . . . is an astonishingly reckless movement."

It did not take the Confederates long to find out that something was up. South Carolina cavalryman U. R. Brooks was riding with Captain Jim Butler when the two spotted a Yankee scout not fifty yards ahead of them. "Captain Butler did not say, 'Halt, surrender,' but merely said, 'Come here to me, sir,' which seemed to paralyze him and he came up to us looking like 'a poor man at a cash sale.' After getting what information we could from him he was sent to Libby Prison."

Wade Hampton later reported, "Hearing on the morning of the 7th of December that the enemy, in heavy force, was moving down the Jerusalem plank road, I came to Stony Creek Depot. . . .'"

The Union infantry column pushed steadily along the Jerusalem Plank Road until it reached Hawkinsville, nearly twenty miles from Petersburg. One weary Maine soldier remembered that the town consisted of a "series of old buildings, in a dilapidated condition, inhabited by a few 'poor white trash,' and surrounded by negro huts."

Warren's men had been moving on a southeasterly track, roughly parallel to but some distance from the Weldon Railroad. The route of the march turned to the southwest at Hawkinsville, crossing the Nottoway River at Freeman's Ford. Once across, Warren would be able to strike directly west to intersect the railroad just below Stony Creek Station.

The span over Freeman's Ford had been destroyed, so Warren's first task was to construct a pontoon bridge for the wagons and artillery. "No sooner was it laid," complained aide Robert Tilney, "than the first wagon that attempted to cross it, upset, and broke the bridge down, causing a delay of an hour." Not until nearly 5:00 p.m. would the infantry begin to cross the Nottoway.

The river was no obstacle for Gregg's cavalrymen, who had already crossed at a "deep ford nearly impassable for wagons" and ridden five miles further west, to Sussex Court House. "Here we found a long building surrounded by a piazza used as a hotel," recalled one New York trooper. "There were plenty of fences, and . . .the boys were soon surrounding cheerful, crackling fires, over which chickens, hams, potatoes, etc., were cooking."

Warren's infantrymen spent this night camped on both sides of the Nottoway. Griffin and Ayres were to the north of the river, and Mott and the supply train were to the south, while Crawford's division trudged on to bivouac at Sussex Court House, arriving there at around 11:00 p.m. There was some confusion. A few units stood by for hours expecting to cross, even though it had already been decided that they would not move farther this night. In the 190th Pennsylvania, several soldiers fell asleep while waiting. One practical-joking lieutenant roused a group of snoring men to tell them they could sleep until 2:00 a.m., when the march would resume.

"Well, what the—did you wake us up for, to tell us that?" someone yelled. "Why, you—lunatic," the smiling lieutenant replied, "aren't two sleeps better than one?"

Not everyone enjoyed an easy slumber. Private John Haley remembered that it was with "dreadful misgivings that we lay down to sleep, having never before been out overnight in such an insecure place where death seems to lurk in every thicket."

Thursday, December 8
Day Two

The infantry north of the Nottoway began moving toward Freeman's Ford before 2:00 a.m. As one foot soldier put it, "we were again on our way toiling through the mud and darkness." This same infantryman also described the pontoon bridge across the Nottoway: "[It was] made by investing boat-shaped frames twenty-four feet in length with canvas, which being anchored above and below the crossing parallel with the current and covered with scantling and boards, sounded and swung beneath the tread of horses and men as the columns passed over. . . ." "It was so dark we had to trust our horses more than ourselves," a nervous artilleryman admitted, "but we crossed safely."

Griffin's command moved to the south bank first, followed by Ayres's. "They were both over by 4:30 a.m.," Warren later recorded, "and the bridge was up and away soon after daylight." "[As soon as] the bright sun appeared," one of Griffin's men remembered, "the warm rays . . . seemed to inspire new life and spirit to the men." They also inspired wholesale divestiture of clothing. "The men threw away their blankets and everything . . . to lighten the load," a Pennsylvania soldier wrote. Units that had crossed the Nottoway on the evening of December 7 were not immune to the contagion. "The day turned out warm and pleasant, overcoats were at a discount, and . . . many thoughtlessly threw them away," commented a New Jersey soldier in Mott's division.

Mott's men, already across the river, began marching by 6:30 a.m. "All were up before daylight," brigade commander Robert McAllister observed, "with campfires burning brightly." The Second Corps column passed through Sussex Court House at about 8:45 a.m. One Maine man described it as a "dilapidated village, consisting of a large brick courthouse, a jail, and several black wooden houses; there was no store or church, nor a single evidence of thrift or enterprise."

The troops in Samuel Crawford's division, who had begun the day encamped about Sussex Court House, were also moving to the west. "The Cavalry started about 4 o'clock and we at daylight," Massachusetts soldier George Fowle recalled.

Gregg's raiders were again out in front, with Brigadier General Henry Davies's brigade leading. "My advance encountered along the road small parties of the enemy's cavalry, apparently placed for purpose of observation, as they fell back readily and without much resistance," Davies reported. By 9:00 a.m., he had reached the Halifax Road, which ran alongside the Weldon Railroad. Coming up behind Davies, Colonel Charles H. Smith's cavalry brigade veered north and moved along the tracks as far as the Nottoway River bridge, which it had been ordered to destroy. "This [destruction] was speedily accomplished," Gregg later wrote, "the enemy having fled upon our approach."

Even as Smith's men were carrying out their mission, Davies's command halted along the tracks, where, as one New York cavalryman remembered, "the work of demolition [was] vigorously begun."

Wade Hampton did not wait for his full command to gather at Stony Creek Station before he acted. Portions of M. C. Butler's division crossed the

Nottoway at Gee's Ford well before dawn, and their commander sent squadrons of riders prowling along the narrow dirt roads that snaked south and east. A section of the Jeff Davis Legion scrapped with Gregg's outriders. "We had a slight skirmish with them," Frederick Waring, the legion's commander, wrote in his diary. A more serious engagement took place east of the rail lines, as a sixty-man squadron from the 9th Virginia Cavalry penetrated the gap between Gregg's last brigade and the van of Warren's infantry. It set off a running fight that spread over miles of backcountry roads.

Hampton deduced from the information he received that the enemy was turning and following the railroad south. The Confederate cavalry chief reasoned that his best move would be to pull back across the Nottoway, and swing around to the west of the Federal advance to get in front of it at the point where the railroad and the wagon road crossed the Meherrin River. The small village of Hicksford lay along the south bank of the river there, while the hamlet of Belfield was nestled along the north side.

Hampton's men were moving according to this design when their commander received a message from Robert E. Lee, "informing me that Lieutenant-General Hill was moving through Dinwiddie toward Belfield and directing me to communicate with him."

Once more Lee was responding aggressively to a challenge. He had detached as much of Hill's corps as could be spared from the Petersburg lines—troops from all three divisions were included—and sent them off to meet Hampton. This time, Hill was well enough to lead his men personally.

In a telegram to the Confederate war secretary, Lee concluded that the enemy column was "moving against Weldon." "Hill and Hampton are following," he added grimly.

December 8 proved an anxious day for Union headquarters at Petersburg. Signal-station reports were carefully analyzed as Grant and Meade tried to determine whether Lee was detaching troops from the Cockade City to intercept Warren.

Should that be the case, Grant was eager to improve his tactical position. "If the enemy send off two divisions after Warren, what is there to prevent completing the investment of Petersburg with your reserves?" he asked Meade at midmorning. George Meade was not one to leap before looking very thoroughly at the situation. His response, written within twenty minutes of his receipt of Grant's question, pointed out that the intelligence reports were inconclusive and that the twenty-two thousand troops available were

June 14, 1864: Hancock's corps crossing the James River. *William Waud*

June 15, 1864: The Confederate Dimmock Line position being overrun by the
Federal Eighteenth Corps. *E. Forbes*

Summer, 1864: Warren's headquarters at the Avery House. *A. Waud*

July 27, 1864: Lieutenant Colonel Henry Pleasants supervising the
loading of powder into the mine. *A. Waud*

July 30, 1864: Explosion of the mine. *A. Waud*

August 9, 1864: Explosion at City Point. *A. Waud*

Summer 1864: U.S.S. *Commodore Perry* on patrol near Port Walthall. *W. Waud*

August 18-21, 1864: General Warren's men fortifying lines
on the Weldon Railroad. *A. Waud*

September 16, 1984: Wade Hampton's "Beefsteak Raid." *A. Waud*

October 27, 1864: Hospital attendants tending the
wounded near Hatcher's Run. *W. Waud*

April 1, 1865: General Warren's Fifth Corps attacking
General Pickett's lines at Five Forks *A. Waud*

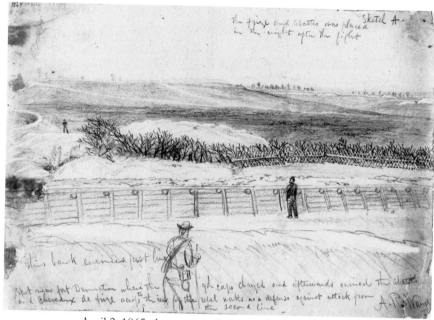

April 2, 1865: A spot near Fort Damnation (Mahone).
Note the *abatis* and *chevaux-de-frise*. *A. Waud*

April 2, 1865: The storming of Fort Damnation (Mahone). *A. Waud*

April 2, 1865: Storming Fort Gregg. *A. Waud*

April 2, 1865: Storming Fort Damnation (Mahone). Note the artist's comment, "Have no time to finish this." *A. Waud*

April 3, 1865: A burned railroad bridge in Petersburg, with troops formed in pursuit of General Lee's army. *A. Waud*

April 3, 1865: The remains of General Lee's Petersburg headquarters. *A. Waud*

insufficient to complete Petersburg's encirclement. "I should therefore be in favor of waiting [for] more positive information before making a movement," Meade opined.

Meade decided not to wait for the information to come to him. Shortly before 11:00 a.m., he ordered a "small command of cavalry down the Vaughan road to endeavor to ascertain the movements of the enemy." Nearly eleven hours would pass before Meade received the results of this reconnaissance. As Meade explained to Grant at 9:40 p.m., the Federal riders "found a force at the crossing of Hatcher's Run by the Vaughan Road, said to be Young's brigade of cavalry, which prevented any farther progress, and . . .the officer withdrew." Meade vowed to send out more men first thing the next morning, but he counseled that the "difficulty of taking advantage of Lee's detaching against Warren is to get positive information of the fact in time."

The first elements of Warren's infantry reached the Weldon Railroad at about noon. For the next six hours, the kinked files of blue-coated soldiers deployed along the tracks, from the Nottoway River bridge south as far as Jarratt's Station. "Thinking the enemy might meet us near the railroad, I delayed destroying it with the infantry until sunset, by which time the whole command was up and the trains parked," Warren later reported.

Then orders went out to begin tearing up the Weldon line. "First the rails were removed," a soldier in the 32nd Massachusetts wrote, "then the sleepers were taken up, piled and fired; when the rails, laid across the burning ties, were heated so as to be pliable, they were doubled and twisted in such manner that they could not be relaid unless rerolled. Then the same operation was repeated on another length of track until several miles in all were ruined. It was a long day's work."

The 198th Pennsylvania arrived on the scene just as the sun was setting. "As far as the eye could reach were seen innumerable glowing fires, and thousands of busy blue-coats tearing up the rails and piling the ties. It was at once a wild, animated scene. . . ."

The weary Federals finished wrecking this portion of the rail line before midnight and then went into bivouac. The weather had turned bitter, and those who had thrown away their overcoats or blankets suffered. Pennsylvanian John L. Smith had managed to hold on to his blanket, though it did not do him much good: "We made big fires. It was awful cold, [the] wind went right through us. We sat by the fire. You could roast in front and freeze behind on your back."

A. P. Hill's infantry also suffered during its march from Petersburg to intercept the Yankee raiders. "In all my experience during the war I do not remember any weather which was so trying to the troops," one officer recalled. "A high wind and cold rain prevailed when we started on the march of forty miles. To these succeeded hail and sleet which, with execrable roads and worn out shoes made our cup of misery full."

Friday, December 9
Day Three

The Yankee boys were up early this morning to complete what some of their officers jokingly referred to as their "contract" with the Weldon Railroad. Aide Robert Tilney, shivering in the bitter cold, nevertheless carefully watched the infantry in action. "The entire Corps was stretched along the road by divisions, and, having stacked arms, went to work . . . The track disappeared fast; the men loosened the ties, all got hold and raised about thirty yards up, until the whole track fell over, which would cause some part of it to break; then the ties were wrenched off the rails and laid in piles, fifteen in each pile, fence rails filled the interstices, and then the iron rails were placed on top; all this was set fire to, and as the rails heated they bent with their own weight . . . Cotton gins, stores, and some houses were burning in all directions . . . As fast as one division destroyed the road in its front it would march some distance further along the road and begin again and so on, each division alternately."

While the infantry pried and burned, the cavalry pushed south toward Hicksford. It was a slow advance, with almost constant skirmishing. The head of Gregg's column drew up before Three Creek at 10:00 a.m., only to find the hundred-foot-long truss-frame railroad bridge wrapped in flames, the wagon bridge knocked apart, and the nearby fords blocked with fallen trees. About two hundred Confederates, dug in along the opposite bank, were backed by a field howitzer that banged away as the blue-coated riders came into sight.

The 10th New York Cavalry was ordered to clear the crossing. "We were drawn up in line just out of the woods," young Nelson Egbert remembered. "After a few minutes the bugles blew the charge and away we went. We kept a fairly good line and with sabers flashing, horses on a dead run, and the men yelling at the top of their voices, it made a good showing of a cavalry charge in the open.

"The Johnnies kept firing . . .and had demolished the [wagon] road bridge on our front except one timber, which reached from one abutment to the other, about 36 feet apart. A part of the regiment was dismounted and I followed Capt. Perry of Co. A across the single timber of the road bridge. We were the first men across."

"A ford was soon cleared," Gregg reported, ". . . and the march continued to Hicksford."

"Marched like Arabs and got to Hicksford early in the morning," noted Frederick Waring, commanding the Jeff Davis Legion. A trooper in the 9th Virginia Cavalry recalled that "never did I see people so glad to see soldiers & friends as those poor people seemed to see us. They rushed out of their houses & shouted with joy & I must confess that, for my part, I never felt more enthusiasm or more energy for the fight."

Wade Hampton found Lieutenant Colonel John J. Garnett in charge of Hicksford's defenses. Garnett led a real patchwork force, consisting of a battalion of Louisiana Zouaves, a few pieces of artillery, some Virginia Reserves, one small company of the 62nd Georgia Cavalry, and portions of three regiments from the North Carolina Junior Reserves. The latter units, raised under a February 1864 act of the Confederate Congress, contained men "between the ages of 17 and 18 and between 45 and 50." These particular North Carolinians had been gathered in Wilmington after Lee gave the alarm, and had been transported to Hicksford on open flatcars. "The weather was intensely cold," one officer remembered. "More than once the train had to be stopped, fires made in the woods and some of the boys lifted from the trains and carried to the fires and thawed out." Despite these difficulties, the troops had arrived at around noon, in plenty of time to meet the Yankee raiders.

Hampton examined Hicksford's defenses. The railroad and wagon bridges were guarded from the south side of the Meherrin River by three large redoubts connected by rifle pits. On the north side of the river, the area between the two bridges was covered by a series of rifle pits fronted by a thick belt of abatis and chevaux-de-frise.

Hampton sent the 5th North Carolina Cavalry across the river to support other units from Garnett's command that were guarding the bridge approaches. Another North Carolina cavalry regiment, the 2nd, was sent to watch a ford one mile up the river, while the Jeff Davis Legion was dispatched to block yet another crossing, this one four miles below town. The rest of Hampton's veterans were deployed where needed to bolster Garnett's forces. Now came the waiting.

"The enemy moved on slowly and cautiously," Hampton stated, "and did not make his appearance before Belfield until 3 p.m."

Before he dismantled the pontoons spanning Freeman's Ford, Gouverneur Warren detailed three cavalry companies to return to Petersburg, gathering up stragglers as they went. "These were already numerous on account of the night movement," Warren wrote, "and sending them back was necessary as they could not follow the column."

The sorry procession arrived within the Union lines shortly before 8:00 a.m. Meade's aide Theodore Lyman watched them stagger into view, "looking[,] in the dusk, like a large brigade." The stragglers were sorted and counted; there were 851 in all, 399 from Mott's division and the rest, 452, from the Fifth Corps. "Their way was not made soft to them," Lyman confided. "They were marched three miles more, making twenty in all, and were then put out on picket on a right frosty night."

Federal troops were again probing the Confederate lines southwest of Petersburg. A force consisting of the First, Third, and Fourth brigades of Nelson Miles's division (Second Corps), three regiments of cavalry, and artillery moved along the Vaughan Road at dawn.

The 6th Ohio Cavalry cleared the way, steadily pushing back Confederate vedettes until it reached Hatcher's Run. Here the enemy made a determined stand in some well-sited earthworks on the opposite side of the run.

Miles rode up and pondered the situation. It would be a tough nut to crack. As he later reported, "[the] run had been dammed about one-eighth of a mile below the crossing, making the water about four feet deep and fifty feet wide. Holes had been dug in the bed of the stream, and trees slashed in it for a considerable distance above and below, making it a most difficult obstruction."

He ordered two of his cavalry regiments (the 6th Ohio and the 13th Pennsylvania) to swing west to Armstrong's Mill and hold that crossing. To the 3rd Pennsylvania Cavalry, he gave the task of capturing a ford a short distance downstream. One trooper grumbled about "General Miles, having a few cavalrymen under his powers, and apparently entertaining a high idea of their powers." The Federal riders found the ford well guarded and sent word back that it "could not be carried by a mounted force."

This meant that Miles's infantry would have to take the Vaughan Road crossing. Skirmishers from the 140th Pennsylvania pushed into the stream, only to reel back under a fusillade of gunfire from the far shore. Miles rode to the next regiment in line, the 2nd New York Heavy Artillery, and asked its commander, Major George Hogg, for "volunteers to take the works at Hatcher's Run." Hogg nominated Captain George Armes of Company E "as the only one whom he thought would volunteer to attempt such a dangerous task." Miles sought out Armes, who declined to volunteer but agreed to lead the attack if Miles ordered it. Miles gave the order.

Armes picked his own company and Company C, the regimental color company, for the mission. The men formed into battle lines, moved closer to the creek bank, and waited for the signal guns to fire.

Then the moment came. Armes jumped up. "Forward, guide center, march!" he shouted. George Macy, commanding the First Brigade, watched as the "assaulting party moved forward, under a sharp fire from the enemy, plunged into the stream, and a portion of them succeeded in gaining the opposite bank."

George Armes recalled, "After reaching the water we charged through it, crawling up and working our bodies through the obstacles placed in the space between the bank of the stream and the breastworks; then over we went into the works, many of our brave boys being shot or bayoneted through while dragging themselves with their heavy wet clothes up the steep embankment."

Captain Armes was clubbed down as he clambered over the earthworks, bayoneted in the jaw and throat, and then left for dead. He would survive his wounds. Supports splashed across Hatcher's Run to secure the lodgment even as the 61st New York marched downstream to take possession of the dam that flooded the ford. Nelson Miles later counted twenty wounded and thirteen missing in this engagement.

Miles now spread his infantry along Hatcher's Run as far west as Armstrong's Mill and sent his cavalry further out to gather information. The Federal riders scooped up a handful of prisoners, including one garrulous mail-carrier from Dearing's cavalry brigade. A preliminary interrogation elicited the information that Wade Hampton's men "had gone after Warren[, and] that Hill's corps was at Dinwiddie Court-house." Later questioning of the mail-carrier prompted him to assert "that he heard yesterday afternoon that Hill's corps had passed through Dinwiddie Court-House yesterday morning, moving against our troops that were on the Weldon railroad."

George Meade shared his conclusions with the Second Corps commander, Andrew Humphreys at 10:45 p.m. "I expect the mail-carrier told about all he knew. Warren will have to look out for himself, but we must be on the *qui vive* to send assistance to him in case we hear of his requiring it. I don't think we can do anything by moving to the left."

The fight for the Meherrin River bridge was beginning nearly 50 miles to the south. The 1st New Jersey Cavalry, leading Gregg's advance along the Weldon Railroad, was the first to test the Confederate defenses above Hicksford. After scattering a Rebel outpost, one squadron "swept forward at the run, until the road took a sudden twist, and lost itself in an abatis of felled trees, perfectly impenetrable for horses." Musketry rippled from the rifle pits guarding the bridge, and horses tumbled, flinging their riders onto the cold, hard ground.

Brigade commander Henry Davies organized a strong attack. "The First New Jersey Cavalry was then dismounted, and led by Colonel [Hugh] Janeway, advanced on either side of the road toward the works, while the First Massachusetts Cavalry charged, mounted. The First Pennsylvania Cavalry (dismounted), on the right, also participated in this movement."

One New Jersey trooper later recalled how they "charged . . .straight into the rifle pits, over ditches and fallen trees, under a heavy fire of musketry and artillery from the woods beyond." The mounted attack by the Massachusetts men took the regiment into an open field, where it was blasted by cannon massed across the river. The officer leading the charge, Lieutenant Colonel Lucius M. Sargent, ordered his men to disperse. As he turned to go, Sargent reeled from his saddle, mortally wounded by a shrapnel burst. "This is the last of me," he gasped as he was carried from the field.

Even as Janeway's men swarmed into the rifle pits, the North Carolinians who had been holding them fell back over the bridge under a covering fire from the other side. Once the wagon bridge had been cleared, a call went out for volunteers to set the structure ablaze. Five local boys, all under eighteen years old, scrambled forward under a brisk peppering from Yankee sharpshooters to torch it. None of the boys was hit.

Gouverneur Warren, accompanied by his artillery chief, Charles Wainwright, and cavalry commander Gregg, arrived on the scene to examine the Confederate defenses. "While Warren and Gregg were sitting on their horses a shell passed over their heads," a New Jersey officer remembered. Wainwright later stated that each of the three, "I believe, disliked to go away and leave [the enemy] unharmed, but it would cost us at least one day's delay, and probably two or three hundred men; half our rations were gone, and the most dangerous part of our work, the getting back, still to do." Warren also worried about the threatening weather and his command's fatigue. "I determined to return [to Petersburg]," he later wrote, "and orders were issued accordingly for the next morning."

Another kind of destruction was being visited upon the farms and homesteads along the tracks well in the rear of the fighting. "[Lucky] was the chicken or other barn-yard game that escaped the ever-vigilant eye of the boys," an officer in the 198th Pennsylvania remarked. "Feathers, sheep and calf-skins, hides and horns, marked the bivouacs of the army."

The foraging parties also uncovered stocks of fermented apple cider. "Many weeks had passed since our boys were on a time," observed Theodore Garrish, a private in the 20th Maine, "and they seemed determined to make the most of it." "About every man in the brigade filled his canteen and coffee pot, and by midnight we had a drunken brigade," Amos Judson, of the 83rd Pennsylvania, declared. The soldiers gathered around roaring bonfires, and according to Garrish, "sham-battles were fought, and the night was one of wild hilarity and mirth." "The boys got lots of apple Brandy on the raid and call it the 'Apple-Jack raid,'" young Waters Braman wrote to his uncle a few days afterward. Warren was furious when he found out, but there was little he could do to stop distribution of the liquor, which, he later reported, "was in almost every house in appreciable quantities."

(Most Union accounts skip over the evidence that several women – white and black – were sexually assaulted by drunken Yankee soldiers of all ranks. According to one statement, the officer commanding a Pennsylvania regiment and his adjutant extorted sexual favors from two women who were "compelled to submit to their infamous proposals or have their house burned down." No charges were brought against any Federal soldiers for such crimes.)

Wade Hampton never worried about Hicksford's security. "The [Federal] assault was a feeble one," he maintained, "and it was not renewed, though a sharp fire was kept up until after night." Cavalryman N. P. Foard had nothing but praise for the North Carolina Junior Reserves, who were "totally unequipped for such service as they were now engaged in, but . . . bore their duty manfully and when the enemy appeared . . . acquitted themselves like little heroes. . . . Some of our own shells exploded prematurely on account of defective fuses, killing and wounding seven or eight of these dear boys." An officer in the 5th North Carolina was a bit more critical: "And oh! how those boys did fire. They seemed to be taking their 'Christmas' then, in fire works at least. They made their lines lurid in the darkness. And a courier had to be sent down to them 'to stop their firing.' "

A. P. Hill, riding ahead of his exhausted infantry, arrived at Hicksford this evening and met with Hampton. It was decided, Hampton later noted, "that I should endeavor to pass the left flank of the enemy and gain his rear, while General Hill would move to Jarratt's Station and strike him there."

The Confederate counterstroke was set to begin at dawn.

Saturday, December 10
Day Four

The harsh weather that had so worried Warren broke shortly before midnight. "A cold storm of sleet and rain began to fall, so that in the morning we were covered with ice and frost," Theodore Garrish recollected. The Philadelphia Inquirer's reporter covering this expedition recorded it as "one of the most potent hail storms this latitude has ever known." "Falling in," added a member of the 189th New York, "our few remaining blankets and tents proved to be so frozen, wet and heavy, our men were generally compelled to abandon them." At least one Federal kept his sense of wonder long enough to observe that the "icicles, before they began to lessen with advancing day, presented a scene of winter grandeur almost unknown to the latitude." Not everyone wore such rose-colored glasses, however. "[Marching] was hard," a Wisconsin soldier remarked. "The ice and snow began to melt[,] making the roads sloshy and muddy."

Warren's withdrawal was planned with the same precision as his advance. John Irvin Gregg's cavalry brigade led the way, followed by Griffin's infantry division (with the supply train) and then Mott, Ayres, and Crawford. Davies's and Smith's brigades covered the rear. The long column began moving northward at 7:00 a.m. Cavalryman C. W. Wiles topped a hill and looked back: "As far as the vision extended[,] the landscape was like shining crystal, suggestive of the home of fairies—in the rear the long column of cavalry and artillery, the brightness of their arms and trappings being reflected by the morning's sun."

Wade Hampton already had his men moving when word came that the enemy was retreating. "Sending this information to General Hill," he noted, "I directed Major-General [Fitzhugh] Lee to push after the enemy, to develop his movement." Switching the forces protecting Hicksford from a defensive posture to an offensive one, though, was easier said than done. "Imagine . . .," complained a South Carolinian in M. C. Butler's division, "anything more trying and dismal than moving out in that hour in such weather to remove the barriers . . .we had so thoroughly placed there during the day before to stop Warren, cross to the north side of the Meherrin River and join in the pursuit of the retreating Yankees." Hampton's men did all of this despite having outrun their food supplies. "We were out three days without anything to eat," attested cavalryman C. M. Calhoun. "One of my mess, Lucius McSwain, said he was living on the fat of his intestines."

A. P. Hill's infantrymen were within seven miles of Hicksford when orders came for them to change direction. "The weather was exceedingly cold," a member of the 33rd North Carolina recalled, "and the sufferings of the men were intense." Another Tarheel remembered that the "ground [was] so slick after the sleet that it was impossible, almost[,] to stand. Men could often be seen marching on the sleety ground with no shoes on." A mounted scout passing through Hill's plodding column never forgot "how I saw the blood spurt from the feet of his barefooted and ragged soldiers marching over the frozen ground." "We had a very rough time," surgeon I. F. Cavaness, with the 46th North Carolina, reflected in a quiet understatement.

Unless Warren's retreating column could be brought to bay, Hill's men would not be able to close the distance between them before the Yankees safely crossed the Nottoway. Hampton therefore pushed out from Hicksford with everything he had, including some of the North Carolina Junior Reserves. One of his cavalrymen later wrote of passing squads of these "boys following in the pursuit, some of them almost absolutely barefooted." E. R. Hampton, a hospital steward in one of those reserve units, stumbled along with "very badly inflamed heels, caused by trying to wear a pair of coarse, stubborn new shoes, drawn from the quartermaster's store just before leaving Wilmington. I . . . . found it more endurable to march all day through the sleet and mud barefoot."

Warren split his column a short distance north of Mill Swamp. The infantry veered to the northeast, on a more direct route to Sussex Court House; the cavalrymen continued north toward Jarratt's Station, where they would turn east to rendezvous with the foot soldiers. The sound of rear-guard combat was constant throughout the morning and afternoon.

The Federal ranks grew throughout the day. "Negroes from all directions left their masters and flocked to the protection of the Union troops," one Pennsylvania soldier wrote, "among them old men and women and little children, and as soon as a wagon of the supply train was emptied of its contents, it was filled with negro mothers with their children."

As the leading Union elements reached Sussex Court House, other blacks came forward with the grisly news that a number of Federal stragglers had been waylaid and killed by Rebel guerrillas. "Detachments were sent out to verify the facts, which were found to be true," General de Trobriand declared angrily. "They found the bodies, the throat cut, the head crushed in by blows of an axe, and the breast pierced by a knife." Another brigade commander, Robert McAllister, went and viewed the bodies. "It was a sad sight," he later told his wife. "From appearances they had been stripped of all their clothing and, when in the act of kneeling in a circle, they were shot in the head."

"This discovery had a peculiar effect upon the soldiers," claimed Robert McBride, of the 190th Pennsylvania. "Even those who were usually undemonstrative gave vent to their feelings in hearty curses on the rebellion, and everything connected with it." "We protected [the] houses, when we advanced," a soldier in the 17th Maine remembered, "but on our return, after witnessing the inhuman acts of the inhabitants, we fired every building on the route . . . . Every home, barn, and building, hay stack, corn crib, and granary, were burned to the ground." One woman, driven from her house and forced to watch as it was set afire, screamed at her persecutors, "Is this what you call subjugating the South? Is this the way you intend to subjugate the noble South?"

The pursuing Confederates were angered and appalled at the destruction they encountered. "It is distressing to see the ruin and desolation these columns inflict upon inoffensive citizens," one artilleryman reflected. "We cannot believe Americans can do these things." The mood of other Southern soldiers was vengeful. One cavalryman related that Confederate scouts were "instructed that when they caught Yankees in the act of robbing and burning to take the vandals by the arms and legs and swing them in the fire, drunk or sober. Such are the terrors of war."

There were deadly rear-guard actions at Three Creek and Jarratt's Station, as well as innumerable smaller clashes. "[The] enemy had been crowding our rear guard all day and kept it up after dark, so the boys concluded to teach them a lesson," wrote a member of the 6th Wisconsin. "[The] Eleventh Pennsylvania, Ninety-seventh New York, and part of the Eighty-eighth Pennsylvania, formed in ambush, on either side and across the road . . . . The strategy was explained to our cavalry, who, first making a show of resistance, quickly retired, pursued by the rebels, fifteen or twenty of whom came within the ambush," added Chaplain William Locke, of the 11th Pennsylvania.

Company K of the 3rd North Carolina Cavalry rode into the trap. "When they had got up about right the Regiment rose up and fired a volley into them which killed and wounded 15 of them," Massachusetts soldier George Fowle later wrote. "If it had not rained a good many more would have got hit, but a good many guns would not go on account of being wet." (Confederate accounts admit to the loss of between twelve and twenty men in the encounter.)

"The mist continued to fall and keep the men cold and wet all night," Warren reported afterward, "so that they got little sleep or rest."

There was action along the Richmond-Petersburg front again as defensive lines were probed. This time, however, it was a Confederate force pushing out to ascertain whether Union garrisons had been weakened.

Federal troops had been spotted massing at Bermuda Hundred and boarding river transports.[2] This might mean either a general evacuation of the lines or a significant weakening of them—James Longstreet determined to find out which.

Brigadier General Johnson Hagood reckoned that some eleven thousand men from Field's and Hoke's divisions took part in the probe. "It was very cold and the roads abominable with frozen slush," he remembered. "Orders to march by daylight," Texan Thomas McCarty scribbled in his diary entry, "ground covered with snow. Advanced and commenced skirmishing with the Yanks and drove them steadily all day, into their works at New Market Heights, where we remained for a few hours, many suffering much from the cold." Another Texas soldier, Edward Crockett, also kept a diary of the affair. "Several men came near freezing to death as we had no fires & it was very cold," he wrote.

Federals from the Army of the James met Longstreet's men. "It was a cold, sleety day, dismal in the extreme," one of them recalled, "but we fell in lively and manned the formidable breastworks in our immediate front. Quickly pushing out a heavy skirmish line, the lost ground was regained. . .

Longstreet's men returned to their starting point before nightfall. Lee summarized the results to War Secretary Seddon:

---

2   These soldiers were earmarked for Butler's Fort Fisher expedition.

GENL. LONGSTREET MADE A RECONNAISSANCE OF ENEMY'S LINES
TODAY ON NORTH SIDE OF JAMES RIVER AS FAR AS NEW MARKET
HEIGHTS, DRIVING IN THE PICKETS, AND FOUND THEM FORTIFIED
ALONG THE WHOLE DISTANCE.

Also this evening, Nelson Miles withdrew his men from Hatcher's Run.
"My troops reached the intrenchments at dark," he reported.

The Union high command at Petersburg decided shortly after midday that
Warren might be in trouble. The sum of the various intelligence reports now
supported the notion that both Hill and Hampton were off after him. U. S.
Grant wired Meade at 1:20 p.m., "I think it advisable to move with all the force
you can to Warren's relief."

Meade selected Robert B. Potter's Ninth Corps division for the job. He
informed Grant at 7:40 p.m. that "General Potter's column moved at 6 p.m. He
has orders to march all night and not to halt till he gets to the Nottoway."

"The road was in a horrible condition, very muddy," Albert Pope, of the
35th Massachusetts, noted in his diary. "It commenced raining in the evening,
and poured nearly all night." "Marched 30 miles to the left through guerrillas
and devil knows what all," groused a soldier in the 200th Pennsylvania.

Sunday, December 11
Day Five

Warren's column was up early and moving toward Freeman's Ford on the
Nottoway. Once there, engineers began work on a pair of pontoon bridges.

"The enemy followed us closely all day," a soldier in Edward Bragg's
brigade—Warren's rear guard—wrote later. "When the enemy emerged . . . and
the familiar zip-zip of the bullets reminded the 'Little General' that it was time
for us to move to the next scene of operations, we would change from deployed
line to column of fours and continue the march. During the day, we formed into
line ten different times to keep the enemy in check."

The stripped bodies of more Federal stragglers were found by Mott's
division when it passed through Sussex Court House. "Some of the residents
were seized, and not being able to prove an alibi or explain certain suspicious
circumstances, they were hung in the Court House yard," claimed Private John
Haley of the 17th Maine. George Giles, marching in Crawford's division,
passed the dangling bodies. "Hung some guerrillas," he wrote to his wife several

days after the raid. "They cut some of our men's throats. They are a pretty bad set of humans anyhow." One soldier in the 120th New York remembered that a "church standing near the road met the same fate as other structures, though some of the men protested and did all they could to save it from the flames."

The destruction continued until dark, by which time all of Warren's men were safely across the Nottoway. "It was a sad sight to see women and children wailing and running about with no shelter in the cold December night," remarked John Haley.

A. P. Hill discontinued the chase today and turned his footsore infantry columns toward Petersburg. "I could not succeed in bringing [Warren] . . . to fight, though I marched 40 miles one day and night," Hill explained in a letter to his wife. "We succeeded however in turning him back from Weldon."

The pugnacious Wade Hampton was not so willing to let go. "Being informed that our infantry had given up the pursuit of the enemy," he later recounted, "I sent one regiment at daylight the next morning to follow to the Nottoway River, while I endeavored with the rest of the command to get across to the Jerusalem plank road in time to intercept the retreating column there. I found this impracticable, so I withdrew my force to Stony Creek."

As Hill's men retraced their bloody footprints back toward Petersburg, one Florida veteran quipped wearily, "Ain't Florida a great place? There the trees stay green all the time, and we have oranges and lemons and figs and bananas and it is the greatest country for taters you ever did see."

Potter's relief column proved unnecessary, though welcome. "The junction of forces was made at Nottoway river on the afternoon of the 11th," a soldier in the 6th New Hampshire recalled, "and the weary men of the Fifth Corps were glad to see us." One of the would-be rescuers, in the 35th Massachusetts, remembered the "raiders . . .coming back in high spirits, after destroying the railroad and trying their hands a little at foraging, of which they had read so much in connection with Sherman's marches, but had so little in their own experience of late."

Meade's aide Theodore Lyman found some humorous irony here: "Poor General Potter! . . . He had a frightful night march and was doubtless buoyed up by the feeling that he . . .could distinguish himself if there was a fight, and slam in on Hill's left flank, and win a great name for himself. What then was his disgust to see, about noon, the head of Warren's column trudging peaceably back, on the other side of the river! There were two decent-sized armies staring at each other, across the stream, each wondering what the other meant by being there; and both wondering why so many men were concentrated against nobody . . . . It was a terrible cold night for a bivouac, with an intensely piercing cold wind and everything frozen up. Warren crossed the river and spent the night on this side of it."

Early the next morning—Day Six of the operation—Warren's command went into winter camps at Petersburg.

* * *

Writing on December 14, Warren estimated that his men had marched "about 100 miles in the six days" and destroyed about seventeen miles of track between the Nottoway and Meherrin rivers. "General Hill's corps, the people thought would attack us, but we saw nothing of it," Warren concluded smugly. In the report he wrote to accompany Warren's, Meade noted that the "result of the expedition was the complete destruction of sixteen miles of the railroad, preventing its use beyond Hicksford, which, unless the damages are repaired, is in effect depriving the enemy from using it beyond Weldon." Northern newspapers declared the operation a success and Warren was praised as an "executive soldier of the highest capacity."

Elias J. Marsh, the U.S. Army's surgeon in chief, tabulated the Union cavalry casualties in this operation as "killed 12; wounded 51; missing 51. Total, 114." The figures for infantry and artillery casualties were incomplete but did not exceed 200 in all categories. Confederate losses were unreported.

Writing to one of his sons on December 13, Robert E. Lee explained that the raid had forced him to cancel plans to visit his family in Richmond. Of the expedition itself, Lee admitted, "We did them little harm I fear. They destroyed about six miles of railroad, so the superintendent reports, & burned some small bridges." Lee's artillery chief, William Nelson Pendleton, was a bit more pointed in his assessment: "We hoped A. P. Hill might destroy the column thus engaged, but either we were too slow or the inclement weather rendered it impossible." Lee Barfield, a Georgia cavalryman in the ranks, wrote to his wife, "We were all really disappointed in letting them escape for we thought we were sure of a capture, but when they found we had a pretty good force, there was no chance to bring them to battle."

Warren's six-day operation (variously referred to as the Weldon, the Belfield, the Hicksford, or the Applejack Raid) dealt Lee's already brittle supply chain a serious though not fatal blow. It exacerbated a difficult food situation and contributed greatly to the hardships that Lee's army would face in the coming months.

Yet, like green sprouts poking through fire-blackened soil, the railroad would not die. The 1866 *Annual Report of the Petersburg Rail Road Company* proudly proclaimed:

> Some how or other the Confederate government and the railroad managed to find the necessary men and materials to re-build the sixteen miles General Warren had destroyed. Early in March (1865) the road was opened all the way from Weldon to Stony Creek, but it was in operation only for a brief period before events at Petersburg led to the abandonment of the whole line.

Chapter Fourteen

"When we weren't killing each other, we were the best of friends"

Siege Life: 1864 -1865

From the Darbytown Road north of the James to Hatcher's Run south of Petersburg, opposing lines of entrenchments rippled across a denuded and shell-scoured landscape. A visitor to the front in July itemized some of the damages when he wrote that the "fences [are] all gone, (as usual,) houses nothing left but chimneys with brick enough in them to build a good sized house – here and there a tree cut off by a solid shot."

The greatest concentration of works was about the Cockade City: "The trenches around Petersburg of the two armies were scarcely a mile apart, and frequently they approached within a few hundred yards and were generally in plain view of each other," one soldier recalled.

Every soldier knew by now that it was suicide to charge well-manned earthworks. Toward the end of the June 18 fighting, the 1st Massachusetts Heavy Artillery had been stopped from taking part in such a charge by veterans in a nearby regiment, who screamed, "Lie down, you damn fools, you can't take them forts." "You can scarce imagine the amount of fighting and loss of Life & Limb [it took] to drive them out [of their works]," a New Yorker noted.

Grant's operational orders reflected this understanding. "I do not want Hancock to attack intrenched lines," he warned Meade in July. Three months and several military operations later, his intent had not changed. "Parke . . . should be instructed that if he finds the enemy intrenched and their works well-manned, he is not to attack," Grant cautioned Meade prior to the first operation to Hatcher's Run. The deadly furrows stretching around Petersburg's perimeter forced the mobile combat out to the flanks of the lines, north and south of the James.

To the casual eye, the competing mounds seemed to wriggle with no rhyme or reason in every conceivable direction—the whole reminding one observer of "an immense prairie dog village." But there was method to this madness. The historian of the 13th New Hampshire provided a word picture of the typical trench system:

CONFEDERATE

Reserve Camps		Reserve Camps
Rear Trenches	Rear Trenches	Rear Trenches
Fort	Covered Ways	Fort

Front Rifle Trenches — "Main Line" — Traverses & Bombproofs

Small Rifle-Pits for C.S.A. Vedettes, Inter-Line Pickets at night

NO-MAN'S LAND

Small Rifle-Pits for U.S.A. Vedettes, Inter-Line Pickets at night

Front Rifle Trenches — "Main Line" — Traverses & Bombproofs

Fort	Covered Ways	Fort
Rear Trenches	Rear Trenches	Rear Trenches
Reserve Camps		Reserve Camps

UNION

"Covered ways" were trenches, sometimes roofed, dug deep enough to allow men to safely walk upright. Some even accommodated supply wagons. "Traverses" were sharply angled turns in the trench line, designed to protect troops from enfilading fire. Bombproofs came in various sizes; a South

Carolina soldier recollected one of the small versions as just "a hole cut in the ground and covered over with logs and dirt, and just high enough to sit up in."

Since it was French military engineers who codified the construction of siege works for 18th Century armies, it was natural that many features would be named in their language. Movement between the rear and front trenches was accomplished by means of zigzagging communication trenches called boyaux. A combination of wooden entanglements protected the main trenches and forts. The most basic of these was abatis, made up of trees chopped down and piled in such a way that their bushy tops were interlocked and pointing toward the enemy. A little more work resulted in fraises, which were sharpened, closely packed rows of stakes embedded in the ground with their points angling upward, chest-high.

Perhaps the most wicked-looking entanglements were the chevaux-de-frise, which, as one Southern officer related, "consisted of square pieces of timber of convenient length, bored through at short intervals alternately from either side of the square, and wooden spikes eight or ten feet long, sharpened at both ends, and driven halfway through these holes so that when placed in position the ends of two rows of spikes would rest on the ground while the ends of the other two presented their sharp points to the front and rear at the height of a man's breast."

The forts were the pillars of Petersburg's trench system. The Confederates were more sparing with the designation than the Federals, and their lines, though bristling with powerful batteries and fortified salients, boasted comparatively few forts. The notable exceptions were Fort Mahone, near the place where Lee's lines crossed the Jerusalem Plank Road, and Forts Gregg and Whitworth, which protected the city's extreme right.

Federal engineers took advantage of the Petersburg siege to test a wide variety of designs. There were forty-one forts constructed along the inner and outer Union trench lines, with an additional eight protecting City Point. Some of these became more famous than others. There was Fort Stedman near Hare's Hill, Fort Wadsworth on the Weldon Railroad, and the crescent of forts on the extreme left—Fort Gregg,[1] Fort Welch, and what became the largest earthen fortification on the Petersburg front, Fort Fisher.[2]

---

1   Not to be confused with Confederate Fort Gregg.

2   Not to be confused with Confederate Fort Fisher in North Carolina.

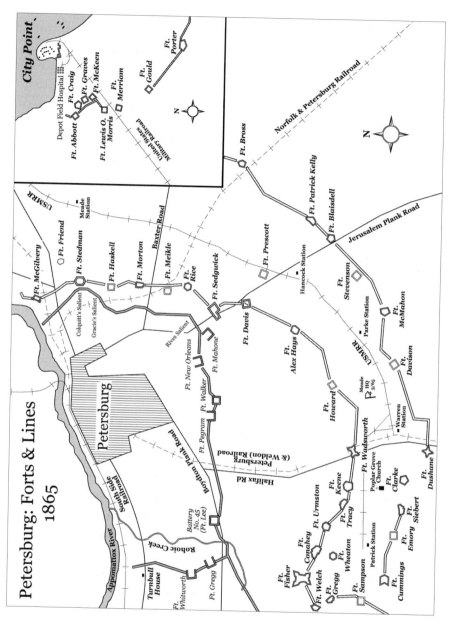

Petersburg: Forts & Lines 1865

Fort Sedgwick was a special case. Located at the spot where the Union line pivoted from north-south to east-west, Sedgwick came under such a steady barrage of artillery and sharpshooter fire that the soldiers manning the position referred to it as Fort Hell. Before long, the enemy strongpoint across the way acquired the corresponding sobriquet of Fort Damnation, while the pickets in between referred to their place as Purgatory. A Union soldier who spent some time in Sedgwick noted wryly, "When the boys desired to jar their friends at home they would start their letters 'between Hell and Damnation.'"

Men loathed their tour of duty at the front. "This life in the trenches was awful—beyond description," a Confederate officer declared. Explained another, "It was endurance without relief; sleeplessness without exhilaration; inactivity without rest; constant apprehension requiring ceaseless watching. . . . Not the least of the evils encountered was the unavoidable stench from the latrines." "For eight months and more," a North Carolina veteran recounted, his regiment "lived in the ground, walked in wet ditches, ate its cold rations in ditches, slept in dirt-covered pits." "We lived and ate and looked like troglodytes," a New York soldier maintained.

Vermin abounded. "During this period we had uninterruptedly two enemies to contend against," a Pennsylvania infantryman grumbled. "General Mahone was in front; myriads of graybacks [i.e., lice] on our rear." "This little enemy was no respecter of persons; and having enlisted for the conflict, went into position in the pants seams of the highest officer as quickly as that of the lowest private," added a Maine artilleryman. In summer, flies were an additional torment. A New Hampshire soldier in the Ninth Corps never forgot those hot days, "the men suffering tortures from the fierce heat and the swarms of flies that seemed to be determined to devour them." Topping it off was the summer dust. A reporter on the scene declared that it was "almost impossible to get a single inhalation of pure air within a quarter mile of any road."

Water was such a precious commodity at the front that men often risked their lives to obtain it. A soldier in the 146th New York decided that he could stand his thirst no longer and resolved to go into some nearby woods, where there was a stream. A few friends loaded him down with empty canteens as he set out. He reached the point of no return, an open space of about a hundred yards, and dashed out. Almost at once, little geysers of earth kicked about his feet as Confederate riflemen found the range. "Men from my regiment and the one next to us. . . .were watching me and they shouted after me words of encouragement and sarcastic advice," the soldier recalled. He made it into the woods and drank deep of his reward. Then came the return trip, this time with full canteens. "The Confederates had been expecting me, I guess. . . . The bullets struck all around me, some of them so close that I could hear them whistle." Somehow he survived to distribute his treasure. "It was the last time I tried the experiment, however," he noted.

Death could come at any time, and men ceased to be surprised by the little tragedies that were played out on a daily basis. "Many is the luckless fellow, who, in an unguarded moment, shows his crown above the works & receives into it a ball that 'settles the hash' with him forever," a North Carolinian grimly observed. They talked for a long time in the 120th New York about Sergeant Melville Hunt, who, on the eve of his discharge, took one last look at the Confederate lines. "[A] sharpshooter's bullet passed through his heart, killing him instantly." An untutored North Carolina soldier described another death in a letter to his wife: "George was shot threw the head. All he said after he was shot was he said that I am shot. That was the last word he said."

The chaplain of the 10th Connecticut told the story of two men from his regiment who were posted in an advanced, exposed rifle pit. One got careless and was shot in the head; his companion then had to suffer hours of agony, "cramped in that close clay pit, by the side of his bleeding, moaning, dying fellow; unable to lift himself for a full change of posture . . . he passed the long hours of the dragging day, longing for darkness and feeling that it would never come. 'I tell you Chaplain,' he said, 'they were long hours.'" "From daybreak to darkness the men in the rifle pits had no other thought except to kill," wrote a Union sergeant after the war. It "was kill, kill, kill."

"We never went into the rifle-pits without some one being killed or wounded," a Rhode Island officer attested. "A feeling prevails that sooner or later this experience will befall us all," a soldier from Maine wrote after another random killing. "So we have an indefinable dread, our nerves subjected to a continual strain which we know cannot end till the war ends, or we are wiped out." Soldiers who broke down under the stress were cared for in so-called convalescent camps. There, the "quiet surroundings enabled many to obtain the much needed renovating sleep."

Most, however, found ways to adapt. "The men became accustomed to it," a New Jersey officer wrote, "and grew reckless." Referring to the sound of an approaching shell, a Ninth Corps man boasted: "I have become so used to their humming that I can tell exactly the course they have selected for their journey." "It was indeed, astonishing to see how men, situated as they, could enjoy life at all," a Mississippian remarked. "Such was life in the trenches around Petersburg."

Soldiers on both sides hated the mortars. "These mortar shells were the most disgusting, low-lived things imaginable," declared W. W. Blackford, a Confederate engineer. "There was not a particle of the sense of honor about them; they would go rolling about and prying into the most private places in a sneaking sort of way." "Mortar shells fly into the works occasionally," a Maine soldier confirmed, "at which times we get out in double-quick time." Added a

Georgia infantryman, "Old veterans can never forget the noise those missiles made as they went up and came down like an excited bird, their shrieks becoming shriller and shriller, as the time to explode approached."

A soldier in the 35th Massachusetts described a mortar attack: "In the daytime the burst of smoke from the Confederate mortars could be seen; a black speck would dart into the sky, [and] hang a moment, increasing in size, rolling over and over lazily, and the revolving fuze [would begin] to whisper audibly, as it darted towards us, at first, softly, 'I'm a-coming, I'm a-coming'; then louder and more angrily, I'm coming! I'm coming!' and, at last, with an explosion to crack the drum of the ear, I'm HERE!'"

Mortar batteries alternated with tubed guns all along the front. Some artillery even acquired nicknames: one seven-gun siege battery just south of Fort Morton was called the Seven Sisters, while Union soldiers referred to several different artillery pieces as The Petersburg Express, most notably the thirteen-inch heavy mortar that was also known as The Dictator. This gun, the only one of its size at Petersburg, went into action on July 9 and remained active until September, firing 218 times, from various positions. "It made the ground quake," one infantryman swore.

"There is incessant vigilance on both sides at the front," a New Yorker wrote in the fall, "and daily casualties; and but few hours pass – I guess not one, night or day,—without the boom of a cannon or a mortar; oftener a continued booming." A Pennsylvanian who signed himself "Gamma" in his numerous letters to his hometown newspaper The Alleghanian, observed in one of them, "October is nearly gone, yet as times the warbling of birds will strike the ear, in strange contrast with the heavy booming of the batteries along the river."

Primary responsibility for manning the siege artillery rested with the 1st Connecticut Heavy Artillery, Colonel Henry L. Abbot commanding. One of his soldiers later calculated that in the course of the campaign against Petersburg, the 1st Connecticut Heavies, posted in positions from north of the James to Petersburg, fired a total of 61,884 rounds, "weighing a trifle over 879 tons."

The image of shells in flight could be almost sublime. "It is a beautiful sight at night to see the bomb shells mount into the air, so high that the boys say they knock a star out of the sky every time," a New York soldier wrote with a touch of awe. "The shells, in their passage through the air, describing luminous curves, resembled rockets and the men would frequently leave the. . . .bomb proofs[,]. . . .even at the risk of their lives, to watch the display of the fireworks." When some of the Yankee boys heard the overhead passage of outbound Federal munitions, they would sing out: "All board for Petersburg."

The impersonal nature of mortars and cannon found a deadly compliment in the work of the sharpshooters, whose actions were anything but impersonal. "Shells can be dodged when one gets used to it," remarked an engineer in the 50th New York, "but there is no use in trying to [dodge] minnie balls, by the time you can wink your eye or bend your head it is either through you or over you." "In many places the two lines are so near together that not a man dares show his head above the breastworks in daylight," a North Carolina soldier wrote to the folks at home. "Still in our holes, for it is dangerous to show our heads out of them," echoed a Massachusetts man across the no-man's land. The instant an unwary soldier on the front line exposed himself, "he immediately became the target of the enemy," declared a New York infantryman.

Almost every memoir or regimental history covering the Petersburg campaign has at least one story of a long distance killing or a near miss. A common theme is the weary veteran, discharge paper in his pocket, who takes a final (and fatal) glance across no-man's land. Mostly it was the unlucky, like the drummer in the 92nd New York, who was killed on June 28. "Hit through the neck," noted a diarist. "Poor fellow." Union officer Stephen Weld was awakened one night early in the siege by two fearful shrieks. A random shot had hit and mortally wounded a sleeping man in a tent. "I tell you it made me shudder to hear these two shrieks breaking the stillness of the night," declared Weld.

For most of those who called themselves sharpshooters it was merely the business of war. "It is queer," admitted one of them, "but we had no feeling of remorse when we saw a gunner topple over and drop." Some had a regular routine – settled in their perch before dawn and back into the main lines after dusk – while others set their own schedules. Some were decided virtuosos of the long range rifle. "I've seen them pick a man off who was a mile away," insisted a Rebel officer. "They could hit so far you couldn't hear the report of the gun." A New Yorker recorded a day's work in his diary as he and three comrades "took our stations. . . . in an old brick cellar wall. We did a good work on the Rebs."

Some had a sense of humor. Confederate artilleryman E. P. Alexander watched as his superior attempted to survey the nearby Federal earthworks using a mirror to peek over the trench top. "In a minute a bullet smashed the glass in his hands," Alexander recalled, and "the marksman in the Federal trenches shouted out to him, 'Set it up again, Johnny!'"

"It is a very dangerous business, but quite an honorable position," Private M. E. Parker of the 81st New York wrote his parents in late June. "A sharpshooter is in a great deal more danger than the regiment is, for they have to go ahead of the regiment and have to fight the best marksmen the rebels have. Yesterday I fired 44 rounds. Two men were wounded in the pit I was in. One, I think, will die, as the ball went in just forward of the right ear and came out just in front of the other. But we made the rebels pay dear for them. We saw six men on horseback. We fired on them, and when the smoke cleared away, there were six horses but no one of them."

For soldiers on the edge of the no-man's-land, life was in some ways kinder. As one literary Maine man remembered, "though we dealt always in the land of Memento Mori,[3] we enjoyed some extraordinary lapses into life." There were times, a Pennsylvanian recalled, when "by tacit consent rather than by formal agreement, the pickets on both sides ceased to fire at each other in the daytime and often saluted or conversed together like comrades or old friends." Noted another, "The pickets soon began to fraternize with probably a greater freedom and familiarity than ever before."

A rear echelon soldier visiting the picket lines during a quiet time was invited to try his hand at swapping. "I began to feel in my pockets to see what I could find to trade," he wrote soon afterwards, "but had nothing but my pocket-knife, so I hallooed to the Johnnies and gave it a throw, and one of them picked it up and after looking it over he threw me two plugs of tobacco worth here $1.50 each, so you see my first trade was a pretty good one." Marveled one Rhode Island veteran, "When we weren't killing each other, we were the best of friends."

These informal truces did not extend into the nighttime (when any movement at all might signal danger), and most officers did what they could to break up the daylight intercourse, but it continued throughout the siege. A New Yorker recounted one incident in early July: "The other day two men of our regiment engaged with a couple of the 'Johnnies' in a game of cards, the stakes being the fate of the country. Of course, our side was victorious." It did not always turn out that way, though, as a Rhode Island soldier reported in late January 1865: "One of our boys invited a reb to come out on neutral ground and have a free fight. . . . The reb whipped the Yank, after which each returned to their respective sides amid loud and prolonged cheers from the rebs."

It was a game that could become deadly without warning. *Philadelphia Inquirer* correspondent E. T. Peters, writing in September, reported an incident

---

3 Very loosely translated: "Think of yourselves as dead men."

involving a pair of New York lieutenants – Robert Green (5th New York Veteran Infantry) and Charles L. Buckingham (146th New York). Wrote Peters: "An arrangement had been entered into between our own and the Rebel pickets to abstain from firing, and depending on this the two officers named had gone out to the Rebel lines to converse with some of the Rebel officers, and were shot while returning to our own lines." A number of surmises were put forth to explain what happened, the most likely one being "the act of the pickets further to the right, who were not cognizant of the arrangement." Green survived but the 22-year old Buckingham did not.

Mutual needs sometimes brought the warring soldiers together. In the summer a stream of cool water between the sunbaked trenches might occasion a momentary ceasefire; in the winter impromptu truces would allow parties from the two sides to chop down firewood in the no-man's land. On one occasion, at least according to Mississippi soldier Thomas Roche, the Yankee fatigue detail took pity on the "worn-out Confederate axes," and "tendered us the use of their sharp axes." For those few minutes, he declared, "Yanks and Rebs were on the best of terms."

Although both high commands took measures to stop these contacts, they also seized the opportunity to obtain the other side's latest newspapers. U. S. Grant's military secretary, Adam Badeau, attested that one "great occupation was the study of the rebel newspapers, which often brought the earliest news from distant commands. They were exchanged for our own on the picket line, almost daily, and the Richmond papers were brought in as regularly as if they had been subscribed for."

Occasionally the old rivalries would reassert themselves. One New Hampshire soldier admitted that "after a time, our men began playing a few of their Yankee tricks, by taking a large New York daily and tearing the pages off, making four papers of each one, which in exchange would bring four Richmond papers." He was quick to add that "most of us were afterwards ashamed of such unfairness on the part of our men."

None of the truces ever held for very long. The relief of a unit on the front lines would bring on a resumption of firing until the two sides could again come to terms. (If the relieving unit was black, however, peace on that section of the picket line was less likely.) Other challenges to the soldierly status quo came in the form of picket-line raids designed to scoop up enemy prisoners for interrogation and unit identification. "We find our life in camp very monotonous, one day being but the repetition of another," wrote a New York artilleryman, "except when the Johnny Rebs make a dash at our lines." These dangerous night actions were known as "gobbling the picket line."

The North Carolina sharpshooters, under Major Thomas J. Wooten, were so good that one fellow Tarheel declared, "Wooten's 'seine-haulings' were proverbial, and he was liberally used by division, corps and army headquarters for ascertaining the enemy's lines or movements." One such action took place in the early morning hours of the last day of 1864 and targeted the picket line maintained by the 9th New York Heavy Artillery. "Imagine yourself roused an hour or so before early daylight, by the shrill din of musketry, and the shouts of an exultant enemy, sounding almost at your very doors," wrote an officer on the receiving end. "200 men of our regiment were on the picket line, and although prepared for an attack, yet so stealthily were the movements executed, that in a few moments two of them were killed, and twenty taken prisoners. . . .[It] was well executed. Within five minutes after the attack commenced, all was quiet, except now and then an occasional yell from the hostile lines."

These little affairs could quickly intensify. In early September, the 124th New York supported a three-regiment raiding party that set out at 1:00 a.m. The raiders returned with more than a hundred prisoners, having suffered only a small loss. "But ten minutes later the work of death began in earnest," a New Yorker remembered, "and the night was made hideous with discordant sounds. Every battery and fort for miles around began a furious cannonade, the pickets opened all along the lines on both sides of us, and three times the enemy in our front charged. . . . determined to retake the lost ground. . . . After this affair the picket firing was incessant and most desperate for over a week. If a man raised his hand, on either side a score of bullets were fired at it."

The Confederates returned the favor in early November with a large scale raid on a section of the picket line held by the Second Corps. "The affair began as Rebel assaults always do," recorded reporter Edward Crapsey. "First that wild peculiar yell, the rush forward, and a discharge of musketry. The immediate result was that the centre of our picket line was broken, and the regiments composing it driven back." Things were just getting started as Union defenders took predetermined countermeasures: a suppressing artillery fire against the Rebel line coordinated with a countercharge by New York and Massachusetts soldiers.

The two sides wound up hunkered down just feet apart on either opposite slopes of an earthwork. As Crapsey described it: "Our boys on one side of a frail field work and the Rebels on the other, added to the darkness, the roar of the guns, the noise and din." The Confederates finally managed to withdraw in the morning "leaving a score of dead bodies" and "everything. . . .in exactly the same condition as before the Rebel assault."

There were also men who moved across the no-man's land with neither friendship nor malice on their minds, but only a driving imperative to escape the killing. These were the deserters.

Desertion had reached crisis proportions within the Army of Northern Virginia by late 1864 and early 1865. Robert E. Lee called attention to the problem on January 27, when he sent a report to Richmond about what he described as "the alarming frequency of desertions from this army." Lee identified the root causes as "insufficiency of food and nonpayment of the troops." On February 9, in his new capacity as general in chief, Lee proposed to Jefferson Davis that a thirty-day grace period be announced, during which all deserters and absentees could return to the army without punishment. "All who may desert after the publication of the order shall receive quick and merited punishment," Lee vowed.[4] Later that same month, he still felt obliged to call to the attention of John C. Breckinridge, the new secretary of war, "the alarming number of desertions that are now occurring in the army." This time, Lee added another cause that drove men to desert: "the representation of their friends at home who appear to have become very despondent as to our success." Lee concluded, "These desertions have a very bad effect upon the troops who remain and give rise to painful apprehension."

Heth's and Wilcox's divisions lost five hundred men this way over two weeks in February, and during the period from February 15 to March 18, nearly three thousand of Lee's soldiers risked being shot by friend or foe in order to scamper across the no-man's-land into captivity. "The (newspaper) accounts (of deserters coming in) are not exaggerated," a Massachusetts artilleryman confirmed. "Almost any day one can spot squadrons of rebels prowling round in our lines." "The rebels come over to us occasionally in numbers from one to three," a Pennsylvania infantryman wrote in late November. "They don't go back. They are well dressed and look good."

An officer in an African-American unit wrote in early February: "The 'Johnnys' continue to come in. . . . A few days since they had a man under guard for some misdemeanor, and sent him under a guard of two men out between

---

4 "Lee's proposal was accepted by Jefferson Davis on February 10 and announced to the troops the next day. It had no appreciable effect.

the picket lines to get some wood; and the prisoner and guard did not stop coming till they got safely into our lines. Good guard duty that." Summing it all up, a New Yorker who met and spoke with some of the deserters, remarked that "it looks to me as if Rebeldom was fast falling to pieces."

The Confederate soldiers who remained were appalled and angered by what was happening. One South Carolinian, writing in February, lamented that "there are such a number who are ready to bring eternal disgrace on themselves & country by their ignominious conduct." But the day after this letter was written, a young Connecticut chaplain recorded in his diary that he "conversed with a S.C. reb who came in this morning, as he did not have sufficiency of food."

They told a story in the 11th New Jersey about the "unusually bright and intelligent-looking man" who deserted and explained to his captors that "the usual number of men on the picket-post was three, but it had recently been increased to four by adding a man who was known to be reliable." When asked how it was, then, that he had gotten away, the soldier replied, "I was the reliable man on my post last night." One New Jerseyman reflected, "Even to the dullest mind the fact was plain that the Confederacy was falling to pieces."

The traffic in the opposite direction, while not at the same level, was not insignificant. "During the fall and winter desertions became alarming in frequency," reporter Sylvanus Cadwallader declared. "I was told that desertions were very heavy; that as high as 1,400 had left in a week," a military visitor to City Point noted in late October. Brigade commander Robert McAllister pointed his finger at bounty men who enlisted for the substantial cash payments and then deserted at the earliest opportunity. "The large bounties are demoralizing," McAllister complained. "Also, they give us a class of worthless men."

The 5th New Hampshire seemed especially prone to deserters, or at least was the butt of most stories about them. A New York artilleryman remembered "the chaffing across the lines which occurred every day about dusk [when] the rebels called on us to send over the flag and the colonel to command the regiment, as the greater part of it had come over to them." Another time, a new Federal unit moved up onto the picket line, and someone called out to the rebels on the other side, "What regiment is that over there?" Back came the answer, "The Fifth New Hampshire!"

Deserters who failed in their efforts and were captured faced the extreme penalties of military justice. Most suffered some form of imprisonment, but a few paid with their lives. As one member of the Union provost guard recalled,

"Those who had simply deserted to the enemy and had been recaptured were shot; while those, who, after deserting had, to avoid imprisonment, enlisted in the Confederate army, and then again had deserted from that army into our lines, were hanged."

Executions became a predictable part of the Union army schedule at Petersburg. Friday was the day most often set aside for the administration of sentences handed down by the military courts. "It has a gruesome sound," one New York soldier wrote after the war, "but the chief diversion of the latter part of 1864 was the attending of hangings in the vicinity." "We are treated to a hanging exhibition every Friday," another remarked, "and the men have grown to enjoy the spectacle. We lose all human feelings towards such dastards and traitors."

In the Ninth Corps they remembered December 10, 1864, the day that two condemned men from the 179th New York were hung:

William Hopkins (7th Rhode Island): "At one p.m. Edward Rowe and Daniel C. Smith, two deserters[,]. . . .were hung . . . just east of Hancock Station. They were comparatively young men, had willfully deserted to the enemy, and a few weeks later, had been recognized among a lot of rebel prisoners captured by their own regiment."

Elisha P. Comstock (186th New York): "There were some 2,000 present."

Albert M. Pope (35th Massachusetts): "Nearly a whole division was formed in a square around the gallows to witness the execution. It was a sad affair."

William Hopkins (7th Rhode Island): "The condemned were brought forth from the guardhouse and escorted to their fate in the following manner: A band playing a dirge, two coffins borne by soldiers, the two culprits good-looking and apparently intelligent, with wrists handcuffed behind them, two chaplains, an infantry guard on either hand, and a cavalry guard surrounding all."

Eugene Beauge (45th Pennsylvania): "One of them, I remember, walked firmly to the gallows smoking a cigar until it was time to pull the black cap over his face. His companion . . . showed more feeling. He tried to be brave, but the expression on his face as he looked up at the dangling rope with a noose already fixed for his neck gave him away."

William Hopkins (7th Rhode Island): "The army overcoats buttoned about their shoulders were not removed, but they could not conceal their violent, though ineffectual efforts to free their hands, the drawing up of the feet, the heaving of their chests, or the spasmodic tremors that frequently darted through their frames, but constantly becoming weaker and more infrequent until they finally ceased."

Joseph Gould (48th Pennsylvania): "The execution was very artistically performed; and, after the division was marched past the suspended bodies, we were conducted to camp."

L. W. Lord (45th Pennsylvania): "Many of the recruits who had recently joined us shed tears."

Unidentified soldier (35th Massachusetts): "The effect upon the men was less impressive than [with] death by shooting. . . . One of the spectators, who had probably been at work fixing up some officer's accounts, wanted to know whether the ropes and slip-nooses would be charged to the condemned men's camp and garrison equipage accounts!"

Life in the army camps about Petersburg took on its own particular character. Following the operations in late October, the pace of activity slowed down, and soldiers on both sides began to think of their encampments in something less than temporary terms. The men built huts of wood and mud, laid out company streets, did their turn of duty in the trenches, and waited for something to happen. The wearisome routine drove some soldiers to distraction. "Dull, duller, dullest," a New Yorker declared. "Nothing can exceed the monotony of camp-life." Added a Pennsylvania man: "There is the usual routine of business, so that before the dawn begins to break, the drums beat reveille, the camp is awaked, and the fortifications lined with troops, to prevent even the possibility of a surprise. A little smart walk, an occasional 'rough and tumble,' or a few embers serve to keep one comfortable until daylight sends him to his quarters."

Some found relief in practical jokes. Soldiers in the Union camps liked to wait until a certain hut or bombproof was filled to capacity on a cold day. "Then would be the time for the circus to commence," a participant in the stunt remembered. "Some rascal having located the crowd would get a rope and tie the door from the outside, then cover up the chimney, himself and his comrades sitting outside, meanwhile, giving advice. It was wonderful the amount of Scripture the boys inside could quote on such occasions."

Other Yankees with time on their hands found an unapproved use for damp rifle cartridges. A reporter on hand explained that "a soldier puts in his [dry] cartridge, and then a second one, the powder of which has been wet. The gun is fired, and the wet powder or the extra cartridge goes flying through the air very much like a comet with an abbreviated but exceedingly brilliant tail. Out of this, although the first bullet, or even the second may carry death of mutilation across the Rebel parapets, out boys extract a prime article of fun."

Amusements weren't limited to the boys in blue. A cannoneer in gray recalled how "during a cold spell of weather some of the more frolicsome veterans managed to pass off instructions on the novices of the night guard 'to blow in the vents of the cannon in order to keep them clear,' which operation brought forth a full budget of experiences and gossip for the next day."[5]

Others found relief from the long wait by decorating their encampments with tree boughs or constructing huts more elaborate than their neighbors'. The clear winner was the winter camp of the 50th New York Engineers, located around Poplar Grove Church. The soldier-engineers built a little village of tidy Gothic-style cottages, crowned by an impressive miniature Gothic church. A Connecticut chaplain described it as a "beautiful rustic chapel built of pine logs and poles with the bark on. . . . It [had] . . . a graceful spire of the same material as the building itself, and was a most attractive and picturesque structure."

Confederates found different ways to pass the time. "Rode ten miles to attend a Virginia Reel or break-down," a South Carolina cavalryman posted near Richmond wrote in February. "Had no supper but plenty of kisses." A North Carolina infantryman, on the other extreme of the Confederate line, noted that "we had a theatre in Davis' Brigade, built of logs with a dirt floor and log seats, and such capers the soldier comedians and tragedians cut by torch light, and music by banjo and the fiddle!"

---

5   The vent was the hole in the closed end of the tube, through which the friction primer was pushed into the powder.

There were also theatrical groups, music ensembles, and card games of all types on the Union side, but perhaps the biggest diversion was an equestrian one. "Horse racing has become quite the rage in all ranks of the army," a telegrapher observed in October. Almost as fast as Union arms could claim new extensions of the line around Petersburg and Richmond, opportunists were staking out fresh racecourses. In September, the venue was a level stretch of the Halifax Road, and the action continued as late as March, when the New Market Road, north of the James, was the scene for a race "between some of the corps and division staff."

Meade staff aide Theodore Lyman attended a festive event held at Peebles Farm on Saint Patrick's day. "There was a judge's stand, flaunting with trefoil flags, and a band beside the same. . . . Then a bugler blows at a great rate and the horses are brought to the line; the bugler blows at a great rate some more, and away they go. . . . [We] had tragic consequences; for one [horse,] scared by the crowd and by the brush hurdle, bolted violently and knocked down [and killed] a soldier."

Christmas day 1864 was observed by both sides. Just as in armies before then and after, some soldiers had better luck this day than others. There are stories of special repasts enjoyed by boys in blue and those in grey, and others who seemed to be left off the delivery list. Thanks to a little creative bookkeeping, most of the U. S. hospitals, reported the *New York Herald's* Sylvanus Cadwallader, "set out a tempting dinner." Some Confederate units posted near to Petersburg received a special meal prepared by townspeople that was "highly appreciated." "But," a soldier added, "it was evident that at many a hearth-stone there was now suffering for food." The war business did not take a break and, as another reporter noted, "Christmas. . . .will bear a very striking likeness to every other day."

The Yankee boys were kept well supplied by what an artilleryman called "one of the curiosities out here"—the U.S. Military Railroad. "[It] ran the whole length of our line at Petersburg and was extended as fast as the line," a Maine soldier testified. "It was an up-and-downhill affair, scarcely any grading except steep rises and across chasms." "There was no pretense of grading," another infantryman agreed. "They just placed ties on top of the ground and laid the rails across them."

"No other such railroad was ever seen before, or ever will be again," a Connecticut man exclaimed. "The soldiers declared that it made them sea-sick to ride on its cars," added an officer. According to Horace Porter, "It ran up hill and down dale, and its undulations were so marked that a train moving along it looked in the distance like a fly crawling over a corrugated washboard." Unconventional it may have appeared, but the U.S.M.R.R. brought the lifeblood of supplies to the Union forces besieging Petersburg. As many as fifteen trains per day carried food and ammunition of all kinds to within easy hauling distance of the front. As one Union soldier put it, the military railroad "proved to be of great service to the investing army."

The most serious attempt to disrupt this smooth supply operation came on the night of January 23, when three Confederate ironclads, accompanied by a small flotilla of wooden torpedo boats and gunboats, moved from Chaffin's Bluff, along the James River, to attack Union shipping at City Point. A combination of Union defensive fire, poor C.S. sailing, and mechanical breakdowns ended the raid well short of its goal.

The important Union successes in the winter of 1864-65 occurred everywhere but Petersburg—in Nashville, Tennessee; Fort Fisher, North Carolina; Columbia and Charleston, South Carolina; and Savannah, Georgia. Each achievement was celebrated by hundred-gun salutes along the Petersburg lines. One young North Carolinian, writing home on December 18, paused in the midst of family gossip to note that "I can hear the Yankee guns now pegging away. . . . It sounds as though they were firing salutes, for they fire very regularly and I suppose they are celebrating a victory gained somewhere."

Another Tarheel, writing on January 15, observed, "The great part of the soldiers seem to be in low spirits and a good many say the Confederacy has 'gone up'. . . . and that we are whipped. I have never seen the men so discouraged before." "We must pass thro' a great crisis before spring," a Virginian wrote five days later, adding, "Much to be done and suffered." "We were waiting for something to explode," a Southern staff officer remarked grimly, "killing time, for time was killing us."

Chapter Fifteen

"Proper subjects for the hangman"

December 20, 1864 - February 9, 1865

Ulysses S. Grant
Final Report of Operations, March 1864-May 1865

Wilmington, N.C., was the most important sea-coast port left to the enemy through which to get supplies from abroad and send cotton and other products out by blockade-runners, besides being a place of great strategic value. The navy had been making strenuous exertions to seal the harbor of Wilmington, but with only partial effect. The nature of the outlet of Cape Fear River was such that it required watching for so great a distance that, without possession of the land north of New Inlet or Fort Fisher, it was impossible for the navy to entirely close the harbor. . . .

[Following the failure of an expedition under Major General Benjamin Butler, I determined to] make another attempt to take the place. This time I selected Bvt. Maj. Gen. A. H. Terry to command the expedition. . . .

The expedition sailed from Fort Monroe on the morning of the 6th [of January], arriving on the rendezvous, off Beaufort, on the 8th, where, owing to the difficulties of the weather, it lay until the morning of the 12th, when it got underway and reached its destination that evening. . . . In the afternoon of the 15th the fort was assaulted, and, after most desperate fighting, was captured, with its entire garrison and armament. . . . This gave us entire control of the mouth of the Cape Fear River.

*   *   *

December 20 1864: Washington, D.C.
First Move

Horace Greeley and Francis P. Blair, Sr., were an odd couple. The fifty-three-year-old Greeley, founder and editor of the powerful *New York Tribune*, was a fearless anti-establishment outsider who was driven by a burning desire to bludgeon his way inside—a rough-and-tumble man who wooed new ideas with the fervor of a religious convert. Greeley's support had given credence to the nascent Republican party, and his crafty maneuvering at the 1860 national convention had helped Abraham Lincoln with the nomination. Seventy-three-year-old Francis Blair was a member in good standing of the American political aristocracy. Perhaps *the* dominant figure in Andrew Jackson's kitchen cabinet, Blair had also edited the politically influential *Washington Globe* and helped found the Republican party. He was the classic insider, a man whose counsel helped to shape the very nature of the establishment. The point of intersection for these two very different men was the simple matter of finding a way to peace.

"*You* have Mr. Lincoln's ear, as I have not, and can exert influence on every side where it is needed," Greeley wrote to Blair early in December. "Do urge and inspire him to make peace among our friends any how, and with our foes so soon as may be." A second letter outlined some specific proposals. Greeley believed that both sides wanted the bloodshed to end; Blair also felt that the time was right for peace, and how better to crown a distinguished career in public service than by ending the Civil War?

In his reply, written on December 20, Blair confided to Greeley that he had a plan for delivering the country once and for all from "*the cause of the war, the war itself, and the men & means* essential to carrying it on against us." He had an appointment with Lincoln two days from then, he added, at which time he would "hint it to" the President. "Meanwhile," Blair closed his note, "you will keep my suggestion a Secret as illicit embryos ought to be & generally are."

December 28, 1864: Washington, D.C.
Second Move

Abraham Lincoln needed some bargaining chips. His public stand on continuing the war was unequivocal. Pressed hard on the peace issue by Horace Greeley in the summer of 1864, Lincoln had issued a statement that promised, "Any proposition which embraces the restoration of peace, the integrity of the whole Union, and the abandonment of slavery…will be met by liberal terms on other substantial and collateral points."

Lincoln admitted to a prominent Peace Democrat in a private conversation that September that he was willing to go "as far 'as any man in America to restore peace on the basis of the Union and further, that he "never has and never will present any other *ultimatum*—that he is misunderstood on the subject of slavery—that it shall not stand in the way of peace."

Lincoln was enough of a pragmatist to recognize that any contact between the two warring sides, however unlikely, might be the means to open face-to-face negotiations, but he was also wary of Radical Republicans against conciliation and dared not move too openly in that direction. Enter Francis P. Blair, Sr. Whatever schemes Blair may have concocted were incidental to the fact that the elder statesman was willing to take the political risk of making public contact with Richmond. Lincoln was careful, however, to keep Blair at arm's length.

"When he applied for a passport to go to Richmond, with certain ideas which he wished to make known to me," Lincoln jotted down in a memorandum of the conversation, "I told him that I did not want to hear them."

Lincoln told Blair to return "after Savannah falls." William Tecumseh Sherman entered that city on December 22; six days later, Lincoln sent Blair a card inscribed, "Allow the bearer, F. P. Blair, Senr. to pass our lines, go South and return. A. Lincoln."

January 12, 1865: Richmond, Virginia
Third Move

The plan that Francis Blair presented to Jefferson Davis was part fantasy and part hopeful delusion. What was needed to reunite the North and South, Blair declared, was a common enemy. He believed that the real threat facing North America was Louis Napoleon's puppet regime in Mexico; accordingly, he proposed that a general amnesty be issued, allowing Davis to lead a Confederate force into Texas and then on to Mexico, where they would unite with Juarez to free the country. "He who expels the Bonaparte-Hapsburg dynasty from our southern flank," Blair said, "…will ally his name with those of Washington and Jackson as a defender of the liberty of the country."

Jefferson Davis found Blair's proposal wild, fantastic, impossible to take seriously. Yet Blair himself was a tangible link to Washington, something that Davis might be able to use to his advantage.

Davis knew that the North and South were divided by one utterly irreconcilable issue—union. The United States would accept no solution that did not include it, and the Confederate States would accept no solution that did. For Davis, the war must end either in total victory or in total defeat, and it was vital that the Southern people come to embrace that fact.

But the years of bloodshed had drained the living spirit of the Southern soul, and morale was slipping throughout the Confederacy. Davis knew his people. Nothing would reignite the fires of Southern nationalism more quickly than an unequivocal Northern declaration against Confederate self-determination. And if some prominent Southern peacemakers were the ones to bring back that message, so much the better.

With the smooth eloquence of a practiced politician, Davis listened to Blair's ideas without endorsing them. He scribbled a note addressed to the erstwhile diplomat: "I have no disposition to find obstacles in forms," it read, "and am willing, as heretofore, to enter into negotiations for the restoration of peace.... I would, if you could promise that a commission, minister, or other agent would be received, appoint one immediately, and renew the effort to enter into a conference with a view to secure *peace to the two countries*." Davis made a point of emphasizing the final words.

He signed the message and gave it to Blair.

January 18, 1865: Washington, D.C.
Fourth Move

Abraham Lincoln kept Davis's note for two days. Blair had added some personal observations to the Confederate president's message: the self-designated emissary was convinced that Southerners, having experienced severe economic hardships, were eager for peace.

Lincoln at last decided that two could play at this game of indirection, and he gave Blair a note to take back to Richmond. In it, he promised to "receive any agent whom [Davis], or any other influential person now resisting the national authority, may informally send to me, with the view of securing peace to the people of our one common country."

He did not emphasize the last three words, but then he knew he did not have to.

Francis Blair could see only his own historical immortality. "My faith is strong that we shall have a happy deliverance, and that soon," he bubbled in a letter to Horace Greeley. "There is good will for it on both sides."

January 24, 1865: Richmond, Virginia
Fifth Move

There was no love lost between Jefferson Davis and his vice president, Alexander H. Stephens. Stephens had been a reluctant convert to the Confederate cause, yet such was the force of his intellect and his esteem among political colleagues that the diminutive, consumptive-looking Georgian had nearly beaten Davis for the presidency. Davis, Stephens said, was not "*great* in any sense of the word. The power of will has made him all that he is." In happier times, Davis had referred to Stephens as "the little pale star from Georgia," but now he recognized that the vice president was a focal point for growing antiwar sentiment in the South. Stephens had loudly proclaimed the total failure of Davis's war program just two months earlier and called for the opening of direct talks with Washington.

The peripatetic Mr. Blair returned to Richmond with Lincoln's note on January 23. Davis immediately focused on the U.S. President's closing reference to "our common country"; when he asked Blair about Lincoln's choice of words, he was told that it related to that part of Mr. Davis's letter that spoke of "the two countries." The yawning gap between the two sides was irrefutable. When Blair left, Davis sent for Mr. Stephens.

As Davis had expected, Stephens saw both the note and Blair's fantastic plan as the means to an end. Recalled Stephens, "I told him that I thought the program suggested by Mr. Blair should be acceded to, at least so far as to obtain, if possible, a conference upon the subject."

Who should take part in such a conference? Davis asked. Stephens at once suggested that Davis himself lead the delegation, but the Confederate president firmly vetoed that idea. Stephens then recommended three men: Judge John A. Campbell, assistant secretary of war; Confederate general Henry L. Benning; and Thomas S. Flourney, a Virginian who was well known to Lincoln. It was a sensible, well-balanced group—and Jefferson Davis rejected it. If there was to be a peace committee, Davis insisted, Stephens would have to head it. He then named the two other members he had in mind: Judge Campbell and Robert M. T. Hunter, president pro tem of the Confederate Senate. Stephens and

Campbell were clearly aligned with those willing to consider a compromise settlement.

Davis told his secretary of state, Judah Benjamin, to draft the necessary authorization. Benjamin drew up a statement that, in accordance "with the letter of Mr. Lincoln," allowed the trio to travel to Washington "for a conference with him upon the subject to which it relates." This phrasing was far too diplomatically vague for Davis's purposes, so he changed the final words to read "for the purpose of securing *peace to the two Countries*."

Armed with this official document, the newly appointed Confederate Peace Commissioners journeyed to Petersburg, where they hoped to cross into the Union lines.

January 29 - 31, 1865: Petersburg, Virginia
First Interlude

It was Sunday, the twenty-ninth of January, a Maine soldier posted near the crater recalled, when "pickets reported a flag of truce to be shown on the enemy's works." An investigation revealed that "the purpose of the flag was to request permission for Messrs. A. H. Stephens, R. M. T. Hunter, and J. A. Campbell to pass through our lines as commissioners to treat with our government on the subject of a cessation of hostilities." Added *New York Times* reporter George F. Williams, "they...would have approached our lines via the James River, but were unable to do so, owing to the ice in the stream."

The message was hurried to City Point, but U. S. Grant was away examining the Confederate defenses around Wilmington preparatory to his next expedition against that place. It took two days for the note to reach him and his reply to reach City Point.

During those two days, observed correspondent Williams, the news that the Confederate commissioners "were awaiting permission to enter our lines flew like wildfire through the camps." "Expectation was a-tip-toe in both armies," one Massachusetts soldier maintained, "and the wearied rank and file hoped the result would be a peace with honor to both parties—with, of course, the Union saved." "There is some talk of piece now," a poor-spelling Tarheel wrote to his father, "the greatest that I ever saw since the war broke out."

The delegation received permission to cross the lines on January 31. According to the *New York Times*, a "deputation, consisting of Col. Babcock of Gen. Grant's staff, Col. Harriman[, commanding the Ninth Corps troops in that sector,] Col. Lyndon, of Gen. Parke's Staff, and Capt. Brackett of Gen.

Wilcox's Staff, were appointed to meet the gentlemen and escort them within our lines." The Federals guided the delegates across the no-man's land. "After a few minutes spent in the interchange of civilities the party came within our lines," continued the *Times* account, "at which moment the troops on both sides united in a simultaneous cheer, which seemed to give them greater confidence than they had before exhibited." "'Peace in the brain' appeared now to have spread like a contagion," added a Pennsylvania artilleryman.

Grant met the commissioners at City Point. According to Horace Porter, the Confederates were "most cordially received. . . . As General Grant had been instructed from Washington to keep them at City Point until further orders, he conducted them in person to the headquarters steamer, the *Mary Martin*, which was lying at the wharf, made them his guests, and had them provided with well-furnished state-rooms and comfortable meals during their stay."

February 1, 1865: Richmond, Virginia
Sixth Move

Another piece of Jefferson Davis's plan fell into place today when the Confederate Congress approved his appointment of Robert E. Lee as general in chief of all Confederate armies. This action had been pushed on Davis by the Confederate Senate and the General Assembly of Virginia. Such a move, the assembly had declared, would "inspire increased confidence in the final success of our arms."

Lee himself was appalled at the prospect. "If I had the ability I would not have the time," he protested when he was informed of his unsolicited promotion. The senate's resolution also called for P. G. T. Beauregard to take charge in South Carolina and for Joseph E. Johnston to be restored to command of the Army of Tennessee. Davis saw these actions as blunt attempts to preempt his executive powers. He made no official comment on the matter, but his outspoken wife, Varina, was not so reluctant. "If I were he," she told one senator, "I would die or be hung before I would submit to the humiliation that Congress intended him."

Yet Davis saw clear advantages to Lee's appointment. He understood his man well enough to know that Lee would never leave his army, so his new powers would be employed seldom, if at all. And there was little doubt that the naming of Lee as commander in chief of all Confederate armies would inspire new confidence in Davis's government.

Davis signed the congressional act that created the post of general in chief on January 26. He submitted Lee's name to the Senate five days later, which quickly approved the appointment.

Davis notified Lee in a February 1 telegram. Lee's reply, which came three days later and was addressed to Adjutant General Samuel Cooper, stated, "I am indebted alone to the kindness of His Excellency the President for my nomination to this high and arduous office, and wish I had the ability to fill it to advantage." Lee also made the telling point that "As I have received no instructions as to my duties, I do not know what he desires me to undertake."

One Southern staff officer later described the appointment as a "mockery of a rank no longer of any value." A wounded Texas soldier added his complaint that "Now it was too late; the Confederacy was gasping for breath, its armies were scattered, disorganized, and, practically, commanderless, and there was no time to gather together and weld the fragments into fighting machines."

February 1, 1865: City Point, Virginia, 10:00 p.m.
Seventh Move

Major Thomas T. Eckert, superintendent of the U.S. Military Telegraph, was highly trusted by the White House. So reticent about confidential matters that one of his colleagues nicknamed him Silent Eckert, the otherwise unknown officer had been sent by Lincoln to City Point to question the Confederate Peace Commissioners on three crucial points. Lincoln insisted that any discussion had to begin with the following non-negotiable items: (1) restoration of the Union; (2) acceptance of all laws against slavery passed by the U.S. Congress; and (3) the goal of the talks to be a total, not partial, cessation of hostilities.

The Confederate commissioners replied that they were willing to meet Lincoln "without any personal compromise on any question in the letter." Eckert felt that this response was "not satisfactory" and, after two conversations with the representatives, refused them permission to continue their journey to Washington. He did this despite the fact that Secretary of State William Seward was waiting downriver at Fort Monroe to greet the trio.

Eckert telegraphed his report to the White House at 10:00 p.m. He tried to send a follow-up message to the Secretary of War thirty minutes later, but was told that the wires were down. Eckert boarded a steamer for Fortress Monroe that very night and arrived there at 9:00 a.m. the next day.

As far as he was concerned, the peace conference was over before it even began.

February 1, 1865: City Point, Virginia, 10:30 p.m.
Eighth Move

Support for the peace process now came from an unexpected quarter—Lieutenant General U. S. Grant. Thirty minutes after Eckert's negative assessment had been transmitted, Grant had a note of his own on the same lines that Eckert had been told were down.[1]

"I am convinced," Grant wrote to Secretary of War Stanton, "upon conversation with Messrs. Stephens and Hunter, that their intentions are good and their desire sincere to restore peace and union…. I fear now their going back without any expression from any one in authority will have a bad influence."

Stanton passed the communication along to Abraham Lincoln, as Grant knew he would.

February 2, 1865: Washington, D.C., 9:00 a.m.
Ninth Move

HON. W. H. SEWARD, FORTRESS MONROE, VA.

INDUCED BY A DISPATCH OF GENL. GRANT, I JOIN YOU AT FORT MONROE AS SOON AS I CAN COME.

A. LINCOLN

LIEUTENANT-GENERAL GRANT, CITY POINT, VA.

SAY TO THE GENTLEMEN I WILL MEET THEM PERSONALLY AT FORTRESS MONROE AS SOON AS I CAN GET THERE.

LINCOLN

---

1 The supposition is that Grant held up Eckert's follow-up note, which would have ended any possibility of a peace conference.

February 2, 1865:
Confederate Camps near Hatcher's Run, Virginia
Second Interlude

Major Henry Kyd Douglas, adjutant general for Brigadier General John Pegram's division, was full to bursting with pride and, perhaps, a touch of envy. He had been on leave in mid-January and so had missed Pegram's marriage to Miss Hetty Carey of Baltimore. Determined to do something special for his commanding officer and friend, Douglas had arranged things so that the review of Pegram's troops by General Gordon, already planned for this day, would also be a tribute to the new bride. All the Confederate brass was invited—including Lee, Longstreet, A. P. Hill, Gordon, Anderson, Heth, and others.

As the reviewing party took its place, Douglas stole a secret glance at Pegram's new wife. "[With] her classic face, her pure complexion, her auburn hair, her perfect figure and her carriage[, she was] altogether the most beautiful woman I ever saw in any land," he thought.

It was quite an occasion. "As the division under General Pegram passed in review before her—General Gordon abdicating in her favor—General Lee was on her right and the other generals with their glittering staff officers about her and in her train. Her rich color emblazoned her face, a rare light illumined her eyes and her soul was on fire with the triumph of the moment, horrors of war forgotten," Douglas recalled. "I rode with her off the field, and as we passed the troops returning to camp, she . . . sitting her horse like the Maid of France and smiling upon them with her marvelous beauty, their wild enthusiasm sought in vain for fitting expression and vent. An excited 'Tar Heel,' whom her horse struck and nearly knocked down, quickly sprang up and, as she reined up her horse and began to apologize, he broke in as he seized his old hat from his head, 'Never mind, Miss. You might have rode all over me, indeed you might!'"

February 3, 1865:
Aboard the *River Queen*, off Fortress Monroe, Virginia
The Conference

(Present were Abraham Lincoln, William Seward, Alexander Stephens, Robert M. T. Hunter, and John A. Campbell. No aides attended the meeting, and no notes were taken.)

The meeting began with small talk. Robert Hunter, a former U.S. senator, asked about the Capitol dome, which had been under construction when he left

Washington in 1861. It was finished, Seward told him, and he went on to describe the new structure. There was some other chatter, and then Stephens got to the point.

"Well, Mr. President," he said, "is there no way of putting an end to the present trouble?"

"There is but one way," Lincoln replied. "Those who are resisting the laws of the Union must cease their resistance."

Stephens sought to introduce Blair's idea of a joint war against the French in Mexico as something that might "divert the attention of both parties for a time." Lincoln closed that avenue fast. "The restoration of the Union is a *sine qua non* with me," he stated bluntly.

Judge Campbell asked what kind of postwar settlement might be possible in the matter of confiscated property, especially slaves. Lincoln stood by the Emancipation Proclamation—which, he reminded the Virginia jurist, had yet to be tested in the courts.

Seward now dropped a bombshell. "The Richmond party were then informed," he later remembered, "that Congress had on the 31st ultimo adopted by a constitutional majority a joint resolution submitting to the several States the proposition to abolish slavery throughout the Union." Lincoln interjected that he was willing to consider paying some form of compensation to slaveholders for their losses, but he added that Congress would have to agree to that as well. The U.S. Secretary of State took this point a step further and suggested to the Confederate commissioners that if the "Southern States will return to the Union…with their own strength and the aid of the connections they will form with other States, this [constitutional] amendment will be defeated."

Other, side issues were discussed, and then Robert Hunter summed things up with a question: "Mr. President, if we understand you correctly, you think that we of the Confederacy have committed treason; that we are traitors to your government; that we have forfeited our rights, and are proper subjects for the hangman. Is that not about what your words imply?"

Lincoln thought a moment before replying. "Yes," he said at last, "you have stated the proposition better than I did. That is about the size of it."

Stephens wondered whether the door to a peace settlement had been completely closed. "Mr. President, I hope you will reconsider," he said.

"Well, Stephens," Lincoln responded, "I will reconsider, but I do not think my mind will change."

In his report to Congress about this meeting, Abraham Lincoln noted, "The Conference ended without result."

February 4, 1865: City Point, Virginia
Tenth Move

```
CONFIDENTIAL
TO MAJ. GEN. G. G. MEADE FROM U. S. GRANT:

I WOULD LIKE TO TAKE ADVANTAGE OF THE PRESENT GOOD WEATHER TO
DESTROY OR CAPTURE AS MUCH AS POSSIBLE OF THE ENEMY'S WAGON
TRAIN, WHICH IT IS UNDERSTOOD IS BEING USED IN CONNECTION WITH
THE WELDON RAILROAD, TO PARTIALLY SUPPLY THE TROOPS ABOUT
PETERSBURG. YOU MAY GET THE CAVALRY READY TO DO THIS AS SOON AS
POSSIBLE. . . .
```

February 5, 1865:
Union Lines, South of Petersburg

The Yankee horsemen began moving at 3:00 a.m. The troopers, all from Gregg's division, "following the Jerusalem plank-road reached Ream's Station at 8 a.m.; thence [west] to Dinwiddie Court-House, passing deserted Confederate camps *en route*, where the fires, like the Confederacy, were still burning, but very low," one New Yorker editorialized.

Two infantry corps, the Second and the Fifth, moved with the cavalry. Gouverneur Warren's Fifth Corps provided close support for the operation; his three divisions, preceded by three squadrons of the 6th Ohio Cavalry, marched at about 7:00 a.m. from camps located between the Halifax Road and the Jerusalem Plank Road. Soon the spiky files began to angle west on the Stage Road, prompting one veteran to remark that they were moving "in light marching order on the old bloody path." Noted another in a New York regiment: "This time, the men were aware that a march in this direction meant business, and it surely did."

There was a delay of several hours at Monk's Neck Bridge, where Warren's line of march crossed Rowanty Creek. A *New York Herald* reporter covering the Fifth Corps described it as "about twenty feet wide, and not conveniently fordable." Here a small enemy detachment was manning rifle pits on the west side of the stream. It required a charge by two Pennsylvania regiments from Brevet Brigadier General James Gwyn's brigade to clear the way.

A soldier who participated in that attack remembered it years later:

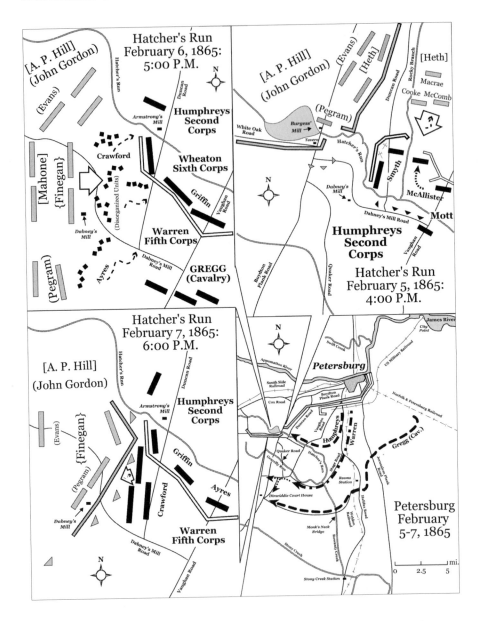

Reaching the stream, we found it covered with ice, on which we hoped to cross. One of the foremost boys stepped upon it, and it at once gave way, and let him into the water. Just the top of his head stuck out above the fragments of ice. He was fished out as expeditiously as possible, and the idea of crossing in that way was abandoned. Men came down with axes, and proceeded to fell trees across the run on which to cross.... Soon the trees were down, and part of the men crossed, while others kept careful watch on the rebels, and fired rapidly to keep them down. When enough had crossed, perhaps forty or fifty, then every body yelled, and those who had crossed charged the pits, and the rest came crowding over. Some of the rebels surrendered, and a few escaped.

The crossing was secured by 11:00 a.m., but it took nearly two more hours to build a rough bridge for the wagons and artillery. Warren's men met little opposition once across the Rowanty, as they pushed west toward their assigned positions—Griffin's division perhaps two miles east of Dinwiddie Court House, Ayres's division at the meeting of the Vaughan and Quaker roads, and Crawford's division holding the intersection of the Vaughan and Stage roads.

Also moving with the blue procession were George Meade and his staff. Meade had profound misgivings about expending so much force for such small gain. In fact, after receiving Grant's orders for him to organize the operation, Meade had asked the lieutenant general, "Are the objects to be attained commensurate with the disappointment which the public are sure to entertain if you make any movement and return without some striking result?" "The objects to be attained are of importance," Grant had answered.

Meade rode into battle with both his personal and his professional life in turmoil. His son Sergeant was so seriously ill that Meade had thought of taking a leave to help his wife care for the boy. On top of that, the Committee on the Conduct of the War—guided by Senator Ben Wade, a powerful friend of Ambrose Burnside's—had just issued its report on the Crater, a report that was decidedly anti-Meade in tone.

George Meade's media relations were acidly antagonistic at best, and he knew he would catch the heat for anything that went wrong during the impending operation. "It is rather hard under these circumstances to be abused," he wrote to his wife a few days after this movement, "but I suppose I must make up my mind to be abused by this set, never mind what happens."

The other blue-coated actors in this particular drama were two divisions of the Second Corps, commanded now by Major General Andrew A. Humphreys. These soldiers had moved out of their camps on the Union left at about 7:00 a.m. and headed south along the Vaughan Road. They, too, ran into a stubborn Rebel roadblock at an important stream crossing; it took a charge by skirmishers from de Trobriand's brigade to break the impasse at Hatcher's Run. The Federal soldiers were firmly in control of the position by 9:30 a.m.

Humphreys's mission was to shield Warren's corps, operating south of Hatcher's Run. Accordingly, the Second Corps column followed the north bank of the run and drew up before the Confederate entrenchments guarding the Boydton Plank Road. These earthworks had blocked Warren's and Parke's probes in late October, resulting in Hancock's fight at Burgess' Mill.

Humphreys had no intention of challenging the enemy's defenses. His orders were to hold the crossings "of Hatcher's Run at the Vaughan Road and at Armstrong's Mill," in order to maintain a connection between the main Petersburg lines and the force pushing toward the Boydton Plank Road.

Guessing that the Confederates opposite him would waste little time before contesting his advance, the former chief of staff of the Army of the Potomac began to set up a defensive position around Armstrong's Mill. Brigadier General Thomas Smyth's division held the left of Humphreys's line, its extreme left anchored in the low, swampy ground just above Hatcher's Run. Smyth's line ran north, parallel to the Duncan Road, for perhaps half a mile before turning east as far as a small stream known as Rocky Branch. Further east, Mott's division took up the line, reaching back to the left flank of the Union entrenchments south of Petersburg, now manned only by Nelson Miles's division.

Humphreys examined his lines and at once detected a problem: there was a large gap between Smyth's right and Mott's left. "It was here that I expected the attack of the enemy," Humphreys later reported.

The first warning that Robert E. Lee gave Richmond of the Union move was brief:

> AT 11 A.M. TO-DAY ENEMY FORCED A PASSAGE ACROSS HATCHER'S RUN, AT VAUGHAN'S ROAD, BELIEVED TO BE SECOND AND FIFTH CORPS, ACCOMPANIED BY CAVALRY; PREPARING TO MEET THEM.

The earthworks confronting Humphreys were manned by North Carolinians and Mississippians from Henry Heth's division of A. P. Hill's corps. Further south, newlywed John Pegram's division (of John Gordon's corps) was blocking the Boydton Plank Road near Burgess' Mill. When the Union movement was first detected, Brigadier General Clement A. Evans's division of Gordon's corps was moved south along the Boydton Plank Road to assist Pegram. As it became apparent that the Yankees were not going to duplicate their October 27 push to the White Oak Road, Evans's men were shunted in behind Heth's line to support a strike force that was being organized to shove back the Federals. Scouts had detected the gap in Humphreys's line, and Heth's men were preparing to exploit it.

Brigadier General John R. Cooke's North Carolina brigade was pulled out of line (Davis's Mississippians spread to cover the emptied position) and marched north and then east, outside the works, and into battle formation. "Somehow whenever there is any flanking or dirty fighting to be done Cooke's Brigade has to take the lead," one officer grumbled. Colonel William McComb's mixed Maryland-Tennessee brigade took station on Cooke's left, with Brigadier General William MacRae's all-North Carolina brigade in support.

The leading battle lines moved toward the gap in the Union lines short after 4:00 p.m.

Brevet Brigadier General Robert McAllister was ordered to plug that hole. His mixed Massachusetts-New Jersey-New York brigade, part of Mott's division, had been holding the eastern shoulder of the gap. Under orders from General Mott, McAllister had placed one regiment—the 7th New Jersey—in the gap itself, "a considerable distance from my left," as he later recalled. At 3:30 p.m., word came that a brigade detached from Nelson Miles's division would relieve McAllister, to enable him to cover the open space between Smyth's right and Mott's left. The detached brigade began to arrive thirty minutes later, and McAllister immediately put his troops in motion. According to the Union officer, "my right regiments were just filling in, when the attack was made on the picket line. I then ordered 'double-quick,' and we were moving in rapidly."

Heavy woods in their front prevented the Union soldiers from seeing the full extent of the enemy force, but there was no doubt that there were plenty of them. "The fire was taken up all along the line as fast as my troops were formed," McAllister reported. All of his regiments save one found cover, either in the woods or behind hastily erected breastworks. Bad luck placed that one regiment—the 8th New Jersey—out in the open, fully exposed to the enemy's fire. "[In] this unprotected position…they stood nobly and fought splendidly," McAllister observed proudly. "Not a man of this regiment, or indeed of the whole brigade, left for the rear." Of the fifty-three casualties suffered by McAllister's men in this affair, forty-eight were from the 8th New Jersey.

From Smyth's position, three hundred yards to McAllister's left, gunners from the 10th Massachusetts Battery blasted shells into the Confederate battle lines. Rifle fire from both flanks swept the ground in front of McAllister's men, who also kept up their own steady shooting.

The engagement lasted ninety minutes. The enemy lines pushed at one point to within a hundred yards, and some Federals began to waver. At that very moment, recalled a New Jersey soldier, "Chaplain Hopkins, of the One Hundred and Twentieth New York, began to sing the 'Battle Cry of Freedom.' The song was taken up by the brigade, and there is no doubt that as the strains of music rose above the battle's din many hearts resolved anew to 'rally 'round the flag' whenever danger menaced it." Added McAllister, "The Rebels replied: 'We will rally round your flag, boys!'"

A Second Corps staff aide who rode along McAllister's line with Andrew Humphreys remembered the end of this fight: "It was about dark and the flash of the muskets was visible. The enemy's fire slackened, and it became apparent that his attack was ceasing."

"All praise to my gallant Brigade," McAllister crowed in a letter to his wife, "and all are willing to award it to us; and well they may, for it saved our army. Had the Rebels succeeded, it would have been a terrible blow to us." "The 3rd Brigade knocked the thunder out of them for a while," seconded a Pennsylvania soldier.

Cooke's North Carolina Brigade caught the brunt of the Yankee fire. Three times the battle lines struggled forward, and three times they fell back, each time more disorganized than before. Finally, as one Tarheel veteran recollected, "some few of the new recruits who had recently joined our brigade, not exactly fancying the shot and shell which were flying around, thought the rear was a safer place, and suiting the action to the thought, 'dusted.' Gen. Lee with several of his staff was seated on horseback in rear of our lines and in proximity to the battle, awaiting the issue, when observing these men crossing the works without their guns, in seeming alarm and haste, he rode toward them, endeavoring to halt and return them to their command, when one of the 'dusters,' in grave alarm, raised his hands and voice in terror, exclaiming: 'Great God, old man, get out of the way, you don't know nothing[!]'"

After Heth's third attack failed, Evans's men were moved up on Heth's left, though it was too late for them to accomplish anything.

In his official report to Richmond, Lee allowed this affair two sentences: "In the afternoon parts of Hill's and Gordon's troops demonstrated against the enemy on the left of Hatcher's Run, near Armstrong's Mill. Finding him intrenched they were withdrawn after dark."

The intensity of the Confederate attacks aroused concern at Meade's headquarters for the safety of the Fifth Corps and Gregg's cavalry. Orders were issued at 9:30 p.m. for both forces to pull back and concentrate near the

Vaughan Road crossing of Hatcher's Run. Charles Griffin's division, posted nearest the Boydton Plank Road, began withdrawing at around ninety minutes later. "The night was very cold and the troops suffered considerably, many having no blankets or overcoats," a correspondent reported. "The troops had little rest and no sleep," a soldier in the 118th Pennsylvania added.

Conditions were scarcely better in the Second Corps. The weary soldiers built fires, only to find that the wet wood produced more smoke than flame, and the heavy air kept the fumes from dispersing. One New York infantryman recalled that "many of the boys went up on the hill above the smoke until they would get so cold they had to come back to the smoke and fire to get warm."

Not until 4:00 a.m. on February 6 did Gregg's worn-out cavalrymen rejoin the infantry. The Federal riders had met little opposition on their mission, reaching Dinwiddie Court House with plenty of daylight to spare. The only thing missing from the otherwise perfect scenario was the Confederate supply wagons: Gregg had sent squadrons galloping up and down the plank road to search in vain for the heavily laden vehicles that were rumored to be there. His total catch for the operation was eighteen wagons and fifty prisoners. The troopers also brought back a copy of an appeal made by Robert E. Lee to local citizens encouraging them to sell their surplus crops to the army. In the words of the *New York Herald* correspondent who saw the message: "This is an unquestionable evidence of short diet in Richmond."

February 6, 1865:
Confederate and Union Lines, near Hatcher's Run

When morning brought nothing more serious than a few halfhearted Yankee probes, Robert E. Lee decided to return some of his troops to their warm camps. All the brigades in Mahone's division (Joseph Finegan covering for an absent Mahone) were put on the road back to Petersburg.

Orders were issued at the same time for John Pegram to march his division out from Burgess' Mill to reconnoiter the corridor east of the Boydton Plank Road, which included the area around Dabney's Mill. One of Pegram's brigades moved "near [Hatcher's] run and the others farther to the right and along the Vaughan Road." It was a little before 1:00 p.m. when Pegram's skirmishers passed Dabney's Mill and continued their slow scout to the east.

There was confusion in high places on the Union side this morning. At 7:15, Meade assured Grant that he had instructed both Humphreys and Warren "to move out at once to determine whether or not Hill's or any portion of the enemy's force is now outside of their works." De Trobriand's brigade carried out Humphreys's assignment and moved cautiously northward at about 9:00 a.m. "Finding we couldn't draw [the enemy] out, we faded into some woods and stayed until noon, when we made a further retrograde movement to our line of works," one of de Trobriand's soldiers remembered.

Gouverneur Warren did nothing while this was happening. He chose to interpret Meade's orders to mean that only Humphreys was to reconnoiter, and that the Fifth Corps and cavalry would be held in readiness to cooperate with the Second Corps if needed. Meade appeared at Warren's headquarters a little after noon and personally straightened out his subordinate. "Consequently," Warren later reported, "at 1:15 p.m. I issued instructions to General Crawford to move out on the Vaughan Road to where it turns to Dabney's Mill, and then follow up that road toward the mill." At the same time, Gregg's cavalrymen were pushing south along the Vaughan Road.

It was not, long after 2:00 p.m. when slight gunfire crackled into the deeper roar of something more serious occurring east of Dabney's Mill. Crawford's division had run into the lone brigade that Pegram had sent scouting along Hatcher's Run. To further complicate matters for Warren, Gregg's cavalrymen now reported enemy infantry (Pegram's other brigades) in their front.

In his brief report of the actions that followed, Confederate corps commander John Gordon wrote that John Pegram's "brigades were vigorously attacked by both cavalry and infantry in heavy force. They were pressed slowly back, bravely resisting the enemy's advance."

The Federal riders along the Vaughan Road had had little trouble overcoming the mounted outposts they had encountered, but it was an altogether different matter when North Carolina infantrymen from Lewis's and Johnston's brigades arrived on the scene. The blue-coated cavalrymen fell back in what one Federal officer described as "considerable confusion," but infantry supports from Winthrop's brigade of Ayres's division were on hand, and the serious fighting here ended by late afternoon.

However, the collision east of Dabney's Mill began to suck in large numbers of reinforcements from both sides. Evans's men, like Mahone's on the march back to Petersburg, were turned around and hustled to assist Pegram. Evans's division, Gordon reported, "formed on Pegram's left, charged and drove the enemy before it, but was finally forced by superior numbers to retire." This "retirement" of some of Evans's troops was less than orderly. The soldiers, according to a Confederate staff officer who was present, "fled precipitately. . . . Nothing we did could stop them."

A Georgian in Evans's command recalled this as being a "very stubborn battle," in which a large mound of sawdust near the mill became the focal point for several attacks and counterattacks. A captain in Walker's Brigade, of Pegram's Division, attested to the intensity of the fighting, declaring that although "I have been in more severe engagements, I am sure I never, in all the battles I was in during the war, had so many shots fired directly at me."

Crawford's Federals had little trouble at first driving the enemy "to the vicinity of Dabney's Mill, where he [took] position under cover of some temporary works, from which he was soon dislodged." Pegram's men abandoned what appeared to be a large fort in their retreat. Color-bearers from the 16th Maine and 97th New York almost at once made a dash for it. "The 97th contestant achieved the victory," noted the unit's historian, "but great was his disappointment when instead of a veritable fort he found it only a huge heap of saw-dust."

Crawford's men were then hit by Evans's counterattack and rocked back from the site of the mill. Now Union reinforcements—consisting of two brigades from Ayres's division—came up on Crawford's left, counterattacked in turn, and retook the sawmill ruins.

Despite their regaining the ground, the Federals were in a bad way; Crawford's division was barely holding together. "The musketry fire on both sides was for a time as terrible as any of the war," the correspondent for the *Philadelphia Inquirer* stated. Regiment after regiment reported ammunition shortages, and as one pragmatic veteran observed, the "best of men will not stand with empty muskets and be shot down." There was also a decided lack of confidence in the wisdom of fighting in this place. "These woods were so dense that it was impossible to see far, and, remembering their rough experiences in a similar position on the Weldon Railroad in August, the men were very reluctant about advancing in such a thicket, unless assured of prompt support," one Pennsylvanian commented.

A full division from the Sixth Corps was on its way, but it was not close enough to help when fresh Confederate troops appeared and charged against the unsteady Fifth Corps line.

An Alabama officer in the 8th regiment recalled that his unit, part of Mahone's Division, "arrived at Hatcher's Run, after General Gordon had been repulsed at that place, in time to check the pursuing enemy." Joseph Finegan, leading the division this day, was an inspiration to his troops. One Virginian remembered how the general, "in command on horse back with a citizen coat, Beaver hat and walking stick[, was] . . . cheering the men [on,] leading them on saying 'On ye go you brave lads. On ye go you brave lads.' " Also inspirational was Nathanial Harris, one of whose men never forgot how he led his men "in his clear, ringing voice, which was heard distinctly above the roll of musketry."

Finegan's men struck the Federals in two waves of two brigades apiece—first the Alabamians of Sanders's Brigade (Colonel William H. Forney in command) and Brigadier General David A. Weisiger's Virginians, then Brigadier General G. Moxley Sorrel's Georgians and Brigadier General Nathaniel H. Harris's Mississippians. "[My] Georgians were hotly engaged . . . and made a handsome, successful charge, which dislodged and forced back the Federals," Sorrel wrote with pride. A Mississippian with Harris later recollected that "the Federals became demoralized and broke in confusion." "We drove them back easily and did it handsomely, nothing easier," an Alabamian under Forney added.

Henry Kyd Douglas was riding near John Pegram when the young brigadier clutched at his side and slumped in his saddle, the victim of an enemy sharpshooter. "I jumped from my horse and caught him as he fell and with assistance took him from his horse," Douglas remembered. "He died in my arms, almost as soon as he touched the ground."

Confusion and panic infected Crawford's and Ayres's men. According to the *New York Herald* man with the Fifth Corps, "the entire line became a wreck." Flanks collapsed, rattled regiments fired at friend and foe alike, and soldiers ran in every direction. A New York artilleryman present observed that "wagons and ambulances were beating a rapid retreat and in a word there was 'demoralization' and a regular stampede." Unengaged units coming up to support Warren's embattled men were almost engulfed by the rout. Brevet Major General Frank Wheaton's Sixth Corps division shuddered under the impact of terrified stragglers scrambling through its battle lines. Some of Wheaton's men "threw down their muskets and ran back," a New Jersey veteran of the Shenandoah Valley campaign later admitted. A chaplain in the 121st New York watched in dumb amazement as provost guards screamed at the stragglers, "Go back, go back!"

More help arrived, this time from Charles Griffin's division. By evening, the collapsed line had been reestablished a short distance east of Dabney's Mill.

Gouverneur Warren played down the final phase of the action in his official report and concluded, "On the whole, it was not a bad fight." Privately, he complained bitterly that "We are getting to have an array of such poor soldiers that we have to lead them everywhere, and even then they run away from us."

Night brought no succor to the suffering Union soldiers. "It was bitterly cold, and we were soaked with rain, which froze and stiffened our clothes under the influence of the wind," a Massachusetts soldier in the Sixth Corps recollected. "We built fires, but they were of little avail. The rain changed into snow and we finally rolled up in our blankets and slept the sleep of exhaustion, wet as we were."

Conditions were scarcely better for the victorious Confederates. A Mississippi man recalled that while huddling near the blazing logs "one side would be thawed out by getting close to the fire, the other side would be freezing." A Virginian in Finegan's division remembered, "During the evening the cooks brought to the men in line of battle a small pone of bread each, the first morsel since early morning; then these hungry soldiers wrapped their shivering frames into wet blankets and slept as best they could under their brush shelters on the frozen ground, while the pickets paced their beats in front to watch the enemy."

Even the dead were not spared indignity this night. A Virginia skirmisher sketched the macabre scene: "Upon the dead bodies, our men plundered them which I did all I could to prevent it yet they did it. It appeared to be an impossibility to prevent men from plundering and taking away the property and even the clothing which hid their naked form as a man. Yet they were so hardhearted as to strip from them every stitch of clothing which they had on and carried it off. Left their manly form stretched out on the cold icy ground without a stitch of garment to hide or shelter their nakedness."

General John B. Gordon sought out Henry Kyd Douglas for a sad personal mission. Someone would have to tell Hetty Pegram that her husband had been killed.

"You must do it, Douglas," Gordon said.

"Heavens! General—I'll lead a forlorn hope—do anything that is war—but not that," Douglas replied in anguish.

Another aide, Major John New, got the assignment and set off to carry it out. "An hour after," Douglas recalled years later, "as the General lay, dead, on my bed, I heard the ambulance pass just outside the window, taking Mrs. Pegram back to their quarters. [Major] New had not seen her yet and she did not know; but her mother was with her. A fiancée of three years, a bride of three weeks, now a widow!"

February 7, 1865:
Confederate and Union Lines, near Hatcher's Run

Gouverneur Warren had sorted out the confusion by 10:00 a.m. and reorganized his command. He then "ordered General Crawford to move out from our right near Armstrong's Mill and attack the enemy." Operations were hampered by a "severe storm which prevailed all day," but the Confederate picket line was nonetheless slowly pressed, and by 6:00 p.m., "General Crawford . . . drove the enemy back to his line near Dabney's Mill, regaining part of the battle-field of the preceding day and burying those killed found there."

Robert E. Lee recognized Crawford's movement for the limited action that it was and mounted no significant countermove. During the night, Warren pulled his men back across Hatcher's Run to conform to a new extension of the Union lines. In a 12:30 p.m. message to Grant, George Meade described this new entrenched line, which ran "from Fort Cummings, our old left, to Armstrong's Mill." "The territory of Hatcher's run, which for months has been a region of controversy between the two forces, now forms part of our lines," proclaimed the *New York Herald's* Fifth Corps man. "Five miles have been added to our lines, and Richmond is so much nearer its downfall."

Union losses in the actions of February 5-7 were 171 killed, 1,181 wounded, and 187 captured or missing, for a total of 1,539. Confederate casualties were estimated at about 1,000.

In the 14th Connecticut (in Smyth's division), they remembered First Lieutenant Franklin Bartlet, the youngest officer in the regiment. He had been promoted to captain, but his commission did not make it through army red tape before this action began. Bartlet was killed during one of the last Confederate attacks on February 5. Sergeant Charles A. Frey, of the 150th Pennsylvania (Crawford's division), eulogized his friend Private John Deihl, who was mortally wounded during the February 6 fighting: "Very few could say as he could: 'I never missed a march or a battle that the regiment took part in; I never missed my turn to go on guard or picket; was never excused from duty on account of sickness; was never home after I entered the service'; and very few could show more rents in their clothing, made by bullets, without drawing blood [,] than he."

They knew the names of their dead on the other side as well. The 2nd Maryland took part in Heth's attack on February 5. According to that regiment's history, "It was here that Lieutenant Charles W. Hodges, of Company C, acting Adjutant, was shot through the head and instantly killed.... A Christian gentleman, kind to all, and fearless in the discharge of his duty, he was universally beloved."

Final Moves

On February 5, Lincoln submitted to his cabinet the draft of a remarkable proclamation that he proposed to make to Congress. Upon reunification of the country, it would authorize him to distribute $400,000,000 in six percent bonds among all sixteen slave states (including the recently created West Virginia), to be used to reimburse slaveholders for property lost because of the Thirteenth Amendment. Lincoln also made it clear that this resolution would be accompanied by an executive pardon for all Southerners willing to return to the fold, and he strongly recommended that the U.S. Congress adopt a position of leniency on "all points not lying within executive control."

Lincoln's cabinet unanimously rejected his proposals, and the matter was dropped.

The three Confederate Peace Commissioners returned to Richmond on February 6. Jefferson Davis promptly sent their brief report of the conference to the Confederate Congress, with a covering note in which he declared, "The enemy refused to enter into negotiations with the Confederate States, or with any of them separately, or to give to our people any other terms or guarantees than those which the conqueror may grant, or to permit us to have [peace] on any other basis than our unconditional submission to their rule."

At a hurriedly called public meeting that same evening in Metropolitan Hall, Robert Hunter decried the Northern position. "Lincoln might have offered something.... What was this but unconditional submission to the mercy of the conquerors?" Davis himself made an unannounced appearance at the meeting and, according to John B. Jones, a clerk working in the war department, "denounced President Lincoln as 'His Majesty Abraham the First' . . . and said before the campaign was over he and Seward might find 'they had been speaking to their masters,' when demanding unconditional submission."

One reporter present watched Davis closely and noted that a "smile of strange sweetness came to his lips[,] as if the welcome assured him that, decried as he was by the newspapers and pursued by the clamor of politicians, he had still a place in the hearts of his countrymen."

All this was but prelude to the grand event—a mass rally on February 9 at the African Church, chosen for the occasion because of its vast capacity. The purpose of this rally, war clerk Jones wrote with cynical clarity, was "to reanimate the people for another carnival of blood." Davis had wanted Alexander Stephens to preside over this public call to arms, but the tired peacemaker would have none of it. "I declined," he later explained, "because I could not undertake to impress upon the minds of the people the idea that they could do what I believed to be impossible."

The rally began around midday. Speaker after speaker hammered home the message that was perhaps best expressed by Secretary of State Judah Benjamin: "We know in our hearts that this people must conquer its freedom or die." Cavalryman Henry Pollard was present that day and "sat for hours under the spell of the eloquent and earnest addresses which were made, and was filled with renewed hope and determination." Another soldier in the audience, artilleryman John W. Stott, wrote in his diary, "Resolutions were passed pledging ourselves to a vigorous prosecution of the war, till our independence be won, be the cost what it may in time, treasure and blood."

This rally was also used by the Davis administration to advance its controversial proposal to enlist black soldiers. "Let us say to every negro who wishes to go into the ranks on the condition of being made free—'Go and fight, you are free,'" Judah Benjamin exhorted the crowd. Such was the momentum generated by this meeting that action on the matter began in the Virginia Assembly the next day. The Confederate Congress took up the issue as well, and black enlistment became a Confederate national law on March 13, 1865.

Soldiers on both sides reacted strongly to the "failed" peace conference. "We saw nothing before us then but starvation, battles, wounds and death as our Government would accept nothing but the recognition of the independence of the Southern states, and the Northern Government would not do that," North Carolinian W. A. Day reflected. The failure of the talks, added David E. Johnston, of the 7th Virginia, was "a great disappointment to the soldiers, who saw plainly nothing short of a bitter fight to the end."

A New York infantryman who read the Confederate speeches in the Richmond and New York papers exclaimed, "What hopeless envy, what wounded pride, what deep despair is necessary to hear, tolerate, indulge or prompt such sentiments! Poor deluded wretches those Confederates, they will never unite with us again until every hope of success is lost!"

Jefferson Davis had won his political war. The peace movement was in disarray; the newspapers that had constantly sniped at him were now loud in their call for a united front to win the war; and that distantly threatening idol, Robert E. Lee, had become a figurehead in the government's propaganda campaign.

Lee, for his part, faced the coming spring with cold realism. Soon after the failed conference, he met with Senator Hunter, who pressed the military chief to proclaim publicly that a victory in the field was out of the question. "To this," Hunter recalled, Lee "made no reply. In the whole of this conversation he never said to me he thought the chances were over; but the tone and tenor of his remarks made that impression on my mind." In late February, Lee admitted to James Longstreet that the Confederate "line is so long, extending nearly from the Chickahominy to the Nottoway, and the enemy is so close upon us[,] that if we are obliged to withdraw we cannot concentrate all our troops nearer than some point on the line of the railroad between Richmond and Danville. Should a necessity therefore arise, I propose to concentrate at or near Burkeville."

Fifteen days later, on March 7, Lee supplied Longstreet with detailed instructions for which routes to take when the time came to retreat from Richmond and Petersburg.

Another run at peace talks came in late February, when Major General E. O. C. Ord, Butler's successor, met with Lieutenant General James Longstreet to discuss prisoner exchanges. The two men believed that a military convention between the two armies might be one means to stop the fighting and get the politicians on both sides talking to each other. Longstreet reported his conversation to Confederate authorities, who, in early March, authorized Lee to write directly to Grant requesting a meeting on that subject. Grant referred the message to Washington and was told that discussions could be held only in regard to "purely military" questions. Grant sent this reply back to Lee. The war would continue.

Part IV

AN END, A BEGINNING

The U.S. Military Railroad. *W. Waud*

Chapter Sixteen

"The tremendous possibility"

March 25, 1865

Ulysses S. Grant
Final Report of Operations, March 1864-May 1865

Anticipating the arrival of Gen. Sherman at Savannah . . . I sent orders on the 6th of December, that after establishing a base on the sea-coast [he was] . . . to come by water to City Point with the balance of his command. On the 18th of December, having [learned] . . . it would take over two months to transport Sherman's army, and doubting whether he might not contribute as much toward the desired result by operating from where he was, I wrote to him . . . for his views as to what would be best to do. A few days after this I received a communication from General Sherman . . . informing me of his preparations to . . . march to Columbia, S.C., thence to Raleigh, and thence to report to me. . . .

By the 1st of February General Sherman's whole army was in motion from Savannah. He captured Columbia, S.C., on the 17th; thence moved on Goldsborough, N.C. . . . Among the important fruits of this campaign was the fall of Charleston, S.C. It was evacuated by the enemy on the night of the 17th of February, and occupied by our forces on the 18th. . . . On the 15th [of March, Sherman] . . . met a force of the enemy at Averasborough, and . . . defeated and compelled it to retreat. . . . On the [19th] the combined forces of the enemy, under Joe Johnston, attacked his advance at Bentonville], N.C., and were defeated]. . . . From there Sherman continued to Goldsborough, which place had been occupied . . . on the 21st. . . .

General Sherman having got his troops all quietly in camp about Goldsborough, and his preparations for furnishing supplies to them perfected, visited me at City Point on the 27th of March and stated that he would be ready to move . . . by the 10th of April . . . if it should become necessary to bring his command to bear against Lee's army . . . in co-operation with our forces in front of Richmond and Petersburg. . . .

I had spent days of anxiety lest each morning should bring the report that the enemy [at Petersburg] had retreated the night before. I was firmly convinced that Sherman's crossing the Roanoke would be the signal for Lee to leave.

* * *

March 24-25
Confederate: Late Night-Early Morning

The soldiers marched silently into Petersburg at around midnight. There were two brigades in all, hard men from North and South Carolina who belonged to Bushrod Johnson's division and who only a few hours earlier had occupied trenches near Burgess' Mill. The march had commenced suddenly, remembered W. A. Day of the 49th North Carolina, after the "long roll beat and Colonel McAfee kept ordering us to fall in just like he was scared half to death." Captain Henry Chambers, in a different company of the same regiment, was as confused as everyone else, noting, "No one knew our destination. There were many conjectures." "Many were the surmises as to what the forced march meant," echoed another captain, William Henry Edwards of the 17th South Carolina, "but we all agreed on one point, that it meant a fight."

One observer, with a touch of prescience, wrote of Petersburg this night, "[The] hum of voices in this city of the dead was low, and the movement of armed bodies through it almost as noiseless and shadowy as the flitting of ghosts, while the strokes of the neighboring clocks sounded on the still night air like the tolling of funeral bells."

The soldiers rested in the city streets for two hours. Then, according to Captain Chambers, "we were aroused and took the line of march towards…the works East of the city. We now began to suspect our object."

The man whose planning had brought these men to the section of the Confederate lines known as Colquitt's Salient was worried. He had been promised all the troops he would need for this operation, and now had nearly a third of the Army of Northern Virginia under him. The stakes were so high, and the payoff potentially so great, that Major General John B. Gordon had to be certain of the outcome. Hours before Bushrod Johnson's soldiers began their night march to Petersburg, the Southern officer had sent a note to Robert E. Lee asking for even more men. Lee's answer came within two hours:

GENL: I HAVE RECEIVED YOURS OF 2:30 P.M. AND TELEGRAPHED FOR PICKETT'S DIVISION, BUT I DO NOT THINK IT WILL REACH HERE IN

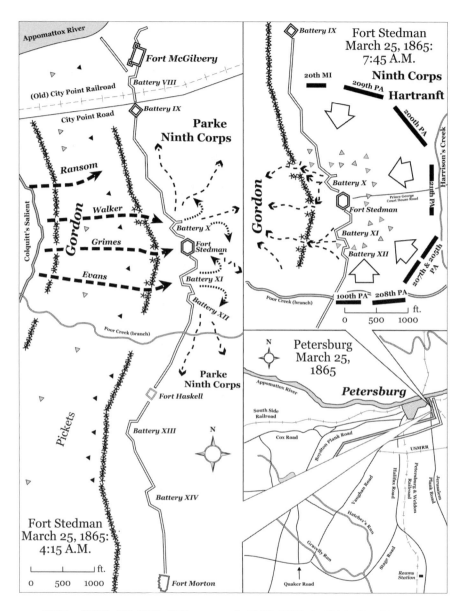

TIME. STILL WE WILL TRY . . . I PRAY THAT A MERCIFUL GOD MAY
GRANT US SUCCESS AND DELIVER US FROM OUR ENEMIES.

Union: Late Night–Early Morning

Captain John C. Hardy, of the 2nd Michigan, had a bad feeling. Hardy's
unit, part of the Ninth Corps's First Division, held the section of trenches just
north of Fort Stedman.

Hardy, a veteran of four years' service, was used to the irregular tattoo of nighttime picket gunshots, but this time it was different. "Desultory firing was kept up that night until about 1 o'clock," he later recalled, "when everything became suddenly still and the unusual silence along the line to the left [toward Stedman] seemed to me very suspicious and I ordered a shot from each of the six posts every three minutes as near as could be judged."

Hardy alerted his listening posts. After a while, "one of the men came in and reported that he had heard a noise in front which sounded as if someone was removing an obstruction, but a thorough investigation failed to reveal any cause for alarm." There were still nearly four hours left before daybreak, and John Hardy could do nothing but wait.

The waiting was already over for Francis Laverty, a private in the 59th Massachusetts. Laverty stood lonely duty along the picket line in advance of Fort Stedman. It was about 2:00 a.m., Laverty remembered, when "eight rebels came in to the videt[te] post. They carried their rifles at reverse as a sign they were deserters. Our videt[te] received them and escorted them to the inner post, but as soon as they reached it they turned their rifles and ordered all to surrender."[1] Without a single shot's being fired, Laverty and his fellow pickets were hustled across the dark, rutted fields into the Confederate lines and captivity. Daylight was still three hours away.

March 4-6
Army of Northern Virginia Headquarters, Petersburg

In the early morning of March 4, John Gordon had looked up from the papers he was reading. The confidential material, outlining the real condition of the Army of Northern Virginia, painted a catastrophic picture. "Each report was bad enough [in itself]," Gordon remarked, "[but] all the distressing facts combined were sufficient, it seemed to me, to destroy all cohesive power and lead to the inevitable disintegration of any other army that was ever marshalled."

Gordon wondered why he—at thirty-three, Lee's youngest corps commander—had been abruptly summoned on this cold March morning for a private conference with the supreme Southern general.

---

1   To encourage Southern troops to desert with their arms, Federal authorities had offered $10 for each gun brought along; armed deserters were consequently not an uncommon sight.

Lee began to talk. He tallied up the various Federal troops that were likely to confront him when spring came and Grant resumed full-scale offensive actions. "This made an army of 200,000 well-fed, well-equipped men which General Grant would soon concentrate upon our force of 50,000, whose efficiency was greatly impaired by suffering," Gordon realized.

Lee finished speaking, paced the room for a few moments to allow his subordinate to gather his thoughts, and then put the question bluntly: What did John Gordon think it best for them to do?

"General," Gordon answered quickly, "it seems to me there are but three courses, and I name them in the order in which I think they should be tried.

"First, make terms with the enemy, the best we can get.

"Second, if that is not practicable, the best thing to do is retreat . . . Unite . . . with General [Joseph E.] Johnston in North Carolina, and strike Sherman before Grant can join him; or,

"Lastly, we must fight, and without delay."

These comments provoked a sharp response from Lee, and the conversation whirled wildly, like a weary moth circling an all-consuming flame. To Gordon's first proposal, Lee replied that it was not his province to advise the civilian government to make peace. Regarding the second point, Lee worried that "it would be attended with the greatest difficulties." The third option was barely mentioned. Gordon left this remarkable interview believing that Lee thought "immediate steps should be taken to secure peace."

Two days later, Gordon was again summoned to Headquarters. In the interim, Lee had met in Richmond with Jefferson Davis, to whom he had confided, as Davis later wrote, "that the evacuation of Petersburg was but a question of time." From Davis, all Lee got was a cold determination to see the war out to its bitter end. Gordon listened Lee's report in grim silence.

"What, then, is to be done, general?" he asked at last.

Lee's reply, Gordon remembered, was that "there seemed to be but one thing that we could do—fight. To stand still was death. It could only be death if we fought and failed."

March 20

HIS EXCELLENCY A. LINCOLN:

CAN YOU NOT VISIT CITY POINT FOR A DAY OR TWO? I WOULD LIKE VERY MUCH TO SEE YOU, AND I THINK THE REST WOULD DO YOU GOOD.

RESPECTFULLY YOURS, ETC.

U. S. GRANT, LIEUTENANT-GENERAL

LIEUT. GEN. GRANT, CITY POINT, VIRGINIA:

YOUR KIND INVITATION RECEIVED. HAD ALREADY THOUGHT OF GOING IMMEDIATELY AFTER THE NEXT RAIN. WILL GO SOONER IF ANY REASON FOR IT. MRS. L. AND A FEW. OTHERS WILL PROBABLY ACCOMPANY ME. WILL NOTIFY YOU OF EXACT TIME, ONCE IT SHALL BE FIXED UPON.

A. LINCOLN

Thursday, March 23
Army of Northern Virginia Headquarters, Petersburg: Night

Following their talk after Lee's return from Richmond, John Gordon had spent a "week of laborious examination and intense thought" seeking a weak point in the Union lines. Three possible plans of attack emerged. One focused on the line fronting the site of the crater, the second targeted Fort Stedman, and the third was aimed at Federal Battery IX, near the Appomattox River. Further consideration reduced the options to one. Wrote Gordon, "I decided that Fort Stedman on Grant's lines was the most inviting point for attack and Colquitt's Salient on Lee's line the proper place from which to sally."

Fort Stedman—named after Connecticut colonel Griffin A. Stedman, who had been killed in August while reconnoitering the ground —was an enclosed field redoubt located on the crest of Hare Hill, near the site of the fatal June 18 charge by the 1st Maine Heavy Artillery. It perched on the eastern rise of a small plateau, the western side of which—some 282 yards away—was the Confederate redoubt known as Colquitt's Salient, after the Georgia general whose troops had first occupied it. Inside Stedman were four cannon manned by the 19th New York Light Artillery, and the fort itself was further supported by batteries—guns placed in smaller, often only partially enclosed positions— located just to its north (Battery X) and south (Batteries XI and XII). Completing the Union defenses here were Fort Haskell, half a mile south of Stedman, and Battery IX, roughly equidistant to the north.

The ground in front of Fort Stedman was crisscrossed with picket trenches and covered ways and protected by what one Federal infantryman boasted was "every…arrangement known to military science and art." In practical terms, this meant a first line of abatis—small, felled trees that were piled up and interlocked to entangle the enemy—and, directly around Stedman and its flanking batteries, a thick seeding of breast-high fraises—angled rows of logs with their ends sharpened to points, placed about six inches apart and strung together with telegraph wire.

Using all his innate guile and resourcefulness to overcome these formidable obstacles, Gordon devised one of the most methodical attack plans of the war. First, while it was still dark, special squads would open avenues through the Confederate defenses by quietly removing the obstructions that had been placed there. Then picked men (identified by strips of white cloth tied around their shoulders) would infiltrate forward to take out the advanced Union picket posts and open pathways through the Federal abatis. Behind this group would come fifty men with axes, who were to chop openings in the fraises protecting Stedman and its batteries.

Right behind the axmen would be three storming parties of a hundred men apiece, whose job it was to rush and secure Fort Stedman and Batteries X, XI, and XII. After the storming parties had achieved their objective, three more groups of a hundred men each were to undertake a special mission. Gordon's careful, albeit long-range, survey of the Union position had revealed several strong points well in the rear (that is, to the east) of Stedman; guided by local people familiar with the ground, the three special-mission groups would press through the gap opened by the storming parties in order to seize and hold these crucial places. As an added touch, Gordon had the officers leading these groups learn the names of their Union counterparts; should any of the advancing parties be challenged, the Southerners would assume the identities of the Yankee officers so as to bluff their way through. Their securing this rear line of entrenchments would effectively hamper any Union efforts to mount a quick counterstrike against Gordon's incursion.

As the special-mission groups headed toward their objectives, the bulk of Gordon's infantry would cross over the no-man's-land to widen the breach by sweeping north and south along the captured trenches. Once the infantry had secured the lodgment, a cavalry division would ride through the pocket to the enemy's rear, cutting communications and raising general havoc.

Lee had heard out Gordon's plan on March 22. He asked a series of probing and sometimes pointed questions and then told Gordon that he would need some time to review the operation. This night, March 23, Robert E. Lee gave John Gordon's plan his approval.

Friday, March 24
Union Army Headquarters, City Point: Evening

The boat carrying Abraham Lincoln, his wife and son, and various staff anchored off City Point two hours after sunset. Grant and his wife greeted the arriving party. As soon as the proper courtesies had been observed, the President and his military chief sat down for a private chat. Grant's principal worry at this moment, as expressed by his military secretary, Adam Badeau, was that some "morning should bring the news that the enemy had retreated the night before. He was firmly convinced that the crossing of the Roanoke by Sherman would be the signal for Lee to leave; and if Johnston and Lee were combined, a long and tedious and expensive campaign, consuming most of the summer, might be inevitable." The discussion turned to Lincoln's peace talks just six weeks earlier; one of the three Confederate commissioners, C.S. Vice President Alexander Stephens (who stood 5'7" and whose weight hovered around 100 pounds), had worn a large, thick overcoat, and Lincoln, his eyes twinkling, asked Grant if he recalled it.

"Oh, yes," Grant replied after a moment's thought.

"Well," Lincoln said, warming to his story, "soon after we assembled on the steamer at Hampton Roads, the cabin began to get pretty warm, and Stephens stood up and pulled off his big coat. He peeled it off just about as you would husk an ear of corn. I couldn't help thinking, as I looked first at the coat and then at the man, 'Well, that's the biggest shuck and the littlest ear I ever did see.'"

Grant greatly enjoyed the story. He then briefly touched upon the current military situation before Petersburg. At the end of the discussion, it was agreed that Lincoln would come ashore the next day to review the troops.

Saturday, March 25
3:30-4:15 a.m.

John B. Gordon stood atop the breastworks fronting Colquitt's Salient, with, as he later recalled, "no one at my side except a single private soldier with rifle in hand, who was to fire the signal shot for the headlong rush."

Either crouching expectantly in the trenches behind him or crowded into the deep ravine directly in rear of the position were the troops chosen for the desperate attack—virtually all of Gordon's corps (Evans's, Walker's, and Grimes's divisions), with two brigades from Bushrod Johnson's division

(Ransom's and Wallace's) ready for close support, and two brigades from Cadmus Wilcox's division on call. Those few of Gordon's units that were not directly involved in the attack were thinly spread to cover the trenches that had been held by the entire Second Corps. Additionally, Gordon was expecting George Pickett's division, of Longstreet's corps, then north of the James, to join him in time to participate in the action. There would be perhaps 11,500 men (from Gordon's corps and Bushrod Johnson's division) involved in the primary assault, with some 1,700 of Wilcox's men nearby and 6,500 from Pickett's command hurrying to the scene.

G. Nash Morton, an artillery lieutenant in Martin's Battery, worried about the morale of some of the officers who were leading the attack. "[During] the preceding month," he later stated, "officers of Lee's army had been given furloughs to visit their desolated homes in the wake of Sherman's march to the sea. They came back to the army whipped men. There was nothing more for them to fight for."

The men selected for the storming parties waited tensely for the signal for them to go. Louisiana troops from Colonel Eugene Waggaman's brigade would pave the way for the rest of Clement Evans's division. "On account of the valor of your troops, you will be allowed the honor of leading off in the attack," Evans told Waggaman, adding, "This you will make with unloaded guns."

North Carolina axmen would clear the opening for the storming party from James Walker's division. To lead the hundred-man party, Walker tapped two Virginia officers "personally known to me to be the bravest of the brave, and in whom the men had confidence."

Bryan Grimes's division made up the last of the three attack columns that Gordon was using in this first phase of the assault. Moving in advance of this command were Georgia sharpshooters under Captain Joseph P. Carson. As Carson visited his men, he was surprised to find his sole surviving brother, Bob, crouched among them. "He did not belong to my command," Carson later explained, "but was serving as courier for General Phil Cook." Captain Carson had no illusions about his prospects of surviving the upcoming action and bluntly told his brother so. "He admitted that he, too, believed that I would be killed, and, for that reason, he was going with me in order to bring back my body. What could I say then? Nothing!"

John Gordon, from his observation point atop the outer earthworks at Colquitt's Salient, noticed some Confederate obstructions that had not yet been removed. He ordered them cleared away, and then froze in horror as the working party's efforts aroused the suspicion of a nearby Yankee picket.

"What are you doing over there, Johnny?" the wary Federal called. "What is that noise? Answer quick or I'll shoot."

Gordon's mind went blank, but the common soldier alongside him responded instantly: "Never mind, Yank. Lie down and go to sleep. We are just gathering a little corn. You know rations are mighty short over here."

The Union guard yelled back his okay. Seconds seemed like hours as the offending obstructions were removed, but at last the moment came.

"Fire your gun," Gordon told the quick-witted soldier. This time, however, the man hesitated, unwilling to return the Union picket's favor with treachery.

"Fire your gun, sir," Gordon repeated.

The soldier came to a decision. "Hello, Yank!" he called. "Wake up; we are going to shell the woods. Look out; we are coming." Then he fired the signal shot.

Division commander James Walker watched his men disappear into the gloom. "The cool, frosty morning made every sound distinct and clear," he recollected, "and the only sound heard was the tramp! tramp! of the men as they kept step as regularly as if on drill." Private Henry London, in Grimes's Division, never forgot how the storming party, "with unloaded muskets and a profound silence, leaped over our breastworks, [and] dashed across the open space in front."

Despite all Gordon's precautions, at least one Yankee picket escaped to spread the alarm. Standing in the wake of his advancing storming party, James Walker could hear the frightened man shouts faded in the distance, "The Rebels are coming! The Rebels are coming!"

In Federal Battery X, perhaps ninety yards northwest of Fort Stedman, the sentinel's cry sent sleepy-eyed gunners racing to their posts. The two three-inch rifled guns placed in the position were kept loaded at all times for just such an emergency, and both were fired within seconds of the alarm. Before the pieces could be reloaded, however, shadowy figures appeared along the battery parapets and dropped in among the frantic gunners. "Small-arms were brought into use, and for a short time the enemy were held in check by a hand-to-hand conflict," one Federal officer later reported. "Owing to the darkness the entire garrison of this advanced battery was captured."

In Stedman itself, Captain Edward W. Rogers, of the 19th New York Light Artillery, was alerted by the fighting at Battery X. "The guard on my pieces immediately discharged the guns, which were kept loaded with canister," he testified. The only problem was that these guns were pointed toward the

Confederate lines, not Battery X. There was an opening in the fort's walls that covered the trenches leading to the battery, and Rogers ordered one gun to be manhandled into that position. The three remaining guns continued to fire to the west, getting off about twelve rounds before they were silenced.

South of Stedman, Battery XI fell without a shot.

The cannon blasts startled Joseph Carson, the Georgia sharpshooter captain. "At the flash of their guns darkness disappeared, and at intervals, as the guns were discharged, it was as light as day," he maintained.

Carson's small force came up against the fraises outside fronting Fort Stedman and its flanking batteries. His younger brother Bob had arrived there ahead of him. "I saw him for an instant by the flash of the cannon tearing apart and dragging aside the wire and logs." Gaps were opened up, and squads squeezed through. "Then the wind from the cannon and flying balls was so strong we could not keep our hats on, while the frightful roar of the guns drowned every other sound," Carson recalled.

Suddenly, men were clambering over the works on both sides of Stedman and dropping into the trenches. Lieutenant R. B. Smith, of the 2nd Louisiana, led an eight-man squad into the ditches just south of it and fought his way to its outer walls. Stalled in front of the bastion, Captain Carson yelled for his group to go to the right. An opening was found, and, he remembered, "we . . . scrambled into the fort."

Security for the forts, batteries, and trenches along this portion of the Union line was provided by units from the 14th New York Heavy Artillery. A few New Yorkers in Stedman fought a brief, desperate battle. "[The] fort was completely surrounded," noted William Clowminger, of that regiment, "and the enemy came swarming in at every possible ingress, and swarmed over the breastworks." One of the cannoneers who was caught in the fray later described the defense of Stedman as "creditable, but entirely unavailing. The fight in the darkness was not very sanguinary." Another New York heavy ruefully admitted that "All this was done so quickly and skillfully that the surprise to the Union troops was simply shocking." The gun that Captain Rogers had ordered into position to fire on Battery X never got there.

Within minutes, Fort Stedman, too, fell to Gordon's men.

Even as Stedman was being overrun by their comrades, other Confederates were crowding into the encampments of two Federal regiments located immediately behind the front line. "It was a complete surprise," declared one North Carolinian. "Many were killed coming out of their tents by our men, using their guns as clubs." In the camp of the 29th Massachusetts, the regiment's commander later reported, "Private W. Klinkler, of Company E, placed himself at the entrance of a bomb-proof, refused all demands for a surrender, and fell fighting gallantly." Another private, Edward Carney, was grabbed, choked, and ordered to surrender. "I don't see it," Carney gasped, and fought on. Despite receiving several blows to the head and a minor gunshot wound, he slipped free and escaped.

Tarheel soldier Hence Proctor stuck his head into a bombproof and "called out with ugly words...'Come out of there. I know you are in there.'" A startled Federal officer in nightclothes burst from the shelter and attacked Proctor with his sword. It took the help of several of Proctor's friends to subdue the Yankee. "As it was," remembered Sergeant Cyrus Watson of Proctor's regiment, the North Carolinian "came out of the fight with many gashes on his head and face."

Some of the assaulting units lost all cohesion as they entered the booty-rich camps. "We were soon in possession," wrote a soldier in Grimes's Division, "and our half-starved men busy searching the bomb proofs and covered ways for rations."

The first phase of Gordon's attack had secured nearly all of its goals. Fort Stedman and Batteries X and XI had been seized, along with the camps of the 29th and 57th Massachusetts regiments, and a hole nearly a thousand feet long had been opened in the Union line, with very small loss. As an added plus, eager hands had torn up the telegraph wires, so U.S. Army headquarters at City Point remained figuratively and literally in the dark.

First light was still forty-five minutes away.

4:15-4:45 a.m.

Brevet Brigadier General Napoleon B. McLaughlen had overall responsibility for the Fort Stedman sector of the Union line. He was awakened this morning by the noise of the attack and instantly sent his aides to spread the warning.

After dressing quickly, McLaughlen rode first to Fort Haskell, which he found "on the alert and ready to resist an attack." Continuing toward Stedman, the Federal officer saw that troops from the 100th Pennsylvania were manning the trenches between Haskell and Battery XII. That latter emplacement was still in Union hands, but just beyond it, McLaughlen met the officer in charge of the 29th Massachusetts, who told him that Battery XI "was in the enemy's hands, and that his command had just been driven from it."

McLaughlen ordered the mortars in Battery XII to open fire on Battery XI and sent instructions for the reserve regiment, the 59th Massachusetts, to counterattack immediately. "On the arrival of the Fifty-ninth I put them into the work with fixed bayonets and recaptured it at once," he later reported. Believing that he had sealed the only break in the U.S. line, McLaughlen rode into Fort Stedman. There was confusion everywhere, so he barked out orders, which were promptly obeyed by the shadowy figures. "In a few minutes I saw a man crossing the parapet," McLaughlen remembered, "whose uniform in the dawning light I recognized to be the enemy's, and I halted him, asking his regiment. This called attention to myself, and the next moment I was surrounded by the rebels, whom I had supposed to be my men, and sent to the rear." The North Carolina soldier who hustled McLaughlen back across the no-man's land recalled that the Union officer "asked permission to surrender his sword to General Gordon." While talking with Gordon, McLaughlen was joined by other Ninth Corps officers—Lieutenant Thomas Sturgis, of his own staff, and Captain Henry L. Swords, of the First Division staff, now also captives.

They joined a queue of what would become several hundred Federal soldiers now prisoners. A number of them passed by a correspondent (who signed himself "A. T.") representing the *Richmond Dispatch*, who dutifully reported everything they said, no matter how outrageous. "They state that it was a perfect surprise," he wrote, "that they had no idea of an attack, and that they had no troops except the Ninth corps...on this side of the Appomattox."

The Union recovery of Battery XI proved to be brief. A battle line had been hastily established at right angles to the main trenches, with the 59th Massachusetts in the battery, the 100th Pennsylvania on its right, and the 29th Massachusetts back in its encampment, but Confederate troops, flooding through the gap on the north side of Stedman and pressing southward, outflanked this line.

J. L. Pounds was part of a thirty-man skirmish line from the 100th Pennsylvania placed near the rear of Fort Stedman. Pounds peered into the smoky gloom and saw a battle line looming closer and closer. "It was so dark we could not distinguish blue from gray," he wrote years afterward. "When the order was given to forward, the line was in bayonet reach of us before we could distinguish them as Johnnies."

The three Federal regiments scattered in the face of this attack and scampered back to Fort Haskell. Pennsylvanian Philip Crowl raced down the hill and, about halfway between Battery XII and Haskell, turned for a parting shot at the Johnnies. "[The] first thing I heard was: 'Surrender, you Yank,'" he remembered. Gathered up with a group of other Federal prisoners, Crowl was pointed back toward the Confederate lines. Hit and wounded as he crossed into the no-man's land, he dropped into a rifle pit about fifty yards in front of the captured Union line. Another soldier from his company was already hiding in the hole, and the two decided to lay low until the fighting around them settled down.

John Gordon entered Fort Stedman a short time after meeting with McLaughlen, the captured Federal. "Up to this point," he later reflected, "the success had exceeded my most sanguine expectations." Fort Stedman was in Confederate hands, as were Batteries X, XI, and XII. The great hole in the enemy line was now serving as a conduit for the infantry brigades that Gordon had so carefully massed in Colquitt's Salient. These fresh troops were spreading the Confederate pocket in all directions—south toward Fort Haskell, north toward Battery IX, and east toward the rear line of works, which should even now be in the hands of the special-mission groups. Also, squads of volunteer cannoneers had come across the no-man's land and were presently working the guns of Fort Stedman against the Yankees.

Gordon believed that he was about to achieve what he had described to Lee as the "tremendous possibility" of this operation—"the disintegration of the whole left wing of the Federal army, or at least the dealing of such a staggering blow upon it as would disable it temporarily, enabling us to withdraw from Petersburg in safety and join Johnston in North Carolina."

The first crack in this fragile dream came when Gordon was handed a note from one of the special-mission groups, reporting its failure to carry out its assignment. The guide had become separated from the group during its rush across the no-man's land, and the men had consequently gotten lost amidst the bewildering crisscrossings of trenches and fieldworks behind Stedman. "I soon received a similar message from the other two [special-mission groups], and so notified General Lee," Gordon wrote.

Brigadier General John F. Hartranft, whose Union Third Division headquarters was at the Avery House, was alerted at 4:20 a.m. that there was trouble near Fort Stedman. Hartranft's division provided the general reserve for the seven-mile-long Ninth Corps front, which stretched from the Appomattox River south to Fort Howard. The six regiments of the division were camped at widely spaced intervals along that front, with the 200th Pennsylvania about a mile east of Stedman and the 209th Pennsylvania perhaps another half a mile east of that, near Meade Station, on the Military Railroad. The next closest regiment to the danger point, the 208th Pennsylvania, was posted near the Avery House itself, almost two miles southeast of Stedman. Hartranft's remaining three regiments were well south of Petersburg and not immediately available.

Even as aides galloped off to determine the extent of the trouble, Hartranft's soldiers began falling into ranks. Miles C. Huyette, in the 208th Pennsylvania, was "awakened by an occasional cannon shot, more intense crackle of musketry—nearly volley firing—and the rebel yell." Then a mounted officer rushed by, bawling, "Form your company, and double-quick for Fort Stedman. Don't wait for anybody." In the 209th, young drummer I. J. Jamison was scared half to death by the eruption of gunfire in the darkness. "I got out in the company street with my drum, and beat the alarm without orders," he remembered. "Everybody seemed panic stricken. Our lieutenants came running along the company quarters, beating the tents with their swords, crying out: 'Men fall in, or we will all be prisoners.... Fall in!'"

The Union defenders were stirring. There was still no overall pattern to their actions, but waves of demoralizing panic, which might have magnified the Confederate success, did not develop.

4:45-5:15 a.m.

Spirits were high in the Confederate ranks as more troops moved up to exploit the gap. Men from Ransom's Brigade, of Johnson's Division—who had marched into Petersburg only five hours earlier—now crossed the no-man's land. "We were under no direct fire as we advanced across the field," recalled W. A. Day. "We took our position in the enemy's works.... Re-inforcements kept crossing over the field and it really looked like we could hold our position." "The enemy were dumbfounded," Henry Chambers exulted. "Our attack, sudden, vigorous, unlooked for, was thus far completely successful."

Once across the no-man's-land, Ransom's Brigade moved purposefully northward along the captured lines, heading toward Union Battery IX.

The blue-coated troops manning the trenches immediately north of Fort Stedman fared little better than their counterparts to the south. Two Michigan regiments were the first victims.

Captain John Hardy, who had never lost his bad feeling about this day, gave in to his fears and ordered the whole regiment into the trenches well before daylight. Sleepy officers looked in vain for signs of trouble and chided Hardy for his nervousness. Then there was a sparkling of gunfire all around Fort Stedman.

"That's what's the matter," Hardy yelled. "They have got Fort Stedman."

But before Hardy's regiment could turn to meet this threat, it was struck by the full force of the enemy. The Michigan soldiers fought a confused action. "We could not tell where to send in our leaden missiles except when we saw the flash of the guns in the hands of the enemy," Hardy noted. He and his men ran north to the protection of Battery IX. Within a very short time, the Union trenches up to that point were under Confederate control.

After being routed out of their camp behind Battery X, the men of the 57th Massachusetts fell back slowly to the northeast. "As they were flanked out of one position they fell back to another, until they made a final stand behind an old abandoned rebel fort known as Dunn House Battery, near the Prince George Court House road," wrote John Anderson of the regiment.[2]

It was light enough to see now, and full sunrise was less than an hour away.

5:15-7:00 a.m.

Lieutenant Valentine H. Stone peered over the parapet of Battery IX toward Fort Stedman. "I could just see in the gray of dawn (it was then about 5:15 a.m.) a line of battle drawn up, moving toward me, their right being inside of our works; this line extended along the ravine between Battery No. IX and Fort Stedman, their left resting near the rebel lines. I immediately ordered my section to open on them with spherical case," he remembered. "They were in easy range, about 400 yards, maybe a little more." Other Federal batteries, advancing from their reserve camps near Meade Station, took "position on the crest of the hill in front of the station [and] opened fire upon the enemy's skirmish line."

---

2   The Dunn House Battery was Battery 11 on the old Dimmock line.

Union gunners on all sides of the Stedman pocket began to pummel Gordon's Confederates. "We lay close to the works to protect ourselves," explained W. A. Day, of Ransom's Brigade. "The smoke from the guns settled low and hid the enemy's movements." Cannon in Fort Haskell, Battery IX, and Fort McGilvery did especially severe damage. "Their fire completely enfiladed our position," Henry Chambers, of the same unit, wrote bitterly. "[With] shrapnel shell from our right beyond Fort Stedman and minnies from the fort near the river on our left, and with shell from the bluffs in our front, our position was made, in the opinion of our commanders, untenable."

Captain R. D. Funkhouser of Virginia tried to organize his men to break out of the pocket that was fast becoming a trap. "[In] my first attempt to lead it, having to jump a ditch, only three men followed me. I was knocked down by the concussion of a shell, and that brave trio started to carry me back, supposing my wound to be mortal, as I was gasping for breath; but when another shell burst near by, they let me fall, which caused my breath to come back all right. So I jumped up and followed them behind a bombproof."

Henry London, of Grimes's Division, refused to let a little artillery fire get in the way of more important things. "I got some crackers and ate them as complacently under an awful shelling as I would at [the] breakfast table, so accustomed have I become to the 'fun,'" he wrote later this day.

John Gordon's elation now turned to despair: "Through the failure of the three guides, we had failed to occupy the three forts in the rear, and they were now filled with Federals. Our wretched railroad trains had broken down, and the troops who were coming to my aid did not reach me. . . . It was impossible for me to make further headway with my isolated corps, and General Lee directed me to withdraw."

Fort Haskell was a rallying point for disorganized Federal troops, and the target of several Confederate attacks. George Kilmer, a member of the 14th New York Heavy Artillery, stood nervously with gun in hand as the first Rebel assault group approached in the darkness soon after Stedman fell.

"A breath seemed an age," he recalled, "for we knew nothing of the numbers before us. Finally, the Confederate leaders called out, 'Steady! We'll have their works. Steady, my men!' Our nerves rebelled, and like a flash the thought passed along the parapet, 'Now!' Not a word was spoken, but in perfect concert the cannon and muskets were discharged upon the hapless band. . . . But this repulse did not end it; the survivors closed up and tried it again. Then they divided into squads and moved on the flanks, keeping up the by-play until there were none left." Wrote another 14th man on the scene: "When they advanced to within 15 rods of our fort, we opened on them with grape and shell that made them waver and fall like grass before a scythe."

An unyielding Federal battle line slowly stretched eastward from Fort Haskell. It included portions of the 100th Pennsylvania, the 29th and 59th Massachusetts, and the 208th Pennsylvania, which had come on the run from the Avery House.

By the time the Pennsylvanians of the 208th arrived, remembered Miles C. Huyette, "Fort Haskell was a ring of fire…. As daylight approached a slight air movement made a rift in the pall of smoke over Fort Haskell, and we could see Old Glory waving from its ramparts. It looked good, and, oh, how we did cheer!"

"Daylight soon gave us perfect aim," George Kilmer added grimly, "and their game was useless."

Captain William H. Edwards, of the 17th South Carolina, was told to take his men "out in front and to the left of the fort, ostensibly to support a North Carolina regiment." This he did, "without accomplishing anything, except to get the regiment mutilated by shot and shell. . . . I did not go more than twenty yards before I was shot down, and I lay there and saw the men of the Seventeenth Regiment falling along down the line."

Union major Theodore Miller huddled in a bombproof with his Confederate captors and listened to the increasingly heavy bombardment outside. The Federal cannon fire, Miller observed, "was most accurate and destructive. Rebel officers came in and reported the effect to be terrible, and stated that their lines could not be held at any point…. The wounded were brought in in great numbers; I noticed among them a large proportion of officers. The number of stragglers and skulkers was astonishingly large; and I saw several instances where the authority of the officers who urged them on was set at defiance."

A correspondent for the *Petersburg Express* tried to describe the "rain of iron, before which the experiences of Malvern Hill and Gettysburg are said by veterans to pale almost into insignificance. It was painfully distinct in this city, where our very dwellings were shaken to their foundations."

Brigadier General John Hartranft was a man possessed. From the instant he received word that Fort Stedman had fallen, Hartranft worked furiously to limit the Confederate penetration and, once that objective had been achieved, to eliminate the pocket. He did much of this on his own initiative, since both Grant and Meade were at City Point with no direct working telegraph to the scene of the action. The success or failure of the Union response to Gordon's assault rested with the officers in the zone of engagement and, fortunately for U.S. fortunes, some of them such as Hartranft rose to the occasion.

His first orders sent the 208th Pennsylvania scurrying off to support Fort Haskell, and other messages alerted the distant Second Brigade (consisting of the 205th, 207th, and 211th Pennsylvania regiments) to stand by for quick movement. Then Hartranft himself, a superb horseman, mounted and galloped north.

A little less than a mile east of the main Union defenses (which included Battery IX and Fort McGilvery) was a rear line of works located along portions of the old Dimmock line. Here was Fort Friend and, alongside the road running from Fort Stedman to Meade Station, the entrenched position known as the Dunn House Battery. Near Fort Friend was the Friend House, where Brevet Major General Orlando Willcox, commanding the First Division of the Ninth Corps, had his headquarters. It was to Willcox's headquarters that Hartranft now rode.

He passed the 209th Pennsylvania, which was following contingency orders, moving away from its Meade Station camp and toward Fort Friend. The 200th Pennsylvania had also fallen into ranks, and had taken up a line on the edge of a ridge overlooking Harrison's Creek. Hartranft saw at once that with the movement of the 209th, only the 200th Pennsylvania stood between the advancing Rebels and their obvious target: Meade Station, with all of its supplies.

Arriving at the Friend House, Hartranft was more than a little surprised to find his superior with, as one officer later wrote, "his staff mounted, baggage packed, and headquarters tent struck, ready for a movement to the rear." Hartranft and Willcox agreed to redirect the 209th to support the 200th, and the junior brigadier took tactical command of all offensive actions. The two had just finished their hurried discussion when Hartranft noticed an enemy line of battle, with skirmishers in front, advancing along the road from Fort Stedman to Meade Station. Racing back to the road, the Union officer ordered the 200th Pennsylvania (which had been joined by portions of the 57th Massachusetts) to drive back the approaching enemy. "It advanced bravely," Hartranft recalled with pride, "but the enemy was too strong to be pushed, and the fire from the supports and Fort Stedman was very severe." The 200th fell back, reorganized itself, and tried again. Once more the regiment breasted a heavy fire, held its advanced position for several bloody minutes, and then reeled back. But the Pennsylvanians had bought their side some time.

Now the 209th Regiment was alongside the 200th, and it, along with the various units that had fallen back toward Battery IX, effectively blocked any further Confederate thrusts north or northeast from Stedman.

John Hartranft galloped back to the south side of the pocket and there found a patchwork line that was firming up more with every passing minute. Also, the three distant regiments of his Second Brigade had marched up and were ready to be deployed. He immediately ordered the 211th Pennsylvania to fill in the three-hundred-yard gap between the defensive lines northeast of Stedman and those southeast of it.

Hartranft had constructed an armed perimeter that completely hemmed in the Stedman pocket. At that instant, the Union posture changed from a defensive to an offensive one.

7:00-8:00 a.m.

John Gordon's only thought now was of getting as many of his men as possible back across the no-man's land and to Colquitt's Salient. "A consuming fire on both flanks and front during this withdrawal caused a heavy loss to my command. I myself was wounded, but not seriously, in recrossing the space over which we had charged in the darkness," Gordon later wrote. According to the captive Union major Theodore Miller, Gordon did not run back, nor did he walk; as Federal officer told the *New York Herald's* correspondent, "he trotted away."

"My dear, it was an awful time," South Carolinian Thomas Brady wrote to his wife the next day. "Our men was shot down by the dozens. I am thankful to God that he spared my life." Henry Chambers legged it across the open ground as if the devil himself were close behind. "Good God what a time!" he exclaimed. "It seemed as if the enemy's artillery opened with redoubled vigor and the minie balls came in showers." Writing afterward to his father, young Henry London confessed, "I…only escaped capture by running as hard as I could a quarter of a mile through an open field swept by their fire, expecting every moment to be knocked over as the dead lay in a long line (being killed attempting to get away as I did) and I can assure you I drew a long breath of relief when I jumped into our works, for it was a miracle almost that I got through safe." Another North Carolinian, Robert D. Graham, later summed up the moment with grim humor: "The enemy[,] regretting their neglect to turn out in time to meet us more handsomely in the early morning, were now doing all in their power to make the procession more interesting as we returned."

John Hartranft had his counterassault in place by 7:45 a.m. "On a semicircle of a mile and a half," he later noted, "five regiments and detachments, nearly 4,000 men, were ready to charge." "They were just enlisted and fresh and strong," observed a New York man. The signal would be the advance of the 211th Pennsylvania. Hartranft watched impatiently as that regiment struggled over the uneven ground; remembered one soldier in the 211th, "Some of our officers and most of the men were under high tension, and were forging ahead to get at something when a halt was called by Gen. Hartranft. He rode along the line, hurling invectives at the officers to dress the line up and be ready for the order to charge."

The young brigadier had just signaled for a general advance when a courier arrived with a message from Major General John Parke, instructing Hartranft to delay any offensive movement until supports could arrive from the Sixth Corps.[3] "I saw that the enemy had already commenced to waver, and that success was certain," Hartranft later reported without apology. "I, therefore, allowed the line to charge; besides this, it was doubtful whether I could have communicated with the regiments on the flanks in time to countermand the movement."

Captain Joseph P. Carson of Georgia, whose brother had tagged along on this operation, saw the Federals coming. "The whole field was blue with them," he recalled. "Their lines must have been ten or fifteen deep." Carson's men were filing back past Fort Stedman when one of them remarked that he thought the captain's brother had been shot nearby. The approaching enemy battle lines meant little to Carson as he ran to the spot and found his brother's body: "He was dead, shot through the heart." The captain called to one of his men to lend a hand, and together they carried the corpse back to Colquitt's Salient. "As I entered our works again, from which we had so hopefully emerged early in the morning, I looked back toward Fort Stedman. Over it, in the sunlight, floated again the stars and stripes," Carson remembered.

---

3 Parke was also having a busy morning. In trying to inform Meade of the breakthrough, Parke had learned that Meade was out of touch and that he, Parke, was in command of the entire army.

Captain Funkhouser made a break for it and ran right into a Yankee captain, who drew a pistol and demanded his surrender. Two other Virginians appeared and took the Union officer prisoner, but by then retreat was out of the question, so all three Confederates handed their guns to the surprised Federal. "We were glad to surrender," Funkhouser reflected, "and fell down in the ditch to avoid being killed by our own shells."

Federal battle lines were closing the Stedman pocket from the north, east, and south. Everyone, it seemed, wanted to be the first to reenter Stedman. "Boys, let's take that fort!" Colonel Robert Cox of the 207th Pennsylvania bellowed to his men.

Captain John C. Hardy led a group of twenty-five Michigan soldiers toward the fort. As they passed one bombproof, Hardy saw a Confederate poke his head out to look around. "Not liking to leave an enemy in our rear" Hardy declared, "I ran over to take him in, but to my surprise, I found the bomb-proof filled with Confederates." One or two raised their guns to shoot this Yankee, but they were stopped by the others, who recognized that the game was up. "There were thirty-five officers and privates in the lot," recalled Hardy, "and their capture made me feel pretty good."

As a squad from the 208th Pennsylvania pushed its way into the fort, one of its members grabbed an enemy flag and waved it for all to see. "In two seconds several lively shells from one of our batteries well toward a mile in the rear crashed on us," a member of the regiment ruefully noted. "Needless to say we ceased to wave that rebel battle flag then and there."

Miles C. Huyette, who had thrilled to the sight of Old Glory over Fort Haskell, joined his comrades in the 208th Pennsylvania in a cheering charge. "In our advance I tripped and fell so that the stump of a slashed small tree took me where [I] had [previously] wounded [my] leg, but in the excitement [I] did not know it until the fighting ended and [I] felt 'something wet in my boot.' " Huyette scrambled into the fort and then drew back in horror; as he later explained, "It was the first place I saw footprints of men in puddles of human blood. Blood was on my boots when the fighting ended. It was hell! When we gained full possession of the works firing ceased."

A Union observer was appalled by the sight of fleeing Confederates being picked off by the dozen as they fled into the deadly no-man's-land. "My mind sickens at the memory of it—a real tragedy in war—for the victims had ceased fighting, and were now struggling between imprisonment and death or home."

After 8:oo a.m.

Petersburg surgeon John Claiborne's view of this battle was a sobering one: "Remaining in the rear of the fight I saw the worst part of it, of course; and while those who participated were cheered & elated with the excitement & glory of the charge, I witnessed only the blood & wounds & mutilation & death agony of the brave. I am heartsick, & I pray each time I may see these things no more."

CITY POINT—8:30 A.M.
ABRAHAM LINCOLN TO EDWIN STANTON:

ARRIVED HERE ALL SAFE ABOUT 9 P.M. YESTERDAY. NO WAR NEWS. . . . ROBERT JUST NOW TELLS ME THERE WAS A LITTLE RUMPUS UP THE LINE THIS MORNING, ENDING ABOUT WHERE IT BEGAN.[4]

Robert E. Lee was returning from Gordon's front, almost alone, when he spotted two riders approaching. It was his sons Rooney and Robert junior, who had ridden ahead of their cavalry division hoping for orders to exploit Gordon's breakthrough. Lee greeted them warmly, but even a smile could not hide the truth of failure. "I have often recalled the sadness of his face," young Robert wrote years afterward, "its creased expression.... He thanked my brother for responding so promptly to his call upon him, and regretted that events had so shaped themselves that the division would not then be needed, as he had hoped it would be."

President Lincoln, General Grant, and their wives and guests left City Point at around midday on a special train that ran them down to Globe Tavern, on the Military Railroad. There the men mounted horses, the women boarded carriages, and the procession continued to General Meade's headquarters.

Lincoln met there with Meade and his staff, including the perspicacious Theodore Lyman. Just before the arrival of the visitors, the provost guard had marched some 1,500 prisoners taken that morning by the Ninth Corps into a nearby holding pen. "These looked brown and athletic," Lyman observed, "but had the most matted hair; tangled beards, and slouched hats, and the most astounding carpets, horse-sheets and transmogrified shelter-tents for blankets, that you ever imagined."

---

4 Robert was Lincoln's eldest son, presently serving as one of Grant's aides.

Meade greeted Lincoln with the comment, "I have just now a despatch from General Parke to show you." In reply, Lincoln pointed to the corralled Rebels. "Ah," he said, "there is the best despatch you can show me from General Parke!"

It fell to Gordon's aide Henry Kyd Douglas to request a truce to allow both sides to bring in their wounded and bury their dead. Douglas met John Hartranft between the lines, under a white flag. "We agreed immediately to have the wounded and dead taken off, each by his own people," Douglas recalled. "Men ran over the field from each side and gathered up their comrades, taking time, when they could, to exchange pipes, tobacco, penknives, hardtack and anything that was tradable."

Reasoning that Lee must have had to strip his lines to assemble Gordon's assault force, Federal corps commanders Horatio Wright and Andrew Humphreys pressed their fronts and successfully overran large sections of the Confederate picket lines. Attempts to storm the main Rebel defenses were turned back when, as Humphreys later wrote, they "proved to be held by a force sufficient to maintain them against assault."

Once they were in possession of the enemy picket lines, the Yankee soldiers labored frantically to turn the works in order to defend them against Lee's almost obligatory counterattack. This came all along the line at about 7:00 p.m. and regained some but not all of the lost ground.

Prisoner Robert Funkhouser wound up in a holding area near Major General Samuel Crawford's Fifth Corps headquarters. Funkhouser was amazed while he was there to observe Lincoln and his retinue calmly review the troops as if nothing special had happened this day. "And all of us Confederates agreed with one accord that our cause was lost," Funkhouser noted.

Following this review, Lincoln and his party proceeded to Fort Wadsworth, where the President was able to watch from a distance some of the fighting over the picket lines.

When the visiting group returned to Globe Tavern for the ride back to City Point, the depot was filled with wounded and dead soldiers. To one aide, Lincoln remarked that "he had seen enough of the horrors of war, that he hoped this was the beginning of the end, and that there would be no more bloodshed or ruin of homes."

In a letter written on March 26 to Jefferson Davis, Robert E. Lee made his only comments about the Stedman operation: "I was induced to assume the offensive from the belief that the point assailed could be carried without much loss and the hope that by the seizure of the redoubts in the rear of the enemy's main line . . . Gen[era]l Grant would . . . be obliged so to curtail his lines that upon the approach of Gen[enar]l Sherman, I might be able to hold our position with a portion of the troops, and with a select body unite with Gen[enar]l Johnston and give him battle. . . . I fear now it will be impossible to prevent a junction between Grant and Sherman, nor do I deem it prudent that this army should maintain its position until the latter shall approach too near. . . ."

Lee's soldiers were blunt in their assessments of the affair. "I have always been able to find some sort of excuse for failures," observed Captain B. F. Dixon, of the 49th North Carolina, "but in this instance I...unhesitatingly say 'Somebody blundered.'" "I can't give you the particulars at present," a Virginia soldier wrote on the day of the battle, "but we have gained nothing." Although limited by the need to keep inside information from the enemy, the reporter "A. T." admitted in his report that the "affair did not prove so favorable as at first augured." For Henry London, the Stedman attack "was only the meteor's flash that illumines for a moment and leaves the night darker than before."

Ninth Corps casualties in the early-morning fighting were 72 killed, 450 wounded, and 522 missing or captured, for a total of 1,044. The actions later in the day against Lee's picket lines cost the Union Second Corps 513 killed or wounded and 177 missing, for a total of 690, and the Sixth Corps about 400 in all categories. Confederate losses, never officially reported, were later estimated by John Hartranft as "a little over four thousand." Andrew Humphreys also accepted the 4,000 figure to represent the "total loss of the enemy in the operations of the 25th of March." Frederick Phisterer, who after the war made a close study of battle casualties, put the total Confederate losses at Fort Stedman, in all categories, at 2,681. A Richmond newspaper account that appeared six days after the assault, in contrast, put Lee's losses at "eight hundred, of whom about 280 were prisoners."

Postscript: 1904

The guest speaker was an old, much-honored American—three times United States senator from Georgia, and governor of that state for four years. He had come to Kansas in the last year of his life to talk about his experiences in the Civil War. During the ride back to the hotel, his escort, a Union veteran of Fort Stedman named Julius E. Henderson, asked the great man, John B. Gordon, why the Fort Stedman assault had failed.

"Why did we fail? I'll tell you why," Gordon replied. "God did not intend that we should succeed. He did not intend that the Southern Confederacy should be an accomplished fact. He caused the axle of the tender of the last section of the train that was to bring the troops from north of Richmond to break, thus delaying that entire body of troops from reaching us. Had they arrived I believe that we should have captured City Point that morning. God did not intend that we should succeed. He was in command."

Chapter Seventeen

"I have ordered a general assault along the lines"

April 2, 1865

Ulysses S. Grant
Final Report of Operations, March 1864-May 1865

General Sheridan moved from Winchester[, Virginia,] on the 27th of February with two divisions of cavalry numbering about 5,000 each. . . . [He] pushed on to Waynesborough, where he found the enemy in force in an intrenched position, under General Early. . . . [An] immediate attack was made, [and] the position was carried. . . . Thence he marched on Charlottesville. . . . On the morning of the 6th [of March] . . . he . . . marched up the James River Canal to New Market, destroying every lock. . . . From New Market he took up his line of march, following the canal toward Richmond. . . . [He] proceeded down the north bank of the Pamunkey to White House, which place he reached on the 19th. . . .

On the 28th [I gave] . . . Instructions . . . to General Sheridan [to move his cavalry] . . . to or through Dinwiddie [Court-House to] reach the right and rear of the enemy as soon as . . . possible . . . [and] cross the South Side [Rail]road between Petersburg and Burkeville, and destroy it to some extent. . . .

On the morning of the 29th the movement commenced. . . . From the night of the 29th to the morning of the 31st the rain fell in such torrents as to make it impossible to move a wheeled vehicle. . . . During the 30th Sheridan advanced from Dinwiddie Court-House toward Five Forks, where he found the enemy in force. General Warren advanced and extended his line across the Boydton plank road to near the White Oak road. . . . General Humphreys drove the enemy from his front into his main line on the Hatcher, near Burgess' Mills. . . . On the morning of the 31st General Warren reported favorably to getting possession of the White Oak road, and was directed to do so. . . . [After heavy fighting] possession of the White Oak road [was] gained. Sheridan advanced [toward] ... Five Forks, but the enemy ... forced him back toward Dinwiddie Court-House. ... General [Ranald] Mackenzie's cavalry [Army of the James] and ... the Fifth Corps were immediately ordered to his assistance. ...

On the morning of the 1st of April General Sheridan, re-enforced by General Warren, drove the enemy back on Five Forks, where, late in the evening, he assaulted and carried his strongly fortified position, capturing all his artillery and between 5,000 and 6,000 prisoners. About the close of this battle [by General Sheridan's order] Bvt. Maj. Gen. Charles Griffin relieved Major-General Warren in command of the Fifth Corps. The report of this reached me after nightfall.

*   *   *

Horace Porter was in a gleeful mood as he brought word of Sheridan's victory at Five Forks to Grant's headquarters, now located near Dabney's Mill. Grant listened attentively, saying little as his exuberant aide spilled out the details. The instant Porter finished his report, Grant walked to his tent and hurriedly scribbled out a series of dispatches. Rejoining his staff, Grant said (as "coolly as if remarking upon the state of the weather"), "I have ordered a general assault along the lines."

Porter put the time at 9:00 p.m., April 1.

The Ninth Corps Story

The Ninth Corps commander, Major General John G. Parke, had the place and the plan. His men held the lines stretching from Fort McGilvery on the Appomattox River to Union Battery XXV, just east of Fort Howard. Parke had first suggested in February that a Union breakthrough might be possible on his front; the comment had brought down scores of engineers, who perched in a tall pine tree near Fort Davis and carefully surveyed the enemy lines. Their reports confirmed Parke's assessment, and assault plans were devised.

Parke was told to put his plan into action at 4:00 a.m., March 31, but these instructions were canceled a few hours later, and the keyed-up troops returned to their camps. Then, late in the afternoon of April 1, a new order arrived, calling for an attack to be made at 4:00 a.m. on April 2.

There followed several hours of confused, unanticipated combat. The Army of the Potomac commander, George Meade (who, by his own admission, was "quite sick" at this time), interpreted Grant's 9:00 p.m. dispatch to mean that he was to mount an immediate all-out attack on Petersburg, and he instructed his corps commanders accordingly. It was past midnight before

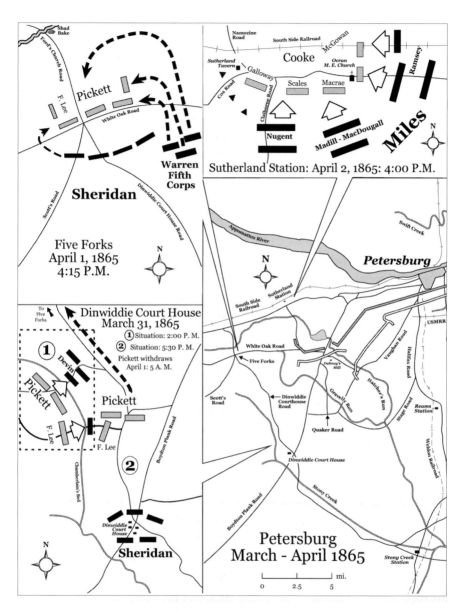

Sutherland Station: April 2, 1865: 4:00 P.M.

Five Forks
April 1, 1865
4:15 P.M.

Dinwiddie Court House
March 31, 1865
① Situation: 2:00 P. M.
② Situation: 5:30 P. M.
Pickett withdraws
April 1: 5 A. M.

Petersburg
March - April 1865

matters were sorted out and the original plan for a 4:00 a.m. assault was confirmed. By that time, however, one of Parke's brigadiers, acting on Meade's misinterpretation, had rushed the Confederate picket line in front of Forts Hays and Howard, capturing eight officers and 241 men. Once they were informed that the initial orders stood, the Federals abandoned their gains and were marched to the assembly point.

This ground action precipitated an artillery exchange that lasted for more than three hours. A Pennsylvania cannoneer in Fort Davis remembered the moment when, "with a flash and roar, the signal gun turned loose the dogs of war." A New York gunner engaged in the affair wrote soon afterwards that the "air was filled with screaming and screeching shells flying in every direction." The Ninth Corps artillery commander, Brevet Brigadier General John C. Tidball, observed in his after-action report that the Union fire "was replied to most vigorously by the whole of the enemy's artillery." Things quieted down again a little after 1:00 a.m.

The position that Parke had selected was one of the toughest facing the Federals on the entire Petersburg front: the Confederate works opposite Fort Sedgwick. The Rebel defenses here consisted of what one Maine officer later described as "several forts, redans, and batteries, near the Jerusalem Plank Road, that swept the approaches in every direction." Directly astride the plank road was the enemy's powerful Battery No. 27, which was supported to its right by Batteries No. 28 and No. 30, and to its left by Battery No. 25. Also part of the defensive scheme was Battery No. 29, located about a quarter of a mile west of the Jerusalem Plank Road and perhaps two hundred yards in advance of the main line. This three-sided bastion, mounting three guns, was variously known as Fort Mahone or Fort Damnation. Further protecting these strong works was a thick zone of wooden entanglements and water-filled ditches.

Parke never explained his reasons for selecting this point of attack. His report of the affair, filed some three months later, merely commented that the enemy's line was not continuous here but rather formed a spur, a separate outer line that extended down to Hatcher's Run. Parke's assumption seems to have been that once he smashed through the hard outer skin of the line opposite Fort Sedgwick, he would also render untenable the rest of Lee's position to the south. An officer who took part in the assault later suggested a secondary reason: since the attack was to begin before it was light enough to discern landmarks, the Union battle lines would be able to use the Jerusalem Plank Road as a guide.

The assault formation began to take shape behind Fort Sedgwick at around 1:00 a.m. Brevet Major General John Hartranft's Third Division, Pennsylvanians all, had the road on their immediate left. On Hartranft's right was Colonel Samuel Harriman's brigade, detached from Willcox's division for this action. Across the road, on Hartranft's left, was Brevet Major General Robert B. Potter's division, with Brigadier General Simon G. Griffin's brigade first, followed by Brevet Brigadier General John I. Curtin's men. Each formation was preceded by a storming party assisted by groups of ax-wielding pioneers, assigned to open passageways through the obstructions.

The Confederate works, one of Harriman's men noted, "bore the reputation of being the strongest and most formidable on the two lines, and it was with rather dubious feelings that we waited for the signal to advance." A Pennsylvanian under Hartranft stared silently at the peaceful night sky, which formed a stark contrast to the earth below, with its sputtering picket and artillery fire. "[Thoughts of] God and eternity rushed through my mind," the soldier recollected. The mood was lightened somewhat in Curtin's brigade when someone remembered that it was now Sunday and called out, "Boys, we're going to early mass."

Promptly at 4:00 a.m., Willcox's division staged a noisy diversion near the Appomattox. Artillery from both sides joined in, and the cannon fire spread all along the Ninth Corps lines. A Pennsylvania gunner in Fort Davis recalled, "From countless muzzles on either side there seemed to flow a constant stream of living fire as the shells, with burning fuzes, screamed and hissed through the night in a semicircle of lurid flame." "The deafening roar and crash were simply appalling," added a waiting infantryman.

It was 4:40 a.m, "just…daybreak," John Hartranft later wrote, when the order to advance was given. "It was yet scarcely grey dawn and a considerable mist hung over the fields, so that objects were quite indistinct at a very short distance and not visible at all a few hundred yards away," one correspondent reported.

The cry "Forward!" fluttered through Hartranft's regiments like a hot wind. "We raised as one man and rushed towards the rebel works," a soldier declared. Once he saw Hartranft's men moving, Colonel Samuel Harriman, commanding the troops on the right, leapt to the top of the Union works and waved his sword. "Go in, boys," he shouted. "It's your last chance for a fight." Potter's division was also on the move, the various regiments guiding themselves with their right on the road. "We moved ahead at a quick step over ground that was fairly good at daylight," one soldier commented, "but in the dusk of morning it seemed rough and uneven. Nothing could be distinguished beyond a few paces in front."

The men pounded over the Union and Confederate picket lines, surging to the very edge of the entanglements before the enemy defenses came alive. Sergeant Miles C. Huyette, with the advance of Hartranft's division, hit the ground as he saw the lanyard primers flash on the Rebel cannon in front of him. An instant later, the "air was full of canister," he remembered. "[I] could hear the thud as it hit men, their cries of agony, curses and cheers, and by the flash of bursting mortar shells could see men falling all about in the rear; then the roll of musketry [came] from their main line of works." While Yankee sharpshooters pinned down enemy cannoneers, the pioneers ripped openings in the abatis and chevaux-de-frise. Then the heavy battle lines were through the barriers and pouring over the works that stretched across the Jerusalem Plank Road. Hartranft's men took Battery No. 27.

Colonel Harriman's battle lines staggered under the fusillade erupting from the dark works ahead. "The cry was raised by our men, 'Let's get there,' and away we went, every man for himself," a New Yorker later wrote. Soldiers clawed up the embankment of a fort and dropped inside. Captain J. G. Harker, of the 109th New York, confronted a Rebel working to reload one of the fort's cannon. "If you discharge that piece you are a dead Johnny," he shouted. The Confederate raised his hands. Battery No. 25, too, had fallen.

On the left of the road, the storming party from Simon Griffin's brigade had scuttled far ahead of the main battle lines. Members of the group huddled against the outer walls of an enemy fort and sniped at Rebel gunners. When the main body of the brigade at last appeared, the Federal pioneers went back to clear openings in the obstructions and then joined in the general scramble up the fort wall. A large water-filled ditch ran around the embankment, and "some of the men fell in as they rushed ahead to climb the high, slanting ascent and were unable to get out and were drowned," a Maine man recalled. Then Griffin's soldiers were in the fort, clubbing down enemy gunners and turning their weapons to aim at the inner line. "Bill Key, give me a match, or your cigar, a pipe or something, so I can touch this darned thing off," a New Hampshire officer yelled to one of his men. Battery No. 28 was now in Union hands.

Moving up behind Griffin's men, John Curtin's brigade veered left and took a bead on Fort Mahone, with the 39th New Jersey leading the way. "Capturing and sweeping away the opposing picket, they pressed up to the fort, some perishing in the ditch as they essayed to cross, but the body of the command reaching the works, heedless of the pitiless fire to which they were exposed," the regiment's historian wrote. Twice, small portions of the regiment fought their way into the three-sided enclosure, only to be blasted back by heavy enemy fire from the inner lines, a few hundred yards away. Then the weary Jerseymen attacked again, and this time they managed to gain a foothold.

Curtin's supporting lines behind them struggled over the fire-swept ground. The 48th Pennsylvania, stalled momentarily before an intact section of enemy obstructions, bunched together while their pioneers worked to clear a

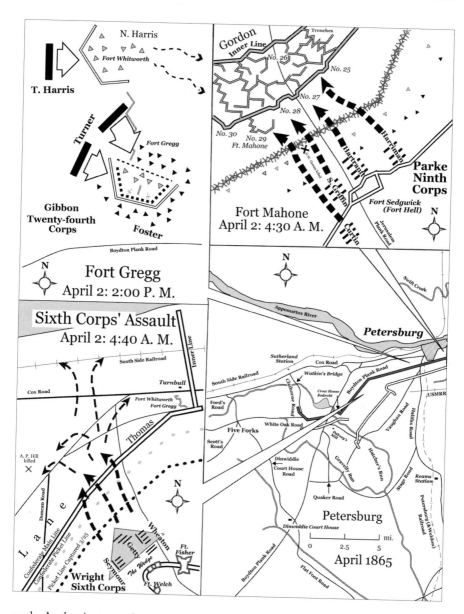

path. At that instant, alert enemy gunners aimed at the regimental flagstaffs, and shells burst over the colors. A piece of shrapnel struck the unit's popular commander, Colonel George W. Gowan, killing him.

John Parke reported to Meade's headquarters at 6:50 a.m., "We have captured 2 redans, 2 forts, and 12 guns, but the enemy hold works in the rear."

John Gordon's corps defended this sector. Battle's Brigade, from Alabama, was the hardest hit, but the Georgians of Cook's Brigade and the North Carolinians of Grimes's Brigade were also sent reeling. "Alabamians! Stand up! Aim low and fire like men!" one officer screamed, in a vain attempt to stem the torrent of bluecoats pouring over the Confederate line. Almost at once, however, a defense began to take shape on the flanks of the Union penetration and along a second line of works, a few hundred yards in rear of the first; Yankee troops attempting to push along the twisting trenches to extend their gains were met with fierce resistance. "The fighting here was most stubborn and desperate, being at close range, almost hand to hand," one North Carolinian recalled. "T. S. Riggsbee…jumped up on top of the breastworks so as to get a better chance to shoot at the advancing enemy, and, after firing his own gun, fired the guns of several of his comrades as they were rapidly handed up to him, until he himself was shot down and killed by the enemy only a few feet distant."

Major General Bryan Grimes organized the first of several counterattacks around 11:00 a.m. Troops from his old brigade and Lieutenant Colonel Fletcher H. Archer's all-Virginia battalion charged the enemy "who were in possession of and protected by our traverses and bomb-proofs, …and continued gradually to [re] gain traverse after traverse of our captured works." Combat was reduced to the squad level as one small group after another rushed to capture a section of trenches, only to be rolled out a few minutes later by an enemy counterthrust. "The fight was from traverse to traverse as we slowly drove them back," one of Grimes's men noted. "The Yankees would get on top of them and shoot down at our men, and as we would re-take them our men did the same thing."

Federal supports stopped this round of attacks, as well as a second one that boiled up from the scarred ground a little after 1:00 p.m. Grimes was not yet finished. More troops were on the way, nd when they were ready, they would launch an all-out attack to eliminate the enemy foothold once and for all.

Parke's attacking formations were all broken up by the combination of enemy obstructions and defensive fire. Confederate batteries on either side of the breach, and along the uncaptured inner line, blasted the pocket and Fort Sedgwick. When one shot struck down division commander Robert B. Potter, responsibility for his men devolved to Simon Griffin. Federal units became mixed together and fought individual battles amidst the smoke and dust. "Several times…the rebels attempt to regain the fort," a Federal defending Battery No. 25 later sketched the scene, "and as often we send them back[,] till the hillside in our front is thick with dead and dying." A New Yorker with

Potter's division recalled having to hug the muddy ground to avoid "the shot and shell hailing so thickly that I wondered if they were being thrown out with a scoop-shovel." One wounded Federal officer who stumbled back across the no-man's-land to Fort Sedgwick later remembered "noticing the water channels along the roadside were tinged red with the blood of our men who had fallen under the fierce fire as they moved up, and some of them were there where they fell."

Several Union cannoneers had volunteered to advance with the infantry and handle the captured Confederate guns, but their effectiveness was hampered by the three-sided design of the Rebel forts, which left the gunners exposed to sharpshooter fire from the rear lines. One Massachusetts artilleryman grumbled that "our men had no protection and might as well have been in the open field."

Grimes's counter strokes worried Parke enough that at a little past 12:30 p.m., he wired Meade's headquarters, "I should have re-enforcements at once."

The third and heaviest Confederate effort came at roughly 3:00 p.m. "My dispositions were soon made to attack the enemy simultaneously at all points," Grimes later wrote. Two brigades pushed in on each of the flanks, while a heavy skirmish line advanced in front. Many of the voltigeurs had just come down on the double-quick from camps north of the Appomattox and had to stand by under a heavy artillery fire while waiting for orders to attack. "[The] shells burst over our heads, or rolled and spun and darted and hissed about our feet in a dreadfully demoralizing way," one of the sharpshooters declared. "Then, too, the wounded men, pale-faced and bloody, some borne on litters, others limping and tottering, and passing us in crowds, had no tendency to enliven our spirits."

Once the counterattack began, the combat again flowed into the ditches like the runoff from a thunderstorm. Confederate sergeant H. C. Wall was with a group that successfully rushed into an undefended section of trenches. "This position we set to work to widen, shooting to right and left along the line," he recollected. "There were traverses along the works at frequent intervals made of timber and earth. The ends of the traverses next to the works were roughly fitted, leaving many holes and openings. Through these holes some of the men fired away at light-blue legs while the bulk of the command fired over the traverses at dark-blue heads." "Every few steps we came upon a dead man, nearly always shot through the head," another sharpshooter wrote.

The Union troops around Fort Mahone began to give way, and the battle-wise Southerners sensed a rout. "The Federals fought us, but not with the spirit which their immense superiority in numbers would have justified," a North Carolina soldier maintained.

When Parke's initial attack lost its momentum amid the maze of trenches, and when his last reserves had been committed, the Ninth Corps operation as a whole began to stall. As the combat bogged down in traverse-to-traverse fighting, all regimental control was lost, as was any semblance of brigade, division, or corps coordination. To make matters worse, Parke's men were running out of ammunition. Soldiers in the Union forts were detailed to carry munitions forward across the no-man's land, and as "the enemy had range of the plain between the two lines, many men were killed and wounded while thus engaged," one officer reported. A Massachusetts gunner observed that "people travelling across…[the] plain between Fort Sedgwick and 'Battery 27…went rather in a hurry."

The last Confederate counterattack drove hard into the Union left, and the fragmented commands that held the outer slopes of Fort Mahone began to fall back. A fresh body of colorfully outfitted Federal troops now appeared and moved purposefully toward the faltering left. This was the provost brigade, which was normally assigned to rear-echelon duties at City Point but had been massed that morning and rushed forward in response to Parke's call for assistance. Most recognizable among these troops were the red-panted Zouaves of the 114th Pennsylvania.

A killing fire ripped into the advancing headquarters guard. "It was a thrilling sight," one mud-caked Ninth Corps soldier recalled. "We battled to hold on and prayed for supports; the thought was 'Can they stand it?'—'will they make it?'" A reporter holed up in Fort Sedgwick wrote, "The fire which rained on the ground and around this fort was of the most terrible and fearful character, and to stand and see our men advance on a run through the very thickest of it, many of them being torn to pieces and lost to sight before they crossed half the distance[,] was a sight not soon to be forgotten."

This attack, by the Independent Brigade commanded by Brevet Brigadier General Charles H. T. Collis, ended the fighting. Another brigade, sent from the Sixth Corps, also arrived on the scene, but it was not sent forward. Parke briefly considered initiating an additional drive to capture the enemy's inner line, "but the exhausted condition of my troops forced me to reluctantly abandon the idea," he later reported.

Parke's assault was over. His men now held a few hundred yards of the enemy's trenches to the right of the Jerusalem Plank Road, and less than that to the left of it. Fort Mahone was controlled by neither side, with Union and Confederate squads both holding sections. Parke's losses in the actions this day exceeded 1,700 killed, wounded, or missing.

Pennsylvanian Miles C. Huyette spoke the thoughts of many a Ninth Corps soldier when he declared, "I never was so glad to see the sun go down."

John Gordon was feverishly preparing yet another Confederate counterattack when an urgent message came from Robert E. Lee directing him to stop. The fighting elsewhere all along the front had been a near disaster for the Southern cause. "In the face of this almost complete crushing of every command defending the entire length of our lines on my right, the restoration of the remaining breach in my front could contribute nothing toward the rescue of Lee's army," Gordon later stated. His losses in defending this sector were never reported.

New orders arrived as the firing ebbed. Lee would abandon Petersburg this night. As Gordon afterward remembered his instructions, "When this withdrawal had been accomplished, my command was to silently evacuate Petersburg, and cover the retreat of Lee's brave but shattered little army."

The Sixth Corps Story

The Sixth Corps commander, Major General Horatio G. Wright, believed he had found the chink in Petersburg's earthen armor. His men held the lines stretching from Fort Howard, about halfway between the Jerusalem Plank Road and the Halifax Road, through the fishhook in the Union defenses formed by Forts Fisher, Welch, Gregg, and Sampson.

Wright had gone over the ground himself several times and carefully interviewed dozens of field officers who were familiar with the terrain. He concluded that there was an opportunity for a breakthrough beyond Forts Fisher and Welch. It would not be easy: "The works in front of the chosen point of attack were known to be an extraordinarily strong line of rifle-pits, with deep ditches and high relief, preceded by one or two lines of abatis," Wright observed, adding that no Federal planner was quite sure what additional obstacles might lie behind these impediments. One of his officers viewed the task with grim humor, noting, "Along and in front of the [enemy] line bristled a heavy fraise, a serried row of heavy sharpened stakes set close together and pointing outward with an unyielding and aggressive air, as if to say, Come and impale yourselves on us."

An offensive operation here was possible only because of actions taken on March 25, when, following the successful Union counterattack at Fort Stedman, Wright had advanced his troops to capture the Confederate picket line. His men had held their gains against furious Rebel counterassaults—taking 547 prisoners and suffering 280 casualties in the process—and now controlled an excellent jump-off point about half a mile from the main enemy positions.

There had been a false alarm on the night of March 30, when an attack was set up only to be later canceled. Then, as Wright later reported, "[on] the evening of the 1st orders were received from Major- General Meade to attack at 4 a.m. the next day."

Acting under subsequent instructions from Meade, which arrived at a little after 9:00 p.m., Wright directed his artillery chief, Brevet Major Andrew Cowan, "to open fire on the enemy's lines with all the batteries." This sparked a three-hour artillery duel that flashed all along the opposing lines, from the Appomattox to Union Fort Gregg. "The night was dark and dismal," one Ohio officer recalled, "and the scene witnessed amid the deafening roar of cannon was indescribably wild and grand."

There was some confusion between Wright's headquarters and Meade's as the Army of the Potomac's commander, misinterpreting Grant's 9:00 p.m. dispatch, contradicted his earlier instructions by ordering the corps to strongly probe the enemy lines and attack if weaknesses were found. Matters were not cleared up until shortly after 1:00 a.m., when the 4:00 a.m. jump-off time was confirmed. "The corps will go in solid, and I am sure will make the fur fly," Wright vowed.

The soon-to-be-famous "wedge-shaped" assault formation began to take form in front of Forts Fisher and Welch. Men from Brevet Major General George W. Getty's division were the first to file out of the main lines. "The night...was dark, damp, chilly and gloomy," one Vermont soldier remembered. "While the Regiment was forming at midnight," a Pennsylvanian in the 93rd Regiment recollected, "knapsacks were flung and placed under guard, ...and in the dark and damp of the early morning, the powder smoke which hung like huge clouds near the ground deepened the obscurity and made our movements somewhat slow."

Getty's first three brigades made up the point of the wedge. The three were discretely arrayed, with Brevet Major General Lewis Grant's all-Vermont brigade closest to the enemy, its left on a swamp, Colonel Thomas Hyde's brigade to Lewis Grant's right and rear, and finally Colonel James M. Warner's brigade to Hyde's right and rear.

After Getty's men had cleared the Union obstructions, Brevet Major General Frank Wheaton's division followed to take station on their right and rear. A Connecticut soldier recalled that it was "about midnight [when] the regiment was…ordered to pack up everything. Knapsacks, however, were to be left behind, and to secure greater silence, canteens were to be worn on the right side." Each of Wheaton's three brigadiers formed a different attack formation: Colonel Oliver Edwards massed his men in a column, Brevet Brigadier General William H. Penrose chose four successive lines of battle, and Brevet Brigadier General Joseph Hamblin placed his troops in two battle lines.

Last to pass beyond the Union forts were the men of Brigadier General Truman Seymour's two-brigade division. "There were no light hearts in the corps that night," one of his brigadiers asserted, "but there were few faint ones. The soldiers of the corps knew the strength and character of the works to be assaulted. . . . The night added to the solemnity of the preparation for the bloody work." One of Seymour's brigades formed into a column, the other into three lines of battle.

Groups of ax-carrying pioneers, assigned to hack pathways through the enemy entanglements, accompanied each of the divisions. According to the recollections of a staff officer present, "Orders were impressed upon both commanders and men to advance without firing, and to force their way through all opposition and obstruction into the enemy's works; and when the works were carried, not to pursue the enemy, but to halt and reform in readiness for any emergency."

Wright stripped his defenses to fill the attacking ranks. The trench details between Forts Howard and Urmston were cut to the bare minimum, as were the garrisons in Forts Gregg, Sampson, and Cummings. Some sections of the earthworks linking these latter strong points were abandoned altogether, and others were manned by one-tenth their normal complement. Horatio Wright was staking everything on the success of a frontal assault against the enemy's hitherto impregnable fortifications.

It was too much to hope that this movement of seventeen thousand men would go unnoticed. Shortly after midnight, even as Truman Seymour's troops were approaching their starting positions, Confederate outpost fire sprinkled flame into the stygian darkness. Some Union pickets disobeyed their orders, returned the fire, and began a briefly violent scrap that threatened the whole operation. If the Rebels were to realize what was happening, they could open fire with everything they had and turn the staging area into a charnel house. "This was a tough place to stay," a Wisconsin soldier observed, "with nothing to do but lie there and take our medicine." Added a nearby New Yorker, "Every once in a while some one would get hit with a ball, and we could hear his cry of anguish as the lead tore through." Among the wounded was the Vermont Brigade's leader, Lewis Grant. Lieutenant Colonel Amasa S. Tracy assumed command.

"Everything was soon quieted down, however, by the exertions of the officers, though many casualties occurred from this contretemps,'" Wright later reported. "The men behaved well during the whole of the severe fire, without returning a shot or uttering a word to indicate their presence to the enemy."

Now came the waiting until it was time to advance. "Would that signal gun never sound! Would daylight never come!" one officer exclaimed. "The silence of the men became painful and almost unendurable," a Pennsylvania veteran recalled.

The portion of the Confederate line targeted by Wright's assault was manned by troops from Major Generals Cadmus M. Wilcox and Henry Heth's divisions of Lieutenant General A. P. Hill's Third Corps. A total of six brigades, most of them undersized, held the six miles of earthworks stretching southward from Petersburg's inner defensive line to Burgess' Mill. Georgians from Brigadier General Edward L. Thomas's brigade connected with the city's perimeter defenses. On Thomas's right—directly opposite the Union Forts Fisher and Welch—were four North Carolina regiments commanded by Brigadier General James H. Lane. Troops from the brigades of Brigadier Generals William MacRae and William McComb and Colonel Andrew M. Nelson completed the thin gray line that shielded the Boydton Plank Road and the South Side Railroad. These works "would have been impregnable if defended by any adequate force," one North Carolinian declared with bitterness, "but . . . in fact were occupied by a mere skirmish line."

A. P. Hill had cut short a much-needed leave of absence to be with his men at this critical time. He had worried over his lines all day and was trying unsuccessfully to sleep this damp night. Feeling anxious about the especially heavy picket and artillery fire, Hill finally got out of bed, quickly dressed, left the house he shared with his wife and two children, and walked across the Cox Road to his headquarters tent. The time was about 3:00 a.m.

Colonel William H. Palmer, Hill's adjutant general, was also awake but had no news to report. The aide did mention that there had been some activity along portions of Gordon's picket line, but he assured his commander that the situation had been stabilized without any serious damage. Hill decided to check with Robert E. Lee's headquarters, and called for his horse. He instructed his aide to "wake up the staff, get everything in readiness, and have the headquarters' wagons hitched up," adding that "as soon as he would have an interview with General Lee, he would return."

Hill rode west for a mile and a half along the Cox Road to the Turnbull House, Lee's headquarters. He found Lee equally exhausted yet equally awake, lying partly clothed on his bed, as if he had not completely undressed the night before. The two discussed the overall situation. Then, at about 4:00 a.m., Lee's First Corps commander, Lieutenant General James Longstreet, arrived in advance of his men, who were marching from Richmond to reinforce the Petersburg lines. "Some members of the staff were up and dressed," Longstreet later wrote. Lee welcomed "Old Pete," the latter recalled, and "gave orders for our march to support the broken forces about Five Forks. He had no censure for any one, but mentioned the great numbers of the enemy and the superior repeating rifles of his cavalry."

Outside the Turnbull House, nearby objects were becoming visible. It was 4:40 a.m.

The appointed hour for the beginning of the assault—4:00 a.m.— came and went, but Horatio Wright did not give the word to advance. Not until forty minutes later, when he felt that it was finally "light enough," did he order the signal gun in Fort Fisher fired.

No one in the Vermont Brigade heard the signal, "owing to the heavy cannonading, which had been kept up at intervals during the night." Everything keyed on Tracy's men, at the apex of the wedge; once they began to move, everyone else would follow. A few tense minutes ticked by before the order to advance was passed to the front.

According to Major Merritt Barber, the Vermont Brigade "immediately moved forward over the works of the [Union] skirmish line and pressed on steadily and silently until they had very nearly reached the first line of the enemy's intrenchments, when they were discovered by their skirmishers, who delivered a weak and scattering volley and then fled." Remembered another Vermont soldier, "Their works were impregnable with big ditches and staked, but they had a small opening through where their pickets passed out and into their front. We broke through this little roadway, driving the rebels before us, and then commenced a run for our lives."

Not all did, however. The Rebel main line looked to be a death trap, and enemy cannoneers laid down a heavy fire. A panic spasm twisted through the brigade as a fair number of the Federals took cover in the Confederate rifle pits, resisting efforts to move them forward. It took the self-sacrificial actions of a number of officers to at last animate the soldiers into renewing the attack. A strong defense might have stopped the Vermont Brigade in its tracks, but there just weren't enough Confederates manning the earthworks and the Granite State men quickly overwhelmed those who attempted such a stand.

Thomas Hyde's brigade moved on Tracy's right. "I remember ordering a lot of rebels to the rear as we crossed their picket pits," Hyde recalled, "for then the black darkness was becoming gray in the coming dawn, and the shot and shell from the enemy's forts were like so many rockets fired horizontally, and they were mostly a few feet over our heads." Coming up on Hyde's right were Warner's men, with the 93rd Pennsylvania, divided into two battalions, in the third and fourth lines. While the first two regiments stalled at the edge of the enemy obstructions, the 93rd passed through them. "The first Battalion of the Regiment reached the abatis, and in an instant the second Battalion was mixed up with it and assisted in the work of making an opening through the abatis, and with a cheer leaped over the breastworks," one Pennsylvanian recollected.

Frank Wheaton's division advanced on Getty's right. The axmen preceding Wheaton's leading brigade—Colonel Edwards's—rushed to the first row of entanglements. "A destructive fire was opened upon the exposed line, which the [Federal] skirmishers returned with interest from their Spencer rifles while the pioneers chopped and wrenched away the obstructions with desperate energy," a Massachusetts officer wrote afterward.

C. F. Barnes was one of those massed in the gloom waiting for openings to be made by the pioneers. "When I started on that charge," he recalled, "I was not feeling very well; there was something the matter with my throat. I thought my heart would jump clear out of my mouth. The boys were yelling and charging all around me. I think I went more than half way across before I yelled, and then I felt so much better that I was sorry I had not yelled when I started. I was much surprised at the great change in my feelings. After that whoop I think I could have tackled the whole so-called Southern Confederacy."

Lieutenant Colonel Elisha H. Rhodes led a party from the 2nd Rhode Island in a wild scramble across the dark, rutted field. "The first I knew I fell into the ditch with a number of my men after me," he remembered. "The Rebels fired their cannon and muskets over our heads, and then we crawled up...onto the parapet of their works, stepping right among their muskets as they were aimed over their works. It was done so quick that the Rebels had no chance to fire again but dropped their guns and ran."

Advancing on Getty's left were Truman Seymour's two brigades. Declared a Maryland man in Brevet Brigadier General J. Warren Kiefer's command, "Not even a temporary check was experienced in passing through and over the double line of abatis, ditch and high, strong earthworks. A hand-to-hand fight ensued within the main works in which many gallant officers and men fell killed and wounded." Added another, "We rushed through like a hurricane."

By 5:00 a.m., or a little after, Wright's Sixth Corps had torn a gap in Lee's defensive line. Triumphant Yankees now spread into what had formerly been Confederate rear-echelon areas.

"My line was pierced by the enemy in strong force," C.S. Brigadier General James Lane later reported. At Robert E. Lee's headquarters, the informal conference among Lee, Longstreet, and Hill was abruptly interrupted when Colonel Charles Venable of Lee's staff burst into the room to warn that panicked teamsters were fleeing past headquarters, and that enemy troops had been spotted in the rear. The generals ran out to the porch and peered toward the southwest. What they saw, James Longstreet later remembered, "as far as the eye could cover the field, [was] a line of skirmishers in quiet march toward us. It was hardly light enough to distinguish the blue from the gray."

A. P. Hill was frantic with anxiety. Before Lee could say a word, Hill mounted his horse and galloped toward the breach, accompanied by two trusted couriers, George Tucker and William Jenkins. The three had gone only a short distance when they were joined by Colonel Venable, who was carrying a message from Lee urging Hill not to expose himself to danger.

Hill asked Venable to thank General Lee for his consideration and explained that he was only trying to establish communication with his right flank. Venable tagged along when the group moved on. Recalled courier Tucker, "We had gone a little more than half [the distance toward a small branch running eastward to Old Town Creek] when we suddenly came upon two of the enemy's armed infantry men. Jenkins and myself...were instantly upon them, when, at the command 'surrender,' they laid down their arms. Turning to the General, I asked what should be done with the prisoners. He said, 'Jenkins, take them to General Lee.' Jenkins started back with his men, and we rode on."

Hill did not realize that his lines had already been overwhelmed. The first wave of the Union assault had in fact pressed on toward the South Side Railroad, leaving behind scattered groups of stragglers and whole companies that had been separated from their regiments. It was into this uncertain situation that Hill, Venable, and Tucker now rode. Before long, they spotted figures milling about the huts that marked the winter camp of Mahone's Division.

"General," Tucker asked, "what troops are there?"

"The enemy's," Hill quickly answered.

Moving ahead, the party saw Lieutenant Colonel William T. Poague's artillery battalion drawn up near the Cox Road. Hill ordered Venable to have the guns placed so as to be able to open upon the enemy. Then Hill, accompanied now only by George Tucker, continued on. The courier was getting worried.

"Please excuse me, General, but where are we going?"

"Sergeant, I must go to the right as quickly as possible," Hill replied, pointing toward the southwest. "We will go up this side of the branch to the woods, which will cover us until reaching the field in rear of General Heth's quarters. I hope to find the road clear at General Heth's." The pair went on and soon lost sight of both friend and foe. For an instant, Hill stopped thinking of the military problems facing him and remembered that he was in personal danger. "Sergeant, should anything happen to me, you must go back to General Lee and report it," he commented. The two men at length came out of a small wood and looked to where the main line had been; groups of soldiers were moving about the position in a seemingly aimless fashion. Hill viewed the scene through his field glasses.

"They are there," he said flatly.

Tucker knew what he meant. "Which way now, General?" he asked. "We must keep to the right," Hill answered, and they spurred on toward a small patch of trees a short distance north of the Boydton Plank Road.

Wright's formations lost much of their cohesion when they crashed through the Confederate line. "The troops were perfectly wild with delight at their success in this grand assault and [only] with difficulty could [they] be restrained," Wright reported. "Then, and there," a Connecticut man recalled, "the long tried and ever faithful soldiers of the Republic saw DAYLIGHT!—and such a shout as tore the concave of that morning sky, it were worth dying to hear."

Groups from all three divisions eventually reached the Boydton Plank Road. "[We] fired into the running Rebs, and also into some wagons which were passing. We also twisted off the telegraph wires with our bayonets, continuing our firing at everything in sight," a soldier in the 121st New York remembered. Another soldier, in Wheaton's division, wrote afterward of "cutting the telegraph wire along the Boydton Plank Road, the men mounting on their comrades' shoulders to better do the work. . . . One part of our regiment met a large crowd of women and old men who said they were going to church."

Other troops pressed over the Cox Road to reach the long-coveted South Side Railroad. Most of these were from Truman Seymour's division; Captain E. S. Norvell, of the 6th Maryland, guessed that nearly five hundred men made it that far. Included among them were Private Daniel Wolford and Corporal John Mauk, both from the 138th Pennsylvania. After getting separated from their regiment and wandering on their own across the battle area, the two soldiers found some crowbars and ripped at the railroad track for a while, then turned back toward the Boydton Plank Road, taking potshots at a distant supply train as it passed near them. Spotting a gathering of Union stragglers who were brewing coffee, Mauk and Wolford moved to join them; at that instant, Mauk later recounted, they saw "two men on horseback coming from the direction of Petersburg, who had the appearance of officers."

George Tucker, the courier accompanying A. P. Hill, caught sight of the two enemy soldiers. The pair, according to Tucker's accounts, "ran quickly forward to the cover of one of the large trees, and, one above the other, on the same side, leveled their guns."

Tucker looked to Hill. "We must take them," the corps commander said, drawing his Navy Colt pistol.

"Stay there, I will take them," called Tucker, pushing his horse ahead of Hill's. By now the two Confederates were less than twenty yards away from the enemy riflemen. "If you fire you will be swept to hell," Tucker shouted to the Federals. "Our men are here—surrender!" Suddenly A. P. Hill was at Tucker's side. "Surrender!" he echoed.

They were now within ten yards of the two blue-coated figures. One lowered his rifle as if to surrender.

Corporal Mauk and Private Wolford ran behind a large oak tree and aimed their guns at the approaching riders. Mauk later recalled that one moved ahead of the other and shouted, "Surrender, or I will shoot you. A body of troops are advancing on our left and you will have to surrender anyway." The second rider drew up even with the first and added his voice to his fellow's, urging, "Surrender your arms."

Wolford hesitated and lowered his gun slightly. "I can't see it," Mauk said to his companion. "Let us shoot them."

The two fired. Wolford missed, but Mauk's aim was true.

George Tucker ducked as Wolford's shot went wide. Next to him, A. P. Hill was punched from his saddle by the impact of a .58-caliber bullet that shot off his left thumb, pierced his heart, and blew out a bloody exit hole in his back.

Tucker caught the bridle of the general's horse and galloped for cover.

Mauk and Wolford decided not to hang around; they hurried southward to rejoin their command without even examining the body.

Some order had been returned to the Sixth Corps formations by this time. "As promptly as possible," Horatio Wright reported, "the lines were reformed, wheeled to the left and moved, with the left of line guiding on the rebel intrenchments, toward Hatcher's Run." A lone brigade was left behind to blunt any enemy interference from Petersburg.

The Confederate defenders were by now fully alerted, and the swing toward Hatcher's Run was not unopposed, but the victorious Federals were possessed of a fierce abandon. "It was most difficult to keep the line formed," one Union officer complained. "The troops in their enthusiasm would break away in bodies of from ten to fifty, heedless of commands, charging this point or that, wherever the enemy attempted to make a stand."

Sporadic Confederate counterattacks and brief holding actions in some of the redoubts slowed but could not halt the Sixth Corp's advance toward Hatcher's Run.

Portions of Lane's, MacRae's, McComb's, and Nelson's brigades were pinned on the north bank of Hatcher's Run. Most made their way across, but not all. The 11th Mississippi scattered in a panic. "A few of the men made their escape by swimming the stream," a member of the regiment recalled. "Frank Hope, the color bearer, tore the flag of the regiment into shreds, tied them to the flag-staff and threw them into Hatcher's Run. About this time the regiment was entirely surrounded and all the members surrendered."

Back at the Turnbull House, Robert E. Lee turned from disaster to disaster. After Hill left, he had dressed quickly, given preparatory orders to move his headquarters, mounted Traveller, and ridden across the road so he could have a clear view of the country. He was pondering his next step when a sad party of Third Corps staff officers arrived with Tucker in tow. Colonel Palmer began to tell Lee of Hill's death but broke down and was unable to finish. It fell to the courier to tell his story. Lee listened with tears in his eyes, and when Tucker had finished talking, he said with great emotion, "He is now at rest, and we who are left are the ones to suffer." The army commander then turned to Palmer and told him to inform Mrs. Hill of what had occurred. "Colonel," Lee cautioned sadly, "break the news to her as gently as possible."

There was just no time for further sentiment. James Longstreet was placed in command of the Third Corps until Henry Heth could be summoned to take charge. The Union battle lines had receded to the west, but for the moment, Petersburg's western defenses were not seriously threatened. Remnants of Lane's and Thomas's brigades had fallen back into those positions, where another of Hill's divisional commanders, Cadmus Wilcox, was organizing the defenses. Sometime before 10:00 a.m, Brigadier General Nathaniel Harris's Mississippi brigade arrived on the scene with its four hundred guns.

Lee sent his first dispatch to Richmond at about that time. It read, in part, "I see no prospect of doing more than holding our position here till night. I am not certain that I can do that. . . . I advise that all preparations be made for leaving Richmond to-night."

The leading elements of the Union Sixth Corps reached Hatcher's Run at about 9:00 a.m. Here Wright "learned from staff officers…that the Second and Fifth Corps and the cavalry were sweeping down in that direction, and that it was not necessary to proceed farther. I therefore turned and moved toward Petersburg."

His men began to arrive near the Cockade City's inner perimeter lines a little before 10:00 a.m. That was none too soon for the lone brigade left behind in the move toward Hatcher's Run; Rebel cannon had kept up a lively fire throughout, and fresh enemy troops had appeared in an extended skirmish line that threatened to overlap the Federal position.

Help came not only from the returning Sixth Corps but from the Twenty-fourth Corps as well. The Twenty-fourth, posted along the Union line on Wright's immediate left, had been ordered into the gap following the breakthrough. Both corps now closed the ring around Petersburg, with the left of the Sixth Corps resting on the Appomattox River and its right a short distance south of the Cox Road. The next section of the line, stretching from there past the Boydton Plank Road, was taken by the Twenty-fourth Corps.

A few stubborn Confederate artillerists delayed Wright's deployment for some time. This unit, Williams's North Carolina battery, made a defiant last stand near Lee's headquarters, which was being abandoned even as the cannoneers unlimbered and opened fire on the approaching bluecoats. Yankee sharpshooters got close enough to kill the battery's horses, and a pell-mell rush by several Union regiments finally captured the pesky guns.

Some Federals believed that it would take only one more advance to carry Petersburg and wreck Lee's army, but Wright felt that his "men were so exhausted as to make an assault upon the enemy's lines inadvisable. The corps had been under arms for nearly eighteen hours, had assaulted the strong lines of the enemy; swept down them several miles and returning had moved upon Petersburg, some miles further."

As one of Wright's soldiers recalled, "Columns of smoke [in Petersburg] during the day announced the burning of the warehouses and public stores in preparation of withdrawal. All that afternoon we lay quietly expecting the order to assault, and spent the night before the works. We could only conjecture what was taking place within the city." Added a staff officer in Getty's division, "The enemy in some disorder were hastily forming behind the works, and I myself saw their officers beating their men with their swords back into the lines. A thousand fresh men could have broken through."

Soon after Wright's men turned back from Hatcher's Run earlier in the day, Lieutenant General Grant had ridden onto the field. "The troops had but commenced moving toward Petersburg," a New Jerseyman remembered, "when a hearty cheer was given by the rear regiments…and as soon as the soldiers saw the Lieutenant-General…the men cheered him with the wildest enthusiasm; he rode with head uncovered, and bowed his thanks for the soldiers' hearty greeting." *New York Herald* correspondent Charles H. Haanam recorded that Grant's "strongly marked and sun-browned face lighted up with stern pleasure as he rode along through the rebel works. On seeing Generals Wright, Getty, Seymour, Wheaton and other Sixth Corps officers, he shook hands with great heartiness." According to his aide Horace Porter, "The general galloped along toward the right, and soon met Meade, with whom he had been in constant communication, and who had been urging the Army of the Potomac with all vigor. Congratulations were rapidly exchanged, and both went to pushing forward the good work."

They were counting the cost of the operation at the Sixth Corps field hospital, which had been set up near Fort Fisher: "By daylight the wounded began to come in, and from this time until four p.m. the surgeons were occupied in dressing wounds, extracting bullets and amputating limbs," a New Jersey soldier observed. "There were the usual sad and terrible scenes of suffering and death." Casualties for the Sixth Corps this day were 123 killed and 958 wounded or missing, a total of 1,081; Confederate losses were unreported, but Getty's division alone claimed more than 2,100 Rebels captured.

Wright had fulfilled his promise. His men had broken Lee's main line, isolated several brigades west of Hatcher's Run, completely cut off Pickett's infantry and Fitz Lee's cavalry near Five Forks, closed the river-to-river circle about Petersburg, and finally, in doing so, doomed Richmond. A soldier in the 2nd Vermont recalled the end of this day: "A happier night I never have seen, as the fires which lit up the whole country were burning, and the city we had fought for for four years was ours. The boys would wake each other up to see the fires burn."

It was with justifiable pride that another Sixth Corps veteran later referred to the assault formation that began this dramatic attack as the "wedge that opened the home of the Confederacy."

The Twenty-Fourth Corps Story

The Twenty-fourth Corps was the by-product of a failed experiment. The mixing of black and white combat units did not work, and the army high command acknowledged that on December 3, when it dismantled the integrated Tenth and Eighteenth corps to create the all-white Twenty-fourth and the all-black Twenty-fifth corps.[1] As part of the command shuffle following Ben Butler's departure, Major General E. O. C. Ord took charge of the Army of the James, while the Twenty-fourth Corps went to Major General John Gibbon and the Twenty-fifth to Major General Godfrey Weitzel.

"It was difficult to conceal my pleasure and satisfaction at the receipt of the news," Gibbon remembered. He had risen through the ranks to the divisional level as the protégé of Winfield Hancock's, but the stresses of the Petersburg campaign had soured their once warm friendship. The ambitious Gibbon had felt further slighted when, after Hancock's departure, command of the Second Corps had been given to Andrew Humphreys. The appointment that arrived on January 13 was just what Gibbon wanted, however, for it "made me more independent and second in command in the Army of the James instead of the seventh as I was in the Army of the Potomac."

---

1   The black troops assigned to the Ninth Corps had been transferred into the Army of the James in November.

The long-awaited orders for the spring offensive had finally come in late March. Ironically, they called for most of the Twenty-fourth Corps to be temporarily joined to the Army of the Potomac. Accordingly, on the night of March 27, Gibbon put his First Division (with Brigadier General Robert S. Foster commanding) and his Independent Division (under the direction of Brevet Major General John W. Turner) on roads leading south. Two days later, his troops were manning a section of trenches near Hatcher's Run, allowing the Second Corps to move farther to the left.

The first testing of the Twenty-fourth Corps occurred along its picket lines on March 31 and April 1, in a series of short, sharp engagements over little points of advantage. There were bigger things in the wind, though, and on the night of April 1, Gibbon was instructed to prepare his corps for an "assault in the morning to co-operate with the Sixth and Ninth Corps on our right."

His men got a real taste of war Petersburg-style when a massive artillery duel erupted along the lines at a little after 10:00 p.m. It was all too much for one West Virginia soldier, who "became a raving maniac on the instant, from the great and unexpected shock to his nervous system caused by the tremendous and sudden roar of cannon and outpour of musketry on that memorable morning."

With daylight came a change of plans. "At 6:50 a.m. an order was received from Major-General Ord directing me to send all my available force to the support of the Sixth Corps, which had broken through the enemy's line near Fort Welch," Gibbon later recalled. He complied at once, ordering "the whole of Foster's division and two of Turner's brigades to move to the right." The remaining brigade in Turner's Independent Division (Brigadier General Thomas M. Harris's) advanced its line at the same time. Harris's men took the Rebel position "without loss" and pivoted to the right, where they soon met the triumphant Sixth Corps on its way down from Petersburg.

Gibbon's other units set out on the double-quick at a little after 7:00 a.m. It took them more than two hours to reach Fort Welch and pass through the gap opened up by the Sixth Corps, after which the advance almost at once engaged with small groups of the enemy.

The Twenty-fourth Corps had cleared out most of the scattered resistance by 11:00 a.m. and wheeled right toward Petersburg. Two obstacles stood in the way of Union entry into the Cockade City. The first of these was Lee's inner line, which stretched northward from Battery 45, roughly following the course of Old Town Creek.[2] Located a short distance outside this inner line was the second obstacle, two redoubts made of earth and wood that barred the western approaches to the city. The Confederate defensive line immediately to the east of these two strong-points was rendered impassable by a dam constructed during the winter by C.S. engineers, which effectively inundated a large section of the low-lying ground.

John Gibbon believed that the critical moment in this day's fighting had arrived. East of Petersburg, cannon fire still boomed and musketry crackled as the Ninth Corps battled for a foothold near Fort Mahone; southwest of the city, almost all resistance had collapsed, with Confederate survivors barely managing rear-guard actions as they tried to fall back to the west. A thrust into Petersburg now would spell catastrophe for the Army of Northern Virginia.

A blast of artillery fire from the two redoubts scattered Yankee scouting parties and showed that here, at least, the Rebels were prepared to fight. "We evidently now had the enemy by the throat," Gibbon observed, "but he still held tenaciously to his line."

Along the Howlett line north of Petersburg the men in Brigadier General Nathaniel H. Harris's all-Mississippi brigade (of William Mahone's division) were put on alert at around midnight to be "ready to move at a moment's warning." The call came one hour later for them "to march at once to Petersburg, cross at the upper pontoon bridge and report to General R. E. Lee."

The Mississippians began at once "to move quietly to the rear, [leaving] …everything but canteens and cartridge boxes." Not everyone was pleased with the assignment. "As we had had a hand in every fracas in front and rear of Petersburg from Richmond to Meherrin River on the line of North Carolina, we set off grumbling and wondering, 'Why in _____ can't Mahone get some other troops to do some fighting?' " one soldier later recalled.

Another remembered, "Not having heard of the disaster at Five Forks the day previous, we could not imagine the cause of alarm, as everything was perfectly quiet on our front." That all changed, however, once the men drew near the Appomattox River. "As the brigade approached Petersburg, deep, heavy and incessant roar of artillery and the sharp rattle of musketry announced

---

2   Sometimes referred to as Indian Town Creek, Old Town is known today as Rohoic Creek.

a more than ordinary conflict on the lines around that devoted city," brigadier Harris noted.

The Sixth Corps's attack had split James Lane's brigade nearly in half. Portions of it were shoved away from Petersburg, while other fragments managed a fighting retreat toward the city. Most of the latter groups passed near the two redoubts that had been constructed to serve as a breakwater should the blue tidal wave engulf the lower trenches. These strongpoints were named after the farms on which they were built— Forts Gregg and Whitworth.[3] Lane had no intention of making a stand in these exposed works, wanting instead to move his men immediately into the inner line, but he was overruled by Cadmus Wilcox, who ordered him to organize some counterattacks. Aided by his fellow brigadier Edward Thomas, Lane rallied a force of about six hundred men and formed them into battle lines before Fort Gregg.

Most of the Yankee columns had turned away from Petersburg by this time, so Lane and Thomas had remarkably little trouble advancing their formation a short distance.

As Nathaniel Harris led his men onto the fields west of Petersburg, he was convinced that the "brigades of Wilcox's occupying the lines had been scattered and there was no other organized body of troops" than his own. Operating on orders from Cadmus Wilcox, Harris deployed his four hundred men in front of Fort Gregg and advanced the line, guiding on the Boydton Plank Road. "We found everything in confusion," one of his soldiers recollected. "Our lines had been ruptured everywhere, and the Union troops were in possession."

Harris's men topped one rise in time to see the Yankee Twenty-fourth Corps march through what had been the main Confederate defenses. "They seemed to be in no hurry, but very deliberately dressed their line and then moved forward," noted one Rebel observer. "It was a grand but awful sight, the Federals moving with the same precision as though on parade." Harris spread his units thin to cover a broad front and sent out skirmishers to harry the slowly advancing enemy; when the Federals got close enough, the Mississippians opened a "brisk fire" that momentarily halted their advance. At about this time, an aide appeared with orders from Wilcox to Harris instructing him "not to suffer himself to be cut off, but to hold the enemy in check as long as possible,

---

3   Period accounts sometimes refer to these two as *Battery* Gregg and *Battery* Whitworth. Whitworth is also on occasion referred to as Fort Baldwin, Fort Alexander, or Fort Anderson.

and when compelled to retire to fall back slowly and to throw two regiments into Battery Gregg and two regiments into Battery Whitworth."

The sight of Gibbon's columns deploying was enough for James Lane, who "withdrew, and sent an officer at once to Fort Gregg with instructions to let a sufficient number of my men enter the fort to man it, and to order the others to the [portion of the inner line] …between Fort Gregg and Battery 45."

Nathaniel Harris also now decided that it was time to pull back. His battle lines retired slowly to Forts Gregg and Whitworth, where Harris was preparing to make his stand. Two Mississippi regiments the 12th and 16th, about 150 men altogether—were detailed into Fort Gregg, and two others—the 19th and 48th—took position in Whitworth. Lieutenant Colonel James H. Duncan of the 19th Mississippi was placed in charge of Gregg, while Harris himself directed the defense of Whitworth. As Harris's men entered Gregg, they found it already occupied by remnants of Lane's and Thomas's brigades and armed with two cannon, manned by detachments from the Washington (Louisiana) Artillery (Lieutenant Francis McElroy commanding) and the 4th Maryland Battery (under Captain Walter S. Chew).

"I rode to the front of Battery Gregg," recalled Harris, "and instructed Colonel Duncan to have plenty of ammunition brought into that work." The brigadier then galloped to Whitworth and immediately ordered out details to set fire to the winter huts near the fort, which obstructed its field of fire. Mounted officer Frank H. Foote accompanied the arson detail, which hurried to do its work even as the enemy approached. "As I came in full view of the Federal skirmishers a volley greeted me that caused my 'Pegasus' to practice all the tricks and acts of the much-vaunted circus horse," Foote remembered. "He showed a strong inclination to go further to the front than was necessary, and in one of his plunging freaks a bullet struck him on one of his legs, breaking it. Fortunately I had him headed toward our line, and after a few frantic plunges he tumbled to the ground, myself with him. I fortunately struck on my feet 'a running,' which I kept up until the lines were reached."

Cadmus Wilcox came out from the inner line for one last visit to Fort Gregg. "Men," he said in a loud, excited voice, "the salvation of Lee's army is in your keeping; you must realize the responsibility, and your duty; don't surrender this fort; if you can hold the enemy in check for two hours, Longstreet…will be here, and the danger to the army in the trenches will be averted."

Wilcox made as if to continue, but an enemy shell burst nearby and cut him short. A soldier in the redoubt finished the speech: "Tell General Lee that Fort Gregg will never be surrendered."

Brigadier General James Lane stood apart from the battle frenzy that coursed through the ranks in Fort Gregg. "I felt satisfied then that every man in the Fort would be killed or captured, & I wanted to save as many as I could," he later explained. He approached Wilcox and obtained permission to withdraw along with his staff officers. Then, on his own volition, Lane sent several aides into Gregg to get out as many of his men as they could. Enemy cannon were already ranging on the redoubt, making it, in Lane's words, "a perfect hell on earth."

Conditions inside the fort were so chaotic that Lane's officers were unable to organize the North Carolinians to carry out an orderly withdrawal. Most of the troops therefore stayed, and the few who left did so only under the baleful glare of their comrades from Mississippi. "They begged to go to the rear; and we hesitated whether to let them go or make them stay to defend the fort; but concluded that in their demoralized condition it was better to let them go, provided they left their guns with us, which they readily consented to do," wrote one soldier who remained.

Lane and his staff galloped to the inner line as enemy shell explosions began to blossom about the doomed fort. For years afterward, there would be anger between Lane and Harris over this affair, but that lay in the future. For the present, there was only the promise of battle and death.

John Gibbon was determined that the attack on Forts Gregg and Whitworth would be solely a Twenty-fourth Corps operation. As the Sixth Corps units came up from Hatcher's Run, they were put into position on Gibbon's left, "extending our line nearly to the river."

Even as his skirmishers peppered the redoubts and his artillery began to pound the position, Gibbon set up his attack. He picked Foster's division to storm Gregg, with two of Turner's brigades in reserve. Turner's other brigade, Harris's—which had come up from Hatcher's Run with the Sixth Corps—was sent to watch over Fort Whitworth. Gregg was the key; capture it and Whitworth would fall.

It was about 1:00 p.m. when Colonel Thomas O. Osborn's brigade (of Foster's division) began advancing across the eight hundred yards of mostly open ground to Fort Gregg. Recalled Osborn, "I moved my command forward about half the distance, in quick time, at right shoulder shift arms, and having passed a deep and difficult slough, gave the command [to] charge, when the brigade, with cheers, swept up the ascent at the double-quick, under a terrible fire of grape, canister, and minie-balls tearing through the ranks." One Illinois survivor wrote afterward of the "destructive fire…which mowed down our men most unmercifully." "A few feet from the ditch, which was deep and broad, the withering fire of the fort became too hot for even the most desperate men, and the whole column recoiled," testified a nearby Ohio soldier.

There was a brief lull as Osborn's line fell back a short distance, reformed, and returned, this time accompanied by another wave of Yankee troops. These were two regiments—the 10th Connecticut and the 100th New York—from Colonel George B. Dandy's brigade. "It was impossible to keep up an unbroken line in crossing the fire-swept plain of death," the chaplain of the Connecticut regiment lamented. The momentum of the new battle line carried the Federals back to the ditch, where they once again staggered under a blast of rifle and cannon fire. This time, however, two Connecticut boys pushed their way out of the pack, plunged into the moat, and jammed the regimental flagstaff into the earthen wall. Nearby, the flag of the 39th Illinois also fluttered from the pitted, muddy slope, put there by a Pennsylvanian who had taken it from a dying Illinois color-bearer.

Swarms of Yankees now plunged into the breast-high ditch water to spread out along the front and side walls. Others rushed around the back to seek a way inside, but the few who made it to the rear found it closed off by a loop-holed stockade, through which Rebel marksmen fired at anything that moved.

The Federals in the moat, meanwhile, had their own problems. "The steepness and slippery nature of the sides of the fort for a time rendered futile all our efforts to scale them," one recounted. "The excitement which now prevailed beggars description. The men were nearly frantic in their attempts to gain the top of the works."

Pennsylvanian Michael Dunn lay wounded in the ditch and watched in horror as its muddy waters became infused with dark tendrils of blood from the injured and dying. Dunn managed to twist about so that Lieutenant Colonel Hughes of the 199th could reach his dry cartridge box, which, Dunn remembered, "he was not slow in using." Dunn continued, "While in the trench a member of Co. B. 199th Pa. named Hess asked if I had seen his brother. I pointed to where a cap was floating on the water, and told him that I thought it was his brother lying dead under the water where the cap was."

"Only by digging with swords and bayonets could footholds be secured on the slippery ascent," an Illinois soldier wrote. Another member of the 39th, Charles W. Ware, found himself next to Colonel Osborn, who was boosting troops up the wall as fast as he could, shouting all the while, "Men, we must take this fort before the enemy receives reinforcement." Ware remembered being shoved up onto the parapet of the work at a point "some 10 or 12 feet from the corner of the fort. As I raised to shoot at a reb to my right (we were only the length of our musket barrels apart) another jumped up in front of me and hastily fired at my head. The charge raked the side of my neck, knocking me senseless, and when I came back to my senses, a dead man was laying across my back. I rolled him off, picked up my gun, and was again ready for business."

The Yankees clustered along Gregg's northern side were blasted by cannon fire from Whitworth, prompting John Gibbon to order Thomas Harris's brigade to attack that fort. At the same time, Gibbon gave instructions for the other two brigades of Turner's division to advance in support of Foster's embattled men.

Robert E. Lee remained calm throughout this crisis. "The deportment of General Lee at that time was such as to excite the admiration of all about him," Colonel Walter Taylor, one of Lee's trusted aides, noted with awe. Lee held his headquarters at the Turnbull House until long lines of blue-clad skirmishers were approaching and enemy artillery was bracketing the handful of Confederate cannoneers who had made a stand in the building's garden.

There was little that Lee could do; every Southern soldier with a gun was either fighting, fleeing, or preparing to defend a likely avenue of approach to Petersburg. "This is bad business, Colonel," Lee remarked to one of his staff officers. The only crack in his personal composure came later in the afternoon, when he was handed a message from Jefferson Davis in which the C.S. president complained that for the Richmond government to "move to-night will involve the loss of many valuables." Lee crumpled the dispatch and then tore it to bits. "I am sure I gave him sufficient notice," he said. To another officer Lee confided, "Well, colonel, it has happened as I told them it would at Richmond. The line has been stretched until it has broken."

As Lee and his staff galloped toward the relative safety of the inner line, a Federal battery lobbed a shell just a few feet behind the white-haired general. "This incident seemed to arouse in General Lee his fighting blood," a nearby aide observed. "He turned his head over his right shoulder, his cheeks became flushed, and a sudden flash of the eye showed with what reluctance he retired before the fire directed upon him."

Lee's only hope now rested with James Longstreet's men and the defenders of Forts Gregg and Whitworth. If the mixed forces in the two redoubts could hold back the blue tide long enough for Old Pete's troops to man the western trenches of the inner line, then it would be possible to withdraw the rest of the army during the night.

Longstreet's men were coming. Two of his brigades—Benning's and Bratton's—had been on the move since early morning and should now be approaching the city, if they were not already across the Appomattox. As Longstreet himself later reported, "I sent back toward the [Petersburg] Depot for our troops, which were expected to hurry forward as rapidly as possible."

The men from Mississippi, North Carolina, Louisiana, and Virginia inside Fort Gregg beat down the first wave of attacking bluecoats. "In these charges there was no shooting but by us, and we did cruel and savage work with them," one officer recalled. A young rifleman helping with the cannon never forgot the third shot fired by his gun, which struck the enemy line "breast high (about 300 feet away) . . . . The shot produced a beautiful panorama."

A Confederate watching from Fort Whitworth confessed his admiration for the enemy troops who "charged gallantly up the parapet in the face of a perfect hail of Minie balls. As they seemed to be badly led, however, after a faint attempt to enter the fort, they appeared to lose courage, dropped down and huddled together in the ditch."

Fresh Unionists then came hustling into the struggle for Gregg. "[We] gave them the same warm welcome that we gave the first," a Rebel defender noted grimly, "and more of it." But there were just too many Yankees, and soon they were swarming against every section of the fort's walls. To one Southerner, it seemed as if "the battle flags of the enemy made almost a solid line of bunting around the fort."

Bolstered by Turner's two brigades, the Federals in the moat now began clambering up the walls of Fort Gregg in such numbers that the struggle moved to the parapet shelf. One man in the 54th Pennsylvania remembered the soldier who scrambled up the slippery wall and held his position at the top by throwing dirt into the defender's eyes even as he "pulled his comrades up with him." A Union officer fighting nearby recollected, "It was the first time since entering the service that I ever thought it necessary to use my revolver in battle, [and] this time I made good use of it, as I stood near our colors and fought the enemy on the parapet." More and more Federals shoved their way up the walls, until, wrote one West Virginia soldier, "there was enough on the parapet to rush in."

"The fighting on both sides at this point was the most desperate I ever witnessed," General Foster later declared, "being a hand-to-hand struggle for twenty-five minutes after my troops had reached the parapet."

"[Fort] Gregg raged like the crater of a volcano emitting its flashes of dead fire, enveloping our flag and honor in flame and in the smoke of death," an artilleryman from Louisiana later recalled. "It was a terrific struggle and slaughter."

Lieutenant General Longstreet watched all this from the inner line and wondered whether his men would arrive in time. "Not venturing to hope," he afterward wrote, "I looked towards Petersburg and saw General Benning, with his Rock brigade, winding in rapid march around the near hill." Quickly Longstreet gave orders for the deployment of Benning's men. There were only six hundred rifles in the brigade, not nearly enough, but it would have to do.

While Benning's Georgians took position along Old Town Creek, James Longstreet rode outside the inner line, turned toward Fort Gregg, "and had a careful view of the enemy's formidable masses. I thought I recognized General Gibbon, and raised my hat, but he was busy and did not see me."

The two artillery pieces deployed inside Fort Gregg managed only a few shots apiece before each guns was disabled by enemy fire. The unemployed gunners now had to find other ways to kill the enemy. Seventeen-year-old Homer Atkinson teamed up with two older men: "I was down behind the breastworks & lit the fuse of the shells & these men rolled them to the Yankees. The powder burned sh-s-s-s. I had a block of Confederate matches . . . & I struck the match on the shell. The sulphur burned blue & the powder s-s-s-s & away she went."

Lieutenant D. M. Rigler remembered that by the time the Federals swarmed across the flat parapet, "the ammunition was almost out, and our men threw bats and rocks at them in the ditch." "The noise outside was fearful, frightful and indescribable," recalled Captain A. K. Jones of Mississippi. "The curses and groaning of frenzied men could be heard over and above the din of our musketry. Savage men, ravenous beasts!"

Suddenly, Federals were across the parapet and pouring into Fort Gregg. A lieutenant in the 12th West Virginia who was among the first inside, a Union soldier testified, "was shot dead by a Confederate who was immediately bayoneted by one of our men." Another officer, who escaped all injury, recollected, "When we rushed over the top the sight was truly terrific—dead men and the dying lay strewn all about, and it was [only] with the greatest difficulty that we could prevent our infuriated soldiers from shooting down and braining all who survived of the stubborn foe."

A New Yorker who was present later wrote, "The interior of the fort was a pool of blood, a sight which can never be shut from memory. The rebels had recklessly fought to the last."

Mississippi general Nathaniel Harris was livid with anger. Just as the last great blue battle formation began to hurl itself at Fort Gregg, he received orders from the Third Corps artillery chief, Brigadier General R. Lindsay Walker, to pull the four guns in Whitworth back to the inner line. Harris believed that Whitworth's artillery had helped to break up the earlier Union attacks on Gregg, and he was convinced that removing them would doom the beleaguered redoubt. Harris protested the order, but, he noted bitterly, "it was of no avail."

Even as two of the Yankee brigades moved against Gregg, another advanced on Whitworth. "Gen. Harris mounted the parapet and waved the flag [of the 48th Mississippi] over our heads, and shouted 'Give 'em hell, boys,' " one of Whitworth's defenders reported.

More orders now arrived for Harris, these "from General Lee to evacuate Whitworth, as time had been gained for Longstreet to arrive…and an inner line formed." There was no time for a properly conducted retreat; Federals were flowing over the fort's front while Confederates scampered out the back. General Harris, one Mississippi soldier observed, "did not relish the 'home stretch,' and [he] soon became tired. The run exhausted him, and while catching his breath he said to me, 'I'll be d——d if I run any more.'" Just then a squad of Yankees fired on the group. "The volley stimulated [us] to renewed exertions," the soldier remembered, "so much so that I believe that we led the boys into the last ditch of Petersburg, spitting into spray the placid waters of Old Town Creek."

Homer Atkinson survived the bloody finale inside Fort Gregg. "More of our men were killed after the Yankees got into the fort than during the fighting," he maintained. "'Tis true," added an officer in the 33rd North Carolina, "that when they rushed into the fort upon us, they were yelling, cursing and shooting with all the frenzy and rage of a horde of merciless barbarians." Young Atkinson owed his life to an enemy officer who protected him. "Is it possible the South has gotten to that point of using such children as you are for soldiers?" the Yankee wondered aloud.

"I forbear to describe the scene inside that work after the surrender," Union colonel George Dandy later wrote, "but I think at least one-fourth of the entire garrison was killed in the assault." His estimate was tragically close to the mark: of Gregg's 300 or so defenders, 56 died and approximately 200 were wounded. John Gibbon later put his losses this day, "most of which occurred around these two forts," at 122 men killed and 592 wounded, for a total of 714.

Among those who lived to fight another day were two small companies of Mississippi troops posted south of Fort Gregg along the Boydton Plank Road. As Gregg was overwhelmed, the veteran soldiers hustled back to the main line, moving around a still occupied residence. The owner appeared as they were passing and yelled at them, "You are all cowards! You are a disgrace to your country; stop and help drive them back!" "My friend, we haven't time," a Mississippian in a hurry shouted back, "and you don't know what you are talking about. Go into the house quick or you will be hurt!"

Advance parties from the 11th Maine now pushed toward Lee's inner line in order to secure, according to one soldier, "a skirmishing position on Indian Town Creek[,] where they remained for some time, anxiously looking for an advancing Union column, and fully determined to head it, and if possible be the first armed Yankees to enter the Cockade City."

Fresh Union columns were in short supply, however. The Ninth Corps was fully committed to holding its gains near Fort Mahone and had even drawn off a brigade from the Sixth Corps to help it. The Sixth Corps itself was exhausted from its sweep through the enemy's lines, and its commander was not prepared to order it forward. Gibbon's command, the Twenty-fourth, had spent its offensive energy taking Gregg and Whitworth. That left the Second Corps, most of which had only engaged the enemy lightly this day near Burgess' Mill. Two divisions of the corps had, in fact, begun marching toward Petersburg to assist in the grand assault, but early in the afternoon they reversed course to Sutherland Station. There was just no organized Federal force that was able or willing to test Lee's final line, drawn along the steep, rugged banks of Old Town Creek. Charles Field, one of Longstreet's division commanders, later noted that "the enemy, finding us not inclined to give way for him, contented himself with forming line in front of us, but out of range."

Even U. S. Grant was satisfied with what had been gained this day. He communicated to City Point at 4:40 p.m., "We...have a continuous line of troops, and in a few hours will be intrenched from the Appomattox, below Petersburg, to the river above. All seems right with us, and everything quiet just now." To his wife he wrote, "Altogether this has been one of the great victories of the war. Greatest because it is over what the rebels have always regarded as their most invincible Army and the one used for the defense of their capital." By 7:40 p.m., Grant's mind was on the pursuit of Lee's army. "I think there is nothing in Petersburg," he mused, "except the remnant of Gordon's corps and a few men brought from the north side to-day. I believe it will pay to commence a furious bombardment at 5 a.m. to be followed by an assault at 6."

The Second Corps Story

For two days the fighting had been constant but inconclusive for Major General Andrew Humphreys and his Second Corps. On March 29, his men extended the line to the left by crossing to the south side of Hatcher's Run and taking a position covering the Vaughan Road. This enabled the corps to connect with the Twenty-fourth Corps on its right, and at the same time maintain a connection with the Fifth Corps operating on its left. There was heavy skirmishing on March 30 as units from the Fifth and Second corps tested Rebel lines west of the Boydton Plank Road while other parts of Humphreys's corps probed the lines near a strongpoint known as the Crow House Redoubt.

Serious fighting erupted on March 31, when two of Gouverneur Warren's divisions got into difficulty while testing the White Oak Road line. It took two of Humphreys's divisions to help restore the status quo. There was more skirmishing and probing on April 1, and preparations were made to assault the Crow House Redoubt position at 4:00 a.m. the next day. These attack orders were superseded during the night, however, by new instructions that called for Humphreys to detach one of his divisions to assist the Fifth Corps near Five Forks. The two remaining divisions were advised to be ready to "take advantage of anything that might arise in the operations of the remainder of the army."

Brigades from four Rebel divisions manned the right of Lee's extended line. The soldiers were, for the most part, North Carolinians from John Cooke's and William MacRae's brigades of Henry Heth's division, and from Scales's Brigade of Cadmus Wilcox's division, with the addition of Samuel McGowan's South Carolina brigade, also of Wilcox's command. Also present were troops from Hunton's Brigade of George Pickett's division, and Wise's and Moody's brigades of Bushrod Johnson's division, with Johnson in overall command.

Combat had been continuous on this flank since March 29, when blue and gray infantry had clashed along the Quaker Road, south of Burgess' Mill. The threat was such that Lee dispatched his only reserve, Pickett's Division, to stop the Yankee move. Sharp fighting broke out April 1 at Five Forks, an important crossroads several miles to the west. No one along or near the White Oak Road on the night of April 1 knew for certain that Pickett had been badly handled at

Five Forks, but everyone suspected as much. If the suspicion proved true, it would mean that the Confederate right flank was wide open for trouble.

Bushrod Johnson's command left the White Oak Road line during the evening and headed north "to Church [Road] Crossing, on the South Side Railroad." Among the soldiers who remained, there was great concern about the integrity of the line toward Petersburg. "Our position . . . was only tenable," observed a member of the 27th North Carolina, "provided the troops on our left held their position."

The signs were not good. "We could hear the keen cracking of muskets away over in the direction of Petersburg," a soldier in the 13th North Carolina recalled. Lieutenant J. F. J. Caldwell, an officer in McGowan's Brigade, was also anxious. "Hundreds of men in our army had predicted long ago, that Grant would continue to stretch, until he forced us to draw out our line as thin as a skirmish, and then storm some point with massed columns. Men listened…and, although they said little, seemed to feel that the end was drawing near."

"Just before sunrise," remembered a Tarheel posted in one of the redoubts along the White Oak Road, "a courier dashed into the fort with news that the lines had been broken and our troops were in retreat." Henry Heth, commanding the sector, later reported, "As soon as I found that the enemy had possession of the Boydton Plank Road and that he was moving down this road—my position being no longer tenable—I gave orders to withdraw to Sutherlands Station on the S[outh] S[ide] Rail Road, crossing Hatcher's Run at Watkins Bridge."

The four brigades under Heth's command began filing up the Claiborne Road around 8:00 a.m. on April 2, abandoning the earthworks that had held the Federals at bay since February.

For the weary troops of Nelson Miles's division of the Union Second Corps, the night of April 1 was filled with marching. Originally posted south of White Oak Road, Miles's men had been temporarily assigned to Sheridan's command and ordered west to Five Forks. The leading elements of the Federal column reached Sheridan at around 1:00 a.m. on April 2, only to find that their help was not needed. Miles let his men rest for a few hours and then moved them out, heading east, back toward the earthworks that had already rebuffed them several times.

Major Seward F. Gould, commanding the 4th New York Heavy Artillery, halted at daylight in sight of "very formidable breastworks." The division commander rode up and ordered Gould to pick a sergeant and two "volunteers" to scout the enemy lines. Gould made his selection and watched as the three "went on and up to the works and then over. They discovered the enemy some ways from the works, and in full retreat." "Without waiting for orders," noted a soldier in the nearby 140th Pennsylvania, "[the rest of] the men dashed forward at a double- quick and with a wild chorus of cheers entered and took possession." The time was about 9:00 a.m.

When Andrew Humphreys learned that Miles's division was returning, he directed his troops near the Crow House Redoubt to move forward. "[We] expected a desperate resistance and great loss," one of his soldiers afterward wrote. "Orders were received to advance up the road and carry the works. . . . But a sudden change came over us, for as we gazed at the point we were to attack, a sight met our eyes that nearly unmanned us. Where two minutes before the Stars and Bars had flown, now floated the glorious old Stars and Stripes. Never before have we thought it so beautiful, and a cheer went up that could have been heard in Petersburg."

The long Confederate line from Fort Gregg to Hatcher's Run was now in Union hands.

The first attempt by Nelson Miles's troops to follow the retreating Confederates along the Claiborne Road was poorly organized and easily stopped by Heth's rear guard. "The sharpshooters…," one member of this elite Southern unit proudly recalled, "held their position on Hatcher's Run…and by a few well directed shots checked the pursuit." The Federals returned shortly, better organized this time, and forced the crossing, but still they were kept at bay. "We threw out first one regiment and then another as skirmishers to retard the enemy, who was pressing us hard," a soldier in the 27th North Carolina remembered.

Henry Heth, riding north toward Sutherland Station, was overtaken by a courier bearing tragic news. Recounted Heth, "Gen. Lee sent him to say to me that Lieutenant General Hill had been seriously disabled and that I must take command of the [Third] corps and report in person to him as soon as possible." Heth spurred ahead to the small railroad depot, where he found Confederate supply wagons gathering in anticipation of a general retreat. "I then turned over the command to Gen. Jno. R. Cooke and directed him as soon as the wagon train withdrew to push on after it, that my desire was not to fight a battle if it could be avoided." As soon as he gave Cooke the instructions, Henry Heth hurried toward Petersburg.

The Sutherland Station location had a natural feature that veteran soldiers took advantage of as they made ready. "We...elected a position on the brow of a slight hill in an open field and rapidly fortified our line as well as we could, with bayonets used to break the earth, and such other means as were at [our] command," declared a North Carolinian in MacRae's Brigade. "The line ran...just on the edge of a highway, and ...was almost parallel with the South Side Railroad," noted Lieutenant Caldwell of McGowan's Brigade. At the foot of the slope leading up to the crest was a small stream, and "beyond the ravine ran a ridge, similar to the one we occupied, but covered partly with large oaks, partly with pines."

Brigadier General Cooke later reported, "Line of battle was formed at 11 o'clock a.m. and every preparation made to check the enemy who were now close on us in heavy force."

McGowan's South Carolinians held Cooke's left, anchored on the Ocran Methodist Church. Next came MacRae's Brigade, then Scales's (Colonel Joseph Hyman commanding), and finally Cooke's own, which rested its flank alongside Sutherland's Tavern, on the west side of the Namozine Road. Also on hand, according to Lieutenant Caldwell, were "a few pieces of artillery, principally on the flanks near the center of the line."

The other two divisions of the Union Second Corps were now astride the lower Boydton Plank Road. General Humphreys had intended to move all his strength up the Claiborne Road "to close in on the rear of that portion of the enemy's troops cut off from Petersburg, while Sheridan would probably strike their front and flank," but his plans were changed following the sudden arrival of Major General George Meade. Meade redirected the two Second Corps divisions to move toward Petersburg and indicated that once the remaining division (Miles's) crossed Hatcher's Run, it was also to turn to the east. Humphreys rode off to find Miles and, as he later reported, instead found Phil Sheridan, who informed him that he "had not intended to return General Miles's division" to Humphreys's control. Humphreys "declined to assume further command of it," and, according to Miles's report, the "pursuit of the enemy was at once commanded."

Miles's Third Brigade, commanded by Brevet Brigadier General Henry J. Madill, was the first to approach Sutherland Station, though portions of Colonel Robert Nugent's Second Brigade also came into line. Major Gould, of the 4th New York Heavies, remembered that "the rebels were seen on an opposite hill across a low piece of land, safely ensconced behind breastworks."

Major John Hyde of the 39th New York, in Madill's brigade, testified that his men "were much exhausted from loss of sleep the previous night and the rapid marching they had gone through." Yet, noted Gould, "the excitement was such that the desire prevailed to charge."

The hastily arranged Federal battle lines guided on the Claiborne Road and advanced toward the Confederate right. "When we came to the point where the final move was to be made on their works," complained Chaplain Ezra Simons of the 125th New York, "our line resembled a line broken by the fire of the enemy, rather than a line about to charge against their works." The time was shortly after noon.

The enemy's advance, asserted a soldier in the 52nd North Carolina, "was met with a well-delivered and telling volley from our rifles." "Lee's veterans…," added Lieutenant Caldwell, "rolled a perfect sheet of lead across the open interval, striking down scores of the enemy, opening great gaps in their line, and destroying all concert and all order." Pockets of blue-coated soldiers were isolated near the Confederate lines when the main Union force recoiled. "As they started back," wrote a soldier in the 27th North Carolina, "our sharpshooters, rushing forward, captured many prisoners." Then, Cadmus Wilcox recollected, "the Confederates…gave vent to a wild and derisive yell."

"General Miles attacked impetuously," one Massachusetts historian later maintained. Flag bearer Herman Fox from the 126th New York was badly wounded in the hand during the retreat and swarmed by Rebels anxious to seize the prize. His struggles sparked an impromptu countercharge that reclaimed both. "The troops were reformed on the crest of a hill opposite [the enemy] …and slight breastworks thrown up," reported Major Hyde. General Madill was wounded and out of action, so Brevet Brigadier General Clinton MacDougall took charge of the second attack. This time the entire Second Brigade formed on the right of the Third, and the axis of advance shifted toward the Confederate left.

The Yankee soldiers moved forward with a grim fatalism. "All were impressed with the uselessness of the charge," declared Chaplain Simons. It was just 1:00 p.m.

This time the blue wave broke against McGowan's South Carolinians. Recalled Confederate lieutenant Caldwell, "We opened upon them at three or four hundred yards and tore fearful rents in their line, covered the ground with dead and dying, and set forth, above all the roar of artillery and musketry, ringing peals of cheers, which proclaimed the last soldiers of the Confederacy still unsubdued."

The Federals, wrote Colonel Nugent, "owing to a terrific enfilading fire of artillery and musketry, were repulsed." Among the wounded was the commander of the second attack, Clinton MacDougall.

Nelson Miles pulled back the battered Third Brigade eight hundred yards to allow it to re-form, and ordered skirmish lines forward to find the enemy flanks. At the same time, he sent a courier toward Petersburg for help.

The victorious Confederates tended their wounded and gathered up Union prisoners. One Federal informed a group of North Carolina soldiers that "the next charge would be made by the negro corps…and that they would show no quarter." Lieutenant Caldwell found the captured Yankees surprisingly confident. "We all know the exact length of your line," bragged one. "We will outstretch you, fall upon your flank, and rout you before an hour passes."

One image haunted Caldwell. Between the first and second attacks, several Confederate skirmishers had come upon a badly wounded Yankee, who told them that he had vowed never to be taken alive, and begged them to shoot him. "They refused to do so," Caldwell related. "He then deliberately cut his throat with his pocketknife."

It was approaching 4:00 p.m. West of Sutherland Station, a mixed force of Bushrod Johnson's infantry and Fitzhugh Lee's cavalry was in full retreat toward Amelia Court House, with Sheridan's riders snapping at its heels. East of the station, the final Federal assaults on Petersburg had overrun Fort Gregg but had not managed to break Lee's defensive perimeter about the city. At Sutherland Station, the four-brigade Confederate battle line waited for the Federals to make their next move.

Having failed in two frontal assaults, Nelson Miles "now determined to flank the position. . . . A strong skirmish line was pushed forward upon the extreme right flank of the enemy, overlapping it and threatening the railroad. . . . The attention of the enemy being thus diverted from his left flank, the Fourth Brigade [Brevet Brigadier General John Ramsey commanding] was moved rapidly around it through a ravine and wood, and massed in the woods without being discovered by the enemy. . . . This time the Union troops would also have artillery support: Captain A. Judson Clark's 1st New Jersey, Battery B, took a position "in [the] edge of the woods near the [Cox] road, and opened fire on the enemy's battery of four guns, which was estimated about 1,200 yards distant."

Confederate troops watched these movements. "It was evidently too late to maneuver," said Lieutenant Caldwell. "We lay still and awaited the awful finale."

Ramsey's attack was decisive. The Federal troops, claimed a Pennsylvania soldier, "went like a pack of wolves turned loose." "Our lines opened fire in full chorus at long range," remembered one Confederate sharpshooter, "and as the enemy closed upon us the vigor of our defense increased, until the entire line was enveloped in one living cloud of blue coats."

McGowan's Brigade was the first to be engulfed. "Now was the most disorderly movement I ever saw among Confederate troops," Caldwell wrote years afterward. In his after-action report, William MacRae noted, "When McGowan...gave way in confusion, I ordered up my sharpshooters to the support of his left, but they arrived too late to effect anything. In a few moments Scales's Brigade on my right gave way, leaving me alone to confront the enemy with 280 men. . . . At length [I] gave the order to fall back." Only Cooke's Brigade, on the extreme Confederate right, avoided serious damage as it fell back toward the river.

Although one of the Federal attackers later dismissed the Confederate defensive works as "rude affairs," few devalued the North's achievement this day. "Never shall I forget the exultation that thrilled my very soul as our troops swept over the line of fortifications . . . on that memorable day of April 2, 1865," Nelson Miles wrote in his postwar memoirs. In his otherwise businesslike official summary, John Ramsey declared that this "success was eminently a happy, a glorious one."

Federal accounts of this action almost unanimously claimed six hundred prisoners, two cannon, and one flag taken. Confederate mortalities probably numbered twenty to thirty. In his report, Andrew Humphreys put his losses at 33 killed, 236 wounded, and 97 missing, for a total of 366.

Those Confederates who joined Cooke's Brigade in its retreat successfully escaped along the south bank of the Appomattox River. Other small groups fell back directly to the water barrier and either swam across it or crossed it in small boats. The remainder, Nelson Miles later remarked, "were driven to the woods near the river where they were picked up the next morning."

There was no rest for Miles's men. Even as a few units mopped up around the station, others began marching toward Petersburg, where they might still be needed. The weary column had gone only a short distance when Miles met Humphreys and the other two divisions of the Second Corps, coming in response to his earlier request for help. Miles's men returned to Sutherland Station for the night, while Humphreys retraced his steps to Petersburg, too late to make a final assault this day on Lee's inner line.

The battle of Sutherland Station marked the last organized combat in the nine-month siege of Petersburg, and the official capture of the South Side Railroad.

*   *   *

The heady taste of total victory was everywhere at Army of the Potomac headquarters. At 11:00 p.m. this night, George Meade's aide Lieutenant Colonel Theodore Lyman expressed the general feelings in a brief note to his wife:

My dear Mimi:

THE
REBELLION
HAS
GONE UP!

Epilogue

A DISTANT THUNDER

Although drawn in June 1864, Waud's image portrays the close-in combat
that marked many Petersburg actions. *A Waud*

Chapter Eighteen

"My kitchen is full of soldiers"

April 3, 1865

April 2-3, 1865
8:00 P.M. – Dawn

Confederate troops began evacuating Petersburg at 8:00 p.m., April 2. Following orders drawn up a few hours earlier, Longstreet's and Hill's corps were to cross to the north side of the Appomattox River, using the Battersea Cotton Factory pontoon bridge, and then take up the westward march along the River Road; John Gordon's men would use the Pocahontas and railroad bridges and then follow the line of Longstreet's march. Other courses were designated for the troops north of Petersburg and in Richmond. "Every officer is expected to give his unremitting attention to cause these movements to be made successfully," Lee's orders stressed. Ammunition and military supplies that could not be carried along were to be destroyed.

A North Carolina soldier named H. C. Wall was among those who refused to believe that things were as bad as rumor made them out to be. Indeed, Wall insisted, "it was not until the march had taken direction to and through the half-deserted streets, and noble women were observed weeping as in the agony of despair, that the realization came forcibly to mind that the once lovely 'Cockade City' was being abandoned to the ruthless invader."

"As we passed through Petersburg," a soldier in Hill's corps remembered, "the sidewalks of the city were filled with weeping women and children, lamenting the fate which they knew daylight would bring upon them." Another infantryman, marching nearby in Gordon's corps, recalled that when "we came on through the town, the people of the place seemed to be under great excitement on account of our leaving." Henry Kyd Douglas, newly appointed to brigade command, waited in the darkness with his men for orders to move. "It was all commotion and bustle," Douglas observed. "Before we got away, shells were bursting at places over the town and the air was now and then illuminated by the baleful light of mortars." Douglas took advantage of the pause to say farewell to friends who lived nearby. He came at last to the house of Mary Tabb Bolling, one of Petersburg's belles. Douglas never forgot the fact that "she uttered not a word of fear or complaint; the infinite sadness of her silence was pathetic beyond words."

The Union army pressed Petersburg from three sides. Brevet Major General Orlando Willcox commanded the Ninth Corps troops east of the Cockade City. It was, Willcox later noted, "about midnight [when] reports came up…that there were signs of the enemy withdrawing from our front, leaving only their picket line."

A captain in the ranks of the 51st Pennsylvania, part of Willcox's First Brigade, recalled that the regimental commander sought out "a daring man, Thomas Troy[,]…at 1 o'clock on the morning of the 3rd, and asked him if he was willing to…go into Petersburg and see if it was evacuated. The man replied 'He would go.' The colonel told him to take off his equipments, and leave them and his gun in his quarters. Tom said 'No; while he had his guns he was sure of pinning one man before they could take him!'"

The scout returned in less than an hour, "with the pleasing intelligence that the enemy hadn't all left yet, but they were getting out of it as fast they could. Tom had certainly been in the city, and long enough to get a leetle tight."

Along another portion of the Union line—this held by the 100th Pennsylvania—a trio of Confederate deserters came into the Federal outposts. Under close questioning by a Yankee sergeant, the three reported "their pickets withdrawn and their army falling back."

At the army field hospital near Hancock Station, *New York Times* reporter J. R. Hamilton stepped outside for some fresh air. He had been working all night at the doleful task of compiling casualty lists for his paper. "A dead and ominous silence rested over everything," he remarked, "and seemed almost awful in contrast with the deafening roar of artillery and musketry to which the ear had been so long acquainted." A glance toward Petersburg revealed the unforgettable sight of a city on fire: "It had been burning during the day, but its appearance now was heightened by its vivid contrast with the darkness of night, and was sublime beyond expression."

Along the lines occupied by Willcox's Second Brigade, the men of the 1st Michigan Sharpshooters and the 2nd Michigan had been waiting in light marching order since 1:30 a.m. After an hour had passed, the brigade commander, Brevet Colonel Ralph Ely, learned that a deserter had come into his outposts claiming that "the rebels had all left except the picket line." Ely's troops held a position astride the City Point Road, a direct route into the heart of Petersburg; when the order came to advance, they would have the advantage.

Ely's scouts probed the enemy lines and reported that things were quiet—"in fact, too much quiet," one stated. The rumble of explosions in town and off to the right, as well as the "rising flames from various points in Petersburg," lent credence to the story told by the deserters.

Ely finally ordered his two Michigan regiments to move forward at 3:10 a.m.

Petersburg's streets were filled with "great clouds of smoke; acrid, stinging smoke" and little else, recollected young Anne Banister. Tobacco warehouses bulging with the valuable leaf were among the first structures to be torched by retreating Confederates. Another resident, Mary E. Morrison, recalled that in the now quiet streets, "the darkness and the hush…wrapped us as a pall."

A few Confederate soldiers, mostly pickets forgotten by their officers, stumbled along the dark avenues, hoping to escape. I. G. Bradwell, a Virginian in Gordon's corps, was one of a group of three soldiers who tramped wearily toward the river. "As we passed the houses in the city the women peeped out and said to us sadly: 'Good-by Rebels; we never expect to see you again,' " he remembered. Confusion and disorganization reigned. Bradwell and his companions came across a soldier lying in a dead drunk alongside the road, but there was nothing they could do to help him, so they moved on. They struck the railroad tracks near the river where they encountered an old man pushing a handcart filled with looted provisions. As he shoved his way past the astonished trio, a barrel rolled off the cart and spilled its contents at their feet. Bradwell grabbed a piece of meat and filled his canteen with sorghum syrup, little realizing that this would be the only food the three of them would have for the next few days.

When the soldiers reached the near end of Campbell's Bridge, they saw a man with a light waving to them from the other side. "Come on boys," he called out. "I am going to blow it up now. Hurry up." Bradwell and his comrades scurried across and begged the man to hold off destroying it for as long as possible, to allow others to escape the doomed city. They had barely reached the top of a nearby hill, Bradwell reflected, when "we heard a tremendous explosion, and, looking back, we saw the timbers of the bridge rising high in the blue sky, now beautifully illuminated by the full moon."[1]

Also among the last to leave Petersburg was Henry T. Bahnson, a North Carolina sharpshooter. "The city was in indescribable confusion," he recalled. "Men and women thronged the; streets in every sort of dishabille—some drinking and cursing, others praying and wringing their hands…. When we reached the Pocahontas bridge, some men were pouring turpentine over the planking. We had hardly crossed when with a hiss and a roar as of a rushing wind, the long structure burst into flames."

Bahnson watched in horror near Dunlop's Station as a mob of women and children ignored the pleas of engineers and clambered over burning railroad cars looking for clothing and food. There were ammunition caches mingled with the supplies, and once they began to explode, Bahnson remembered, "we could see women and children blown about in every direction over the ground."

Captain John C. Gorman marched with the Confederate army's rear guard, now a few miles west of the Richmond-Petersburg corridor. "The whole heavens in our rear were lit up in lurid glare that added intensity to the blackness before us," he noted. "It was as if the gases chained in the earth had at last found vent and the general conflagration of the world was at hand."

Members of Petersburg's Common Council met early in the morning at the home of Councilman D'Arcy Paul to figure out how to surrender their city. A capitulation proclamation was drawn up, copies were made, and the council was divided into squads of two or more, each of which was to head out of the city in a different direction and deliver the document to the highest-ranking Union officer encountered.

It was still dark as the various groups made their way west, south, and east.

Picket James Ford, of the 60th Ohio, crawled up to the Confederate lines in front of Fort McGilvery and found them empty. "Come on, boys, the Johnnies are gone," he shouted back to his companions on the outpost line.

---

1 Bradwell was waxing poetic as the next full moon would not occur until April 10.

A great cheer swelled up from the Union lines, spreading like a wave to the south and west. Near Fort McGilvery, Jacob Roemer, an artillery officer, ordered "Cease firing" and asked if all the guns had been discharged. One sergeant reported that his was still loaded. Roemer gave the command, and the last gun was fired. The officer pulled out his watch and made note of the time; it was 3:40 a.m. "Petersburg is ours," he shouted to his men. "The war is over; and to-day is my 47th birthday. Boys, you have done nobly."

All along the bitterly contested city perimeter, groups of Federal soldiers were filtering into the now abandoned Rebel positions. Skirmishers from the 51st Pennsylvania and the 38th Wisconsin pushed through Colquitt's Salient and into the town's residential outskirts. Closer to the Crater, parties from Colonel James Bintliff's brigade occupied Cemetery Hill and the Blandford Church area. From positions south of Petersburg, elements of John Hartranft's division poked into the suburbs, the 200th Pennsylvania later laying claim to being the first organized regiment to cross the city limits. In the 121st New York, part of the Sixth Corps, soldiers hauled a flag with them and raised it on the first public building they entered.

Brevet Colonel Ely's two Michigan regiments, moving west along the City Point Road, had their formations broken up when they passed through the main enemy fortifications. As the lines were being reformed, Major Clement A. Lounsberry sought out the 1st Michigan Sharpshooters' color guard, telling the men that the 2nd Michigan was planning to forge ahead in order to claim the honor of getting into the city first. Instantly a flying squad formed about the 1st Michigan colors, and the small group, led by Major Lounsberry, raced ahead, their route "lighted by the glare from burning tobacco warehouses."

The squad reached the short street leading up to the courthouse and its dominating clock tower. Here one of the Common Council's surrender teams was waiting, but Lounsberry waved the civilians away, saying that he "could listen to no proposition until the 'old flag' was floating from the highest point of the court-house steeple and proper pickets had been established in the vicinity."

Color Sergeant William T. Wixcey was part of the group that entered the building. "It was yet dark when we made our way into the courthouse and up the winding stairs into the clock tower," he recollected. "For want of a better place to display our colors we opened the door of the clock face and thrust them out through it, and there, for the first time in years, floated the dear old flag.... Our hearts were too full for utterance, so we clasped hands and shed tears of joy, for we knew that the beginning of the end had come."

Down below, Major Lounsberry looked at his watch. It was 4:28 a.m. The next flag on the scene, that of the 2nd Michigan, went up on the customs house, followed by the 20th Michigan's colors, also raised on the courthouse steeple.

Daylight

Dawn was breaking as Petersburg's mayor, W. W. Townes, and Councilman Charles Collier made their way west. Townes was carrying a white handkerchief fastened to his walking stick.

The two had just reached Old Town Creek—Lee's final defensive position west of town—when they were stopped by the sound of a signal gun off to their left. "Instantaneously," recalled Collier, "there sprang forth, as from the bowels of the earth, it seemed to me, a mighty host of Federal soldiers, and there followed such a shout of victory as seemed to shake the very ground on which we stood." Squads of blue-coated infantrymen rushed past the pair of civilians, who tried in vain to attract their attention. Someone finally escorted Townes and Collier to Colonel Oliver Edwards, who, as he later wrote, "received the surrender of Petersburg."

One of the *New York Herald's* intrepid band of reporters, Thomas Cook, rode into town right behind the first foot soldiers, after carefully navigating his horse through the maze of entrenchments spun about the Crater. "The civilian cannot better understand [the site] than by conceiving a vast system of sunken roads sufficient to maneuver armies of a hundred thousand men, without exposing any above the level of the ground," he commented. The reporter's mount plunged awkwardly as it picked out a path across the gouged and pitted landscape.

Cook reached the Jerusalem Plank Road and turned toward Petersburg. "The streets at first seemed deserted," he recorded, "but the cheers of the excited soldiers, as they marched through the town, soon brought out swarms of negroes—men, women and children—who manifested their gladness by every conceivable demonstration." The *Herald* man was one of the few mounted figures in view, and crowds of happy blacks were drawn to him. "It was somewhat embarrassing, as well as a little annoying, to be compelled to explain at every street corner that I was no very great personality after all," Cook wryly reflected.

The newsman now made his way down to the river, where two bridges— one for wagons and foot traffic, the other for the railroad—spanned the

Appomattox. The railroad structure had been destroyed, but the other, though in flames, still stood. Cook at once began barking out orders. Some black civilians ran and fetched the fire engines, while others formed a bucket brigade. When an engine finally arrived, it was accompanied by a white man who proclaimed himself a fireman, so Cook happily delegated the bridge rescue operation to the man and moved on. (Various Ninth and Sixth corps units also took part in the firefighting, and several of Petersburg's bridges were saved and later used by the Union army.)

Gazing at the smoldering timbers of burned warehouses and the scattered debris left by Lee's men, Cook mused, "Good by to the rebel army of Northern Virginia. It has been a noble army, worthy of a better cause and a more honorable death."

George Meade had been monitoring events since before dawn. He rode into Petersburg at a little after 8:00 a.m., determined, as one of his aides put it, to "take a look at the place we so long had seen the steeples of." Meade and his staff toured the main part of the city, moved down along the river, and then went back up to the heights near Blandford Church. From this vantage point, the whole city was spread out before them in one direction, and the crazy-quilt trench network in another. Meade's aide Theodore Lyman stared silently across the now unoccupied Confederate earthworks. "Upon these parapets, whence the riflemen have shot at each other, for nine long months, in heat and cold, by day and by night, you might now stand with impunity and overlook miles of deserted breastworks and covered ways!" he marveled. "It was a sight only to be appreciated by those who have known the depression of waiting through summer, autumn, and winter for so goodly an event!"

Meade and company returned to Petersburg to find that U. S. Grant had ridden in about an hour after them and set up headquarters at No. 21 Market Street, the home of Thomas Wallace.

The two generals discussed their next moves. While they were talking, a prisoner was brought to them, who volunteered that Lee was falling back only a short distance and would make a stand in a prearranged defensive position. Meade believed the man and suggested that the Union forces be concentrated in order to assault the position. Grant, however, discounted this piece of intelligence. "I knew that Lee was no fool," he later declared. He thought it highly unlikely that the Southern commander would turn to fight with fordable rivers on either flank; instead, he was convinced, Lee would retreat along the

Danville Road. If that was the case, Meade responded, then the army should be organized to pursue.

But trailing Lee was the last thing on Grant's mind. "My reply was that we did not want to follow him," Grant recalled years afterward, "we wanted to get ahead of him and cut him off." The Federal commander in chief worried that Lee might slip from his grasp, turn south, and link up with Joseph E. Johnston's army in North Carolina.

While the officers continued their discussion, Theodore Lyman circulated among the crowd that had gathered to view the celebrities. In this way, he learned of A.P. Hill's death and also encountered "crowds of nigs [who] came about to sell Confederate money, for which they would take anything we chose to give." Meade gathered up his officers around noon and rode west to join the chase of Lee's army.

Most of Petersburg's white citizens, a *New York Times* reporter observed, "did not show themselves during the fore part of the day, but after discovering that our soldiers were orderly and well behaved…they began to make their appearances at the doors and windows of their residences, and later in the day, even [entered] familiarly into conversation."

A member of Petersburg's Simpson family later wrote of this day, "[We] discovered our streets literally filled with soldiers, thousands being drawn up in regular order along the main avenue, while some regiments were marching in this direction & some in that, all accompanied by Bands which continually discoursed music of the most lively and exciting character to them, but to us the very reverse. Yankee Doodle was never a favorite air with me, but on this occasion it sounded most execrably."

Not every blue-coated soldier was on his best behavior. One of them, in the army's provost guard, remembered that during his unit's brief stay in town, "a good many of us were bent on an inspection of the place and what had been left. Some things we inspected and others we 'sampled.'"

Other squads, meanwhile, were busy rounding up stragglers and running afoul of Southern womanhood. "Some of the women whose houses we entered, to get the Johnnies the darkies told us were hidden there, gave us a strong exhibition of their ability to blackguard us," wrote one New York soldier.

Yankee enterprise was also in evidence this morning. Squads of newsboys from City Point came into town, staked out street corners, and immediately began hawking copies of the latest New York papers. With them came another curiosity: black soldiers. Reporter Sylvanus Cadwallader watched with admiration as the U.S.C.T. columns entered the town: "A negro regiment passing seems to take special pride and pleasure in maintaining the dignity becoming soldiers, and are neither boisterous nor noisy," he noted. Observers in the Simpson household admitted afterward that the black soldiers were "smartly dressed and well drilled" and that they "really looked [like] good soldiers."

One small group of civilians who ventured outdoors in the morning discovered the body of a young Rebel artilleryman propped up against the wall of the Second Presbyterian Church. They wrapped the body in a blanket, laid it in a churchyard grave, and were preparing for a brief burial service when a crowd of Yankee soldiers came by.

"Putting Johnnie in an ice-house, eh?" one of them jeered.

A Federal officer arrived and chased the soldiers away. "A brave soldier, no doubt," he said to the funeral party.

"Yes, a brave soldier whom you killed," one of the group said, passing forward a shovel. "Would you like to throw the first shovelful of earth upon him?"

The Federal stared at the tool for a moment. "My God! this brings war home to a man," he exclaimed.

Another Union squad then came marching past, and the officer halted it. "Present arms," he commanded, removing his hat and nodding to the Southerners to finish the burial service.

This was an eventful day for Sarah Pryor's household, which had recently been transferred from Petersburg's western outskirts to a rented house on Washington Street. Well before dawn, Mayor Townes had called to ask if ex-Congressman Pryor would help surrender the city. Sarah told him she would not hear of it, and the mayor left. Just a few hours later, she watched cautious Yankee pickets enter the town, and a little after that, a group of them arrived to arrest her husband, a Confederate officer who had been released on parole.

Then another group of Union soldiers broke into her kitchen, and when she tried to shoo them out, one threatened her with his bayonet. This was an indignity that Sarah Pryor would not endure; she ran outside and found a young Federal officer.

"Is it your pleasure we should be murdered in our houses?" she demanded. "My kitchen is full of soldiers."

The officer dismounted, followed Sarah into her house, and used the flat of his sword to drive the soldiers out. Before riding off, he posted a sentry to prevent it from happening again.

Sarah Pryor's brief moment of triumph was dashed to dust, however, when she looked up the street and saw a Yankee column approaching with a captured Confederate standard at its head. She knew that particular flag well, having helped to sew it at the start of the war. "It was coming back—a captive!" she thought bitterly.

Abraham Lincoln left City Point for Petersburg a little after 9:00 a.m. He was accompanied by his young son Tad, Admiral David Porter, military aide Captain Charles Penrose, and another naval officer, Captain John S. Barnes.

So far, Lincoln's visit to the Petersburg front had been anything but uneventful. On March 26, he traveled up the James and saw Admiral Porter's fleet, festooned with flags and manned by cheering sailors. The President, a military aide recalled, "waved his high hat as if saluting old friends in his native town, and seemed as happy as a schoolboy."

The party went ashore at Aiken's Landing and then rode inland a few miles to review the Army of the James. On March 27, Lincoln visited Point of Rocks and there toured a hospital for wounded officers. General Sherman arrived at City Point that same day to meet with Grant. The next morning he joined Grant and Admiral Porter to discuss unfolding events with the President. "It was in no sense a council of war," maintained Horace Porter, "but only an informal interchange of views between the four men who, more than any others, held the destiny of the nation in their hands." It was during this discussion that Lincoln outlined for the military men his plans for a humane reconstruction of the South.

The next five days were anxious ones for Lincoln as he followed reports of the fighting about Petersburg. The first clear sign of success came on the evening of April 1, when the President was shown a captured Confederate battle flag. "Here is something material—something I can see, feel, and understand," he exclaimed. "This means victory. This is victory." Another twenty-four hours would pass before Lincoln could truly savor the achievement.

Lincoln and his staff now boarded a special train that was to run them down to Hancock Station, where they would be met by the President's older son, Robert. The train was halted near its destination to allow a column of Confederate POWs to cross the tracks. "If they only knew what we are trying to do for them they would not have fought us and they would not look as they do," Lincoln exclaimed softly, as if to himself.

The group arrived at Hancock Station at around 10:00 a.m. to find Robert, now a captain on Grant's staff, waiting with a small escort from the 5th U.S. Cavalry. They had been expecting just the President, and the additional guests necessitated dismounting several of the cavalrymen to provide their horses.

The party turned onto the Jerusalem Plank Road and passed through the area of fighting for Fort Mahone. Burial squads had yet to finish their job, and the carnage of the previous day's vicious fighting was only too visible. A cavalryman in the escort long remembered one soldier who had been killed in the muddy moat girding the bastion: "He was stone dead, but being over knee-deep in the mud and mire of the ditch, could not fall over." The same horseman observed that "big tears ran down the President's cheeks." Captain Penrose likewise noted that Lincoln's face had once again "settled into its old lines of sadness."

Lincoln's mood changed abruptly as his party drew abreast of a column of troops from First Brigade of the Second Division (Ninth Corps) which had halted to draw rations in a field near Cemetery Hill. The men forgot about any military formation and happily crowded along the road as the President's party rode past. When soldiers from the 39th New Jersey saw the President, they "cheered him to the echo." The infantrymen of the 45th Pennsylvania joined in the impromptu greetings as the Chief Executive rode by. "Mr. Lincoln seemed very content that morning as he bowed and smiled in response to our cheering," a Pennsylvania soldier recollected.

The boisterous Pennsylvanians alerted the next regiment along the plank road, the 7th Rhode Island: "'That's Old Abe coming,' was the cry, and men swung their caps and cheered and cheered," one remembered.

Lincoln's group made its way to Grant's temporary headquarters at the Wallace House. A Pennsylvania artilleryman who watched the two men meet noted that "Grant walked down the steps [and] reached the edge of the pavement as Mr. Lincoln dismounted. General Grant's extended hand was eagerly seized by the President in both of his, and with more feeling than I ever saw in any face." "Do you know, general, I had a sort of sneaking idea all along that you intended to do something like this," Lincoln said.

The two drew aside and talked for a while. Grant shared his thoughts on the upcoming campaign, while Lincoln reflected on the civil complications that would follow the collapse of the Confederacy. Once again, the President hinted at his plans for Reconstruction.

Young Tad Lincoln fidgeted while the two conversed. Brevet Brigadier General George H. Sharpe, who oversaw most of the Union army's intelligence-gathering operations, fished some sandwiches out of a pouch and offered them to the boy with the comment, "You must be hungry."

Tad took the sandwiches gratefully. "Yes I am, that's what's the matter with me," he replied. The adults smiled.

Sometime during this informal discussion, the owner of the house appeared and invited his "guests" inside. Lincoln recognized him as an old political colleague from the time when both were Whigs. Grant declined the man's offer, and he and the President remained on the porch. Lincoln did accept a straight-backed chair from his host, setting it so that his feet dangled off the edge of the porch as he sat and jawed with Grant.

The pair lingered on at the Wallace House, hoping to hear word of Richmond's capture, but when ninety minutes passed with no news, they parted company—Grant riding west after Lee's army and Lincoln returning to City Point.

The Presidential party came across scattered bundles of tobacco leaves, and several in the group, including Lincoln himself, grabbed a few souvenirs. The President now passed along Bollingbrook Street and through some of the hardest hit neighborhoods, sights that vividly displayed the terrible cost of the war. Located directly in line with massed Union batteries, just two miles east, the area had been heavily damaged in some nine months of constant shelling. Northern photographers would soon document the worst of the destruction, with several damaged houses that Lincoln rode past this day being especially prominent in the gallery of images that emerged. According to a young resident named Charles Clark, the "house that attracted his attention more than any other was the old Dunlop Mansion,…which had been struck more than one hundred times by shells, and fragments of shells. He stopped at this place for a moment, looked and shook his head and rode off."

When he reached City Point at 5:00 p.m., Abraham Lincoln learned that Richmond had fallen that morning. He was also handed a telegram that had arrived shortly after his departure for Petersburg. It was from Secretary of War Stanton, who strongly urged the President not to risk his safety by visiting the Rebel city. "Thanks for your caution," Lincoln wired back, "but I have already been to Petersburg…. It is certain now that Richmond is in our hands, and I think I will go there tomorrow. I will take care of myself."

Most of the Union troops were out of Petersburg by late afternoon. Only Orlando Willcox's division, of the Ninth Corps, was left behind to garrison the city. Correspondents for the dailies who had chronicled each step in the nine-month investment of this place now scribbled down their last impressions of it before riding off after the big story—the end of Lee's army.

"The city presents a very clean and respectable appearance, and there are many residences here that would do no discredit to Fifth-avenue," a *New York Times* reporter observed. The *Herald's* S. T. Bulkley visited the lower part of the town, where the effect of the long Union bombardment was most pronounced. "Here the houses are literally knocked to pieces," he informed his readers. "[There is] scarcely a building but has been perforated with shell and damaged more or less, and some of them entirely destroyed."

Bulkley also told of two Ninth Corps officers who had taken possession of the intact facilities of the *Petersburg Express*. The pair set to work and by evening turned out a special edition of what they proudly called *Grant's Petersburg Progress*. Its motto proclaimed, "[We] believe in the United States one and indivisible; in Abraham Lincoln, our adopted father; in U.S. Grant captain of the host." Wrote Bulkley, "It is a decided improvement in sentiment, at least, on the *Express*, and will, we doubt not, soon convert the inhabitants into good loyal people."

Not every reporter was the bearer of joyous news. J. R. Hamilton, of the *New York Times*, could not forget the price that had been paid to achieve this moment: "I came upon a youth, laying flat upon his back, his upturned face exhibiting an expression very like a smile. He had cautiously buttoned to his vest the envelope of an old letter, which gave the following address: 'Wm. B. Adair, Co. K., Two Hundred and Eleventh Pennsylvania Volunteers, Second Brigade, Third Division, Ninth Corps.' Brave boy! he, for one, had died while doing his duty, for I found him close to the very edge of the second line of rebel works."

A young survivor of the Petersburg campaign struggled to find the right expression for his feelings. He ended his diary entry for this day, "I can write no more now. Everybody shouting. My heart overflows with happiness too deep for words."

Chapter Nineteen

"I hoped to capture them soon"

Events after April 3, 1865

Ulysses S. Grant
Final Report of Operations, March 1864-May 1865

On the morning of the 3d pursuit was commenced. General Sheridan [with his cavalry and the Fifth Corps] pushed for the Danville road, keeping near the Appomattox, followed by General Meade with the Second and Sixth Corps, while General Ord [with portions of the Army of the James] moved for Burkeville along the South Side [Rail]road; the Ninth Corps stretched along that road behind him. ... On the 4th General Sheridan struck the Danville road near Jetersville, where he learned that Lee was at Amelia Court-House. He immediately intrenched himself and awaited the arrival of General Meade, who reached there the next day. . . .

On the morning of the 6th it was found that General Lee was moving west of Jetersville toward Danville. General Sheridan moved with his cavalry (the Fifth Corps having been returned to General Meade on his reaching Jetersville) to strike his flank, followed by the Sixth Corps, while the Second and Fifth Corps pressed hard after. . . . General Ord advanced from Burkeville toward Farmville. . . . In the afternoon General Sheridan struck the enemy south of Sailor's Creek . . . and detained him until the Sixth Corps got up, when a general attack of infantry and cavalry was made, which resulted in the capture of 6,000 or 7,000 prisoners. . . . On the morning of the 7th the pursuit was renewed. . . . It was soon found that the enemy had crossed to the north side of the Appomattox; but so close was the pursuit that the Second Corps got possession of the common bridge at High Bridge before the enemy could destroy it. . . . The Sixth Corps and a division of cavalry crossed at Farmville to its support. . . .

Early on the morning of the 8th the pursuit was resumed. . . .

On the morning of the 9th General Ord's command and the Fifth Corps reached Appomattox Station just as the enemy was making a desperate effort to break through our cavalry. The infantry was at once thrown in. Soon after a white flag was received, requesting a suspension of hostilities pending negotiations for a surrender.

* * *

U. S. Grant was not one to linger when there was a job to be finished. "I was sure Lee was trying to make his escape and I wanted to push immediately in pursuit…," he later wrote. "I hoped to capture them soon."

While Willcox's division stayed in Petersburg, the rest of three armies—the Army of the Potomac, the Army of the James, and the Army of the Shenandoah—hurried after Lee's forces. Willcox's men were relieved on April 5 by a small independent division led by an officer who would carry the specter of the Crater to this grave: Brevet Major General Edward Ferrero. Another career casualty of the campaign, Major General Gouverneur K. Warren, commanded the Petersburg district. After being relieved under controversial circumstances at Five Forks, Warren would dedicate his life to correcting the historical record. Tragically, vindication would come only posthumously.

Ferrero's garrison troops enjoyed their assignment. "Co. E's first quarters were in a machinist's shop near Sycamore street next to a tobacco warehouse," a member of the 6th New York Heavy Artillery remembered, "and 10 minutes after taking possession every man had a board across his knee rolling cigars from as good a supply of long green as we ever saw."

"Crowds of soldiers, citizens, ladies, boys and children, not forgetting the inevitable 'darkies,' filled the sidewalks, and made that part of the town appear quite busy," *New York Times* reporter George F. Williams wrote of Sycamore Street on April 5. "Patrols pace up and down the different streets, and guards are distributed throughout the city in order to keep the large crowds of stragglers and furloughed officers and men within due bounds," he added.

Town officials adapted quickly to their changed circumstances. On April 12, the members of the Common Council and the city administration took the Union oath of allegiance. Five days later, their salaries were set to U.S. currency. The U.S. Christian Commission established a relief station for indigent blacks, while white residents faced a small army of sutlers who operated from vacant stores. Sarah Pryor was among those who had to pawn their family possessions to obtain the new legal tender.

Events tended to blur in the memory when the time came to review the ten months of warfare about Petersburg—or at least that was how Confederate staff officer John Esten Cooke saw it. "At Petersburg the fighting seemed to decide little," he declared, "and the bloody collisions had no names…. It was one long battle, day and night, week after week, and month after month—

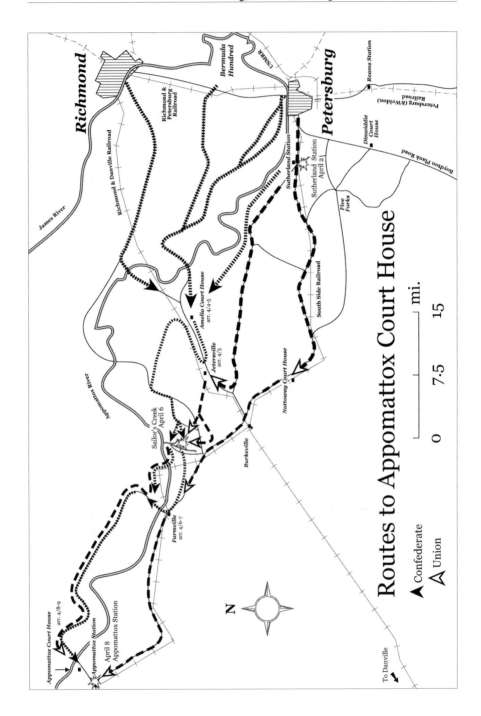

Routes to Appomattox Court House

during the heat of summer, the sad hours of autumn, and the cold days and nights of winter."

For forty-one weeks, the big stories of the war had been everywhere but in Petersburg—in the Shenandoah Valley, along the Atlantic and Gulf coasts, with Thomas in Tennessee or Sherman on his march to the sea. Compared to operations in these dynamic theaters of the conflict, the Petersburg campaign advanced with glacial languor.

The soldiers who survived those siege months recognized the many pieces of the puzzle that was Petersburg, even as they doubted that the whole picture would ever be assembled. Warned one veteran, "The story of Petersburg will never be written; volumes would be required to contain it, and even those who went through the trying ordeal, can not recall a satisfactory outline of the weird and graphic occurrences of that stormy period."

Indeed, the Petersburg campaign need never have occurred at all. Grant's brilliant move to disengage at Cold Harbor, cross the James, and capture the Cockade City in one quick rush should have succeeded but did not. "The Army of the Potomac…was a blunt tool when it reached Petersburg," one field officer claimed. "The Wilderness, Spottsylvania, and especially Cold Harbor, had killed out the men who, in a charge, run ahead; and the remainder were discouraged by incessant fighting and toil, and by want of success." "Why is the Army kept continually fighting until its heart has sickened within it?" a staff officer lamented. "Grant has pushed his Army to the extreme limit of human endurance."

Still, these explanations might have been moot had P. G. T. Beauregard not been there to direct the city's defense. "He promptly took every man he had, flung them into Petersburg where the enemy were making great progress, and beyond doubt by this wise and vigorous movement saved that City from capture," wrote a Richmond official.

There followed a series of engagements that began on June 22 and continued, with varying intervals of quiet, until late October. No single plan or consistent goal guided these, though a factor in all—sometimes in the foreground, others times as a backdrop—was the desire to cut the rail lifelines to Petersburg and, through it, to Richmond. A young Yankee artilleryman explained the situation to his wife this way: "The rebs get their supplies from here as it is the center of railroads our folks want to destroy them but the rebs fight like tigers [but] if we get them the folks will see hard times in richmond."

Grant, however, did not pursue this end single-mindedly. His attention was sometimes diverted by events elsewhere, and his planning sometimes subverted by nonmilitary considerations. Nevertheless, each lunge and each repulse or limited victory sharpened Grant's ability to effectively employ the combined Federal armies against Petersburg and Richmond. "Grant is a man of such infinite resource and ceaseless activity," an officer stationed at City Point marveled, "scarcely does one scheme fail before he has another on foot; baffled in one direction he immediately gropes round for a vulnerable point elsewhere."

Grant understood that relatively few troops were required to hold strongly entrenched lines. This freed up units for use as a mobile column. According to Horace Porter, "General Grant...now began to take measures looking to the investment of that place by leaving a portion of his forces to defend our works, while he moved out with the other portion against the railroads, with the design of cutting off Lee's communications in that direction."

Even when the various operations failed to achieve their often overly ambitious goals, there was always the inevitable benefit of stretching out Lee's defenses. "More than once . . . ," wrote *Philadelphia Inquirer* reporter Edward Crapsey in late October, "we have failed in gaining what we had good grounds for expecting, but the great fact remains that we have never taken a step backward." "The siege had now settled down to the arithmetical process of killing us off little by little, and the slow but sure one of compelling us to lengthen our lines until they became too weak to hold," a Confederate officer stated.

One of the great myths of the Petersburg siege was that the Confederate army steadily wasted away while the Federal ranks swelled with a constant supply of fresh recruits. The facts reveal a far different picture. At the end of August, for instance, the effective strength of the Army of the Potomac (including cavalry and artillery) was 37,827. The Army of the James added just 22,340 men to that, for a grand total of 60,167. Confederate returns for the same period totaled out at little better than 35,600. On April 2, 1865, the number of Union troops taking part in the pursuit of Lee's army was about 112,500, while Lee had 58,400 men. Lee still faced a disparity of better than 2 to 1, but the odds, while long, were not hopeless.

The quality of the recruits was a problem on both sides. In October, a New Hampshire soldier in the Ninth Corps noted, "The regiments in the Second Brigade were being made larger in numbers by the arrival of conscripts and bounty jumpers, but few of whom were of any worth as soldiers." After reviewing one set of newcomers, a Virginia cavalryman declared with disgust, "They are a sick looking set of fellows." "These recruits did much to dispirit the veteran Confederates," an artilleryman insisted.

Events elsewhere also affected actions at Petersburg. Difficulties in the Shenandoah Valley inspired a series of operations that resulted in the extension of the Union lines to the Weldon Railroad, and in the west, Confederate general Joseph E. Johnston's slow retreat before Sherman's advance damaged the morale of Lee's men. "Much uneasiness is felt in regard to General Johnstone Army retreating and leaving our butiful country to be desolated," one Georgian wrote in July.

Atlanta's fall, a Petersburg doctor observed, was "a serious blow to us." "We have had bad news to day from Georgia which casts a gloom over every one," agreed another Rebel. Sherman's subsequent sweep to the east brought disquiet to men from South and North Carolina, with the burning of Columbia, South Carolina, providing a particularly ominous portent for troops from the Tarheel state. "The hearts of the people and soldiers began to sink. Deserters increase and many commit desperations about home. Our prospects getting more gloomy fast," a member of the 48th North Carolina recorded in his diary.

Sherman's methodical march to the sea also had the dangerous effect of driving the Confederacy's other major army closer and closer to Lee's, thus raising the unnerving possibility of a linkup. "For four long years we had tried to drive the Confederates away from Richmond," one of Meade's division commanders reflected. "Now we were most anxious to keep them there."

Throughout the vexations and vicissitudes of this seemingly unending campaign (which would cost the North about 42,000 casualties, and the South about 28,000), U. S. Grant never lost sight of his goal, nor faith in his eventual success. "Think Richmond will fall before we quit here but cannot say how soon," he wrote in mid-July. In December, he could still assert, "I have great hope this will be the last Winter of the War." Even when he waffled, he was confident. "I will not predict a day when we will have peace again, with a Union restored," he wrote in January 1865, "but that that day will come is as sure as the rising of to-morrow's sun. I have never doubted this in the darkest days of this dark and terrible rebellion." Then, on April 3, as he sat in the heart of the city that had defied him for so long, Grant's only thoughts were of winding things up. "We may have some more hard work but I hope not," he told his wife.

Grant "stood still" at Petersburg to allow others to move. Robert E. Lee and the Army of Northern Virginia were the only combination in the Confederacy that, if given the freedom to seize the initiative, could strike blows that might seriously shake public confidence in Lincoln's administration and upset Grant's grand plan for victory. By maintaining an aggressive, threatening posture at Petersburg, Grant ensured that Lee was never far away. This was the dirtiest task he had to undertake in order to end the war—and the most critical. By keeping his headquarters at Petersburg, Grant made absolutely certain that this vital job would be accomplished.

For Robert E. Lee, the ultimate tragedy of Petersburg was his own knowledge of the certainty of his defeat. Even before the armies were entrenched around the Cockade City, Lee predicted, "If [Grant] ...gets there it will become a siege, and then it will be a mere question of time." Lee's obsession with duty, however distasteful, and his instinctive combative spirit shaped his handling of Confederate arms at Petersburg. "Never forget me or our suffering country," he wrote to his wife in June, fully anticipating the trials that were yet to come.

Lee's once magnificent Army of Northern Virginia had been badly bled during the Overland campaign and was further weakened by his decisions to detach portions of it to other theaters of the war. Jubal Early's expedition into the Shenadoah Valley, a gamble to divert Grant's attention, never repaid its costs. Then, in January 1865, Lee reluctantly allowed Kershaw's Brigade, M. C. Butler's cavalry division, and the capable Wade Hampton to depart for South Carolina in an attempt to tip the balance against Sherman.

Just how much Lee's army had changed for the worse he discovered in the course of the Petersburg campaign. It could still react defensively to strike short, fiercely hard blows that turned back or blunted Union feelers, but when Lee tried to put it into an offensive mode—as he did on June 24 along the south bank of the Appomattox, or on September 30 at Fort Harrison—his careful plans completely unraveled.[1]

Lee could read the writing on the wall. He was heard to exclaim in October, "If we can't get the men, all that is left for us is to make peace on the best terms we can." During a closed hearing before a joint C. S. congressional committee in January, Lee complained that his obligation to defend Petersburg and Richmond severely limited his options and forced him to "permit the enemy to make my plans for me."

Lee assessed the effect of Sherman's operations upon his own in a letter he wrote in 1868: "As regards the movements of General Sherman, it was easy to see that unless they were interrupted I should be compelled to abandon the defense of Richmond, and with a view of arresting his progress, I so weakened

---

1   The result was the same on October 7 along the Darbytown Road, east of Richmond.

my force by sending reinforcements to South and North Carolina, that I had not sufficient men to man the lines. Had they not been broken, I should have abandoned them as soon as General Sherman reached the Roanoke [River]."

Another of the great Petersburg myths, propagated in scores of postwar memories and unit histories, was that Lee's army was starved out of the city. There is little question that the months of January and February 1865 were especially harsh ones, leading Lee to declare, "My army is starving." The appointment of General I. M. Saint John as commissary general, on February 16, however, provided almost immediate relief, as Saint John moved quickly to improve and streamline the supply delivery system. The new Confederate secretary of war was soon able to report that "General St. John's conduct of the department was so satisfactory that a few weeks afterwards I received a letter from General Lee, in which he said his army had not been so well supplied for many months."

Throughout the Petersburg ordeal, Lee maintained a poise that profoundly inspired his men. One weary Virginia soldier noted in late March, "If there was ever a man, the very sight of whom could fill despaired men with the determination to win or die, that man was Lee." Privately, though, Lee acknowledged that his reward for duty done at Petersburg would be defeat and perhaps even death. "We must suffer patiently to the end," he wrote to his wife in August, "when all things will be made right." To a C.S. legislator, Lee vowed, "I intend to die sword in hand."

New York Times correspondent E. A. Paul sat down in Petersburg on April 25 to write out his impressions of the defeated Confederacy. After witnessing Lee's surrender at Appomattox on April 9, Paul "traveled through portions of Appomattox, Prince Edward, Nottoway, Dinwiddie and Prince George Counties." The roads were filled with defeated Confederate soldiers, and Paul spoke with many of them, reporting, "The one absorbing idea with all was that the country was at peace again; and they were intensely gratified at the prospect of immediately returning to civil life…and no power on this earth…can ever force these men from their homes again to fight against the Union cause." Reflecting upon the course of events in the final years of the conflict, Paul singled out Robert E. Lee for special censure. The Virginian's successes had been amplified by an adoring Rebel press, Paul charged, "until the people, and the rank and file of his army began to believe him something more than a human being."

For the past two years, the Times reporter declared, "the Confederate armies have been held together mainly through the influence of this one man." Paul astutely zeroed in on the winter of 1865, when Lee "testified before a committee of the rebel Senate that the cause of which he was the military head was a failure. For every drop of blood shed since that time Robert E. Lee should be held answerable."

Paul's strident opinion was not shared by the South itself. On May 5, 1865, William H. Platt, rector of Saint Paul's Church in Petersburg, where Lee often worshiped during the siege, wrote the general a personal note that at once identified the core of what would become the Lee legend and the essence of the Lost Cause:

> The grateful hearts of millions will ever bless you for struggling so long and so nobly for their right of self government. You, no more than Napoleon, and other great commanders, could do impossibilities. The enemy exceeded us vastly in numbers and other resources of war and exhaustion was inevitable. The Powers of the world, misunderstanding us, coldly left us to expire. Our Confederate nationality is gone, but not the glory of its brief existence and history. Whatever we have lost, our honor is safe.

Petersburg survived the siege with its honor intact; events were moving so swiftly toward the end that there was no longer any need for "examples" to be made, so the city was spared the fate of Atlanta and Columbia. But although the Federal occupation was not accompanied by wholesale destruction or arson, nine months of steady bombardment had already taken their toll: a survey completed in the summer of 1865 listed more than eight hundred buildings that had been hit by Yankee shells. (The Cockade City's civilians fared better: although no comprehensive count was ever made, it seems that less than half a dozen citizens died as a direct result of the siege.)

Petersburg, like most of the South, was slow to fully recover. A Northern reporter who visited the city in late September 1865 wrote, "Its business was shattered. Its well-built, pleasant streets rising upon the south bank of the Appomattox, were dirty and dilapidated." Nevertheless, its spirit was unbroken. Petersburg's women organized a memorial association to supervise the gathering of Confederate dead from area battlefields and their reburial in Blandford Cemetery, and it soon became a town tradition to honor those who had fallen in its defense with special ceremonies held on June 9. These commemorative activities so impressed Mrs. John A. Logan, the wife of a Federal general, that she returned north determined to establish a national memorial day. The holiday now celebrated by all Americans owes its beginnings, in part, to the remembrance of Confederate valor by the citizens of Petersburg.

Abraham Lincoln's sojourn in the area lasted until April 8. On the day after his Petersburg visit, Lincoln walked the streets of Richmond. He returned to City Point on April 5 and remained there for three more days, hoping in vain to hear news of Lee's surrender before he had to return to Washington. During those days the President met with several Southern notables, made another tour of Petersburg, and spent some time with wounded Union soldiers.

The presidential visit climaxed with a grand soiree held aboard the River Queen. Among those present was a young nobleman, the Marquis de Chambrun. Lincoln playfully asked the military band serenading the guests to perform the "Marseillaise," a revolutionary anthem banned in France by the royalist government. "You have to come over to America to hear it," he joked to the marquis, and then he asked the young aristocrat if he had ever heard "Dixie." When de Chambrun replied that he had not, Lincoln requested the surprised musicians to play it. "That tune is now Federal property," Lincoln said, "and it is good to show the rebels that, with us in power, they will be free to hear it again."

The *River Queen* began her return journey to Washington shortly after 10:00 p.m. Lincoln stood almost alone on the deck, watching the lights of City Point recede in the darkness. Ahead lay his next and perhaps greatest battle—the fight with Congress for a merciful reconstruction of the nation. "Mr. Lincoln's mind seemed absorbed in the many thoughts suggested by the scene," reminisced de Chambrun, "and we saw him still pursue his meditation long after the quickened speed of the steamer had removed it forever from him."

Notes

(See the bibliography for full citations for this and all other sources listed. Citations are generally given in the order of their appearance within the text.)

Chapter 1: "Petersburg is to be and shall be defended"

The best modern history of 1861-65 Petersburg is A. Wilson Greene's *Civil War Petersburg: Confederate City in the Crucible of War*. Also of value are James G. Scott and Edward A. Wyatt IV's *Petersburg's Story*, as well as William D. Henderson's 1981 study. "Petersburg, Virginia, Confederate City," published in the *Confederate Historical Institute Journal*. Less valuable is M. Clifford Harrison's *Home to the Cockade City!*

For a complete strategic, tactical, and anecdotal account of the June 9 fighting, see William G. Robertson's *Battle of Old Men and Young Boys*. August Kautz defended his efforts in a piece written for the *National Tribune* that appeared in its issue for May 18, 1899.

Bessie Callender's recollections of this day can be found in two accounts, one on deposit at the Petersburg Battlefield Park, the other published in George Bernard's *War Talks*. Also in Bernard's collection and used here were accounts by Virginia Davidson, William Hinton, and Anthony Keiley. Anne Banister's "Incidents in the Life of a Civil War Child" comes from the Virginia State Library. The letters of Dr. John Herbert Claiborne may be found in the University of Virginia Library; I used a transcription in the Virginia Historical Society. A copy of Charles Friend's "My Father and his household, before, during and after the war" is among the valuable materials collected at the Petersburg Battlefield Park. Sarah Pryor's *Reminiscences* has been reprinted several times since it first appeared, in 1908. The United Daughters of the Confederacy collection at the North Carolina Department of History and Archives yielded the typescript "Diary of Mrs. Charles Waddell." Margaret Stanly Beckwith's pithy summary is in her "Reminiscences, 1844-1865" in the Virginia Historical Society.

Chapter 2: "It was a marvel of a move"

The following northern accounts were used in this chapter: Albert, *45th PA*; Baker, *9th MA Battery*; Billings, *10th MA Battery*; Brinton, *Personal Memoirs*; Buck, *Brief Sketch*; F. Burr, *James Beaver*; Child, *5th NH*; Charles E. Davis, *Three Years*; Dusseault, *Company E*; Gibbs, *187th PA*; A. Haines, *15th NJ*; Hopkins, *7th RI*; Kirk, *Heavy Guns*; G. Lewis, *Battery E*; O. Lewis, *138th PA*; Mulholland, *116th PA*; Murphey, *1st DE*; Nevins, ed., *Diary of Battle*; Page, *14th CT*; Pickerill, *3rd IN Cavalry*; Roback, *Veteran Volunteers*; A. Small, *16th ME*; G. Stevens, *Three Years*; T. Vaill, *2nd CT*; Washburn, *108th NY*; and Wilson, *Under Old Flag*. Also useful was the coverage appearing in the June 18 issues of the *New York Herald* and the *New York Tribune*. The case of Lieutenant Swan was first recounted in a June 14 letter appearing in the *Batavia Republican Advocate* for June 28, 1864. It was still a topic of discussion at the regiment's 74th reunion as recounted in the *Syracuse Daily Courier and Union* for August 23, 1938.

Union headquarters perspective came from Agassiz, ed., *Meade's Headquarters*; Lowe, ed., *Meade's Army;* Catton, *Grant*; Grant, *Personal Memoirs*; H. Porter, *Campaigning*; and Sumner, ed., *Diary of Comstock*. Also helpful were Holstein, *Three Years*; Humphreys, *Virginia Campaign*; and Page, *Letters*.

The Southern perspective was drawn from Caldwell, *South Carolinians*; Clark, *Histories*; Dowdey, *Lee's Last*; Dowdey and Manarin, eds., *Wartime Papers*; Early, *Memoir*; Freeman, *Lee*; Fuller, *Diary*; Hunton, *Autobiography*; and Stiles, *Four Years*.

Chapter 3: "Hold on at all hazards!"

In my opinion, there was no other period of fighting at Petersburg during which the decisions of the officers in command exerted so decisive an influence over events. The battles of June 15-18 were won and lost as much in the minds and actions of the field generals as by the soldiers actually fighting; accordingly, I have shaped this chapter along those lines. A finely detailed tactical study of this period is Thomas J. Howe's *Wasted Valor*.

The Grant material was obtained from his *Personal Memoirs*; his Petersburg Campaign report in the *Official Records*, vol. 46, part 1; Badeau, *Military History*; Porter, *Campaigning*; Simon, ed., *Papers of Grant*, vol. 11; and Wilson, *Life of Rawlins*. William Kent's observations appeared in the *New York Tribune* for June 24, 1864.

"Baldy" Smith wrote extensively after the war, often in defense of his reputation. I drew upon his articles "The Eighteenth Corps at Cold Harbor" (in *Battles and Leaders,* vol. 4) and "The Movement Against Petersburg: June, 1864" (in *Papers of Massachusetts Historical Society*, vol. 5), his published memoir *Chattanooga to Petersburg*, and his 1897 letter to the editors of *Century Magazine*, printed under the title "General W. F. Smith at Petersburg." Valuable as well was Smith's autobiography, written for his daughter and published, in an edition edited by Herbert M. Schiller. Also helpful was Clarence E. Macartney's *Grant and His Generals*. The *New York Tribune* article praising Smith at the expense of both Hancock and Meade can be found in the paper's June 28, 1864, edition. The remarkable odyssey of Lieutenant Davenport is contained in a letter published in one of the many appendices of *Butler's Book*, Ben Butler's postwar defense of his military career. The memoirs of George T. Ulmer were published under the title *Adventures of a Drummer Boy*. Another useful overview of Smith's career with details about the Petersburg assaults appeared in a syndicated column that was published in various newspapers, among them the *New York Evening Post* for May 16, 1903.

I stepped outside Smith's point-of-view with help from E. P. Alexander's *Military Memoirs* and letters from "Old Vet" of the 8th Connecticut published in the November 1864 edition of *The Connecticut War Record*, and from "J. R." which appeared in the *Sacramento Daily Union* for August 18, 1864.

Indispensable to an understanding of the excessively self-promoting Beauregard is Harry T. Williams's biography, *P. G. T. Beauregard*. Like Smith and Butler, Beauregard spent much of his postwar years defending his honor in print. The most extensive defense of his achievements is Alfred Roman's two-volume study, *Military Operations*, which was personally approved, if not largely dictated, by its subject. Also useful to me were Beauregard's letter to General Cadmus Wilcox of about June 15-18, 1864 (included in the MHSM papers cited above), and the article he wrote for *Battles and Leaders*, titled "Four Days of Battle at Petersburg." A good understanding of Beauregard's successes during Butler's Bermuda Hundred expedition can be gleaned from William Glenn Robertson's excellent study of the campaign, *Back Door to Richmond*.

John Gibbon's assessment of George Meade's command dilemma can be found in Gibbon's *Personal Recollections*. Meade's letters, edited by his son and published in *Life and Letters*, are remarkably revealing. Always invaluable for a close look at Meade are Theodore Lyman's letters, published in Agassiz, ed., *Meade's Headquarters*, and his contemporary notebook printed in Lowe, ed., *Meade's Army*. The other biographies of Meade consulted were by Cleaves and Pennypacker.

Tucker's *Hancock the Superb* and Jordan's *Winfield Scott Hancock* are the basic biographies of the Union Second Corps commander at Petersburg. Also of value is Walker's *General Hancock*. Some of the "snapshots" of this officer at Petersburg were found in Livermore, *Days and Events*; Smith, *19th ME*; and Walker, *Second Corps*.

Chapter 4: "I have determined to try to envelop Petersburg"

Union scenes of June 19 came from Drake, *9th NJ*; Roback, *Veteran Volunteers*; White, Memoir; Kent, ed., *Three Years*; Sparks, ed., *Inside Lincoln's Army*; Agassiz, ed., *Meade's Headquarters*; and Comstock, *Diary*. The Confederate side was drawn from

Stewart, *Pair of Blankets*; Macrae, *Americans at Home*; and Dowdey and Manarin, eds., *Wartime Papers*.

The execution of William Johnson is based on the following accounts: W. F. Parish, "A Notable Execution," and W. E. Webster, "The Petersburg Execution," both in the *National Tribune*, November 18 and December 15,1915; Rauscher, *Music on March*; Tilney, *My Life*; Frassanito, *Grant and Lee*; and the *Boston Evening Transcript* for June 30, 1864.

Other accounts consulted on the events of June 20 were Weygant, *History of 124th*; Jones, *Rebel War Clerk*; and Albright, Diary.

A very helpful source for the events of June 21-23 is Bryce A. Suderow's article "Confederate Casualties near the Jerusalem Plank Road, June 21—23, 1864." In addition to the reports in the *Official Records*, the following materials were used for the Union side of the story: Gilbert, *Story of Regiment*; Page, *14th CT*; Haley, *Rebel Yell*; Stevens, *Berdan's Sharpshooters*; Child, *5th NH*; Meade, *Life and Letters*; Armes, *Ups and Downs*; Lockley, "Letters"; Ford, *Story of 15th MA*; Morgan, comp., *Narrative*; Adams, *Reminiscences*; Kirk, *Heavy Guns*; *History of 57th PA*; Shaw, *1st ME*; Landis, Letter of July 26, 1864; Carter, *Four Brothers*; Ward, *106th PA*; Waitt, comp., *19th MA*; Gibbon, *Personal Recollections*; Vaill, *2nd CT*; Haines, *15th NJ*; Roe, *9th NY*; Simons, *125th NY*; Humphreys, *Virginia Campaign*; Simon, ed., *Papers of Grant*, vol. 11; Houghton, *17th ME*; Benedict, *VT in the Civil War*; Perry, *Letters from Surgeon*; Menge, ed., *Notebook*; and a letter from a member of the 125th New York named "C" that was printed in the June 30, 1864 edition of the *Troy Daily Times*.

Confederate accounts of these events include Gordon, Diary; D.B.R., "Barringer's North Carolina Brigade of Cavalry," in *The Daily Confederate*, February 22, 1865; Wilcox, Report of Actions and letter to General Mahone of about June 22; Report of Actions on June 22 from the 28th NC (Auburn University); Phillips, Journal and Diary; McCabe, "The Defence of Petersburg"; L. H. Carter, Letter about the 10th Georgia Battalion, in the *Macon Daily Telegraph*, July 9, 1864; Couture, *Charlie's Letters*; Wise, *End of an Era*; and Herbert, "History of 8th Alabama." Also very helpful was William Mahone's account of this affair, which can be found in Mulholland, *116th PA*.

For the June 24 affair, I utilized (for the Union side) Thompson, *13th NH*; Kreutzer, *Notes*; and the *New York Tribune* for June 28, 1864; as well as (for the Confederate side) Field, "Campaign of 1864 and 1865"; Anderson, Report of Actions; and Hagood's letter, reprinted in the July 2, 1864, edition of the *Petersburg Express*, as well as in his *Memoirs*.

Lincoln's two-day visit is recounted in Porter, *Campaigning*; Catton, *Grant*; Meade, *Life and Letters*; Corbin, Diary; Cadwallader, *Three Years*; Cadwell, *Old 6th*; Eldredge, *3rd NH*; Palmer, *48th NY*; and Wilson, *Life of Rawlins*; as well as in reports in the *New York Herald* for June 26 and 27, 1864, the *New York Times* for June 26, 1864, and the *Syracuse Daily Journal* for June 29, 1864.

For information about the Wilson Raid, I turned to Starr, *Union Cavalry*; Wilson's two reports in the Official Records; and Johnston II's dissertation "Virginia Railroads in the Civil War, 1861—65."

Chapter 5: "The destructive work of the shells was visible on every hand"

The first "official" shelling of Petersburg (there were doubtless unofficial ones preceding this incident) is recounted in Billings, *10th MA Battery*. The United Daughters of the Confederacy collection at the North Carolina Department of History and Archives yielded the typescript "Diary of Mrs. Charles Waddell." The officer who found Petersburg "exceedingly depressing" is Wise, writing in his *End of an Era*.

The exodus from Petersburg is described in the Albright diary, Pryor's *Reminiscences*, the diary of William Wiatt, the letters of Dr. Claiborne and the Charles Campbell diary. The report from the *Mobile Daily Advertiser* was reprinted in Andrew's *South Reports the Civil War*.

The comments of Lee's artillery chief may be found in Lee, ed., *Memoirs of Pendleton*; the remarks of the cavalryman who likened the shells to "hawks of perdition" are in Myers, *Comanches*.

All records concerning the Petersburg Common Council come from the council minutes, which are on file in the office of the Petersburg city clerk. Comment on the Council's effort to ban alcohol came from a column in the *Richmond Daily Dispatch* for November 8, 1864.

The pastor who sought to spare General Lee the sound of Sunday church bells is so quoted in Greene, *Civil War Petersburg*. The fact of the trains' running on schedule is related in MacDonald, *Laurel Brigade*.

Accounts of soldier visits to Petersburg come from Coles, "History of 4th Alabama," and the Alexander letters. Napier Barlett's praise of Petersburg womanhood comes from his *Soldier's Story*, while the romances at the cotton factories are related in Herbert, "History of 8th Alabama."

In addition to sources cited above, accounts of the shelling of Petersburg may be found in Macrae, *Americans at Home*; the A. J. Leavenworth papers, the Brown letters, and Blackford, *War Years*. The *Petersburg Express* account comes from a reprinting in the September 22, 1864 edition of the *New York Evening Express*.

The fires in Petersburg are described in many Union sources, including Lord, *9th NH*; Everts, *9th NJ*; Bartlett, *12th NH*; Roemer, *Reminiscences*; and Cleveland, "Civil War Journal." Confederate sources are Albright, *Diary*; and Dickert, *Kershaw's Brigade*.

The heavy bombardment of July 28 is attested to by Babcock, *Diary*; Carter, *Four Brothers*; and Drake, *9th NJ*. The artilleryman who was angry over Grant's failure to notify the noncombatants is quoted in Marcus, ed., *Memoirs of American Jews*.

Dawson's observations appear in his *Reminiscences*, while those of Varin may be found in his Diary. The editorial on dodging can be found in the *Petersburg Daily Register* for June 24, 1864.

Union reflections on Petersburg are included in Cleveland (cited above); Clark, *Iron Hearted Regiment*, Twitchell, *7th ME Battery*; and Albert, *45th PA*.

Chapter 6: "The saddest affair I have ever witnessed in the war"

For many students of the Civil War, the Battle of the Crater *is* the Siege of Petersburg. Henry Pleasants's observations may be found in his report in the *Official Records* and in his testimony before the Committee on the Conduct of the War. The first significant modern study of this fighting appeared in 1989: coauthored by Michael A. Cavanaugh and William Marvel, *Battle of the Crater* is a well-balanced, evenhanded study that cuts through much of the postwar rhetoric surrounding this controversial action. There have been several more since then, most notably Richard Slotkin's *No Quarter*. A rich selection of Confederate reminiscences of the fighting appears in Bernard, ed., *War Talks*.

The official Court of Inquiry on the Mine Explosion convened on August 6, 1864, and questioned witnesses between August 6 and September 8. The court delivered its findings on September 9. A full transcript of the inquiry can be found in the *Official Records*, Series 1, Volume 40, Part 1. The *Joint Congressional Committee on the Conduct of the War* investigated a curious variety of wartime incidents, including the Battle of the Crater, and published its findings in 1865.

Regimental histories used in this chapter were Anderson, *57th MA*; Andrews, *23rd SC*; Cutcheon, *20th MI*; Cutchins, *Richmond Light Blues*; Herbert, "History of 8th AL"; Houston, *32nd ME*; Jackman, *6th NH*; Lord, *9th NH*; Osborne, *29th MA*; Rhodes, *Battery B, 1st RI*; and Day, *49th NC*.

Personal accounts consulted were Amory, *Brief Record*; Binion, Letter of August 10, 1864; Burbank, "The Battle of the Crater"; Coit, "Letter from Major J. C. Coit"; Govan, ed., *Haskell Memoirs*; Hall, "Mine Run to Petersburg"; Hudson, *Sketches*; Kenfield, "Captured by the Rebels"; Kilmer, "The Dash into the Crater"; McAlister, Letter of July 31, 1864; McClendon, *Recollections*; McMaster, "The Battle of the Crater"; Mahone, "The Crater" (pamphlet); Russell, *Diary*; Scott, *Memoirs*; Stewart, *Pair of Blankets*; Stinson, Letters; and Stephen M. Weld, "The Petersburg Mine." A New Yorker identified only as "N" wrote of the "incessant concussions" in a letter printed in the August 10, 1864 edition of the *Albany Atlas & Argus*. The "awfullest sight" was penned by an unidentified soldier whose letter appeared in the *Buffalo Daily Courier* for the same date. Helpful as well was the recollection of Charles A. Taylor published in the *Oswego Daily Times* for August 12, 1911. The extended piece on the fight printed in the *Petersburg*

Express was used as copied by the *Edgefield* (South Carolina) *Advertiser* in its August 10, 1864 issue.

Also of useful were the following articles and letters published in the postwar newspaper the *National Tribune*: Delevan Bates, "A Day with the Colored Troops" (January 30, 1908); Freeman S. Bowley, "The Crater" (November 6, 1884); John C. Featherston, "Battle at Crater thru Southern Eyes" (November 19, 1925); Squire D. Rhodes, "The Battle of the Crater" (October 8, 1903); Benjamin Spear, "Fighting Them Over" (June 20, 1889); Charles W. Walton, "The Battle of the Mine" (November 20, 1884); Clarence Wilson, "Exploding a Mine" (May 14, 1896); and "The Petersburg Mine" (July 3, 1919).

Chapter 7: "It was terrible—awful—terrific"

Basic information about City Point during the Union occupation of 1864-65 can be found in a study prepared in 1978 for the National Park Service, "Appomattox Manor-City Point, A History," by Harry Butowsky. (The Eppes House itself and an adjacent area encompassing the site of Grant's headquarters is now administered by the National Park Service as part of the Petersburg Battlefield Park.) Also helpful were the pertinent sections of Robertson's *Back Door*. The observant July visitor wrote of his City Point trip to the *Batavia Republican Advocate*, where it was published on July 19, 1864.

John Maxwell's report can be found in the *Official Records*, Volume 42, Part 1, pages 954-955. Various observations about City Point were drawn from Livermore, *Days and Events*; Miller, *Drum Taps*; de Trobriand, *Four Years*; Allen, *Down in Dixie*; Palmer, *Story of Aunt Becky*; Chase, *Memoir*; Tilney, *My Life*; and Gilbert, *Story of Regiment*.

A good standard article about the City Point explosion is Rayburn's "Sabotage at City Point." Memoirs and reminiscences used in my account include Freeman, *Letters from Two Brothers*; O. K. Harvey, "Explosion at City Point," in the *National Tribune Scrapbook*, Volume 2; James Otis Moore's letter, published in O'Donnell, "The 'Accidental' Explosion at City Point"; Porter, *Campaigning*; Fay, *War Papers*; Schaff, "The Explosion at City Point"; Lane, *Soldier's Diary*; Morgan, *Memoir*, and a letter from a Ninth Corps soldier published in the *Union County and Lewisburg Chronicle* (Pennsylvania) for August 23, 1864. From the New York State Library came the letters of Hamlin, Burnham, and Babcock, and from the *National Tribune* came Catharine van Wicks, "Explosion at City Point" (November 30, 1930); Ebenezer Cook, "Explosion at City Point" (July 3, 1913); Charles Porter, various reminiscences (December 12, 1887, December 4, 1913, and August 19, 1915); and John W. Porter, "Close Call in Virginia" (June 25, 1925).

Contemporary newspaper accounts used appeared in the *Philadelphia Inquirer* for August 12, 1864, *Harper's Weekly* for August 27, 1864, and the *Syracuse Daily Courier and*

Union for August 12, 1864. Mention of the Maltby House opening was found in the October 19, 1864, issue of the *Philadelphia Inquirer.*

Chapter 8: "Fire low! Low! Low!"

This chapter on the August fighting at Deep Bottom, the Weldon Railroad, and Reams Station was greatly facilitated by three studies: Bryce A. Suderow, "The Second Deep Bottom Expedition"; and Edward C. Bearss, "Battle of the Weldon Railroad" and "The Battle of Reams' Station." The latter two have been collected into a collection of Bearss' Petersburg works titled *The Petersburg Campaign: The Eastern Front Battles* (2012). The former was provided by its author.

Specific sources used in addition to the *Official Records* for the Deep Bottom portion of the chapter are:

Union: Catton, *Grant*; Cleaves, *Meade*; Meade, *Life and Letters*; Grant, *Personal Memoirs*; Jaquette, ed., *South after Gettysburg*; Lockley, "Letters"; Ford, ed., *Cycle of Adams Letters*; Houghton, *17th ME*; Walker, *Second Corps*; Dickey, *85th PA*; Little, *7th NH*; Eldredge, *3rd NH*; Stowits, *100th NY*; Marino, "General Alfred Howe Terry"; Kirk, *Heavy Guns*; Cunningham, *Irish Brigade*; Brady, *11th ME*; Porter, *Campaigning*; Copp, *Reminiscences*; Hyndman, *History of Cavalry Company*; Simon, ed., *Papers of Grant*, Vol. 12; Frederick, *Story of Regiment*; Paxton, *Sword and Gown*; Willson, *Disaster, Struggle, Triumph*; Hays, *Under Red Patch*; de Trobriand, *Four Years*; Robertson, ed., *Letters of McAllister*; Comstock, *Diary;* and a letter from "Charlie B." appearing in the September 27, 1864 edition of the *Batavia Republican Advocate.* Also consulted was the August 18, 1864, issue of the *New York Herald.*

Confederate: Lee, *General Lee*; Pickett, *Soldier of the South*; Krick, *Parker's Virginia Battery*; Freeman, *Lee;* Dowdey and Manarin, eds., *Wartime Papers*; Field, "Campaign of 1864 and 1865"; Bratton, Letters; Polly, *Hood's Texas Brigade*; Taylor, *General Lee*; Oates, *War Between Union & Confederacy*; Beale, *9th VA Cavalry*; and Lee, ed., *Memoirs of Pendleton.* Also useful were the *Richmond Dispatch* for August 24, 1864, the *Richmond Enquirer* for August 31, 1864, and the *Charleston Daily Courier* for August 27, 1864.

For the Weldon Railroad I used:

Union: Porter, "Operations Against the Weldon Railroad"; Smith, *Corn Exchange Regiment*; Humphreys, *Virginia Campaigns*; White, "From the Union Side"; Cutcheon, *20th MI*; McBride, *In the Ranks*; Vautier, *88th PA*; Roe, *39th MA*; Wilson, *Life of Rawlins*; Locke, *Story of Regiment*; Coco, ed., *Through Blood*; Crater, *50th PA*; Walcott, *21st MA*; *History of 35th MA*; Cheek, *6th WI*; Hall, *97th NY*; Brainard, *146th NY*; Harvey, *Recollections*; Judson, *83rd PA*; Gibbs, *187th PA*; van Vleck, Letters; Garrish, *Army Life*; Small, ed., *Road to Richmond*; Baker, *9th MA Battery*; Agassiz, ed., *Meade's Headquarters*; and Badeau, *Military History.* Contemporary newspapers provided "Our Army Correspondence" by "Alpha" (*Detroit Advertiser and Tribune* for October 26, 1864). Also helpful were the following articles from the postwar newspaper the *National Tribune*: Richard N. Bowerman, "Cutting Off Lee" (June 26, 1902); Thomas F. McCoy, "At the Weldon Road" (March 13,1890); Grove H. Dutton, "Weldon Railroad" (April 15, 1886, and January 23, 1890); and A. Wentz, "Closing Days of the War" (February 4, 1904).

The story of Medal of Honor winner Frederick C. Anderson can be found in a two piece article published in the *Taunton* (Massachusetts) *Daily Gazette*, beginning on July 28, 2009.

Confederate: Dunn, Diary; Thrasher, Letter; Goldsborough, *MD Line*; Clark, *Histories from North Carolina*; Heth, *Memoirs*; Stewart, "The No Name Battle"; Bernard, "Notes Relating to the Battle of the Weldon Railroad"; de Peyster, "Military Memoir of Mahone"; Croom, *6th GA*; Ferguson, Letters; Day, *49th NC*; Heth, Report of Actions (Lee Headquarters Papers); Izler, *Edisto Rifles*; Mackey, "Bravest Deed of the War"; Hagood, *Memoirs*; Freeman, *Lee's Lieutenants*; Robertson, Jr., *General A. P. Hill*; Todd, "Reminiscences"; Smith- wick, Letters; Greer, Letters; and Krick, *Fredericksburg Artillery*. Newspaper articles of use came from the *Weekly Confederate* for August 24, 1864, and the *Charleston Mercury* for August 26, 1864. Also useful was the postwar recollection of Mississippi soldier Thomas T. Roche that appeared in the May 5, 1883, issue of the *Philadelphia Weekly Times*.

For Reams Station:

Union (in addition to the above Deep Bottom citations): Page, *14th CT*; Walker, *General Hancock*; Bruce, *20th MA*; Mohr, ed., *Cormany Diaries*; Preston, *10th NY Cavalry*; Miers, ed., *Ride to War*; Tobie, *1st ME Cavalry*; Billings, *10th MA Battery*; Dauchy, "Battle of Ream's Station"; Menge, ed., *Notebook of Chisholm*; Stewart, *140th PA*; Muffley, *Story of Our Regiment*; and Child, *5th NH*. Also helpful was Starr, *Union Cavalry*.

Confederate (in addition to the Deep Bottom citations): Beale, *Lieutenant of Cavalry*; Beale, *9th VA Cavalry*; Calhoun, *Liberty Dethroned*; MacDonald; *Laurel Brigade*; Myers, *Comanches*; Wade Hampton's letter of March 29, 1884 (in the Francis C. Walker Papers at the MOLLUS Library, Philadelphia); Wells, *Hampton and His Men*; Brooks, *Butler and His Cavalry*; Krick, *9th VA Cavalry*; Sloan, "North Carolina in the War"; Mullen, Diary; Dunlop, *Lee's Sharpshooters*; Cavness, Diary; Justice, Letters; and Gordon, Diary. Contemporary newspapers used included the *Charleston Mercury* for September 2, 1864, the *Richmond Daily Dispatch* for August 30, the *Weekly Confederate* for September 7, and the *Columbus Daily Sun* for September 10. The quotation from the *Petersburg Express* reporter was from the September 2, 1864, reprint edition of the *New York Herald*.

Chapter 9 "Hello! Yanks! want any fresh beef?"

The naval side of the raid-and-ambush war at Petersburg is detailed in reports in the naval *Official Records*, especially in volumes 10, 11, and 12. Also helpful was David D. Porter's *Naval History*.

Union cavalry accounts of service behind the lines appear in *History of 3rd PA Cavalry*; Hyndman, *History of a Cavalry Company*; *History of 11th PA Cavalry*; and Mohr, ed., *Cormany Diaries*. Also helpful was Volume 2 of Starr's *Union Cavalry*, pages 400-401.

Boykin's *Beefsteak Raid* is a book-length treatment of the main subject of this chapter. Boykin's narrative is heavily overdramatized, however, and his sources are not always clear. Far more concise and satisfying are Richard W. Lykes's "The Great Civil War Beef Raid," and Horace Mewborn's "Herding Yankee Cattle: The Beefsteak Raid, September 14-17, 1864."

The best single Confederate account of the irregular activities behind the lines and the Beef Raid itself is John S. Elliott's reminiscence "Scouts with Wade Hampton," published in the May 3, 1884, issue of the *Philadelphia Weekly Times*. Shadburne's meticulous report can be found in the *Official Records*, Volume 42, No. 2, pages 1235-1236, while Hampton's report is on page 945 of No. 1 of the same volume. Also useful were Baylor, *Bull Run*; G. Beale, *Lieutenant of Cavalry*; R. L. T. Beale, *9th VA Cavalry*; Calhoun, *Liberty Dethroned*; MacDonald, *Laurel Brigade*; D. Cardwell's "A Brilliant Coup" in the *Southern Historical Society Papers*; L. H. Davis' "Famous Cattle Raid" in the *Confederate Veteran*, and Myers, *Comanches*. Also valuable were the appropriate regimental entries in Clark's *Histories from North Carolina*. The *Petersburg Express* account was used as copied in the *Richmond Daily Dispatch* for August 20, 1864.

For the Union side, Kautz defended his reputation in a set of unpublished memoirs. A printed account used in the narrative was in Edward P. Tobie's *1st ME Cavalry*. The editorial quoted came from the September 24, 1864, edition of the *New York Evening Express*.

Southern reaction to the raid was culled from Wilson, *Confederate Soldier*; Reid, *4th SC*; and Krick, *Parker's VA Battery*. Northern comments came from Comstock, *Diary*; Washburn, *108th NY*; Haines, *Company F*, and a letter from an army man posted to headquarters who signed himself "B. W. W.," and whose letter was printed in the September 29, 1864, edition of the *Watkins Express*.

Chapter 10: Dateline: Petersburg

The best single-volume study of Union combat correspondents (at least in my humble opinion) is Starr's *Reporting the Civil War*. The soldier perspectives on Civil War newspapers came from Corby, *Memoirs*; Cleveland, "Civil War Journal"; Bruce, *20th MA*; Boston, *Diary*; Holmes, *Horse Soldiers*; and Valentine, *23rd MA*.

The story of the coverage war at City Point was principally gleaned from Cadwallader's memoir *Three Years* and the J. R. Hamilton letters, which may be found at Chapel Hill.

The definitive strategic-, tactical-, and regimental-level study of Grant's fifth offensive is Sommers's *Richmond Redeemed*. It well repays careful and repeated readings.

With the exception of Swinton's observations (which were published in his *Campaigns of the Army of the Potomac*), all correspondent accounts came from period newspapers. Those used were the *New York Herald* for September 30 and October 2-7, 1864, the *New York Times* for October 1 and 3-5, and the *Philadelphia Inquirer* for October 3. Southern points of view came from the *Columbia Daily South Carolinian* for October 14 and the *Richmond Examiner* for October 1,3, and 6.

Chapter 11: "Everything now hinges on the election"

Observations on the pending elections came from Jones, *Rebel War Clerk*; Garrish, *Army Life*; Braman, *War of the Rebellion*; Haynes, Letters; William Wiatt, Diary; Person, Letters; Hyndman, *History of a Cavalry Company*; Krick, *30th VA*; Catton, *Grant Takes Command*; "Gamma" in the November 24 edition of *The Alleghanian*, Welch, *Confederate Surgeon's Letters*; Stewart, *Pair of Blankets*; and Simon, ed., *Papers of Grant*, Vol. 12. The letter quoted from the soldier's hometown newspaper was found in the October 4, 1864, edition of the *Long Island Farmer*, while the letter from the soldier who was against fighting for black equality (and who did not identify himself) was published in the *Syracuse Daily Courier and Union* for October 28, 1864.

The account of the genesis of what became the October 27 operations north and south of the James is drawn from the *Official Records*, Vol. 42, Part 3, pages 316-319, 328, 331-332, and 340-342, as well as from Meade, *Life and Letters*. The analysis of Grant's right-left strategy in Sommers's *Richmond Redeemed* was very helpful.

At the time this chapter was written, no published study of the October 27 actions had appeared. I did benefit from the unpublished work done by two students of the fighting south of the James. John Horn's "The Diamond and the Clover" was valuable for pointing out the Third Corps' internal dissent, while Bryce A. Suderow's "October 27, 1864 — Burgess Mills, Va." provided a succinct overview of the action, along with essential information about Confederate casualties.

For activities north of the James (Union side), the following materials were used, in addition to numerous reports published in the *Official Records*: Hyde, *112th NY*; Thompson, *13th NH*; Comstock, *Diary*; Tourtellotte, *7th CT*; Porter, *76th PA*; Price, *97th PA*; Califf, *7th U.S.C.T.*; Eisenschiml, ed., *Vermont General*; Haynes, *2nd NH*; Cunningham, *Three Years*; Jackson, ed., *Back Home*; Nesbitt, Letters; Clarke, *Iron Hearted Regiment;* and James H. Estes, "Second Fair Oaks" (in the *National Tribune* for August 5, 1909). Merriam's tribute to a fallen officer was published in the *New York Herald*'s October 31, 1864 edition.

The Confederate perspective on the north side of the James came from Longstreet, *Manassas to Appomattox*; Hagood, *Memoirs*; Polley, *Hood's Texas Brigade*; McFall, Letters; Coward, *South Carolinians*; McCarty, Diary; Crockett, Diary; and Hinson, "Diary."

For south of the James (Union), my sources included Coco, ed., *Through Blood*; Sparks, ed., *Inside Lincoln's Army*; de Trobriand, *Four Years*; McBride, *In the Ranks*; Tilney, *My Life*; Badeau, *Military History*; Porter, *Campaigning*; Crater, *50th PA*; Chandler, Letters; C. Humphreys, *Andrew Atkinson Humphreys*; A. Humphreys, *Virginia Campaign*; Cowtan, *10th NY*; Page, *14th CT*; Mohr, ed., *Cormany Diaries*; King, *93rd NY*; the Francis C. Walker Papers; Robertson, ed., *Letters of General McAllister*; Agassiz, ed., *Meade's Headquarters*; Livermore, *Days and Events*; Roback, *Veteran Volunteers*; Nelson, *Nuggets of Experience*; and a letter from Captain J. R. Cooper published in the November 15, 1864, edition of the *Batavia Republican Advocate*.

For south of the James (Confederate), my sources were Wise, *End of an Era*; "Letter from Virginia," by "Delta," in the *Charleston Daily Courier* for November 4, 1864; Brooks, ed., *Stories of the Confederacy*, and *Butler and His Cavalry*; Hassler, *A. P. Hill*; Heth, Report of Actions (Lee Headquarters Papers); Thurston, Letter; Phillips, Journal and Diary; Calhoun, *Liberty Dethroned*; *Final Report of the Wade Hampton Monument Commission*; Bartlett, *War Record*; the Bernard Papers; and Freeman, *Lee's Lieutenants*. Also valuable were the appropriate regimental entries in Clark's *Histories from North Carolina*.

Campaign assessments were drawn from Hopkins, *7th RI*; Nevins, ed., *Diary of a Battle*; the *Petersburg Express* for October 29, 1864, and the *Columbus* (Georgia) *Daily Sun* for November 9, 1864. Appreciation of the October 28 sunrise came from Edward Crapsey's account in the *Philadelphia Inquirer* published on October 31.

Election results, reflections, and anecdotes came from Roe, *1st MA Heavy Artillery*; Cutcheon, *20th MI*; Gould, *Story of 48th*; Aubery, *36th WI*; Smith, *76th NY*; Younger, ed., *Inside Confederate Government*; and Johnston, *Story of a Confederate Boy*.

Chapter 12: "Starvation parties"

A large portion of this chapter was based on information found in various siege editions of the *Petersburg Daily Express*. Issues of this paper, one of the most often quoted in other news sheets (both north and south) during the war, are extremely hard to locate. I drew upon the incomplete collections in the Virginia Historical Society and the Library of Congress. Specific editions used here were those for July 23; August 9; September 17, 2.1, 23, 28, and 30; October 15; and November 30, 1864; and March 3, 23, 24, and 25, 1865. It was not unusual for excerpts from the *Petersburg Daily Express* to appear in Richmond and Northern newspapers. Also useful was the *Petersburg Daily Register* for June 30, 1864.

Other accounts utilized were Pryor, *Reminiscences*; Claiborne, Letters and *75 Years*; Scarbrough, Letters; Conolly, *An Irishman*; Chambers, *Diary*; Archer, Letters; Leavenworth, Papers; the Keen-Armistead Letters; Harder, Memoir; and Heptinstall, Letter of February 26, 1865.

All records concerning the Petersburg Common Council come from the council minutes, which are on file in the office of the Petersburg city clerk.

Also helpful was Scott and Wyatt IV's *Petersburg's Story, A History*.

Chapter 13: "We cannot believe Americans can do these things"

Winter perspectives, north and south, came from the letters of Dr. Claiborne; Aubery, *36th WI*; and Tilney, *My Life*.

For the strategy and background of the Weldon Raid, see Woodward, *198th PA*; the *Official Records* (especially Vol. 42, No. 3, pages 798-799 and 804- 828); Houghton, *17th ME*; Judson, *83rd PA*; and *Under the Maltese Cross*.

For the longest time the only published study of the raid itself was Watkin's *The Hicksford Raid*, prepared in 1978 for the Greensville County Historical Society. It was joined in 2005 by Calkins, "The Apple Jack Raid, December 7-12, 1864: 'For This Barbarism There Was No Real Excuse.'" The only daily newspaper that covered the expedition in detail was the *Philadelphia Inquirer*, whose correspondent Edward Crapsey's report appeared in the December 14, 1864 issue. Also helpful in the matter of Confederate supply was Calkins, *Final Bivouac*.

Northern accounts used in my re-creation were Preston, *10th NY Cavalry*; Miers, ed., *Ride to War*; Locke, *Story of the Regiment*; Cheek, *Sauk County Riflemen*; Rogers, *189th NY*; McBride, *In the Ranks*; de Trobriand, *Four Years*; Haley, *Rebel Yell*; Garrish, *Army Life*; J. Smith, Letters and *Corn Exchange Regiment*; Marbaker, *11th NJ*; Robertson, ed., *Letters of General McAllister*; Greenleaf, ed., *Letters to Eliza* (Fowle Letters); Parker, *32nd MA*; Agassiz, ed., *Meade's Headquarters*; *History of 3rd PA Cavalry*; Stewart, *140th PA*; Crowninshield, *1st MA Cavalry*; Braman, *War of the Rebellion*; Jackman, *6th NH*; *History of 35th MA*; Giles, Letters; and Baker, *9th MA Battery*.

The view from the Southern side came from Brooks, *Butler and His Cavalry*; Waring, Diary; Todd, Reminiscences; Willis, Diary; Calhoun, *Liberty Dethroned*; Foard, Reminiscences; Cavaness, Diary; Hagood, *Memoirs*; Hassler, *A. P. Hill*; Lee, ed., *Memoirs of Pendleton*; and Barfield, Letters. Also valuable were the appropriate regimental entries in Clark's *Histories from North Carolina*.

For actions tangential to the Weldon Raid, I used Armes, *Ups and Downs*; the *Official Records*; Longstreet, *Manassas to Appomattox*; McCarty, Diary; Crockett, Diary; and Little, *7th NH*.

Chapter 14: "When we weren't killing each other, we were the best of friends"

Information for this chapter on the miscellany of the Petersburg siege was drawn from many sources.

Comments about the trench systems and forts came from Thompson, *13th NH*; Steedman, Letters; Wright, Letters; Walker, "Gordon's Assault on Fort Stedman"; Elliott, "Martin's Brigade, 1863-64"; Huyette, *Reminiscences*; Hagood, *Memoirs*; Clark, *Histories from North Carolina*; Kreutzer, *Notes*; Albert, *45th PA*; Twitchell, *7th ME Battery*; Lord, *9th NH*; Brainard, *140th NY*; Justice, Letters; Santvoord, *120th NY*; Trumbull, *War Memories*; Shearman, "Battle of the Crater"; Mowris, *117th NY*; J. W. Mitchell, "From New Jersey to Appomattox," in the *National Tribune* for March 11, 1915; and Haley, *Rebel Yell*; as well as the *Philadelphia Weekly Times* for April 9, 1881; the *Cold Spring Recorder* for December 28, 1894; and the *Batavia Republican Advocate* for July 19, 1864, and January 17, 1865; and the *Union County and Lewisburg Chronicle* for August 23, 1864. Also added for this edition was the postwar recollection of Mississippi soldier Thomas T. Roche that appeared in the May 5, 1883, issue of the *Philadelphia Weekly Times*. The first time trader wrote of his adventure to the editor of the *Dansville Advertiser,* who printed the letter on March 23, 1865. The complaint about the dust came from the *Philadelphia Inquirer* for June 29, 1864, and the unofficial use of wet cartridges in the same paper on October 24, and the account of the picket line fight appeared on November 10.

Life under artillery fire was recounted in Blackford, *War Years*; Bowden, "My Experiences as a Confederate Soldier"; *History of 35th MA*; Cuffel, *Durrell's Battery*; Allen, *4th RI*; Walter F. Sage, "Before Petersburg," in the *National Tribune* for December 25, 1902; Aubery, *36th WI*; Gilder, Letters; Hays, *Under the Red Patch*; Small, ed., *Road to Richmond*; Stewart, *140th PA*; J. Smith, *Corn Exchange Regiment*; D. Smith, *24th MI*; Badeau, *Military History*; Little, *7th NH*; Weygant, *History of 124th*; Dowdey and Manarin, eds., *Wartime Papers*; *History of 5th MA Battery*; Hinson, "Diary"; Phelps, "Chaplain's Life in the Civil War"; Marbaker, *11th NJ*; Cadwallader, *Three Years*; Rose, Diary; Robertson, ed., *Letters of General McAllister*; and Dauchy, "The Battle of Ream's Station." Also useful were comments by an unnamed New York soldier whose letter appeared in the October 1, 1864, edition of the *Schenectady Evening Star*; one from a New York artilleryman calling himself "Ginger," to *The Rockland County Journal* appearing on February 25, 1865; "Gamma," whose October 26 letter was published in the November 10 edition of *The Alleghenian;* and the postwar recollection of Charles A. Taylor printed in the *Oswego Daily Times* for August 12, 1911.

Featured in the sharpshooter section (the term sniper had yet to gain general acceptance) are: T. M. Blythe, "From the 50th Regiment," in the *Corning Journal* for August 18, 1864; Justice, Letters (Emory University); Kent (ed.), *Three Years*; Smith, *76th NY*; *Potsdam Courier Freeman*, February 18, 1925; Weld, *Diary and Letters*; *Bolivar Breeze*, May 28, 1903; Stevens, Berdan's *United States Sharpshooters*; Gallagher (ed.), *Fighting for the Confederacy*; a diary entry from New Yorker Richard Treat that appeared in the *Naples Record* for June 3, 1927; and Private Parker's letter which was published in the July 15, 1864 edition of the *Oswego Commercial Advertiser*.

E. T. Peters' account of the picket incident involving the two New York lieutenants appeared in the September 9, 1864, issue of the *Philadelphia Inquirer.*

Deserters and executions at Petersburg were followed through the accounts in History of *3rd PA Cavalry*; Roe, *9th NY*; Lockley, "Letters"; Hopkins, *7th RI*; Elisha P. Comstock, "Soldier's Letter" by M. L. McHenry in December 2, 1864 edition of *Star of the North;* "Extract from an Army Letter" in the *Huntington Long-Islander* for February 24, 1865; "Army Correspondence," in the March 9, 1865, issue of the *Watkins Express*; "Some Notable Executions," in the *National Tribune* for February 17, 1916; Pope, Diary; and Gould, *Story of the 48th.*

Comments about camp life, supply transportation, and entertainment were derived from material in Kirk, *Heavy Guns*; Daniel, *Richmond Howitzers*; Story *of 21st CT;* Agassiz, ed., *Meade's Headquarters*; Isaiah Simpson, "Campaigning with the 1st Maine H.A.," in the *National Tribune* for September 15, 1927; Miller, *Drum Taps*; Vaill, *2nd CT*; Meyers, *Ten Years*; Porter, *Campaigning*; and Graham, *Papers, 1861—1864.*

Christmas Day events noted came from Wagstaff (ed.), *James A. Graham Papers*; Thompson, *Thirteenth Regiment of New Hampshire Volunteer Infantry*; the *New York Herald* for January 2, 1865; Robert D. Graham, "Fifth-Sixth [NC] Regiment," in Walter Clark, *Histories*; and the *Philadelphia Inquirer* for December 29, 1864.

Expressions of Confederate morale in the waning weeks of the Petersburg siege came from Battle, *Forget-me-nots*; Chamberlayne, *Ham Chamberlayne*; and Douglas, *I Rode with Stonewall.*

Two articles that were especially helpful in the preparation of this chapter were Sylvester, "The U.S. Military Railroad and the Siege of Petersburg," and Savas, "Last Clash of the Ironclads."

Chapter 15: "Proper subjects for the hangman"

With their mix of political intrigue and military action, the various moves surrounding the Hampton Roads Peace Conference seemed to me like a modern thriller. Background material on the conference came from E. Smith, *Francis Preston Blair*; Johnson, "Lincoln's Solution to the Problem of Peace Terms, 1864—1865"; McElroy, *Jefferson Davis*; Foote, *The Civil War*; Hendrick, *Statesmen of the Lost Cause*; Nevins, *The War for the Union*, Volume IV; and Jones, *Rebel War Clerk.*

The account of events immediately prior to the conference was derived from Houston, *32nd ME*; History *of 35th MA*; Freeman, *Letters*; Porter, *Campaigning*; and Bates, *Lincoln in the Telegraph Office.* Also helpful were the February 1 and 3, 1865, issues of the *New York Times* and event reconstructions developed in McFeely, *Grant*, and Westwood, "The Singing Wire Conspiracy."

All three Confederate participants left accounts of the conference. Campbell's "Memo on Hampton Roads Conference" is at Chapel Hill, Hunter's "The Peace

Commission of 1865" was published in the *Southern Historical Society Papers*, Vol. 3, and Stephens's report is in Vol. 2 of his *Constitutional View of the War Between the States*. Both Lincoln and Seward left public accounts, which can be found in the *Official Records*.

The military review for Pegram's young bride is recounted in Douglas, *I Rode with Stonewall*.

Union cavalry accounts for Second Hatcher's Run were Preston, *10th NY Cavalry*; Miers, ed., *Ride to War*; and Tobie, *1st ME Cavalry*. Also helpful was Starr's *Union Cavalry*.

The Union story from the infantry side was told by Woodward, *198th PA*; *Baldwinsville Messenger*, November 29, 1945; McBride, *In the Ranks*; Menge, ed., *Notebook of Chisholm*; Marbaker, *11th NJ*; Robertson, ed., *Letters of General McAllister*; J. Smith, *Corn Exchange Regiment*; Haley, *Rebel Yell*; Hall, *97th NY*; Curtis, *24th MI*; Vautier, *88th PA*; Haines, *15th NJ*; John Ripley Adams, *Memorial and Letters*; Taylor, *Warren*; Tyler, *Recollections*; Kreutzer, *Notes*; Meade, *Life and Letters*; Livermore, *Days and Events*; Page, *14th CT*; Chamberlin, *150th Regiment*; Chase, Memoir; Stross, Letters; and Cuffel, *Durrell's Battery*. Additionally helpful were the February 12 and 13, 1865, issues of the *New York Herald*. The quotation from the New York artilleryman (signing himself "G. B.") came from a letter he wrote to the February 17, 1865, edition of the *Rochester Daily Union and Advertiser*.

Materials consulted on the Southern side were Graham, Papers, 1861-1864; Clark, *Histories*; Sloan, *Reminiscences*; Nichols, *Soldier's Story*; Buck, *With Old Confeds*; Herbert, "History of 8th AL"; Phillips, Journal and Diary; Sorrel, *Recollections*; Stewart, *A Pair of Blankets*; Pollard, *Memoirs and Sketches*; Stott, Diary; Day, *49th NC*; D. Johnston, *Story of a Confederate Boy*; Dowdey and Manarin, eds., *Wartime Papers*; Cooke, *Life of Lee*; Polley, Hood's *Texas Brigade*; Goldsborough, *MD Line*; Cooke, Diary; Forney, Letter of February 9, 1865; Thomas T. Roche, "Fighting for Petersburg," from the *Philadelphia Weekly Times* for May 5, 1883; and the diary of an unknown Confederate soldier in the Paris Papers at Chapel Hill.

Chapter 16: "The tremendous possibility"

My account of the midnight march of the North and South Carolinians into Petersburg was based on details in Andrews, *23rd SC*; Day, *49th NC*; Chambers, *Diary*; and Stevens, *Captain Bill*; as well as in Clark's *Histories*. Also helpful was T. Jones's "Last Days of the Army of Northern Virginia."

Union picket accounts of this night came from John C. Hardy, "The Final Effort —Last Assault of the Confederates at Petersburg," and Francis Laverty, "The Fight at Fort Stedman," in the *National Tribune* for September 20, 1923.

Gordon's story of the genesis and execution of the Stedman operation comes from two sources: a letter published in Davis, *Rise and Fall of the Confederate Government*, and the account in Gordon's own *Reminiscences*. Also of value was Freeman's *R. E. Lee*.

For communications and episodes relating to Lincoln's visit to City Point at this time, Pfanz's *Abraham Lincoln at City Point* is highly recommended.

Two examinations of the Fort Stedman affair were particularly helpful. They are Steere, "A Study of Fort Stedman," and Hodgkins, "The Battle of Fort Stedman." Since *The Last Citadel* first appeared, William C. Wyrick wrote a study of this battle for *Blue & Gray Magazine* titled "Bursting of the Storm: Action at Petersburg, March 25, 1865."

The order and composition of the Confederate units taking part in the Fort Stedman assault remains a subject of controversy. The unpublished diary of Bushrod Johnson (in the National Archives) clearly places the brigades of Ransom and Wallace in the second wave. Cadmus Wilcox's unpublished after-action report (in the Virginia Historical Society) states that two of his brigades were in support but not used. Of Gordon's corps, I was able to find accounts that suggested the following participation: in Grimes's (sometimes listed as Rodes's) Division, Grimes's Brigade and Cook's Brigade were definitely involved, with Battle's Brigade possibly and Cox's Brigade likely not participating; in Walker's (sometimes listed as Early's) Division, Pegram's Brigade, Johnston's Brigade, and Lewis's Brigade all took part; and in Evans's Division, Evans's Brigade, Terry's Brigade, and York's Brigade were all involved. In my reconstruction, all of Gordon's corps went across in the first "wave" (consisting of a storming party followed by a special-mission group followed by an infantry division), and Bushrod Johnson's two brigades (which suffered nearly a thousand casualties) went over in the second "wave." It is worth noting that despite Gordon's often-quoted statements about the non-arrival of Pickett's Division, he did not call upon the two brigades of Wilcox's that were on hand for just such a reason.

Confederate accounts of the assault used in my reconstruction were (in addition to those cited above) Walker, "Gordon's Assault on Fort Stedman"; Thomas, *Doles-Cook Brigade*; Funkhouser, "Fort Steadman — So Near and Yet So Far"; London, Letter of March 25, 1865; Devereux, "From Petersburg to Appomattox"; Brady, Letters; the letters of Dr. Claiborne; Robert E. Lee, Jr., *My Father, General Lee*; Douglas, *I Rode with Stonewall*; and G. Nash Morton, "A Johnny Reb at Petersburg," in the *National Tribune* for December 21, 1922. Secondary works of value were Jones, *Lee's Tigers*; Driver, *52nd VA*; and Iobst, *Bloody Sixth*. The article "The Louisiana Troops in the Battle Near Petersburg," in the *Richmond Whig* for April 1, 1865, was also useful, as was the *Petersburg Express* account reprinted in the *Whig* edition of March 28, and the report of "A. T." which was printed in the *Richmond Dispatch* for March 27, 1865.

Union accounts came from the *Official Records* and from Anderson, *57th MA*; Sidney Dobbins, "An Accurate Account of the Capture of Fort Stedman," from the June 10, 1916 edition of the *Utica Saturday Globe;* Henry Purcell, "Sterlingville Boy at Fort Stedman," from the April 18, 1915 issue of the *Waterville Daily Times;* a letter from Curtis F. Sheldon printed in the April 13, 1865, edition of the *Mexico* (New York) *Independent*; Hartranft, "Recapture of Fort Stedman," and Kilmer, "Gordon's Attack at

Fort Stedman" (both in Johnson and Buel, eds., *Battles and Leaders*); Huyette, *Reminiscences*; and Agassiz, ed., *Meade's Headquarters*. Helpful as well were the reporter accounts in the *Philadelphia Inquirer* for March 28, 1865. A secondary source that was helpful was Stern, *End to Valor*.

Also of great value were the following articles and letters published in the postwar newspaper the *National Tribune*: William Clowminger, "History of the 14th N.Y.H.A." (March 10, 1904); W. C. Beck, "Fort Steadman" (September 24, 1885); Philip Crowl, "At Fort Stedman" (February 23, 1913); Miles C. Huyette, "Fight at Fort Stedman" (February 29,1912); I. J. Jamison, "Fort Stedman" (September 26, 1912); W. B. Reynolds, "Raw Keystone Boys Took Fort Stedman" (June 2, 1904); J. L. Pounds, "Fort Steadman" (September 16, 1909); Julius E. Henderson, "Fort Stedman" (February 12, 1920); "Dad," "The Charge at Fort Stedman" (October 6, 1910); and F. M. Smith, "Recapture of Fort Stedman" (March 25, 1920).

Chapter 17: "I have ordered a general assault along the lines"

An excellent source for the fighting at Quaker Road (March 29), Dinwiddie Court House (March 31), White Oak Road (March 31), and Five Forks (April 1) is *Battle of Five Forks* by Bearss and Calkins. Porter's "preface" came from his *Campaigning*.

For the Fort Mahone section, the sources used (in addition to the Official Records) were:

Union: Jackman, *6th NH;* Beales, "In a Charge near Fort Hell, Petersburg"; Eden, *Sword and Flag;* "Cooper's Battery Before Petersburg"; Gould, *Story of the 48th;* Huyette, *Reminiscences*; Foster, *NJ; History of 5th MA Battery;* and Hopkins, *7th RI*. Also valuable were accounts found in the postwar newspapers, the *National Tribune* (B. S. Philbrick, "Fort Mahone" [September 13, 1906]; William H. Thompson, "Fort Mahone" [October 23, 1884]; Jack Crawford, "Fort Mahone" [July 7, 1887]; Right General Guide, "The Mine Explosion" [March 10, 1892]; and G. H. Holden, "Fort Mahone" [October 20, 1887]) and the *Philadelphia Weekly Press* (John Hartranft, "The Third Division of the Ninth Corps in the Assault of Petersburg, April 2, 1865" [September 15,1886]). An April 3 letter from a cannoneer named "J. R. C." describing the action can be found in the April 18, 1865, edition of the *Batavia Republican Advocate*. Additionally helpful were the accounts published in the *New York Herald* and the *New York Times* on April 5, 1865.

Confederate: Gordon, Report of Actions (Lee Headquarters Papers) and his later *Reminiscences*; Grimes, *Extracts of Letters;* Clark, *Histories;* Devereux, "From Petersburg to Appomattox"; and Bahnson, *Last Days of the War*.

For the Sixth Corps assault on the Petersburg lines, I was greatly helped by a study prepared by the indefatigable National Parks chief historian, Ed Bearss, titled "The VI Corps Scores a Breakthrough, April 2, 1865" (at the Petersburg Battlefield Park). Since this book was first published historian A. Wilson Greene has written a fine full-length study of this phase of the day's fighting titled *Breaking the Backbone of the Rebellion: The Final Battles of the Petersburg Campaign*. He managed to condense it for an issue of *Blue & Gray Magazine* in a piece titled "April 2, 1865, Day of Decision at Petersburg."

Other accounts consulted were:

Union: Stevens, "Storming of the Lines of Petersburg by the Sixth Corps"; Anson, "Assault on the Lines of Petersburg, April 2"; Mark, *Red, White, and Blue Badge*; Vaill, *2nd CT;* Keifer, *Slavery and Four Years of War*; Best, *121st NY*; Bowen, *37th MA*; Rhodes, *All for the Union*; Hyde, *Following the Greek Cross*; Abbott, *Personal Recollections*; Haines, *15th NJ*; Terrill, *14th NJ*; and Westbrook, *49th PA*. Also valuable were the following accounts published in the postwar newspaper the *National Tribune*: C. F. Barnes, "Petersburg" (July 27, 1883); George Flagg, "Marching to Appomattox" (May 30, 1918); John R. King, "Sixth Corps at Petersburg" (April 15, 1920); G. M. Eichelberger, "Who Took My Flag?" (December 22, 1910); William W. Perry, "At Petersburg" (August 20, 1891); and E. S. Norvell, "Petersburg" (June 11, 1891).

Confederate: Clark, *Histories*; Hassler, *A. P. Hill*; Robertson, *General A. P. Hill*; Dowdey, *Lee;* Longstreet, *Manassas to Appomattox*; Love, *Prairie Guards*; Freeman, *R. E. Lee*; Wilcox, Report of Actions (Lee Headquarters Papers); and Poague, *Gunner with Stonewall*. I also drew upon the following accounts of A. P. Hill's death published in the Southern Historical Society Papers: G. W. Tucker, "Death of Lieutenant General A. P. Hill" (Volume 11); and James P. Matthews, "How General A. P. Hill Met His Fate" (Volume 27).

A useful account of the Fort Gregg affair is Skoch's "The Last Ditch."

Other accounts consulted were:

Union: Gibbon, *Personal Recollections*; Egan, *Flying, Gray-Haired Yank*; Clark, *39th IL*; Dalzell, *Private Dalzell*; Trumbull, *War Memories*; Stowits, *100th NY*; Maxfield, *Roster and Statistical*; and Simon, ed., *Papers of Grant*, Vol. 14. From the *National Tribune* came Charles W. Ware, "Fort Gregg Again!" (February 19, 1891); Michael Dunn, "Fort Gregg Again" (June 16, 1891), William Bennett, "Fort Gregg" (May 12, 1904); F. H. Patton, "Fort Gregg Again" (March 3, 1892); and Daniel Maxwell, "Also at Fort Gregg" (November 14, 1912).

Confederate: Harris, *Movements of the Confederate Army*; Sloan, "North Carolina in the War Between the States"; Taylor, *General Lee*; Atkinson, "Statement"; Pipes, "First Twenty-three Years"; and McClendon, *Recollections*. Also useful were accounts in the postwar newspapers the *National Tribune* (Frank H. Foote, "Front of Petersburg" [May 1, 1890]) and the *Philadelphia Weekly Times* (Thomas Roche, "Fighting for Petersburg" [May 5, 1883]). Fort Gregg became the subject of quite a lot of ink in the pages of the postwar *Southern Historical Society Papers*. Included were James Lane, "Defence of Fort Gregg" (in Vol. 3); Cadmus Wilcox, "Defence of Batteries Gregg and Whitworth, and the Evacuation of Petersburg" (in Vol. 4); Nathaniel Harris, "Battery Gregg" (in Vol. 8); and A. K. Jones, "The Battle of Fort Gregg" (in Vol. 31).

For Sutherland Station, the last organized combat occurring on April 2 at Petersburg, I used:

Union: Humphreys, *Virginia Campaign*; Miles, Report of Actions (*Official Records*, Vol. 46, No. 1) and *Serving the Republic*; Kirk, *Heavy Guns*; Stewart, *140th PA*; Simons, *125th NY*; Hanifen, *Battery B. 1st NJ Artillery*; and Haley, *Rebel Yell*. Helpful as well was a short piece appearing in the April 14, 1880, edition of the *Geneva Courier*.

Confederate: Clark, *Histories*; Caldwell, *South Carolinians*; Sloan, *Reminiscences*; Dunlop, *Lee's Sharpshooters*; and Henry Heth, Report of Actions, April 1-9, 1865; John N. Cooke, Report of Actions, April 1-9, 1865; and William MacRae, Report of Actions, April 1-9, 1865 (all in Lee Headquarters Papers).

Chapter 18: "My kitchen is full of soldiers"

The Confederate evacuation of Petersburg is drawn from these accounts: Taylor, *General Lee*; Wall, *Pee Dee Guards*; Clark, *Histories;* Bone, Reminiscences; Bradwell, "Fort Steadman and Subsequent Events"; Bahnson, *Last Days of the War*; Gorman, *Lee's Last Campaign;* and Douglas, *I Rode with Stonewall.*

For civilian accounts, I turned to Banister, "Incidents of the Life of a Civil War Child"; the W. S. Simpson Papers; Collier, "War Recollections"; Morrison, Memoirs; and Pryor, *Reminiscences*. The observation by Charles Clark comes from a letter he wrote to Lincoln biographer Ida Tarbell and is part of her papers at Allegheny College.

The stories of the Union troops in the early-morning hours of April 3 came from Parker, *51st PA*; Best, *121st NY*; Roemer, *Reminiscences*; Bowen, *37th MA*; Rhodes, "Second Rhode Island Volunteers at the Siege of Petersburg"; Agassiz, ed., *Meade's Headquarters*; Grant, *Personal Memoirs*; Porter, *Campaigning*; Albert, *45th PA*; Hopkins, *7th RI*; and Lane, *Soldier's Diary*. Also useful was William McClelland's article "A Brave Battery" in the June 13, 1883, issue of the *Philadelphia Weekly Times*.

An excellent study of Lincoln's Petersburg visit can be found in Donald Pfanz's *Abraham Lincoln at City Point*. In research recently undertaken for a book about Lincoln's visit I came to the conclusion that the often quoted recollections by William H. Crook are either pure fiction or lifted from conversations with eye-witnesses who were present. The evidence I've seen indicates that the earliest he might have been at City Point was April 5, so I have either expunged quotations I originally used in this chapter or assigned them to someone else. I also replaced Crook in the Lincoln party with the President's military aide, who certainly was present.

Newspapers of the period consulted were the *New York Times* for April 6 and 7, 1865, and the *New York Herald* for April 5, 6 and 7. Information about the *Petersburg Express* came from an article in the *Watkins Express* for September 1, 1904.

Also of great value were the following articles and letters published in the postwar newspaper the *National Tribune*: J. L. Pounds, "The Fall of Petersburg" (January 20, 1910); William T. Wixcey, "First Flag in Petersburg" (July 4, 1907); J. E. Henderson, "Entering Petersburg" (August 10, 1911); George A. Beck, "The Occupation of Petersburg" (December 23, 1886); J. H. Hoffman, "Petersburg" (March 3, 1887); Levi Huntley, "The 37th Mass. First in Petersburg" (July 28, 1887); Alonzo P. Lenox, "Lincoln at City Point" (February 10, 1910); Jacob Burch, "Lincoln at City Point" (October 23, 1890); and Hiram Oldboyd, "The Union Colors at Petersburg" (November 11, 1886).

Chapter 19: "I hoped to capture them soon"

The final scenes in Petersburg were drawn from Grant, *Personal Memoirs*; Pryor, *Reminiscences*; the *New York Times* for April 9, 1865; the minutes of the Petersburg Common Council; and the reminiscence of a soldier in the 6th New York Heavy Artillery, printed in the December 22, 1910, edition of the *National Tribune*.

The comment by the North Carolina soldier about Petersburg's story never being written comes from Clark, *Histories*.

The quotes about the army's heart being sickened within it and Grant's infinite resources are from Ford, ed., *Cycle of Adams Letters*, while the anecdote of June 18 comes from Morgan, comp., *Narrative*. Edward Crapsey's assessment appeared in the October 31, 1864 issue of the *Philadelphia Inquirer*. Beauregard's praise is sung in Younger, ed., *Inside Confederate Government*.

Union observations on the importance of Petersburg's railroads are made in Brett, *My Dear Wife*; and Clark, Diary.

Reflections upon Grant's changing tactics are derived from Porter, *Campaigning*; and Alexander, *Fighting for the Confederacy*. For the careful calculations of Lee's strength at the beginning of the Appomattox Campaign, I am indebted to Chris Calkins, who set down the figures in his study *Final Bivouac*.

Concerning the quality of new recruits, I consulted Cogswell, *11th NH*; Clark, *39th IL*; Balfour, *13th VA Cavalry*; and Figg, *Where Men Only*.

On matters of Confederate morale, I used Stillwell, Letters; Rees/Reese, Letters; Claiborne, Letters; the York Family Papers; and Walkup, Letters.

The changing Union strategic outlook is reflected in comments found in Miles, *Serving*; Badeau, *Military Memoirs*; and Simon, ed., *Papers of Grant*.

Lee's comments were found in Vandiver, *Ploughshares*; and Catton, *Grant*. His 1868 letter is in the collection of the Virginia Historical Society, as is William Platt's letter of 1865.

The reminiscence of Adolphe de Chambrun comes from an article by him in the January 1893 issue of *Scribner's Magazine*, titled "Personal Recollections of Mr. Lincoln."

Note on the Organization of Forces

This table of organization is designed to assist readers in becoming oriented to the units and leaders described in the text. For reasons of space, the table does not go below brigade level. The double-column layout reflects the major reorganization of forces at Petersburg that took place on December 3, 1864, when the integrated Tenth and Eighteenth Corps became the all-white Twenty-fourth Corps and the all-black (officers excepted) Twenty-fifth Corps.

The names following each unit name indicate the various successors to that command over the time span. Names enclosed in brackets ([]) are interim replacements, while those without brackets represent longer-term appointments. On those occasions when an officer commanding a unit was temporarily incapacitated or away on leave, his temporary replacement is noted but his eventual return to the unit is not. Readers should therefore consider the name lists to be roughly chronological but not absolutely so.

The rank preceding an officer's name is the highest he achieved while commanding that unit in the time-period. Promotions that followed reassignment to other outfits are reflected within those other unit lists.

Provisional-force regroupings and temporary command assignments for special operations (such as the Confederate battle groups created for the August fighting around the Weldon Railroad) are not shown in this table.

Organization of Forces
(1864-1865)

UNION

LT. GEN. ULYSSES S. GRANT
(Commanding U.S. Armies in the Field)

The Army of the Potomac

Maj. Gen. George Gordon Meade
Provost Guard: Brig. Gen. Marsena R. Patrick
Engineer Brigade: Brig. Gen. Henry W. Benham
Artillery: Brig. Gen. Henry J. Hunt

Second Army Corps

Maj. Gen. Winfield S. Hancock
[Maj. Gen. David B. Birney]
Maj. Gen. Andrew A. Humphreys

Maj. Gen. Andrew A. Humphreys

1st Div.: Brig. Gen. Francis C. Barlow
Brig. Gen. Nelson A. Miles

Bvt. Maj. Gen. Nelson A. Miles

1st Brig.: Brig. Gen. Nelson A. Miles
[Col. James C. Lynch]
Lt. Col. H. P. Rugg
Col. William Wilson

Bvt. Brig. Gen. George N. Macy
Col. George W. Scott

Consolidated Brig.[1]:
[Col. Clinton D. MacDougall]
[Col. Levin Crandell]
[Lt. Col. James E. McGee]
[Capt. Nelson Penfield]
[Lt. Col. William Wilson]

2nd Brig.: Col. Patrick Kelly

Col. Robert Nugent

---

1 Consisting of the 2nd and 3rd brigades, in operation June 27-November 1, 1864.

3rd Brig.: Brig. Gen. Thomas A. Smyth
Col. Clinton MacDougall

Col. Clinton MacDougall
Bvt. Brig. Gen. Henry J. Madill

4th Brig.: Col. James A. Beaver
[Lt. Col. John Hastings]
Col. John Fraser
Lt. Col. K. Oscar Broady
Lt. Col. William Glenny
Col. Saint Clair A. Mulholland

Lt. Col. William Glenny
Gen. John Ramsey

2nd Div.: Maj. Gen. John Gibbon
[Brig. Gen. Thomas W. Egan]
[Brig. Gen. William Hays]

Maj. Gen. John Gibbon
Brig. Gen. Thomas A. Smyth

1st Brig.: Brig. Gen. Byron R. Pierce
[Maj. William F. Smith]
Lt. Col. Francis E. Pierce
Col. George N. Macy
Brig. Gen. Thomas W. Egan

Col. James Willett
Col. William A. Olmsted

2nd Brig.: Col. John Fraser
Col. James M. Willett
[Maj. Timothy O'Brien]
Col. Mathew Murphy

Col. Mathew Murphy
Col. James P. McIvor

3rd Brig.: Brig. Gen. Thomas A. Smyth[2]
[Lt. Col. Henry A. Cook]
[Lt. Col. Samuel A. Moore]
[Lt. Col. Francis E. Pierce]

Brig. Gen. Thomas A. Smyth
[Lt. Col. Francis E. Pierce]
[Col. Daniel Woodall]

4th Brig.[3]: Col. John Ramsey
[Col. James P. Ivor]
Col. William Blaisdell

3rd Div.: Maj. Gen. David B. Birney
Brig. Gen. Gershom Mott

Brig. Gen. Gershom Mott

2   Promoted from colonel as of October 1, 1864.

3   June 15-26, changed to 2nd Brigade.

1st Brig.: Col. Thomas W. Egan   Brig. Gen. Regis de Trobriand
[Col. Henry J. Madill]   [Bvt. Brig. Gen. George W. West]
Brig. Gen. Regis de Trobriand

2nd Brig.: Col. Thomas R. Tannatt   Brig. Gen. Byron R. Pierce
[Col. Daniel Chaplin]   [Bvt. Brig. Gen. George W. West]
[Maj. Levi B. Duff]
[Maj. John Willian]
Col. Robert McAllister
Brig. Gen. Byron R. Pierce
[Col. Henry J. Madill]
[Col. Calvin A. Craig]
[Col. John Pulford]

3rd Brig.: Brig. Gen. Gershom Mott   Bvt. Brig. Gen. John Ramsey
Col. Robert McAllister   Bvt. Brig. Gen. Robert McAllister

4th Brig.: Col. William R. Brewster[4]

Artillery Brig.: Col. John C. Tidball   Bvt. Lt. Col. John G. Hazard
Maj. John G. Hazard   [Maj. Robert H. Fitzhugh]
[Capt. A. Judson Clark]

Fifth Army Corps

Maj. Gen. Gouverneur K. Warren   Maj. Gen. Gouverneur K. Warren
[Brig. Gen. Samuel W. Crawford]   [Brig. Gen. Joseph J. Bartlett]
Bvt. Maj. Gen. Charles Griffin

1st Div.: Brig. Gen. Charles Griffin   Brig. Gen. Charles Griffin
[Brig. Gen. Joseph J. Bartlett]   [Bvt. Maj. Gen. Joseph J. Bartlett]

1st Brig.: Col. Joshua L. Chamberlain   Bvt. Brig. Gen. Horatio Sickel
Col. William S. Tilton   Brig. Gen. Joshua L. Chamberlain
[Lt. Col. William A. Throop]
Col. Horatio Sickel

2nd Brig.: Col. Jacob B. Sweitzer   Col. Allen L. Burr
Col. Edgar M. Gregory   Bvt. Brig. Gen. Edgar M. Gregory

---

4   Discontinued July 5, 1864.

3rd Brig.: Brig. Gen. Joseph J. Bartlett　　Bvt. Maj. Gen. Joseph J. Bartlett
[Col. Norval E. Welch]　　Bvt. Brig. Gen. Alfred L. Pearson
[Col. James Gwyn]

2nd Div.: Brig. Gen. Romeyn B. Ayres　　Bvt. Maj. Gen. Romeyn B.Ayres
[Bvt. Brig. Gen. James Gwyn]

1st Brig.: [Col. Edgar M. Gregory]　　Bvt. Brig. Gen. Frederick Winthrop
Brig. Gen. Joseph Hayes　　[Col. James Grindlay]
[Col. Frederick Winthrop]　　Brig. Gen. Joseph Hayes
[Col. Charles P. Stone]
[Lt. Col. Elwell S. Otis]
[Maj. James Grindlay]

2nd Brig.: Col. Nathan Dushane　　Col. Richard N. Bowerman
[Col. Samuel A. Graham]　　Bvt. Brig. Gen. Andrew W. Denison
[Col. Andrew W. Denison]
[Col. David L. Stanton]

3rd Brig.: [Col. J. Howard Kitching]　　Bvt. Brig. Gen. James Gwyn
[Lt. Col. Michael Wiedrich]　　[Col. William Sergeant]
[Col. Arthur H. Grimshaw]

3rd Div.: Brig. Gen. Samuel W. Crawford　　Bvt. Maj. Gen. Samuel W. Crawford
Brig. Gen. Henry Baxter

1st Brig.: [Col. Peter Lyle]　　Brig. Gen. Edward S. Bragg
Brig. Gen. Edward S. Bragg　　Bvt. Brig. Gen. Henry A. Morrow
[Col. Thomas F. McCoy]
[Col. John A. Kellogg]

2nd Brig.: [Col. J. William Hofmann]　　Brig. Gen. Henry Baxter
[Col. James I. Bates]
Brig. Gen. Henry Baxter
[Col. Charles Wheelock]
[Col. Richard Coulter]

3rd Brig.: Col. James Carle　　Bvt. Brig. Gen. J. William Hofmann
Col. William R. Hartshorne　　Bvt. Brig. Gen. Henry A.Morrow
[Col. J. William Hofmann]
Bvt. Brig. Gen. Richard Coulter

4th Div.: Brig. Gen. Lysander Cutler[5]
1st Brig.: Brig. Gen. Edward S. Bragg
2nd Brig.: Col. J. William Hofmann

Artillery Brig.: Col. Charles S. Wainwright   Bvt. Brig. Gen. Charles S. Wainwright

Sixth Army Corps[6]

Maj. Gen. Horatio G. Wright

1st Div.: Brig. Gen. David A. Russell   Bvt. Maj. Gen. Frank Wheaton

1st Brig.: Col. William H. Penrose   Bvt. Brig. Gen. William H. Penrose
[Capt. Baldwin Hufty]

2nd Brig.: Brig. Gen. Emory Upton   Brig. Gen. Ranald MacKenzie
Bvt. Brig. Gen. Joseph E. Hamblin

3rd Brig.: Lt. Col. Gideon Clark   [Col. Thomas S. Allen]
Col. Oliver Edwards   Col. Oliver Edwards

4th Brig.: Col. Nelson Cross[7]
Col. Joseph E. Hamblin

2nd Div.: Brig. Gen. Thomas H. Neill   Bvt. Maj. Gen. George W. Getty
[Brig. Gen. Frank Wheaton]   [Bvt. Maj. Gen. Lewis A. Grant]
Brig. Gen. George W. Getty

1st Brig.: Brig. Gen. Frank Wheaton   Col. James M. Warner
[Col. John F. Ballier]   [Col. George P. Foster]
[Lt. Col. Charles Hunsoon]

3rd Brig.: Col. Daniel D. Bidwell   Col. Thomas W. Hyde

4th Brig.: Col. Oliver Edwards[8]

---

5   Consolidated with 3rd Division in September.

6   On detached service in the Shenandoah Valley from mid-July to early December. Command changes occurring in that period are not tracked here.

7   Discontinued July 6, 1864.

8   Discontinued July 6, 1864.

3rd Div.: Brig. Gen. James B. Ricketts   Brig. Gen. Truman Seymour

1st Brig.: Col. William S. Truex   Col. William S. Truex

2nd Brig.: Col. Benjamin F. Smith   [Col. Benjamin F. Smith]
Bvt. Brig. Gen. J. Warren Keifer

Artillery Brig.: Col. Charles H Tompkins   Bvt. Col. Andrew Cowan

Ninth Army Corps

Maj. Gen. Ambrose E. Burnside   Maj. Gen. John G. Parke
Maj. Gen. John G. Parke   [Bvt. Maj. Gen. Orlando B. Willcox]

1st Div.: Brig. Gen. James H. Ledlie   Bvt. Maj. Gen. Orlando B. Willcox
Brig. Gen. Julius White
Brig. Gen. Orlando B. Willcox

1st Brig.: Col. Jacob P. Gould   Bvt. Gen. Napoleon B. McLaughlen
Brig. Gen. William F. Bartlett   Col. Samuel Harriman
Lt. Col. Joseph H. Barnes
Brig. Gen. John F. Hartranft

2nd Brig.: Col. Ebenezer W. Peirce   Col. Byron M. Cutcheon
[Lt. Col. Joseph H. Barnes]   Bvt. Col. Ralph Ely
Col. Elisha G. Marshall
Lt. Col. Gilbert P. Robinson
Col. Byron M. Cutcheon

3rd Brig.: Col. Elisha G. Marshall   Bvt. Brig. Gen. Napoleon B. McLaughlen
[Lt. Col. Benjamin G. Barney]   Bvt. Col. Gilbert P. Robinson
Col. Napoleon B. McLaughlen

2nd Div.: Brig. Gen. Robert B. Potter   Bvt. Maj. Gen. Robert B. Potter
[Brig. Gen. Simon G. Griffin]

1st Brig.: Col. John I. Curtin   Bvt. Brig. Gen. John I. Curtin
[Lt. Col. Henry Pleasants]
[Col. William H. P. Steere]
Col. Zenas R. Bliss

2nd Brig.: Brig. Gen. Simon G. Griffin   [Col. Herbert B. Titus]
Brig. Gen. Simon G. Griffin

3rd Div.: Brig. Gen. Orlando B. Willcox   Bvt. Maj. Gen. John F. Hartranft
Brig. Gen. Edward Ferrero

1st Brig.: Brig. Gen. John F. Hartranft   Col. Charles W. Diven
Col. Ozora P. Stearns   Lt. Col. William H. H. McCall
[Col. Delevan Bates]
[Col. Alfred B. McCalmont]

2nd Brig.: Col. Benjamin C. Christ   Col. Joseph A. Mathews
[Col. William C. Raulston]
[Lt. Col. George W. Travers]
[Lt. Col. Walter C. Newberry]
Col. William Humphrey
Col. Henry G. Thomas

4th Div.: Brig. Gen. Edward Ferrero[9]   Independent Brig.:
[Brig. Gen. Julius White]   Bvt. Brig. Gen. Charles H. T. Collis

1st Brig.: Col. Joshua K. Sigfried

2nd Brig.: Col. Henry G. Thomas

Artillery Brig.: Lt. Col. J. Albert Monroe   Bvt. Brig. Gen. John C. Tidball

Cavalry Corps   Army of the Shenandoah

Maj. Gen. Philip H. Sheridan   Maj. Gen. Philip H. Sheridan
Maj. Gen. Wesley Merritt

1st Div.[10]: Brig. Gen. Alfred T. A. Torbert   Brig. Gen. Thomas C. Devin

1st Brig.: Brig. Gen. George A. Custer   Col. Peter Stagg

2nd Brig.: Col. Thomas Devin   Col. Charles L. Fitzhugh

Reserve Brig.: Brig. Gen. Wesley Merritt   Brig. Gen. Alfred Gibbs

---

9   Became the 3rd Division in November.

10 On detached service in the Shenandoah Valley from mid-July to late March. Command changes occurring in that period are not tracked here.

2nd Div.:[11] Brig. Gen. David McM. Gregg
[Brig. Gen. Henry E. Davies, Jr.]

Brig. Gen. David McM. Gregg
Maj. Gen. George Crook

1st Brig.: Brig. Gen. Henry E. Davies, Jr.
[Col. William Stedman]
[Lt. Col. Walter C. Newberry]

Brig. Gen. Henry E. Davies, Jr.
[Col. Hugh H. Janeway]

2nd Brig.: Col. J. Irvin Gregg
[Col. Michael Kerwin]
Col. Charles H. Smith

Col. J. Irvin Gregg

3rd Brig.:[12] Bvt. Brig. Gen. Charles H. Smith
[Col. Oliver B. Knowles]

Bvt. Brig. Gen. Charles H. Smith

3rd Div.[13]: Brig. Gen. James H. Wilson

Bvt. Maj. Gen. George A. Custer

1st Brig.: Col. John B. McIntosh

Col. Alexander C. M. Pennington

2nd Brig.: Col. George H. Chapman
[Col. John J. Coppinger]

Col. William Wells

3rd Brig.: Col. Henry Capehart

Artillery Brig.: Capt. James M. Robertson

The Army of the James

Maj. Gen. Benjamin F. Butler
Maj. Gen. Edward O. C. Ord

Maj. Gen. Benjamin F. Butler

Tenth Army Corps

Brig. Gen. Alfred H. Terry
Brig. Gen. William T. H. Brooks
Maj. Gen. David B. Birney
Bvt. Maj. Gen. Alfred H. Terry

Twenty-fourth Army Corps

Maj. Gen. Edward O. C. Ord
[Bvt. Maj. Gen. Alfred H. Terry]
Maj. Gen. John Gibbon

11 Part of the Army of the Potomac.

12 Organized October 24, 1864.

13 On detached service in the Shenandoah Valley from mid-July to late March. Command changes occurring in that period are not tracked here.

1st Div.: Brig. Gen. Robert S. Foster
Brig. Gen. Alfred H. Terry
Brig. Gen. Adelbert Ames

Brig. Gen. Robert S. Foster

1st Brig.: Col. Joshua B. Howell
Col. Francis B. Pond
Col. Alvin C. Voris

Col. Thomas O. Osborn

2nd Brig.: Col. Joseph R. Hawley
Col. Joseph C. Abbott

Brig. Gen. Joseph R. Hawley

3rd Brig.: Col. Harris M. Plaisted
Brig. Gen. Robert S. Foster

Col. Harris M. Plaisted
Col. George B. Dandy

4th Brig.: Bvt. Brig. Gen. James Jourdan
Col. Harrison S. Fairchild

2nd Div.: Brig. Gen. Adelbert Ames
Brig. Gen. John W. Turner
Brig. Gen. Robert S. Foster

Independent Div.: Bvt. Maj. Gen.
Thomas M. Harris
Bvt. Maj. Gen. John W. Turner

1st Brig.: Col. N. Martin Curtis
Col. Rufus Daggett

Lt. Col. Thomas F. Wildes
Lt. Col. Andrew Potter

2nd Brig.: Col. William B. Barton
[Maj. Edward Eddy, Jr.]
Lt. Col. William B. Coan
Col. Galusha Pennypacker

Col. William B. Curtis

3rd Brig.: Col. Louis Bell
Col. Francis A. Osborn
[Maj. Ezra L. Walrath]
[Capt. Frank W. Parker]
[Capt. Robert J. Gray]

[Col. Milton Wells]
[Lt. Col. Moses S. Hall]
Brig. Gen. Thomas M. Harris

3rd Div.: Brig. Gen. Orris S. Ferry
Brig. Gen. William Birney
Brig. Gen. Joseph R. Hawley

Brig. Gen. Charles Devens

1st Brig.: Brig. Gen. Gilman Marston
Col. Alvin C. Voris
Col. James Shaw, Jr.

Lt. Col. John B. Raulston
Col. Edward M. Cullen
Col. Edward H. Ripley

2nd Brig.: Col. Samuel C. Armstrong
Col. Ulysses Doubleday
[Col. Elias Wright]

Col. Joseph H. Potter
Col. Michael T. Donohoe
Col. John E. Ward

3rd Brig.: [Col. Samuel H. Roberts]
Bvt. Brig. Gen. Guy V. Henry

Artillery Brig.: Lt. Col. Richard H. Jackson

Maj. Charles C. Abell

Eighteenth Army Corps

Twenty-fifty Army Corps

Maj. Gen. William F. Smith
[Brig. Gen. John H. Martindale]
Maj. Gen. Edward O. C. Ord
[Brig. Gen. Charles A. Heckman]
Bvt. Maj. Gen. Godfrey Weitzel

Maj. Gen. Godfrey Weitzel

1st Div.: Brig. Gen. George F. Stannard
[Col. Edgar M. Cullen]
Brig. Gen. James Jourdan
Brig. Gen. Hiram Burnham
Brig. Gen. Gilman Marston

Brig. Gen. Charles J. Paine
Brig. Gen. Edward A. Wild
Bvt. Maj. Gen. August V. Kautz

1st Brig.: Brig. Gen. Gilman Marston
Col. Edgar M. Cullen
Col. Aaron F. Stevens
Lt. Col. John B. Raulston

Bvt. Brig. Gen. Delevan Bates
Bvt. Brig. Gen. Alonzo G. Draper

2nd Brig.: Brig. Gen. Hiram Burnham
Col. Edgar M. Cullen
[Col. Michael T. Donohoe]
Russell

Col. John W. Ames
Brig. Gen. Edward A. Wild
Bvt. Brig. Gen. Charles S.

3rd Brig.: Col. Guy V. Henry
Col. Samuel H. Roberts
Col. Edgar M. Cullen
Lt. Col. Joab N. Patterson

Col. Elias Wright
Brig. Gen. Henry G. Thomas

2nd Div.: Brig. Gen. John H. Martindale
Brig. Gen. Adelbert Ames
Brig. Gen. Charles A. Heckman
Brig. Gen. George J. Stannard

Brig. Gen. William Birney
[Col. James Shaw, Jr.]

1st Brig.: Brig. Gen. George F. Stannard

Col. James Shaw, Jr.

Col. Alexander Piper   [Col. Orion A. Bartholomew]
Col. James Stewart, Jr.
[Lt. Col. William H. McNary]
Col. George M. Guion
2nd Brig.: Col. Griffin A. Stedman, Jr.   Col. Ulysses Doubleday
Col. Edward H. Ripley

3rd Brig.: [Col. Augustus A. Gibson]   Col. Henry C. Ward
Brig. Gen. Adelbert Ames   Col. William W. Woodward
Col. Harrison S. Fairchild
Col. Edward Martindale

3rd Div.: Brig. Gen. Edward W. Hincks   Brig. Gen. Edward A. Wild
[Col. John H. Holman]
Brig. Gen. Joseph B. Carr
[Bvt. Brig. Gen. Alonzo G. Draper]
Brig. Gen. Charles J. Paine

1st Brig.: Brig. Gen. Edward A. Wild   Bvt. Brig. Gen. Alonzo G. Draper
Col. John H. Holman
[Col. Jeptha Garrard]
[Lt. Col. Abial G. Chamberlain]

2nd Brig.: Col. Samuel A. Duncan   Col. Edward Martindale
Col. John W. Ames
Col. Alonzo G. Draper
[Lt. Col. Dexter E. Clapp]

3rd Brig.: Col. John W. Ames   Brig. Gen. Henry G. Thomas

Artillery Brig.: Col. Henry S. Burton   Capt. Loomis L. Langdon
Col. Alexander Piper   Lt. Col. Richard H. Jackson
Maj. George B. Cook

Cavalry Div.: Brig. Gen. August V. Kautz   Brig. Gen. August V. Kautz
Col. Robert M. West
Brig. Gen. Ranald S. Mackenzie

1st Brig.: Col. Simon H. Mix   Col. Simon H. Mix
Col. Robert M. West
[Col. George W. Lewis]

2nd Brig.: Col. Samuel P. Spear   Bvt. Brig. Gen. Samuel P. Spear
[Col. Andrew W. Evans]

3rd Brig.:[14] Col. Andrew W. Evans
[Col. Edwin V. Sumner, Jr.]

Nineteenth Army Corps[15]   **Bermuda Hundred Defensive Force**

Bvt. Maj. Gen. Edward Ferrero

1st Brig.: Brig. Gen. Henry W. Birge   Col. William Heine
Bvt. Brig. Gen. Gilbert H. McKibbin

2nd Brig.: Col. Edward L. Molineux   Lt. Col. G. de Peyster Arden
Col. George C. Kibbe

Provisional Brig.: Col. William M. McClure

CONFEDERATE

The Army of Northern Virginia

Gen. Robert E. Lee

First Army Corps

Lt. Gen. Richard H. Anderson   Lt. Gen. James Longstreet
Lt. Gen. James Longstreet

Kershaw's Div.: Maj. Gen. Joseph B Kershaw.   Maj. Gen. Joseph B.Kershaw

Kershaw's Brig.: Col. John W. Henagan   *Conner's Brig.*: Col. John D. Kennedy
Col. John D. Kennedy

Humphreys's Brig.:   Maj. G. B. Gerald
Brig. Gen. Benjamin G. Humphreys   Lt. Col. H. Fitzgerald
Maj. G. B. Gerald

Wofford's Brig.:   *Du Bose's Brig.*:
Brig. Gen. William T. Wofford   Brig. Gen. Dudley M. Du Bose
Col. C. C. Sanders

14 Discontinued in late March.

15 Attached to the Army of the James, July 21-31.

Bryan's Brig.: Col. James P. Simms
Brig. Gen. Goode Bryan
Col. James Dickey
Col. Peter McGlashan

Simms's Brig.: Brig. Gen. James P. Simms

Field's Div.: Maj. Gen. Charles W. Field
[Brig. Gen. Henry L. Benning]

Gregg's Brig.: Brig. Gen. John Gregg
Col. Frederick S. Bass

Col. Frederick S. Bass

Benning's Brig.: Col. Dudley M. Dubose
[Maj. Peter J. Shannon]

Brig. Gen. Henry L. Benning

Anderson's Brig.: Brig. Gen. George T. Anderson
Col. Francis H. Little
Col. Jack Brown

Law's Brig.: Col. William F. Perry
Col. Pinckney D. Bowles

Perry's Brig.: Brig. Gen. William F. Perry

Bratton's Brig.: Brig. Gen. John Bratton

Pickett's Div.: Maj. Gen. George E. Pickett

Terry's Brig.: Brig. Gen. William R. Terry
Maj. William W. Bentley

Hunton's Brig.: Brig. Gen. Eppa Hunton
Col. Henry Gantt
Maj. Michael P. Spessard

Barton's Brig.: Brig. Gen. Seth M. Barton
[Col. W. R. Aylett]
Brig. Gen. George H. Steuart

Steuart's Brig.: Brig. Gen. George H. Steuart

Corse's Brig.: Brig. Gen. Montgomery Corse
Col. Arthur Herbert

Provisional Brig.: Col. Edgar B. Montague
Artillery Brig.: Brig. Gen. Edward Porter Alexander

Second Army Corps

Lt. Gen. Jubal Early[16]   Maj. Gen. John B. Gordon

Gordon's Div.: Brig. Gen. Clement A. Evans

Evans's Brig.: Col. John H. Baker
Col. John H. Lowe

Terry's Brig.: Brig. Gen. William Terry
Col. Titus V. Williams

York's Brig.: Col. William R. Peck
Col. Eugene Waggaman

Grimes's Div.: Maj. Gen. Bryan Grimes

Battle's Brig.: Col. Charles Forsyth
Col. Samuel B. Pickens
Col. Edwin L. Hobson

Grimes's Brig.: Col. David G. Cowand
Col. John R. Winston

Cox's Brig.: Brig. Gen. William R. Cox

Cook's Brig.: Col. Edwin A. Nash
Col. William H. Peebles

Archer's Batln.: Lt. Col. Fletcher H. Archer

Early's Div.: Brig. Gen. John Pegram
Brig. Gen. James A. Walker

Johnston's Brig.: Brig. Gen. Robert D. Johnston
Col. John W. Lea

Lewis's Brig.: Brig. Gen. William G. Lewis
Capt. John Beard

---

16 On detached service in the Shenandoah Valley.

Walker's Brig.: Col. John S. Hoffman
Maj. Henry Kyd Douglas
Col. John G. Kasey

Artillery Brig.: Brig. Gen. Armistead L. Long

Third Army Corps

Lt. Gen. Ambrose P. Hill
[Maj. Gen. Henry Heth]

Heth's Div.: Maj. Gen. Henry Heth
Brig. Gen. John R. Cooke

MacRae's Brig.: Brig. Gen. William MacRae

Cooke's Brig.: Brig. Gen. John R. Cooke

Davis's Brig.: Brig. Gen. Joseph R. Davis
Col. Andrew M. Nelson

Archer's Brig.: Brig. Gen. James J. Archer   *McComb's Brig.*: Brig. Gen. William McComb

Walker's Brig.: Brig. Gen. Birkett D. Fry
Col. Robert M. Mayo

Wilcox's Div.: Maj. Gen. Cadmus M. Wilcox
[Brig. Gen. James Conner]

Lane's Brig.: Brig. Gen. James H. Lane
[Col. John D. Barry]
[Col. Robert Cowan]
[Col. William M. Barbour]
[Col. William H. A. Speer]

McGowan's Brig.: Brig. Gen. Samuel McGowan
[Lt. Col. Isaac F. Hunt]

Scales's Brig.: Brig. Gen. Alfred M. Scales
Col. Joseph H. Hyman
Col. William L. J. Lowrance

Thomas's Brig.: Brig. Gen. Edward L. Thomas
[Col. Thomas J. Simmons]

Mahone's Div.: Maj. Gen. William Mahone
[Brig. Gen. Joseph Finegan]

Mahone's Brig.: Col. David A. Weisiger
[Col. George T. Rogers]

Harris's Brig.: Brig. Gen. Nathaniel H. Harris
[Col. Joseph M. Jayne]

Finegan's Brig.: Brig. Gen. Joseph Finegan   Col. David Lang

Sanders's Brig.:   *Forney's Brig.*: Brig. Gen. William H. Forney
Brig. Gen. John C. C. Sanders
Col. J. Horace King
Col. William H. Forney

Wright's Brig.: Brig. Gen. Ambrose R. Wright   *Sorrel's Brig.*: Col. George E. Taylor
[Lt. Col. Matthew R. Hall]
Brig. Gen. Victor J. B. Girardey
Col. William Gibson
Brig. Gen. G. Moxley Sorrel

Artillery Brig.: Col. R. Lindsay Walker   Brig.: Brig. Gen. R. Lindsay Walker

Cavalry Corps

Maj. Gen. Wade Hampton   Maj. Gen. Fitzhugh Lee

Lee's Div.: Maj. Gen. Fitzhugh Lee   Brig. Gen. Thomas T. Munford
Maj. Gen. Fitzhugh Lee

Wickham's Brig.:   *Munford's Brig.*: Brig. Gen. Thomas T. Munford
Brig. Gen. Williams Wickham
Col William B. Wooldridge

Lomax's Brig.: .   *Payne's Brig.*: Brig. Gen. William H. Payne
Brig. Gen. Lunsford L. Lomax
Col. Reuben B. Boston

Butler's Div.: Maj. Gen. M. C. Butler   *Rosser's Div.*: Maj. Gen. Thomas L. Rosser

Dunovant's Brig.:Brig. Gen. James Dunovant   *Dearing's Brig.*: Brig. Gen. John Dearing
Col. Richard H. Dulany

Young's Brig.:
Brig. Gen. Pierce M. B. Young
Col. J. Fred Waring
Col. Gilbert J. Wright

McCausland's Brig.: Brig. Gen. John McCausland

Rosser's [Laurel] Brig.: Brig. Gen. Thomas L. Rosser
Col. Richard H. Dulany

W. H. F. Lee's Div.: Maj. Gen. William H. F. Lee

Barringer's Brig.: Brig. Gen. Rufus Barringer
Col. William H. Cheek

Chambliss's Brig.: Brig. Gen. John R. Chambliss
Col. J. Lucius Davis
Col. Richard L. T. Beale

Beale's Brig.: Capt. Samuel H. Burt

Dearing's Brig[17] Brig. Gen. James Dearing
Col. Joel R. Griffin

Roberts's Brig.: Brig. Gen. William P. Roberts

Horse Artillery: Maj. R. Preston Chew

Petersburg Defensive Force

Gen. P. G. T. Beauregard

Fourth Army Corps

Lt. Gen. Richard H. Anderson

Johnson's Div.: Maj. Gen. Bushrod R. Johnson

Gracie's Brig.:
Brig. Gen. Archibald Gracie, Jr.

Moody's Brig.: Brig. Gen. Young M. Moody

Elliott's Brig.:
Brig. Gen. Stephen Elliott
Col. Fitz William McMaster
Brig. Gen. William H. Wallace

Wallace's Brig.: Brig. Gen. William H. Wallace

Ransom's Brig.: Brig. Gen. Matthew W. Ransom
Col. Lee M. McAfee
Lt. Col. John L. Harris
[Col. Henry M. Rutledge]

17 Often operated as an Independent Brigade.

Wise's Brig.: Brig. Gen. Henry A. Wise   Col. John T. Goode
Col. Powhatan R. Page   Brig. Gen. Henry A. Wise
Col. John T. Goode

Hoke's Div.: Maj. Gen. Robert F. Hoke

Clingman's Brig.: Brig. Gen. Thomas L. Clingman
Col. Hector McKethan

Colquitt's Brig.: Brig. Gen. Alfred H. Colquitt

Martin's Brig.: Brig. Gen. James G. Martin
Col. Charles T. Zachry
Brig. Gen. William W. Kirkland

Hagood's Brig.: Brig. Gen. Johnson Hagood

Artillery Brig.: Col. Hilary P. Jones

Richmond Defensive Force

Gen. P. G. T. Beauregard   Lt. Gen. Richard S. Ewell
Brig. Gen. Henry A. Wise

G. W. C. Lee's Div.: Maj. Gen. G. W. Custis Lee

Walker's Brig.: Brig. Gen. James A. Walker   *Barton's Brig.*: Col. M. Lewis Clark
Brig. Gen. Henry H. Walker

Garnett's Brig.: Lt. Col. John J. Garnett   *Crutchfield's Brig.*: Col. Stapleton
Crutchfield

Independent Cavalry Brig.: Brig. Gen.
Martin W. Gary

Unattached Units

B. R. Johnson's Brig.: Col. John M. Hughs

Cavalry Brig.: Maj. Edward M. Boykin

Virginia Res.: Brig. Gen. Patrick I. Moore

Bibliography

Manuscripts

ALABAMA DEPARTMENT OF ARCHIVES AND HISTORY
  Crater Reminiscence by a soldier in the 11th Alabama, 1909.
  Coles, R. T. History of Fourth Regiment Alabama Volunteer Infantry, n.d. Stinson, Thomas Austin. War Reminiscences, n.d.

ALLEGHENY COLLEGE SPECIAL COLLECTIONS
  Ida Tarbell Papers: Charles Clark letter, April 28, 1898.

AUBURN UNIVERSITY
  Denson, Hugh. Letters and Diary, 1864-1865.
  Lane, James H. Papers, 1864-1865.
  Mason, Benjamin. Letters, 1864-1865.
  York Family. Papers: Diary, 1864.

CITY OF PETERSBURG
  Petersburg Common Council Meeting Minutes, 1864-1865.

CITY OF PETERSBURG: CENTRE HILL MANSION
  Archer, Fletcher. Letters, 1864.

CIVIL WAR MUSEUM AND LIBRARY, PHILADELPHIA
  Walker, Francis. Papers

COLLEGE OF WILLIAM AND MARY, WILLIAMSBURG, VIRGINIA: EARL GREGG
SWEM LIBRARY
  Campbell, Charles. Diary

DUKE UNIVERSITY
  Allen, C. Tacitus. Memoirs, n.d.

Bernard, John Gross. Letter, April 2, 1865.

Biddle, Samuel S. Letters, 1864.

Biggs, William. Letters, 1864.

Charles. Letters, 1864.

Ewell, Richard S. Letterbook, 1862-1865.

G.A.S. Letters, 1864.

Haderman, M. T. Letter, December 18, 1864.

Hampton, Caleb. Papers. Letters, 1864.

Haynes, Joseph N. Letters, 1864.

Leavenworth, A. J. Papers. "Journal of a Petersburg Civilian," 1864.

Love Family. Letters, 1864-1865.

McLeroy, S. J. Letter, July 3, 1864.

Moore, James Otis. Letters, 1864.

Penn, Green W. Letter, December 4, 1864.

Person, Presley Carter. Letters, 1864.

Russell, William. Diary, 1864.

Sill, Edward B. Letter, July 6, 1864.

Smith, William T. Letter, September 21, 1864.

Smithwick, Edgar. Letters, 1864.

Steedman, A. W. Letters, 1864-1865.

Taintor, Henry E. Letters, 1864.

Tuttle, Daniel. Letter, June 28, 1864.

Unidentified Confederate soldier. Letter, August 30, 1864.

Unidentified Confederate soldier. Letter, January 13, 1865.

Walkup, Samuel Hoey. Diary, 1865.

Welch, S. E. Letter, August 4, 1864.

Wingard, Simon P. Papers, 1864-1865.

Wright, Joseph. Letters, 1864-1865.

EAST CAROLINA UNIVERSITY

Bacon, Charles D. Diary, 1864.

Carlton, Cornelius Hart. Diary, 1864-1865.

Eberstein, William Henry. Memoir, n.d.

Hill, Jesse. Papers: Letter, February 25, 1865.

Jones, Abraham G. Letter, December 13, 1864.

Knowles, Francis W. Journal, n.d.

McMillen, F. M. Diary, 1865.

Rodman, William Blount. Letters, 1864-1865.

EMORY UNIVERSITY

Adams, W. H. Reminiscences of the Civil War, n.d.

Bennage, Enos. Diary, 1865.

Binion, Dorsey. Letter, August 10, 1864.

Craig, James C. Letter, January 1, 1865.

Everett, John A. Letters, 1864-1865.
Gourdin, Robert. Collection: Letters, 1864.
Justice, Benjamin Wesley. Letters, 1864-1865.
Keen-Armistead. Letters, 1864.
LaFayette, Jonathan. Diary, 1864-1865.
McFall, William. Letters, 1864.
Plummer, David. Letters, 1864.
Scarbrough, R. P. Letters, 1864-1865.
Shore, Augustine E. Letter, 1864.
Workman, Willie. Letters, 1864-1865.

FREDERICKSBURG-SPOTSYLVANIA NATIONAL BATTLEFIELD PARK
Corbin, Elbert. Diary, 1864.
Luttrell, Thomas J. Diary, 1864.
McConnell, John D. Recollections, 1918.
Morton, N. G. Letters, 1864-1865.
Pattison, Alexander. Diary, 1864.
Shaner, Joe. Letter, August 2, 1864.
Snyder, T. A. "Recollections of Four Years with the Union Cavalry," 1927.
Uber, Edwin. Diary, 1864-1865.

GEORGIA DEPARTMENT OF ARCHIVES AND HISTORY
Barfield, Lee. Letters, 1864.
Bowden, John M. "Some of My Experiences as a Confederate Soldier," 1910.
Carson, Joseph P. "Personal Experiences…Capture of Ft. Stedman," n.d.
Carter, Grant Davis. Letters, 1864.
Dunn, Washington. Diary, 1864.
Graham, Ezekiel D. Letters, 1864-1865.
Lee, Robert E. Letter, August 29, 1864.
Marshall, Thomas J. Diary, 1864.
Martin, J. H. "My Experience as a Confederate Soldier," n.d.
Perkins, Andrew J. Letter, August 2, 1864.
Rees/Reese, A. J. Letters, 1864-1865.
Stillwell, William Ross. Letters, 1864.
Thrasher, Albert M. Letter, August 22, 1864.
Tomlinson, William. Letter, June 23, 1864.
Wellborn, Jesse M. Letter, January 23, 1865.
Wright, Gilbert J. Letters, 1864.

GERMAN MSS.
[Unpublished material owned by Mr. Andrew German of Mystic, Connecticut]
Bevan, John H. Letters, 1864.

HISTORICAL SOCIETY OF PENNSYLVANIA
Clarke, Thomas. Letters, 1864.
Cornett, John. Letters, 1864-1865.
Irvin, John. Diary, 1864.
Smith, John L. Letters, 1864.

LIBRARY OF CONGRESS
Alvord, Augustus V. Letter, June 25, 1864.
Arnold, John Carvel. Letters, 1864.
Brinckle, John Rumsey. Journal and Diary, 1864—1865.
Cooke, Giles Buckner. Diary, 1865.
Coon, David. Letters, 1864.
Fleetwood, Christian A. Papers, 1864.
Hamilton, William. Letters, 1864-1865.
Hancock, Winfield Scott. Letter, August 6, 1864.
Hatton, John William Ford. Memoir, n.d.
Kautz, August V. Diary, 1864, and Reminiscences of the Civil War, 1936.
Landis, Allen. Letter, July 26, 1864.
Lewis, Lothrop Lincoln. Journal, 1864-1865.
Mordecai, Alfred. Letter, August 2, 1864.
Newburger, Alexander. Diary, 1864.
Phelps, Winthrop Henry. "A Chaplain's Life in the Civil War," 1864.
Proctor, Wilbur H. Diary, 1864.
Reed, Charles W. Diary, 1864, and Papers.
Rose, Luther A. Diary, 1864.
Smith, Howard Malcolm. Letters, 1864-1865.
White, John Chester. Memoir, n.d.
Wilcox, Cadmus M. "Notes on the Richmond Campaign, 1864-65," n.d.

MINNESOTA HISTORICAL SOCIETY
Caswell, Arthur D. Papers. Notebook of John W. Pride, Sergeant Major,
1st Minnesota Battalion, n.d.
Smith, George B. Diary, 1864-1865.
Stewart, Thomas Rice. Memoirs, 1865.

MUSEUM OF THE CONFEDERACY
Gordon, John W. Diary, 1864-1865.
Harding, Hiram W. Diary, 1864-1865.
Lewis, William F. Diary, 1865.
Sorrel, G. Moxley. "Field Note Book," 1864.
Tanner, J. S. Register of Casualties for Hoke's Division, 1864.

MISSISSIPPI DEPARTMENT OF ARCHIVES AND HISTORY
Abernathy, Wm. M. "Our Mess: Southern Army Gallantry & Privations," 1902.

NATIONAL ARCHIVES
Hayes, Joseph. Official Report, Battle of Weldon Railroad, 1867.
Johnson, Bushrod. Diary, 1864-1865.

NEW YORK PUBLIC LIBRARY
Clark, Albion W. Diary, 1864.
Edwards, Samuel. Letters, 1864.
Galloway, Joseph D. Diary, 1864.
Harris, William H. Journal, 1864.
Muchmore, Henry S. Diary, 1864-1865.
Sargent, Ransom. Diary, 1864-1865.

NEW YORK STATE LIBRARY
Ames, Albert N. Letters, 1864.
Babcock, Allen. Diary, 1864-1865.
Baum, A. Clark. Letters, 1864.
Burnham, Uberto A. Letters, 1864.
Gilder, William H. Letters, 1864.
Gilmore, Horace O. Letters, 1865.
Hamlin, Charles. Letters, 1864.
Vleck, Jacob van. Letters, 1864.

NORTH CAROLINA DEPARTMENT OF ARCHIVES AND HISTORY
Alexander, Jonathan S. "My Experiences in the War, 1861-1865," n.d.
Bahnson, Henry T. "The Last Days of the War," n.d.
Bone, J. W. Reminiscences, n.d.
Clifton, J. B. Diary, 1864.
Ferguson, G. S. Letters, 1864.
Foard, N. P. Reminiscences, n.d.
Harper, Samuel Finley. Letters, 1864-1865, and Reminiscences, 1923.
Lewis, W. G. "Sketch of the Life of W. G. Lewis," n.d.
Mabry, Robert C. Letters, 1864.
Scales, Alfred M. Letters, 1864.
Sherrill, James A. Reminiscences, 1913.
Shuford, Lowry. "My War Story," n.d.
Sill, J. G. Letter, October 23, 1864.

PETERSBURG NATIONAL MILITARY PARK
Adkins, E. (compiler). "Civilian Accounts of Petersburg Siege," n.d.
Alexander, T. J. Letter, July 6, 1864.
Barbour, Joseph. Letters, 1864.
Hearne, George H. Diary, 1865.
Morgan, George. Letters, 1864-1865.
Morgan, Michael. Memoir, n.d.

Morgan, Timothy. Letter, July 1, 1864.
Nye, Ephraim B. Diary, 1864.
Russell, William. Diary, 1864-1865.
Smith, [?]. Diary, 1864-1865.
Wiatt, William. Diary, 1864-1865.

RICHMOND NATIONAL BATTLEFIELD PARK
Paine, Charles J. Letters, 1864.

SOUTH CAROLINIANA LIBRARY, UNIVERSITY OF SOUTH CAROLINA
Boozer, Alice. Collection: Letters, 1864.
Elliott, Stephen. Letters, 1864.
Lowry, Samuel Catawba. Diary, 1864.
McMaster, Fitz William. Letters, n.d.
Rootes, Thomas R. Letters, 1864.
Thomas, W. M. "Letter to the Editor of *The State*," n.d.

SOUTHERN HISTORICAL COLLECTION, UNIVERSITY OF NORTH CAROLINA
Albright, James W. Diary, 1864-1865.
Alexander, William D. Diary, 1864.
Baker Papers. Letters, 1864.
Bartlett, J. S. "War Record of J. S. Bartlett," n.d.
Bernard, George S. Papers, n.d.
Brooke, N. J. Diary and Letters, 1864.
Dean, Henderson. Reminiscence, 1920.
Devereux, Thomas P. "From Petersburg to Appomattox," n.d.
Forney Papers. Letter, February 9, 1865.
Hamilton, J. R. Letters to John Swinton, 1864-1865.
Haskell, John Cheves. Reminiscences, n.d.
Iredell, Cadwallader J. Letters, 1864-1865.
London, Henry Armand. Letter, March 25, 1865.
Lyons, Jacob. Diary, 1864-1865.
Paris Papers. Diary, 1865.
Shaffner, John Francis. Letter, January 23, 1865.
Sloan, John A. "North Carolina in the War Between the States," n.d.
Todd, Westwood A. Reminiscences, n.d.
Turrentine, John R. Reminiscence of the Crater, n.d.
Walkup, Samuel H. Diary, 1865.
Waring, J. Frederick. Diary, 1864-1865.
Wells, Henry D. Letter, August 28, 1864.

SUDEROW MSS., Washington, D.C.]
Elder, Thomas C. Letters, 1864.
Hall, W. C. Diary, 1864.

Hicks, Robert W. Diary, 1864.
Petty, J. Thomas. Diary, 1864.

TENNESSEE STATE LIBRARY AND ARCHIVES
Beard, James. Letters, 1864.
Coleman, Ben W. Letter, November 29, 1864.
Harder, William Henry. Memoir, n.d.
Massenburg, A. C. Letter, December 1864.
Stay, Charles. Diary, 1865.
Trimmer, Theodore. Letters, 1864-1865.
Vassy, John. Letters, 1864.

UNIVERSITY OF TEXAS
Brady, Thomas. Letters, 1865.
Cavaness, I. F. Diary, 1864-1865.
Crockett, Edward R. Diary, 1864—1865.
McCarty, Thomas. Diary, 1864, and Reminiscence of September Z9, 1864, n.d.
McDonald, Wilfred. Diary, 1864-1865.
Pomeroy, Nicholas. "Reminiscences of the American War," n.d.
Ramsey, James G. "Gettysburg and Petersburg," n.d.

U.S. ARMY HERITAGE AND EDUCATION CENTER: MILITARY HISTORY INSTITUTE
Chamberlain Papers:
Henry, Isaiah. Letter, October 26, 1864.
Ramsey, W. R. History of the 150th Pa. Regiment, n.d.
Civil War Times Illustrated Collection:
Barnes, Jim. "Autobiography of an Ex-Confederate Soldier," 1941.
Bowden, John M. "Some of My Experiences as a Confederate Soldier," 1910.
Brion, Daniel. Diary, 1864.
Cartwright, James W. Letter, December 19, 1864.
Chase, Stephen P. Memoirs, n.d.
Clendening, William A. Memoir, n.d.
Coleman, John Kennedy. Diary, 1864-1865.
DeGraff, Nicholas. Memoir, 1862-1865.
Foskett, Liberty. Letter, August 2, 1864.
Gardner, Charles. Memoir, n.d.
Huff, William Thomas. Letters, 1864—1865.
Jones, Peleg Gardner. Diary, 1864, and Letter, March 13, 1865.
Parsons, Charles Moses. Reminiscences, 1864.
Pope, Albert A. Diary, 1864-1865.
Porter, John A. "Personal Recollections," 1977.
Resser, Isaac H. Diary, 1864.
Scott, David J. Letter, April 10, 1865.
Smith, James. Diary, 1864.

Stott, John W. Diary, 1864-1865.

Stout, David B. Letter, August 24, 1864.

Stross, Ellis C. Letters, 1865.

Civil War Miscellaneous Collection:

Beard, James. Letters, 1864.

Beddall, Samuel A. Diary, 1864-1865.

Breneman, Amos. Letter, November 27, 1864.

Burn, Christian M. Letter, January 1, 1865.

Chandler, George C. Letter, November 5, 1864.

[?], Charles. Letter, July 2, 1864.

Cram, Oscar. Letters, 1864.

Giles, George. Letter, December 15, 1864.

McAlister, T. S. Letter, July 31, 1864.

Morrison, John W. Reminiscences of the Mine Explosion, n.d.

Nesbitt, Harrison. Letters, 1864.

Reily, John Young. "Fort Gregg: Confederates' Desperate Stand," n.d.

Root, Samuel H. Memoir, n.d.

Shuman, Joshia. Diary, 1864-1865.

Harrisburg Civil War Round Table Collection:

Bakeman, George Albert. Letters, 1864.

Cauler, Samuel Y. Letters, 1864.

Covell, Harvey. Letter, June 20, 1864.

Hardeman, John. Letter, March 28, 1865.

Keiser, Henry. Diary, 1864-1865.

Knox, Andrew. Letters, 1864.

Madill, Henry J. Diary, 1864-1865.

Metzger, Henry C. Letters, 1864.

Potter, Jared J. Diary, 1864.

Seibert, Jacob. Letters, 1864-1865.

Lewis Leigh Collection:

Burr, Henry D. Letter, March 7, 1865.

Buterbaugh, Elias L. Letters, 1864.

Lobb, William T. Letter, October 17, 1864.

Phelps, Frank M. Letter, August 24, 1864.

Smith, Charles W. Letters, 1864-1865.

Stinson, Charles F. Letters, 1864.

White, Ansell L. Letter, March 11, 1865.

Michael Musick Collection:

Binion, Dorsey. Letter, August 10, 1864.

Chick, Wade G. Letter, July 14, 1864.

Funkhouser, Robert D. Account of Fort Stedman, 1894.

Save the Flag Collection:

Inch, William. Diary, 1865.

Perry, William L. Diary, 1864.

Murray J. Smith Collection:
Paul, Charles R. Diary, 1865.
Wiley Sword Collection:
Greene, William B. Diary, 1864-1865.

U.S. MILITARY ACADEMY CADET LIBRARY
    Gibbon, John. Letters, 1864.

VIRGINIA HISTORICAL SOCIETY
    Anderson, Richard H. "Narrative of Services: May 7, 1864-April 1865," n.d.
    Atkinson, Homer. Statement, n.d.
    Bagley, Edward. Letter, July 9, 1864.
    Beckwith, Margaret Stanly. Recollections, n.d.
    Brown, Alexander G. Letters, 1864.
    Clark, George. "History of My Life," n.d.
    Cooke, Giles Buckner. Diary, 1864-1865.
    Cooke, John R. Official Report of the Appomattox Campaign, 1865.
    Cox, Leroy W. Memoirs, n.d.
    Davis, Jefferson. Letters, 1865.
    Dearing, James. Letter, October 29, 1864.
    Freaner, George. Letter, October 6, 1864.
    Gary, Louella Pauline. "Biography of General M. W. Gary," 1910.
    Gordon, John. Official Report of the Appomattox Campaign, 1865.
    Hamilton, J. R. Letters to John Swinton, 1864-1865.
    Heth, Henry. Official Reports: May-December 1864 and April 1-9, 1865.
    Howard, Conway R. Official Report, 1865.
    Kay, A. H. Letters, 1864-1865 [in Baylor Family Papers].
    Lee, Fitzhugh. Dispatch, March 24, 1865.
    Lee, Robert E. Letter, July 27, 1868.
    Lee Headquarters Papers, 1864-1865.
    Longstreet, James. Official Report of the Appomattox Campaign, 1865.
    McComb, William M. Official Report of the Appomattox Campaign, 1865.
    Macrae, William. Official Report of the Appomattox Campaign, 1865.
    Mahone, William. Official Report of the Appomattox Campaign, 1865.
    Martin, John Marshall. Letter, July 31, 1864.
    Morrison, Mary E. Memoirs, n.d.
    Nattall, James. Letter, 1864.
    Pegram, Willie. Letter, October 28, 1864.
    Pickett, George. Official Report of the Appomattox Campaign, 1865.
    Platt, William H. Letter, May 5, 1865.
    Scott, Alfred Lewis. Memoirs, 1910.
    Stephenson, Jennie F. "My Father and His Household," 1897.
    Vincent, F. N. Diary, 1864.
    Willis, Bird. Diary, 1865.

VIRGINIA STATE LIBRARY

Banister, Anne A. "Incidents in the Life of a Civil War Child," n.d.

Bragg, Robert Richard. Reminiscences, 1913.

Davis, Creed T. Diary, 1884.

Dobie, David F. Letter, August 3, 1864.

Harris, Nathaniel. Letter to William Mahone, 1866.

Parker, Ezra S; Letter, September 23, 1864.

Simpson, W. S. Papers. Letter, May 20, 1865.

Thurston, E. N. Letter to William Mahone, 1889.

White, William S. "A Diary of the War, or, What I Saw of It," 1883.

Williams, James Peter. Letter, March 16, 1865.

Dissertations and Theses

Johnston, Angus James II. "Virginia Railroads in the Civil War, 1861-65."
Ph.D. diss., Northwestern University, 1959.

Marino, Carl W. "General Alfred Howe Terry: Soldier from Connecticut."
Ph.D. diss., New York University, 1968.

Newspapers

Albany (New York) Atlas & Argus

The Alleghanian (Ebensburg, Pennsylvania)

Atlanta (Georgia) Constitution

Baldwinsville (New York) Messenger

Baltimore American & Courier Advertiser

Bangor (Maine) Whig & Courier

Batavia (New York) Republican Advocate

Bolivar (New York) Breeze

Boston Evening Transcript

Boston Journal

Buffalo Daily Courier

Charleston Daily Courier

Charleston Mercury

Cold Spring (New York) Recorder

Columbia Daily South Carolinian

Columbus (Georgia) Daily Enquirer

Columbus (Georgia) Times

Columbus (Ohio) Daily Sun

Connecticut War Record

Corning (New York) Journal

Daily Confederate (Macon, Georgia)

Daily Constitutional (Raleigh, North Carolina)
Dansville (New York) Advertiser
Detroit Advertiser & Tribune
Geneva (New York) Courier
Harper's Weekly
Hillsborough (North Carolina) Recorder
Huntington Long-Islander
Long Island Farmer (Jamaica, New York)
Macon Daily Telegraph
Montgomery (Alabama) Daily Mail
Naples (New York) Record
National Tribune
New Haven Journal & Courier
New York Evening Express
New York Herald
New York Times
New York Tribune
Oswego (New York) Commercial Advertiser
Oswego (New York) Daily Times
Petersburg Daily Express
Petersburg Daily Register
Philadelphia Inquirer
Philadelphia Ledger
Philadelphia Weekly Press
Philadelphia Weekly Times
Potsdam (New York) Courier Freeman
Richmond Enquirer
Richmond Examiner
Richmond Whig
Rochester Daily Union & Advertiser
Rockland (New York) Country Journal
Rutland (Vermont) Herald
Sacramento Daily Union
Schenectady (New York) Evening Star
Star of the North (Bloomsburg, Pennsylvania)
Syracuse (New York) Daily Courier & Union
Syracuse (New York) Daily Journal
Tobacco Plant (Durham, North Carolina)
Troy (New York) Daily Times
Union County and Lewisburg Chronicle (New York)

Utica (New York) Saturday Globe
Washington Post
Watertown (New York) Daily Times
Watkins (New York) Express
Weekly Confederate (Raleigh, North Carolina)
Western Democrat (Charlotte, North Carolina)
Wyndham Co. Transcript (Connecticut)

Newspaper Reporters' and Correspondents' Accounts

Andrews, J. Cutler. *The South Reports the Civil War.* 1970.
Blackett, R. J. M., ed. *Thomas Morris Chester: Black Civil War Correspondent.* 1989.
Cadwallader, Sylvanus. *Three Years with Grant.* 1956.
Coffin, Charles Carleton. *Four Years of Fighting.* 1896.
Starr, Louis M. *Reporting the Civil War.* 1962.
Townsend, George Alfred. *Rustics in Rebellion.* 1950.

Official Documents

The Official Military Atlas of the Civil War. 1978.
The War of the Rebellion: A Compilation of the Official Records of the Union and Confederate Armies. 1880-1901.

Published Autobiographies, Biographies, Diaries, Letters, Memoirs, and Personal Narratives (Military)

Abbott, Lemuel. *Personal Recollections and Civil War Diary.* 1908.
Adams, John Ripley. *Memorial and Letters.* 1890.
Agassiz, George R., ed. *Meade's Headquarters 1863-1865.* 1922.
Alexander, E. Porter. *Military Memoirs of a Confederate.* 1907.
———. (Gary Gallagher, ed.). *Fighting for the Confederacy.* 1989.
Allen, Stanton P. *Down in Dixie: Life in a Cavalry Regiment.* 1893.
Ames, Blanche. *Adelbert Ames, 1835-1933.* 1964.
Amory, Charles B. *Brief Record of Army Life.* 1902.
Armes, George Augustus. *Ups and Downs of an Army Officer.* 1900.
Armstrong, Hallock. *Letters from a Pennsylvania Chaplain at the Siege of Petersburg.* 1961.
Armstrong, Nelson. *Nuggets of Experience.* 1906.
Austin, Aurelia. *Georgia Boys with "Stonewall" Jackson.* 1967.
Bache, Richard Meade. *Life of General George Gordon Meade.* 1898.
Badeau, Adam. *Grant in Peace.* 1887.

———. *Military History of Ulysses S. Grant.* 1885.

Bahnson, Henry T. *Last Days of the War, 1863-1865.* N.d.

Barrett, Eugene A. "The Civil War Services of John F. Hartranft," *Pennsylvania History*, 32, (1965), no. 2.

Bartlett, William H., ed. *Aunt and the Soldier Boys.* N.d.

Battle, Laura Elizabeth. *Forget-me-nots of the Civil War.* 1909.

Baylor, George. *Bull Run to Bull Run.* 1900.

Beale, George William. *A Lieutenant of Cavalry in Lee's Army.* 1918.

Beauregard, P. G. T. "Four Days of Battle at Petersburg." *Century Magazine*, 1889.

Bernard, George, ed. *War Talks of Confederate Veterans.* 1892.

Bevier, Robert S. *History of the 1st and 2nd Missouri Confederate Brigades.* 1879.

Blackford, Susan Leigh. *Letters from Lee's Army.* 1947.

Blackford, William W. *War Years with Jeb Stuart.* 1945.

Blake, Henry Nichols. *Three Years in the Army of the Potomac.* 1865.

Blake, Nelson Morehouse. *William Mahone of Virginia.* 1935.

Bloodgood, John D. *Personal Reminiscences of the War.* 1893.

Bolton, Horace. *Personal Reminiscences of the Late War.* 1892.

Bouton, John Bell. *A Memoir of General Louis Bell.* 1865.

Bowley, Freeman S. *A Boy Lieutenant.* 1906.

Brett, David. *My Dear Wife.* 1964.

Brinton, John H. *Personal Memoirs.* 1914.

Brown, Augustus. *The Diary of a Line Officer.* 1906.

Brown, Joel F. "The Charge of the Heavy Artillery." *Maine Bugle*, campaign 1 (1894), call 1.

Brown, Philip Francis. *Reminiscences of the War of 1861-1865.* 1912.

Burr, Frank A. *Life and Achievements of James Addams Beaver.* 1882.

Burrage, Henry. "My Capture and What Came of It." *Maine MOLLUS 1* (1898).

Butler, Benjamin. *Butler's Book.* 1892.

Butler, Jason. Letter, March 27, 1865. In *Lincolnian* (1987).

Calhoun, Charles M. *Liberty Dethroned.* 1903.

Carter, Robert G. *Four Brothers in Blue.* 1913.

Carter, Solon A. "Fourteen Months' Service with Colored Troops." *Maine MOLLUS 3* (1908).

Case, Leverette N. "Personal Recollections of Siege of Petersburg." *Michigan MOLLUS 2* (1898).

Catton, Bruce. *Grant Takes Command.* 1968.

Cauthen, Charles, ed. *Family Letters of Three Wade Hamptons.* 1953.

Chamberlain, Joshua. *The Passing of the Armies.* 1915.

———. "Reminiscences of Petersburg & Appomattox." *Maine MOLLUS 3* (1908).

Chamberlaine, William W. *Memoirs of the Civil War.* 1912.

Chamberlayne, John H. *Ham Chamberlayne -Virginian.* 1932.

Chamberlin, George E. *Letters of George E. Chamberlin.* 1883.

Chambers, Henry A. *Diary of Captain Henry A. Chambers.* 1983.

Clark, Charles A. "Campaigning with the Sixth Maine." *Iowa MOLLUS 2.* (1892).

Clark, George. *A Glance Backward.* 1914.

Cleaves, Freeman. *Meade of Gettysburg,* 1960.

Cleveland, Edmund. "Civil War Journal." *Proceedings of the New Jersey Historical Society* 66 (1948).

Coco, Gregory A., ed. *Through Blood and Fire.* 1982.

Cole, Jacob H. *Under Five Commanders.* 1906.

Colston, R. E. "Repelling the First Assault on Petersburg." *Century Magazine,* 1889.

Connelly, Thomas L. *The Marble Man: Robert E. Lee and His Image.* 1977.

Cooke, John Esten. *A Life of Gen. Robert E. Lee.* 1873.

———. *Wearing of the Gray.* 1867.

Copp, Elbridge J. *Reminiscences of the War of the Rebellion.* 1911.

Corbin, Richard W. "Letters of a Confederate Officer." *Magazine of History* no. 24 (1913).

Corby, William. *Memoirs of Chaplain Life.* 1893.

Couture, Richard T. *Charlie's Letters: Correspondence of Charlie DeNoon.* 1982.

Coward, Asbury. *South Carolinians: Colonel Asbury Coward's Memoirs.* 1968.

Crawford, Robert F., ed. "Civil War Letters of S. Rodman and Linton Smith." *Delaware History* 21 (1984), no. 2.

Cronin, David Edward. *Evolution of a Life . . . Memoirs of Seth Eyland.* 1884.

Cummins, Simon. *Give God the Glory.* 1979.

Daggett, Monroe. "A Cavalryman in the Eleventh Maine Infantry." *Maine Bugle,* campaign 1 (1894), call 1.

Daly, Louise Haskell. *Alexander Cheves Haskell - Portrait of the Man.* 1834.

Dalzell, James McCormick. *Private Dalzell, His Autobiography.* 1888.

Davidson, Victor. *History of Wilkinson County.* 1930.

Davies, A. M. "Petersburg - The Battle of the Crater." *Blue and Gray Magazine 3* (1894), no. 5.

Davis, Burke. *Gray Fox.* 1956.

Davis, Charles E. *Three Years in the Army.* 1894.

Davis, Charles L. "Signal Officer with Grant." *Civil War History* 8 (1961).

Davis, Oliver W. *Life of David Bell Birney.* 1867.

Davis, T. A. "Company F, 35th Regiment — History of the Company." N.d. [Pamphlet]

Davis, W. M. "Diary, 1865." *46th Annual Reunion of the 6th Ohio Cavalry,* 1911.

Dawes, Rufus R. *Service with the Sixth Wisconsin Volunteers.* 1890.

Dawson, Francis W. *Reminiscences of Confederate Service*. 1882.

Day, David L. *My Diary of Rambles with the 25th Mass*. 1884.

DeForest, Bartholomew. *Random Sketches and Wandering Thoughts*. 1866.

de Peyster, J. Watts. "A Military Memoir of William Mahone." *Historical Magazine* 10 (1871), no. 1.

de Trobriand, Regis. *Four Years with the Army of the Potomac*. 1889.

Dobbins, Austin C., ed. *Grandfather's Journal - Co. B 16th Mississippi Volunteers*. 1988.

Dodge, Grenville M. *Personal Recollections*. 1914.

Dollard, Robert. *Recollections of the Civil War*. 1906.

Dority, Orin G. "The Civil War Diary of Orin G. Dority." *Northwest Ohio Quarterly*, 1965.

Dorman, G. H. *Fifty Years Ago*. 1911.

Douglas, Henry Kyd. *I Rode with Stonewall*. 1940.

Dowdey, Clifford. *Lee*. 1965.

Dowdey, Clifford, and Manarin, Louis H., eds. *Wartime Papers of R. E. Lee*. 1961.

Doyle, W. E. "A Confederate Prisoner." *Confederate Veteran* 34 (1926).

Drake, James Madison. *Historical Sketches*. 1908.

Draper, William. *Recollections of a Varied Career*. 1908.

Dunovant, Adelia. "Gen. John Dunovant, Houston, Tex." *Confederate Veteran*, 16 (1908).

Eckert, Ralph Lowell. *John Brown Gordon*. 1989.

Edwards, John Frank. *Army Life of Frank Edwards*. 1911.

Egan, Michael. *The Flying, Gray-Haired Yank*. 1888.

Eisenschiml, Otto, ed. *Vermont General*, 1960.

Elliott, James Carson. *The Southern Soldier Boy*. 1907.

Fatout, Paul, ed. *Letters of a Civil War Surgeon*. 1961.

Fewell, Alexander F. *Dear Martha - Confederate War Letters*. 1976.

Field, Charles. "Campaign of 1864 and 1865." *Southern Historical Society Papers*, 14 (1886).

Figg, Royal W. *Where Men Only Dare To Go!* 1885.

Final Report of Wade Hampton Monument Commission. 1907.

Fleetwood, Christian A. "Letter (June 8, 1864)." *Civil War Times Illustrated*, 16 (1977), no. 4.

Ford, Worthington, ed. *A Cycle of Adams Letters, 1861-1865*. 1920.

Fowler, Philemon H. *Memorials of William Fowler*. 1875.

Freeman, Benjamin H. *Confederate Letters*. 1974.

Freeman, Douglas S. *R. E. Lee: A Biography*. 1944, 1949.

Freeman, Walker Burford. *Memoirs of Walker Burford Freeman*. 1978.

Freeman, Warren Hapgood. *Letters from Two Brothers*. 1871.

Fulton, William F. H. *War Reminiscences*. 1986.

Gerrish, Theodore. *Army Life: A Private's Reminiscences*. 1882.

Gibbon, John. *Personal Recollections of the Civil War*. 1928.

Gilmore, Pascal. *Civil War Memories*. 1928.

Goodson, Joab. "Letters." *Alabama Review* 10 (1957).

Gordon, Armistead C. *Memories & Memorials of William Gordon McCabe*. 1925.

Gordon, John B. Reminiscences of the Civil War. 1903.

Gordon, Marquis L. *M. L. Gordon's Experiences in the Civil War*. 1922.

Goss, Warren Lee. *Recollections of a Private*. 1890.

Govan, Gilbert E. *The Haskell Memoirs*, 1960.

Graham, James A. (ed. H. M. Wagstaff). *James A. Graham Papers, 1861-1884*. 1928.

Grant, Ulysses S. *Personal Memoirs of U. S. Grant*. 1885.

Greenleaf, Margery, ed. *Letters to Eliza*. 1970.

Grimes, Bryan. *Extracts of Letters of Major-General Bryan Grimes*. 1883.

Hagood, James R. "Report of Campaign of 1864." *Southern Historical Society Papers*
    13 (1885).

Hagood, Johnson. *Memoirs of the War of Secession*. 1910.

———. "Hagood's Brigade: In Trenches of Petersburg." *Southern Historical Society
    Papers*, 16 (1888).

Haley, John W. *The Rebel Yell & the Yankee Hurrah*. 1985.

Hall, Henry Seymour. "Mine Run to Petersburg." *Kansas MOLLUS*, 1894.

Hamilton, D. H. *History of Co. M, 1st Texas Volunteer Infantry*. 1925.

Hamlin, Percy Gatling. *Old Bald Head*. 1940.

Hardy, John C. "Final Effort - Last Assault of Confederates at Petersburg."
    Michigan MOLLUS 2 (1898).

Harrill, Lawson. *Reminiscences, 1861-1865*. 1910.

Harris, Nathaniel H. *Movements of the Confederate Army in Virginia*. 1901.

Harrison, Walter. *Pickett's Men - A Fragment of War History*. 1870.

Hartranft, John F. "Recapture of Fort Stedman." In Johnson and Buel, eds., *Battles
    and Leaders of the Civil War*. 1889.

Harvey, Marshall. *Recollections of 1864-65*. 1904.

Hassler, William Woods. *A. P. Hill: Lee's Forgotten General*. 1957.

Heslin, James J., ed. "From the Wilderness to Petersburg." *New York Historical
    Society Quarterly*, 41 (1961).

Heth, Henry. *The Memoirs of Henry Heth*. 1974.

Hinson, William G. "Diary." *South Carolina Historical Magazine* 75 (1974), no. 1.

Hoffman, John Bacon. *Civil War Diary and Letters*. 1979.

Holland, Lynwood M. *Pierce M. B. Young - The Warwick of the South*. 1964.

Holmes, Oliver W., Jr. *Touched with Fire*. 1946.

Horrocks, James. *My Dear Parents*. 1982.

Houghton, Charles H. "In the Crater." In Johnson and Buel, eds., *Battles and*

Leaders of the Civil War, 1889.

Houghton, William R. *Two Boys in the Civil War and After*. 1912.

Howard, McHenry. *Recollections of a Maryland Confederate Soldier*. 1914.

——. "Closing Scenes of the War about Richmond." *Southern Historical Society Papers* 31 (1903).

Hudson, Joshua H. *Sketches and Reminiscences*. 1903.

Humphreys, Charles A. *Field, Camp, Hospital and Prison*. 1918.

Humphreys, Henry H. *Andrew Atkinson Humphreys: A Biography*. 1924.

Hunton, Eppa. *Autobiography*. 1933.

Huyette, Miles Clayton. *Reminiscences of a Soldier in the American Civil War*. 1908.

Hyde, Thomas Worcester. *Following the Greek Cross*. 1894.

Jackson, Harry F. *Back Home in Oneida: Hermon Clarke Letters*. 1965.

James, Henry B. *Memories of the Civil War*. 1898.

Jewett, Albert. *A Boy Goes to War*. 1944.

John K. McIver Chapter UDC. *Treasured Reminiscences*. 1911.

Johnson, Mary, ed. *This They Remembered*. 1986.

Johnson, Robert, and Buel, Clarence, eds. *Battles and Leaders of the Civil War*. 1889.

Johnson, Thomas Scott. "Letters from a Civil War Chaplain." *Journal of Presbyterian History*, 1968.

Johnston, David E. *Story of a Confederate Boy in the Civil War*. 1914.

——. *Four Years a Soldier*. 1887.

Johnston, Nathaniel B. *Civil War Reminiscences*. 1972.

Jones, Evan Rowland. *Four Years in the Army of the Potomac*. 1881.

Jones, J. William, ed. *Army of Northern Virginia Memorial Volume*. 1880.

Jordan, David M. *Winfield Scott Hancock: A Soldier's Life*. 1988.

Jordan, William C. *Some Events and Incidents During the Civil War*. 1909.

Kautz, August V. "How I Won My First Brevet." *Ohio MOLLUS 4 (1896)*.

Keifer, Joseph Warren. *Slavery and Four Years of War*. 1900.

Kenfield, Frank. "Captured by the Rebels: A Vermonter at Petersburg." *Vermont History* 36 (1968), no. 4.

Kent, Arthur A., ed. *Three Years with Company K*. 1976.

Kieffer, Henry Martyn. *Recollections of a Drummer-Boy*. 1883.

Kilmer, George L. "Gordon's Attack at Fort Stedman." In Johnson and Buel, eds., *Battles and Leaders of the Civil War*. 1889.

Kingman, Eugene. *Tramping Out the Vintage*. 1983.

Klein, Maury. *Edward Porter Alexander*. 1971.

Lane, David. *A Soldier's Diary*. 1905.

Lane, James H. "Glimpses of Army Life in 1864." *Southern Historical Society Papers*, 18 (1890).

Lang, David. "Civil War Letters." *Florida Historical Quarterly* 54 (1976).

Lapham, William B. "With the Seventh Maine Battery." *Maine MOLLUS 1* (1898).

——. My Recollections of the War of the Rebellion. 1892.

Lee, Fitzhugh. *General Lee*. 1894.

Lee, Robert E., Jr. *My Father, General Lee*. 1960.

Lee, Susan P. *Memoirs of William Nelson Pendleton*. 1893.

Lewis, Richard. *Camp Life of a Confederate Boy*. 1883.

Lightsey, Ada. *The Veteran's Story*. 1899.

Linn, George Wilds. *An Echo of the Civil War*. 1911.

Livermore, Thomas L. *Days and Events, 1860-1866*. 1920.

Lockley, Frederick. "Letters." *Huntington Library Quarterly* 16 (1952).

Long, A. L. *Memoirs of Robert E. Lee*. 1886.

Longstreet, James. *From Manassas to Appomattox*. 1903.

——. "Report of Affair of October 27th, 1864." *Southern Historical Society Papers*, 7 (1879).

Lowe, David W., ed. *Meade's Army: The Private Notebooks of Lt. Col. Theodore Lyman*. 2007.

Lyman, Theodore. SEE Agassiz, George R. and Lowe, David. W.

Macartney, Clarence E. *Grant and His Generals*. 1953.

McBride, Robert. *In the Ranks, from Wilderness to Appomattox*. 1881.

McCarthy, Carlton. *Detailed Minutiae of Soldier Life in the Army of Northern Virginia*. 1882.

McClendon, William. *Recollections of War Times*. 1909.

McDonald, Edward H. "We Drove Them from the Field." *Civil War Times Illustrated*, 6 (1967), no. 7.

McElroy, Robert. *Jefferson Davis: The Unreal and the Real*. 1937.

McFarlane, Carrington. *Reminiscences of an Army Surgeon*. 1912.

McFeely, William S. *Grant: A Biography*. 1981.

Mackey, T. J. "The Bravest Deed of the War." 1899.

McKim, Randolph. *A Soldier's Recollections*. 1910.

McKinney, Edward. *Life in Tent and Field*. 1922.

McWhiney, Grady. "The Union's Worst General." CWT, Ill. 6 (1975).

Martin, Samuel J. "Campbell Brown." *The Kepi* 3 (April-May 1985), no. 2.

Matthews, James P. "How General A. P. Hill Met His Fate." *Southern Historical Society Papers*, 27 (1899).

Meacham, Henry H. *The Empty Sleeve*. 1869.

Meade, George Gordon. *Life and Letters of George Gordon Meade*. 1913.

Melville, Dorothy. *Tyler-Browns of Brattleboro*. 1973.

Menge, W. Springer, ed. *Civil War Notebook of Daniel Chisholm*. 1989.

Mereness, George. "Letters, 1864." *The Kepi* 3 (February-March 1985), no. 1.

Meyers, Augustus. *Ten Years in the Ranks*. 1914.

Miles, Nelson. *Serving the Republic.* 1911.

Miller, Delavan S. *Drum Taps in Dixie.* 1905.

Mills, Luther Rice. "Letters." *North Carolina Historical Review* 4 (1927).

Mixson, Frank M. *Reminiscences of a Private.* 1910.

Mohr, James C., ed. *The Cormany Diaries.* 1982.

Montgomery, Horace. "A Union Officer's Recollections of the Negro. . . ." *Pennsylvania History,* 27 (1961), no. 2.

Moore, Edward. *Story of a Cannoneer Under Stonewall Jackson.* 1907.

Moore, Josiah S. *Reminiscences.* 1903.

Munroe, James Phinney. *A Life of Francis Amasa Walker.* 1923.

Newhall, Fred C. "With Sheridan in Lee's Last Campaign." *Maine Bugle,* campaign 1 (1894), call 4.

Newton, Alexander H. *Out of the Briars.* 1910.

Nichols, G. W. *A Soldier's Story of His Regiment.* 1898.

Nichols, Samuel Edmund. *Your Soldier Boy Samuel.* 1929.

Nichols, Wesley. *Autobiography and Civil War Recollections.* 1915.

Norton, Oliver. *Army Letters, 1861-1865.* 1903.

O'Brien, John Emmet. *Telegraphing in Battle.* 1910.

Oates, William C. *War Between the Union and the Confederacy.* 1905.

Owen, Thomas James. "Dear Friends at Home -Letters and Diary 1864-65." 1985.

Palfrey, Francis Winthrop. *Memoir of William Francis Bartlett.* 1878.

Park, Robert Emory. "Diary." *Southern Historical Society Papers* 1 (1876).

Parker, David B. *A Chautauqua Boy in '61 and Afterward.* 1912.

Partridge, Sylvester B. "With the Signal Corps from Fortress Monroe to Richmond." *Maine MOLLUS* 3 (1908).

Paxton, John Randolph. *Sword and Gown.* 1926.

Peck, George B., Jr. "A Recruit Before Petersburg." *Rhode Island Soldiers' and Sailors' Narratives,* series 2 (1880).

Peck, Rufus H. *Reminiscences of a Confederate Soldier.* 1913.

Pennypacker, Isaac R. *General Meade.* 1901.

Perry, John Gardner. *Letters from a Surgeon of the Civil War.* 1906.

Phillips, Marion G., ed. *Richard and Rhoda - Letters from the Civil War.* 1981.

Pickett, George E. *Soldier of the South.* 1928.

Pipes, David Washington. *First Twenty-three Years, 1845-1868.* N.d.

Piston, William Garrett. *Lee's Tarnished Lieutenant: James Longstreet.* 1987.

Poague, William Thomas. *Gunner with Stonewall.* 1957.

Poe, Clarence, ed. *True Tales of the South at War.* 1961.

Pollard, Henry R. *Memoirs and Sketches.* 1923.

——. *Address Delivered . . . Memory of Edward Bagby.* 1912.

Polley, J. B. *A Soldier's Letters to Charming Nellie.* 1908.

Porter, Horace. *Campaigning with Grant*. 1897.

——. "Five Forks and the Pursuit of Lee." In Johnson and Buel, eds., *Battles and Leaders of the Civil War*. 1889.

Powell, Junius L. "A Memory of Our Great War." *Journal of the Military Service Institution*, 1911.

Powell, William H. "Battle of the Petersburg Crater." In Johnson and Buel, eds., *Battles and Leaders of the Civil War*. 1889.

Price, George. *Across the Continent with the 5th Cavalry*. 1883.

Rhodes, Elisha Hunt. *All for the Union*. 1985.

Rhodes, James E. "The Sixth Maine Battery Before Petersburg." *Maine Bugle*, campaign 1 (1894), call 3.

Rickard, James H. "Services with Colored Troops." *Rhode Island Soldiers' and Sailors' Narratives*, series 5 (1894), no. 1.

Robbins, Walter Raleigh. *War Record and Personal Experiences*. 1923.

Robertson, James I. *General A. P. Hill: Story of a Confederate Warrior*. 1987.

——, ed. *Civil War Letters of Gen. Robert McAllister*. 1965.

Rockwell, Alphonso. *Rambling Recollections*. 1920.

Rodenbough, Theo., comp. *From Everglade to Canyon with the 2nd Dragoons*, 1875.

Roemer, Jacob. *Reminiscences of the War of the Rebellion*. 1897.

Roman, Alfred. *Military Operations of General Beauregard*. 1884.

Rosenblatt, Emil, ed. *Anti-Rebel: Civil War Letters of Wilbur Fisk*. 1983.

Royall, William. *Some Reminiscences*. 1909.

Sallada, William. *Silver Sheaves*. 1879.

Sanford, George Bliss. *Fighting Rebels and Redskins*. 1969.

Schiller, Herbert M., ed. *Autobiography of Major General William F. Smith*. 1990.

Scott, J. Z. H. *Memoirs*. 1901.

Scroggs, Joseph J. "The Earth Shook and Quivered." *Civil War Times Illustrated* 11 (1972), no. 8.

Sheridan, Philip. *Personal Memoirs*. 1888.

Simon, John Y., ed. *Papers of Ulysses S. Grant*. 1984-1985.

Slater, Thomas Ogden. *Incidents of Personal Experience*. 1916.

Small, Harold Adams, ed. *The Road to Richmond*. 1939.

Smith, William F. *Autobiography of Major Gen. William F. Smith*. 1990.

——. "General W. F. Smith at Petersburg." *Century Magazine* 54 (1897).

——. *From Chattanooga to Petersburg*. 1893.

Snyder, Charles M. "A Teen-Age G.I. in the Civil War." *New York History* 35 (1954)

Sorrel, G. Moxley. *Recollections of a Confederate Staff Officer*. 1905.

Sparks, David S., ed. *Inside Lincoln's Army*. 1964.

Stevens, George T. *Three Years in the Sixth Corps*. 1866.

Stevens, Robert J. *Captain Bill.* 1985.

Stewart, Alexander M. *Camp, March and Battle-field.* 1865.

Stewart, William H. *A Pair of Blankets.* 1911.

Stiles, Robert. *Four Years Under Marse Robert.* 1903.

Stoddard, Henry Luther. *Horace Greeley.* 1946.

Stoddard, William O. *Ulysses S. Grant.* 1886.

Stone, James Madison. *Personal Recollections of the Civil War.* 1918.

Strayhorn, Thomas Jackson. "Letters." *North Carolina Historical Review* 13 (1936).

Sulivane, Clement. "Fall of Richmond." In Johnson and Buel, eds., *Battles and Leaders of the Civil War.* 1889.

Sumner, Merlin E., ed. *The Diary of Cyrus B. Comstock.* 1987.

Talbot, Edith. *Samuel Chapman Armstrong.* 1904.

Taylor, Emerson Gifford. *Gouverneur Kemble Warren.* 1932.

Taylor, Walter H. General Lee: *His Campaigns in Virginia.* 1906.

———. *Four Years with General Lee.* 1877.

Tenney, Luman. *War Diary.* 1914.

Thomas, Hampton Sidney. *Personal Reminiscences of Service in the Cavalry.* 1889.

Thomas, Henry G. "The Colored Troops at Petersburg." In Johnson and Buel, eds., *Battles and Leaders of the Civil War.* 1889.

Thomas, Howard. *Boys in Blue from the Adirondack Foothills,* 1960.

Tilney, Robert. *My Life in the Army.* 1912.

Toney, Marcus. *Privations of a Private.* 1905.

Trumbull, Henry Clay. *War Memories of an Army Chaplain.* 1906.

———. Knightly Soldier. 1865.

Tucker, Glenn. *Hancock the Superb,* 1960.

Tyler, Mason. *Recollections of the Civil War.* 1912.

Ulmer, George T. *Adventures & Reminiscences of a Volunteer.* 1892.

Urwin, Gregory J. W. *Custer Victorious.* 1983.

Vaill, Dudley. *County Regiment: A Sketch of 2nd Regiment Connecticut Heavy Artillery.* 1908.

Vandiver, Frank E. *Ploughshares into Swords.* 1952.

Venable, Charles. "Campaign from the Wilderness to Petersburg." *Southern Historical Society Papers* 14 (1886).

Venable, M. S. "In the Trenches at Petersburg." *Confederate Veteran* 34 (1926).

Vredenburgh, Peter. *Letters of Major Peter Vredenburgh.* N.d.

Walker, Cornelius I. *Life of Lieutenant General Richard Heron Anderson.* 1917.

Walker, Francis A. *General Hancock.* 1894.

Wallace, Willard M. *Soul of the Lion.* 1960.

Watson, James A. *Diary, 1864-65.* 1865.

Welch, Spencer Glasgow. *Confederate Surgeon's Letters to his Wife.* 1911.

Weld, Stephen M. *War Diary and Letters.* 1979.

Wellman, Manly Wade. *Rebel Boast: First at Bethel - Last at Appomattox.* 1956.

West, Richard S., Jr. *Lincoln's Scapegoat General.* 1965.

White, Whitman V. "From the Union Side." *Blue and Gray Magazine,* 5 (1895), no. 1.

Whitehorne, J. E. "Seventeen Days of Sunset." *Military Engineer* 31 (1939), no. 177.

Wilkeson, Frank. *Recollections of a Private Soldier.* 1887.

Willcox, Orlando B. "Actions on the Weldon Railroad." In Johnson and Buel, eds., *Battles and Leaders of the Civil War.* 1889.

Williams, T. Harry. *McClellan, Sherman and Grant.* 1962.

———. *P. G. T. Beauregard: Napoleon in Gray.* 1955.

Wilson, James H. *A Life of John A. Rawlins.* 1916.

———. "Major General Andrew A. Humphreys." *Massachusetts MOLLUS* 10 (1893).

Wilson, LeGrand James. *The Confederate Soldier.* 1902.

Winkler, A. V. (Mrs). *The Confederate Capital & Hood's Texas Brigade.* 1894.

Wise, John Sergeant. *The End of an Era.* 1902.

Wood, William N. *Reminiscences of Big I.* 1956.

Woodbury, Augustus. *Major General Ambrose E. Burnside & the Ninth Army Corps.* 1867.

Wright, J. E. M. "From Petersburg to Appomattox Court House." *Maine Bugle,* campaign 1 (1894), call 2.

Yeary, Mamie, comp. *Reminiscences of the Boys in Gray, 1861-1865.* 1912.

Published Autobiographies, Biographies, Diaries, Letters, Memoirs, and Personal Narratives (Civilian and Medical)

Adams, George Washington. *Doctors in Blue.* 1961.

Bates, David Homer. *Lincoln in the Telegraph Office.* 1907.

Campbell, John A. *Reminiscences & Documents Relating to the Civil War.* 1889.

Carpenter, C. C. "President Lincoln in Petersburg." *Century Magazine* 57 (1890).

Chesnut, Mary Boykin. *A Diary from Dixie.* 1949.

Claiborne, John Herbert. *Letters, 1864-1865.* 1961.

———. *Seventy-five Years in Old Virginia.* 1904.

Collier, Charles F. "War Recollections." *Southern Historical Society Papers* 22. (1894).

Collis, Septima M. *A Woman's War Record.* 1889.

Conolly, Thomas. *An Irishman in Dixie.* 1988.

Crook, William H. "Lincoln's Last Day." *Harper's Monthly Magazine.* 1907.

Dana, Charles A. *Recollections of the Civil War.* 1898.

Davis, Jefferson. *The Rise and Fall of the Confederate Government.* 1881.

de Chambrun, Adolphe. *Impressions of Lincoln and the Civil War.* 1952.

———. "Personal Recollections of Mr. Lincoln." *Scribner's Magazine* 13 (1893), no. 1.

DeLeon, Thomas Cooper. *Four Years in Rebel Capitals.* 1962.

Fay, Franklin B. *War Papers of Frank B. Fay.* 1911.

Friend, Embrey E. "My Father and His Household." 1897. [Pamphlet]

Harrison, Mrs. Burton. *Recollections Grave and Gay.* 1911.

Jaquette, Henrietta, ed. *South after Gettysburg: Letters of Cornelia Hancock.* 1956.

Jones, John B. *A Rebel War Clerk's Diary.* 1961.

Keckley, Elizabeth Hobbs. *Behind the Scenes.* 1868.

Keyes, Edward L. *Lewis Atterbury Stimson, M.D.* 1918.

Laugel, Auguste. "Auguste Laugel Visits the Army of the Potomac." *Virginia Magazine of History & Biography,* 1961.

McKay, Charlotte E. *Stories of Hospital and Camp.* 1876.

Palmer, Sarah A. *Story of Aunt Becky's Army-Life.* 1867.

Pember, Phoebe Yates. *A Southern Woman's Story.* 1959.

Potter, William Warren. *Reminiscences of Field-Hospital Service.* 1889.

Pryor, Mrs. Roger A. (Sarah). *Reminiscences of Peace and War.* 1908.

Reagan, John H. *Memoirs.* 1906.

Segal, Charles M., ed. *Conversations with Lincoln.* 1961.

Smith, Adelaide. *Reminiscences of an Army Nurse.* 1911.

Smith, Elbert B. *Francis Preston Blair.* 1980.

Younger, Edward, ed. *Inside the Confederate Government.* 1957.

Unit Histories

Adams, John G. B. *Reminiscences of the Nineteenth Massachusetts Regiment.* 1899.

Albert, Allen Diehl, ed. *History of the Forty-fifth Regiment Pennsylvania Veteran Volunteer Infantry.* 1912.

Allen, George H. *Forty-six Months with the 4th Rhode Island Volunteers.* 1887.

Ames, Nelson. *History of Battery G, New York Light Artillery.* 1900.

Anderson, John. *Fifty-seventh Regiment of Massachusetts Volunteers.* 1896.

Andrews, Welburn. *Sketch of Co. K, 23rd South Carolina Volunteers.* 1909.

Aston, Howard. *History and Roster of the ... 13th Regiment Ohio Volunteers.* 1902.

Aubery, James Madison. *Thirty-sixth Wisconsin Volunteer Infantry.* 1900.

Aycock, Burnell L. *A Sketch of the Lone Star Guards.* N.d.

Baker, Levi. *History of the Ninth Mass. Battery.* 1888.

Balfour, Daniel T. *13th Virginia Calvary.* 1986.

Banes, Charles H. *History of the Philadelphia Brigade.* 1876.

Baquet, Camille. *History of the First Brigade, New Jersey Volunteers.* 1910.

Bartlett, Asa W. *History of the Twelfth Regiment New Hampshire Volunteers.* 1897.

Bartlett, Napier. *A Soldier's Story of the War.* 1874.

Bates, Samuel. *Brief History of the 100th Regiment (Roundheads).* 1884.

———. *History of Pennsylvania Volunteers.* 1869.

Beach, William H. *The First New York (Lincoln) Cavalry.* 1902.

Beale, R. L. T. *History of the Ninth Virginia Cavalry.* 1899.

Beaudry, Louis Napoleon. *Historic Records of the Fifth New York Cavalry.* 1868.

Bedel, John. "Historical Sketch of the 3rd Regiment New Hampshire Volunteers." *Granite Monthly* 3 (1880), no. 12.

Beecher, Herbert W. *History of the 1st Light Battery Connecticut Volunteers.* 1901.

Bell, Robert E. *11th Virginia Infantry.* 1985.

Benedict, George G. *Vermont in the Civil War.* 1886.

Bennett, Andrew J. *Story of the 1st Massachusetts Light Battery.* 1886.

Bennett, Edgar. *First Connecticut Heavy Artillery, Historical Sketch.* 1889.

Best, Isaac O. *History of the 121st New York State Infantry.* 1921.

Bidwell, Frederick, comp. *History of the Forty-ninth New York Volunteers.* 1916.

Billings, John D. *History of the Tenth Massachusetts Battery.* 1909.

Bird, W. H. *Stories of the Civil War.* 1910.

Bosbyshell, Oliver. *The 48th in the War.* 1895.

Bowen, James Lorenzo. *Massachusetts in the War, 1861-1865.* 1889.

———. *History of the Thirty-seventh Regiment Massachusetts Volunteers.* 1884.

Bowen, James Riley. *Regimental History of the 1st New York Dragoons.* 1900.

Brady, Robert. *Story of One Regiment, 11th Maine Volunteers.* 1896.

Brainard, Mary G. *Campaigns of the 146th Regiment, New York State Volunteers.* 1915.

Brewer, Abraham T. *History Sixty-first Regiment Pennsylvania Volunteers.* 1911.

Brewer, Willis. *Alabama: Her History, Resources, War Record.* 1872.

Brief History of the Fourth Pennsylvania Veteran Cavalry. 1891.

Brooks, U. R. *Butler and His Cavalry in the War of Secession.* 1909.

———, ed. *Stories of the Confederacy.* 1912.

Brown, Henri le Fevre. *History of the . . . 72d New York Volunteer Infantry.* 1902.

Brown, Maud. *University Greys: Co. A, Eleventh Mississippi.* 1940.

Bruce, George Anson. *Twentieth Regiment of Massachusetts Volunteer Infantry.* 1906.

Buck, Samuel D. *With the Old Confeds.* 1925.

Buford, T., comp. *Lamar Rifles: History of Co. G, 11th Mississippi Regiment.* 1903.

Burnett, William G. *Better a Patriot Soldier's Grave.* 1982.

Burrage, Henry. *History of the 36th Regiment Massachusetts Volunteers.* 1884.

Burton, Joseph Q. *Historical Sketch of the Forty-seventh Alabama Regiment.* N.d.

Cadwell, Charles K. *The Old Sixth Regiment.* 1875.

Caldwell, J. F. J. *History of a Brigade of South Carolinians.* 1866.

Califf, Joe M. *Record of the Services of the 7th Regiment United States Colored Troops.* 1878.

Camper, Charles, comp. *Historical Record of the 1st Regiment Maryland Infantry.* 1871.

Cavanaugh, Michael A. *6th Virginia Infantry.* 1988.

Chamberlayne, Edwin H. *War History and Roll of the Richmond Fayette Artillery.* 1883.

Chamberlin, Thomas. *History of the One Hundred and Fiftieth Regiment.* 1905.

Chapla, John. *42nd Virginia Infantry.* 1983.

Chase, Philip S. *Battery F, 1st Regiment Rhode Island Light Artillery.* 1892. Cheek, Philip. History of the Sauk County Rifleman. 1909.

Cheney, Newel. *History of the 9th Regiment New York Volunteer Cavalry.* 1901.

Child, William. *History of the Fifth Regiment New Hampshire Volunteers.* 1893.

Clark, C. M. *History of the Thirty-ninth Regt. Illinois Volunteer Veteran Infantry.* 1889.

Clark, James H. *The Iron Hearted Regiment.* 1865.

Clark, Walter. *Histories of the Several Regiments & Battalions from North Carolina.* 1901.

Cleveland, Mather. *New Hampshire Fights the Civil War.* 1969.

Coates, Earl J. "The Bloody First Maine." *Civil War Times Illustrated* 11 (1972), no. 4.

Cogswell, Leander. *History of the Eleventh New Hampshire Regiment.* 1891.

Coker, James Lide. *History of Co. G, 9th South Carolina, & Co. E, 6th South Carolina Regiment.* 1899.

Collier, Calvin L. *They'll Do to Tie To!* 1959.

Company D of the 11th Regiment Maine Infantry Volunteers. 1890.

Conyngham, D. P. *The Irish Brigade and Its Campaigns.* 1867.

Cook, Benjamin F. *History of the 12th Massachusetts Volunteers.* 1882.

"Cooper's 'Battery B' Before Petersburg." *Blue and Gray Magazine* 4 (1894), no. 1.

Cowtan, Charles. *Services of the Tenth New York Volunteers.* 1882.

Craft, David. *History of the 141st Regiment Pennsylvania Volunteers.* 1885.

Crater, Lewis. *History of the 50th Regiment, Penna. Vet. Volunteers.* 1884.

Croom, Wendell D. *War History of Co. C, 6th Georgia Regiment.* 1879.

Crotty, Daniel G. *Four Years Campaigning in the Army of Potomac.* 1874.

Crowninshield, Benjamin. *History of the 1st Regiment of Mass. Cavalry.* 1891.

Cuffel, Charles A. *History of Durrell's Battery in the Civil War.* 1903.

Cunningham, John. *Three Years with the Adirondack Regiment.* 1920.

Curtis, O. B. *History of the Twenty-fourth Michigan.* 1891.

Cushman, Frederick E. *History of the j8th Regt. Massachusetts Volunteers.* 1865.

Cutcheon, Byron M. *Story of the Twentieth Michigan Infantry.* 1904.

Cutchins, John A. *A Famous Command - Richmond Light Blues.* 1934.

Daniel, Frederick S. *Richmond Howitzers in the War,* 1891.

Day, W. A. *A True History of Co. I, 49th Regiment, North Carolina Troops.* 1893.

Denison, Frederic. *Sabres and Spurs: The 1st Regiment Rhode Island Cavalry.* 1876.

Dennett, George M. *History of the Ninth U.S.C. Troops.* 1866.

Denny, Joseph. *Wearing the Blue in the Twenty-fifth Massachusetts.* 1879.

Derby, William P. *Bearing Arms in the Twenty-seventh Massachusetts Regiment.* 1883.

Dickert, D. Augustus. *History of Kershaw's Brigade.* 1899.

Dickey, Luther. *History of the Eighty-fifth Regiment Pennsylvania Volunteer Infantry.* 1915.

Divine, John E. *35th Virginia Cavalry Battalion.* 1985.

———. *8th Virginia Infantry.* 1983.

Drake, James Madison. *History of the Ninth New Jersey Veteran Volunteers.* 1889.

Driver, Robert J., Jr. *52nd Virginia Infantry.* 1986.

DuBose, Henry Kershaw. *History of Company B, 21st South Carolina Regiment.* 1909.

Dunlop, W. S. *Lee's Sharpshooters.* 1899.

Eden, Robert C. *Sword and the Gun, History of the 37th Wisconsin.* 1865.

Edwards, W. H. *Condensed History of 17th Regiment S.C.V., C.S.A.* 1909.

Eldredge, Daniel. *The Third New Hampshire.* 1893.

Elliott, Charles G. "Martin's Brigade, 1863-64," *Southern Historical Society Papers* 23 (1895).

Embick, Milton, ed. *Military History of the 3rd Division, 9th Corps.* 1913.

Emmerton, James. *Record of the Twenty-third Regiment Massachusetts Volunteer Infantry.* 1886.

Everts, Hermann. *Complete and Comprehensive History 9th New Jersey.* 1865.

Fields, Frank E., Jr. *28th Virginia Infantry.* 1985.

Fifty-second Reunion of the 10th New York Cavalry. 1913.

Fleming, Elvis E., ed. "Some Hard Fighting." *Military History of Texas & the Southwest.* 1971.

Floyd, Frederick. *History of the Fortieth (Mozart) Regiment.* 1909.

Fontaine, Clement R. *Complete Roster of the . . . 57th Virginia Regiment of Infantry.* N.d.

Ford, Andrew E. *Story of the Fifteenth Regiment Massachusetts Volunteer Infantry.* 1898.

Foster, Alonzo. *Reminiscences and Record of the 6th New York Veteran Volunteer Cavalry.* 1892.

Foster, John Young. *New Jersey and the Rebellion.* 1868.

Frederick, Gilbert. *Story of a Regiment.* 1895.

Frye, Dennis E. *2nd Virginia Infantry.* 1984.

Fuller, Edward H. *Battles of the Seventy-seventh New York.* 1901.

Galloway, G. Norton. *Ninety-fifth Pennsylvania Volunteers in the Sixth Corps.* 1884.

Garrett, James Jackson. "Forty-fourth Alabama Regiment." *Transactions of the Alabama Historical Society* 2 (1898).

Gates, Theodore B. *Ulster Guard and the War of the Rebellion.* 1879.

Gibbs, James M. *History of the . . . 187th Regiment Pennsylvania Volunteer Infantry.* 1905.

Goldsborough, William W. *The Maryland Line in the Confederate Army.* 1900.

Goolsby, John. "The Crenshaw Battery." *Southern Historical Society Papers* 28 (1900).

Gould, Joseph. *Story of the Forty-eighth.* 1908.

Gracey, Samuel. *Annals of the Sixth Pennsylvania Cavalry.* 1868.

Graves, Joseph A. *History of the Bedford Light Artillery.* 1903.

Gregory, G. Howard. *38th Virginia Infantry.* 1988.

Gunn, Ralph White. *24th Virginia Infantry.* 1987.

Haines, Alanson A. *History of the Fifteenth Regiment New Jersey Volunteers.* 1883.

Haines, William P. *History of the Men of Co. F. 1897.*

Hale, Laura V., and Phillips, Stanley S. *History of the Forty-ninth Virginia Inf.* 1981.

Hall, Harry H. *Johnny Reb Band from Salem.* 1963.

Hall, Henry and James. *Cayuga in the Field.* 1873.

Hall, Isaac. *History of the 97th Regiment New York Volunteers.* 1890.

Hanifen, Michael. *History of Battery B, First New Jersey Artillery.* 1905.

Hanks, O. T. *History of Captain B. F. Benton's Company.* 1984.

Harris, James S. *Historical Sketches of the 7th Regiment North Carolina Troops.* 1893.

Haynes, Edwin M. *History of the Tenth Regiment Vermont Volunteers.* 1870.

Haynes, Martin A. *History of the Second Regiment, New Hampshire Volunteers.* 1896.

Hays, Gilbert, comp. *Under the Red Patch.* 1908.

Henderson, William D. *41st Virginia Infantry.* 1986.

——. *12th Virginia Infantry.* 1984.

Herbert, Hilary A. "History of the Eighth Alabama Volunteer Regiment." *Alabama Historical Quarterly* 39 (1977).

Hill, Isaac J. *Sketch of the 29th Regiment of Connecticut Colored Troops.* 1867.

A Historical Sketch of the Quitman Guards. 1866.

History of the Eighteenth Regiment of Cavalry. 1909.

History of the Eleventh Pennsylvania Volunteer Cavalry. 1902.

History of the Fifth Massachusetts Battery. 1902.

History of the Fifty-seventh Regiment, Pennsylvania Veteran Volunteer Infantry. 1904.

History of the Fourth Maine Battery. 1905.

History of the One Hundred Twenty-first Regiment Pennsylvania Volunteers. 1893.

History of the Sixth New York Cavalry. 1908.

History of the Third Pennsylvania Cavalry. 1905.

History of the Thirty-fifth Regiment Massachusetts Volunteers. 1884.

Holmes, Torlief S. *Horse Soldiers in Blue.* 1985.

Hopkins, William. *Seventh Regiment Rhode Island Volunteers.* 1903.

Houghton, Edwin B. *The Campaigns of the Seventeenth Maine.* 1866.

House, Charles J. "How the 1st Maine Heavy Artillery Lost 1,179 Men in 30 Days." *Maine Bugle,* campaign 2 (1895), call 2.

Houston, Henry. *Thirty-second Maine Regiment of Infantry.* 1903.

Howell, H. *Chronicles of the 151st Regiment New York State Volunteer Infantry.* 1911.

Hutchinson, Gustavus B. *Narrative of the Formation . . . 11th MA Volunteers.* 1893.

Hutchinson, John G. *Roster of the Fourth Regiment of New Hampshire Volunteers.* 1896.

Hyde, William. *History of the 112th Regiment N.Y. Volunteers.* 1866.

Hyndman, William. *History of a Cavalry Company.* 1872.

Iobst, Richard W. *The Bloody Sixth.* 1965.

Irby, Richard. *Historical Sketch of the Nottoway Grays.* 1878.

Izlar, William. *Sketch of the War Record of the Edisto Rifles.* 1914.

Jacklin, Rufus W. "The Famous Old Third Brigade." *Michigan MOLLUS* 2 (1898).

Jackman, Lyman. *History of the Sixth New Hampshire Regiment.* 1891.

Jago, Frederick W. *12th New Jersey Volunteers:* 1862-65. 1967.

Jenkins, W. H. "The Thirty-Ninth Illinois Volunteers." *Transactions of the Illinois State Historical Society,* 1914.

Jones, Benjamin W. *Under the Stars and Bars.* 1909.

Jones, Samuel C. *Reminiscences of the 22nd Iowa Volunteer Infantry.* 1907.

Judson, Amos M. *History of the Eighty-third Regiment Pennsylvania Volunteers.* 1865.

Keyes, Charles M. *Military History of the 123d Regiment Ohio Volunteer Infantry.* 1874.

King, David H. *History of the 93rd Regiment, New York Volunteer Infantry.* 1895.

Kirk, Hyland C. *Heavy Guns and Light.* 1890.

Kreutzer, William. *Notes and Observations.* 1879.

Krick, Robert E. L. *40th Virginia Infantry.* 1985.

Krick, Robert K. *The Fredericksburg Artillery.* 1986.

———. *30th Virginia Infantry.* 1985.

———. *9th Virginia Cavalry.* 1982.

———. *Parker's Virginia Battery C.S.A.* 1975.

Lane, James H. "History of Lane's North Carolina Brigade." *Southern Historical Society Papers* 9 (1881).

Laughton, John E. "The Sharpshooters of Mahone's Brigade." *Southern Historical Society Papers* 22 (1894).

Levstik, Frank R. "The Fifth Regiment, U.S. Colored Troops." *Northwest Ohio Quarterly,* 1970.

Lewis, George. *History of Battery E, 1st Regiment Rhode Island Light Artillery.* 1892.

Lewis, Osceola. *History of the 138th Regiment, Pennsylvania Volunteers.* 1866.

Lindsley, John B., ed. *Military Annals of Tennessee.* 1886.

Little, Henry F. W. *Seventh Regiment New Hampshire Volunteers.* 1896.

Livermore, Thomas L. *History of the Eighteenth New Hampshire Volunteers.* 1904.

Lloyd, William Penn. *History of the First Regiment Pennsylvania Reserve Cavalry.* 1864.

Locke, William. *The Story of the Regiment.* 1868.

Loehr, Charles T. War *History of the Old 1st Virginia Infantry Regiment.* 1884.

Lord, Edward Oliver. *History of the Ninth Regiment, New Hampshire Volunteers.* 1895.

Love, D. C. *The Prairie Guards.* 1890.

McAlpine, Charles R. "Sketch of Co. I, Sixty-first Virginia Infantry." *Southern Historical Society Papers* 24 (1896).

McBrien, Joe Bennett. *The Tennessee Brigade.* 1977.

McDermott, Anthony. *Brief History of the 69th Regiment Pennsylvania Veteran Volunteers.* 1889.

McDonald, William N. *A History of the Laurel Brigade.* 1907.

Manarin, Louis H. *Richmond Volunteers:* 1861-1865. 1969.

Marbaker, Thomas. *History of the Eleventh New Jersey Volunteers.* 1898.

Marcus, Jacob Rader, ed. *Memoirs of American Jews: 1775-1865.* 1955.

Mark, Penrose G. *Red, White, and Blue Badge.* 1911.

Marvel, William. *Race of the Soil-9th New Hampshire Regiment in the Civil War.* 1988.

———. *The First New Hampshire Battery: 1861-1865.* 1985.

Maxfield, Albert. *Roster & Statistical Record of Company D.* 1890.

Mickley, Jeremiah M. *Forty-third Regiment U.S. Colored Troops.* 1866.

Miers, Earl Schenck, ed. *Ride to War: History of the 1st New Jersey Cavalry.* 1961.

Mills, George H. *History of the 16th North Carolina Regiment.* 1901.

Minnesota in the Civil and Indian Wars. 1890.

Morgan, William H., comp. *Narrative of the Service of Company D.* 1907.

Mowris, James A. *History of the 117th Regiment N.Y. Volunteers.* 1866.

Moyer, Henry P. *History of the 17th Regiment Pennsylvania Volunteer Cavalry.* 1911.

Muffly, Joseph. *Story of Our Regiment.* 1904.

Mulholland, Saint Clair A. *Story of the 116th Regiment, Pennsylvania Infantry.* 1899.

Murphey, Thomas G. *History of the 1st Regiment of Delaware Veteran Volunteers.* 1866.

Murray, Thomas H. *History of the Ninth Regiment, Connecticut Volunteer Infantry.* 1903.

Myers, Frank M. *The Comanches.* 1871.

Nash, Eugene Arus. *History of the Forty-fourth Regiment New York Volunteers.* 1910.

Newell, Joseph, ed. *Ours: Annals of 10th Regiment Massachusetts Volunteers.* 1875.

Nichols, James M. *Perry's Saints.* 1886.

Norton, C. S. *Red Neck Ties, or History of 15th New York Volunteer Cavalry.* 1891.

Norton, Henry. *Deeds of Daring - History of 8th New York Volunteer Cavalry.* 1889.

Oehmig, B. A. "Gen. B. R. Johnson's Tennessee Brigade." *Confederate Veteran* 9 (1901).

Osborne, Wm. H. *History of the 29th Regiment of Massachusetts Volunteer Infantry.* 1877.

Owens, Ira S. *Greene County Soldiers in the Late War.* 1884.

Page, Charles D. *History of the Fourteenth Regiment, Connecticut Volunteer Infantry.* 1906.

Palmer, Abraham. *History of the Forty-eighth Regiment New York State Volunteers.* 1885.

Parker, Francis J. *Story of the 32nd Regiment Massachusetts Infantry.* 1880.

Parker, John Lord. *Henry Wilson's Regiment.* 1887.

Parker, Thomas H. *History of the 51st Regiment of Pennsylvania Volunteers and Veteran Volunteers.* 1869.

Pickerill, William N. *History of the Third Indiana Cavalry.* 1906.

Polley, J. B. *Hood's Texas Brigade.* 1910.

Porter, John A. *76th Regiment Pennsylvania Volunteer Infantry.* 1988.

Powell, William H. *The Fifth Army Corps.* 1895.

———. *History of the Organization & Movements of the 4th Regiment.* 1871.

Powelson, Benjamin. *History of Company K of the 140th Regiment Pennsylvania Volunteers.* 1906.

Preston, Noble D. *History of the 10th Regiment of Cavalry New York State Volunteers.* 1892.

Price, Isaiah. *History of the 97th Regiment Pennsylvania Volunteer Infantry.* 1875.

Prowell, George. *History of the Eighty-seventh Regiment Pennsylvania Volunteers.* 1901.

Pullen, John J. *The Twentieth Maine.* 1957.

Putnam, Samuel. *Story of Company A, Twenty-fifth Regiment Massachusetts.* 1886.

Rankin, Thomas M. *23rd Virginia Infantry.* 1985.

Rauscher, Frank. *Music on the March.* 1892.

Reid, Jesse Walton. *History of the Fourth Regiment of South Carolina Volunteers.* 1892.

Reidenbaugh, Lowell. *33rd Virginia Infantry.* 1987.

Rhodes, Elisha H. "2nd Rhode Island Volunteers at Siege of Petersburg." *Rhode Island Soldiers' and Sailors' Narratives,* series 7 (1915).

Rhodes, John H. *History of Battery B, First Regiment Rhode Island Light Artillery.* 1894.

Richards, Donald H. "The Fifth New Hampshire Volunteers." *Historical New Hampshire* 28 (1973), no. 4.

Riggs, David F. *7th Virginia Infantry.* 1982.

Ripley, William Y. W. *Vermont Riflemen in the War for the Union.* 1883.

Roback, Henry. *Veteran Volunteers of Herkimer & Otsego.* 1888.

Roberts, Agatha. *As They Remembered.* 1964.

Robertson, Frederick L. *Soldiers of Florida.* 1909.

Robertson, James I. *18th Virginia Infantry.* 1984.

———. *4th Virginia Infantry.* 1982.

Robertson, Jno., comp. *Michigan in the War.* 1882.

Roe, Alfred. *History of the 1st Regiment of Heavy Artillery Massachusetts Volunteers.* 1917.

———. *Thirty-ninth Regiment Massachusetts Volunteers.* 1914.

———. *Tenth Regiment Massachusetts Volunteer Infantry.* 1909.

———. *Twenty-fourth Regiment Massachusetts Volunteers.* 1907.

———. *The Ninth New York Heavy Artillery.* 1899.

Rogers, William H. *History of the 189th Regiment of New York Volunteers.* 1865.

Ruffner, Kevin Conley. *44th Virginia Infantry.* 1987.

———. *From Aguia to Appomattox: History of 30th Virginia.* 1978.

Salley, A. S., comp. *South Carolina Troops in Confederate Service.* 1930.

Santvoord, C. Van. *One Hundred and Twentieth Regiment New York State Volunteers.* 1983.

Schneider, Frederick. *Incidental History of the Flags ... of 2nd Michigan.* 1905.

Scott, Kate M. *History of the 105th Regiment of Pennsylvania Volunteers.* 1877.

Seville, William P. *History of the First Regiment, Delaware Volunteers.* 1884.

Shaver, Lewellyn A. *History of the Sixtieth Alabama Regiment.* 1867.

Shaw, Horace H. *The First Maine Heavy Artillery.* 1903.

Simmes, J. P. "Official Report of Operations 6/2-12/30." *Southern Historical Society Papers* 13 (1885).

Simons, Ezra. *Regimental History the 125th New York State Volunteers.* 1888.

Simpson, Harold. *Gaines' Mill to Appomattox.* 1963.

Sloan, John A. *Reminiscences of the Guilford Grays.* 1883.

Small, Abner. *The Sixteenth Maine Regiment.* 1886.

Smith, A. P. *History of the Seventy-sixth Regiment New York Volunteers.* 1867.

Smith, Donald L. *Twenty-fourth Michigan of the Iron Brigade.* 1962.

Smith, John Day. *History of the Nineteenth Regiment of Maine Volunteers.* 1909-

Smith, John L. *History of the Corn Exchange Regiment.* 1888.

Smith, W. A. *The Anson Guards.* 1914.

Spencer, John. *From Corsicana to Appomattox.* 1984.

Stevens, C. A. *Berdan's United States Sharpshooters.* 1892.

Stevenson, James H. *Boots and Saddles: History of the ...1st New York Cavalry.* 1879.

Stewart, Robert L. *History of the 140th Regiment Pennsylvania Volunteers.* 1912.

Stiles, Kenneth L. *4th Virginia Cavalry.* 1985.

Story of the Twenty-first Regiment Connecticut Volunteer Infantry. 1900.

Stowits, George H. *History of the One Hundredth Regiment New York State Volunteers.* 1870.

Sublett, Charles W. *57th Virginia Infantry.* 1985.

Sutton, Joseph J. *History of the 2nd Regiment West Virginia Cavalry.* 1892.

Swinfen, David B. *Ruggles' Regiment: The 122nd New York Volunteers in the Civil War.* 1982.

Tennessee Civil War Centennial Committee. *Tennesseans in the Civil War.* 1964.

Terrill, John. *Campaigns of the Fourteenth Regiment, New Jersey Volunteers.* 1866.

Thomas, Henry Walter. *History of the Doles-Cook Brigade.* 1903.

Thompson, James Monroe. *Reminiscences of the Autauga Rifles.* 1879.

Thompson, S. Millett. *Thirteenth Regiment of New Hampshire Volunteer Infantry.* 1888.

Tobie, Edward P. *History of the First Maine Cavalry.* 1887.

Todd, William. *Seventy-ninth Highlanders New York Volunteers.* 1886.

Tompkins, Daniel Augustus. *Company K, Fourteenth South Carolina Volunteers.* 1897.

Tourtellotte, Jerome. *History of Company K of the 7th Connecticut Volunteer Infantry.* 1910.

Trask, Benjamin H. *9th Virginia Infantry.* 1984

———. *16th Virginia Infantry.* 1986.

———. *61st Virginia Infantry.* 1988.

Under the Maltese Cross: Antietam to Appomattox. 1910.

Underwood, George C. *History of the Twenty-sixth Regiment of North Carolina Troops.* 1901.

Vaill, Theodore. *History of the 2nd Connecticut Volunteer Heavy Artillery.* 1868.

Valentine, Herbert E. *Story of Company F, 23 d Massachusetts Volunteers*. 1896.

Vautier, John D. *History of the 88th Pennsylvania Volunteers*. 1894.

Waitt, Ernest L., comp. *History of the Nineteenth Regiment Massachusetts Volunteer Infantry*. 1906.

Walcott, Charles. *History of the 21st Regiment Massachusetts Volunteers*. 1882.

Walker, Francis A. *History of the Second Army Corps*. 1887.

Walkley, Stephen, comp. *History of the 7th Connecticut Volunteer Infantry*. 1905-

Wall, H. C. *Historical Sketch of the Pee Dee Guards*. 1876.

Wallace, Lee A., Jr. *3rd Virginia Infantry*. 1986.

———. *5th Virginia Infantry*. 1988.

Ward, George W. *History of the 2nd Pennsylvania Veteran Heavy Artillery*. 1904.

Ward, Joseph Ripley. *History of the 106th Regiment Pennsylvania Volunteers*. 1883.

Warren, Horatio N. *Two Reunions of the 142d Regiment, Pa. Volunteers*. 1890.

Washburn, George H. *Complete Military History & Record 108th New York*. 1894.

Webb, Edward P. *History of the 10th Regiment N.Y. Heavy Artillery*. 1887.

Wells, Edward L. *Hampton and his Cavalry in '64*. 1899.

———. *Sketch of the Charleston Light Dragoons*. 1888.

Westbrook, Robert S. *History of the 49th Pennsylvania Volunteers*. 1898.

Weygant, Charles H. *History of the One Hundred and Twenty-fourth*. 1877.

Whitman, William. *Maine in the War for the Union*. 1865.

Willson, Arabella M. *Disaster, Struggle, Triumph*. 1870.

Wilson, Joseph T. *Black Phalanx: History of the Negro Soldiers of the United States*. 1888.

Wise, George. *History of the Seventeenth Virginia Infantry*. 1870.

Wise, Henry A. "The Career of Wise's Brigade." *Southern Historical Society Papers* 25 (1897).

Woodbury, Augustus. *The Second Rhode Island Regiment*. 1875.

Woodward, Evan M. *History of the 198th Pennsylvania Volunteers*. 1884.

Wray, William James. *History of the 23rd Pennsylvania Volunteer Infantry*. 1904.

Zierdt, William. *Narrative History of the 109th Field Art*. 1932.

Campaign and Battle Studies

Alexander, E. P. "The Movement Against Petersburg." *Century Magazine* 41 (1907).

Allen, Cornelius T. "Fight at Chaffin's Farm, or Fort Harrison." *Confederate Veteran* 13 (1906).

Anson, Charles H. "Assault on the Lines of Petersburg, April 2." *Wisconsin MOLLUS* 1 (1891).

"Battle at Fort Gregg—Louisiana Survivors Tell." *Southern Historical Society Papers* 28 (1900).

Beals, Thomas P. "In a Charge near Fort Hell, Petersburg." *Maine MOLLUS* 2 (1902).

Bearss, Edwin C. "Sergeant Major Hawkins & Black Heroes." 1980. [Pamphlet]

———. "Deep Bottom Report." 1978. [Pamphlet]

———. "The Battle of Reams' Station." N.d. [Pamphlet]

———. "Battle of the Weldon Railroad." N.d. [Pamphlet]

———. "The VI Corps Scores a Breakthrough." N.d. [Pamphlet]

———, and Bruce Suderow, ed. *The Petersburg Campaign: The Eastern Front Battles.* (2012)

———, and Bruce Suderow, ed. *The Petersburg Campaign: The Western Front Battles.* (2014)

Beaudot, William J. K. "The Bravest Act of the War." *Virginia Country's Civil War Quarterly,* 1986.

Boykin, Edward. *Beefsteak Raid.* 1960.

———. Falling Flag—The Evacuation of Richmond. 1874.

Bradwell, I. G. "Fort Steadman and Subsequent Events." *Confederate Veteran* 23 (1915).

Breckinridge, G. W. "Story of a Boy Captain." *Confederate Veteran* 13 (1906).

Bruce, George A. "Petersburg, June 15 - Fort Harrison, Sept. 29." *Massachusetts MOLLUS,* 1917.

———. "The Capture and Occupation of Richmond." *Massachusetts MOLLUS,* 1915.

Burbank, Horace H. "The Battle of 'The Crater.'" *Maine MOLLUS* 1 (1898).

Calkins, Chris M. "The Apple Jack Raid, December 7-12, 1864: 'For This Barbarism There Was No Real Excuse'." *Blue & Gray Magazine,* Volume XXII/Issue 3, 2005.

Calkins, Chris M., and Bearss, Edwin C. *Battle of Five Forks.* 1985.

Cardwell, David. "A Brilliant Coup." *Southern Historical Society Papers* 22 (1894).

Case, Ervin T. "Battle of the Mine." *Rhode Island Soldiers' and Sailors' Narratives,* series 1 (1879).

Cavanaugh, Michael A., and Marvel, Wm. *Battle of the Crater: "The Horrid Pit."* 1989.

Chase. James J. "The Charge at Day-Break." 1875.

Clay, Cecil. "Narrative of the Capture of Fort Harrison." *District of Columbia MOLLUS* 1 (1891), no. 7.

Coit, J. C. "The Battle of the Crater, July 30, 1864." *Southern Historical Society Papers* 10 (1882).

Committee on Conduct of War. "Report ... on the Attack on Petersburg." 1882.

Cryer, Matt. H. "The Last Fighting Campaign: Dinwiddie Court House." 1911.

Cullen, Joseph P. "Petersburg." In Editors of *Civil War Times Illustrated,* eds., *Great Battles of the Civil War.* 1984.

Dauchy, George K. "The Battle of Ream's Station." *Illinois MOLLUS*, 3 (1899).

Davis, Burke. *To Appomattox: Nine April Days*, 1865. 1959.

Davis, L. H. "Famous Cattle Raid." *Confederate Veteran* 26 (1918).

Davis, William C. *Death in the Trenches*. 1986.

"Defenders of Fort Gregg." *Confederate Veteran* 25 (1917).

Driver, William R. "Siege of Petersburg After the Weldon Railroad." *Massachusetts MOLLUS* 5 (1906).

Flanigan, W. A. "That Fight at Fort Gilmer." *Confederate Veteran* 13 (1906).

Fossen, Robert D. Van. "Sketch of Happenings at the Davis Farm, 1864." 1911.

Funkhouser, Robert D. "Fort Steadman — So Near and Yet So Far." *Confederate Veteran* 19 (1911).

Granberry, J. A. H. "That Fort Gilmer Fight." *Confederate Veteran*, 13 (1906).

Greene, A. Wilson. *Breaking the Backbone of the Rebellion: The Final Battles of the Petersburg Campaign*. 2000.

———. "April 2, 1865: Day of Decision at Petersburg." *Blue & Gray Magazine*, Volume XVIII/Issue 3, 2000.

Harvey, O. K. "Explosion at City Point." *National Tribune Scrapbook*, vol. 2. N.d.

Hodgkins, William H. *The Battle of Fort Stedman*. 188[?].

Hoehling, A. A. *The Last Days of the Confederacy*. 1981.

Howe, Thomas J. Wasted Valor: *The Petersburg Campaign, June 15-18. 1988.*

Humphreys, Andrew A. *The Virginia Campaign of 1864 and 1865*. 1883.

Johnston, Charles. "Attack on Fort Gilmer, September 29th, 1864." *Southern Historical Society Papers 1* (1876).

Jones, A. C. "Texas and Arkansas at Fort Harrison." *Confederate Veteran* 25 (1917)-

Jones, A. K. "The Battle of Fort Gregg." *Southern Historical Society Papers* 31 (1903)-

Jones, Thomas G. "Last Days of the Army of Northern Virginia." 1893.

Kilmer, George L. "The Dash into the Crater." *Century Magazine* 46 (1887).

Klein, Frederic S. "Lost Opportunity at Petersburg." *Civil War Times Illustrated* 5 (1966), no. 5.

Korn, Jerry. *Pursuit to Appomattox*. 1987.

Lane, James H. "Defence of Battery Gregg — Reply to N. Harris." *Southern Historical Society Papers* 9 (1881).

Longacre, E. "The Petersburg Follies." *Civil War Times Illustrated* 18 (1980), no. 9.

Lott, Jess B. "Two Boys of the Fifth Texas Regiment." *Confederate Veteran* 13 (1906).

Lykes, Richard W. "The Great Civil War Beef Raid." *Civil War Times Illustrated* 5 (1967), no. 10.

Lyman, Theodore. "Crossing of the James & the Advance on Petersburg." *Massachusetts MOLLUS* 5 (1906).

McCabe, William Gordon. "The Defence of Petersburg." 1876.

McMaster, Fitz William. "The Battle of the Crater, July 30, 1864." *Southern Historical Society Papers* 10 (1882).

Mahone, William. "The Battle of the Crater." N.d. [Pamphlet]

Martin, Judge H. "The Assault Upon Fort Gilmer." *Confederate Veteran* 13 (1906).

Mewborn, Horace. "Herding Yankee Cattle: The Beefsteak Raid, September 14-17, 1864." *Blue & Gray Magazine*, Volume XXII/Issue 3, 2005.

Miers, Earl Schenck, ed. *The Last Campaign*. 1972.

Moore, James B. "The Attack of Fort Harrison." *Confederate Veteran* 13 (1906).

Newberry, Walter C. "The Petersburg Mine." *Illinois MOLLUS* 3 (1899).

Osborn, Francis A. "Bermuda Hundred, June 16 and 17, 1864." *Massachusetts MOLLUS* 5 (1906).

Owen, William M. "The Artillery Defenders of Fort Gregg." *Southern Historical Society Papers* 19 (1891).

Perry, Herman H. "Assault on Fort Gilmer." *Confederate Veteran* 13 (1906).

"Petersburg's Ninth of June." *Virginia Cavalcade*, Summer 1958.

Pickens, J. D. "Fort Harrison." *Confederate Veteran* 21 (1913).

Pleasants, Henry, Jr. *Inferno at Petersburg*. 1961.

Porter, Charles H. "Fifth Corps at the Battle of Five Forks." *Massachusetts MOLLUS* 6 (1907).

———. "Operations of the Fifth Corps on the Left." *Massachusetts MOLLUS* 6 (1907).

———. "Operations Against the Weldon Railroad." *Massachusetts MOLLUS* 5 (1906).

———. "The Petersburg Mine." *Massachusetts MOLLUS* 5 (1906).

Rhea, Gordon. "The Move to the James and the Battle of Riddell's Shop." *North and South Magazine*, vol. 10, no. 6 (2008).

Reese, George. "What Five Confederates Did at Petersburg." *Confederate Veteran* 11 (1904).

Richards, George W. "Fort Gregg Again—A Surgeon's Defense." *Southern Historical Society Papers* 31 (1903).

Robertson, William Glenn. *Battle of Old Men and Young Boys*. 1989.

Savas, Theodore P. "Last Clash of the Ironclads: The Bungled Affair at Trent's Reach." *Civil War Quarterly* 16 (February 1989).

Schaff, Morris. "The Explosion at City Point." *Massachusetts MOLLUS* 1 (1900).

Shearman, Sumner U. "Battle of the Crater." *Rhode Island Soldiers' and Sailors' Narratives*, series 5 (1898).

Sherman, George R. "Assault on Fort Gilmer." *Rhode Island Soldiers' and Sailors' Narratives*, series 5 (1898).

Skoch, George. "The Last Ditch." *Civil War Times Illustrated* 27 (1989), no. 9-

Slotkin, Richard. *No Quarter*. 2009.

Smith, William F. "The Movement Against Petersburg, June 1864." *Massachusetts MOLLUS* 5 (1906).

Sommers, Richard J. *Richmond Redeemed.* 1981.

——. "The Dutch Gap Affair." *Civil War History* 21 (1975), no. 1.

——. "The Battle No One Wanted." *Civil War Times Illustrated* 14 (1975), no. 5.

Stedman, Charles M. "Battle at Reams' Station." *Southern Historical Society Papers* 19 (1891).

Stern, Philip van Doren. *An End to Valor.* 1958.

Stevens, Hazard. "The Storming of the Lines of Petersburg by the Sixth Corps." *Massachusetts MOLLUS* 6 (1907).

Stewart, William H. "The Hardships of Hatcher's Run." *Confederate Veteran* 19 (1911).

——. "The Charge of the Crater." *Southern Historical Society Papers* 25 (1897).

——. "The 'No Name' Battle," *Blue and Gray Magazine* 5 (1895), no. 1.

Suderow, Bryce A. "Confederate Casualties near the Jerusalem Plank Road." *The Kepi* 3 (1985), no. 5.

——. "Confederate Casualties at the Crater." *The Kepi* 3 (1985), no. 3.

Swinton, William. *Campaigns of the Army of the Potomac.* 1866.

Thomas, Henry Goddard. "The Colored Troops at Petersburg." *Century Magazine* 12 (1887).

Thomas, William M. "The Slaughter at Petersburg —June 18, 1864." *Southern Historical Society Papers* 25 (1897).

Walker, D. N. "Capt. D. N. Walker's Notes on 'Crater Fight.'" 1892.

Walker, Francis A. "Expedition to the Boydton Plank Road." *Massachusetts MOLLUS* 5 (1906).

——. "Reams' Station." *Massachusetts MOLLUS* 5 (1906).

Walker, James A. "Gordon's Assault on Fort Stedman." *Southern Historical Society Papers* 31 (1903).

Wall, Edward. "The First Assault on Petersburg." *Proceedings of New Jersey Historical Society* 3 (1918), no. 4.

Watkins, Raymond W. "The Hicksford Raid." 1978.

Weld, Stephen M. "The Petersburg Mine." *Massachusetts MOLLUS* 5 (1906).

Wells, Stephen F. "Forts Harrison and Gilmer." *The National Tribune Scrap Book*, vol. 3. N.d.

Wickham, Williams C. "Battle of Reams's Station — Official Report." *Southern Historical Society Papers* 9 (1881).

Wilcox, Cadmus M. "Battery Gregg — Reply to Gen. N. H. Harris." *Southern Historical Society Papers* 9 (1881).

Winder, J. R. "Judge Martin's Report Approved." *Confederate Veteran* 13 (1906).
Wright, Marcus J. "Bushrod Johnson's Men at Fort Harrison." *Confederate Veteran* 14 (1906).
Wyrick, William C. "Bursting of the Storm: Action at Petersburg, March 25, 1865." *Blue & Gray Magazine,* Volume XXVIII/Issue 5, 2012.

Miscellaneous Works

Adams, Michael C. C. *Our Masters the Rebels.* 1978.
Beringer, Richard, et al. *Why the South Lost the Civil War.* 1986.
Bill, Alfred Hoyt. *The Beleaguered City.* 1946.
Binder, Frederick M. "Pennsylvania Negro Regiments in the Civil War." *Journal of Negro History* 37 (1952).
Butowsky, Harry. "Appomattox Manor — City Point: A History." 1978.
Calkins, Chris M. *Final Bivouac - Surrender Parade at Appomattox.* 1988.
——. "Geographic Description of the Petersburg Battlefield." *Virginia Geographer* 16 (Spring-Summer 1984).
Carr, Julian S. "The Hampton Roads Conference." 1917.
Catton, Bruce. *A Stillness at Appomattox.* 1954.
Cornish, Dudley Taylor. *The Sable Arm.* 1956.
Croffut, W. A. *Military & Civil History of Connecticut.* 1868.
Foote, Shelby. *The Civil War: A Narrative.* 1974.
Frassanito, William A. *Grant and Lee: The Virginia Campaigns.* 1983.
Freeman, Douglas S. *Lee's Lieutenants.* 1944.
Furness, William Eliot. "The Negro as a Soldier." *Illinois MOLLUS* 2 (1894).
Harrison, M. Clifford. *Home to the Cockade City!* 1942.
Greene, A. Wilson. *Civil War Petersburg: Confederate City in the Crucible of War.* 2006.
Heaps, W. A. and P. W. *The Singing Sixties,* 1960.
Henderson, William D. "Petersburg, Virginia, Confederate City." *Confederate History Institute Journal* 2 (1981), no. 3.
——. *Unredeemed City: Reconstruction in Petersburg.* 1977.
Hotchkiss, Jedidiah. *Confederate Military History: Virginia.* 1899.
Johnson, Ludwell H. "Lincoln's Solution to the Problems of Peace." *Journal of Southern History* 34 (1968), no. 4.
Jones, Terry L. *Lee's Tigers.* 1987.
Jones, Virgil Carrington. *Civil War at Sea: July 1863— November 1865.* 1962.
Kirkland, Frazar. *Pictorial Book of Anecdotes of the Rebellion.* 1889.
Leech, Margaret. *Reveille in Washington: 1860-1865.* 1941.
Linderman, Gerald F. *Embattled Courage.* 1987.
Livermore, Thomas L. *Numbers & Losses in the Civil War in America.* 1900.

Longacre, Edward. "Black Troops in the Army of the James 1863-65." *Military Affairs* 45 (1981), no. 1.

McPherson, James M. *The Negro's Civil War.* 1965.

Macrae, David. *The Americans at Home.* 1952.

Miles, Wyndham. "Suffocating Smoke at Petersburg." *Armed Forces Chemical Journal*, 1959.

Minick, Rachel. "New York Ferryboats in the Union Navy." *New York Historical Society Quarterly* 47 (1963), no. 2.

Mitchell, Joseph B. *The Badge of Gallantry.* 1968.

Naisawald, L. Van Loan. *Grape and Canister*, 1960.

Nevins, Allan. *War for the Union: Organized War to Victory.* 1971.

Niven, John. *Connecticut for the Union.* 1965.

O'Donnell, J. H. "The 'Accidental' Explosion at City Point." *Virginia Magazine of History & Biography* 72 (1964), no. 3.

Pfanz, Donald C. *Abraham Lincoln at City Point.* 1989.

Powell, C. Percy. *Lincoln Day by Day.* 1960.

Preisser, Thomas M. "The Virginia Decision to Use Negro Soldiers in the Civil War." *Virginia Magazine of History & Biography* 83 (1975), no. 1.

Rayburn, E. S. "Sabotage at City Point." *Civil War Times Illustrated* 22 (1983), no. 2.

Robertson, William Glenn. *Back Door to Richmond.* 1987.

Schiller, Herbert M. *The Bermuda Hundred Campaign.* 1988.

Scott, James G., and Wyatt, Edward A., IV. Petersburg's Story: A History. 1960.

Sherman, George R. "The Negro as a Soldier." Rhode Island Soldiers' and Sailors' Narratives, series 7 (1915).

Sommers, Richard J. "Petersburg Beseiged,"iIn William C. Davis, ed., *Image of War.* 1984.

Starr, Stephen Z. *The Union Cavalry in the Civil War.* 1981.

Stine, James Henry. *History of the Army of the Potomac.* 1892.

Sylvester, Robert Bruce. "The U.S. Military RR & Siege of Petersburg." *Civil War History* 10 (1964), no. 3.

Weber, Thomas. *Northern Railroads in the Civil War.* 1952..

Westwood, H. C. "The Singing Wire Conspiracy." *Lincoln Herald* 81 (Winter 1979).

Whyte, James H. "Maryland's Negro Regiments — How, Where." *Civil War Times Illustrated* 1 (1962), no. 4.

Williams, T. Harry. *Lincoln and His Generals.* 1952.

Wise, Jennings Cropper. *Long Arm of Lee.* 1915.

Wood, W. B. *Military History of the Civil War.* 1960.

Acknowledgments (1991)

This book is the product of many solitary hours spent arranging material, poring over notes, scribbling rough drafts, typing, revising, and revising again. It is also the result of many kindnesses extended to the author by others, both in the line of duty and above and beyond the call.

The staffs of the manuscript archives noted in the bibliography were, with few exceptions, fully professional and unfailingly helpful. A special acknowledgment must go to Dr. Richard J. Sommers, Archivist/ Historian at the U.S. Army Military History Institute at the War College, Carlisle Barracks, Pennsylvania. The Civil War manuscript collection housed at Carlisle Barracks is a must-see for any student of the conflict, and Dr. Sommers is a superb guide to its treasures.

Michael A. Cavanaugh, coauthor of the most detailed study to date of the Crater fiasco, kindly read that portion of my manuscript and cheerfully shared the fruits of his extensive research. Thanks also to Steven J. Wright, expert on Reams Station and helpful guide to the Civil War Museum and Library in Philadelphia.

I was fortunate to be able to make one of my first reference stops at the Fredericksburg-Spotsylvania National Military Park, where Chief Historian Robert K. Krick presides over an impressively organized collection of primary and secondary materials. Bob's willingness to open his door for a project clearly outside his park's domain is much appreciated. In Richmond, historian Mike Andrus of the Richmond National Battlefield Park helped out with matters north of the James with tours, advice, and a sharp-eyed review of pertinent sections of my manuscript.

It would be impossible to put a value on the assistance rendered by the staff at the Petersburg National Battlefield Park. James H. Blankenship, Jr., who generally holds forth at City Point, graciously allowed me access to his research files and provided a detailed critique of the chapter on the August 9, 1864, explosion. The words "thank you" seem a terribly inadequate recompense for the time, effort, and sound advice received from Petersburg Park historian Chris M. Calkins. No one working on any aspect of this complex campaign can fail to benefit from Chris's extraordinary knowledge of the ground and the prime source information. Despite his multiple full-time jobs as park historian, battlefield preservation activist, and writer/cartographer, Chris still found the time to guide this bewildered author to many obscure portions of the battlefield and to review the entire manuscript, making countless valuable suggestions. Thank you, Chris.

This project owes much to the faith of two individuals and two organizations: the author's agent, Lisa DiMona of the Sagalyn Agency, and the author's editor at Little,

Brown, Colleen Mohyde. Also, a tip of the hat to Little, Brown's ace copyeditor Dorothy Straight, whose blue pencil was wielded with an aim that was fair and true.

The historian Bryce A. Suderow made innumerable contributions to this book. His knowledge of and enthusiasm for period newspapers opened the eyes of this writer to the wealth of information and accounts to be discovered there. Bryce's encyclopedic knowledge of Civil War print materials enriched my bibliography with items to be found in few indices. In his grasp of campaign casualty figures, he has few peers, and he was unselfishly generous with the results of years of dedicated research. His astute understanding of the personalities and strategies of this campaign provided the stuff of many hours of intense conversation. It is safe to say that without his assistance, this book would be far less than it is.

Once again I was fortunate to be able to call upon Christine Malesky, who passed up many a sunny afternoon to patiently read through the text, making certain I did not stray from the proper grammatical road. I'm proud to say that her editorial marks were fewer for this book than for the last, though no less welcome. The dedication of this volume to her is a small enough payment for the hours freely given.

With all these helpful guides and all this assistance, it was still ultimately my call when it came down to deciding which of two (or more!) conflicting sources to believe. For all the choices made—and there were many—I bear full responsibility.

Acknowledgments (2014)

While I am happy to say that everyone cited by name in the original edition is still around to (I hope) enjoy this reissue, many have changed jobs, or job titles, or entered the realm of retirement. It seemed wrong to make the changes in the original, and there's nothing to be gained at this point in individually tracking them. I'll make one exception for Chris Calkins, who can at this writing be found presiding over the Sailor's Creek Battlefield Historical State Park operated by the state of Virginia. My appreciation of all their efforts remains undiminished.

I will note for the record that the U.S. Army Military History Institute is now part of the U. S. Army Heritage and Education Center, still in Carlisle, Pennsylvania, but no longer within the Carlisle Barracks area; also that the Civil War Museum and Library in Philadelphia changed locations (as well as a few other things) and is now part of the Civil War Museum of Philadelphia.

Thanks, previously stated, to Theodore P. Savas, managing director at Savas Beatie LLC, for accepting this project are repeated now. And thanks to the folks at the Sagalyn Agency in Washington, D.C. for facilitating rights issues involving this new edition.

Index

Abbot, Henry L., 292

Adair, William B., 415

Adams, John G. B., 72

African-American civilians, 280

Agawam, U.S.S., 148

Aiken House, 163, 165-166

Aiken's Landing, 412

Alabama troops: infantry (8th Regiment, 92, 323) (10th Regiment, 92)

Albert, Allen, 22

Albright, James, 60, 90

Alexander, Edward Porter, 23, 41, 76, 97-98, 100

Alexander, William D., 91

Allen, George, 104

Ames, Adelbert, 227

Amory, Charles, 121

Anderson, Finley, 74, 204

Anderson, Frederick C., 170-171

Anderson, John, 108, 121, 348

Anderson, Richard H., 76, 83, 145

Appomattox campaign, 416; Dinwiddie Court House (March 31), 359; Five Forks (April 1), 359-360, 383, 391, 410; White Oak Road (March 31), 393

Appomattox Court House, 171

Appomattox River, 8, 79, 130, 132, 356, 383, 399, 403

Archer, Fletcher H., 8-9, 366

Archer Rifles, 2; see also, Virginia troops: infantry (12th Regiment)

Armes, George, 46, 61, 73, 275

Armstrong's Mill, 177, 226, 231, 234, 242, 247, 275, 318, 320, 322, 326

Army of Northern Virginia, 409, 422; brigades (Battles's, 365, 442) (Benning's, 389-390) (Bratton's, 237-238, 389) (Christian's, 159) (Colquitt's, 159, 163) (Cook's, 365, 442) (Cooke's, 168, 235, 319-320, 393-399) (Davis's, 159, 235-236, 244, 319) (Dearing's, 8, 194, 196, 235-236, 244, 275)

(Gregg's, 237, 239) (Hagood's, 79, 81-82, 168-170) (Harris's, 168, 236, 324, 379, 383-384) (Hunton's, 393) (Jayne's, 168) (Johnston's, 322) (Kershaw's, 91, 93, 422) (Kirkland's, 168) (Lane's, 235, 378-379, 384-386) (Lewis's, 322, 442) (MacRae's, 168, 234, 242, 244, 246, 319, 378, 393, 396) (Mahone's, 68-69, 115, 163, 236, 244, 246, 324) (McComb's, 319, 378) (McGowan's, 17, 235, 393-399) (Nelson's, 81, 378) (Perry's, 78) (Ransom's, 168, 341, 348-349) (Rosser's, 194-199) (Sanders's, 69, 169, 236, 324) (Scales's, 168, 393, 396, 399) (Sorrel's, 324) (Thomas's, 372, 379, 385) (Weisiger's, 71, 115-116, 118, 163, 236, 243, 246, 324) (Wright's, 69, 70-71, 115, 168) (P. M. B. Young's, 194, 271); divisions (Evans's, 318, 320, 322-323, 340-341, 442) (Field's, 50, 79-82, 145, 148, 154, 212, 237, 281) (Hoke's, 23, 32, 36, 45, 48, 79, 82, 83, 125, 212, 281) (Kershaw's, 50, 141, 145) (W. H. F. Lee's, 161, 232, 242, 244) (Mahone's, 55, 68, 70-71, 86, 115, 125, 152, 163, 165, 168, 169-170, 171, 242-245, 321, 323-324, 376, 383) (Wilcox's, 65, 68, 73-74, 77, 152, 182, 213, 235, 298, 341, 384, 393); morale, 421; strength, 418; supply, 423

Army of the James: Bermuda Hundred campaign, 5; corps (Tenth Corps, 145, 149, 172-173, 213-214, 223, 227, 241) (Eighteenth Corps, 16, 35, 80, 209, 223, 246-247) (Twenty-fourth Corps, 381, 393)

Army of the Potomac, 12; election returns, 251-252; corps (Second Corps, 11, 16, 18, 21, 26, 34, 47, 54, 58, 66-67, 143-144, 147, 167-168, 173, 187, 222, 264-265, 393-400) (Third Corps, 225) (Fifth Corps, 11-12, 14-18, 48, 50, 55, 211, 222, 226, 263) (Sixth Corps, 11-12, 16, 18, 22, 57, 67-68, 74-75, 77, 140, 264, 369-381) (Ninth Corps, 11, 16, 18, 43, 46-47, 50, 124-125, 163, 211,

220, 229-230, 299-300, 360-369); strength, 420

Arthur's Swamp, 207

Atkinson, Homer, 390

Atlanta campaign, 96

Atlanta, Georgia, 218, 262, 421; capture, 192

Avery House, 346, 347, 350; image in picture section

Ayres, Romeyn, 156, 214, 231, 267

Babcock, Orville, 41, 241, 309

Badeau, Adam, 52, 190, 226, 240-241, 295, 340

Bahnson, Henry T., 406

Bailey's Creek, 142, 143, 147, 148, 149

Baker, John A., 61

Baltimore, U.S.S., 62

Banister, Anne, 6, 9, 405

Banister, William C., 7, 9

Barber, Merritt, 373

Barfield, Lee, 284

Barlow, Francis, 66-67, 70, 148-149, 157, 175-176

Barnes, C. F., 374

Barnes, John S., 412

Barringer, Rufus, 64

Barth, Charley, 74-75

Bartlet, Franklin, 326

Bartlett, William F., 108, 120, 122

Bates, Delevan, 114

Battersea Cotton Factory, 403

Baxter Road, 40

Baylor, George, 194, 197

Baylor's Farm, Battle of (June 15), 35

Beauge, Eugene, 299-300

Beauregard, P. G. T., 23, 31-32, 36-37, 40-41, 45, 48-50, 60, 64, 79, 157-158, 160, 162-163, 166-167, 227, 310, 419; opinion of Robert E. Lee, 31

Beckwith, Margaret Stanley, 10

Bermuda Hundred campaign, 5

Belches Mill, 199

Belfield, Virginia, 270

Benham, Henry, 22

Benjamin, Judah, 309, 328

Bennett, James Gordon, 202

Benning, Henry L., 308

Bentonville, Battle of (1865), 333

Bermuda Hundred, 14, 16, 23, 40, 47-49, 145-146, 172, 206

Bermuda Hundred campaign, 3-4, 7-8, 30, 31-32, 129; Chester Station (May 10), 5; Port Walthall (May 7), 5; Swift Creek (May 9), 5

Billings, John D., 88

Bintliff, James, 407

Birney, David B., 21, 51, 58, 67, 73, 74, 152, 172-173, 206, 213-214; promoted to command Tenth Corps, 150; temporarily assumes command of Second Corps, 49

Birney, William, 227

Blackford, W. W., 92, 94, 291

black troops: C.S., 328; U.S., 9, 35, 39, 63, 103, 113-114, 121-122, 208-209, 227, 236, 239, 381, 410-411

Blackwater Swamp, 193, 194, 199

Blair, Francis P., 305-308

Blandford Cemetery, 5, 424

Blandford Church, 407-409

Blick Station, 157

Bliss, Zenas R., 110, 123, 125

Bollingbrook Street, Petersburg, 8, 260

Bosbyshell, Oliver, 101, 102, 106

Boston Evening Transcript, 57

Bowers, Theodore S., 137, 188, 219

Bowley, Freeman S., 114, 117, 119, 121

Boydton Plank Road, 193, 206, 210-212, 215, 222, 224, 230-233, 234-236, 240, 242, 246, 318, 321, 359, 372, 376, 377, 379, 384, 392-394, 396

Bradwell, I. G., 405, 406

Brady, John A., 204, 209, 212

Brady, Matthew, 58

Brady, Thomas, 352

Bragg, Braxton, 33, 36, 64

Bragg, Edward, 162, 163

Braman, Waters, 218, 277

Breckinridge, John C., 15, 297

Brinton, John H., 22

Brooks, U. R., 267

Brooks, William T. H., 35

Brower, Henry D., 183-184

Brown, Alexander, 94

Brown, Jerry Z., 249

Buck, George, 16

Buckingham, Charles L., 295
Bulkley, Solomon T., 204-207, 214, 415
Bull Pen (Hatcher's Run expedition, October 27), 244
Bull Pen (Union Prison), 130
Bull Ring (Hatcher's Run expedition, October 27), 244
Bull Run, Battle of (1861), 31
Burbank, Horace, 117
Burgess, William, 233
Burgess' Mill, 233, 236, 242, 243, 244, 249, 250, 318, 321, 334, 359, 372, 392, 393
Burke, D. F., 249
Burkeville, Virginia, 329
Burnham, Hiram, 209
Burnham, Uberto, 135
Burnside, Ambrose, 16, 48, 51, 98, 102-103, 105-106, 112, 115-117, 118, 123-124
Butler, Benjamin F., 1, 5, 14, 44-45, 47, 64, 67, 150, 218, 222-224, 228-229, 240, 247, 253
Butler, Jim, 267
Butler, M. C., 234, 242, 245, 270, 279, 422
Cadwallader, Sylvanus, 63, 202-204, 298, 302, 411
Caldwell, J. F. J., 17, 394, 396-399
Calhoun, C. M., 197, 279
Callender, Bessie, 5-7
Callender, David, 7, 11
Campbell, John A., 308-310, 313-315
Campbell, Thomas, 8, 10
Campbell Bridge, 91, 405-406
Carey, Hetty, 313, 325-326
Carney, Edward, 344
Carson, Joseph P., 341-343, 353
Carter, L. H., 70
Casualties: Beefsteak Raid (September 14-17), 199; Crater (July 31), 125; final assaults (April 2/Sixth Corps, 381) (April 2/Ninth Corps, 369); Fort Gregg (April 2), 391-392; Fort Harrison (September 29-30), 216; Fort Stedman (March 25), 357; Hagood's assault (June 24), 83; Hatcher's Run expeditions (February 5-7, 326) (October 27, 249-250); Jerusalem Plank Road (June 22), 74-75, 77; Peebles Farm (September 30-October 1), 216; Petersburg assaults

(June 15-18), 52; Petersburg campaign, 421; Reams Station (August 25), 187; Second Deep Bottom expedition (August 13-20), 167-168; Sutherland Station (April 2), 399; Weldon Raid (December 7-12), 284; Weldon Railroad (August 18-21), 172; Williamsburg Road expedition (October 27), 247
Cavaness, I. F., 279
Cemetery Hill, 108-109, 115, 407, 413
Chaffin's Bluff, 151, 157, 171, 226
Chambers, Henry, 334, 347, 349, 352
Chambersburg, Pennsylvania, 97
Chambliss, John R., 86, 152, 155
Chandler, George C., 230
Chapman, George H., 12, 14-15
Charles City Road, 17, 20, 149, 151, 153, 157, 175, 223, 228-229, 240, 246
Charleston, South Carolina, 31, 303
Charleston Mercury, 83
Charlotte Bulletin, 245-246
Chattanooga, Tennessee, 30
Chester, Thomas M., 208
Chew, Walter S., 385
Chickahominy River, 12, 14-20
Chubb, O. P., 109
Church Road, 206, 235, 394
Cincinnati (horse), 413
City Point, Virginia, 5-6, 8, 14, 28, 35, 43, 62, 67, 129-132, 139, 151, 154, 156, 192, 193, 200, 202, 210, 288, 303, 310-312, 340, 368, 412, 414, 418; explosion (August 9), 129-139
City Point Railroad (spur of South Side Railroad), 4, 35, 38, 40
City Point Road, 8, 79, 405, 407
Claiborne, John H., 9, 90, 92-93, 259, 263, 355
Claiborne Road, 394-397
Clark, A. Judson, 74, 398
Clark, George, 120
Clarke, Hermon, 239-240
Clements House, 229
Clingman, Thomas, 172
Clowminger, William, 343
Cocke's Mill, 192, 194-196
Coggins Point, 192, 193, 194

Coit, J. C., 109, 110
Cold Harbor, Battle of (June 1-3), 12, 14, 28, 30, 32, 33, 34, 37, 72, 419
Cold Harbor, Virginia, 12, 17, 35, 36, 60, 419
Cole's Ferry, 21
Collier, Charles, 408
Collis, H. T., 368
Colquitt's Salient, 334, 338-339, 340-342, 346, 352-353, 407
Colston, Raleigh, 7, 9
Columbia, South Carolina, 303, 333, 421
Columbia Daily South Carolinian, 208, 209
Columbus (Georgia) *Daily Sun*, 251
Commodore Perry, U.S.S., 190
Comstock, Cyrus, 14-15, 115, 199, 224, 247, 251
Comstock, Elisha P., 299
Confederate States troops: cavalry (7th Regiment, 9)
Connecticut troops: artillery, heavy (1st Regiment, 292); infantry, (6th Regiment, 67) (10th Regiment, 291, 387) (14th Regiment, 326)
Cook, Ebenezer, 134, 135-136
Cook, Thomas M., 204, 207-208, 209-210, 212-213, 214-216, 408-409
Cook's (aka Cooke's) Bridge, 194, 197-199
Cooke, John E., 416
Cooke, John R., 319, 393
Cooke's Bridge, 194, 197-199
Cooper, Samuel, 311
Corbin, Elbert, 63
Corby, William, 202
correspondents and artists, 18, 35, 39, 63, 67, 74, 423-424
Cowan, Andrew, 367
Cox, Robert, 354
Cox Farm, 228
Cox Road, 236, 372-373, 376-377, 379
Crapsey, Edward, 296, 420
Crater, The, 249, 408; construction begins, 99-100; construction problems, 100-101; fuse problems, 106; packing with explosives, 104-105
Crawford, Samuel W., 16, 156, 231, 242-243
Crockett, Edward, 239, 281
Crow House Redoubt, 393, 395

Crowl, Philip, 346
Cullen, Edgard M., 238
Culpeper, Virginia, 175
Curles Neck, 147
Curtin, John I., 362-364
Cutcheon, Byron, 107
Cutler, Lysander, 156
Dabney's Mill, 232, 248-249, 317-319, 326, 324, 356, 366, 378, 390
Dabney's Mill Road, 236, 246, 248
Dailey, Dennis, 170
Dana, Charles, 25
Dandy, George B., 387, 391
Danville Road, 87, 410, 416
Darbytown Road, 208, 210, 223, 227-229, 286
Davenport, John, 42-43
Daves, Graham, 20
Davies, Henry E., Jr., 194, 198-199, 206, 214, 269, 276, 278
Davis, Charles E., 15
Davis, Jefferson, 15, 31, 56, 252, 297, 306, 307, 308, 310, 327-328, 329, 357, 388
Davis, Varina, 310
Davis House, 159, 163, 168
Dawson, Francis W., 93
Day, W. A., 328, 334, 347, 349
Dearing, James, 8, 234-236
de Chambrun, Marquis, 425
Deep Bottom, 55, 120, 142-143, 145-148, 150-154, 167-168, 172-173, 188, 206-208
Deep Run, 150
Depot Road, 181, 184-185
desertions, 297-298
de Trobriand, Regis, 225, 245-246, 248-249, 251, 267, 280
Dictator, The, 292
Dillard, R. K., 129, 132-135, 139
Dimmock, Charles H., 4
Dimmock line, 2-3, 6, 8-9, 37, 41-43, 48, 348
Dinwiddie Court House, 85, 275-276, 315-317, 321, 359-360
Dinwiddie Stage Road. See Stage Road
District of Columbia troops: cavalry (1st Regiment, 192, 196-198)
Dixon, B. F., 357
Dobbs, Lemuel D., 121
Douglas, Henry K., 313, 324-326, 356, 404

Douty, Jacob, 106
Drake, J. Madison, 54
Duane, James C., 14, 16, 101
Duncan, James H., 385
Duncan Road, 230, 318
Dunlop House, 36
Dunlop's Station, 91, 257, 406
Dunn, Michael, 387
Dunn, Moncena, 69, 72
Dunn House Battery, 348, 355
Dunn's Hill, 79
Dunovant, John, 232
Dushane, Nathan, 159, 169
Dusseault, John H., 18
Dutch Gap, 146, 155, 253
Early, Jubal, 15, 23, 51, 141, 359
Ebenezer Church, 199
Eckert, Thomas T., 311
Edwards, Oliver, 371, 374, 406
Edwards, William H., 334, 350
Egan, Thomas, 232-233
Egbert, Nelson, 271-272
Egolf, Joseph, 186
Elliott, John S., 197
Elliott's Salient, 97, 102
Ely, Ralph, 405, 407
entrenchments, 190, 286, 287-288
Estes, James, 238
Etheredge, W. H., 117
Evans, Clement A., 318, 338
Ewell, Richard S., 145
executions, 57-58, 261, 299-300
Fairchild, Harrison S., 238
Farley, Henry, 234
Fay, Frank B,, 134, 135, 137
Featherston, John C., 120
Ferebee, Dennis D., 10
Ferrero, Edward, 103, 109, 113, 123-124, 224, 417
Field, Charles, 80, 81-82, 149, 151, 229, 238, 392
Finegan, Joseph, 78, 321, 324
Fitzhugh, Robert H., 21
Fitzpatrick, James C., 204-206, 208, 210-211, 212-213
Flourney, Thomas S., 308
Foard, N. P., 277
Foote, Frank H., 385

Ford, George W., 12
Ford, James, 406
Forrest, Nathan B., 3
Fort Alexander, 384
Fort Anderson, 384
Fort Archer, 211-212
Fort Baldwin, 384
Fort Brady, 223
Fort Burnham, 215
Fort Cummings, 224, 326, 368
Fort Damnation. See Fort Mahone
Fort Davis, 360, 362, 363
Fort Dushane, 169, 206, 231
Fort Fisher, 288, 366-367, 369, 380
Fort Fisher campaign (North Carolina), 253, 281, 304
Fort Friend, 355
Fort Gilmer, 209, 229
Fort Gregg (C.S.), 288, 384-386, 390-394, 392
Fort Gregg (U.S.), 288, 369-371
Fort Harrison, 209-212, 214-216, 223, 227, 239, 422
Fort Haskell, 344-346, 349-350, 354
Fort Hays, 361
Fort Hell. See Fort Sedgwick
Fort Howard, 356, 361, 368
Fort McGilvery, 349, 351, 360, 404-405
Fort Mahone, 289, 362, 361, 367-369, 380, 413
Fort Monroe, 5, 134, 311, 310
Fort Morton, 249, 292
Fort Sampson, 369, 368
Fort Sedgwick, 249, 252, 289-290, 362, 366-368
Fort Stedman, 288, 332-335, 342-344, 346-347, 352-357
Fort Urmston, 371
Fort Wadsworth, 211, 288, 356
Fort Welch, 288, 369-370, 372, 382
Fort Whitworth, 288, 384-386, 390-394
Foster, Robert S., 227, 240, 382, 389
Fowle, George, 269, 281
Franklin, Battle of (1864), 262
Freeman, Warren, 132, 138
Freeman's Ford, 267, 268, 274, 282
Frey, Charles A., 326
Friend, Charles, 4, 9
Friend, John E., 9
Friend House, 351

Fuller, Joseph, 17
Funkhouser, R. D., 349, 354, 356
Fussell's Mill, 142, 148, 149, 150, 152, 157
Gage, E. Darwin, 247
Garnett, John J., 273
Garrish, Theodore, 218, 277-278
Gary, Martin W., 20, 145, 149, 240
Gee House, 120
Gee's Ford, 270
Georgia troops: cavalry (Jeff Davis Legion, 191, 270, 273) (62nd Regiment, 273); infantry (10th Battalion, 70)
Getty, George W., 370, 380
Gettysburg, Battle of (1863), 225, 350
Gibbon, John, 32, 66, 74-75, 185-187, 381-383, 386-388
Gillmore, Quincy A., 2, 9, 64
Gilly (executed slave), 261
Girardey, Victor, 153
Globe Tavern, 157-160, 163, 164, 165, 167, 173, 177, 181, 182, 355, 356
Goldsboro, North Carolina, 333
Gordon, John B., 191, 313, 322-323, 325, 334, 338-339, 340-342, 344, 346, 349, 352, 357-358, 365, 369, 403
Gordon, John W., 64
Gorman, John C., 406
Gould, Joseph, 300
Gould, Seward F., 394, 396
Gowan, George W., 362
Graham, Edward, 8
Graham, Robert D., 352
Grant, Julia, 41, 75, 219, 222
Grant, Lewis, 77, 370-371
Grant, Ulysses S., 15-16, 18-20, 24, 28, 30, 33, 41-48, 52, 55, 58, 62-63, 68, 75, 78, 114-115, 124-125, 129, 133, 137, 141, 142, 148-151, 154-156, 161, 171, 173-174, 188, 200, 210, 219-224, 229, 231, 240-242, 250-252, 263-264, 270, 282, 286-287, 310, 315, 337-338, 340, 353, 360, 380, 392, 409-410, 410-412, 417-419; assessment, 420; decides to cross James River, 14; described, 52; final report of operations, 1-2, 11-12, 27, 54, 96-97, 140, 190, 201, 217, 262-263, 304, 333-334, 359-360, 416

Grant's Petersburg Progress, 415
Gravelly Run, 178, 233, 235
Greeley, Horace, 305, 308
Gregg, David McM., 149, 157, 175, 185-186, 194, 206, 232-233, 248, 273, 276-277
Gregg, Henry H., 196
Gregg, John, 239
Gregg, John I., 278
Green, Robert, 295
Griffin, Charles, 156, 164, 231, 360, 362-364
Griffin, Simon G., 110, 118, 362, 363
Grimes, Bryan, 366
Grover's Farm, 206
guerrilla activities, 191, 280, 282, 283
Gurley House, 155, 156, 173
Gwyn, James, 315
Haanam, Charles H., 380
Hagood, Johnson, 83, 170, 281
Haley, John, 28, 72, 267-268, 283
Halifax Road, 159, 163, 165, 168, 177, 180, 182-183, 206, 225, 231, 264, 269, 302, 315, 369
Hall, H. Seymour, 103
Hall, Matthew R., 115
Halleck, Henry, 14, 30, 53, 78, 151
Hamblin, Joseph, 368
Hamilton, J. R., 203-204, 215, 404, 415
Hamlin, Charles, 135
Hampton, E. R., 279
Hampton, Preston, 245
Hampton, Wade, 15, 60, 86, 145, 149, 157, 175-177, 178-181, 192, 193, 197-198, 199, 207, 214, 232-236, 242-243, 245, 250, 270, 273, 277-278, 283
Hampton, Wade, Jr., 245
Hancock, Cornelia, 143, 188
Hancock, Winfield S., 16, 33-34, 37, 38, 40, 44, 143-144, 148, 150, 152, 153-154, 161, 166, 167-168, 175-176, 178-179, 181-187, 222, 224-226, 233, 240-244, 246, 248-249, 251-252, 381; command abilities, 40, 47; illness, 46-47, 62, 73; temporarily relinquishes command of Second Corps, 49
Hancock Station, 299, 404, 412, 413
Hannaford, Roger, 65
Harder, William H., 260

Hardy, John C., 335-336, 348, 354
Hare House Hill, 51, 88
Harker, J. G., 364
Harriman, Samuel, 309, 362, 363
Harris, Nathaniel H., 379, 383-386, 391
Harris, Thomas M., 382
Harrison's Creek, 40, 45, 48, 351
Harrison's Landing, 21
Hart, James F., 235
Hartranft, John F., 111, 120, 346-347, 350-353, 356, 357-360, 363, 405
Harvey, O. K., 132, 134, 136
Haskell, John C., 119
Hastings, Jo., 238
Hatcher's Run, 175, 177, 220, 222, 225, 226, 231-232, 234-236, 241, 242, 244, 246, 271, 274, 275, 282, 286, 287, 313, 317, 318, 320-321, 322, 323, 326, 362, 378-379, 380, 381, 382, 386, 393-394, 395, 396
Hawkinsville, 268
Hayes, Joseph, 159, 165
Henderson, Julius E., 358
Hendrick, L. A., 204, 211, 214-215
Henry, Guy V., 80-81, 86-87
Heptinstall, P. B., 261
Herbert, Hilary, 76, 92
Herring Creek, 21
Heth, Henry, 159-160, 163, 168-169, 183-184, 187, 235, 242, 245, 250, 318, 379, 394
Hicksford, Virginia, 174, 264, 270, 272-273, 276-277, 278, 279, 284, 285
Hill, Ambrose P., 73, 159, 168-169, 176-177, 178-179, 181, 186-187, 212, 226, 242, 278, 283-284, 372-373, 375-376, 393, 408; death, 378; illness, 183, 235, 270
Hill, Lossie, 8
Hill, W. T., 239
Hincks, Edward W., 35
Hinson, William, 239
Hinton, E. O., 8
Hodges, Charles W., 326
Hogg, George, 275
Hoke, Robert F., 32, 79-80, 83, 229
Holibaugh, J. R., 124
Holly Point Church, 177, 178
Holman, John, 236, 239

Holstein, Anna, 22-23
Hood, John B., 262-263
Hope, Frank, 378
Hopkins, William, 300
"horological torpedo," 129, 131, 133-135
horse racing, 302
hospitals, 2, 54, 90, 130, 132, 134, 186, 259, 302, 380, 404, 412
Howlett House, 36
Howlett Line, 172, 383
Hughes, Robert P., 387
Humphreys, Andrew A., 20-21, 43, 52, 58, 75, 78, 106, 111-112, 117, 178, 226, 230-231, 242, 252, 276, 317-318, 356, 393, 395
Hunt, Melville, 291
Hunter, David, 27, 140
Hunter, Robert M. T., 308-310, 314-315, 327, 329
Hunton, Eppa, 17
Huyette, Miles C., 347, 346, 354, 363-364, 369
Hyde, John, 397
Hyde, Thomas, 370, 374
Hyman, Joseph, 393
Hyndman, William, 218
Illinois troops: infantry (39th Regiment, 387)
Indiana troops: cavalry (3rd Regiment, 14, 20)
Indian Town Creek, 260, 383, 392
Ingals, Rufus, 203
Jackson, Andrew, 305
James River, 12, 15, 18, 43, 129-132, 190-191, 196; pontoon bridge, 22, 41
Jamison, I. J., 347
Janeway, Hugh, 276
Jarrett's Station, 87, 279-281
Jeffords, Robert J., 244
J. E. Kendrick, 133, 135
Jenkins, William, 375
Jerusalem Plank Road, 7-10, 45, 49, 61-62, 64, 66-68, 76, 97, 103, 108, 110, 116, 120, 156, 162, 166, 173, 179, 183, 186, 264-267, 319, 362, 368-369, 408, 413
Johnson, Andrew, 218
Johnson, Bushrod, 40, 118, 250
Johnson, William, 57-58
Johnson House, 68, 70
Johnson Road, 163

Johnston, Albert S., 31
Johnston, David E., 252, 328
Johnston, Joseph E., 1, 31, 310, 410, 421
Joint Committee on the Conduct of the War, 98, 103-105, 111-113, 313, 317
Jones, A. K., 390
Jones, George, 9
Jones, George B., 7
Jones, John B., 60, 64, 217, 327
Jones, William F., 152
Jones Bridge, 16, 18
Jones House, 62, 67
Jones Neck, 142, 143, 206
Jordan House, 56
Jordan Point Road, 9, 35, 39, 44
Kautz, August V., 2, 9, 35, 86, 155, 191-193, 198, 208, 210
Keiley, Anthony, 7, 9
Keiley, J. D., 261
Kent, William H., 52
Kiefer, J. Warren, 375
Kilmer, George, 346
Kingsland Road, 228
Klinkler, W., 340
Lafayette Guards, 2; see also: Virginia troops: infantry (12th Regiment)
Landis, Alien, 71
Lane, David, 134, 136
Lane, James H., 372, 378, 384-386
Laverty, Francis, 336
Lawley, Francis, 100
Leavenworth, A. J., 260
Ledlie, James H., 106, 109, 123-124
Lee, Fitzhugh, 60, 144, 279
Lee, Robert E., 1, 21, 23, 52-53, 56, 60, 65, 68, 76, 79, 83, 86, 110, 120, 122, 141, 144-145, 149, 151, 155, 161, 171, 175-176, 193, 210-212, 227, 234, 270, 282, 284, 297, 318, 316-317, 322, 326, 332-334, 339, 355, 357, 373, 375, 379, 388, 393, 403, 407, 419, 422-423; appointed commander in chief of Confederate armies, 310-311; assessment, 422-423; learns Union army has left Cold Harbor, 17
Lee, Robert E., Jr., 355
Lee, Samuel P., 41, 46, 67
Lee, W. H. F., 161, 232, 234, 242-244, 355

Lee's Mill, 266
Libby Prison, 186
Lieutenant Run, 8
Lincoln, Abraham, 67-68, 141, 156, 218, 270, 302-305, 326-327, 337-338, 340, 355-356, 412-414, 419, 425; Hampton Roads Peace Conference, 314-315, 326; reelection, 251-252; visits Richmond-Petersburg front, 62-63, 67-68
Lincoln, Robert, 412
Lincoln, Tad, 412, 414
Livermore, Thomas, 129
Locke, William, 266, 281
Lockley, Fred, 61
Logan, Mrs. John A., 424
Lombard Street, Petersburg, 8, 260
London, Henry, 349, 352, 357
Long Bridge, 12, 14, 16, 18
Longstreet, James, 226, 229, 237, 281, 329, 373, 375, 390
Lord, L. W., 300
Loring, Charles, 113
"Lost Cause," 424
Louisiana troops: artillery (Washington Artillery, 385); infantry (2nd Regiment, 343)
Lyman, Theodore, 41-44, 46, 49, 67, 78, 118, 162, 188-189, 251, 274, 284, 302, 355, 400, 409-410
Lynchburg, Virginia, 27, 96
McAllister, Robert, 72, 245, 269, 280, 298, 319-320
McBride, Robert, 267, 280
McCabe, W. Gordon, 70-71
McCarty, Thomas L., 239, 281
McClellan, George B., xiii, 21, 217, 218, 225, 237, 251-252
McComb, William, 319, 372
MacDougall, Clinton, 397-398
McDowell family, 207
McGregor, William D., 204, 211, 215-216
Mackenzie, Ranald, 360
McKnight, George F., 70
McLaughlen, Napoleon B., 345
McSwain, Lucius, 279
MacRae, William, 245, 372, 399
Macy, George, 275

Madill, Henry J., 396-397

Mahone, William, 68-69, 73-74, 116, 118-119, 164-165, 169-170, 236, 242, 244; described, 115

Maine troops: artillery, heavy (1st Regiment, 51-52, 72, 251, 338); cavalry (1st Regiment, 232); infantry (9th Regiment, 241) (11th Regiment, 392) (16th Regiment, 323) (17th Regiment, 77, 267, 280) (20th Regiment, 277) (32nd Regiment, 116, 123)

Major, Francis, 9

Malone's Crossing, 177, 178, 180

Marsh, Elias J., 284

Marshall, Elisha, 107

Marston, Gilman, 236

Martindale, John H., 35, 51

Maryland troops (C.S.): artillery (4th Battery, 385); infantry (2nd Regiment, 327)

Maryland troops (U.S.): infantry (5th Regiment, 238) (6th Regiment, 377)

Mary Martin, 310

Massachusetts troops: artillery, heavy (1st Regiment, 286); artillery, light (10th Battery, 88, 319; cavalry (1st Regiment, 276); infantry (13th Regiment, 15, 55) (15th Regiment, 66, 72) (19th Regiment, 69, 72) (29th Regiment, 344-346, 350) (35th Regiment, 282-283, 292, 299-300) (57th Regiment, 107, 344, 348, 351) (59th Regiment, 336, 345, 350)

Mauk, John, 377-378

Maxwell, John, 129, 132-135, 139

Meade, George G., 1, 11, 14, 28, 41-45, 47-48, 53-54, 60-64, 67, 77-78, 83, 100-102, 105, 112, 116, 119, 141, 149, 161, 170, 173-174, 182-183, 188, 200, 214-215, 220, 229, 231, 240-242, 248, 264, 271, 276, 315-318, 322, 355, 360, 394, 409-410; relationship with Grant, 33; temper, 49, 55, 219-220

Meade, George, Jr., 248

Meade, Sergeant, 317

Meade Station, 347, 348, 355

Mechanic's Hall, 260

medicine and nursing, 143

Meherrin River, 270, 273, 276, 279, 284, 383

Merriam, William H., 204-206, 208, 212-213, 216, 247

Michigan troops: infantry (1st Regiment Sharpshooters, 405, 407) (2nd Regiment, 335, 405, 407) (16th Regiment, 211) (20th Regiment, 107, 109, 251, 408)

Michler, Nathaniel, 19, 21-22

Miles, Nelson, 174-176, 179-180, 184-185, 249, 274-275, 282, 394, 394-397, 398

Miller, Lovick P., 193

Miller, Theodore, 350

Mills, Charles, 224

Mill Swamp, 279

Mine. See Crater, The

Mississippi troops: infantry (11th Regiment, 378) (12th Regiment, 385) (16th Regiment, 385) (19th Regiment, 385) (48th Regiment, 385, 391)

Mitchell, William G., 144, 157, 167

Mobile Daily Advertiser and Register, 90

Monk's Neck Bridge, 181, 226, 232, 234, 315

Monocacy, Battle of (1864), 97

Moore, James Otis, 133, 135-136

Morgan, Charles, 66

Morgan, Michael R., 137

Morrison, Mary E., 405

Morton, G. Nash, 341

Mott, Gershom, 66, 215, 241

Mount Sinai Church, 58

Myers, Frank, 197

Namozine Road, 396

Napier, Bartlett, 92

Nashville, Battle of (1864), 263, 303

Nelson, Andrew M., 372

Nelson, Patrick H., 81

Nesbitt, Harrison, 240

New Hampshire troops: cavalry (1st Regiment, 20); infantry (2nd Regiment, 252) (3rd Regiment, 67, 172) (5th Regiment, 61, 249-250, 298) (6th Regiment, 283) (7th Regiment, 146-147) (10th Regiment, 238) (13th Regiment, 247, 288)

New Jersey troops, 63: artillery, light (1st Battery, 398) (5th Battery, 244); cavalry (1st Regiment, 276); infantry (7th Regiment, 319) (8th Regiment, 319) (9th Regiment, 54) (11th Regiment, 72, 298) (39th Regiment, 230, 364, 411)

New Market, Battle of (1864), 27

New Market Heights, 147, 207, 281

New Market Road, 143, 208, 223, 227, 228, 239, 302

newspaper operations at Petersburg, 202-204

New York Herald, 74, 202-203, 205-206, 208, 210-216, 247, 315, 321, 324, 380, 408, 415

New York Independent, 220

New York Times, 34, 67, 192, 203-208, 210, 212-214, 215, 309, 404, 410, 415, 417, 423-424

New York Tribune, 35, 39, 52, 80, 133, 135, 203, 305

New York troops: artillery, heavy (2nd Regiment, 275) (4th Regiment, 394) (6th Regiment, 417) (7th Regiment, 61) (8th Regiment, 18) (14th Regiment, 108, 343, 349); artillery, light (12th Battery, 70, 73-76) (19th Battery, 342); cavalry (3rd Regiment, 196) (8th Regiment, 20) (10th Regiment, 266, 271) (22nd Regiment, 14); engineers (50th Regiment, 301); infantry (5th Regiment, 295) (10th Regiment, 249) (39th Regiment, 397) (48th Regiment, 67) (57th Regiment, 61) (61st Regiment, 185, 275) (66th Regiment, 17) (88th Regiment, 202) (96th Regiment, 238) (97th Regiment, 280, 323) (100th Regiment, 387) (108th Regiment, 21) (109th Regiment, 364) (112th Regiment, 241) (115th Regiment, 241) (117th Regiment, 241) (118th Regiment, 238) (120th Regiment, 283, 291, 320) (121st Regiment, 324, 376-377, 407) (124th Regiment, 58, 296) (125th Regiment, 186, 397) (146th Regiment, 290, 295) (148th Regiment, 247) (152nd Regiment, 72, 233) (186th Regiment, 299) (189th Regiment, 278)

New York World, 203

Nine Mile Road, 236, 239

Norfolk & Petersburg Railroad, 4-5

North Anna, Battle of (May 23-26), 11, 28, 33

North Carolina troops: cavalry (2nd Regiment, 65, 274) (3rd Regiment, 61, 281) (4th Regiment, 8) (5th Regiment, 273, 277-278); infantry (11th Regiment, 245) (13th

Regiment, 391) (22nd Regiment, 20) (26th Regiment, 184, 246) (27th Regiment, 394, 395) (28th Regiment, 68) (33rd Regiment, 279, 391) (46th Regiment, 279) (47th Regiment, 246) (49th Regiment, 334, 357) (52nd Regiment, 397)

Norvell, E. S., 377

Nottoway River, 267-268, 269, 271, 282-284, 329

Nugent, Robert, 396, 398

Oates, William, 153

Ocran Methodist Church, 396

Official Court of Inquiry on the Mine, 100-101, 109-113, 116, 118-120, 122-124

Ohio troops: cavalry (6th Regiment, 232, 274); infantry (60th Regiment, 406)

Old Street, Petersburg, 260

Old Town Creek, 383, 390-391, 408

Ord, E. O. C., 111, 118, 209, 329, 381-382

Osborn, Thomas O., 386

O'Sullivan, Timothy, 57

Overland campaign, 11-12, 28, 33-34, 141

Page, Charles, 18

Paine, Charles, 208

Palmer, William H., 372, 374

Pamunkey River, 60, 359

Parish, W. F., 56, 57

Parke, John G., 124, 221-222, 224, 244, 353, 360, 362, 365, 368-369

Patrick, Marsena, 55, 57-58

Patterson, Joab, 237

Paul, D'Arcy, 406

Paul, E. A., 423-424

Pawnee, U.S.S., 3

Peebles Farm, 211, 212-215, 219, 220, 221, 224-226, 302

Pegram, John, 313, 318, 321, 322, 324-326

Pegram, Richard, 107

Pegram, William J., 183-84

Pendleton, George H., 218

Pendleton, William N., 90, 157, 284

Pennsylvania troops: artillery, heavy (2nd Regiment, 108); artillery, light (1st Artillery, 236-237); cavalry (1st Regiment, 276) (3rd Regiment, 274) (4th Regiment, 191) (11th Regiment, 191, 196) (13th Regiment, 196,

274); infantry (11th Regiment, 281) (45th Regiment, 299, 413) (48th Regiment, 98, 100, 106, 252, 300, 364) (50th Regiment, 230) (51st Regiment, 404, 407) (54th Regiment, 389) (57th Regiment, 70) (63rd Regiment, 244) (88th Regiment, 281) (93rd Regiment, 370, 370-371) (100th Regiment, 344-345, 346, 404) (105th Regiment, 244) (114th Regiment, 368) (116th Regiment, 17, 74-75) (138th Regiment, 377) (140th Regiment, 274) (148th Regiment, 249) (150th Regiment, 326) (155th Regiment, 266) (190th Regiment, 267-268, 280) (198th Regiment, 271) (199th Regiment, 387) (200th Regiment, 282, 347, 351-352) (203rd Regiment, 241) (205th Regiment, 351) (207th Regiment, 347, 350-351, 354) (208th Regiment, 347, 350-351, 354) (209th Regiment, 347, 351-352) (211th Regiment, 351-352, 415)

Penrose, William H., 371

Peters, E. T., 204, 208-209, 294

Petersburg, Virginia, 20, 30, 36, 44, 88-95, 123, 166, 176-177, 186, 211, 257-261, 334, 369, 384, 392, 417; before the war, 2; capture of, 405-408; Christmas 1864, 259; Cockade monument, 4; food prices, 4, 94; fuel supplies, 94; health concerns, 94; population, 4; railroad system, 4; siege damage, 93, 424; slave population, 4

Petersburg & Weldon Railroad, 4, 5, 56, 58, 61, 67, 77-78, 83, 86, 155, 157-158, 172, 188, 269, 276

Petersburg campaign, 417; Beefsteak Raid (September 14-17), 192-200; Crater (July 31), 97-125; crossing of James (June 12-16), 12-24; final assaults (April 2/Sixth Corps, 369-381) (April 2/ Ninth Corps, 360-369); First Deep Bottom expedition (July 27-30), 104, 142, 153-154; Fort Gregg (April 2), 384-395; Fort Harrison (September 29-30), 205-216; Fort Stedman (March 25), 334-358; Hagood's assault (June 24), 80-83; Hatcher's Run expeditions (October 27, 219-246) (February 5-7, 315-327); Jerusalem Plank

Road (June 22), 66-77; June 15-18, 27-53; June 9, 8-9, 10-12; Peebles Farm (September 30-October 1), 205-216; Reams Station (August 23-25), 174-187; Second Deep Bottom expedition (August 13-20), 142-167; Sutherland Station (April 2), 393-400; Weldon Raid (December 7-12), 266-285; Weldon Railroad (August 18-21), 155-170; Williamsburg Road expedition (October 27), 222-247; Wilson-Kautz Raid (June 22-30), 65, 84-87; siege artillery rounds fired, 292

Petersburg Common Council, 91-93, 258-259, 261, 410, 417

Petersburg Express (newspaper), 78, 187, 197, 251, 257-260, 350, 415

Petersburg Express (Union artillery piece), 292

Petersburg Grays, 2; see also: Virginia troops: infantry (12th Regiment)

Petersburg Rifles, 2; see also: Virginia troops: infantry (12th Regiment)

Philadelphia Inquirer, 135, 204, 208-209, 278, 294, 323, 420

Philadelphia Ledger, 203

Philadelphia Press, 208

Phillips, James E., 76

Phisterer, Frederick, 357

Pickett, George, 17, 151

Piedmont, Battle of (1864), 27

Pierce, Byron, 74, 243-244

Platt, William H., 424

Pleasants, Henry, 98, 101-102, 105-106

Po River, Battle of (1864), 33

Poague, William T., 376

Pocahontas Bridge, 403, 406

Point of Rocks, 8, 35, 412

Pollard, Henry, 328

Pope, Albert, 282, 299

Poplar Grove Church, 301

Poplar Spring Road, 211

Porter, Charles, 134, 135

Porter, David, 191, 412

Porter, Horace, 14-16, 23-24, 45, 51, 62, 67-68, 114-115, 137, 139, 156, 188, 226, 229, 231, 240-241, 302-303, 310, 360, 412

Port Walthall, 5, 10

Potter, Robert B., 98, 214, 224, 282, 362-364
Prince George Court House, 194
Prince George Court House Road, 44-45, 51, 348
Proctor, Hence, 344
Proctor's Mill, 266
Pryor, Roger A., 411, 412, 413
Pryor, Sarah, 4, 8, 258-259, 411-412, 417
Quaker Bridge, 232-235
Quaker Road, 232, 248, 317, 393
Queen's Creek, 22
Rains, G. J., 138
Raleigh, North Carolina, 333
Ramsey, John, 398
Randall, George M., 109
Rauscher, Frank, 57
Rawlins, John, 44, 55
Reams Station, 65, 85-86, 175-187, 315; fortifications, 179
Reese, Henry, 106
Reilly, John E., 17
Renfro, J. D. D., 92
Reynolds, Francis, 207
Rhode Island troops: infantry (2nd Regiment, 374) (4th Regiment, 104) (7th Regiment, 16, 123, 300, 413)
Rhodes, Elisha H., 374
Rhodes, J. L., 204
Rhodes, John H., 107
Richards, R. G., 121
Richardson, Emmet, 117
Richardson, Nathaniel A., 193
Richmond, Virginia, 15, 17, 21, 59-60, 76, 214-215, 224, 229, 310-311, 321, 379, 388, 423
Richmond & Danville Railroad, 85
Richmond & Petersburg Railroad, 94, 257
Richmond Dispatch, 345
Richmond Examiner, 210, 212, 215, 216, 246
Richmond Whig, 214
Riddell's Shop, Battle of (1864), 20-21
Riggsbee, T. S., 366
Rigler, D. M., 390
Ripley, Edward H., 224, 238
River Queen, 313, 425
Rives's Farm, 9
Roanoke River, 85

Robinson, W. D., 70
Rocky Branch, 318
Roebling, Washington, 243
Roemer, Jacob, 93, 407
Rogers, Edward W., 342
Roman, Alfred, 36, 48-49, 50
Rowanty Creek, 174, 177, 181, 193, 199, 315-317
Rowe, Edward, 299
Ruffin, Julian, 5
Saint John, I. M., 87, 423
Sanders, John, 172
Sargent, Lucius M., 276
Savannah, Georgia, 303, 306, 333
Savannah Republican, 88
Scannel, Mike, 72
Scarbrough, R. P., 258, 260
Schaff, Morris, 134, 137, 138, 139
Scott, Alfred L., 120
Scott, Tom, 196-197
Second Presbyterian Church, 411
Seddon, James, 21, 65, 122, 226, 282
Seven Sisters, 292
Seward, William, 311, 314-315
Seymour, Truman, 371, 375, 380
Shadburne, George D., 192
sharpshooters, 12, 61, 77, 98, 100, 181, 186, 191, 237, 239, 276, 289, 291, 293-294
Sharpe, George H., 133, 414
Shenandoah Valley, 15, 27, 48, 60
Shenandoah Valley campaign, 141, 201, 217, 324
Sheridan, Philip H., 12, 14-15, 140-141, 201, 217, 219, 264, 359-360
Sherman, William T., 1, 96, 190, 306, 357, 412, 419
Shiloh, Battle of (1862), 31
Sickles, Daniel E., 225
Siegel, Franz, 27
Sigfried, Joshua K., 114
Signal Hill, 155-156
Simons, Ezra, 397
Simpson family, 410
Six Mile House, 157
Smith, Charles H., 206-207, 269
Smith, Daniel C., 299

Smith, John D., 38
Smith, John L., 271
Smith, R. B., 343
Smith, William C., 117
Smith, William F. "Baldy," 13-14, 16, 28, 30-31, 35-39, 42-43, 49, 64; relieved of command, 55
Smyth, Thomas, 318
snipers. See sharpshooters
Solomon Rumage, 134, 136
Sorrel, G. Moxley, 115
Soule, Pierre, 92
South Carolina troops: cavalry (6th Regiment, 196); infantry (Palmetto Sharpshooters, 238) (11th Regiment, 81) (13th Regiment, 94) (17th Regiment, 334, 350) (21st Regiment, 81) (27th Regiment, 81, 170)
South Side Railroad, 4, 5, 54, 58, 85, 87, 91, 220, 222, 233, 235, 241, 252, 359, 372, 375, 377, 394, 396, 400, 416
Spaulding, Albert, 196
Spaulding, Ira, 12
Spear, Benjamin, 122
Spear, Samuel P., 175, 177, 180, 228
Spiers House, 185
Spotsylvania Court House, Battle of (May 8-21), 11, 33, 226
Squirrel Level Road, 177, 211, 212
Stage Road, 175, 181, 317
Stanton, Edwin, 24, 312, 414
Stearns, Austin, 55
Stedman, Griffin A., 338
Stephens, Alexander H., 308-309, 314-315, 327, 340
Stevens, George, 18
Stewart, William H., 55-56, 69, 73, 219, 246
Stiles, Robert, 17
Stone, Valentine H., 348
Stony Creek Station, 86, 176, 263, 270
Stott, John W., 328
Stowall, John, 171
Stowall, Robert, 171
Strawberry Plains, 143, 150, 154
Stuart, J. E. B., 233
Sturgis, Thomas, 345
Summer, A. C., 252

Sussex Court House, 268-269, 279-280, 283
Sutherland Station, 392, 394-397, 398, 400
Sutherland's Tavern, 396
Swan, Henry R., 18
Swift Creek, 36
Swinton, William, 204, 210
Swords, Henry L., 345
Sycamore Church, 192, 194, 198
Sycamore Street, Petersburg, 8, 260, 417
Taylor, Walter, 151, 388
Tennessee troops: infantry (23rd Regiment, 260)
Terry, Alfred H., 145, 147, 223, 227, 229, 247, 304
Texas troops: infantry (5th Regiment, 239)
Thomas, Edward L., 372, 381
Thomas, George H., 263
Thomas, Henry, 114
Thrasher, A. M., 171
Three Creek, 271, 281
Tidball, John C., 74, 362
Tilney, Robert, 57, 231, 263, 266, 268, 272
Todd's Tavern, Battle of (1864), 33
Townes, W. W., 408, 411
Tracy, Amasa S., 372
Traveller (horse), 110, 378
trenches, 2, 5, 79, 97, 114, 222, 286-297; images 25, 127
Trent's Reach (naval engagement), 303
Trevallian Station, Battle of (1864), 60
Troy, Thomas, 404
Tucker, George, 375-376
Turnbull House, 373, 378, 388
Turner, John W., 382
Tyler's Mill, 22
Ulmer, George, 39
United States Military Railroad, 302-303, 347, 355
United States troops: artillery (1st Artillery, 207); cavalry (5th Regiment, 413); infantry (1st Regiment U.S.C.T., 239) (7th Regiment U.S.C.T., 227) (19th Regiment U.S.C.T., 121) (22nd Regiment U.S.C.T., 239) (30th Regiment U.S.C.T., 114, 117, 119, 121) (37th Regiment U.S.C.T., 239) (43rd Regiment U.S.C.T., 103)

United States Christian Commission, 417
Van Wicks, Catharine, 134, 136, 138
Varin, A. L. P., 94
Varina Road, 223
Vaughan Road, 159, 168, 175, 177, 178, 206, 214, 222, 225, 231, 234, 271, 275, 317-318, 321-322, 393
Venable, Andrew R., 235-236
Venable, Charles, 76, 83, 100, 110, 115
Vermont Brigade, 373-375
Vermont troops: cavalry (1st Regiment, 20); infantry (2nd Regiment, 381) (4th Regiment, 77) (11th Regiment, 77, 134)
Virginia Central Railroad, 60
Virginia Hospital, 260
Virginia troops: artillery (Graham's Battery, 2, 7-8); cavalry (7th Regiment, 196) (11th Regiment, 196) (12th Regiment, 194, 196) (35th Battalion, 197); infantry (7th Regiment, 252, 324) (12th Regiment, 2, 76, 117, 243, 246) (26th Regiment, 111) (41st Regiment, 73, 117) (46th Regiment, 9) (61st Regiment, 56, 69, 73, 246)
Waddell, Fanny, 8-9, 56, 88, 92
Waggaman, Eugene, 341
Wainwright, Charles, 22, 164, 250-251, 276-277
Waitt, William, 218
Walker, Francis, 37-38, 40, 47, 50, 143-144, 147-148, 178, 252; captured, 186
Walker, James, 341-342
Walker, R. Lindsay, 391
Wall, H. C., 367, 403
Wallace, Thomas, 409
Ware, Charles W., 388
Waring, Frederick, 270, 273
Warner, James M., 370
Warren, Gouverneur K., 11-12, 14-16, 48, 53-54, 112, 155-156, 159, 161, 164-169, 171, 173, 222, 225-226, 231, 243-244, 248, 264, 266, 274, 276-277, 281, 284, 322, 325-326, 417; relieved of command, 360
Warwick Swamp Creek, 266
Washburne, Elihu B., 154
Washington Globe, 305
Washington Street, 411
Watkins Bridge, 394

Watson, Cyrus, 344
Way, D. L., 103
Webster, W. E., 57-58
Weisiger, David, 69, 115
Weitzel, Godfrey, 228-229, 236-238, 240, 252-253, 381
Welch, Norval E., 211
Welch, Spencer, 94, 219
Weld, Stephen, 121
Weldon, North Carolina, 263
Weldon Raid, atrocities, 277
Weldon Railroad. See Petersburg & Weldon Railroad
West Virginia troops: infantry (12th Regiment, 390)
West, Robert, 228
Wheaton, Frank, 324, 371, 374, 380
White, Elijah, 196-199
White, John Chester, 55
White, Julius, 163, 165
White House, Virginia, 12, 16, 60-61, 359
White Oak Bridge, 18
White Oak Road, 233, 235, 242, 244, 394
White Oak Swamp, 15, 20, 238
White's Tavern, 151, 153
Wiedrich, Michael, 159
Wilcox, Cadmus, 65, 68, 73-74, 182, 379, 384, 395
Wilcox's Landing, 18, 21, 25
Wilderness, Battle of the (May 5-6), 11, 27, 28, 31, 33, 45, 419
Wiler, C. W., 266, 278
Wilkinson's Bridge, 193
Willcox, Orlando B., 111, 123, 125, 183, 224, 230, 351, 404
Williams, George F., 204, 213, 309, 417
Williamsburg, Battle of (1862), 225
Williamsburg Road, 228-229, 236, 238
Wilson, Clarence, 109
Wilson, James H., 12, 16, 21, 58, 65, 84-87, 141
Windmill Point, 21
Windsor Shades, 20
Winser, Henry J., 34, 67, 204-208, 212-215
Wisconsin troops: infantry (6th Regiment, 266, 281) (36th Regiment, 252) (38th Regiment, 407)
Wise, Henry A., 6, 8, 9, 10, 36

Wise, John S., 115
Wixcey, William T., 407
Wolford, Daniel, 377-378
Wooten, Thomas J., 296
Wright, Horatio G., 16, 63, 66-67, 77-78, 356,
      369-370, 373-375, 377, 378-381
Wright, Samuel T., 109, 110
Wyatt's Crossing, 231
Wyanoke Neck, 21
Yellow Tavern, 157
York River Railroad, 237
Young, Pierce M. B., 193

Robert Malesky

About the Author

Noah Andre Trudeau is a history graduate of the State University of New York at Albany. His first book, *Bloody Roads South*, won the Civil War Round Table of New York's prestigious Fletcher Pratt Award, and enjoyed a cameo appearance in the hit web television series *House of Cards*. His fourth book, *Like Men of War*, a combat history of black troops in the Civil War, was honored with the Grady McWhiney Research Foundation's Jerry Coffey Memorial Book Prize. His other books include a best-selling history of the Battle of Gettysburg, Sherman's "March to the Sea," and a compact biography of Robert E. Lee.